D0036061

SAXONY-ANHALT
Pages 142–157

RG

ERN
ANY

Dresden

NY

EYEWITNESS TRAVEL

GERMANY

EYEWITNESS TRAVEL

GERMANY

MAIN CONTRIBUTORS: JOANNA EGERT-ROMANOWSKA
AND MAŁGORZATA OMILANOWSKA

LONDON, NEW YORK,
MELBOURNE, MUNICH AND DELHI
www.dk.com

PRODUCED BY Wydwnictwo Wiedza i Życie, Warsaw
CONTRIBUTORS Małgorzata Omilanowska, Marek Stańczyk,
Tomasz Torbus, Hanna Köster, Teresa Czerniewicz-Umer
CARTOGRAPHERS Kartographie Huber (Munich),
Magdalena Polak, Dariusz Romanowski
PHOTOGRAPHERS Adam Hajder, Dorota and Mariusz Jarymowiczowie,
Wojciech Mędrzak, Tomasz Myśluk, Paweł Wójcik
ILLUSTRATORS Lena Maminajszwili, Paweł Marczak,
Andrzej Wielgosz, Bohdan Wróblewski, Magdalena Żmudzińska
DTP DESIGNERS Paweł Pasternak, Paweł Kamiński
EDITORS Teresa Czerniewicz-Umer, Joanna Egert-Romanowska
PRODUCTION Anna Kożurno-Królikowska
DESIGNERS Ewa Roguska, Piotr Kiedrowski
Dorling Kindersley Limited
EDITORS Sylvia Goulding, Irene Lyford
TRANSLATORS Magda Hannay, Ian Wisniewski
DTP DESIGNERS Jason Little, Conrad Van Dyke
PRODUCTION Marie Ingledew

Printed and bound by South China Printing Co. Ltd., China

First American Edition 2001
07 08 09 10 9 8 7 6 5 4 3 2

Published in the United States by DK Publishing, Inc.,
375 Hudson Street, New York, New York 10014

Reprinted with revisions 2003, 2004, 2005, 2006, 2007
Copyright © 2001, 2007 Dorling Kindersley Limited, London

Published in Great Britain by Dorling Kindersley Limited.

ISSN 1542-1554

ISBN 978-0-75662-635-8

Front cover main image:
Rheinstein Castle, Rheingau, Hessen, Germany

THROUGHOUT THIS BOOK, FLOORS ARE REFERRED TO IN ACCORDANCE WITH
EUROPEAN USAGE, I.E., THE "FIRST FLOOR" IS THE FLOOR ABOVE GROUND LEVEL.

**The information in this
Dorling Kindersley Travel Guide is checked regularly.**

Every effort has been made to ensure that this book is as up-to-date
as possible at the time of going to press. Some details, however,
such as telephone numbers, opening hours, prices, gallery hanging
arrangements and travel information are liable to change.
The publishers cannot accept responsibility for any consequences
arising from the use of this book, nor for any material on third party
websites, and cannot guarantee that any website address in this book
will be a suitable source of travel information. We value the views
and suggestions of our readers very highly. Please write to:
Publisher, DK Eyewitness Travel Guides, Dorling Kindersley,
80 Strand, London WC2R 0RL, Great Britain.

◁ **Church in Bavaria nestled at the foothills of the Alps**

CONTENTS

Picturesque landscape in Mecklenburg

Statue of a dancing figure, Stadtmuseum in Munich *(see p214)*

Mainz Cathedral
(see pp350–51)

HOW TO USE THIS GUIDE

This guide will help you to get the most out of a visit to Germany, providing expert recommendations as well as thoroughly researched practical information. The first section, *Introducing Germany*, locates the country geographically and provides an invaluable historical and cultural context. Succeeding sections describe the main sights and attractions of the different regions and major cities. Feature spreads, with maps and photographs, focus on important sights. Information on accommodation and restaurants is provided in *Travellers' Needs*, while the *Survival Guide* has useful tips on everything you need to know from money to getting around.

BERLIN

This section is divided into two parts: East and West. Sights outside the centre are described in the section *Around Berlin*. All sights are numbered and plotted on a map of the region. Detailed information for each sight is given in numerical order to make it easy to locate within the chapter.

Pages marked with red refer to Berlin.

A locator map shows where you are in relation to the city plan.

1 Area Map
For easy reference the sights in each area are numbered.

Sights at a Glance describes, by category, buildings in a particular area: Historic Streets and Buildings, Museums and Galleries, Churches, Parks and Gardens.

2 Street-by-Street Map
gives a bird's-eye view of each sightseeing area described in the section.

Stars indicate the sights that no visitor should miss.

A suggested route for a walk is marked with a broken red line.

3 Detailed Information
All the sights of Berlin are described individually. Addresses, telephone numbers, opening hours, admission charges and information on how to get there are given for each sight. The key to symbols is shown on the back flap.

1 Introduction
The landscape, history and character of each region are described, showing how the area has changed through the ages. It also outlines the sights on offer for visitors.

GERMANY AREA BY AREA
In this guide, Germany is divided into 13 areas, each of which is covered in a separate section. The most interesting cities, towns, villages and sights in the area are marked on the Area Map.

2 Regional Map
This shows the main roads and the general topography of the area. All sights are numbered, and there are also details on how to get there.

Boxes contain additional information about sights.

Colour coding at the edge of every page makes it easy to find each particular region.

3 Detailed Information
All major towns, places of interest and other tourist sights are listed in order and numbered according to the Regional Map. Each entry contains information on important sights.

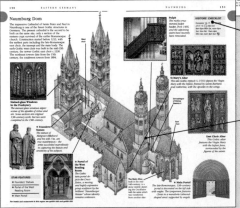

A **Visitors' Checklist** for each of the main sights provides practical information to help you plan your visit.

4 Major Sights
At least two pages are dedicated to each major sight. Historic buildings are dissected in order to show their interiors. Interesting towns or town centres have street maps with the main sights indicated and described.

INTRODUCING
GERMANY

DISCOVERING GERMANY

ermany is a country of marked contrasts and this is nowhere more apparent than in its geographic diversity. Modern cities of glass and steel sit only a few minutes-drive from ancient forests populated with ruined castles. From the windswept coasts of the northern part of the

Sculpture on a Berlin bridge

country to the alpine splendour of the southern states, Germany's natural beauty is multi-faceted. The same is true at the cultural level, where many regional differences can be seen in the architecture, dress and food. Visitors are certain to be impressed with the variety that Germany has to offer.

The imposing steel and glass dome of the Reichstag in Berlin

BERLIN

- **Checkpoint Charlie and the Kaiser-Wihelm-Gedächtnis-Kirche**
- **The Reichstag and Unter den Linden**
- **Shopping at KaDeWe**

In terms of its museums, other cultural attractions, architecture and shopping, Berlin is on a par with Paris, London and New York. **Checkpoint Charlie** (see p80) and the **Kaiser-Wilhelm-Gedächtnis-Kirche** (see p86) are two of Berlin's most famous memorials to the aftermath of World War II and are not to be missed. As the political epicentre of Germany, Berlin hosts a variety of diplomatic visitors throughout the year and provides a home to the country's parliament, the Bundestag, in the newly renovated **Reichstag** (see p93) building. A stroll along **Unter den Linden** (see pp66–7)

boulevard reveals a host of architectural and historical landmarks. Shopping opportunities abound, not least at **KaDeWe** (see pp106–7), one of the largest and most exclusively stocked shopping centres in Europe.

BRANDENBURG

- **Spreewald Biosphere Preserve**
- **Potsdam's royal splendour**
- **Schloss Sanssouci**

The federal state of Brandenburg is located in eastern Germany and surrounds the vibrant city of Berlin. The region has long been the country asylum for weary Berliners and it is well-known for its crystal-clear lakes and waterways, broad expanses of countryside, verdant tree-lined roads, fruit orchards and unspoilt natural scenery. Its sleepy villages and cultural attractions are

historically significant and the UNESCO protected **Spreewald Biosphere Preserve** (see p141) is geographically and culturally unique in Europe. Here you can punt between the island farmsteads of the area. The regional capital and former garrison town, **Potsdam** (see pp134–5), is one of Europe's most magnificent royal cities, filled with baroque architectural wonders commissioned by the Prussian kings, like **Schloss Sanssouci** (see pp136–9).

SAXONY-ANHALT

- **Historic Magdeburg**
- **Lutherstadt Wittenberg**
- **Wörlitz Park**

Located close to the geographic centre of Germany is the Eastern German state of Saxony-Anhalt. Few other German regions offer a similar variety of historical tourist

Schloss Sanssouci in Potsdam, Brandenburg

A bridge over one of the many waterways in Wörlitz Park

attractions in such a small area. Prehistoric, medieval, Reformation and Renaissance sights are all within close visiting distance and often within the same towns. In **Magdeburg** *(see p152)*, the Monastery of Our Lady and the Cathedral are typical of the Romanesque architecture found in the area. Saxony-Anhalt is the birthplace of the Reformation with Martin Luther's hometown of Eisleben and the city of **Wittenberg** *(see pp154–5)* where he first posted his 95 propositions. The region also has some beautiful rural areas with a number of parks and gardens, most notably **Wörlitz Park** *(see pp156–7)* which is well worth a visit.

SAXONY

- **Meissen porcelain**
- **Erzgebirge mountain region**
- **Dresden's restored grandeur**

Divided by the river Elbe, Saxony is considered Germany's gateway to the East with borders to both Poland and the Czech Republic. Saxony is also known for its unique craft traditions, the most famous of which is porcelain from **Meissen** *(see p167)*. The **Sächsische Silberstraße** *(see p166)*, which runs through the old silver mining route in the Erzgebirge mountains,

offers delightful scenery, while the beautiful buildings of **Dresden** *(see pp168–77)* continue to enchant. The city was all but destroyed in the war, but much has been done in recent years to restore it to its former glory.

A tree-lined hiking trail in the Thuringian Forest

THURINGIA

- **Thuringian Forest**
- **The mighty Wartburg**
- **Weimar's literary culture**

Thuringia is one of the least known regions of Germany, but should not be missed. Home to several natural reserves encompassing extensive walking trails in the **Thuringian Forest** *(see pp190–91)*, it is one of Germany's top destinations for hiking enthusiasts. In **Eisenach** *(see pp186–7)*, the Wartburg fortress dominates

the city – Wagner immortalized it in his opera *Tannhäuser* and Martin Luther translated the New Testament into German here. The city of **Weimar** *(see pp194–5)*, meanwhile, offers a glimpse into the lives of German authors Goethe and Schiller, who resided in this UNESCO heritage site, famous for its classical architecture.

MUNICH

- **Museums and architecture**
- **Hofbräuhaus Beer Hall**
- **Home to Oktoberfest**

"Munich nestles between art and beer like a village between hills," wrote Heinrich Heine some 150 years ago. Munich has much more to offer than just great beer, however. Composed of five central districts, the city manages to marry old Bavarian tradition with a vibrant modern life. The **Marienplatz** *(see pp210–11)* in the city's old town is a prime jumping-off point for seeing the city's beautiful architecture and numerous museums. There is a diverse music scene and a plethora of excellent restaurants. Visitors will also want to visit the renowned **Hofbräuhaus** *(see p215)* beer hall and experience Munich at its most traditional, and, in October, the city hosts the world-famous **Oktoberfest** *(see p227)*, the biggest folk and beer fair in Europe.

Revellers enjoying beer and music at the annual Oktoberfest

BAVARIA

- Fairytale castles
- German alpine heartland
- Medieval towns

Bavaria is Germany's top tourist destination due to its mix of urban and rural landscapes. To the south, nestled among hills and lakes, is the eccentric King Ludwig II's 18th-century **Schloss Neuschwanstein** *(see pp282–3)*. The castle was built according to Ludwig's particular tastes in the style of a medieval fairytale castle.
Berchtesgadener Land *(see pp276–7)* is a region of impressively spectacular alpine scenery, while to the east there are tranquil river valleys, miles of forest and an abundance of lakes. Besides the magnificent display of natural wonders is a multitude of well-preserved medieval Bavarian towns.
Rothenburg ob der Tauber *(see pp262–3)* is foremost among these with its tiny cobbled alleyways, gabled houses and towers that form a picturesque skyline.

BADEN-WURTTEMBERG

- Stuttgart and Heidelberg
- Black Forest spa towns
- The Bodensee (Lake Constance)

Pristine and stately, **Stuttgart** *(see pp308–13)* is the regional capital with many parks and beer gardens to enjoy despite the high concentration of industry. However, **Heidelberg** *(see pp296–9)* is by far the most picturesque town in the region, with its mix of medieval and Baroque architecture. Baden Wurttemberg's **Black Forest** *(see pp326–7)* is renowned internationally for its spas, with elegant and exclusive **Baden-Baden** *(see p301)* topping this list. **The Bodensee** *(see pp320–21)*, or Lake Constance as it is more

The Bodensee (Lake Constance) from the Altes Schloss in Meersburg

commonly known, is on the border with Switzerland and is a favoured weekend spot, especially for sailing and caravanning enthusiasts.

RHINELAND-PALATINATE AND SAARLAND

- Palatinate and Mosel wine regions
- Saarbrücken's varied architecture
- Trier's Porta Nigra

These two regions bordering France account for much of Germany's wine production. These wines are best sampled by following the **Deutsche Weinstraße** *(see p347)* driving route where there are also many beautiful castles to be seen along the way *(see pp354–5)*. With a history of changing nationality, both states share a wonderful cultural mix unlike anywhere

A sun-drenched vineyard in the Mosel Valley

else in Germany. This is most apparent in **Saarbrücken** *(see p344)* which was ruled in turn by the Celts, Romans and Franks. The city's resulting range of architecture is now its main attraction. The region's Roman heritage is evident in many cities, particularly in **Trier** *(see pp340–43)*, with its Porta Nigra, the oldest defensive structure in Germany.

HESSE

- The picturesque Waldecker Land
- Bustling Frankfurt
- Historic Wiesbaden

Hesse lies at the heart of western Germany and is home to the beautiful **Waldecker Land** *(see pp366–7)*, which is full of wooded hills ideal for long rambles and cycling tours. At the heart of Hesse is **Frankfurt** *(see pp374–9)*, Germany's ultramodern financial city which has some of Europe's tallest skyscrapers. The banking district's glass and steel architecture is a famous post-card skyline but only a few minutes' walk away is the lovely Römerberg square and the banks of the river Main with its fascinating Museum Mile. In contrast to Frankfurt, many of Hesse's other cities are full of history, and none more so than **Wiesbaden** *(see pp372–3)* with its spa town heritage.

NORTH-RHINE WESTPHALIA

- Gothic cathedral of Cologne
- Düsseldorf: fashion capital
- Modern culture in Dortmund and Essen

North Rhine-Westphalia is the most densely populated federal state in Germany. The city of **Köln (Cologne)** *(see pp398–403)* with its famous Gothic cathedral, Roman ruins and enchanting old city is better known as a tourist destination than the state capital of **Düsseldorf** *(see pp392–3)*, but the latter has excellent shops. Once the centre of the German mining industry and steel production, the Ruhr area, incorporating **Dortmund** *(see p376)* and **Essen** *(see p376)*, is now renowned for its thriving arts scene.

Fischmarkt in Köln, overlooked by the Groß St Martin church

LOWER SAXONY, HAMBURG AND BREMEN

- Pristine Hannover
- Windswept East Frisian Islands
- City-states of Hamburg and Bremen

The regional capital of Lower Saxony, **Hannover** *(see pp444–5)*, is well known as a trade fair city, but it has much more to offer. There are several parks, the magnificent Baroque Herrenhäuser Gardens and the unusual town hall, built on more than 6,000 beech pillars with Neo-Gothic and Secessionist detail. To the north are the seven **East Frisian Islands** *(see p428)* which line up like pearls on a string just off the North Sea coast. They are popular holiday destinations and home to a unique ecosystem. The city-states of **Hamburg** *(see pp434–8)* and **Bremen** *(see pp430–33)* are located in this region. Being port cities, both Hamburg and Bremen have a strong international flavour, seen in the diversity of shops and restaurants. In Bremen, the Bremen Town Musicians monument is a must-see if you have read the famous Grimm fairytale.

SCHLESWIG-HOLSTEIN

- Sandy beaches on Sylt
- Flensburg's waterfront
- Gothic architecture in Lübeck

Schleswig-Holstein is the most northerly-situated state of Germany and possesses a distinct Nordic feel. With long stretches of coastline and the rugged sandy beaches of the North Frisian Islands, most particularly **Sylt** *(see p459)*, this region makes an attractive holiday destination, especially for families. **Flensburg** *(see p459)* was once a trading centre with 200 ships; today there are some beautiful walks to be had around the harbour. **Lübeck** *(see pp462–5)* was the most important town in the area at

Bremen's most famous residents, the Bremen Town Musicians

the end of the Middle Ages and many of its superb Gothic buildings remain.

MECKLENBERG-LOWER POMERANIA

- Hanseatic city Rostock
- State capital Schwerin
- Rugged Rügen

The Mecklenberg-Lower Pomeranian region is full of towns with verdant, tree-lined avenues. Its Hanseatic towns, in particular **Rostock** *(see p476)*, are filled with richly decorated townhouses, cathedrals, abbeys and town halls. Over 800 years old, it is the largest town in the region, but it is the smaller **Schwerin** *(see pp470–71)* that is the state capital. It is home to one of the most beautiful Neo-Renaissance castles in Germany. The stretches of Baltic coastline here are unspoilt natural attractions and the island of **Rügen** *(see pp478–9)* boasts miles of untouched sandy beaches.

The picturesque harbour in Flensburg

Putting Germany on the Map

Located in the centre of Europe, between the North and Baltic Seas and the Alps, Germany covers an area of nearly 360,000 sq km (139,000 sq miles). Its neighbouring countries are Poland and the Czech Republic to the east, Austria and Switzerland to the south, France, Belgium, Luxembourg and Holland to the west, and Denmark to the north. The capital is Berlin. Its largest river is the Rhine. Germany is inhabited by over 81 million people.

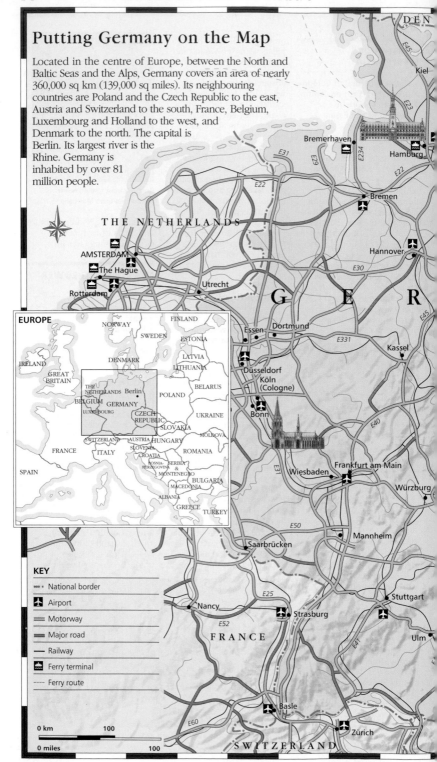

KEY

- --- National border
- ✈ Airport
- ▬ Motorway
- ▬ Major road
- — Railway
- ⛴ Ferry terminal
- ---- Ferry route

0 km   100
0 miles   100

◁ **Grapevines stretching as far as the eye can see in the North Rhine-Palatinate**

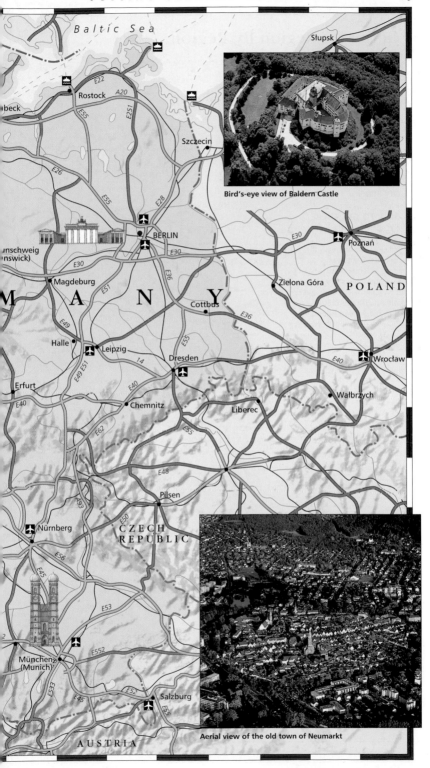

Baltic Sea

Słupsk

Rostock

E22

A20

E251

E55

beck

E26

E55

Szczecin

E28

Bird's-eye view of Baldern Castle

unschweig
nswick)

BERLIN

E30

Poznań

E30

E36

Magdeburg

Zielona Góra

POLAND

E49

E51

Cottbus

E36

Halle

Leipzig

E55

Dresden

14

E40

Wrocław

E40

Erfurt

E49 E51

E40

Chemnitz

Liberec

Wałbrzych

E62

E55

E48

Pilsen

E50

Nürnberg

CZECH
REPUBLIC

E56

E45

E53

München
(Munich)

E552

E533

E52

Salzburg

E45

AUSTRIA

Aerial view of the old town of Neumarkt

Germany: Region by Region

The Federal Republic of Germany is made up of
16 states. Bremen is the smallest state, with
around 700,000 inhabitants; North Rhine-
Westphalia is the most densely populated
state, with 18 million inhabitants. The
largest state, Bavaria, covers an
area of 70,531 sq km
(27,232 sq miles).
Berlin, Bremen and
Hamburg are
self-governing
city-states.

HOW TO GET THERE

Germany has an excellent transport system. There are 14 international airports with flights to
all parts of the world; a
comprehensive network of toll-
free motorways that make
travelling by car easy and fast;
and an efficient railway system,
with high-speed InterCity
Express (ICE) link between
major cities.

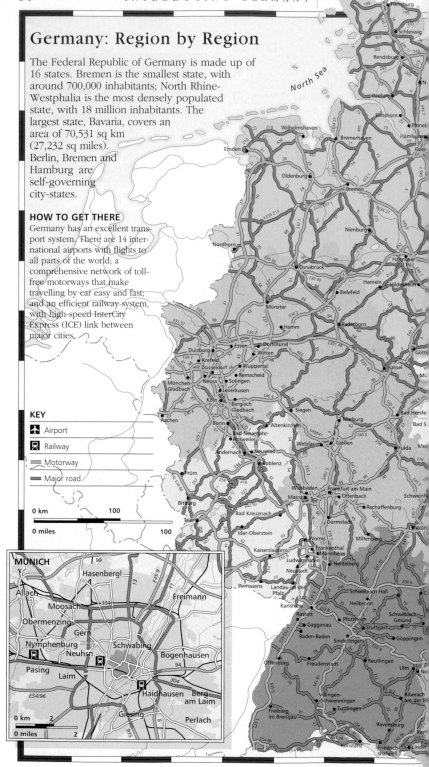

KEY

✈	Airport
🚉	Railway
▬	Motorway
▬	Major road

0 km   100

0 miles   100

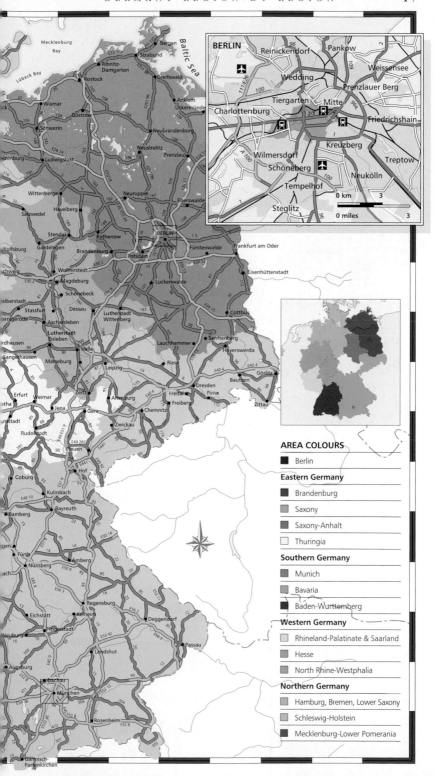

BERLIN

Reinickendorf   Pankow
Wedding   Weissensee
Tiergarten   Prenzlauer Berg
Charlottenburg   Mitte
                    Friedrichshain
Wilmersdorf   Kreuzberg
Schöneberg   Treptow
Tempelhof   Neukölln
Steglitz

0 km   3
0 miles   3

AREA COLOURS

Berlin

Eastern Germany

Brandenburg

Saxony

Saxony-Anhalt

Thuringia

Southern Germany

Munich

Bavaria

Baden-Württemberg

Western Germany

Rhineland-Palatinate & Saarland

Hesse

North Rhine-Westphalia

Northern Germany

Hamburg, Bremen, Lower Saxony

Schleswig-Holstein

Mecklenburg-Lower Pomerania

A PORTRAIT OF GERMANY

Germany is a wealthy country, whose people are generally regarded as hard-working, determined and efficient. This view stems from the country's industrial might and the smooth functioning of its economy, but it overlooks other important aspects of Germany. These include its important contributions to art and culture, its breathtaking scenery and excellent tourist facilities.

Contemporary Germany is far removed from the traditional, stereotyped view of the country. In the last 50 years, it has developed into a multi-ethnic, multi-cultural melting pot. Over 7 million of Germany's inhabitants are immigrants; the majority of these are Turks, with more recent guest workers arriving from the former Yugoslavia, Italy and Greece. In the city of Stuttgart, every third inhabitant is a foreigner; in Frankfurt it is one in four. Hamburg has more mosques than any other city in Europe and, in some schools in Berlin, German children are in the minority. Almost every town has a selection of Italian, Chinese, Greek and Turkish restaurants and cafés, testifying to the multi-ethnicity of its population.

The colourful Bavarian coat of arms

HISTORY AND ROMANCE
For many, the river Rhine epitomizes tourist Germany, particularly the romantic stretch between Mainz and Cologne. The country has far more than this to offer in the way of scenery, however. There is the ever-changing Baltic coastline, the sandy islands of the North Sea, the lakes of Mecklenburg, lonely castles perched on crags in Baden and Thuringia, mountain ranges including the Alps, the vast Bodensee lake, medieval cities and fairy-tale villages. Not all of the latter are original, as countless towns were destroyed by bombs during World War II, but many have been meticulously rebuilt to the original plans, and now it is difficult to tell the difference between the old and the new.

Verdant Alpine meadow against a backdrop of majestic, snowy peaks

◁ Alter Flecken – Freudenberg's quarter of traditional-style houses

Procession during the Plärrer Fest, a beer festival in Augsburg

TRADITIONS

Today's German nation has evolved over the past thousand years, mainly from various Germanic tribes, notably the Franks, Saxons, Swabians and Bavarians. Traditions and dialects have developed within regional ethnic groups that emerged as a result of historical alliances. There is no such thing as a single German tradition. Even the assumption that Germany is a country of beer-drinkers is belied by the large numbers of wine-lovers. These groups, along with consumers of stronger beverages, have given Germany a high position in the world league table for alcohol use. Nevertheless, drunks are rarely seen in Germany.

Bavarian scene on a beer glass

A Bavarian dressed in regional costume

Various ethnic groups in the country are ascribed different characteristics. The people of Mecklenburg, for example, are seen as introspective, while Swabians are regarded as thrifty; the Saxons are seen as disciplined and cunning, while Bavarians are typified as a people bound by rustic traditions, quick to quarrel and fight. Indeed, one of the most pop-ular Bavarian men's folk-dances ends with them slapping each other in the face. Bavaria, of course, is home to the traditional Oktoberfest, a beer festival that brings millions of people to Munich every year from virtually all over the world.

The people of the Rhineland have a reputation for enjoying life. Their favourite season is the Carnival period, and they spend practically the entire year preparing for this week-long event. It begins on the last Thursday before Lent, with "town soldiers", helped by the huge crowds, storming the town hall. The town councillors surrender and power passes to the masked revellers. On the Monday, the Carnival proceeds through the thronged streets of the towns on the Rhine, and the pubs are busy until the end of Shrovetide.

Carnival is rooted in ancient rituals marking the banishment of winter. This custom was most common in the south of Germany, but it also reached the Rhineland, the Palatinate and Hessen. There is a special enthusiasm for the festival among the inhabitants of the former East Germany, where Carnival used to be banned, as it had been during the Third Reich.

ART AND CULTURE

Germany is a land of sagas and legends that tell of woodland spirits, beautiful princesses, magicians and sirens such as the Lorelei. These legends have had a strong influence on German art. An example is the German epic poem, the *Nibelungenlied*, which was written around 1200 on the basis of old legends. This poem was the inspiration for Richard Wagner's cycle of operas, *The Ring of the Nibelungen*, as well as for a trilogy of plays by Christian Friedrich Hebbel and a film by Fritz Lang.

Germans have won eight Nobel Prizes for Literature. The most recent prize-winner was Günter Grass, whose *Tin Drum* brought him world renown. More recently a film adaptation of the book was made by Volker Schlöndorff, which won the Golden Palm at the Cannes Film Festival. After a relatively stagnant period, the German film industry became revitalized around 1995 with a number of hits, albeit only at the national level. German cinemas are now always full and traditional cinemas are increasingly being replaced by multiplexes.

Germans read widely, even in today's age of television and the internet. Every year 70,000 new books are published in Germany and eight times that many titles are on sale. Germany is second only to the United States in the number of books published annually, while the number of bookshops per square kilometre is the highest in the world. The same applies to museums and art galleries.

Germany has over 2,000 national, provincial and local history museums,

The historical Frohnauer hammer forge near Annaberg in Saxony

as well as numerous church museums, folk museums and former royal palaces. This variety and choice owes much to the fact that, in the past, local dukes acquired collections of art in order to impress others and to demonstrate their wealth. The Bavarian dukes also built up extensive collections of machines, artisans' tools, musical instruments and minerals. As early as the 16th century, Munich was an international centre of the arts and the Grünes Gewölbe in 17th-century Dresden was one of the largest treasuries for storing fine art in Europe. Of the many art galleries to be found throughout Germany, the finest are in Cologne, Frankfurt, Stuttgart, Munich and Berlin.

Lorelei overlooking the Rhine

Music also flourishes in Germany. Most large cities have their own symphony orchestra and opera company and every year some 100 regional and local music festivals take place. Musical comedies are especially popular.

The imposing Schönburg Castle, near Oberwesel on the Rhine

SOCIETY AND POLITICS

The scars of World War II are more evident in Eastern Germany, although they are gradually disappearing there, too. Görlitz, Bautzen, Leipzig and Weimar have now acquired a splendour that was previously hidden behind the grim façade of East Germany. The mental, social and political scars of the war and subsequent division of Germany have, however, left deeper scars. Although reunification took place on 3 October 1990, unity among the people themselves has been longer in coming. East Germans are the poor

The Reichstag building, where the *Bundestag* sessions are held

relations: the region has high unemployment rates and its people tend to regard their western counterparts as arrogant and self-assured. The latter, for their part, claim that the inhabitants of the "new states" are jealous and ungrateful despite the billions of marks that have been poured into the region to equalize living standards.

Germany has almost always been divided regionally into states with fluctuating borders. The present-day states were, for the most part, created after 1945 while those in East Germany were not created until forty years later. In all cases, old territorial and historical ties were taken into account. That is the reason for their evocative names, such as the "Free State of Bavaria" or the "Free State of Saxony".

There are now 16 federal states, or provinces. North Rhine-Westphalia, Baden-Wurttemberg and Bavaria are the largest and are like economically powerful countries. At the other end of the scale, the tiny province of Saarland has only 1.1 million inhabitants, while the Free Hanseatic City of Bremen has fewer than 700,000. The former East German states are also relatively small but all play an important role in the *Bundesrat*, or Federal Council, where they are instrumental in enacting legislation. All laws, apart from those relating to the Federation as a whole, such as defence or foreign policy, require the agreement of the *Bundesrat*, which is made up from current local governments. Depending on the number of inhabitants, each federal state has from four to six votes.

The skyline of Frankfurt am Main, reminiscent of New York

A government with a majority in the *Bundestag* (parliament) cannot always count on support in the *Bundesrat*, even if it has a majority there. Each state looks after its own interests and often makes alliances with other states to achieve its own aims, without regard for party loyalty. The complex working of German federalism is based on the compromises that this system makes necessary.

Bathers on the sandy beaches of Norddeich

DAILY LIFE

The traditional image of German women used to be summed up in the "three Ks": *Küche, Kinder, Kirche* (kitchen, children, church). As in other Western European countries, however, this stereotype no longer holds true. Although cookery is fashionable and there are countless TV cookery programmes starring celebrity chefs, for everyday meals, ready-prepared dishes are eaten, either at the work canteen or from the supermarket. The German birthrate is declining, while the antiauthoritarian model of education that was introduced in the 1960s has to some extent relieved parents of many of the more onerous duties of child-rearing. As a result, many young people show little respect for their elders. The churches, for their part, are usually empty. Although the largest churches (Catholic and Protestant) have many adherents, the vast majority are not practising believers and limit themselves to the payment of church dues.

Participant in a parade marking the Reunification celebrations

Germans speak of themselves as a high-performance society *(Leistungsgesellschaft)*, which gives the highest rewards to those who devote almost all their energies to their careers. As a result, stress is often a factor in people's lives, from schooldays onwards. In Germany today there are increasing numbers of people who live alone.

Single-person households are most common in the cities and even young people regard their careers as of paramount importance. Increasingly large numbers say that they are not interested in having a family.

Nevertheless, Germans enjoy mass events such as public holidays and popular festivals. The country has the highest number of public holidays in Europe and German workers have the longest annual holidays. Its citizens are Europe's most enthusiastic travellers, each year spending over 35 million euros on foreign holidays. When they return there is a tendency to long for the southern climes they have just visited – perhaps this explains why restaurants offering Mediterranean food are so popular.

The Bodensee, a popular tourist destination

Flora and Fauna

Black-headed gull

Germany is a vast country whose varied geography has given rise to a great diversity of flora and fauna. It is famous for its forests, many of mixed deciduous trees, including oak, beech and birch. Around 31 per cent of the country is forested. The Alpine regions have a rich variety of wild flowers, with meadow species a particular feature in spring and summer. On the northern peat moors, heaths and heathers are common. Germany is home to a wide range of wildlife, including wild boar, lynx and marmots. Many valuable wildlife areas have now been placed under protection.

GERMAN WILDLIFE

The fauna of Germany is typical of central Europe, with a variety of woodland, wetland and Alpine birds. Of the larger mammals, visitors are most likely to see deer, squirrels and foxes. Small populations of rarer species such as lynx and European beaver exist, but these are threatened with extinction.

Alpine raven

COASTAL REGIONS

Germany's coasts vary considerably: the North Sea coast is predominantly flat with drained land, dikes and islands; the Baltic Sea coast is hillier with sandy inlets and cliffs. Together with differences in tides and temperature, these variations determine the variety of species found along coastal regions.

LAKES

Most of Germany's lakes are grouped in the northern part of the country, mainly in the Mecklenburg region, where they are divided from the south by the mountain ranges, rifts and valleys of the Central Uplands. However, the largest lake in Germany – the Bodensee (Lake Constance) – is situated in the south, on the border with Austria and Switzerland.

Cross-leaved heath *is a species of heath that is commonly found growing on the moors and peat bogs and in the damp coastal forests of northern Germany.*

Yellow floating heart *grows in shallow, fertile water. Its habitats are disappearing but it still survives in the Rhine basin and on the lower Elbe.*

Sea lavender *is one of the salt-tolerant species that grow along Germany's North Sea coast.*

Sea holly *is a beautiful thistle-like plant with an amethyst hue. It is commonly found growing in sand dunes.*

The white water lily, *with its elegant floating flowers and lush foliage, adorns lakes and reservoirs.*

Yellow flag *is a protected species of iris that is found amongst reeds and in damp woodlands, particularly in older, mixed species forests.*

Wild boars *are mammals of the pig family, living in boggy forests. They feed mainly on acorns, beechnuts and the small animals that live in the ground cover of the forest.*

Deer *live in leafy and mixed forests and are one of the most common mammals seen in Germany.*

Marmots *live on vegetation growing in the high Alpine meadows. Rodents of the squirrel family, they sleep in burrows at night and whistle loudly when anxious.*

Lynx *are distinguished by small tufts of hair on the tips of their ears. These mammals are becoming ever rarer.*

UPLANDS

Upland landscapes dominate the southern part of Germany, including Bavaria. Here, the climate is mild, and forests cover nearly a third of the region. In this picturesque and popular part of the country, winter-sports centres and spa resorts are common.

MOUNTAINS

Mountain ranges in Germany vary both in age and in height above sea level. Older, not very high mountains covered with forests predominate. The Bavarian Alps are higher and more recent. Here sub-alpine plants grow, with alpine plants at higher altitudes.

Beech *is one of the commonest trees found in Germany's forests of mixed deciduous species.*

Gentian, *with its intensely blue trumpet-like flowers, is one of the most impressive plants to be seen in the Alps. It is pollinated by bumblebees.*

Holly, *the symbol of Christmas with its glossy leaves and scarlet berries, is found in forests of beech or beech and fir in the west of the country.*

Edelweiss *is a small flowering plant with flat, white flowers and grey-green woolly leaves. It grows high up in the Alps.*

Hepatica *is a protected plant in Germany. It blooms in early spring and the seeds of the blue, star-like flowers are distributed by ants.*

Rhododendron hirsutum *is a low, dense variety of rhododendron, one of a group of plants that grow at sub-Alpine levels.*

German Literature

The first known examples of written German date from the 8th century. German literature flourished in the Renaissance, although it was mainly later writers who entered the world's canon of great literature. Goethe and Schiller, who wrote many of their most famous works in the *Sturm und Drang* (Storm and Stress) era, in the late 18th century, count among the greatest. Germany also produced many dramatists, poets and novelists in the 19th and 20th centuries. German writers have won eight Nobel Prizes for literature, awarded to Nelly Sachs, Thomas Mann, Heinrich Böll and Günter Grass among others.

Schleswig-Holstein

Gotthold Ephraim Lessing
(1729–81), the most famous German writer of the Age of Enlightenment, wrote dramas such as Nathan the Wise, *reviews of plays performed in Hamburg as well as essays on literary and cultural theory.*

Lower Saxony, Hamburg, Bremen

Erich Maria Remarque
(1898–1970) emigrated from Germany in 1931. His pacifist writings, including All Quiet on the Western Front *and* L'Arc de Triomphe, *brought him acclaim around the world.*

North Rhine-Westphalia

Hesse

The Brothers Grimm,
Jacob Ludwig Karl (1785–1863) and Wilhelm Karl (1786–1859), were university professors and philologists, but better known as writers of some of the world's favourite fairy-tales.

Rhineland-Palatinate & Saarland

Baden-Württemberg

Friedrich Schiller
(1759–1805) wrote about the concept of individual freedom in his great dramas, such as The Robbers *and* Wallenstein. *He also wrote ballads and songs, including* Ode to Joy.

0 km 75
0 miles 75

Thomas Mann *(1875–1955) was awarded the Nobel Prize in 1929. The best-known of his novels is* Buddenbrooks, *which chronicles the life of a Lübeck family.*

Gerhart Hauptmann *(1862–1946), dramatist, novelist and winner of the Nobel Prize in 1912, lived and worked mainly in Silesia.* The Weavers *is his most famous drama.*

Mecklenburg-Lower Pomerania

Theodor Fontane *(1819–98) was born in Neuruppin, although his literary activities were chiefly connected with Brandenburg. He was the author of realistic novels such as* Effi Briest, *and he wrote excellent theatre reviews.*

Berlin

Saxony-Anhalt

Brandenburg

Bertolt Brecht *(1898–1956), the great dramatist, poet and director, wrote* The Threepenny Opera, *and was a co-founder of the Berliner Ensemble theatre company.*

Saxony

Thuringia

Karl May *(1842–1912) was known around the world as the author of travel books but his great popularity stems from a cycle of stories featuring the Indian chief* Winnetou, *which he wrote in Radebeul.*

Bavaria

Johann Wolfgang von Goethe *(1749–1832) was the most highly acclaimed German poet and writer of the* Sturm und Drang *period. Born in Frankfurt, he spent most of his life in Weimar. His most famous work is* Faust.

Lion Feuchtwanger *(1884–1958) lived in Munich until his opposition to the National Socialists forced him to emigrate in 1933. He wrote in exile, alluding to contemporary events in his historical novels.*

Munich

Music in Germany

German composers have made an enormous contribution to the world's cultural heritage. Many great musical geniuses were born and worked here, including Johann Sebastian Bach and Ludwig van Beethoven. Today their work, and that of other German composers, continues to be performed to enthusiastic new generations of music-lovers in concert halls and opera houses around the world. In Germany, their work is celebrated regularly at hugely popular music festivals.

Richard Strauss

Renowned composer, Johann Sebastian Bach (1685–1750)

EARLY MUSIC

During the early Middle Ages, music evolved in the courts and monasteries of Europe. The basis of sacred music was the Gregorian chant, which was introduced by Pope Gregory I in the late 6th century. An influential role in medieval court music was played by roving poets (*Minnesänger*), who sang love verses to a lute accompaniment. From the 14th century, German singing guilds known as *Meistersinger* emerged. Unlike the *Minnesänger*, these artistes adopted a settled lifestyle. In the succeeding centuries, both vocal and instrumental music continued to evolve, with many new forms appearing.

In the second half of the 17th century, interest in organ music developed and organ schools were established in many towns. One of the best

was in Nuremberg. This was directed by Johann Pachelbel (c.1653–1706), who worked in Vienna, Stuttgart, Erfurt and Nuremberg as a church organist. He is best known for his organ work *Canon*, a set of variations on a theme.

The first German opera, *Dafne*, was composed by Heinrich Schütz (1585–1672). Completed in 1627, the opera has unfortunately been lost.

THE 18TH CENTURY

A huge flowering of musical talent took place in Germany during the 18th century, when divisions both in German politics and religion led to the development of several important artistic and cultural centres. The most renowned figure in

Georg Friedrich Händel (1685–1759)

German music in the 18th century was undoubtedly Johann Sebastian Bach who, until 1717, was associated with the Weimar court. From 1723 until his death, he was associated with Leipzig, where he was the choir master at the church of St Thomas. Bach's output as a composer is vast and embraces most of the musical forms known at that time. His Passions are today performed in many countries during Holy Week, and his Brandenburg Concertos are among his most frequently performed works. His sons – Wilhelm Friedemann, Carl Philipp Emanuel, Johann Christoph Friedrich and Johann Christian – also became acclaimed composers and made significant contributions to German classical music.

Georg Friedrich Händel was another great composer of late Baroque music. Before forging a prestigious career in England, he began as the cathedral organist in Halle, from where he transferred to the opera house in Hamburg. A friend of Händel and another important composer, Georg Philipp Telemann (1681– 1767) was employed as conductor at many German courts. His work includes chamber music, operas and church music.

MUSIC FESTIVALS

The Bach festival in Leipzig's Church of St Thomas

Germany is a country of musical festivals, which are usually held in the summer and early autumn. Among the most popular are the festivals dedicated to the works of a single composer, such as Wagner in Bayreuth, Bach in various cities of Thuringia, Handel in Halle and Beethoven in Bonn. Apart from these specialized festivals, opera festivals with a broader repertoire are also popular. These include the outdoor opera festival in Berlin and the Sommerfestspiele in Xanten.

Son of a court musician and arguably the greatest figure in classical music, Ludwig van Beethoven (1770–1827) was born in Bonn, although he worked mainly in Vienna. Among his best-known works are his nine symphonies, as well as piano and violin concertos, two masses, various chamber works and the opera *Fidelio*.

The life of this great composer, is shrouded in legend. Succeeding generations have been fascinated not just by his music, but also by the fact that he began to lose his hearing at the age of 30. During his final years, when totally deaf, he composed from memory.

Statue of Ludwig van Beethoven

THE 19TH CENTURY

Romanticism brought about the flowering of opera in Germany. One of the leading creators in this tradition was the composer Ernst Theodor Amadeus Hoffmann (1776–1822), whose opera *Undine* was staged for the first time in 1816 in Berlin. Carl Maria von Weber (1786–1826) rose to prominence following the success of his opera *Der Freischütz*, which was the first opera in the German Romantic tradition. Another

Composer Felix Mendelssohn-Bartholdy (1809–47)

major figure from this time was Felix Mendelssohn-Bartholdy, whose "Wedding March" from *A Midsummer Night's Dream* accompanies wedding celebrations around the world. As well as this famous piece of music, however, Mendelssohn left a legacy that includes five symphonies, piano music, chamber music and oratorios. In 1843, Mendelssohn founded Germany's first musical conservatory, in Leipzig.

The master of chamber music was Robert Schumann (1810–56), a poet and composer whose miniature works for piano, violin sonatas and song cycles all remain popular. The Hungarian composer Franz Liszt, who worked in Weimar from 1848 to 1861, also made a significant contribution to the evolution of German music.

In the second half of the 19th century, Richard Wagner was the major influence on German opera. During his early years, he composed traditional operas such as *Tannhäuser*. He later developed his own creative synthesis, integrating lyrics with the music. This found its finest expression in his Ring cycle, which was based on medieval sagas.

Wagner's ideas about musical theatre, including his use of *leitmotifs* (recurring phrases), were adopted by Richard Strauss (1864–1949), who composed many operas, symphonies and songs. The first bars of his symphonic poem *Zarathustra* became a guiding musical motif in Stanley Kubrick's 1968 film *2001: A Space Odyssey*. Johannes Brahms (1833–97) composed in traditional forms and was

Composer and pianist Johannes Brahms (1833–97)

unsympathetic to the progressive ideas of Wagner and Liszt. From 1872 to 1875, Brahms was the musical director of the *Gesellschaft der Musikfreunde* (Society of Friends of Music).

THE 20TH CENTURY

During the 20th century, many contemporary composers continued the traditions of the earlier masters. One renowned figure was Paul Hindemith (1895–1963), whose work includes opera, ballet and concertos. His music was banned by the Nazis in 1933 and Hindemith emigrated to the USA in 1939.

Another important figure in German musical life was Carl Orff (1895–1982) whose best-known work is the oratorio *Carmina Burana*, based on 13th-century Latin and German poems found in a Benedictine monastery in Bavaria. The Austrian composer Arnold Schönberg (1874–1951) lived in Berlin during the 1920s and exerted great influence on German music.

Richard Wagner (1813–83)

Among the most important composers living and working in Germany today, mention should be made of Hans Werner Henze, Dieter Schnebel, Helmut Lachenmann, Moritz Eggert and Jörg Widmann.

German Painting

The diversity in German painting has its roots in the political and religious divisions that existed in the country in the past. The Old Masters working in the north, for example, were more likely to be influenced by the Netherlandish school, while artists working in the south leaned towards Italian styles. German art reached the peak of its individuality during the late-Gothic, late-Baroque and Expressionist periods – all periods when one of the chief characteristics of artistic style was strength of expression.

Emil Nolde *(1867–1956), one of Germany's foremost Expressionists, painted landscapes of his native region. Pictured above is his* North Friesian Landscape.

Schleswi... Holstei...

Master Francke *(14th– 15th century) was the leading representative of the North German Late-Gothic style, working in Hamburg c.1410–24. He painted religious scenes and his works include* St Thomas's Altar, *of which this is a detail.*

Bremen, Hamburg and Lower Saxony

North Rhine-Westphalia

Hesse

Rhineland-Palatinate and Saarland

Peter von Cornelius *(1783–1867) joined the Nazarenes during the anti-academic rebellion. He later became director of the academy in Dusseldorf and others. He painted the picture* The Wise and Foolish Maidens *at that time.*

Baden-Wurttemburg

Adam Elsheimer *(1578–1610) was born in Frankfurt am Main but spent most of his life in Rome. His poignant landscapes, such as* The Flight to Egypt *shown here, greatly influenced the development of 17th-century painting.*

Caspar David Friedrich
(1774–1840) was one of the most prominent exponents of Romanticism. He created poignant images, such as this Traveller above the Sea of Clouds, *in which Man contemplates the power of Nature as created by God.*

Mecklenburg-Lower Pomerania

Max Liebermann
(1847–1935) is considered one of the leading representatives of Impressionism. His Man with Parrots *was painted during his association with the Berlin Secession.*

Berlin

Saxony-Anhalt   *Brandenburg*

Lionel Feininger
(1871–1956) was born in the USA but spent much of his life in Germany. He lectured at the Bauhaus and painted Cubist-inspired scenes of architectural subjects, such as this Gelmeroda IX.

Saxony

Thuringia

Albrecht Dürer *(1471–1528) is one of the best-known German painters. This great master of the Renaissance period was also an outstanding engraver and art-historian. His* Paumgärtners' Altar *was made for St Catherine's Church in Nuremberg.*

Bavaria

Munich

Wilhelm Leibl *(1844–1900) painted this scene of women praying in a village church in Bavaria,* Three Women in a Church, *which is regarded as one of the outstanding works of German Realism.*

0 kilometres 80

0 miles 80

Castles in Germany

In a number of German regions, medieval castles are among the most character-istic features of the landscape. Some have survived only in the form of picturesque ruins, but many others, refurbished and modernized over the years, continue to be the main residence for the families for whom they were built. The most impressive grouping of great fortresses is to be found along the banks of the Mosel and the central Rhine, while, in the Münster area, you will see the most beautiful moated castles to have survived in the lowlands.

Crest from the castle portal in Gotha

The Great Knights' Hall, where knights ate, drank and entertained, was a feature of every castle.

The 15th-century Michaels-kapelle

Marburg Castle *is one of the best-preserved fortresses in Hesse. At its core is a 12th-century building, but the castle's current appearance is the result of work carried out between the 14th and 16th centuries* (see p369).

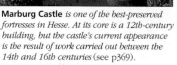

The Royal Room was an apartment specially designated for the use of important guests.

The Wartburg *in Eisenach is one of the most important monu-ments in Thuringia, not only because of its excellently preserved architecture but also for its association with Martin Luther* (see pp186–7).

Heidelberg Castle *has survived as a picturesque ruin. A Gothic-Renaissance structure of imposing proportions, it continues to captivate with its commanding position and fascinating architecture* (see pp298–9).

Gardens were laid out in the 19th century in an area between the castle walls and the site of the farm buildings.

Raesfeld *is one of the most beautiful castles in Münsterland, a region of Westphalia that is renowned for its historic moated castles. The castle was extended in the mid-17th century for Alexandra II von Velen (see p388).*

19TH-CENTURY CASTLES

In the 19th century, many ruined castles in Germany were rebuilt in a wave of nostalgia for the Middle Ages. A number of completely new castles were built, which were modelled on medieval designs.

The Schwerin castle, *built on an island, has a 16th-century chapel, but the rest, dating from 1843–57, was inspired by the French castles along the river Loire (see p470).*

Lichtenstein castle
owes its fame to the novel Lichtenstein *by Wilhelm Hauff and its beauty to the Romantic-style remodelling that was carried out in 1840–41 (see p315).*

Evangelical Chapel

The main entrance to the castle leads through a gate house – here in the form of a tower.

Wernigerode's *castle dominates the entire city. Despite later extensions, it has retained a late-Gothic tower, a beautiful staircase dating from 1495 and some valuable furnishings (see p146).*

BURG HOHENZOLLERN

The family seat of the Hohenzollern family, Burg Hohenzollern in Hechingen, is set on a clifftop in the Swabian Jura. The first building was established here in the 13th century and rebuilt many times over the years. The current medieval appearance is the result of work that was carried out in 1850–67 in the spirit of romantic historicism *(see p314).*

Burg Eltz, *set high above the Mosel, is one of the most beautiful castles in Germany. Built between the 12th and 16th centuries, it has survived with very few alterations (see p345).*

German Scientists and Inventors

Germany is popularly regarded as a nation of practical people, so it is hardly surprising that the history books abound with the names of Germans who have made important contributions to technological progress and the development of science. They include Johann Gutenberg (c.1400–68), who invented printing with movable type, and Karl Benz (1844–1929) and Gottlieb Daimler (1834–1900) who developed the first petrol-driven car. In terms of Nobel Prize winners alone (and not counting those who received the prize for achievements in other fields), there is currently a total of 69 Germans. One of the most illustrious of these is physicist Albert Einstein (1879–1955).

1791 Alexander von Humboldt, a naturalist and geographer, discovers the presence of carbon dioxide in the air

c.1600 Johann Schult invents the dental mirror.

1645 Athanasius Kircher constructs the magic lantern – the first projector

1671 Gottfried Wilhelm Leibniz, philosopher and mathematician, is known for his important philosophical works and his (disputed) claim to have invented differential calculus

c.1707 Johann F Böttger produces the first European porcelain

1718 Jacob Leupold constructs the first decimal scale

1747 Andreas Marggraf succeeds in extracting sugar crystals from sugar beet

1600	1650	1700	1750

1600	1650	1700	1750

1669 Hennig Brand discovers phosphorus

1694 Rudolph Jacob Camerarius discovers the existence of gender in plants, and explains the role of stamens and pollen in fertilization

1781 Martin H Klaproth, chemist, discovers uranium

1740 Johann Pott, porcelain pioneer, discovers manganese

1609, 1619 Johannes Kepler discovers the principal laws of planetary movement

1650 Otto von Guericke, researching air pressure and electrostatic phenomena, develops the vacuum pump

1745 Ewald G Kleist invents the first electric condenser

GERMAN PHILOSOPHERS

German intellectuals have played a major role in the history of philosophy. Gottfried Leibniz (1646–1716), for example, was one of the most renowned exponents of modern rationalism. At the turn of the 18th and 19th centuries, Germany was a fertile source of new ideas, with the work of philosophers such as Immanuel Kant and G W Friedrich Hegel. Karl Marx and Friedrich Engels expounded materialism, while Friedrich Nietzsche developed his cultural and human philosophy. Martin Heidegger and Karl Jaspers were leading existentialists.

Georg Wilhelm Friedrich Hegel (1770–1831)

1813 Karl Freiherr von Drais invents the first two-wheeled vehicle – a kind of bicycle

1989 Wolfgang Paul and Hans Dehmelt receive the Nobel prize for research into nuclear and molecular physics and for their work in the 1950s developing the "Paul trap" – a device for capturing ions

1991 Erwin Neher and Bert Sakmann receive the Nobel prize for research into defining the process of communication between cells

1874 Otto Lilienthal constructs the first glider for engineless flights

1876 Nikolaus Otto invents the internal combustion engine

1987 Georg Bednorz and Karl A Müller receive the Nobel prize for discovering high temperature super-conductivity in metal oxides

1831 Justus von Liebig develops a new method of chemical analysis

1841 Julius Mayer formulates the principle of con-servation of energy

1865 Rudolf J E Clausius formu-lates the second law of thermo-dynamics

1882 Robert Koch discovers the tuber-culosis bacillus (Nobel prize in 1905)

1922 The Nobel Prize is awarded to Albert Einstein, who developed the theory of relativity

1999 Günter Blobel is awarded the Nobel prize for discovering the process that determines the direction of movement and the location of proteins within cells

1850	1900	1950	2000
1850	1900	1950	2000

1885 Karl Benz and Gottlieb Daimler construct the first petrol-driven car

1963 Nobel Prize awarded to Karl Ziegler for his work on industrial production of polymers

1886 Heinrich Hertz discovers radio waves

1918 Nobel Prize awarded to Max K Planck who founded the principles of quantum theory

1944 Nobel Prize awarded to Otto Hahn for discovery (with Lise Meitner) of the process of nuclear fission

1903 Arthur Korn demonstrates how to transmit a photograph from a distance

1866 Ernest W Siemens develops the dynamo

1938 Ernst Ruska and Max Knoll construct the first electron microscope

1850 Wilhelm Bauer constructs a submarine

1841 Christian Schönbein discovers ozone

1941 Konrad Zuse constructs the Z3 calculator – the first digital "computer"

1826 Georg S Ohm shows that the ratio of a steady current to voltage is a constant

1901 Nobel Prize awarded to Wilhelm C Röntgen, for his discovery of X-rays and their uses

German Beer

Although fine wines are produced in Germany, beer is unquestionably the country's favourite alcoholic drink. Germans drink an average of 140 litres of beer annually and Bavarians lead the world in consumption, drinking an average of 240 litres each per annum. Beer is drunk on every occasion, but it tastes best in the summer when it is poured straight from a barrel at one of the numerous festivals or public holidays.

Hop flower cones

The mass *is a tankard that is used to serve beer in Bavaria. It holds a litre, but waitresses are used to carrying eight or nine such tankards at a time.*

Historic brewing facilities in Freising *(see p251)*

GERMAN BREWERIES

In Germany most towns and the larger villages have a brewery. The country's oldest brewery, established in 1040, is the Weihenstephan Benedictine monastery in Freising, which is believed to be the oldest working brewery in the world. Many large breweries and consortiums produce beer that is known throughout the world, but beers produced by small operators, which are available only in a few regional pubs, are in no way inferior. When visiting Germany, do try the produce of small local breweries as well as the beer produced by the giants, such as Paulaner and Löwenbräu.

Logo of the famous Munich brewery, Paulaner

STYLES OF BEER

One of the most popular styles of beer is *Pils* (short for *Pilsener*) a light, bottom-fermented beer of the lager type. Of the seasonal beers, it is worth trying spring beers such as *Maibock* or *Doppelbock*, and in autumn the strong beer that is brewed especially for the Oktoberfest. In the lower Rhine valley, *Altbier* is still produced; this is a top-fermented beer, prepared by traditional methods. In the south, *Weizenbier*, a wheat beer, is also produced. The Berlin version, *Berliner Weisse* (white beer), is served with fruit juice. Dark beers, such as *Dunkel* and *Schwarzbier*, also enjoy great popularity. Breweries have their own specialities. In Bamberg, they produce *Rauchbier*, which has a light smokiness; in Kulmbach it is *Eisbock*, which gains its thicker consistency through a freezing process.

Wheat beer, Berliner Weisse

Seasonal autumn beer, Bock

DRINKING BEER

In Germany, beer is served with a head. Pouring lager from a barrel is supposed to take about 10 minutes, so the head sinks to the regulation level and has a thick consistency. A small beer is normally 0.3 litre, a large one 0.5 litre. In Bavaria, however, a large beer is served in a *Mass*, a tankard holding 1 litre. When travelling in Germany, order the brew of the local brewery, ideally in a *Bierkeller* or *Bierstube* (pub) and, in summer, in a *Biergarten* (beer garden). The largest beer gardens are in Bavaria – Munich's *Hirschgarten* caters for 8,000 beer drinkers. The Oktoberfest, which is celebrated each year in Munich *(see p227)*, is the largest beer festival in the world.

The largest pub in the world, created during the Oktoberfest

HOW BEER IS BREWED

The method of brewing beer that is now virtually standard dates from the 19th century, when Czech brewers first produced bottom-fermented beers at lower temperatures. The method was perfected by Gabriel Sedlmayr. Each brewery has its secrets, but the initial stages of production are the same.

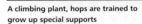

A climbing plant, hops are trained to grow up special supports

Mashing vat

Barley and hops

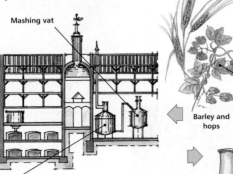

1 *The main ingredients in the production of beer are barley, hops and crystal-clear water. Other grains, including wheat and rice, can also be used – for example Weizenbier is made from wheat rather than barley. The first stage of brewing is malting, when the grains are soaked and left to germinate. After a few days, these are dried and then milled.*

2 *The milled barley is mixed with warm water and placed in a copper mashing vat. During the mashing process, the starches in the grain turn into fermentable sugars. The mash is then filtered to separate out a liquid, known as the wort, from the mash.*

3 *The wort is put into a copper vessel with the hops and then cooked. Depending on the amount of hops added, the beer will be more or less bitter. Traditionally the hops are added to the vessel by hand, in carefully measured proportions. Sometimes, however, they are added, as required, during the cooking process.*

4 *The wort is filtered again, cooled and combined with yeast. Fermentation then takes place. At temperatures above 20° C (68° F), the liquid reaches "top fermentation", which takes 3–5 days. "Bottom fermentation", where the temperature is below 12° C (54° F), takes 7–10 days.*

5 *The young beer produced by fermentation is left to rest in special containers that enable a higher pressure to be maintained. During this resting stage, which can last from a couple of weeks to a year or even longer, the beer matures. The effect of resting the beer is to make it stronger. Resting takes place in metal or traditional wooden barrels.*

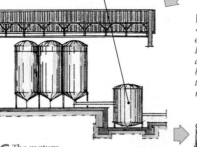

6 *The mature beer, which is ready to be sold, is then transferred to bottles or cans and pasteurized. This process removes micro-organisms that threaten the quality of the beer.*

Traditional wooden barrels containing resting beer

Sport in Germany

Sport has long enjoyed a significant role in German life both for active participants and spectators. The country regularly produces world champions in a variety of activities, including football, tennis and motor racing. Excellent facilities exist throughout the country for taking part in sporting activities, including sailing, swimming, climbing and skiing as well as in field- or track-based events. Southern Germany plays host to a variety of winter sports and competitions.

The German Open in Hamburger Rothenbaum

FOOTBALL

The largest sports organization in the country, the German Football Association has over 6 million registered members in some 25,000 clubs. The national team has won the World Cup three times – in 1954, 1974 and 1990 – and the European Cup in 1972, 1980 and 1996.

One of the outstanding figures in German football is Franz Beckenbauer, who was a member of the team that won the European Cup in 1972 and the World Cup in 1974. He trained the team that took second place in the 1986 World Cup and first place in 1990. Beckenbauer was twice named the best footballer in Europe.

The best-known club is Bayern München, which has won the German Cup a record 16 times. Matches between teams in the elite *Bundesliga* enjoy a great following. League matches are held on Saturday afternoons while European Cup games are usually held on Wednesday evenings. The club teams include a significant number of professionals from abroad. The 2006 World Cup will be held in Germany.

Competing in Hamburg's annual Deutsches Spring Derby

SHOW-JUMPING AND EQUESTRIAN EVENTS

Show-jumping is another sport at which Germany excels. Since it was introduced to the Olympic Games in 1912, German riders have won 32 gold, 18 silver and 21 bronze medals. Major equestrian events are held in Hamburg and Aachen in June. Hamburg's Derby Week is popular with racing fans.

LAWN TENNIS

The German Tennis Association is the largest in the world with over 2 million members, belonging to some 10,200 clubs. From the mid-1980s, Germany became one of the world's most successful tennis nations thanks to some outstanding players. In 1985, aged 18, Boris Becker was the youngest player to win the Wimbledon championships. He repeated his achievement in 1986 and 1989 and was runner-up to fellow-German Michael Stich in 1991. From 1987–91 Steffi Graf was ranked number one among the world's female tennis players.

ATHLETICS

During the Cold War period, East and West German athletes competed against each other for the glory of their rival political systems as much as for the love of their sport. The extraordinary achievements of the East German athletes during that time have since been tarnished by revelations of systematic drug abuse. Since reunification, some athletes have managed to maintain their reputations, but the majority have not.

Germany's most important event, the International Stadionfest (ISTAF), is held each year in Berlin, as the climax of the season.

***Bundesliga* football match (Hertha BSC Berlin v FC Bayern München)**

FORMULA ONE

Back in the 1930s, motor-racing was dominated by the famous "Silver Arrows", made by Mercedes-Benz. Formula One has been a decidedly German discipline since its beginnings in 1950. In all the events there have always been at least three German drivers taking part. The German Formula One Grand Prix is held each July at the Hockenheim-Ring, near Heidelberg. In most years there is a second Grand Prix at the Nürburgring circuit close to the Belgian border. This is dubbed the European Grand Prix or the Luxembourg Grand Prix.

Germany's leading Formula One driver, Michael Schumacher, won the World Championship in 1994, 1995 and 2000. He has also twice achieved second place and been twice in third place.

The Hockenheim race track near Heidelberg

Markus Eberle during the slalom in Ofterschwang in the Allgäu

SKIING

Since 1953, the last week of December and the first week of January have been dominated by the Four Ski Jumps Championship for ski jumpers. This classic event, which is held in Oberstdorf and Garmisch-Partenkirchen in Germany, as well as in Innsbruck and Bischofshofen in Austria, attracts several thousand spectators and millions of television viewers. German athletes have gained first place in this competition 15 times over the years.

As well as in the German Alps, which have the most popular ski resorts, excellent conditions exist for downhill and cross-country skiing in the less glamorous and less expensive Black Forest and the Harz Mountains.

CYCLING

Cycling enjoys a great following in Germany. The Tour de France is broadcast simultaneously by two television stations, and ever-increasing numbers of people are taking part in the sport, both for pleasure and competitively. Success on the cycle track has long been a German tradition, but Jan Ullrich exceeded all expectations when he won gold in the long distance and silver in a time trial at the Sydney Olympics in 2000.

SAILING

Kieler Woche is the most important regatta in the world, according to Paul Henderson, the President of the International Sailing Federation. On 1 September 1881, five officers of the Emperor's navy held a yachting race in the Bay of Kiel, as it was then called. The following year 20 yachts competed while thousands of spectators watched from the shore. The championship went on to become an international event, which gained in prestige as the Emperor took part in each race from 1894 until 1914.

Today it is traditional for the president of the German Federal Republic to formally open the regatta (in the last week of June) in which thousands of yachts from many countries take part.

SWIMMING

Swimming, more than any other sport in Germany, has seen a decline in success since reunification and the subsequent cessation of competition between East and West. At the 1988 Olympics in Seoul, for example, Kristin Otto won 6 gold medals. In 2000, the reunified German team returned from Sydney having gained only three bronze medals. Two figures who rose to the top in the past are Michael Gross, who was a member of the West German team, and Franziska van Almsick, a member of the East German team.

Franziska von Almsick during the German Swimming Championships

GERMANY THROUGH THE YEAR

Germans love to have fun and this is evident from the huge number of light-hearted events that are held throughout the year. Virtually every town has a calendar of festivals and fairs. These include folk festivals connected with local traditions – for example celebrating the asparagus or grape harvest.

A festival mascot

Many towns preserve the tradition of an annual fair – or *Jahrmarkt* – known in Westphalia as *Kirmes* and in Bavaria as *Dult*. Germany is also known for its music and film festivals, which attract an international audience, as well as for organizing major international trade fairs, such as the annual Frankfurt Book Fair.

Witches participating in the Walpurgisnacht celebrations in Thale

Hannover Messe *(2nd half of April)* Hanover. International industrial trade fairs.

Hamburger Dom *(April, August and November)* Hamburg. The largest folk festival in northern Germany, held three times a year.

Walpurgisnacht *(30 April/ 1 May).* On the witches' sabbath, witches gather on Brocken Mountain and in several other places in the Harz mountains.

SPRING

Spring is an idyllic time to arrive in Germany. In the high mountains, conditions are still ideal for skiing, while in the valleys everything is already in bloom. In April and May the first spring fairs and festivals are held. Spring is also time for the traditional solemn observance of Easter and its associated celebrations. May Day, which is also International Labour Day, is marked both by traditional festivities and, in some cities, by demonstrations.

MARCH

Sommergewinn *(3 weekends before Easter)* Eisenach. The largest folk festival in Thuringia, linked with a fair.

CeBIT *(end of March)* Hanover. International trade fairs dedicated to information technology, telecommunications and automation.

Easter During Holy Week, Passion concerts are held throughout the country and colourful church services take place, particularly in

rural Catholic areas. On Easter Sunday, in cities in the Luzyce region, horse races and a gala take place.

Leipziger Buchmesse *(end of March)* Leipzig. International book fair, with antiquarian books.

Thüringer Bach-Wochen Celebration of the life and works of Johann Sebastian Bach with concerts and lectures: held in Arnstadt, Eisenach, Erfurt, Gotha, Mühlhausen and Weimar.

APRIL

Kurzfilmtage Oberhausen. The International Festival of Short Films has been held here since 1955.

The International Dixieland Festival, held annually in Dresden in May

MAY

Maibaumaufstellen *(1 May).* In Bavarian villages, maypoles are decorated with highly ornamental wreaths.

Rhein in Flammen *(1st Saturday in May).* Festival with firework displays, in towns in the Rhine Valley.

Hafengeburtstag *(7 May)* Hamburg. A huge festival with fireworks, regatta and a parade of sailing boats.

Ruhrfestspiele *(May–July)* Recklinghausen. Cultural festival with a number of concerts, performances and exhibitions.

International Dixieland Festival *(2nd week of May)* Dresden. A traditional jazz festival has been held here since 1971.

Blutritt *(Friday after Ascension)* Weingarten. A horseback procession carrying religious relics around the town – held here for 450 years,

Leineweber Markt *(end of May)* Bielefeld. Street theatre, jazz and folk concerts.

SUMMER

In Germany the summer is a time of great open-air festivals and other outdoor events and activities. Nearly every town and village has its festival with a parade, street shows, concerts and fairs. In many places there are colourful illuminations and firework displays. Banquets and knights' tournaments are held in historic castles, while concert series are organized in palaces and castles with the tourist particularly in mind. In June, a number of classical music festivals take place, while July is a popular month for wine and beer festivals.

Yacht race during the annual Kieler Woche regatta in Kiel

JUNE

Spreewaldfest *(June)* Spreewald. Folk festivals are held throughout the summer in Lübbenau and other villages in Spreewald.
Fronleichnam. Observed in states with a Catholic majority. Magnificent processions take place in towns in Bavaria and in Cologne.
Christopher Street Day *(mid-June)*. Gay and lesbian parades held in many cities, including Berlin and Köln.
Kieler Woche *(3rd week in June)* Kiel. Huge yachting regatta with concerts and street fairs.
Open-Air-Saison *(4th week in June, beginning of July)* Berlin. Opera festival held on outdoor stages and in squares in the city.

A wedding couple during the Landshuter Hochzeit festival

Schützenfest *(June)* marks the traditional start of the hunting season. Celebrated in many north German cities.

JULY

Landshuter Hochzeit *(every 4th summer: 2005; 2009)* Landshut. Re-enactment of the wedding feast of Georg, son of Duke Ludwig the Rich and Polish Princess Jadwiga. Costumed wedding procession and medieval tournament.
Love Parade *(2nd Saturday)* Berlin. A parade for fans of techno music, who dance throughout the day and night in all the city's discos and around vehicles equipped with sound systems.

Internationaler Johann-Sebastian-Bach Wettbewerb Leipzig. International music competition dedicated to Johann Sebastian Bach.
Schwörmontag *(penultimate Monday)* Ulm. Folk festival with a parade by the Danube.
Kinderzeche *(3rd Monday)* Dinkelsbühl. Ten-day folk festival commemorating the events of the Thirty Years' War (1618–48).
Richard-Wagner-Festspiele *(last week July/August)* Bayreuth. Festival dedicated to the works of Richard Wagner.

AUGUST

Zissel *(beginning of August)* Kassel. Picturesque folk festival with parades, markets and concerts.
Mainfest. Frankfurt am Main. Feast of the river Main.
Gäubodenfest *(mid-August)* Straubing. Folk festival with a market and beer tasting.
Rhein in Flammen *(2nd Saturday)* Koblenz. Huge firework display on the Rhine and a flotilla of illuminated passenger ships.
Wikingerfest *(even years)* Schleswig. Historical festival with costumed participants, tournaments and regattas.
Weindorf *(end August)* Stuttgart. Huge wine festival with wines served along with typical Swabian cuisine.

Performance of *Tannhäuser* at Richard-Wagner-Festspiele, Bayreuth

AUTUMN

Autumn is a popular time for tourism in Germany, especially September and early October when many cities, including Berlin and Munich, organize cultural events and important festivals. The autumn is also the time when the most significant trade fairs and great sporting events take place. At this time, also, conditions in the mountains and countryside continue to be ideal for outdoor activities such as walking and cycling.

SEPTEMBER

Berliner Festwochen, Berlin. Lasting all month, this is a major series of cultural events, opera performances, exhibitions and various literary events.
Beethovenfestival, Bonn. A musical festival of the works of Beethoven in the city where he was born.
Heilbronner Herbst *(1st Saturday)* Heilbronn. Wine festival, including parades and firework displays.
Berlin-Marathon *(Last Sunday)* Berlin. Marathon through the streets of the city centre, with runners in various age groups and the participation of the disabled in wheelchairs.
Oktoberfest *(last Saturday)* Munich. Beer festival held

Pumpkin race during Dorffest

over 16 days, beginning with a parade through the city's streets. Ceremonial removal of the bung from a new barrel of beer brewed for the festival.
Plärrer *(May and September)* Augsburg. Festival held twice a year, considered one of the most important in Swabia.
Dorffest im Spreewald *(end)* Lehde. Folk festival.
Cannstatter Wasen *(end September/beginning October)* Stuttgart. The second largest beer festival in the world.
Internationales Stadionfest (ISTAF), *(1st Sunday of September)* Berlin. The largest athletics event at the end of the season.

OCTOBER

Tag der Deutschen Einheit *(3 October).* National holiday, established after re-unification. Concerts, parades and meetings.
Frankfurter Buchmesse *(2nd week in October)* Frankfurt am Main. The world's largest book fair, which attracts publishers from around the world.
Freimarkt *(mid-October)* Bremen. Two-week folk festival beginning with a procession.
Liszt-Tage Weimar. Celebration of the life and work of Franz Liszt, with concerts at which world-class musicians are invited to perform.
Ost-West Jazz Festival *(end October)* Nuremberg. International jazz folk festival.
Colmansfest *(2nd Sunday)* Schwangau. Religious festival featuring hundreds of horses and decorated carriages.

NOVEMBER

St Leonard's Day *(1st Sunday in November).* Folk festival in Bavaria, which is held in conjunction with horse parades.
Kasseler Musiktage *(beginning of November)* Kassel. One of Europe's longest-established classical music festivals.
Weinfest *(1st weekend in November)* Cochem. Festival celebrating the removal of the bung from the first barrel of young Mosel wine.
Martinsfest *(11 November).* St Martin's Day is celebrated in northern Baden and the Rhineland with fairs and the essential roast goose. In the Rhine Valley, St Martin's Day signifies the beginning of the Carnival season.
Internationales Film-festival *(2nd week in November)* Mannheim-Heidelberg. Annual festival of short, documentary and educational films.

The International Book Fair in Frankfurt am Main

Berlinale – the grand festival of world cinema

WINTER

December is synonymous with Christmas festivities. Every city has fairs where you can buy Christmas-tree decorations, delicacies and presents. In December, shops have longer opening hours and the skiing season begins in the Alps. January and February are a time for parties and balls (the Carnival season), with enjoyment reaching a peak in the last few days of the season. Then the fun continues all weekend from Thursday, reaching a height on *Rosenmontag* then diminishing on the last Tuesday of Carnival.

DECEMBER

Christkindelsmarkt and **Weihnachtsmarkt**. Christmas fairs are held from the

The famous Christmas market in the city of Nuremberg

beginning of the month until Christmas Eve. The most beautiful are in Baden-Wurttemberg and in Bavaria, while the most renowned is held in Nuremberg.

Christmas *(25/26 December)*. Traditionally celebrated throughout Germany. A Christmas tree is considered essential, together with presents and delicacies.

New Year's Eve *(31 December)*. The New Year is greeted at balls, opera galas, in restaurants, clubs, private houses and in the streets and squares of city centres.

JANUARY

Four Ski Jumps Tournament *(begins 1 January)*. Renowned tournament for ski-jumping held annually in Garmisch-Partenkirchen.

Sechs-Tage-Rennen *(begins 1 January)* Berlin. Spectacular cycle races with associated events, held in Berlin Velodrome.

Grüne Woche *(last week)* Berlin. International trade fairs dedicated to agriculture, animal breeding and the food processing industry. Producers from all over the world offer specialities from their own national cuisines.

FEBRUARY

Berlinale–Internationale Filmfestspiele *(2nd and 3rd weeks)* Berlin. International film festival in which major stars participate.

Fastnacht, also known as **Fasnet, Fasching** or **Karneval** (Shrovetide). Carnival is celebrated enthusiastically in virtually every region of Germany. The most interesting events are held in the Rhine Valley, and particularly in Cologne. *Karneval am Rhein*, which marks the lasts three days of the Carnival, begins on the Thursday of the week before Ash Wednesday with a women's parade, known as *Weiberfastnacht*. On the Monday there is a superb costume parade, known as *Rosenmontagsumzug*.

Costumed revellers on the streets of Cologne during Carnival

PUBLIC HOLIDAYS

Neujahr *New Year* (1 Jan).

Hl. Dreikönige *Three Kings* (6 Jan: Bavaria, Baden-Wurttemberg, Saxony-Anhalt).

Karfreitag *Good Friday.*

Ostern *Easter.*

Maifeiertag/Tag der Arbeit *Labour Day.*

Christi Himmelfahrt *Ascension.*

Pfingsten *Pentecost.*

Fronleichnam *Corpus Christi* (Bavaria, Baden-Wurttemberg, Hesse, North Rhine Valley-Westphalia, Rhine Valley-Palatinate and Saar).

Mariä Himmelfahrt *Assumption of the BVM* (15 Aug: Bavaria, Saar).

Nationalfeiertag *Reunification of Germany Day* (3 Oct).

Allerheiligen *All Saints* (1 Nov: Bavaria, Baden-Wurttemberg, North Rhine Valley-Westphalia, Rhine Valley-Palatinate).

Weihnachten *Christmas* (25/26 Dec).

The German Climate

Germany lies in a temperate climatic zone. In the north of the country, with marine influences predominating, summers tend to be quite cold and winters mild, with relatively high rainfall. In the eastern part of the country, however, the climate is more continental and this produces harsher winters and hotter summers. Germany's highest rainfall and the lowest temperatures are recorded in the Alps.

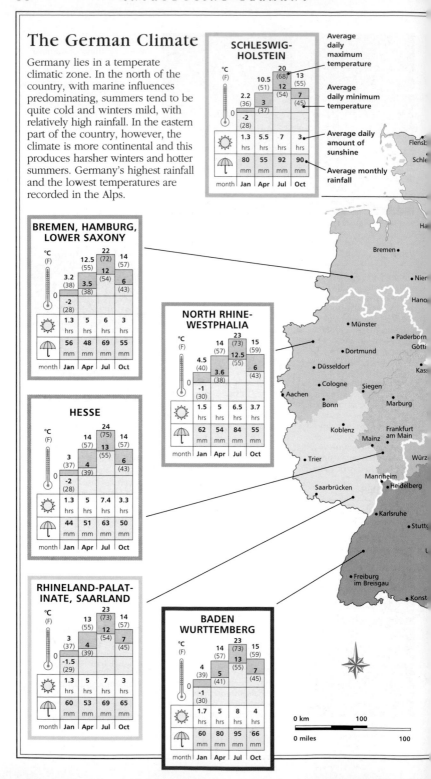

SCHLESWIG-HOLSTEIN

	Jan	Apr	Jul	Oct
max temp °C (F)	2.2 (36)	10.5 (51)	20 (68)	13 (55)
min temp °C (F)	-2 (28)	3 (37)	12 (54)	7 (45)
sunshine	1.3 hrs	5.5 hrs	7 hrs	3 hrs
rainfall	80 mm	55 mm	92 mm	90 mm
month	Jan	Apr	Jul	Oct

- Average daily maximum temperature
- Average daily minimum temperature
- Average daily amount of sunshine
- Average monthly rainfall

BREMEN, HAMBURG, LOWER SAXONY

	Jan	Apr	Jul	Oct
°C (F) max	3.2 (38)	12.5 (55)	22 (72)	14 (57)
°C (F) min	-2 (28)	3.5 (38)	12 (54)	6 (43)
sunshine	1.3 hrs	5 hrs	6 hrs	3 hrs
rainfall	56 mm	48 mm	69 mm	55 mm
month	Jan	Apr	Jul	Oct

NORTH RHINE-WESTPHALIA

	Jan	Apr	Jul	Oct
°C (F) max	4.5 (40)	14 (57)	23 (73)	15 (59)
°C (F) min	-1 (30)	3.6 (38)	12.5 (55)	6 (43)
sunshine	1.5 hrs	5 hrs	6.5 hrs	3.7 hrs
rainfall	62 mm	54 mm	84 mm	55 mm
month	Jan	Apr	Jul	Oct

HESSE

	Jan	Apr	Jul	Oct
°C (F) max	3 (37)	14 (57)	24 (75)	14 (57)
°C (F) min	-2 (28)	4 (39)	13 (55)	6 (43)
sunshine	1.3 hrs	5 hrs	7.4 hrs	3.3 hrs
rainfall	44 mm	51 mm	63 mm	50 mm
month	Jan	Apr	Jul	Oct

RHINELAND-PALATINATE, SAARLAND

	Jan	Apr	Jul	Oct
°C (F) max	3 (37)	13 (55)	23 (73)	14 (57)
°C (F) min	-1.5 (29)	4 (39)	12 (54)	7 (45)
sunshine	1.3 hrs	5 hrs	7 hrs	3 hrs
rainfall	60 mm	53 mm	69 mm	65 mm
month	Jan	Apr	Jul	Oct

BADEN WURTTEMBERG

	Jan	Apr	Jul	Oct
°C (F) max	4 (39)	14 (57)	23 (73)	15 (59)
°C (F) min	-1 (30)	5 (41)	13 (55)	7 (45)
sunshine	1.7 hrs	5 hrs	8 hrs	4 hrs
rainfall	60 mm	80 mm	95 mm	66 mm
month	Jan	Apr	Jul	Oct

Flensb
Schle
Ha
Bremen
Nier
Hano
Münster
Paderborn
Götti
Dortmund
Düsseldorf
Kass
Cologne
Siegen
Aachen
Bonn
Marburg
Koblenz
Frankfurt am Main
Mainz
Würz
Trier
Mannheim
Saarbrücken
Heidelberg
Karlsruhe
Stutt
Freiburg im Breisgau
Konst

0 km   100

0 miles   100

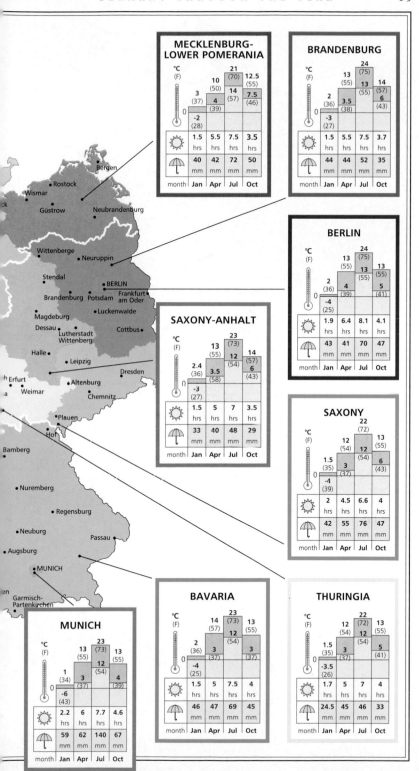

MECKLENBURG-LOWER POMERANIA

month	Jan	Apr	Jul	Oct
°C (F) max	3 (37)	10 (50)	21 (70)	12.5 (55)
°C (F) min	-2 (28)	4 (39)	14 (57)	7.5 (46)
☼	1.5 hrs	5.5 hrs	7.5 hrs	3.5 hrs
☂	40 mm	42 mm	72 mm	50 mm

BRANDENBURG

month	Jan	Apr	Jul	Oct
°C (F) max	2 (36)	13 (55)	24 (75)	14 (57)
°C (F) min	-3 (27)	3.5 (38)	13 (55)	6 (43)
☼	1.5 hrs	5.5 hrs	7.5 hrs	3.7 hrs
☂	44 mm	44 mm	52 mm	35 mm

BERLIN

month	Jan	Apr	Jul	Oct
°C (F) max	2 (36)	13 (55)	24 (75)	13 (55)
°C (F) min	-4 (25)	4 (39)	13 (55)	5 (41)
☼	1.9 hrs	6.4 hrs	8.1 hrs	4.1 hrs
☂	43 mm	41 mm	70 mm	47 mm

SAXONY-ANHALT

month	Jan	Apr	Jul	Oct
°C (F) max	2.4 (36)	13 (55)	23 (73)	14 (57)
°C (F) min	-3 (27)	3.5 (58)	12 (54)	6 (43)
☼	1.5 hrs	5 hrs	7 hrs	3.5 hrs
☂	33 mm	40 mm	48 mm	29 mm

SAXONY

month	Jan	Apr	Jul	Oct
°C (F) max	1.5 (35)	12 (54)	22 (72)	13 (55)
°C (F) min	-4 (39)	3 (37)	12 (54)	6 (43)
☼	2 hrs	4.5 hrs	6.6 hrs	4 hrs
☂	42 mm	55 mm	76 mm	47 mm

BAVARIA

month	Jan	Apr	Jul	Oct
°C (F) max	2 (36)	14 (57)	23 (73)	13 (55)
°C (F) min	-4 (25)	3 (37)	12 (54)	3 (37)
☼	1.5 hrs	5 hrs	7.5 hrs	4 hrs
☂	46 mm	47 mm	69 mm	45 mm

THURINGIA

month	Jan	Apr	Jul	Oct
°C (F) max	1.5 (35)	12 (54)	22 (72)	13 (55)
°C (F) min	-3.5 (26)	3 (37)	12 (54)	5 (41)
☼	1.7 hrs	5 hrs	7 hrs	4 hrs
☂	24.5 mm	45 mm	46 mm	33 mm

MUNICH

month	Jan	Apr	Jul	Oct
°C (F) max	1 (34)	13 (55)	23 (73)	13 (55)
°C (F) min	-6 (43)	3 (37)	12 (54)	4 (39)
☼	2.2 hrs	6 hrs	7.7 hrs	4.6 hrs
☂	59 mm	62 mm	140 mm	67 mm

Bergen
Rostock
Wismar
Güstrow
Neubrandenburg
Wittenberge
Neuruppin
Stendal
BERLIN
Brandenburg
Potsdam
Frankfurt am Oder
Magdeburg
Luckenwalde
Dessau
Lutherstadt Wittenberg
Cottbus
Halle
Leipzig
Dresden
Erfurt
Altenburg
Weimar
Chemnitz
Plauen
Hof
Bamberg
Nuremberg
Regensburg
Neuburg
Passau
Augsburg
MUNICH
Garmisch-Partenkirchen

THE HISTORY OF GERMANY

*G*ermany is a country of cultural and religious contrasts. Regional differences in culture, language and traditions arose from the historical division of the country into many small states. Such differences have been further accentuated by the recent experience of generations of Germans who, until 1990, grew up under two conflicting social systems: capitalism and communism.

EARLY HISTORY

In the 1st millennium BC, the basins of the Rhine, Danube and Main rivers were settled by Celts, who had been largely displaced by Germanic tribes by the 2nd century BC. In the 1st century BC the Roman legions waged wars with the Germans, and conquered the territories west of the Rhine. The settlements they founded there later developed into towns like Trier, Mainz, Cologne and Xanten. The Romans made numerous attempts to conquer the eastern regions between the Rhine and the Elbe rivers. They eventually reached the Elbe at the end of the 1st century BC, but the Germans, under the leadership of Arminius, also known as Germanus, defeated the Roman armies in the Teutoburg Forest in AD 9, and so ended their presence in this region. A system of fortifications, or *limes,* built in the 2nd century along the course of the Danube and the Rhine, divided the region into two: *Germania Romana,* the Roman province, and *Germania Libra,* free Germany. The free German tribes,

Heinrich I, from the house of Liudolf

notably the Goths, often entered into alliances with the Romans. In the 5th century, however, they took advantage of Rome's weakness to appropriate parts of the empire for themselves.

EARLY MIDDLE AGES

After the collapse of the Roman Empire, the area between the Rhine and the Elbe was ruled by Franks, who gradually converted to Christianity from the 6th century. One of the most important figures in this process was the 8th-century missionary, St Boniface. When Charlemagne was crowned Emperor in 800, the territory of present-day Germany became part of the Frankish Empire. The Empire was partitioned by the Treaty of Verdun in 843, with the eastern part going to Ludwig the German. In the 10th century the kingdom, which was made up of numerous tribal states, passed to the house of Liudolf. Otto I, son of Heinrich I and the first king from this Saxon family, was crowned Emperor in 962 after several political and military victories, in particular his defeat of the Magyars.

TIMELINE

Golden Roman mask

754 Death of St Boniface

785 Baptism of Widukind, Duke of Saxony

800 Charlemagne crowned Emperor of the Franks

814 Death of Charlemagne

843 Treaty of Verdun and dissolution of the Frankish state

936 Otto I crowned King

955 Otto I defeats the Magyars at the Lech River near Augsburg

919 Coronation of the Saxon Heinrich I

962 Otto I crowned Emperor

700   800   900   1000

8th-century reliquary

◁ **Germany's Awakening,** a patriotic 19th-century work by Christian Köhler

Stained-glass window in Augsburg cathedral

CONSOLIDATING POWER

With Otto being crowned emperor, the dynasty of the Saxon house of Liudolf acceded to power. It gave the country three further rulers – Otto II, Otto III and Heinrich II. In the year 925 Otto I annexed Lotharingia (present-day Lorraine). On the eastern frontier he created two "marks", the Nordmark and the Ostmark, as buffer states designed to subjugate the Slav-populated regions east of the Oder River. After Heinrich II's death, the house of the Salian Franks took the imperial throne and used their authority to limit the power of the local feudal dukes.

THE INVESTITURE CONTROVERSY

In the 11th century the empire came into conflict with the papacy. Matters came to a head in the so-called "investiture controversy". Pope Gregory VII asserted the church's right to appoint bishops. Emperor Heinrich IV meanwhile, who had been relying on the support of the clergy he had appointed, called his bishops together and asked the Pope to step down. Pope Gregory VII excommunicated Heinrich.

The dukes of Saxony used the opportunity to appoint a king in opposition to Heinrich, and the Pope attempted to intervene in the dispute. Heinrich IV saw himself forced to march to Canossa in Italy, where the Pope had sought refuge, in order to stop his empire from falling apart. Doing penance in this way forced the Pope to withdraw his excommunication. However, the dispute did not end there, but continued for several years, finally ending with the Signing of the Concordat of Worms in 1122.

Enamelled Romanesque medallion, dating from c.1150

HOHENSTAUFENS AND WELFS

After the Salian dynasty died out in 1125 and the brief reign of Lothar III of the Saxon dynasty, another long drawn-out conflict broke out, between the houses of Hohenstaufen and Welf (known in Italian as Ghibellines and Guelphs). Imperial power went to the Hohenstaufens, while the greatest political victories were scored by Friedrich I Barbarossa (meaning "red beard"). He intended gradually to break up his subject principalities and to rule them under a feudal system. The 12th century also saw further expansion eastwards and northwards into areas inhabited by the northwestern Slavic tribes. From the start of the 13th

12th-century reliquary from the Welf family vaults

TIMELINE

1027 Coronation of Konrad II, first Emperor of the Salians

1138 Coronation of Konrad III, first Hohenstaufen Emperor

1155 Coronation of Friedrich I Barbarossa as Emperor

| 1000 | 1050 | 1100 | 1150 |

11th-century reliquary cross

1074 Beginning of Investiture Struggle

1077 Heinrich IV does penance at Canossa

1122 The Concordat of Worms

Portable altar from the vaults of the Welfs

century Barbarossa also conquered territories occupied by the Baltic peoples and the Estonians, which involved armed expeditions by the North German cities and orders of knights.

Friedrich II, crowned Emperor in 1220, was also King of Sicily and his Italian interests brought further conflict with the papacy. Ultimately his policies brought about the collapse of imperial power. After his death in 1250, his successor was unable to find any support, which led to the period known as the Great Interregnum.

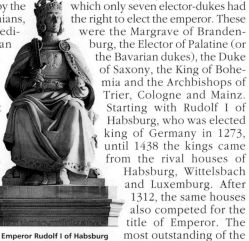
Emperor Rudolf I of Habsburg

13th century a system evolved by which only seven elector-dukes had the right to elect the emperor. These were the Margrave of Brandenburg, the Elector of Palatine (or the Bavarian dukes), the Duke of Saxony, the King of Bohemia and the Archbishops of Trier, Cologne and Mainz. Starting with Rudolf I of Habsburg, who was elected king of Germany in 1273, until 1438 the kings came from the rival houses of Habsburg, Wittelsbach and Luxemburg. After 1312, the same houses also competed for the title of Emperor. The most outstanding of the 14th-century rulers of Germany was Karl IV of Luxemburg, who resided permanently in Prague. In 1338 the electors had rejected the requirement for the Pope to confirm election results. In 1356 Karl IV issued the "Golden Bull" which underlined the federal nature of the state, and clarified the rules for electing its leader.

THE INTERREGNUM

The fall of the Hohenstaufens marked the end of the old imperial system. The absence of an overall ruler led to a breakdown in law and order, and resulted in the rise of the *Raubritter* (robber barons). To protect their common interests, the trading cities set up alliances. The collapse of imperial power, and the decline in the power of the dukes thus gradually led to an increase in the power of the German cities.

From the beginning the imperial throne had been elective, with dukes electing the emperor from the male members of the dynasty. There was also no capital city, as the emperors moved from one city to another, thus spreading the costs of maintaining the imperial court among different duchies. In the

A "Minneteppich" – part of a medieval tapestry, depicting a variety of human traits and a griffin, the mythical beast

1250 Beginning of the Great Interregnum

1312 Heinrich VII crowned Emperor

Silver coin from 1369

| 1200 | 1250 | 1300 | 1350 |

1273 End of the Great Interregnum and coronation of Rudolf I

1348 Prague University founded

1356 Golden Bull issued

1386 Heidelberg University founded

The Hanseatic League

The German Hanseatic League, or Hanse, was only one of many guilds of traders or cities that existed in the Middle Ages, but its important historical role made it one of the best known. Established in the 13th century, it reached its peak in the 14th century and declined again in the 16th century. Over 160 cities, primarily the trading cities of northern Germany, but also including Baltic ports as far afield as Visby, Riga and Tallinn, joined the League. It exercised total control over trade from the Baltic in the east to England in the west. The Hanseatic cities were among the wealthiest in Europe, and crafts and the arts flourished there.

Madonna of the Roses
15th-century painting by Stefan Lochner of the Cologne School.

The Wise and Foolish Maidens
The flowering of art in the Hanseatic cities brought about works such as this portal of Magdeburg Cathedral.

Hanse ships, loaded with merchandise, entering the harbour

Revenue officials awaiting the cargo

Round wooden cranes with swivelling arms were used to unload ships. One example still survives in Lüneburg.

Crucifix in Lübeck Cathedral
This crucifix is one of only few painted woodcarvings made by Bernt Notke of Lübeck that have survived until today.

Cogs
Cogs – heavy, flat-bottomed sailing ships with limited manoeuvrability – were fishermen's and merchants' boats or navy vessels in the North Sea and the Baltic from the 12th to the 14th centuries.

Panoramic view of Lübeck
The vast port town of Lübeck was the largest Hanseatic city. This 15th-century woodcut shows a view of the city with its numerous church spires.

THE HANSEATIC CITIES

In the major Hanseatic cities, the most prominent buildings grew up around the *Markt* (market square) and along the streets that led to the port. The market square would contain the *Rathaus* (town hall), with its multi-functional interiors, and the equally splendid banqueting halls and ballrooms, such as the Gürzenich in Cologne. The main cathedrals in the cities were dedicated either to St Mary or St Nicholas. The gabled residential houses had narrow façades with distinctive portals. The townscape of the port areas was dominated by granaries, warehouses and numerous cranes. The cities were all enclosed and protected by solid fortifications.

Harbour officials in their offices

The Leichter was a harbour boat used to carry cargo from the ships to the warehouses.

Hamburg merchants

Russian merchants, recognizable by their distinctive clothing, are engrossed in intense negotiations.

The town hall in Brunswick, *with its open upper arcades and statues of the Welfs, is one of the finest surviving Hanseatic secular buildings.*

The Kröpeliner Tor *in Rostock* (see p476) *is one of 22 towers on the defensive walls around the medieval city centre.*

THE PORT OF HAMBURG

Hamburg, along with Bremen, Lübeck and Gdansk, was one of the leading Hanseatic cities. In the 14th century, it was the main centre for trade between the North Sea and the Baltic. This miniature, showing the port of Hamburg, dates from the 15th century.

Jan Hus being burned at the stake

THE HUSSITE WARS AND THE HABSBURG DYNASTY

The last king and emperor of the house of Luxemburg, Sigismund, brought an end to the "Great Schism" in the Western church that had persisted since 1378. The Council of Constance, which he called in 1414, led to the election of a single, rather than two rival popes. However, new religious controversy was provoked by the death sentence for heresy passed in 1415 on Jan Hus, a religious reformer from Bohemia. The ensuing Hussite Wars ravaged the northern and western regions of Germany.

From 1482 the imperial crown went to the Habsburgs, who retained it

Title page of the first German edition of the Bible

until 1740. Attempts at political reform in the second half of the 15th century failed. The most ambitious reformer was Maximilian I. He called an Imperial Tribunal in 1495 which set about transferring part of the king's authority to the judiciary; however, it did not result in any great practical changes, although it gave slightly more power to the *Reichstag*, the imperial parliament

THE REFORMATION

Germany entered the 16th century as a country simmering with social conflict, gradually becoming steeped in the ideas of humanism, thanks to the writings of Erasmus of Rotterdam and others. The rise of Martin Luther, who in 1517 nailed his 95 Theses to the door of the Castle Church in Wittenberg, and who opposed the trade in

Lion-shaped water jug (1540)

indulgences conducted by the clergy, set the Reformation in motion *(see pp126–7)*. The idea of ecclesiastical reform propounded by Luther gained a growing following. His supporters included princes who hoped to profit from the secularization of church property, as well as other social classes that simply saw an opportunity to improve their lot. In 1519 Maximilian I died, and Karl V was elected to succeed him. Karl's interests were focused on Spain and the Netherlands, and he was unable to prevent the spread of Lutheranism.

TIMELINE

1419–36 Hussite Wars	**c.1450** The first printing press	**1540** The first stock exchanges are s up in Augsburg and Nürnbe
		Maximilian I **1517** Luther's Theses and the start of the Reformation
1400	**1450**	**1500**
1414–18 Council of Constance	**1438** Coronation of Albrecht II, first Emperor of the House of Habsburg	**1495** Edict banning the waging of private wars **1522** The Knights' War **1524–25** Peasants'

Urban life in Germany in the early 16th century, in a painting by Jörg Breu the Elder (c.1475–1537)

The unrest led to rebellions such as the Knights' War of 1522 and the Peasants' War of 1524, and these were followed by continuous religious conflict. In 1530 the Protestants set up the League of Schmalkalden, which was finally broken up by the Emperor in the war of 1546–7. These basically religious clashes ultimately led to the division of Germany into a northern Protestant part and a Catholic south, a situation that was sanctioned in 1555 by the Peace of Augsburg. This established the principle of *cuius regio, eius religio*, which meant that each ruler had the right to decide on the faith of the region, and the only option left for anyone of a different persuasion was to move elsewhere.

THE THIRTY YEARS' WAR

The second half of the 16th century was relatively stable for Germany, despite the religious conflicts. However, the influ-ence of the Counter-Reformation in the early 17th century ended this stability. The Protestant Union and Catholic League were established in 1608 and 1609 respectively. Unrest in Prague, where the states with a Protestant majority opposed the election of the Catholic Ferdinand II as king of Bohemia, began the Thirty Years' War. This religious war quickly spread throughout Germany, and also drew in Denmark, Spain, Sweden and France. Much of the country and many towns were laid waste, and vast numbers of people died. Finally, in 1648, the German states, France and Sweden signed the Peace of Westphalia in Münster, resulting in major losses of territory for Germany, mainly in the north. A new political system emerged, with the German princes enjoying complete political independence, under a weakened emperor and pope. The second half of the 17th century was marked by the rebuilding of towns and the hard work of restoring the ruined economic infrastructure.

A scene in the Thirty Years' War, in a painting by Wilhelm von Diez

Goethe in the Roman Campagna by Johann H. W. Tischbein (1787)

ABSOLUTISM AND
THE RISE OF PRUSSIA

In the second half of the 17th century and throughout the 18th century, Germany was a loose federation of small, politically weak states in the west, and much more powerful states in the east and the south – Saxony, which was ruled by the house of Wettin, and Bavaria, ruled by the Wittelsbachs. However, the rising star was the state of Brandenburg, ruled by the house of Hohenzollern, which from 1657 also ruled Prussia. In 1701 the Elector Friedrich III crowned himself King of Prussia (as Friedrich I), and subsequently the name "Prussia" was applied to all areas ruled by the house of Hohenzollern. During the 18th century Prussia became the greatest rival to Habsburg Austria. In 1740, Friedrich II, also known as Frederick the Great,

Portrait of Frederick the Great as successor to the throne

was crowned King of Prussia. Under his rule, Berlin became a major European city and a centre of the Enlightenment. In 1740–42, in the Seven Years' War, Frederick the Great took Silesia from the Habsburgs without major losses. In 1772 he took part in the first partition of Poland.

In the second half of the 18th century Germany produced a succession of great poets and playwrights – figures such as Gotthold Ephraim Lessing, Friedrich Schiller and Johann Wolfgang von Goethe.

THE NAPOLEONIC WARS, RESTORATION AND REVOLUTION

From 1793 onwards the German states were involved in the Napoleonic Wars. After France's occupation of the lands west of the Rhine, a territorial reform was carried out by the Reichsdeputationls Hauptschluss in 1803. This resulted in the secularization of most church property, and the total of 289 states and free cities was reduced to 112 larger states. States that gained from this supported Napoleon in his defeat of Austria in the war of 1805–7. In 1806 the Holy Roman Empire of German Nations was dissolved, and Bavaria, Saxony and Wurttemberg were given the status of kingdoms. Napoleon defeated Prussia at Jena and the country was occupied by France.

TIMELINE

1701 The first king of Prussia is crowned

1702–14 Germany joins the War of Spanish Succession

1740–42 The Silesian War

Leopold Hermann von Boyen, Prussian army general

1813 Battle c the Nation at Leipzi

1700	1730	1760	1790

1710 Meißen porcelain factory opened

1700 Academy of Sciences founded in Berlin

1756–63 The Seven Years' War

1740 Frederick the Great crowned King of Prussia

1803 Territorial reform of the German states

1806 Dissolution of the Empire

1814–15 The Congress of Vier

The tide turned for Germany at the Battle of Leipzig in 1813, when Russia, Austria and Prussia defeated the French. After Napoleon's final defeat at Waterloo in 1815, the Congress of Vienna established a German Confederation under Austrian control. Its supreme body was the Bundestag (federal parliament), which met at Frankfurt am Main.

Victory Report at the Battle of Leipzig by Johann Peter Krafft (1839)

The wars of liberation against Napoleon had led to a growth in nationalism and democratic awareness, as well as a desire for unification. In 1848 the March Revolution broke out in Berlin. Its main driving force was the urban middle class, but the revolt was finally put down by Prussian troops in 1849.

Vase with portrait of Kaiser Wilhelm II

In the 1820s and 1830s, Germany underwent rapid industrialization, and the establishment of the Zollverein (customs union) in 1834 marked the first step towards a united Germany. Uniting Germany was the main goal of the Prussian premier Otto von Bismarck. Prussia's victories over Austria in 1866 and France in 1871 resulted in the proclamation of a German Empire on 18 January 1871.

THE SECOND REICH

The Second Reich was a federation of 25 states, and its first Chancellor was Otto von Bismarck. The unification of Germany led to a widespread confrontation between the state and the Catholic Church (known as the "Kulturkampf"). The economy, however, flourished, due to the boom in industry, in particular mining, metallurgy, electrical and chemical engineering. This led to the rise of a workers' movement, inspired by the ideas of Karl Marx. In 1875 the workers' parties united and formed the Social Democratic Party of Germany (SPD). Although the party was banned between 1878 and 1890, it rapidly gained support, and a system of social welfare for workers was gradually introduced.

At the beginning of the 20th century, Germany was a powerful state with overseas colonies. Imperialist tendencies grew, and increased tensions in European politics, particularly in the Balkans, led inevitably to war.

Fighting on the Barricades in May 1848, a fanciful picture of the revolution in Berlin by Julius Scholz

1834 German Customs Union (Zollverein) is established	1848 The Communist Manifesto is published	1871 Proclamation of the German Empire with Prussian king as Emperor Wilhelm I	1898 Construction of the German navy begins
	1848–49 The March Revolution		
1820	1850	1880	1910
	1844 Silesian weavers' uprising	1870–71 Franco-Prussian War	1890 Fall of Bismarck
Neo-Gothic chalice designed by K.F. Schinkel		1866 Prussian-Austrian War	*Abandoned, bas-relief by Ernst Barlach*

Bismarck's Germany

The establishment of a Reich headed by the King of Prussia on 18 January 1871 ensured Prussia's prominent role over the following decades. The Chancellor was the Prussian Prime Minister Otto von Bismarck. Thanks to large reparations paid by France and a favourable economic situation, the economy flourished throughout the Reich. This in turn fostered the development of science and culture. The cities grew rapidly, and the housing shortage led to the development of huge *Miets-kasernen*, blocks of apartments for renting.

GERMANY IN 1871

▨ *The Second German Reich*

Kaiser Wilhelm I
Mosaics, depicting a procession of members of the house of Hohenzollern, decorate the vestibule of the Kaiser-Wilhelm Gedächtnichskirche (memorial church) in Berlin.

The Kaiser's Family Taking a Walk in Sanssouci Park
"Happy family" portraits such as this one were often painted for propaganda purposes.

The Reichstag
The monumental Reichstag (parliament building), was built in the centre of the capital, Berlin, by the architect Paul Wallot.

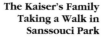

Members of
Parliament

Heads of the
federal states

A Steel Mill in Königshütte
Germany's economic progress was achieved through a high degree of industrialization. Adolf von Menzel's painting depicts a steel mill in Königshütte, Upper Silesia.

Officer's helmet
The characteristic spiked helmet worn by German soldiers was known as a Pickelhaube.

Ludwig II of Bavaria
The federal states, which made up the Reich, enjoyed complete autonomy. Their rulers, however, for instance King Ludwig II of Bavaria, patron of Richard Wagner and builder of "fantastic" castles and palaces, had little real political influence.

The Kaiser's wife, Augusta Victoria

Wilhelm, the heir to the throne

Mourning dress was worn by the women and black ribbons by the men as a mark of respect for the two previous Kaisers who had died in 1888 – the father and grandfather of Wilhelm II.

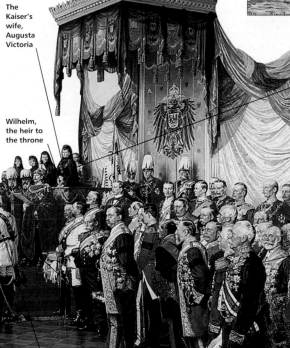

The Diplomatic Corps

Otto von Bismarck

Kaiser Wilhelm II

INAUGURATION OF THE REICHSTAG

This vast canvas by Anton von Werner (1893) shows the opening ceremony for the Reichstag after the coronation of Kaiser Wilhelm II on 25 June 1888 in the Kaiser's Palace in Berlin. The painter depicts the moment when the Kaiser delivers his speech.

Otto von Bismarck
Originating from a Pomeranian family of Junkers, the Prussian Premier and Chancellor of the Reich was one of the most prominent political figures of his time.

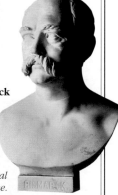

WORLD WAR I

When Germany entered World War I in 1914, the Kaiser's generals hoped for a quick victory, but their invasion of France was halted on the Marne. The war dragged on for the next four years, devastating much of Europe, and ending in Germany's defeat. The Allied offensive in the summer of 1918 forced Germany to the negotiating table – it also led to the November revolution in Germany. Within days the state monarchs were toppled from power, Kaiser Wilhelm II abdicated, and on 9 November 1918 a republic was proclaimed. The form of government had not been decided, and at first the political advantage was held by the socialists. But the Workers' Uprising in Berlin in 1919 was defeated.

Ein Volk, ein Reich, ein Führer!

Propaganda poster for
Adolf Hitler

THE WEIMAR REPUBLIC

The Treaty of Versailles of 1919 imposed many unfavourable conditions on Germany. The country lost a great deal of her territory, mainly to Poland, France and Lithuania, and she was obliged to pay huge reparations, undergo partial demilitarization and limit arms production.

During the Weimar Republic, Germany was riddled with instability. The economy collapsed under the heavy burden of reparation payments and the onset of hyperinflation. Constant changes of government failed to stabilize the political situation, which led to the rise both of left-wing revolutionaries and of right-wing nationalists, and to a general dissatisfaction with the country's status after the humiliating Treaty of Versailles. It is perhaps remarkable that at this time German culture flourished.

Cover of a Socialist
magazine attacking
the book-burning

However, this was not sufficient to stave off the political disaster that led to the rise of the Nazi Party (the NSDAP or National Socialist German Workers' Party).

THE THIRD REICH

Adolf Hitler was appointed Chancellor by President Hindenburg on 30 January 1933 and immediately started to get rid of potential opponents. A fire that burned down the Reichstag served as a pretext for persecuting the communists,

A Berlin synagogue burning during Kristallnacht, 1938

TIMELINE

1914 World War I breaks out	**1919** Signing of the Treaty of Versailles		**1926** Germany accepted in League of Nations
	1921 Adolf Hitler becomes leader of the NSDAP		
1915	**1920**	**1925**	
			1926 Hitler Youth set up
Poster of Marlene Dietrich	**9 Nov 1918** Declaration of the Republic	**1923** Hitler's Putsch in Munich	**1925** Hitler writes *Mein Kampf*

BLONDE VENUS

while in April 1933 a boycott of Jewish businesses began. Trade unions were banned, as were all parties apart from the Nazis. Books by "impure" authors were burned, and the work of "degenerate" artists was exhibited as a warning, marking the start of the persecution of artists and scientists, many of whom decided to emigrate. At the same time, Hitler attempted to present to the world a face of openness and success, particularly with the Berlin Olympics of 1936. Germany broke almost all the demilitarization conditions of the Versailles Treaty. The growth in arms production brought with it an improved economic situation, increasing Hitler's popularity. All his opponents who had not managed to emigrate were either killed or sent to concentration camps.

In 1935 the Nuremberg Laws were passed, which officially sanctioned the persecution of Jews. During the *Kristallnacht* (crystal night) of 9 November 1938, synagogues throughout Germany were burned and Jewish shops and homes were looted, resulting in streets littered with broken glass. Hitler's plans to conquer Europe were realized in March 1938, with the "Anschluss" (annexation) of Austria, then in 1939 German forces occupied Czechoslovakia. After obtaining peace guarantees from the USSR, Germany invaded Poland on 1 September 1939, thus starting World War II.

Pieta, sculpture by Käthe Kollwitz (1937–8)

The centre of Dresden after Allied carpet-bombing

WORLD WAR II

The first two years of World War II were marked by one victory after another for the German Army, which managed to occupy half of Europe. Great Britain was the only country that succeeded in fending off Hitler. In 1941 the Wehrmacht occupied large swathes of the Soviet Union. Terror and genocide were instigated in all occupied territories. The decision to exterminate all Jews in Europe was taken at the Wannsee Conference in Berlin in January 1942. Attempts to oppose Hitler in Germany were crushed. The course of the war did not change until 1943, when on 31 January Germany suffered a major defeat in the Battle of Stalingrad.

The Allied landings in Normandy and the creation of the second front helped bring the war to an end. When Soviet forces reached Berlin in 1945 the city lay in ruins and the populace was starving. During five and a half years, 55 million people had lost their lives.

1935 Enactment of law to build up army	**1938** Anschluss with Austria; occupation of Czechoslovakia **9/10 Nov 1938** "Kristallnacht"	**1 Sep 1939** German invasion of Poland; the beginning of World War II *The Enigma Code machine*
30 Jan 1933 Hitler appointed Chancellor of the Reich		

1930   1935   1940   1945

Poster for the Berlin Olympics in 1936

1936 Berlin Olympics

1935 November laws sanction persecution of Jews

22 Jun 1941 Germany invades USSR

20 Jan 1942 Wannsee conference

30 Apr 1945 Hitler commits suicide as Soviet troops enter Berlin

Nazi war criminals on trial at Nuremberg

THE AFTERMATH OF WORLD WAR II

Germany's unconditional surrender was signed on 8 May 1945, ending the bloodiest war in human history. Peace negotiations began which were to shape the new face of Europe for decades to come. In fact, discussions on Germany's future had already taken place at the Tehran and Yalta Conferences, where the leaders of the Big Three Powers met. But it was not until the Potsdam Conference that the terms were finally agreed.

The Berlin Airlift in 1948–9

Germany lost large parts of its territory to the east, displacing the German population there. It was decided to demilitarize Germany. The four Allied powers – the USA, the USSR, Britain and France – divided Germany into zones of occupation which they would rule until democratic structures were in place. The main perpetrators of war crimes were tried in Nuremberg and sentenced to death. Unfortunately, tensions increased between the Western powers and the Soviet Union, rapidly escalating in the "Cold War", which was largely played out in occupied Germany. In 1948 the three western zones introduced a new currency, which led the Soviets to blockade the western part of Berlin. Thanks to the Berlin Airlift, which supplied the population with food and fuel, the blockade was abandoned. On 23 May 1949 the Federal Republic (Bundesrepublik) of Germany was established in the three western zones, and on 7 October 1949 the German Democratic Republic (DDR) was set up in the Soviet zone. West Berlin, as it was then known, became an enclave inside East Germany.

GERMANY 1949–90

■ *Federal Republic*
□ *DDR*

GERMANY DIVIDED

The German Democratic Republic was democratic only in name. It became one of the satellites of the Soviet Union, and as the westernmost outpost of the Eastern Bloc it was subject to great restrictions. Attempted pro-

Graffiti-covered section of the Berlin Wall

TIMELINE

4–11 Feb 1945 Yalta Conference **8 May** Germany capitulates

17 Jun 1953 Workers' uprising in East Berlin

13 Aug 1961 Building of the Berlin Wall

1973 West and East Germany accepted into UN

1945	1950	1955	1960	1965	1970	1975

24 Jun 1948 Blockade of West Berlin starts

1949 Federal Republic and DDR established

1955 Federal Republic and German Democratic Republic gain sovereignty

Konrad Adenauer

1968 Student riots

1972 Official relations established between East and West Germany; Munich Olympics

Reunification ceremony outside the Reichstag in Berlin in 1990

tests, such as the Workers' Uprising of 17 June 1953 in Berlin, were ruthlessly suppressed. For many people the only solution was to leave the country. As the exodus of skilled workers to the West continued, on 13 August 1961 a wall with barbed wire was built to contain them. Many attempts to cross the frontier between the two Germanies ended in death. A highly efficient apparatus was set up in East Germany to watch over citizens' activities by the infamous Stasi secret police.

The first Chancellor of the Federal Republic of Germany, Konrad Adenauer, had Germany's integration into Western Europe as his main objective. Thanks to aid under the Marshall Plan, the economy rapidly recovered. Willy Brandt, first elected as Chancellor in 1969, pursued a policy of openness to the East, and recognized the German Democratic Republic.

REUNIFICATION

German reunification was made possible by a number of political events, in particular those going on in Eastern Europe. The Soviet premier Gorbachev's policy of *glasnost* led to the loosening of political constraints throughout the

Eastern Bloc. Democratic changes in Poland set off a chain reaction. In 1989, people started to flee the German Democratic Republic en masse via its embassy in Prague and across the Austro-Hungarian border. Then, on 9 November 1989, the Berlin Wall fell and East Germans were free to leave. When, only three weeks later, Chancellor Helmut Kohl presented a ten-point plan for German reunification, few believed that it would happen, but the country was officially reunified on 3 October 1990. Since then, Germany has been undergoing a process of integration.

Crowds visiting the giant Expo 2000 exhibition in Hannover

1982 Helmut Kohl becomes German Chancellor	3 Oct 1990 Reunification of Germany	Helmut Kohl and Richard von Weizsäcker at the reunification ceremony	2002 Floods cause havoc across Germany
1980	**1985**	**1990**	**1995**	**2000**	**2010**

8 Nov 1989 Fall of the Berlin Wall

The Trabant, a trademark of East German industry

1994 Withdrawal of last Russian military units from Berlin

1998 Gerhard Schröder becomes Chancellor

2000 Expo 2000 World Fair in Hannover

2005 Angela Merkel is the first female chancellor in a "Grand Coalition" government

BERLIN
AREA BY AREA

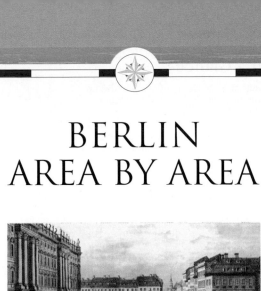

Berlin at a Glance

Since the reunification of Germany in 1990, Berlin
has become an increasingly popular destination
for visitors. The following pages provide a useful
guide to places of interest both in the town centre
and the outskirts, including historic monuments
such as Nikolaikirche *(see p80)*, museums, modern
developments, such as the Potsdamer Platz, as
well as places of recreation and amusement, such
as the Botanical Gardens *(see p104)*. In the guide,
we have divided central Berlin into two parts (east
and west); these, however, do not correspond with
the city's former partition into East and West Berlin.

LOCATOR MAP

The Tiergarten *was once
a royal hunting estate
but, after 1818, it was
converted into a land-
scaped park by Peter
Joseph Lenné (see p87)
with lakes and streams.*

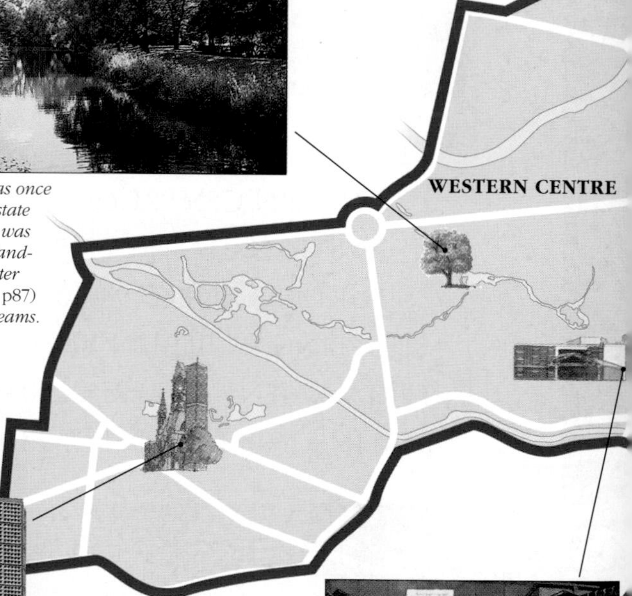

WESTERN CENTRE

The Gemäldegalerie
(see pp90–91) *houses an
exceptional collection of
European masters, including
Hans Holbein's Portrait of
George Gisze (1532).*

**The Kaiser-Wilhelm-
Gedächtnis-Kirche** *was
almost totally destroyed by
bombs during World War II.
However it was rebuilt in
1963 to a design by Egon
Eiermann (see p86).*

◁ **Aerial view of Berlin**

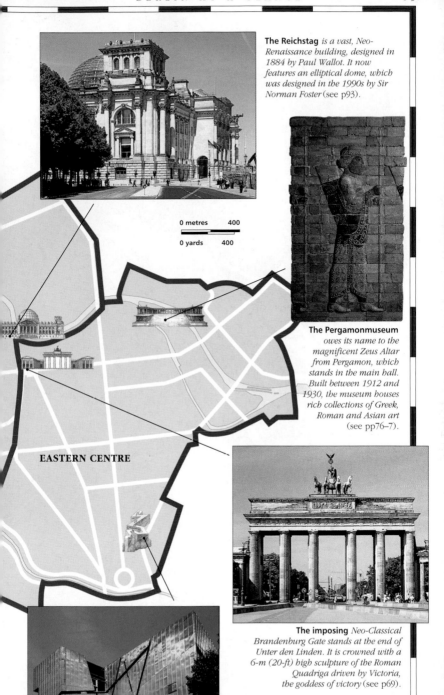

The Reichstag *is a vast, Neo-Renaissance building, designed in 1884 by Paul Wallot. It now features an elliptical dome, which was designed in the 1990s by Sir Norman Foster* (see p93).

0 metres 400

0 yards 400

The Pergamonmuseum *owes its name to the magnificent Zeus Altar from Pergamon, which stands in the main hall. Built between 1912 and 1930, the museum houses rich collections of Greek, Roman and Asian art* (see pp76–7).

EASTERN CENTRE

The imposing *Neo-Classical Brandenburg Gate stands at the end of Unter den Linden. It is crowned with a 6-m (20-ft) high sculpture of the Roman Quadriga driven by Victoria, the goddess of victory* (see p69).

The Jüdisches Museum *(Jewish Museum) is housed in a building designed by Daniel Libeskind. It features a symbolic projection of a broken Star of David* (see p80).

EASTERN CENTRE

This part of Berlin is the historic centre of the city, and includes the Mitte district and parts of Kreuzberg. Its beginnings date back to the 13th century when two

Relief on Schadow-Haus

settlements were established on the banks of the river Spree. One was the former Cölln, situated on an island, and the other its twin settlement, Berlin. Berlin's first church, the Nikolaikirche, survives to this day.

This part of the city features most of its historic buildings, which are located mainly along Unter den Linden. It also includes Museumsinsel, the location of the vast Berliner Dom as well as of the impressive collection of museums that gives the island its name. These include the Pergamonmuseum.

During the city's partition, Mitte belonged to East Berlin while Kreuzberg was in West Berlin.

SIGHTS AT A GLANCE

Museums and Galleries
Alte Nationalgalerie **17**
Altes Museum **15**
Bodemuseum **19**
Checkpoint Charlie **26**
Deutsches Technikmuseum Berlin **29**
Jüdisches Museum **27**
Märkisches Museum **25**
Neues Museum **16**
Pergamonmuseum **18**
Topographie des Terrors **28**
Zeughaus **7**

Streets and Squares
Alexanderplatz **22**
Bebelplatz **2**
Nikolaiviertel **24**
Schlossplatz **13**
Unter den Linden **4**

Churches
Berliner Dom **14**
Deutscher Dom **11**
Französischer Dom **9**
Friedrichswerdersche Kirche **8**
Marienkirche **20**
St Hedwigs-Kathedrale **3**

Historic Buildings and Monuments
Brandenburger Tor **1**

Fernsehturm **23**
Humboldt-Universität **5**
Konzerthaus **10**
Neue Wache **6**
Rotes Rathaus **21**
Schlossbrücke **12**

GETTING THERE
This part of Berlin is served by S-Bahn 1, 2, 3, 5, 7, 9, 75 and U-Bahn 2, 5 & 6. Busses 100 & 200 run along Unter den Linden and Karl-Liebknecht-Strasse.

KEY

▢	Street-by-Street map See pp68–9
▢	Street-by-Street map See pp74–5
🚇	Railway station
Ⓢ	S-Bahn station
Ⓤ	U-Bahn station

◁ *Personification of History* adorning the monument of Friedrich Schiller

Street-by-Street: Around Bebelplatz

Eagle from Altes Palais

The section of Unter den Linden between Schlossbrücke and Friedrichstrasse is one of the most attractive areas in central Berlin. As well as some magnificent Baroque and Neo-Classical buildings, many of them designed by famous architects, there are also some restored palaces that are now used as public buildings. Of particular interest is the beautiful Baroque building of the Zeughaus (the former Arsenal), which now houses the German History Museum.

Neue Wache
Now serving as a memorial to all victims of war and dictatorship, this monument was designed by Karl Friedrich Schinkel 6

Humboldt University
The university courtyard teems with life all year round. Second-hand book-sellers set up their stalls in front of the gate 5

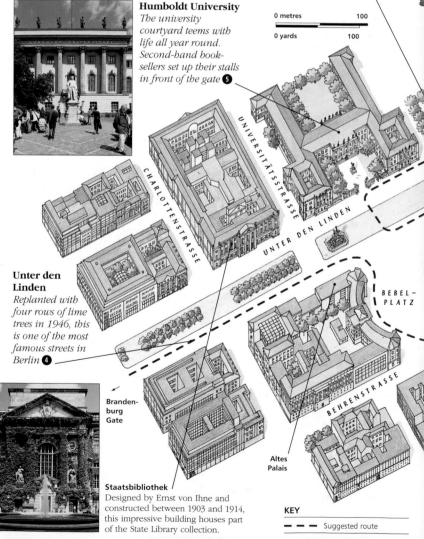

0 metres   100
0 yards   100

CHARLOTTENSTRASSE

UNIVERSITÄTSSTRASSE

UNTER DEN LINDEN

BEBEL-PLATZ

BEHRENSTRASSE

Unter den Linden
Replanted with four rows of lime trees in 1946, this is one of the most famous streets in Berlin 4

Branden-burg Gate

Altes Palais

Staatsbibliothek
Designed by Ernst von Ihne and constructed between 1903 and 1914, this impressive building houses part of the State Library collection.

KEY

- - - Suggested route

★ **Zeughaus (Deutsches Historisches Museum)**
Minerva, goddess of wisdom, decorates this beautiful Baroque building, which has a new wing designed by I M Pei ❼

LOCATOR MAP
See Street Finder, maps 1, 4 & 5

Staatsoper Unter den Linden

★ **Friedrichs-werdersche Kirche**
In this Neo-Gothic church, designed by Karl Friedrich Schinkel, is a museum devoted to the great architect ❽

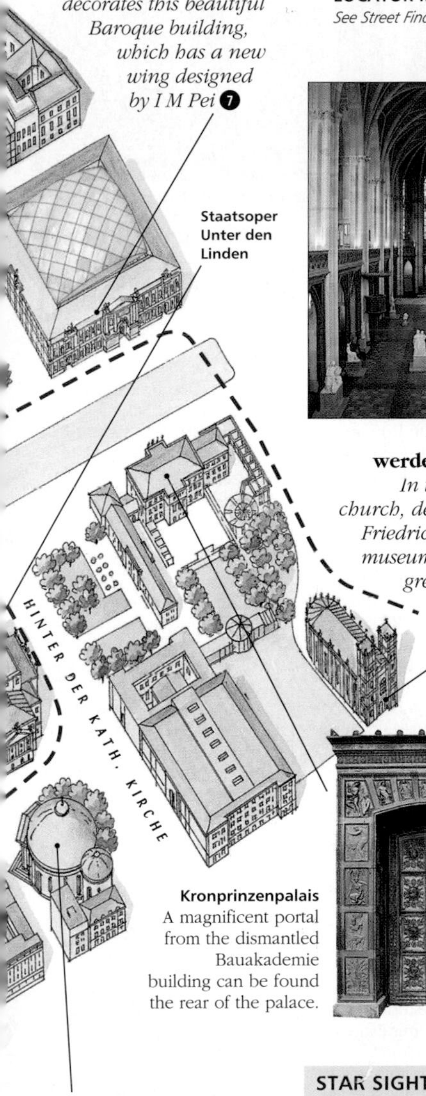

Rotes Rathaus

HINTER DER KATH. KIRCHE

Kronprinzenpalais
A magnificent portal from the dismantled Bauakademie building can be found the rear of the palace.

St-Hedwigs-Kathedrale
Bas-reliefs (1837) by Theodore Wilhelm Achtermann adorn the cathedral's supports ❸

STAR SIGHTS

★ Friedrichswerdersche Kirche

★ Zeughaus

Brandenburger Tor ❶
Brandenburg Gate

Pariser Platz. **Map** 4 A2, 15 A3.
Ⓢ *Unter den Linden.* 🚌 *100.*

The Brandenburg Gate is the quintessential symbol of Berlin. A magnificent Neo-Classical structure, modelled on the Athenian Propylaea (the entrance to the Acropolis), it was constructed between 1788 and 1791. Its sculptured decorations were completed in 1795. A pair of pavilions, once used by guards and customs officers, frames its powerful Doric colonnade and entablature. The bas-reliefs depict scenes from Greek mythology and the whole structure is crowned by Johann Gottfried Schadow's famous sculpture, *Quadriga*. In 1806, during the French occupation, the sculpture was dismantled, on Napoleon's orders, and taken to Paris. On its triumphal return in 1814, it was declared a symbol of victory, and the goddess received a staff bearing the Prussian eagle and an iron cross adorned with a laurel wreath.

Throughout its history, the Brandenburg Gate has borne witness to many of Berlin's important events. Located in East Berlin, the gate was restored between 1956 and 1958, when the damaged *Quadriga* was rebuilt in West Berlin. Over the next 40 years it stood watch over the divided city, until 1989, when the first section of the Berlin Wall came down.

Frieze and sculpture, *Quadriga*, on the Brandenburg Gate

Bebelplatz ❷

Map 4 C2. Ⓢ & Ⓤ *Friedrichstraße.*
🚌 *100, 157, 348.*

Once named Opernplatz
(Opera Square), Bebelplatz
was intended to be the
focal point of the Forum
Fridericianum – an area
designed to mirror the
grandeur of ancient Rome.
Although the plans were only
partly implemented, many
important buildings were
eventually erected here.

On 10 May 1933, the square
was the scene of the infamous
book-burning act organized
by the Nazi propaganda
machine. Some 25,000 books,
written by authors considered
to be enemies of the Third
Reich, were burned.

Today, a monument in the
square commemorates this
dramatic event. A translucent
panel inserted into the road
surface provides a glimpse of
a room filled with empty
bookshelves, while a plaque
bears the tragically prophetic
words of the poet Heinrich
Heine, written in 1820:
"Where books are burned, in
the end people will burn."

**Relief on the façade of the Staats-
oper (Opera House), Bebelplatz**

St-Hedwigs-
Kathedrale ❸
St Hedwig's Cathedral

Bebelplatz. **Map** 4 C2. **Tel** *(030) 203
48 10.* Ⓢ & Ⓤ *Friedrichstraße.* 🚌
100, 157, 348. ⬚ *10am–5pm Mon–
Fri, 10am–4:30pm Sat,1pm–5pm Sun
& holy days.*

This huge church, set back
from the road and crowned
with a dome, is the Catholic
Cathedral of the Roman Arch-

The façade of St-Hedwigs-Kathedrale, with beautiful bas-relief sculptures

diocese of Berlin. It was built
to serve the Catholics of Silesia
(part of present-day Poland),
which became part of the
kingdom of Prussia in 1742
following defeat in the
Silesian Wars.

The initial design, by Georg
Wenzeslaus von Knobelsdorff,
was similar to the Roman
Pantheon. Construction began
in 1747 and the cathedral was
consecrated in 1773, although
work continued on and off
until 1778. Later work was
carried out from 1886 to 1887.

The cathedral was damaged
during World War II and
subsequently rebuilt between
1952 and 1963. The building
received a reinforced concrete
dome and its interior was
refurbished in a modern style.

The crypt holds the tombs
of many of the bishops of
Berlin. It also contains a 16th-
century Madonna.

Unter den Linden ❹

Map 1 C4, 4 A2, B2, C2, 5 D2.
Ⓢ *Unter den Linden.* 🚌 *100,
157, 348.*

One of the most famous
streets in Berlin, Unter den
Linden starts at Schlossplatz
and runs down to Pariser Platz
and the Brandenburg Gate. It
was once the route to the
royal hunting grounds, which
were later transformed into
the Tiergarten.

In the 17th century, the
street was planted with lime
trees, to which it owes its
name. Although the original
trees were removed around
1658, four rows of limes were
planted in 1820.

During the 18th century,
Unter den Linden became the
main street of the westward-
growing city and gradually
came to be lined with

WILHELM AND ALEXANDER VON HUMBOLDT

The Humboldt brothers rank among the
most distinguished Berlin citizens. Wilhelm
(1767–1835) was a lawyer and politician on
whose initiative the Berlin University (later
renamed Humboldt University) was
founded in 1810. At the university,
he conducted studies in comparative
and historical linguistics. His
brother Alexander (1769–1859), a
professor at the university,
researched natural science,
including meteorology, ocean-
ography and agricultural science.

Alexander von Humboldt

prestigious buildings, which have been restored in the years following World War II.

Since the reunification of Germany in 1990, Unter den Linden has acquired several cafés and restaurants, as well as many smart new shops. The street has also become the venue for interesting outdoor events. It is usually crowded with tourists and students browsing the bookstalls around the Humboldt Universität and the Staatsbibliothek (State Library).

Humboldt Universität **❺**

Humboldt University

Unter den Linden 6. **Map** 4 C2. **Ⓢ** & **Ⓤ** *Friedrichstraße.* 🚌 *100, 157, 348.*

The university building was constructed in 1753 for Prince Heinrich of Prussia. The overall design of the palace, with its main block and the courtyard enclosed within two wings, has been extended many times. Two marble statues by Paul Otto (1883) stand at the entrance; these represent Wilhelm and Alexander von Humboldt.

Many famous scientists have worked at the university, including physicians Rudolf Virchow and Robert Koch and physicists Max Planck and Albert Einstein. Among its graduates are Heinrich Heine, Karl Marx and Friedrich Engels.

After World War II, the university was in the Russian sector and the difficulties encountered by the students of the western zone led to the establishment in 1948 of the Freie Universität.

Neue Wache **❻**

Unter den Linden 4. **Map** 7 A3, 16 E2. **Ⓢ** *Hackescher Markt.* 🚌 *100, 157, 348.* ⬜ *10am–6pm daily.*

Designed by Karl Friedrich Schinkel and built between 1816 and 1818, this monument is considered to be one of the finest examples of Neo-Classical architecture in Berlin. The front of the

monument is dominated by a huge Doric portico with a frieze made up of bas-reliefs depicting goddesses of victory.

In 1930–31 the building was turned into a monument to soldiers killed in World War I. Following its restoration in 1960, Neue Wache became the Memorial to the Victims of Fascism and Militarism. It was rededicated in 1993 to the memory of all victims of war and dictatorship. Inside is an eternal flame and a granite slab over the ashes of an unknown soldier, a resistance fighter and a concentration camp prisoner. In the roof opening is a copy of the sculpture *Mother with her Dead Son,* by Berlin artist Käthe Kollwitz.

Zeughaus **❼**

Unter den Linden 2. **Map** 5 D2. **Tel** 20 30 40. **Ⓢ** *Hackescher Markt.* 🚌 *100, 157, 348.* **New wing** ⬜ *10am–6pm daily.*

This former arsenal was built in the Baroque style in 1706 under the guidance of Johann Arnold Nering, Martin Grünberg, Andreas Schlüter and Jean de Bodt. A magnificent structure, its wings surround an inner courtyard. Its exterior is decorated with Schlüter's sculptures, which include masks of dying warriors.

Home to the German History Museum since 1952, it was renovated in 2005. A modern, glass and steel wing, designed by architect I M Pei, now houses temporary exhibits, and there is a new and extensive exhibition on German history.

Friedrichswerdersche Kirche (Schinkel-Museum) **❽**

Werderstraße. **Map** 5 D2. **Tel** (030) 2081 323. **Ⓤ** & **Ⓢ** *Friedrichstrasse.* 🚌 *100, 147, 157, 257, 348.* ⬜ *10am– 6pm Tue–Sun.* 📷 ♿

The first Neo-Gothic church to be built in Berlin, this small, single-nave structure with its twin-tower façade was designed by Karl Friedrich Schinkel and built between 1824 and 1830.

Schinkel's original interior was largely destroyed in World War II. Following its reconstruction, the church was converted to a museum. It currently houses the Nationalgalerie's permanent sculpture exhibition. Highlights include a model of the famous sculpture by Johann Gottfried Schadow, depicting the princesses Friederike and Luise (later Queen of Prussia).

Princesses Luise and Friederike in the Schinkel-Museum

Part of the façade of the Zeughaus on Unter den Linden

Side elevation of the Französischer Dom, built for Huguenot refugees

Französischer Dom **9**
French Cathedral

Gendarmenmarkt 6. **Map** 4 C2.
Tel *(030) 204 15 07.* **U** *Stadtmitte or Französische Straße.* **Museum** ☐ *noon–5pm Tue–Sat, 11am–5pm Sun.* 🏛 **Viewing Platform** *9am–7pm daily.* 🏛 **Church** ☐ *noon–5pm Tue–Sun.* 🛐 *Sun 10am.*

Although the two churches standing on opposite sides of Schauspielhaus seem identical, their only common feature is their matching front towers. The French cathedral was built for the Huguenot community, who found refuge in protestant Berlin following their expulsion from France after the revocation of the Edict of Nantes in 1598. The modest church, built between 1701 and 1705 by Louis Cayart and Abraham Quesnay, was modelled on the Huguenot church in Charenton, France, which was destroyed in 1688. The interior features a late-Baroque organ from 1754.

The structure is dominated by a massive, cylindrical tower, which is encircled by Corinthian porticos at its base. The tower and porticos were designed by Carl von Gontard and added around 1785. It houses the Huguenot Museum, which charts the history of the Huguenot community in France and in Brandenburg.

A viewing platform (temporarily closed), 66 m (216 ft), above the ground is the city's highest historic observation platform and offers stunning views of Berlin's skyline.

Konzerthaus **10**
Concert Hall

Gendarmenmarkt 2. **Map** 4 C2.
Tel *(030) 203 09 21 01.* **U** *Stadtmitte.*

A late Neo-Classical jewel, this magnificent theatre building, known until recently as the Schauspielhaus, is one of the greatest achievements of Berlin's best-known architect, Karl Friedrich Schinkel. It was built between 1818 and 1821 around the ruins of Langhan's National Theatre, destroyed by fire in 1817. The portico columns were retained in the new design. Following bomb damage in World War II, it was reconstructed as a concert hall and the exterior was restored to its former glory. The Konzerthaus is now home to the Berlin Symphony Orchestra.

The whole building is decorated with sculptures alluding to drama and music. The façade, which includes a huge Ionic portico with a set of stairs, is crowned with a sculpture of Apollo riding a chariot pulled by griffins.

In front of the theatre stands a shining white marble statue of Friedrich Schiller, which was sculpted by Reinhold Begas and erected in 1869. Removed by the Nazis during the 1930s, the monument was returned

Interior of the Konzerthaus, formerly the Schauspielhaus

to its rightful place in 1988. The statue is mounted on a high pedestal surrounded by allegorical figures representing Lyric Poetry, Drama, Philosophy and History.

Deutscher Dom **11**
German Cathedral

Gendarmenmarkt 1. **Map** 4 C3.
Tel *(030) 227 30431.* **U** *Stadtmitte or Französische Straße.* **Exhibition** ☐ *10am–10pm Tue, 10am–6pm Wed–Sun (Jun–Aug 10am–7pm).*

The cathedral at the southern end of the square is an old German Protestant-Reformed church. Based on a five-petal shape, it was designed by Martin Grünberg and built in 1708 by Giovanni Simonetti. In 1785 it acquired a dome-covered tower identical to that of the French cathedral.

Burned down in 1945, it was rebuilt in 1993, with its interior adapted as exhibition space. On display is the popular "Fragen an die Deutsche Geschichte" ("Questions on German History"), which was formerly on show in the Reichstag building.

Sculpture from Deutscher Dom

Schlossbrücke **12**

Map 5 D2. **S** *Hackescher Markt.* 🚌 *100, 157, 348.*

This is one of the city's most beautiful bridges, connecting Schlossplatz with Unter den Linden. It was built in 1824 to a design by Karl Friedrich Schinkel. Statues were added to the top of the bridge's sparkling red-granite pillars in 1853. These figures, made of white Carrara marble, were also created by Schinkel. The statues depict tableaux from Greek mythology, such as Iris, Nike and Athena, training and looking after their favourite young warriors. The elaborate wrought-iron balustrade is decorated with intertwined sea creatures.

The surviving Stadtschloss portal fronting a government building

Schlossplatz ⑬

Map 5 D2. Ⓢ *Hackescher Markt.* 🚋 *100, 157, 348.*

This square was once the site of a huge residential complex known as Stadtschloss (City Castle). Built in 1451, it served as the main residence of the Brandenburg Electors. It was transformed from a castle to a palace in the mid-16th century when Elector Friedrich III (later King Friedrich I) ordered its reconstruction in the Baroque style. The building works, which lasted from 1698 until 1716, were overseen initially by Andreas Schlüter and then by Johann von Göthe and Martin Heinrich Böhme.

The three-storey residence, designed around two courtyards, was the main seat of the Hohenzollern family for almost 500 years until the end of the monarchy. The palace was partly burned during World War II but, after 1945, it was provisionally restored and used as a museum.

In 1950–51, despite protests, the palace was demolished and the square was renamed Marx-Engels-Platz under the GDR.

Now all that remains of the palace is the triumphal-arch portal that once adorned the façade on the Lustgarten side. This is now incorporated into the wall of the government building, the Staatsratgebäude, which was erected in 1964 on the square's south side. The building's decor features the remaining original sculptures, including the magnificent atlantes by the famous Dresden sculptor, Balthasar Permoser. Their inclusion was not due to their artistic merit, but rather to their propaganda value: it was from the balcony of the portal that in 1918 Karl Liebknecht proclaimed the birth of the Socialist Republic.

In 1989 the square reverted to its original name. In 1993, a spectacular model of the palace was made out of cloth stretched over a scaffolding frame. After much debate, it has been decided not to rebuild the palace instead to incorporate the remaining elements into a new museum.

Berliner Dom ⑭

Am Lustgarten. **Map** 5 D1. **Tel** *(030) 20 26 91 36.* Ⓢ *Hackescher Markt.* 🚋 *100, 200, TXL.* ☐ *Oct–Mar: 9am–7pm Mon– Sat, noon–7pm Sun; Apr–Sep: 9am–8pm Mon–Sat, noon–8pm Sun.* 📷 ✝ *10am, 6pm Sun.*

The original Berliner Dom was based on a modest Baroque design by Johann Boumann. Built between 1747 and 1750 on the site of an old Dominican church, the cathedral included the original crypt of the Hohenzollern family, one of the largest of its kind in Europe. The present Neo-Baroque structure is the work of Julius Raschdorff and dates from 1894 to 1905. The central copper dome is 98 m (321 ft) high. Following severe World War II damage, the cathedral has been restored in a simplified form. The Hohenzollern memorial chapel, which adjoined the northern walls, has been dismantled.

The Neo-Baroque interior of the Berliner Dom

BERLIN'S BRIDGES

Despite wartime damage, Berlin's bridges are still well worth seeing. The Spree river and the city's canals have some fine, exemplary architecture on their banks, while many of the bridges were designed and decorated by famous architects and sculptors. Probably the most renowned bridge is the Schlossbrücke designed by Karl Friedrich Schinkel. Further south along the Kupfergrabenkanal, the Schleusenbrücke, dating from c.1914, is decorated with reliefs of the early history of the city's bridges and sluices. The next bridge, heading south, is the Jungfernbrücke (1798), which is the last drawbridge in Berlin. The next bridge along is the Gertraudenbrücke. Where Friedrichstrasse crosses the Spree river is the Weidendammer Brücke, built originally in 1695–7 and subsequently rebuilt in 1923, with an eagle motif adorning its balustrade. On the Spree near the Regierungsviertel is the magnificent Moltkebrücke (1886–91). The bridge is guarded by a huge griffin wielding a shield adorned with the Prussian eagle, while cherubs dressed in a military fashion hold up lamps. On the arches of the bridges are portraits of leaders, designed by Karl Begas.

Ornamental feature of a bear on the Liebknechtbrücke

Street-by-Street: Museum Island

The long island that nestles in the tributaries of the Spree river is the cradle of Berlin's history. It was here that the first settlements appeared at the beginning of the 13th century: Cölln is mentioned in documents dating back to 1237, and its twin settlement, Berlin, is mentioned a few years later, in 1244. The island's character was transformed by the construction of the Brandenburg Electors' palace, which served as their residence from 1470. Although it was razed to the ground in 1950, some interesting buildings on the north side of the island have survived, including the Berliner Dom (Berlin Cathedral) and the impressive collection of museums that give the island its name, Museuminsel.

LOCATOR MAP
See Street Finder, maps 4 & 5

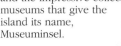

Bode Museum
A rounded corner of the building, crowned with a dome, provides a magnificent end-piece to the tip of the island ⑲

★ Pergamonmuseum
The museum is famous for its reconstruction of fragments of ancient towns, as well as the original friezes from the Pergamon altar ⑱

AM KUPFER-GRABEN

Neues Museum
This museum houses a number of exhibitions on antiquities and ancient Egyptian art after having undergone major renovations ⑯

Alte Nationalgalerie
The equestrian statue of King Friedrich Wilhelm IV in front of the building is the work of Alexander Calandrelli ⑰

KEY

 Suggested route

★ Altes Museum
The corners of the central building feature the figures of Castor and Pollux, heroes of Greek mythology **⑮**

| 0 metres | 400 |
| 0 yards | 400 |

Lustgarten
A 70-ton granite bowl, the biggest in the world, was placed in the garden in 1828 **⑤**

LUSTGARTEN

STAR SIGHTS

★ Pergamonmuseum

★ Altes Museum

Altes Museum ⑮
Old Museum

Am Lustgarten (Bodestraße 1–3).
Map 5 D1. **Tel** (030) 20 90 55 77.
Ⓢ *Hackescher Markt.* 🚌 *100, 157, 348.* ⬜ *10am–6pm Tue–Sun.* 📷

Designed by Karl Friedrich Schinkel, this museum building is one of the world's most beautiful Neo-Classical structures, with an impressive 87-m (285-ft) high portico supported by 18 Ionic columns. Officially opened in 1830, the museum was purpose-built to house the royal collection of art and antiquities.

In the years that followed World War II, the museum building was used only to display temporary exhibitions. Since 1998, however, it has housed the Antikensammlung, with a magnificent collection of various Greek and Roman antiquities.

Many sculptures, sarcophagi, murals and architectural fragments of various eras are on display, including the famous bust of Nefertiti. Most popular is the collection from 19th-century archaeological digs by Richard Lepsius and Johann Ludwig Burckhardt at Tell al-Amarna, Egypt. Tell al-Amarna was the capital founded by Pharaoh Amenhotep IV in the 14th century BC. In a break with tradition, Amenhotep and his wife, Nefertiti, are depicted in a more naturalistic manner.

Neues Museum ⑯
New Museum

Bodestraße 1–3. **Map** 5 D1.
Ⓢ *Hackescher Markt or Friedrichstraße.*
🚌 *100, 147, 257, 348.* 🚊 *1, 2, 3, 4, 5, 13, 53, 58.* ⬛ *until 2009.*

The Neues Museum was built on Museum Island between 1841 and 1855 to a design by Friedrich August Stüler. Until World War II, it housed a collection of antiquities, mainly ancient Egyptian art. The rooms in the museum building were decorated specifically to complement the exhibitions they contained, while wall paintings by Wilhelm von Kaulbach depicted key events in world history.

The building was damaged in 1945 and is currently under reconstruction. The work is expected to be complete in 2009, when it will house the collection of Egyptian art once again as well as the Museum of Early History.

Alte Nationalgalerie ⑰
Old National Gallery

Bodestraße 1–3. **Map** 5 D1.
Tel *(030) 20 90 55 77.* Ⓢ
Hackescher Markt or Friedrichstraße.
🚌 *100, 147, 257, 348.* 🚊 *1, 2, 3, 4, 5, 13, 53, 58.* ⬜ *10am–6pm Tue–Sun, 10am–10pm Thu.*

Pericles' Head

The Nationalgalerie building, designed by Friedrich August Stüler, was erected between 1866 and 1876. It was originally intended to house the collection of modern art that had been on display in the Akademie der Künste (Art Academy). After World War II, however, the collection was split up into several sections and part of it was shown in West Berlin, where the Neue Nationalgalerie was specifically erected for this purpose *(see p88)*. This building was then renamed Alte Nationalgalerie.

Following the reunification of Germany, the modern art collections were merged again. Two new exhibition halls now show paintings from the German Romantic era, including work by Caspar David Friedrich and Karl Friedrich Schinkels. The famous 19th-century marble sculpture of the two Prussian princesses by Johann Gottfried Schadow is also on display, as is a significant collection of works by Adolf Menzel, including his most famous painting, *The Balcony Room*.

Pergamonmuseum ⑱

The Pergamonmuseum was built between 1912
and 1930 to a design by Alfred Messels and
Ludwig Hoffmann. It houses one of the most
famous collections of antiquities in Europe and
owes its name to the famous Pergamon Altar,
which takes pride of place in the main hall. The
three independent collections – the Museum of
Antiquities (Greek and Roman), the Museum of
Near Eastern Antiquities and the Museum of
Islamic Art – are the result of intensive archaeological excavations by German expeditions to the
Near and Middle East at the end of the 19th and
beginning of the 20th century.

★ Pergamon Altar *(170 BC)*
*This scene, featuring the goddess
Athena, appears on the large
frieze illustrating a battle between
the gods and the giants.*

Roman Mosaic
*(3rd or 4th century AD)
This ancient mosaic was
found at Jerash, Jordan.
A second part of it is in
the collection of the Stark
Museum of Art, Texas.*

Non-exhibition
rooms

First
floor

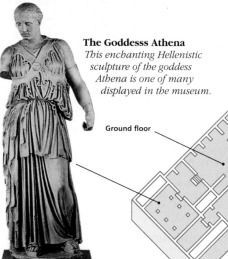

The Goddesss Athena
*This enchanting Hellenistic
sculpture of the goddess
Athena is one of many
displayed in the museum.*

Ground floor

Main
entrance

Assyrian Palace
*Parts of this beauti-
fully reconstructed
palace interior,
from the ancient
kingdom of Assyria,
date from the 12th
century BC.*

Aleppo Zimmer
(c.1603)
This magnificent panelled room comes from a merchant's house in the Syrian city of Aleppo.

VISITORS' CHECKLIST

Bodestraße 1–3 (entrance from Am Kupfergraben). **Map** 4 C1, 5 D1. **Tel** (030) 20 90 55 55. Ⓢ *Friedrichstraße or Hackescher Markt.* 🚌 100, 200, 348. ◯ *10am–6pm Tue–Sun, 10am–10pm Thu.* ● *1 Jan, Tue after Easter and Pentecost, 24, 25, 31 Dec.* 🎫 📷 🛆 👥 🏼 🧥 🛗 🛒 📷 *without flash.*

GALLERY GUIDE
The central section of the ground floor houses reconstructions of ancient monumental structures, while the left wing is devoted to the Antiquities of Greece and Rome. The right wing houses the Museum of Near Eastern Antiquities; the first floor of the right wing houses the Museum of Islamic Art.

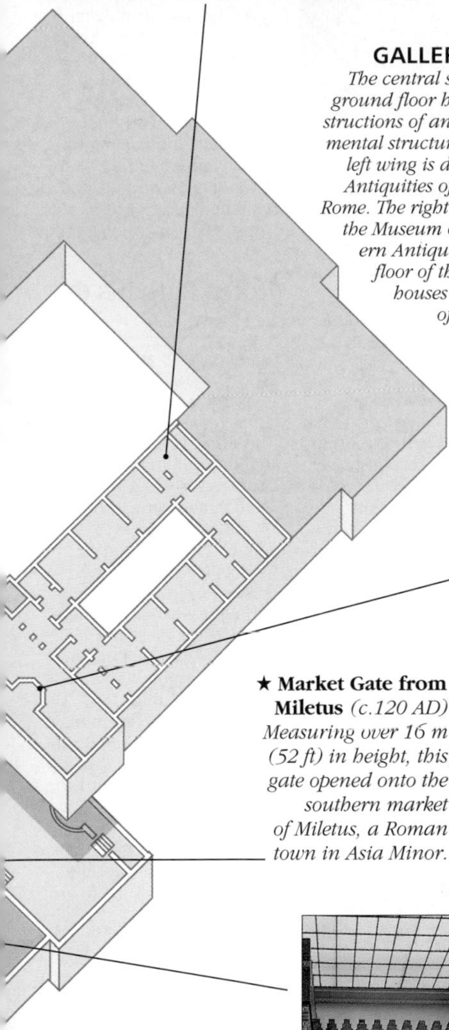

Façade of the Mshatta Palace *(AD 744)*
This fragment is from the southern façade of the Jordanian Mshatta Palace, presented to Wilhelm II by Sultan Abdul Hamid of Ottoman in 1903.

★ **Market Gate from Miletus** *(c.120 AD)*
Measuring over 16 m (52 ft) in height, this gate opened onto the southern market of Miletus, a Roman town in Asia Minor.

★ **Ishtar Gate from Babylon**
(6th century BC)
Original glazed bricks decorate both the huge Ishtar gate and the impressive Processional Way that leads up to it.

STAR EXHIBITS

★ Ishtar Gate from Babylon

★ Market Gate from Miletus

★ Pergamon Altar

KEY

◻ Antiquities (Antikensammlung)

◼ Near Eastern antiquities (Vorderasiatisches Museum)

◻ Islamic art (Museum für Islamische Kunst)

◼ Non-exhibition rooms

The Bodemuseum designed by Ernst von Ihne

Bodemuseum ⑲

Monbijoubrücke (Bodestraße 1–3).
Map 4 C1. **Tel** (030) 20 90 57 01.
Ⓢ Hackescher Markt or Friedrichstraße.
🚌 100, 147, 257, 348. 🚋 1, 2, 3,
4, 5, 13, 53, 58. ⬤ until Oct 2006.

The fourth museum building
on Museuminsel was
constructed between 1897 and
1904. It was designed by Ernst
von Ihne to fit the wedge-
shaped northwestern end of
the island. The interior was
designed with the help of an
art historian, Wilhelm von
Bode, who was the director
of the Berlin state museums
at the time.

The museum displayed a
rather mixed collection that
included some old masters. Its
original name, Kaiser Friedrich
Museum, was changed after
World War II. Following the
reassembling of the Berlin
collections, all the paintings
were rehoused in the Kulturforum *(see pp84–5)*, while
the Egyptian art and the
papyrus collection were
moved to the Ägyptisches
Museum (Egyptian Museum)
at Charlottenburg *(see p96)*.

Following its current
refurbishment, the building
will once again house its
collection of coins, medals
and Byzantine art. It will also
be home to the reassembled
collection of sculptures, which
includes the works of Tilman
Riemenschneider, Donatello,
Gianlorenzo Bernini and
Antonio Canova. A copy of
the magnificent equestrian
statue of the Great Elector,
Friedrich Wilhelm, by Andreas
Schlüter, will once again take
its place in the old hall.

Marienkirche ⑳

Karl-Liebknecht-Straße 8. **Map** 5 E1.
Tel (030) 242 44 67. Ⓢ Hackescher
Markt. 🚌 100, 157. ◻ Apr–Oct:
10am–6pm daily; Nov–
Mar: 10am–4pm daily. 🕂 4:30am
Sat, 10:30am & 6pm Sun.

St Mary's Church, or the
Marienkirche, was first
established as a parish church
in the second half of the 13th
century. Started around 1280,
construction was completed
early in the 14th century.
During reconstruction works
in 1380, following a fire, the
church was altered slightly,
but its overall shape changed
only in the 15th century when
it acquired the front tower. In
1790, the tower was crowned
with a dome, designed by
Carl Gotthard Langhans,
which includes both Baroque
and Neo-Gothic elements.

The Marienkirche was once
hemmed in by buildings, but
today it stands alone in the
shadow of the Fernsehturm
(Television Tower). The early

Baroque altar in the Marienkirche,
designed by Andreas Krüger

Gothic hall design and the
lavish decorative touches
make this church one of the
most interesting in Berlin. An
alabaster pulpit by Andreas
Schlüter, dating from 1703, is
decorated with bas-reliefs of
St John the Baptist and the
personifications of the Virtues.

The Baroque main altar was
designed by Andreas Krüger
around 1762. The paintings
with which it is adorned
include three works by
Christian Bernhard Rode.

A Gothic font, dating from
1437, is supported by three
black dragons and decorated
with the figures of Jesus
Christ, Mary and the Apostles.

Rotes Rathaus ㉑
Red Town Hall

Rathausstraße 15. **Map** 5 E2.
Ⓤ & Ⓢ Alexanderplatz. Ⓤ Klosterstraße, 🚌 TXL, 148.

This impressive structure is
Berlin's main town hall. Its
predecessor was a much
more modest structure that,
by the end of the 19th
century, was inadequate
to meet the needs of the
growing metropolis.

The present building was
designed by Hermann
Friedrich Waesemann, and
the construction works went
on from 1861 until 1869. The
architect took his main inspiration from Italian Renaissance
municipal buildings, but the
tower is reminiscent of Laon
cathedral in France. The walls
are made from red brick and
it was this, rather than the
political orientation of the
mayors, that gave the town
hall its name.

The whole building has a
continuous frieze known as
the "stone chronicle", which
was added in 1879. The frieze
features scenes and figures
from the city's history and
traces the development of
its economy and science.

The Rotes Rathaus was
severely damaged during
World War II but, following
its reconstruction between
1951 and 1958, it became the
seat of the East Berlin
authorities. The West Berlin
magistrate was housed in the

Fernsehturm ㉓

The television tower, called by the locals *Telespargel*, or toothpick, remains to this day the city's tallest structure at 365 m (1,197 ft). It is also the second-tallest structure in Europe. The tower was built in 1969 to a design by a team of architects including Fritz Dieter and Günter Franke, with the help of Swedish experts. However, the idea for the tower originated much earlier from Hermann Henselmann (creator of the Karl-Marx-Allee development) in the Socialist-Realist style.

VISITORS' CHECKLIST

Panoramastrasse. **Map** 5 E1.
Tel *(030) 242 33 33* Ⓢ & **U**
Alexanderplatz. 🚌 *100, 157.* 🔲
Nov–Feb: 10am–midnight daily;
Mar–Oct: 9am–midnight daily.

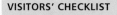

The television antenna is visible all over Berlin.

Transmitter aerial

The metal sphere is covered with steel cladding.

View from the Tower
On a clear day the viewing platform offers a full view of Berlin. Visibility can reach up to 40 km (25 miles).

Concrete structure rising to 250 m (820 ft)

The concrete shaft contains two elevators that carry passengers to the café and viewing platform.

Tele-Café
One of the attractions of the tower is the revolving café. A full rotation takes about half an hour, so it is possible to get a bird's-eye view of the whole city while sipping a cup of coffee.

The monumental, red-brick town hall, known as the Rotes Rathaus

Schöneberg town hall *(see p103)*. Following the reunification of Germany in 1990, the Rotes Rathaus became the centre of authority, housing the offices of the mayor and the Berlin cabinet.

The forecourt sculptures by Fritz Kremer, which depict Berliners helping to rebuild the city, were added in 1958.

Alexanderplatz ㉒

Map 5 E1, F1. **U** & Ⓢ *Alexanderplatz.* 🚌 *200, 257, 348.*

Alexanderplatz, or "Alex" as it is called locally, has a long history, although it would be hard now to find any visible traces of the past. Once known as Ochsenmarkt (oxen market), it was the site of a cattle and wool market. It was later renamed after Tsar Alexander I who visited Berlin in 1805. At that time, the square boasted a magnificent monumental colonnade, which was designed by Carl von Gontard.

In time, houses and shops sprang up around the square and a market hall and urban train line were built nearby.

"Alex" became one of the city's busiest spots. Its frenzied atmosphere was captured by Alfred Döblin (1878–1957) in his novel *Berlin Alexanderplatz*.

In 1929, attempts were made to develop the square, though only two office buildings were added – the Alexanderhaus and the Berolinahaus, both by Peter Behrens.

World War II erased most of the square's buildings and it is now surrounded by characterless 1960s edifices, including the Forum Hotel (formerly Hotel Stadt Berlin) and the Fernsehturm. Now Alexanderplatz awaits its next transformation, to be based on the winning design chosen from a competition for the square's redevelopment.

Riverside buildings of the Nikolaiviertel

Nikolaiviertel ㉔

Map 5 E2. 🅄 & Ⓢ *Alexanderplatz.*
🅄 *Klosterstraße.* 🚌 *100, 142, 157, 257, 348.*

This small area on the bank of the Spree is a favourite place for both Berliners and tourists. Some of Berlin's oldest houses stood here until they were destroyed in World War II. The redevelopment of the area, which was carried out by the GDR government between 1979 and 1987, was an interesting attempt to recreate a medieval village. Now, with the exception of one or two restored buildings, the Nikolaiviertel consists entirely of newly built replicas of historic buildings.

The **Nikolaikirche** was destroyed by bombing in 1945 and rebuilt in 1987. All that remains of the original structure, which was probably built around 1230, is the base of the two-tower façade of the present church, which dates from around 1300.

The only Baroque building in Nikolaiviertel to escape damage during World War II was the **Knoblauchhaus**, a small townhouse built in 1759 for the Knoblauch family. The current appearance of the building is the result of work carried out in 1835 when the façade was given a Neo-Classical look.

Ephraim-Palais was built in 1766 for Nathan Veitel Heinrich Ephraim, Frederick the Great's mint master and court jeweller. Parts of the original structure, which were saved from demolition, were used in the reconstruction.

Märkisches Museum ㉕

Am Köllnischen Park 5. **Map** 5 F2.
Tel *(030) 24 00 21 62.* 🅄 *Märkisches Museum.* Ⓢ *Jannowitzbrücke.* 🚌 *147, 265.* ◻ *10am–6pm Tue, Thu–Sun, noon–8pm Wed.* 🎟 *(free Wed).* *Presentation of mechanical instruments 3pm Sun.*

Built between 1901 and 1908, this complex of red brick buildings was inspired by the brick-Gothic style popular in the Brandenburg region. The museum, founded in 1874, is dedicated to the cultural history of Berlin from the first settlements to today. The department "Berliner Kunst" (art), for example, presents a remarkable collection of paintings, sculpture, textiles, faiences, glass and porcelain. The main hall features the original Gothic portal from the sculpture *Quadriga*, which once crowned the Brandenburg Gate *(see p69).* A further collection is devoted to the Berlin theatre from 1730 to 1933. One of the galleries houses some old-time mechanical musical instruments.

The exterior of the Märkisches Museum, echoing a medieval monastery

Surrounding the museum is the Köllnischer Park, home to three brown bears – the city mascots.

Checkpoint Charlie ㉖

Friedrichstraße 43–45. **Map** 4 C4.
Tel *(030) 253 72 50.* 🅄 *Kochstraße.* 🚌 *129.* **Haus am Checkpoint Charlie** ◻ *9am–10pm daily.* 🎟

The name of this notorious border crossing between the American and Soviet sectors comes from the word that signifies the letter C in the international phonetic alphabet: Alpha, Bravo, Charlie.

Between 1961 and 1990, Checkpoint Charlie was the only crossing for foreigners between East and West Berlin. It came to represent a symbol of both freedom and separation for the many East Germans trying to escape Soviet communism.

Today, a single watchtower is all that remains, and this houses a museum – **Haus am Checkpoint Charlie**. Its rich collection details the years of the Cold War in Berlin.

Jüdisches Museum ㉗

Lindenstraße 14. **Map** 4 C5.
Tel *(030) 25 99 33 00.* 🅄 *Hallesches Tor or Kochstraße.* 🚌 *M29, M41, 265.* ◻ *10am–10pm Mon, 10am–8pm Tue–Sun.*

The building housing the city's recently opened Jewish Museum is an exciting and imaginative example of 20th-century architecture. Designed by a Polish-Jewish architect based in the United States, Daniel Libeskind, the plan, shape, style, and interior and exterior arrangement of the building are part of a profoundly complicated philosophical programme. The museum's architecture itself is intended to convey something of the tragic history of the millions of Jews who perished in the Holocaust. For example, the zig-zag layout recalls a torn Star of David.

The interior arrangement is dominated by a gigantic empty crack, which cuts a swathe through the building. Several corridors lead to a windowless Holocaust tower.

The collection focuses on Jewish history and art. Also on display are artifacts that were once part of everyday Jewish life in Berlin.

The new museum is accessible only through an underground passageway in the former Berlin-Museum building next door.

The austere, steel-clad walls of the Jüdisches Museum

Topographie des Terrors ㉘

Stresemannstraße 110 (enter on Niederkirchner Straße). **Map** 4 B4.
Tel (030) 25 48 67 03. Ⓢ &
Ⓤ Potsdamer Platz. 🚌 129, 248, 341. 🕐 Oct–Apr: 10am–5pm daily; May–Sep: 10am–8pm daily.

During the Third Reich, Prinz-Albrecht-Straße was probably the most frightening address in Berlin: here, three of the most terrifying Nazi political departments had their headquarters. The Neo-Classical Prinz-Albrecht palace,

which stands at Wilhelmstraße No. 102, became the headquarters of Reinhard Heydrich and the Third Reich's security service. The school of arts and crafts at Prinz-Albrecht-Straße No. 8 was occupied by the head of the Gestapo, Heinrich Müller, while the Hotel Prinz Albrecht at No. 9 became the headquarters of the Schutzstaffel or SS.

After World War II, the buildings were pulled down. In 1987, however, in cellars that were once used as torture cells, an exhibition documenting Nazi crimes was mounted.

A new museum building is currently under construction.

Deutsches Technikmuseum Berlin ㉙

Trebbiner Straße 9. **Map** 4 A5.
Tel (030) 90 25 40. Ⓤ Gleisdreieck.
🚌 140. 🕐 9am–5:30pm Tue–Fri, 10am–6pm Sat–Sun. & 📷

The Technical Museum was first established in 1982 with the intention of grouping more than 100 smaller, specialized collections under one roof. The current collection is arranged on the site of the former trade hall, the size of which allows many of the

Exhibition documenting Nazi crimes at the Topographie des Terrors

museum's exhibits, such as locomotives, water towers and storerooms, to be displayed full-size and in their original condition.

Of particular interest in the collection are the dozens of locomotives and railway carriages from different eras, as well as vintage cars. There are also exhibitions dedicated to flying, the history of paper manufacture, printing, weaving, electro-technology and computer technology. There are also two windmills, a brewery and an old forge. The section called Spectrum is especially popular with children as it allows them to try the "hands-on" experiments. A new hall for aircraft and engines will open at the end of 2003.

A special attraction of the Technical Museum is the Historical Brewery, which opened in 1995. The building was once used by the brewery Tucker Bräu for storing beer, but it was destroyed in World War II. Decades later, the brewery was rebuilt on four levels. Some visitors claim they can smell roasted malt.

One of dozens of locomotives displayed in the Deutsches Technikmuseum

WESTERN CENTRE

This part of Berlin includes the areas of Tiergarten, Charlottenburg and parts of Kreuzberg, as well as a small section of Mitte, which used to belong to East Berlin.

Tiergarten, which was once a royal hunting estate, became a park in the 18th century. It survives as a park to this day, although in an altered form.

To the south of Tiergarten is the Kulturforum – a large centre of museums and other cultural establishments, which was created after World War II. The neighbouring Potsdamer Platz is now an ultra-modern development, built in recent years on the wasteland that formerly divided East and West Berlin.

Although the eastern part of Charlottenburg does not feature a great number of historic buildings, it is one of the city's most attractive districts, which, after World War II, became the commercial and cultural centre of West Berlin. Kreuzberg is a lively area that is now populated by immigrants, artists and affluent young professionals.

Detail from Theater des Westens façade

SIGHTS AT A GLANCE

Museums and Galleries
Bauhaus-Archiv ❼
Bendlerblock ❽
Gemäldegalerie ❾
Hamburger Bahnhof ⓱
Käthe-Kollwitz-Museum ❸
Kunstgewerbemuseum ⓬
Kupferstichkabinett und Kunstbibliothek ❿
Museum für Naturkunde ⓲
Musikinstrumenten-Museum ⓮
Neue Nationalgalerie ⓫

Streets and Squares
Kurfürstendamm (Ku'damm) ❷
Potsdamer Platz ⓯

Tiergarten ❺
Zoologischer Garten ❹

Churches
Kaiser-Wilhelm-
Gedächtniskirche ❶

Historic Buildings and Monuments
Philharmonie ⓭
Reichstag ⓰
Siegessäule ❻

GETTING THERE

This part of town is served by S-Bahn lines 3, 5, 7, 9, 75 and by U-Bahn lines 1, 2, 9, 15.

KEY

- ▦ Street-by-Street map See pp84–5
- 🚉 Railway station
- Ⓢ S-Bahn station
- Ⓤ U-Bahn station

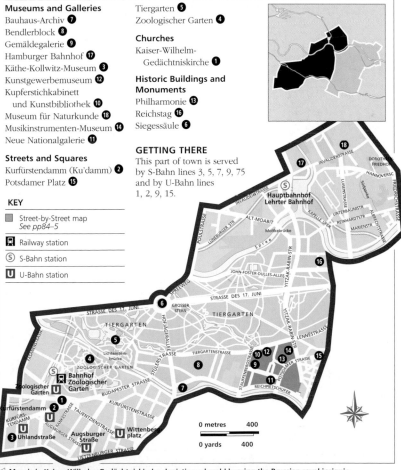

◁ **Mosaic in Kaiser-Wilhelm-Gedächtniskirche depicting a herald bearing the Prussian royal insignia**

Street-by-Street: Kulturforum

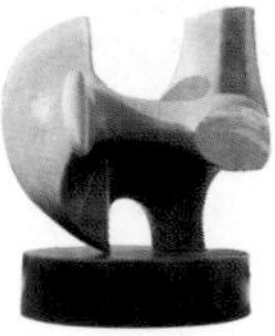

Sculpture by Henry Moore

The idea of creating a new cultural centre in West Berlin was first mooted in 1956. The first building to go up was the Berlin Philharmonic concert hall, built to an innovative design by Hans Scharoun in 1961. Most other elements of the Kulturforum were realized between 1961 and 1987, and came from such famous architects as Ludwig Mies van der Rohe. The area is now a major cultural centre that attracts millions of visitors every year.

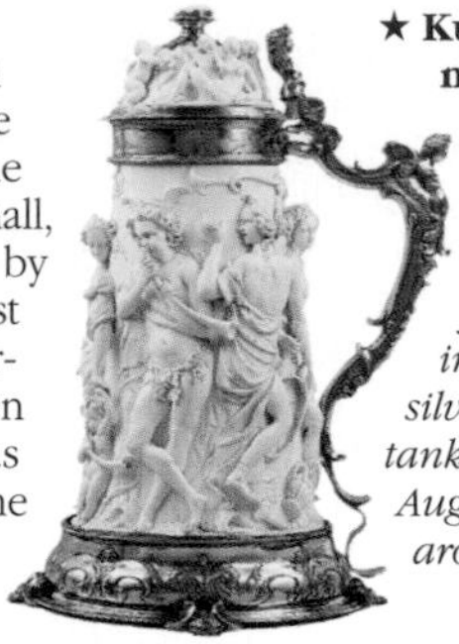

★ Kunstgewerbemuseum
Among the collection at the Museum of Arts and Crafts you can see this intricately carved silver and ivory tankard, made in an Augsburg workshop around 1640 ⓬

Kupferstichkabinett
The large collection of prints and drawings owned by this gallery includes this portrait of Albrecht Dürer's mother ❿

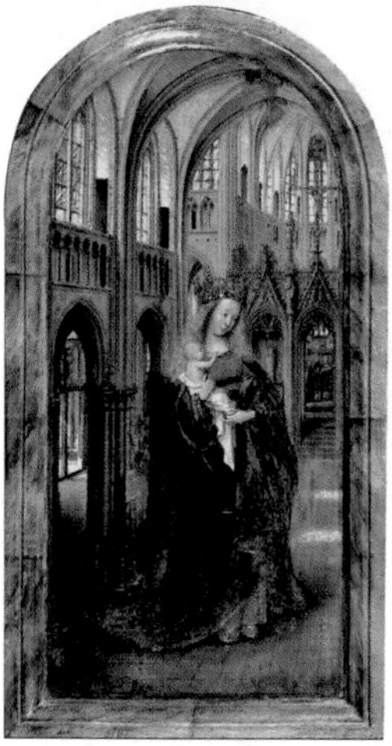

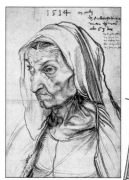

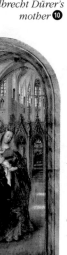

★ Gemäldegalerie
Among the most important works of the old masters exhibited in this gallery of fine art is this Madonna in Church *by Jan van Eyck (c.1425)* ❾

REICHPIETSCHUFER
LANDWEHRKANAL

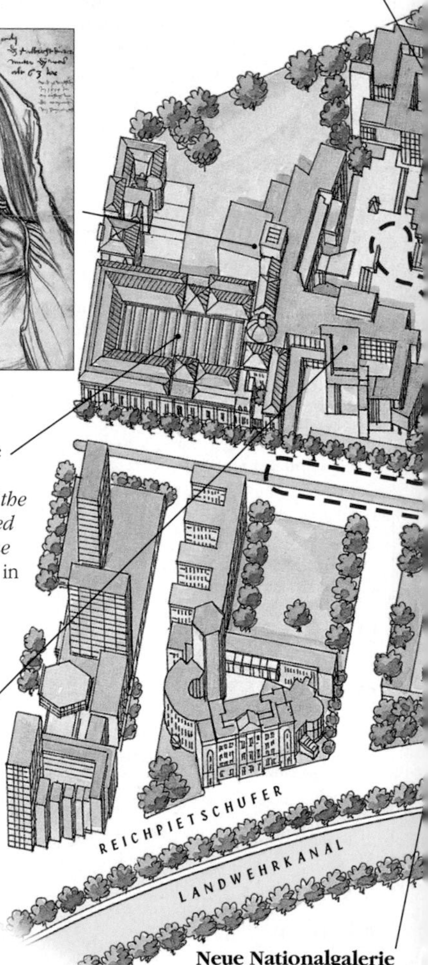

Kunstbibliothek
The Art Library boasts a rich collection of books, graphic art and drawings.

Neue Nationalgalerie
Sculptures by Henry Moore and Alexander Calder stand outside this streamlined building, designed by Ludwig Mies van der Rohe ⓫

STAR SIGHTS

- ★ Gemäldegalerie
- ★ Kunstgewerbemuseum
- ★ Philharmonie

KEY

— — — Suggested route

For hotels and restaurants in this region see pp488–90 and pp526–8

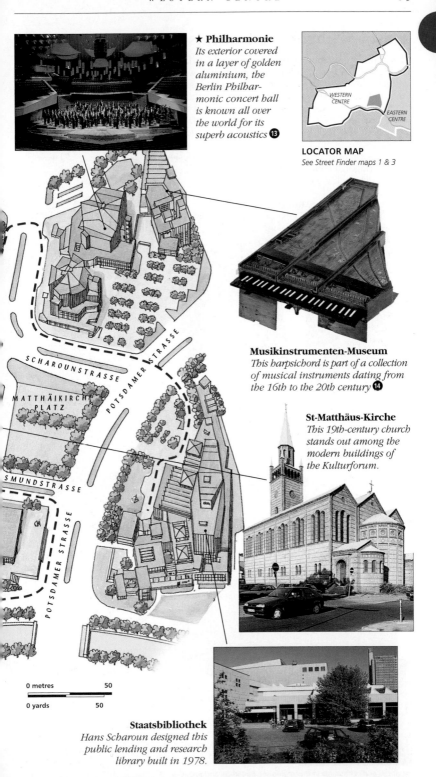

★ **Philharmonie**
Its exterior covered in a layer of golden aluminium, the Berlin Philharmonic concert hall is known all over the world for its superb acoustics ⑬

LOCATOR MAP
See Street Finder maps 1 & 3

Musikinstrumenten-Museum
This harpsichord is part of a collection of musical instruments dating from the 16th to the 20th century ⑭

St-Matthäus-Kirche
This 19th-century church stands out among the modern buildings of the Kulturforum.

SCHAROUNSTRASSE

POTSDAMER STRASSE

MATTHÄIKIRCH
PLATZ

SMUNDSTRASSE

POTSDAMER STRASSE

0 metres 50
0 yards 50

Staatsbibliothek
Hans Scharoun designed this public lending and research library built in 1978.

Kaiser-Wilhelm-Gedächtnis-Kirche ❶

This church-monument is one of Berlin's most famous landmarks. The vast Neo-Romanesque church was designed by Franz Schwechten. It was consecrated in 1895 and destroyed by bombs in 1943. After the war the ruins were removed, leaving only the front tower, at the base of which the Gedenkhalle (Memorial Hall) is situated. This hall documents the church's history and contains some original ceiling mosaics, marble reliefs and liturgical objects. In 1963, Egon Eiermann designed a new octagonal church in blue glass and a new freestanding bell tower.

VISITORS' CHECKLIST

Breitscheidplatz. **Map** 2 B4.
Tel (030) 218 50 23.
Ⓢ & Ⓤ Zoologischer Garten
or Ⓤ Kurfürstendamm.
🚌 100, 200, X-9. ◻ **Church**
9am–7pm daily. **Gedenkhalle**
10am–6:30pm Mon–Sat. 🔒
10am & 6pm Sun. 🖼 **www.**
gedaechtnis-kirche.com

Tower Ruins
The damaged roof of the former church has become one of the best-known symbols of Berlin.

Tower Clock

★ Kaiser's Mosaic
Kaiser Heinrich I, seated on his throne, is depicted in this elaborate mosaic.

Figure of Christ
This vast sculpture by Hermann Schaper once decorated the church altar. It survived World War II damage.

Main entrance

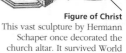

Main Altar
The massive figure of Christ on the Cross is the work of Karl Hemmeter.

STAR SIGHTS

★ Kaiser's Mosaic

Ku'damm ❷

Plan 2 A5, 2 B4. 🇺 *Kurfürsten-damm.* 🚌 *109, 110, X10, M19, M29, M46.*

The eastern area of the Charlottenburg region, around the boulevard known as Kurfürstendamm (the Ku'damm), was developed in the 19th century. Luxurious buildings were constructed along the Ku'damm, while the areas of Breitscheidplatz and Wittenbergplatz filled up with hotels and department stores. After World War II, with the old centre (Mitte) situated in East Berlin, Charlottenburg became the centre of West Berlin. After the war the area was transformed into the heart of West Berlin, with dozens of new company headquarters and trade centres being built.

Mother and Child, from the Käthe-Kollwitz-Museum

Käthe-Kollwitz-Museum ❸

Fasanenstraße 24. **Map** 2 A5. *Tel (030) 882 52 10.* 🇺 *Uhlandstraße or Kurfürstendamm.* 🚌 *109, 110, X10, M19, M29, 249.* 🕐 *11am–6pm Wed–Mon* 🈂 🅿

This small private museum provides a unique opportunity to become acquainted with the work of Käthe Kollwitz (1867–1945). Born in Königsberg, the artist settled in Berlin where she married a doctor who worked in Prenzlauer Berg, a working-class district. Her drawings and sculptures portrayed the social

A tranquil area within the Tiergarten

problems of the poor, as well as human suffering.

This museum displays the work of Käthe Kollwitz and includes posters, drawings and sculptures as well as documents, such as letters and photographs.

Zoologischer Garten ❹

Zoological Garden

Hardenbergplatz 8 / Budapester Str. 34. **Map** 2 B3, C3, 2 B4, C4. *Tel (030) 25 40 10.* 🆂 & 🇺 *Zoo-logischer Garten.* 🚌 *M46, X9, X10, X34, 100, 109, 149, 200, 245, 249.* 🕐 *Apr–Sep: 9am–6:30pm daily; Oct–Mar: 9am–5pm daily.* 🈂

The zoological garden is actually part of the Tiergarten and dates from 1844, making this one of the oldest zoos in Germany. It offers a number of attractions, including the monkey house, which contains a family of gorillas, and a specially darkened pavilion for observing nocturnal animals. A glazed wall in the hippopotamus pool enables visitors to observe these enormous animals moving through the water. The large aquarium contains sharks, piranhas and unusual animals from coral reefs. There is also a huge terrarium with an overgrown jungle that is home to a group of crocodiles. Just to the west of the zoological garden on Jebenstraße is the **Newton-Sammlung**. This gallery houses photographs by Berliner Helmut Newton.

Tiergarten ❺

Map 2 C3, 3 D3, E3, F3. 🆂 *Tiergarten or Bellevue.* 🚌 *100, 187, 341.*

Once a forest used as the Elector's hunting reserve, the Tiergarten was transformed into a landscaped park by Peter Joseph Lenné in the 1830s. A Triumphal Avenue, lined with statues of the country's rulers and statesmen, was built in the eastern section at the end of the 19th century.

World War II inflicted huge damage, but replanting has now restored the Tiergarten and its avenues are bordered with statues of figures such as Johann Wolfgang von Goethe and Richard Wagner.

Near the lake and the Landwehrkanal are memorials to Karl Liebknecht and Rosa Luxemburg, the leaders of the Spartakus movement who were assassinated in 1918.

Siegessäule ❻

Triumphal Column

Großer Stern. **Map** 3 D2. 🆂 *Bellevue.* 🚌 *100, 187.* 🕐 *Apr–Oct: 8:30am–6:30pm daily; Nov–Mar: 8:30am–5:30pm daily.*

The triumphal column, based on a design by Johann Heinrich Strack, was built to commemorate victory in the Prusso-Danish war of 1864. After further Prussian victories in wars against Austria (1866) and France (1871), a gilded figure representing Victory, known as the "Goldelse", was added to the top of the column. It originally stood in front of the Reichstag building but was moved to its present location by the Nazi government in 1938. The base is decorated with bas-reliefs commemorating battles, while higher up a mosaic frieze depicts the founding of the German Empire in 1871. An observation terrace at the top offers magnificent vistas over Berlin.

Siegessäule (Triumphal Column)

The captivating, streamlined buildings of the Bauhaus-Archiv

Bauhaus-Archiv ❼

Klingelhöferstraße 14. **Map** 3 D4,
E4. **Tel** *(030) 254 00 20.* **U**
Nollendorfplatz. 🚌 *100, 187, M29.* ⭕
10am– 5pm Wed–Mon. 💷 *(free
Mon.)* **Library** *9am–1pm Mon–Fri.* ♿

The Bauhaus school of art,
started by Walter Gropius in
1919, was one of the most
influential art institutions of
the 20th century. Originally
based in Weimar, it inspired
many artists and architects.
Staff and students included
Mies van der Rohe, Paul Klee
and Wassily Kandinsky. The
school moved to Berlin in
1932 from Dessau, but was
closed by the Nazis in 1933.
   After the war, the Bauhaus-
Archiv was relocated to Darmstadt. In 1964 Walter Gropius
designed a building to house
the collection but, in 1971, the
archive was moved to Berlin
and the design was adapted to
the new site. As Gropius had
died in 1969, Alexander
Cvijanovic took over the
project. Built between 1976
and 1979 the gleaming white
building with its glass-panelled
gables houses the archive,
library and exhibition halls.

Bendlerblock (Gedenkstätte Deutscher Widerstand) ❽

Stauffenbergstraße 13–14. **Map** 3
E4, F4. **Tel** *(030) 26 99 50 00.* **U**
Mendelssohn-Bartholdy-Park. 🚌 *148,
M29.* ⭕ *9am–6pm Mon–Wed,
9am–8pm Thu, 10–6pm Sat–Sun.*
🔴 *1 Jan, 24, 25 & 31 Dec.* 💷

The collection of buildings
known as the Bendlerblock
was built during the Third
Reich as an extension to the

German State Naval Offices.
During World War II they
were the headquarters of the
Wehrmacht (German Army).
It was here that a group of
officers planned their assassination attempt on Hitler on 20
July 1944. When the attempt
led by Claus Schenk von
Stauffenberg failed, he and
his fellow conspirators were
arrested and death sentences
passed. Stauffenberg, Friedrich
Olbricht, Werner von Haeften,
and Ritter Mertz von Quirn-
heim were shot in the Bendlerblock courtyard. A monument
commemorating this event,
designed by Richard Scheibe
in 1953, stands where the
executions were carried out.
   On the upper floor of
the building there is an
exhibition which documents
the history of the German anti-
Nazi movements.

Gemäldegalerie ❾

See pp90–91.

Kupferstichkabinett und Kunst-bibliothek ❿

Matthäikirchplatz 8. **Map** 3 F3. **Tel**
(030) 266 20 02. Ⓢ & **U** *Potsdamer
Platz or* **U** *Mendelssohn-Bartholdy-
Park.* 🚌 *148, 100, 123, 200, M29,
M41.* **Kupferstichkabinett:
Exhibitions** *10am–6pm Tue–Fri,
11am–6pm Sat–Sun.* **Studio gallery**
9am–4pm Tue–Fri. **Kunstbibliothek:
Exhibits** *10am–6pm Tue–Fri,
11am–6pm Sat–Sun.* **Library** *2–8pm
Mon, 9am– 8pm Tue–Fri.* 💷 ♿ 🚫

The print collections of
galleries in the former East
and West Berlin were united
in 1994 in the Kupferstichkabinett (Print Gallery), whose

collection includes around
2,000 engraver's plates, over
520,000 prints and 80,000
drawings and watercolours.
   The **Kunstbibliothek** (Art
Library) is not only a library
with a range of publications
about the arts; it is also a
museum with an extensive
collection of posters,
advertisements and other
practical forms of design.

Munch's lithograph *Girl on a
Beach*, Kupferstichkabinett

Neue Nationalgalerie ⓫

Potsdamer Straße 50. **Map** 3 F4.
Tel *(030) 266 26 51.* **U** & Ⓢ
Potsdamer Platz or **U** *Mendelssohn-
Bartholdy-Park.* 🚌 *148, 100, 123,
200, M29, M41.* ⭕ *10am–6pm Tue
& Wed, 10am–10pm Thu, 10am–8pm
Fri–Sun.* 💷 ♿

After World War II, when
this magnificent collection
of modern art ended up in
West Berlin, the commission
to design a suitable building to
house it was given to Mies van
der Rohe. The result is a
striking building with a flat
steel roof over a glass hall,
which is supported only by
six slender interior struts.
   The collection comprises
largely 20th-century art, but
begins with artists of the late
19th century, such as Edvard
Munch. German art is well
represented: as well as the
Bauhaus movement, the
gallery shows works by exponents of a crass realism, such

Karl Schmidt-Rottluff's *Farm in Daugart* **(1910), Neue Nationalgalerie**

as Otto Dix. The most celebrated artists of other European countries are included, as are examples of post-World War II art.

Kunstgewerbe-museum ⑫

Tiergarten-Str. 6. **Map** 3 F3. *Tel (030) 266 29 02.* Ⓢ *Potsdamer Platz.* Ⓤ *Potsdamer Platz or Mendelssohn-Bartholdy-Park.* 🚌 *100, 123, 148, 200, M29, M41.* ⭕ *10am–6pm Tue–Fri, 11am–6pm Sat & Sun.* ⚫ *Tue after Easter, Whitsun, 1 Oct, 24, 25 & 31 Dec.* 📷 ♿ 🚫

This museum holds a rich collection embracing many genres of craft and decorative art, from the early Middle Ages to the modern day. Goldwork is especially well represented, as are metal items from the Middle Ages. Among the most valuable exhibits is a collection of medieval goldwork from the church treasures of Enger and the Guelph

treasury from Brunswick. The museum also takes great pride in its collection of late Gothic and Renaissance silver from the civic treasury in the town of Lüneberg. In addition, there are fine examples of Italian majolica, and 18th- and 19th-century German, French and Italian glass, porcelain and furniture.

Philharmonie ⑬

Philharmonic and Chamber Music Hall

Herbert-von-Karajan-Straße 1. **Map** 3 F3. *Tel (030) 25 48 80.* Ⓢ & Ⓤ *Potsdamer Platz or* Ⓤ *Mendelssohn-Bartholdy-Park.* 🚌 *129, 148, M41.*

Home to one of the most renowned orchestras in Europe, this unusual building is among the finest postwar architectural achievements in

Europe. Built between 1960 and 1963 to a design by Hans Scharoun, the Philharmonie pioneered a new concept for concert hall interiors, with a podium occupying the central section of the pentagonal hall, around which are galleries for the public. The exterior is reminiscent of a circus tent. The gilded exterior was added between 1978 and 1981.

Between the years 1984 to 1987 the Kammermusiksaal, which was designed by Edgar Wisniewski on the basis of sketches by Scharoun, was added to the Philharmonie. This building consolidates the aesthetics of the earlier structure by featuring a central multi-sided space covered by a fanciful tent-like roof.

Musikinstrumenten-Museum ⑭

Tiergartenstraße 1. **Map** 1 A5. *Tel (030) 25 48 11 78.* Ⓢ & Ⓤ *Potsdamer Platz or* Ⓤ *Mendelssohn-Bartholdy-Park.* 🚌 *200.* ⭕ *9am–5pm Tue, Wed, Fri, 9am–10pm Thu, 10am–5pm Sat–Sun.* **Wurlitzer Organ demonstration** *noon, first Sat of the month.* 📷 ♿

Behind the Philharmonie, in a small building designed by Edgar Wisniewski and Hans Scharoun between 1979 and 1984, the fascinating Museum of Musical Instruments houses a collection dating from 1888. Intriguing displays trace each instrument's development from the 16th century to the present day. Most spectacular of all is a working Wurlitzer cinema organ dating from 1929. Saturday demonstrations of its impressive sounds attract enthusiastic crowds. There is also an archive and a library.

The tent-like gilded exterior of the Philharmonie and Kammermusiksaal

Gemäldegalerie 9

Woman in a Bonnet by Rogier van der Weyden

The Gemäldegalerie collection is exceptional in the consistently high quality of its paintings. Unlike those in other collections, they were chosen by specialists who, from the end of the 18th century, systematically acquired pictures to represent all the major European schools. Originally part of the Altes Museum collection (see p75), the paintings achieved independent status in 1904 when they were moved to what is now the Bodemuseum (see p78). After the division of Berlin in 1945, part of the collection was kept in the Bodemuseum, while the majority ended up in the Dahlem Museum (see p104). Following reunification, and with the building of a new home as part of the Kulturforum development, this unique collection has finally been united again.

★ **Cupid Victorious** (1602)
Inspired by Virgil's Omnia vincit Amor, *Caravaggio depicted a playful god trampling over the symbols of Culture, Fame, Knowledge and Power.*

Madonna with Child (c.1477)
A frequent subject of Sandro Botticelli, the Madonna and Child are depicted here, surrounded by singing angels holding lilies to symbolize purity.

Circular lobby leading to the galleries

Birth of Christ (c.1480)
This beautiful religious painting is one of the few surviving paintings on panels by Martin Schongauer.

Portrait of Hieronymus Holzschuher (1526)
Albrecht Dürer painted this affectionate portrait of his friend, who was the mayor of Nuremberg.

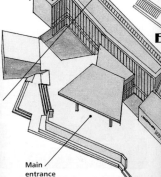

Main entrance

The Glass of Wine
(1661/62)
Jan Vermeer's carefully composed picture of a young woman drinking wine with a young man gently hints at the relationship developing between them.

VISITORS' CHECKLIST

Matthäikirchplatz. **Map** 3 F3.
Tel *(030) 266 29 51.*
Ⓢ & Ⓤ *Potsdamer Platz.*
Ⓤ *Mendelssohn-Bartholdy-Park.*
M29, M41, 123, 200.
◯ *10am–6pm Tue, Wed, Fri–Sun; 10am–10pm Thu.*
first Tue after Easter and Whitsun, 1 May, 24, 25 & 31 Dec.

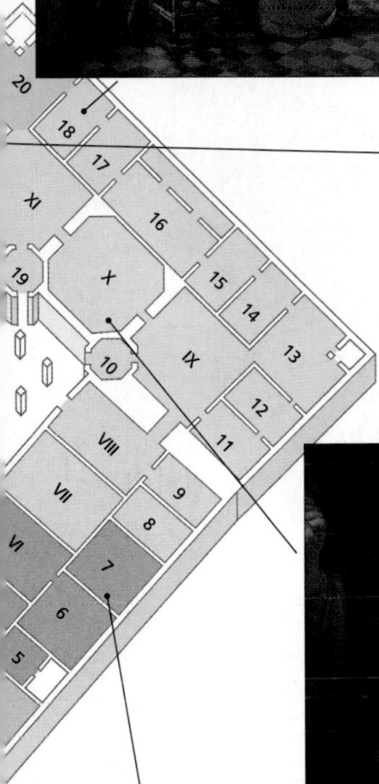

Love in the French Theatre
This picture has a companion piece called Love in the Italian Theatre. *Both by French painter, Jean-Antoine Watteau (1684–1721).*

★ Portrait of Hendrickje Stoffels *(1656–57)*
Rembrandt's portrait of his lover, Hendrickje Stoffels, is typical of his work in the way it focuses on the subject and ignores the background.

KEY

◻ 13th–16th-century German painting

◻ 14th–16th-century Dutch and French painting

◻ 17th-century Flemish and Dutch painting

◻ 18th-century French, English and German painting

◻ 17th–18th-century Italian painting, 17th-century German, French and Spanish painting

◻ 13th–16th-century Italian painting

◻ 16th–18th-century miniatures

◻ Digital gallery

GALLERY GUIDE
The main gallery contains over 900 masterpieces grouped by period and country of origin. These are comple-mented by around 400 works in the educational gallery on the lower floor and by a computerized digital gallery.

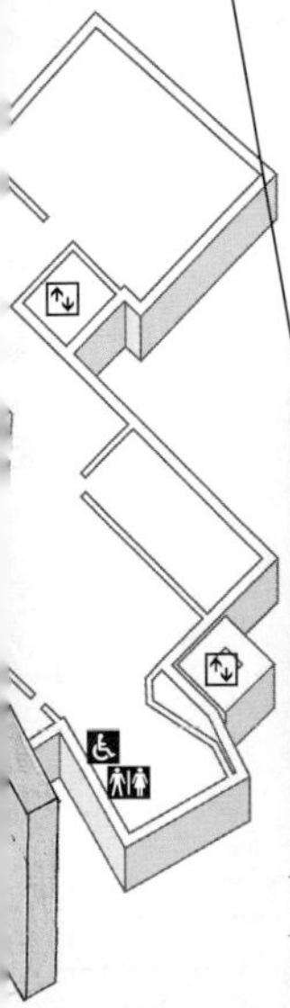

★ Dutch Proverbs *(1559)*
Pieter Brueghel managed to illustrate more than 100 proverbs in this painting.

STAR EXHIBITS

★ Cupid Victorious

★ Dutch Proverbs

★ Portrait of Hendrickje Stoffels

Potsdamer Platz ⑮

In the short space of a few years a new financial and business district has sprung up on the vast empty wasteland surrounding the Potsdamer Platz. It boasts splendid constructions designed by Renzo Piano, Arata Isozaki and Helmut Jahn. As well as office blocks, the area has many public buildings, including cinemas and a theatre, as well as a huge shopping centre – the Arkaden, plus luxury hotels, restaurants and several bars.

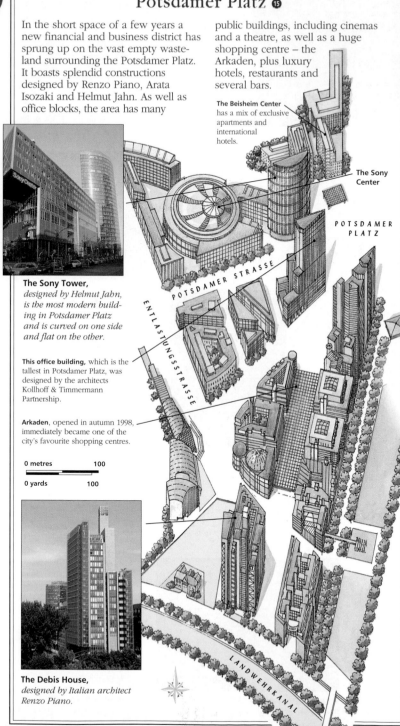

The Beisheim Center has a mix of exclusive apartments and international hotels.

The Sony Center

POTSDAMER PLATZ

POTSDAMER STRASSE

ENTLASTUNGSSTRASSE

LANDWEHRKANAL

The Sony Tower,
designed by Helmut Jahn, is the most modern building in Potsdamer Platz and is curved on one side and flat on the other.

This office building, which is the tallest in Potsdamer Platz, was designed by the architects Kollhoff & Timmermann Partnership.

Arkaden, opened in autumn 1998, immediately became one of the city's favourite shopping centres.

| 0 metres | 100 |
| 0 yards | 100 |

The Debis House,
designed by Italian architect Renzo Piano.

The Reichstag, crowned by a dome designed by Sir Norman Foster

Reichstag ⑯

Platz der Republik. **Map** 1 B4, 4 A1, A2. **Tel** *(030) 22 73 21 52.* Ⓢ *Unter den Linden.* 🚌 *100, 123.* **Dome** ◻ *8am–midnight daily.* **Assembly Hall** ◻ *9am–5pm Mon–Fri, 10am–4pm Sat–Sun, holidays by appointment only.* 🔊 *noon Tue (in English).* ⬤ *1 Jan, 24–26 & 31 Dec.*

Built to house the German Parliament, the Reichstag was constructed between 1884 and 1894 to a New-Renaissance design by Paul Wallot. Capturing the prevailing spirit of German optimism, it became a potent symbol to the populace.

In 1918, from the Reichstag, Philipp Scheidemann declared the formation of the Weimar Republic. The next time the world heard about the building was in February 1933, when a fire destroyed the main hall. The Communists were blamed, accelerating a political witch-hunt driven by the Nazis, who then came to power.

With the onset of World War II, the building was not rebuilt, yet its significance resonated beyond Germany, as shown by a photograph of the Soviet flag flying from the Reichstag in May 1945, which became a symbol of the German defeat.

Following rebuilding work between 1957 and 1972, the Reichstag provided a meeting-place for the lower house of the German Parliament as well as a spectacular backdrop for festivals and rock concerts. After German reunification in 1990, the Reichstag was the first meeting place of a newly elected Bundestag. The latest rebuilding project, to a design by Sir Norman Foster, transformed the Reichstag into a modern meeting hall in which the first parliamentary meeting took place on 19 April 1999.

Hamburger Bahnhof ⑰

Invalidenstraße 50/51. **Map** 1 A2, B2. **Tel** *(030) 397 834-11.* Ⓢ *Lehrter Stadtbahnhof.* 🚌 *147, 245.* ◻ *10am–6pm Tue–Fri, Sun, 10am–8pm Sat.* ⬤ *1 Jan, Tue following Easter and Whitsun, 24, 25 & 31 Dec.* ♿ 📷 📷

This museum is situated in a Neo-Renaissance building, formerly the Hamburg Railway station, which dates from 1847. The building stood vacant after World War II but, following refurbishment by Josef Paul Kleihues, it was opened to the public in 1996. The neon installation surrounding the façade is the work of Dan Flavin. The museum houses a magnificent collection of contemporary art, including the work of Erich Marx and, from 2004, the world-renowned Flick collection. The result is one of the best modern art museums to be found in Europe, which features not only art, but also film, video, music and design.

Jeff and Ilona (1991), **Hamburger Bahnhof**

Museum für Naturkunde ⑱

Natural History Museum

Invalidenstraße 43. **Map** 1 E2. **Tel** *(030) 20 93 85 91.* Ⓤ *Zinnowitzer straße.* 🚌 *147, 240, 245.* 🚃 *6, 8.* ◻ *9:30am–5pm Tue–Fri, 10am–6pm Sat–Sun.* 📷

Occupying a purpose-built Neo-Renaissance building constructed between 1883 and 1889, this is one of the biggest natural history museums in the world, with a collection containing over 60 million exhibits. Although it has undergone several periods of extension and renovation, it has maintained its unique old-fashioned atmosphere.

The highlight of the museum is the world's largest dinosaur skeleton, which is housed in the glass-covered courtyard. The colossal brachiosaurus measures 23 m (75 ft) long and 12 m (39 ft) high. It was discovered in Tanzania, in 1909, by a German fossil-hunting expedition.

The adjacent rooms feature collections of colourful shells and butterflies, as well as stuffed birds and mammals. A favourite with children is Bobby the Gorilla, who lived in Berlin Zoo from 1928 until 1935. The museum also boasts an impressive collection of minerals and meteorites.

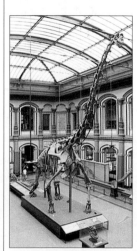

Brachiosaurus skeleton in the Museum für Naturkunde

FURTHER AFIELD

Berlin is a huge city with a unique character that has been shaped by the events in its history. Until 1920 the city consisted only of the districts that now comprise mainly Mitte, Tiergarten, Wedding, Prenzlauer Berg, Friedrichshain and Kreuzberg. At that time the city was surrounded by satellite towns and villages that had been evolving independently over many centuries.

In 1920, as part of great administrative reform, seven towns, 59 parishes and 27 country estates were incorporated into the city, thus creating an entirely new city covering nearly 900 sq km (350 sq miles), with a population of 3.8 million. This metropolis extended to small towns of medieval origin, such as Spandau, as well as to private manor houses and palaces, towns and smart suburban districts. Although the 20th century has changed the face of many of these places, their unique characters have remained undiminished. Because of this diversity, a trip to Berlin is like exploring many different towns simultaneously.

Detail from Schloss Charlottenburg

SIGHTS AT A GLANCE

Museums and Galleries
Brecht-Haus ⑪
Bröhan-Museum ❶
Brücke-Museum ㉔
Gedenkstätte Berlin-
　Hohenschönhausen ⑮
Gedenkstätte Plötzensee ❾
Museum für Ur- und
　Frühgeschichte ❹
Sammlung Berggruen ❷
Stasi-Museum ⑯

Places of Interest
Flughafen Tempelhof ⑲
Klein Glienicke ㉘
Köpenick ⑰
Muzeumszentrum Dahlem ㉒
Nikolskoe ㉗

Olympiastadion ❼
Pfaueninsel ㉖
Prenzlauer Berg ⑬
Strandbad Wannsee ㉕

Streets, Squares and Parks
Karl-Marx-Allee ⑭
Schlosspark ❸
Treptower Park ⑱
Victoriapark ⑳

**Historic Buildings and
Monuments**
Jagdschloss Grunewald ㉓
Messegelände ❻

Neue Synagoge ⑫
Rathaus Schöneberg ㉑
Schloss Charlottenburg ❺
Schloss Tegel ⑩
Zitadelle Spandau ❽

KEY

▨	Central Berlin
▢	Outskirts of Berlin
✈	Airport
▬	Motorway
▬	Main road
=	Secondary road
—	Railway line

0 metres　　400

0 yards　　400

MAP OF GREATER BERLIN

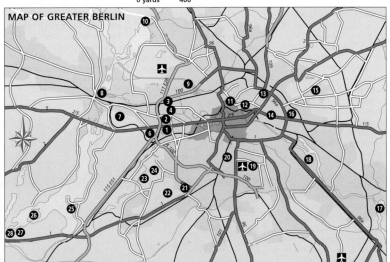

◁ **Façade of Schloss Charlottenburg**

Pablo Picasso's *Woman in a Hat* (1939), Sammlung Berggruen

The museum opened in 1996, in what was once the west pavilion of the barracks, using space freed up by moving the Antikensammlung to Museum Island *(see p74)*. The exhibition halls were modified according to the designs of Hilmer and Sattler, who also designed the layout of the Gemäldegalerie.

The Sammlung Berggruen is well known for its large collection of paintings, drawings and gouaches by Pablo Picasso. In addition to these, the museum displays more than 20 works by Paul Klee and paintings by other major artists – Van Gogh, Braque and Cézanne. The exhibition is supplemented by some excellent sculptures, particularly those of Henri Laurens and Alberto Giacometti.

Bröhan-Museum ❶

Schlossstraße 1a. **Tel** *(030) 32 69 06 00.* Ⓤ *Richard-Wagner-Platz & Sophie-Charlotte-Platz.* Ⓢ *Westend.* 🚌 *145, 309.* ⏱ *10am–6pm Tue–Sun.* ⏺ *24 & 31 Dec.* ♿ *(free 1st Wed)*

Located in a late-Neo-Classical building is this interesting, small museum. The collection was amassed by Karl H Bröhan who, from 1966, collected works of art from the Art Nouveau (Jugendstil or Secessionist) and Art Deco styles. The paintings of artists who were particularly connected with the Berlin Secessionist movement are especially well represented. Alongside the paintings are fine examples of other media and crafts including furniture, ceramics, glassware, silver-work and textiles.

Each of the main halls features an individual artist, often employing an array of media. There is also a display of furniture by Hector Guimard, Eugène Gaillard, Henri van de Velde and Joseph Hoffmann, glasswork by Emile Gallé, and porcelain from the best European manufacturers.

Sammlung Berggruen ❷

Schlossstraße 1. **Tel** *(030) 326 95 80.* Ⓤ *Richard-Wagner-Platz & Sophie-Charlotte-Platz.* Ⓢ *Westend.* 🚌 *145, 309.* ⏱ *10am–6pm Tue–Sun.* ♿ *(free 4pm–8pm Thu.)* 🚻 ♿

Heinz Berggruen assembled this tasteful collection of art dating from the late 19th and first half of the 20th century. Born and educated in Berlin, he emigrated to the US in 1936, spent most of his life in Paris, but finally entrusted his collection "Picasso and his Time" to the city of his birth.

Schlosspark ❸
Palace Park

Luisenplatz (Schloss Charlottenburg). Ⓤ *Richard-Wagner-Platz & Sophie-Charlotte-Platz.* Ⓢ *Westend.* 🚌 *109, 145, 309.* **Neuer Pavillon Tel** *(030) 32 09 14 43.* ⏱ *year-round: 10am–5pm Tue–Sun.* **Mausoleum** ⏱ *Apr–Oct: 10am–5pm Tue–Sun.* **Belvedere Tel** *(030) 32 09 14 45.* ⏱ *Apr–Oct: 10am–5pm Tue–Sun; Nov–Mar: noon–4pm Tue–Fri, noon–5pm Sat & Sun.*

This extensive royal park surrounding Schloss Charlottenburg is a favourite place for Berliners to stroll. The park is largely the result of work carried out after World War II, when 18th-century prints were used to help reconstruct the layout of the original grounds. Just

French-style garden in the Schloss Charlottenburg park

behind Schloss Charlottenburg is a French-style Baroque garden, constructed to a strict geometrical design with a vibrant patchwork of flower beds, carefully trimmed shrubs and ornate fountains adorned with replicas of antique sculptures. Beyond the curved carp lake is a less formal English-style landscaped park, the original layout of which was created between 1819 and 1828 under the direction of the renowned royal gardener, Peter Joseph Lenné.

Designed by Karl Friedrich Schinkel and completed in 1825, the Neo-Classical **Neuer Pavillon** is a charming two-storey building with rooms ranged around a central staircase. A cast-iron balcony encircles the entire structure.

The **Mausoleum** in which Queen Luise, wife of Friedrich Wilhelm III, was laid to rest, was designed by Karl Friedrich Schinkel in the style of a Doric portico-fronted temple. After the death of the king in 1840, the mausoleum was refurbished to create room for his tomb. The tombs of the king's second wife and those of Kaiser Wilhelm I and his wife were added later.

Built as a summerhouse for Friedrich Wilhelm II, with a mixture of Baroque and Neo-Classical elements, the **Belvedere** now houses the Royal Porcelain Workshop, with pieces ranging from the Rococo period up to late Biedermeier.

Museum für Ur- und Frühgeschichte ❹

Luisenplatz (Schloss Charlottenburg). **Tel** (030) 20 90 55 66. Ⓤ Richard-Wagner-Platz. 🚌 109, 145, 309. ◯ 10am–6pm Tue–Fri, 11am–6pm Sat, Sun. ♿ ✍

This Neo-Classical pavilion was designed by Carl Gotthard Langhans and added to the orangery wing of the Schloss Charlottenburg (see pp98–9) between 1787 and 1791. It was originally used as the court theatre but now houses a museum which documents cultures and

civilizations from the Stone Age to medieval times. There is a magnificent collection of items excavated at Troy by Heinrich Schliemann, including the "Treasure of Priam".

Schloss Charlottenburg ❺

See pp98–9.

The Funkturm (radio tower) in Berlin's Messegelände

Messegelände ❻

Hammarskjöldplatz. Ⓢ Witzleben. Ⓤ Kaiserdamm. 🚌 104, 149, 204, 219, X34, X49.

The pavilions of the vast exhibition and trade halls south of Hammarskjöldplatz cover more than 160,000 sq m (1,700,000 sq ft). The original

exhibition halls were built before World War I, but nothing of these buildings remains. The oldest part is the Funkturm and the pavilions surrounding it. The building at the front (Ehrenhalle) was built in 1936 to a design by Richard Ermisch, and is one of the few surviving buildings in Berlin designed in a Fascist architectural style.

The straight motorway at the rear of the halls is the famous Avus, the first German autobahn, built in 1921. At one point adapted as a car-racing track, it now it forms part of the autobahn system.

Olympiastadion ❼

Olympischer Platz. 🚆 & Ⓤ Olympia-Stadion. **Tel** (030) 25 00 23 22. ◯ Nov–late Mar: 10am–4pm daily; late Mar–Aug: 10am–7pm daily; Sep–Oct: 10am–6pm daily. ♿ ✍ **www**.olympiastadion-berlin.de

Olympiastadion, originally known as Reichssportfeld, was built for the 1936 Olympic Games in Berlin. It was designed by Werner March in the Nazi architectural style and was inspired by the architecture of ancient Rome. To the west of the stadium lie the Maifeld and what is now called the Waldbühne. The former is an enormous assembly ground surrounded by grandstands and fronted by the Glockenturm, a 77 m (250 ft) tower, while the latter is an open-air amphitheatre. A four-year high-tech modernization project on the stadium was completed in 2004. It now features a sweeping, illuminated roof.

Newly modernized and ever impressive Olympiastadion

Schloss Charlottenburg

Detail from the main gate

The palace in Charlottenburg was intended as a summer home for Sophie Charlotte, the wife of Elector Friedrich III. Construction began in 1695 to a design by Johann Arnold Nering. Johann Eosander von Göthe enlarged the palace between 1701 and 1713, adding the orangery wing. Further extensions were undertaken between 1740 and 1746 by Frederick the Great (Friedrich II) who added the new wing.

The palace was restored to its former elegance after World War II and its richly decorated interiors are unequalled in Berlin.

GALLERY GUIDE
The ground floor of the main building can only be visited by guided tour. The upper floor and the Neuer Flügel can be visited independently.

First floor

Ground floor

Museum für Vor- und Frühgeschichte
The museum is housed in a pavilion that served formerly as the court theatre, designed by Carl Gotthard Langhans.

★ **Porzellankabinett**
This exquisite mirrored gallery has walls lined from top to bottom with a fine display of Japanese and Chinese porcelain.

Main entrance

Monument to the Great Elector

Schlosskapelle
Only the pulpit in the court chapel is original. All the remaining furniture and fittings, including the splendid royal box, are reconstructions.

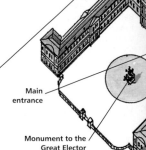

Palace Façade
The central section of the palace is the oldest part of the building. It is the work of Johann Arnold Nering.

Fortuna
A new sculpture by Richard Scheibe crowns the palace, replacing the original statue destroyed during World War II.

VISITORS' CHECKLIST

Luisenplatz. **Altes Schloss (Nering-Eosanderbau)** *Tel* (030) 32 09 11. **U** Richard-Wagner-Platz & Sophie-Charlotte-Platz. **S** Westend. 🚌 109, 145. 🕙 9am–5pm Tue–Fri, 10am–5pm Sat & Sun. 🎦 (compulsory on ground floor only). 🖼 **Neuer Flügel (Knobelsdorff-Flügel)** *Tel* (030) 32 09 442. 🕙 Apr–Oct: 10am–5pm Tue–Sun; Nov–Mar: 11am–5pm Tue–Sun. 🖼

KEY

- ☐ Official reception rooms
- ☐ Sophie-Charlotte's apartments
- ☐ Neuer Flügel or Knobelsdorff-Flügel exhibition space
- ☐ Friedrich Wilhelm II's apartments
- ☐ Mecklenburg apartments
- ☐ Friedrich Wilhelm IV's apartments
- ☐ Friedrich Wilhelm II's apartments
- ☐ Frederick the Great's apartments
- ☐ Non-exhibition space

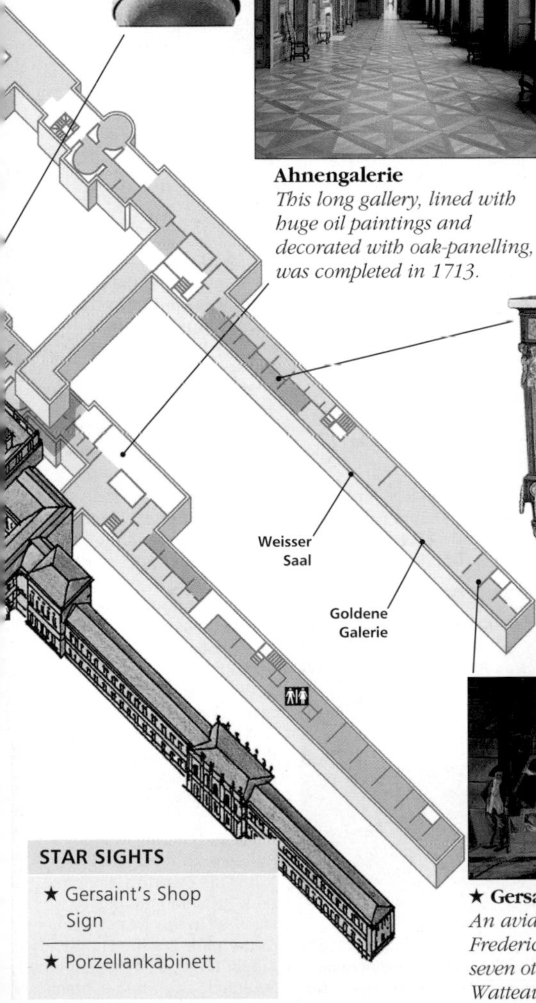

Ahnengalerie
This long gallery, lined with huge oil paintings and decorated with oak-panelling, was completed in 1713.

Weisser Saal

Goldene Galerie

Frederick the Great's Apartments
Located in the new wing, these elegant living quarters feature the king's exquisite furniture.

STAR SIGHTS

- ★ Gersaint's Shop Sign
- ★ Porzellankabinett

★ **Gersaint's Shop Sign** (1720)
An avid collector of French painting, Frederick the Great bought this and seven other fine canvases by Antoine Watteau for his collection.

Hohenzollern coat of arms above the main gate of Spandau's citadel

Spandau **8**

Zitadelle Spandau Am Juliusturm. **Tel** (030) 354 94 42 00. **U** Zitadelle. **■** X33. ○ 9am–5pm Tue–Fri, 10am–5pm Sat & Sun. **✉**

Spandau is one of the oldest towns within the area of greater Berlin, and it has managed to retain its own distinctive character. Although the town of Spandau was only granted a charter in 1232, evidence of the earliest settlement here dates back to the 8th century.

The area was spared the worst of the World War II bombing, so there are still some interesting sights to visit. The heart of the town is a network of medieval streets with a picturesque market square and a number of the original timber-framed houses. In the north of Spandau, sections of the town wall dating from the 15th century are still standing.

In the centre of town is the magnificent Gothic St-Nikolai-Kirche, dating from the 15th century. The church holds many valuable ecclesiastical furnishings, such as a splendid Renaissance stone altar from the end of the 16th century, a Baroque pulpit from around 1700 that came from a royal palace in Potsdam, a Gothic baptismal font and many epitaphs.

A castle was first built on the site of the Zitadelle Spandau (citadel) in the 12th century, but today only the 36 m (120 ft) Juliusturm (tower) remains. In 1560 the building of a fort was begun

here, to a design by Francesco Chiaramella da Gandino. It took 30 years to complete and most of the work was supervised by architect Rochus Graf von Lynar. Although the citadel had a jail, the town's most infamous resident, Rudolf Hess, was incarcerated a short distance away in a military prison after the 1946 Nuremberg trials. In 1987, when the former deputy leader of the Nazi party died, the prison was torn down.

Gedenkstätte Plötzensee **9**

Plötzensee Memorial

Hüttigpfad. **Tel** (030) 344 32 26. **U** Jakob-Kaiser-Platz, then **■** 123, 126. ○ Mar–Sep: 9am–5pm; Nov–Feb 9am–4pm.

A narrow street leads from Saatwinkler Damm to the site where nearly 2,500 people convicted of crimes against

Memorial to concentration camp victims at Gedenkstätte Plötzensee

the Third Reich were hanged. The Gedenkstätte Plötzensee is a simple memorial in a brick hut, which still retains the iron hooks from which the victims were suspended.

Claus Schenk von Stauffenberg and the other main figures in the assassination attempt against Hitler on 20 July 1944 were executed in the Bendlerblock *(see p88)*, but the rest of the conspirators were executed here at the Plötzensee prison.

Count Helmut James von Moltke, one of the leaders of the German resistance movement, was also killed here. He was responsible for organizing the Kreisauer Kreis – a political movement that gathered and united German opposition to Hitler.

Schloss Tegel **10**

Adelheidallee 19–21. **Tel** (030) 434 31 56. **U** Alt Tegel. **■** 124, 123, 133, 222. ○ May–Sep: 11am–noon & 3–4pm Mon. **✉** compulsory.

Schloss Tegel is one of the most interesting palace complexes in Berlin. The site was occupied in the 16th century by a manor house. In the second half of the 17th century, this was rebuilt into a hunting lodge for the Elector Friedrich Wilhelm. In 1766 the ownership of the property passed to the Humboldt family and, between 1820 and 1824, Karl Friedrich Schinkel thoroughly rebuilt the palace, giving it its current style.

Decorating the elevations on the top floor of the towers are tiled bas-reliefs designed by Christian Daniel Rauch, depicting the ancient wind gods. Some of Schinkel's marvellous interiors have survived, along with several items from what was once a large collection of sculptures. The palace is still privately owned by descendants of the Humboldt family, but guided tours are offered on Mondays.

It is also worth visiting the park in which the palace stands. On the western limits of the park lies the Humboldt family tomb, also designed by Schinkel. The tomb contains a

The elegant Neo-Classical façade of Schloss Tegel

copy of a splendid sculpture by Bertel Thorwaldsen. The original piece stands inside the Schloss Tegel.

Bertolt Brecht's study in his former apartment

Brecht-Weigel-Gedenkstätte ⓫
Brecht-Weigel Memorial

Chausseestraße 125. **Tel** *(030) 283 05 70 44.* Ⓤ *Zinnowitzer Straße or Oranienburger Tor.* 🚌 *340.* 🚊 *M6, 12.* 🕐 *10am–noon Tue–Fri, also 5–7pm Thu, 9:30am–noon, 12:30–2pm Sat, 11am–6pm Sun.* 🎧 *compulsory. Every half hour (every hour on Sun).* ⚫ *Mon, public holidays.* 📷

Playwright Bertolt Brecht was associated with Berlin from 1920, but emigrated in 1933. After the war, his left-wing views made him an attractive potential resident of the newly created German socialist state. Lured by the promise of his own theatre, he returned to Berlin in 1948 with his wife, the actress Helene Weigel.

In 1953, Brecht moved into Chausseestraße 125 and lived there until his death in 1956. His wife founded an archive of his work, which is located on the second floor.

Neue Synagoge ⓬
New Synagogue

Oranienburger Straße 30. **Tel** *(030) 880 28 451.* Ⓢ *Oranienburger Straße.* 🚊 *M6, M12.* 🕐 *May–Oct: 10am–8pm Sun–Thu, 10am–5pm Fri; Nov–Apr: 10am–6pm Sun–Thu, 10am–2pm Fri.* 📷 🚫

Construction of the New Synagogue was begun in 1859 by architect Eduard Knoblauch, and completed in 1866. The design was a highly sophisticated response to the asymmetrical shape of the plot of land, with a narrow façade flanked by a pair of towers and crowned with a dome containing a round vestibule. A series of small rooms opened off the vestibule, including an anteroom and two prayer rooms – one large and one small. The two towers opened onto a staircase leading to the galleries, while the main hall had space for around 3,000 worshippers. An innovative use of iron in the construction of

The Neue Synagoge with its splendidly reconstructed dome

the roof and galleries put the synagogue at the forefront of 19th-century civil engineering.

With its gilded dome, this was Berlin's largest synagogue, until 9 November 1938 when it was partially destroyed during the infamous *Kristallnacht.* The building was damaged further by Allied bombing in 1943 and was eventually condemned and demolished in 1958 by government authorities.

Reconstruction began in 1988 and was completed in 1995. Public exhibitions by the Centrum Judaicum are held in the front of the building.

Prenzlauer Berg ㉜

Sammlung Industrielle Gestaltung Kulturbrauerei entrance, Knaackstraße 97. **Tel** *(030) 443 17868.* Ⓢ *Senefelderplatz or Eberswalderstraße.* 🕐 *1pm–8pm Wed–Sun.*

Towards the end of the 19th century this was one of the most impoverished, densely populated districts of Berlin, which became a centre for anti-Communist opposition.

After 1989, however, artists, journalists and students began to gather here from all parts of Berlin, creating a colourful, vibrant community.

Schönhauser Allee is the main thoroughfare of Prenzlauer Berg. A former old brewery was transformed into the "Kulturbrauerei", a centre for cultural events. It also houses a museum – **Sammlung Industrielle Gestaltung** – with a collection of industrial designs from East Germany.

Heading along Sredzkistraße you reach Husemannstraße. At No. 12 was the former Museum Berliner Arbeiterleben; its collection of period interiors has been transferred recently to the Märkisches Museum *(see p80).* Amid the greenery around Belforter Straße is a water tower built in the mid-19th century. Nearby, on Schönhauser Allee, there is an old Jewish cemetery dating from 1827. Among those buried here is the renowned painter Max Liebermann.

Fragment of Socialist Realist decoration from Karl-Marx-Allee

Karl-Marx-Allee ⑭

Map 5 F1. Ⓤ *Strausberger Platz or Weberwiese.*

The section of Karl-Marx-Allee between Strausberger Platz and Frankfurter Tor is effectively a huge open-air museum of Socialist Realist architecture. The route to the east was named Stalinallee in 1949 and chosen as the site for the showpiece of the new German Democratic Republic. The avenue was widened to 90 m (300 ft) and, in the course of the next ten years, huge residential tower blocks and a row of shops were built. The designers, led by Hermann Henselmann, succeeded in combining three sets of architectural guidelines. They used the style known in the Soviet Union as "pastry chef" according to the precept: "nationalistic in form but socialist in content", and linked the whole work to Berlin's own traditions. Hence there are motifs taken from famous Berlin architects Schinkel and Gontard, as well as from the renowned Meissen porcelain.

The buildings on this street, renamed Karl-Marx-Allee in 1961, are now considered historic monuments.

Gedenkstätte Berlin-Hohen-schönhausen ⑮

Genslerstraße 66. *Tel (030) 9860 82 30.* Ⓢ *Landsberger Allee, then* 🚊 *M5, M6.* 🚌 *256.* 🎦 *11am & 1pm Mon–Fri, 11am, 1pm & 3pm Sat–Sun.* 🈂️

This museum was established in 1995 within the former custody building of the Stasi.

The building was part of a huge complex built in 1938. In May 1945, the occupying Russian authorities created a special transit camp here, in which they interned war criminals and anyone under political suspicion. From 1946 the buildings were refashioned into the custody area for the KGB; in 1951, it was given over to the Stasi.

The prisoners' cells and interrogation rooms are on view, two of which have no windows and are lined with rubber. Housed in the cellars was the "submarine" – a series of cells without daylight to which the most "dangerous" suspects were brought.

Forschungs- und Gedenkstätte Normannenstraße (Stasi-Museum) ⑯

Ruschestraße 103 (Haus 1). *Tel (030) 553 68 54.* Ⓤ *Magdalenenstraße.* 🈂️ *11am–6pm Mon–Fri, 2–6pm Sat–Sun.* 🈂️

Under the German Democratic Republic, this huge complex of buildings at Ruschestrasse housed the Ministry of the Interior. It was here that the infamous Stasi (GDR secret service) had its

headquarters. The Stasi's "achievements" in infiltrating its own community were without equal in the Eastern block.

Since 1990 one of the buildings has housed a museum that displays photographs and documents depicting the activities of the Stasi. Here, you can see a model of the headquarters, and equipment that was used for bugging and spying on citizens suspected of holding unfavourable political views. You can also walk around the office of infamous Stasi chief Erich Mielke.

Köpenick ⑰

Ⓢ *Spindlersfeld, then* 🚌 *167 or* Ⓢ *Köpenick, then* 🚌 *164, 167.* 🚋 *27, 60, 61, 62, 67, 68.* **Kunstgewerbemuseum** *Schloss Köpenick, Schlossinsel. Tel (030) 20 90 55 66.* 🈂️ *10am–6pm Tue–Fri (from 11am Sat & Sun).*

Köpenick is much older than Berlin. In the 9th century AD, this island contained a fortified settlement known as Kopanica. In about 1240 a castle was built on the island, around which a town began to evolve. Craftsmen settled here and, after 1685, a large colony of Huguenots also settled.

In the 19th century Köpenick recreated itself as an industrial town. Despite wartime devastation it has retained its historic character and, though there are no longer any 13th-century churches, it is worth strolling around the old town. By the old market square and in the neighbouring streets, modest houses have survived that recall the 18th century, alongside buildings from the end of the 19th century.

At Alt Köpenick No. 21 is a vast brick town hall built in the style of the Brandenburg Neo-Renaissance. In 1906, a famous swindle took place here and the event became the inspiration for a popular comedy by Carl Zuckmayer, *The Captain from Köpenick.*

Köpenick's greatest attraction is a three-storey Baroque palace, built between 1677 and

Office of the infamous Stasi chief Erich Mielke at the Stasi Museum

A reconstructed drawing room from 1548 in the Kunstgewerbemuseum

1681 for the heir to the throne Friedrich (later King Friedrich I), to a design by the Dutch architect Rutger van Langfield. In 2003, the **Kunstgewerbemuseum** *(see p88)* opened a suite of Renaissance and Baroque rooms to the public in the Köpenick Palace.

Gigantic wreath commemorating the Red Army in Treptower Park

Treptower Park ⑱

Archenhold-Sternwarte, Alt-Treptow.
Ⓢ *Treptower Park.* 🚌 *166, 265, 365.* **Archenhold Sternwarte** *Tel (030) 534 80 80.* 📷 *compulsory: Sternwarte 8pm Thu, 3pm Sat–Sun; astronomical museum 2pm–4:30pm Wed–Sun; astronomical observations Oct–Mar: 8pm Fri; sun observations Jul–Aug: 3pm Wed.*

The vast park in Treptow was laid out in the 1860s on the initiative and design of Johann Gustav Meyer. In 1919 it was where revolutionaries Karl Liebknecht, Wilhelm Pieck and Rosa Luxemburg assembled 150,000 striking workers.

The park is best known for the colossal monument to the Red Army. Built between 1946 and 1949, it stands on the grave of 5,000 Soviet soldiers killed in the battle for Berlin in 1945. The gateway, which leads to the mausoleum, is marked by a vast granite sculpture of a grieving Russian Motherland surrounded by statues of Red Army soldiers.

In the farthest section of the park is the astronomical observatory, **Archenhold Sternwarte**, built for a decorative arts exhibition in 1896. Given a permanent site in 1909, the observatory was used by Albert Einstein for a lecture on the Theory of Relativity in 1915. It is also home to the longest reflecting telescope in the world (21 m or 70 ft), and a small planetarium.

Beyond Treptower Park lies another park, Plänterwald.

Flughafen Tempelhof ⑲

Platz der Luftbrücke. Ⓤ *Platz der Luftbrücke.* 🚌 *104, 184.*

Situated beyond Kreuzberg, the Tempelhof was once Germany's largest airport. Built in 1923, the structure is typical of Third Reich architecture. The additions to the original structure were completed in 1939.

In 1951, a monument was added in front of the airport. Designed by Edward Ludwig, it commemorates the airlifts

of the Berlin Blockade. The names of those who lost their lives during the Blockade appear on the plinth.

Viktoriapark ⑳

Ⓤ *Platz der Luftbrücke.* 🚌 *104, 140.*

This rambling park, with several artificial waterfalls, short trails and a small hill, was designed by Hermann Mächtig and built between 1884 and 1894. The Neo-Gothic Memorial to the Wars of Liberation at the summit of the hill is the work of Karl Friedrich Schinkel and was constructed between 1817 and 1821. The monument commemorates the Prussian victory against Napoleon's army in the Wars of Liberation. The monument's cast-iron tower is well ornamented.

In the niches of the lower section are 12 allegorical figures by Christian Daniel Rauch, Friedrich Tieck and Ludwig Wichmann. Each figure symbolizes a battle and is linked to a historic figure – either a military leader or a member of the royal family.

Rathaus Schöneberg ㉑
Schöneberg Town Hall

John-F-Kennedy-Platz.
Ⓤ *Rathaus Schöneberg.*

The Schöneberg town hall is a gigantic building with an imposing tower, which was built between 1911 and 1914. From 1948 to 1990 it was used as the main town hall of West Berlin, and it was outside here, on 26 June 1963, that US President John F Kennedy gave his famous speech. More than 300,000 Berliners assembled to hear the young president say *"Ich bin ein Berliner"* – "I am a Berliner", intended as an expression of solidarity from the democratic world to a city defending its right to freedom.

While Kennedy's meaning was undoubtedly clear, pedants were quick to point out that what he actually said was "I am a small doughnut".

Japanese woodcut from the Museum für Ostasiatische Kunst

Museumszentrum Dahlem ㉒

Lansstraße 8, Dahlem. *Tel (830) 14 38.* ⓤ *Dahlem Dorf.* 🚌 *X111, X83.* **Museum für Indische Kunst. Museum für Ostasiatische Kunst, Ethnologisches Museum (formerly Museum für Völkerkunde), Museum für Kunst Afrikas & Nordamerika Ausstellung** ◯ *10am–6pm Tue–Fri, 11am–6pm Sat & Sun.* 🖼

Dahlem's first museums were built between 1914 and 1923, but the district was confirmed as a major cultural and education centre after World War II with the establishment of the Freie Universität and completion of the museum complex. With many of Berlin's collections fragmented, a miscellany of art and artifacts was put on display here. In the 1960s the museums were extended and the new Museumszentrum was created to rival East Berlin's Museum Island.

German reunification in 1990 meant that the collections could be reunited and reorganized. Paintings were moved to the Kulturforum *(see pp84–5),* and sculptures to the Bode-museum *(see p78).*

Five museums are now housed at Dahlem: the Ethnologisches Museum (Museum of Mankind); the Museum für Indische Kunst (Museum of Indian Art); the Museum für Ostasiatische Kunst (Museum of Far Eastern Art); the Museum für Kunst Afrikas (Museum for African Art) and the Nord-amerika Ausstellung (Exhibition of Native North American Cultures).

Highlights include bronzes from Benin at the Museum of African Art, gold Inca jewellery at the Museum of Mankind, and Japanese woodcuts from Chinese Turkestan at the Museum of Far Eastern Art. The Exhibition of Native North American Cultures, opened in 1999, includes a collection of 600 ceremonial objects.

Jagdschloss Grunewald ㉓

Am Grunewaldsee 29. *Tel (030) 813 35 97.* ◯ *mid-May–mid-Oct: 10am–5pm Tue–Sun; mid-Oct–mid-May: 11am, 1pm, 3pm Sun (tours only).* 🖼

Jagdschloss Grunewald is one of the oldest surviving civic buildings in Berlin. Built for the Elector Joachim II in 1542, it was rebuilt around 1700 in a Baroque style.

In this small palace on the edge of the Grunewaldsee is Berlin's only surviving Renaissance hall, which currently houses a collection of paintings that includes canvases by Rubens and van Dyck, among others.

In the east wing is the small Waldmuseum, which has illustrations depicting forest life and the history of forestry. Opposite the Jagdschloss, a hunting museum (Jagdmuseum) houses a collection of historic weapons and equipment.

Brücke-Museum ㉔

Bussardsteig 9, Dahlem. *Tel (030) 831 20 29.* 🚌 *115.* ◯ *11am–5pm Wed–Mon.*

This elegant Functionalist building hosts a collection of German Expressionist painting linked to the Die Brücke group. It is based on almost 80 works by Schmidt-Rottluff bequeathed to the town of Dahlem in 1964. In addition to other works of art contemporary to Die Brücke, there are paintings from the later creative periods of these artists, as well as works of other closely associated artists. Nearby lie the foundation's headquarters, established in the former studio of the sculptor Bernhard Heliger.

Strandbad Wannsee ㉕

Wannseebadweg. ⑤ *Nikolassee.* 🚌 *513.*

The vast lake Wannsee, on the edge of Grunewald, is a popular destination for Berliners seeking recreation. The most developed part is the southeastern corner where there are yachting marinas and harbours. Further north is one of the largest inland beaches in Europe, Strandbad Wannsee, which was devel-oped between 1929 and 1930 by the construction of shops, cafés and changing rooms on man-made terraces. It is also pleasant to walk around Schwanenwerder island, with its many elegant villas.

Boarding point for lake cruises on the Wannsee

The Schloss Pfaueninsel designed by Johann Brendel

Pfaueninsel ㉖

Pfaueninsel. **Tel** (030) 805 86 830. Ⓢ Wannsee, then take 🚌 218. 🚢 Schloss Pfaueninsel. ⊙ Apr–Oct: 10am–5pm Tue–Sun. 📷

This picturesque island, named for the peacocks that inhabit it, is now a nature reserve, reached by ferry across the Havel river. It was laid out in 1795 according to a design by Johann August Eyserbeck. Its final form, which you see today, is the work of the landscape architect Peter Joseph Lenné.

One of the most interesting sights on the island is the small romantic palace of **Schloss Pfaueninsel**. Dating from 1794, it was designed by Johann Gottlieb Brendel for Friedrich Wilhelm II and his mistress Wilhelmine Encke (the future Countess Lichtenau). The palace was built of wood, with a façade fashioned in the form of a ruined medieval castle. The cast-iron bridge that links the towers was built in 1807. The palace is open to the public in the summer months, when you can see the 18th- and 19th-century furnishings.

Other sights worth visiting include **James's Well**, which was built to resemble an ancient ruin. Towards the northeast corner of the island is the **Luisentempel** in the form of a Greek temple. Its sandstone portico was relocated to the island from the mausoleum in Schlosspark Charlottenburg (see pp98–9) in 1829. Nearby is a stone commemorating Johannes Kunckel, an alchemist who lived on Pfaueninsel in the 17th century. During his quest to discover how to make gold, he discovered a method of producing ruby-coloured glass. Near the **Aviary**, home to multicoloured parrots and pheasants, is a tall fountain that was designed by Martin Friedrich Rabe in 1824.

Nikolskoe ㉗

Nikolskoer Weg. Ⓢ Wannsee, then take 🚌 A16 or 316.

Across the river from Pfaueninsel (Peacock Island) is Nikolskoe. Here you'll find the Blockhaus Nikolskoe, a Russian-style *dacha* (country house) that was built in 1819 for the future Tsar Nicholas I and his wife, the daughter of King Friedrich Wilhelm III.

The house was built by the German military architect Captain Snethlage, who was responsible for the Alexandrowka estate in Potsdam

Guests on the terrace of the Blockhaus Nikolskoe in summer

(see p134). Following a fire in 1985, the *dacha* was reconstructed. It currently houses a restaurant.

Close by is the church of St Peter and Paul, which was built between 1834 and 1837, to a design by Friedrich August Stüler. The body of the church is completed by a tower crowned by an onion-shaped dome, reflecting the style of Russian Orthodox sacral architecture.

Klein Glienicke ㉘

🚌 316. **Tel** (030) 805 30 41. ⊙ mid-May– mid-Oct: 10am–5pm Sat–Sun. 📷

The palace in the palace-park of Klein Glienicke was built in 1825 according to a design by Karl Friedrich Schinkel for Prince Karl of Prussia. The charming parkin which it is located was created by Peter Joseph Lenné. Beyond the Neo-Classical palace extends an irregular cluster of buildings, grouped around a courtyard, including a pergola and staff cottages. Passing by the palace, you approach the **Coach House**, also designed by Schinkel and now housing a restaurant.

Nearby are an orangery and greenhouses designed by Ludwig Persius. Also by Persius is the **Klosterhof**, a mock monastery with pavilions, on whose walls are many Byzantine and Romanesque architectural elements from Italy. Towards the lake is the **Grosse Neugierde**, a circular pavilion based on the Athenian monument to Lysikrates from the 4th century BC. From here there are beautiful views across the Havel river and **Glienicker Brücke** (known under the East German regime as the bridge of unity). The border with West Berlin ran across this bridge where, during the Cold War, the exchange of spies was conducted.

Karl Friedrich Schinkel's Neo-Classical Schloss Klein Glienicke

SHOPPING IN BERLIN

With a shopping centre in every district, each selling a variety of merchandise, Berlin is a place where almost anything can be bought, so long as you know where to shop. The most popular areas are Kurfürstendamm and Friedrichstrasse, but the smaller shops in Wedding, Friedrichshain, Schöneberg and the Tiergarten are also worth a visit. Small boutiques selling flamboyant Berlin-style clothes crop up in unexpected courtyards, while the top fashion houses offer the latest in European elegance. Early on Saturday morning is often the best time to visit the city's various markets, the most popular of which – with their colourful stalls full of hats, bags and belts – can be found on Museum Island and at the Tiergarten. The Galeries Lafayette, KaDeWe and any of the city's numerous bookshops all make ideal venues for a pleasant afternoon's window shopping.

A shop-floor display in the lobby of KaDeWe

PRACTICAL INFORMATION

The majority of shops are open Monday to Friday from 10am to 8pm (10am to 4pm on Saturday). At Christmas, shops stay open until 8pm on Saturdays and the **Berliner Verkehrs-Betriebe**, or BVG, runs a useful service where you can leave your purchases on a special bus while you continue shopping. Some smaller stores do not accept credit cards, so be sure to have some cash, and if Berlin's options seem over-whelming, you can employ someone as a **Shopping Guide**.

DEPARTMENT STORES AND SHOPPING CENTRES

Kaufhaus Des Westens, better known as **KaDeWe** at Wittenbergplatz, is undoubtedly the biggest and the best department store in Berlin, while **Galeries Lafayette** on Friedrichstrasse is nothing less than a slice of Paris placed in the heart of Berlin. Perfumes, domestic accessories and clothing attract an enormous clientele.

Another very popular store is **Wertheim** on the Ku'damm. Although its range of goods is not as broad as the range at Galeries Lafayette, there is still an enormous choice and the top-floor restaurant offers excellent views over the city.

One of the newest shopping centres is the **Potsdamer Platz Arkaden**, which is a very popular meeting place. On a slightly smaller scale is **Galleria** in Steglitz, and the **Gesundbrunnencenter** is the biggest shopping passage in Berlin with stalls and tables covered in bargains. **Europa-Center** is the most visually stunning with its beautiful sculpted fountains.

FASHION

The Ku'damm area plays host to all the best known high street names and department stores, as well as most of the top fashion houses in Berlin. **Escada** and **MaxMara** are two of the best known of the German designers, but Berlin also has a wealth of young designers and their lines are mainly to be seen in the northern part of the Mitte area. **NIX**, for example, offers timeless clothes made from heavy, dark fabrics, while **Tagebau** sells everything from evening dresses to casual wear and accessories. These are all only available in strictly limited numbers so you can be assured that what you are buying is unique.

For men's fashions, once again the Ku'damm area is the

The spacious Wertheim department store on Kurfürstendamm

Store front of German fashion house Escada

place to look. **Patrick Hellmann** is certainly worth a visit with its wide choice of the best designer labels around.

ANTIQUES

The antiques trade in Berlin is booming, and there are many markets and galleries opening all the time. Berlin's most prestigious auction house is **Gerda Bassenge**, while **ART 1900** and **Galeries Splinter** offer endless trinkets and knick-knacks from various periods. Many Berliners spend their Saturday and Sunday mornings at flea markets browsing the stalls. In particular, the **Antik & Trödelmarkt am Ostbahnhof** is considered one of the best places to pick up bargains.

FOOD PRODUCTS

All manner of foods and wine are available in Berlin, and they make excellent gifts and souvenirs. Kaffee und Kuchen (coffee and cakes) is a strong German tradition, so why not head to **Buchwald** and purchase one of their delicious cakes to take home. You will also find that bakeries all over the city sell traditional *Berliners* (doughnuts) along with a good value range of delicious pastries and breads.

Wine-fans will love **Viniculture**, which offers one of the best selections of German wine around or, if you've become a fan of the many local meats, pick from a bewildering range of sausages at **Fleischerei Bachhuber**.

Berlin also plays host to a number of food markets. The **Winterfeldmarkt** is probably the most popular, but the **Wochenmarkt** on Wittenberg-platz also has a particularly loyal following.

SEASONAL SALES

Twice a year (January and July) all the shops in Berlin empty their shelves in the end of season *Schlussverkauf*. Goods bought in a sale are officially non-returnable, though sometimes you may find you are able to negotiate with the shop assistant.

A number of shops sell "second season" items – these are new, but they were stocked for the previous season and as such are generously reduced in price and make great bargain buys.

The central "glass cone" of the Galeries Lafayette department store

DIRECTORY

PRACTICAL INFORMATION

Berliner Verkehrs-Betriebe
Hardenbergplatz.
Tel 194 49.
www.bvg.de

Shopping Guide
Claudia Barthel.
Tel (030) 28 59 86 22.

DEPARTMENT STORES AND SHOPPING CENTRES

Europa-Center
Breitscheidplatz
Map 2 B4. www.europa-center-berlin.de

Galeries Lafayette
Französische Straße 23.
Map 4 C2.
Tel (030) 20 94 80.

Galleria
Schlossstraße 101.
Map 2 E3.

Gesundbrunnen-center
Gesundbrunnen S-Bahn.

KaDeWe
Tauentzienstraße 21.
Map 2 C5. *Tel (030) 21 21 00.* www.kadewe-berlin.de

Potsdamer Platz Arkaden
Debis Gelände.
Map 4 A3. www.potsdamerplatz.net/arkaden

Wertheim
Kurfürstendamm 231.
Map 2 B4. *Tel (030)80 00 30.* www.karstadt.de

FASHION

Escada
Friedrichstr. 176–179.
Tel (030) 238 64 04.
Map 4 C2.

MaxMara
Kurfürstendamm 178.
Map 2 B4.
Tel (030) 885 25 45.

NIX
Oranienburger Str. 32.
Map 5 D1.
Tel (030) 31 50 98 82.

Patrick Hellmann
Fasanenstr. 26.
Map 2 A5.
Tel (030) 882 42 01.

Tagebau
Rosenthaler Str. 19.
Tel (030) 28 39 08 90.

ANTIQUES

Antik & Trödelmarkt am Ostbahnhof
Erich-Steinfurth-Straße.
🕐 *9am–3pm Sat,*
10am–5pm Sun.

ART 1900
Kurfürstendamm 53.
Map 2 A5.
Tel (030) 881 56 27.

Galeries Splinter
Sophienstraße 20–21.
Tel 28 59 87 37. 🔴 *Mon*

Gerde Bassenge
Erdener Straße 5a.
Tel (030) 89 38 02 90.
🕐 *9am–6pm Mon–Fri.*

FOOD PRODUCTS

Buchwald
Bartningallee 29.
Map 3 D2.
Tel (030) 391 59 31.

Fleischerei Bachhuber
Güntzelstraße 47.
Tel (030) 873 21 15.

Viniculture
Grolmanstraße 44–45.
Tel (030) 883 81 74.

Winterfeldmarkt
Wittenbergplatz.
🕐 *8am-noon Wed & Sat.*

Wochenmarkt
Wittenbergplatz.
🕐 *8am-2pm Tue & Fri.*

ENTERTAINMENT IN BERLIN

With so much on offer, from classical drama and cabaret to variety theatre and an eclectic nightclub scene, it is possible to indulge just about any taste in Berlin. During the summer months many bars and restaurants set up outdoor tables and the areas around Unter den Linden, the Kurfürstendamm, Kreuzberg and Prenzlauer Berg in particular, seem to turn into one large social arena. The city really comes into its own at night, when its clubs, all-night cafés and cocktail bars give you the chance to dance till dawn. The city has many night-life centres, each with a slightly different character. Prenzlauer Berg is the best choice for mainstream bars, cafés and clubs, while Friedrichs-hain is more exclusive, and Kreuzberg has a vibrant gay scene. The Mitte district in the Eastern Centre offers a true mixture with its opera house and classical theatre surrounded by lively and inexpensive bars. On a Sunday, a quiet trip down the river or along the canals offers a pleasant way to unwind.

Flute player in costume

The Berlin Philharmonic Orchestra

PRACTICAL INFORMATION

There are so many things going on in Berlin that it can be difficult to find what you are looking for. Listings magazines like *Tip* or *Zitty* are invaluable aids and offer the widest range of suggestions. Information on festivals, sports events, cinema programmes, theatre schedules, cabarets and concerts can be found on the following websites: www.berlinonline.de and www.berlin.de.

For visitors who have just arrived in town, however, and have not made it yet to an Internet café or a kiosk, the chances are the local bar or your hotel foyer has leaflets on the wall to point you in the right direction. There are also lots of posters around town telling you what is on offer. In addition, the free magazine *Flyer* is full of news about nightclubs and discos, and it should be available in most restaurants.

Tickets for events should be bought in advance, though last-minute tickets are available from **Hekticket Theaterkassen**. The disabled, pensioners and students with the appropriate ID are often entitled to a discount. All major venues will provide good wheelchair access.

CLASSICAL MUSIC

The Berlin Philharmonic Orchestra is one of the world's finest orchestras and it performs regularly at the beautiful **Philharmonie**, with its awe-inspiring architecture and fantastic acoustics. Chamber orchestras perform in the smaller **Kammermusiksaal** attached to the bigger hall. **Konzerthaus Berlin**, formally known as the Schauspielhaus, is another important venue for classical music having been magnificently restored after World War II.

Opera lovers will find themselves well catered for in Berlin as there are three major opera houses. The **Staatsoper Unter den Linden**'s impressive, yet conservative repertoire includes traditional German classics and Italian opera, while the **Komische Oper** is known for its broad range of lighter opera and, because its operas frequently have a long run, there are

Prokofiev's *The Love of Three Oranges* staged at the Komische Oper

Traditional jazz music at Berlin's Jazzfest

often last-minute tickets available. The **Deutsche Oper** on Bismarckstrasse is housed in a somewhat plainer building than the other opera venues, but it boasts performances ranging from Mozart to Wagner.

MUSIC FESTIVALS

The **Berliner Festwochen** takes place throughout the month of September and top orchestras and performers come from all over the world to put on classical music concerts around the city.

Also in September, pop fans will love **Popkomm**, one of Europe's biggest music festivals, which hosts a mix of talks, parties and concerts in venues throughout Berlin.

Jazzfest Berlin takes place in July and tends to attract lovers of more traditional styles of jazz, but it also focuses on the more experimental and innovative styles of the genre in its accompanying Total Music Meeting.

ROCK, POP & JAZZ

Whether it is a major event by a world-famous band or a small-scale evening of jazz improvisation, you need not look too far to find what you want. The biggest concerts tend to take place in sports halls and stadiums, like the **Max-Schmeling-Halle** and the **Olympia-Stadion** (see p97), whilst smaller venues like **Café Swing** and **SO 36** play host to the best new talent in popular music. In addition, a lot of the action tends to take

place in the city's many bars, discos and clubs or, if you are looking for particularly atmospheric concerts, why not try those put on at the **Passionskirche**, a converted church in Kreuzberg.

Jazz clubs abound in Berlin, as the style remains very popular amongst locals. The **A-Trane** and **b-flat** are classical jazz bars where you can listen to small bands just about every night of the week, and **Flöz** is famous for its excellent acoustics and atmosphere.

Apart from the typical classical jazz clubs, jazz can also be heard in many of the city's smaller bars, like **Schlot** on Kastanienallee or **Harlem** in Prenzlauer Berg. If it is a mixture of soul, rap and jazz you want to listen to, then

One of the many concerts at Berlin's annual Popkomm festival

head for the **Junction Bar** in Kreuzberg. The **pipapo**, near Nollendorfplatz, is a worthy choice on a Sunday and the **Badenscher Hof Jazzclub** is always a good bet.

WORLD MUSIC

With an increasingly multi-national population, Berlin is home to a wide variety of world music. The Haus der Kulturen der Welt organizes all kinds of concerts at its own **Café Global**, and is one of the best Saturday evening music venues in Berlin.

Latin American discos are becoming ever more popular and **Havanna** in Schöneberg is one of the city's best.

Irish music is also well represented in Berlin's pubs – **Wild at Heart** is very popular.

Rosa's Dance Co. at the "Tanz" dance festival, organized by the Theater am Halleschen Ufer

CLASSICAL AND MODERN DANCE

There are three major ballet groups in Berlin and they work within Berlin's opera houses. The Komische Oper has a modern repertoire, whilst the Staatsoper Unter den Linden focuses on more classical work.

The **Hebbel-Theater** stages avant-garde pieces and welcomes troupes from all over the world. Together with **Theater am Halleschen Ufer**, it organizes the dance festival "Tanz" every August. The seating at both theatres is rather limited, so you need to book well in advance.

Tanzfabrik, based on Möckernstrasse in Kreuzberg, is an excellent stage for all kinds of modern dance and it also organizes dance work-shops as well as popular body-work courses.

NIGHTLIFE

Among its many artistic claims, Berlin is also the techno capital of Europe, with over a million devotees celebrating the genre at a number of annual festivals.

One of the best clubs for techno lovers is **Tresor**, situated in the old vault of a defunct department store. The best DJs in town can be heard here. The clubs **Matrix** and **Columbia Club** are also guaranteed to provide what you are after, and so too is the special techno-room known as Subground, which is located in the subways of **Pfefferbank**. Techno dominates the menu here, but Subground also caters for music lovers of all kinds.

If it is a good old-fashioned disco you are looking for, with happy tunes and a little less techno, the **Far Out** and **Metropol** are the places to go. The Metropol was famous before the fall of the Wall and attracts a teenage crowd every weekend. Tuesdays are devoted to thirtysomethings, who come here to dance to classic funk, soul and pop. For a crowded house with 2000 Watts for 2000 people, head for **Loft** which is always packed, but, if you are no longer a teenager and fancy a bit of retro, then a night at the **Tränenpalast** could be the choice. It is based in the pavilion that served as the former passport control between East and West Berlin.

During the summer, you can dance to pop music in the open air at **Golgatha** in Kreuzberg's Viktoriapark, or in **Die Insel**, a café built on an island in Treptow.

Delicious Doughnuts is one of the best places in town for ambient, house and acid-jazz, while lovers of soul and reggae should head for the lively **Lumumba Tanzcafé**. For something a little more intimate, the romantic atmosphere of **Sophienclub** might be worth investigating.

The city also has a vibrant gay and lesbian scene. **SchwuZ**, **Ostgut** and **Ackerkeller** are among the best gay venues in Berlin.

The reconstructed medieval settlement at the Museumdorf Düppel

SPECTATOR SPORTS

As a rule, Berlin's sports teams tend to be among the country's best, and rank highly in each of their respective leagues. Hertha BSC's football matches take place in the **Olympia-Stadion** and Alba Berlin's basketball games are on at the **Max-Schmeling-Halle**. For international events it is usually best to book in advance.

Lovers of horse racing have two tracks to choose from in Berlin. **Trabrennbahn** in Mariendorf is open all year and the races held here are strictly commercial. **Galopprennbahn Hoppegarten**, on the other hand, has a much more friendly, approachable feel.

CHILDREN'S ACTIVITIES

People of all ages are catered for in Berlin, and children are no exception. **Berlin Tourismus Marketing GmbH** can offer details of special children's discounts for many different activities. The **Zoologischer Garten** is very popular, with its extensive parkland and many animal enclosures. Small children will love the **Kinderbauernhof Görlitzer Bauernhof**, which has a collection of domestic animals. In addition, Berlin's museums are well set up for children. The **Deutsches Technikmuseum** *(see p81)* allows children to take part in all kinds of experiments, while the **Ethnologisches Museum** prepares special exhibitions for children. A visit to the **Museumsdorf Düppel** is an excellent way to show a child life in a medieval village and the **Puppentheatermuseum** offers a chance for children to take part in minor performances.

Another option is one of the city's many lively circuses, such as **Circus Cabuwazi**, or, if it is sport that your child enjoys, it is possible to swim in many rivers, lakes and, of course, swimming pools (the **Berliner Bäderbetriebe** hotline offers useful information). Also, each district has its own ice-skating rink, but the **Eisstadion Berlin Wilmersdorf** is by far the best, whilst **FEZ Wuhlheide** offers a special daily programme for kids.

The Story of Berlin is a fun way to experience the history of Berlin in a multi-media exhibit, and the **Berliner Gruselkabinett** (Room of Fear) is suitably scary.

The **Zeiss-Planetarium** or the **Planetarium am Insulaner** offer kids the opportunity to explore the universe in a fun, yet educational, way.

Flamingos in the beautiful Zoologischer Garten

DIRECTORY

PRACTICAL INFORMATION

Hekticket Theaterkassen
Hardenbergstraße 29d.
Map 2 B4.
Tel 230 99 30.

CLASSICAL MUSIC

Deutsche Oper
Bismarckstraße 34–37.
Tel 34 10 249.

Philharmonie & Kammermusiksaal
Herbert-von-Karajan-Str. 1.
Map 3 F3.
Tel 25 85 23 74.

Komische Oper
Behrenstraße 55–57.
Map 1 F4.
Tel 47 99 74 00.

Konzerthaus Berlin
Gendarmenmarkt 2.
Map 4 C2.
Tel 203 09 21 01/02.

Staatsoper Unter den Linden
Unter den Linden 7.
Map 4 C2.
Tel 20 35 45 55.

MUSIC FESTIVALS

Berliner Festwochen
Schaperstraße 4.
Map 2 B5.
Tel 25 48 91 00.

Jazzfest Berlin
Schaperstraße 24.
Map 2 B5.
Tel 25 48 90.

Popkomm
Messe Berlin.
Tel 303 830 09.

ROCK, POP & JAZZ

A-trane
Pestalozzistraße 105.
Map 2 A3.
Tel 313 25 50.

b-flat
Rosenthaler Straße 13.
Map 5 D4.
Tel 28 38 68 35.

Badenscher Hof Jazzclub
Badensche Straße 29.
Tel 861 00 80.

Café Swing
Nollendorfplatz 3–4.

Flöz
Nassauische Straße 37.
Tel 861 10 00.

Harlem
Rodebergstraße 37.
Tel 444 56 54.

Junction Bar
Gniesenaustraße 18.
Tel 694 66 02.

Max-Schmeling-Halle
Am Falkplatz.
Tel 44 30 44 30.

Olympia-Stadion
Olympischer Platz.
Tel 25 00 23 22.

Passionskirche
Marheineckeplatz.
Tel 69 40 12 41.

pipapo
Grossgörschenstraße 40.
Tel 216 15 43.

Schlot
Chausseestraße 18.
Tel 448 21 60.

SO 36
Oranienstraße 190.
Tel 61 40 13 06.

WORLD MUSIC

Café Global
John-Foster-Dulles-Allee 10. **Map** 3 F2.
Tel 39 78 71 75.

Havanna
Hauptstraße 30.
Tel 784 85 65.

Wild at Heart
Wiener Straße 20,
Kreuzberg.
Tel 611 92 31.

CLASSICAL AND MODERN DANCE

Hebbel-Theater
Stresemannstraße 29.
Tel 25 90 04 27.

Tanzfabrik
Möckernstraße 68
Tel 786 58 61.

Theater am Hallenschen Ufer
Hallesches Ufer 32.
Tel 251 09 41.

NIGHTLIFE

Ackerkeller
Ackerstraße 12, Mitte.

Columbia Club
Columbiadamm 9–11,
Kreuzberg.

Delicious Doughnuts
Rosenthaler Straße 9.
Map 5 D1.
Tel 28 09 92 74.

Die Insel
Alt Treptow 6.
Tel 53 60 80 20.

Far Out
Kurfürstendamm 156.
Map 2 A5.
Tel 32 00 07 23.

Golgatha
Dudenstraße 48–64.
Tel 785 24 53.

Loft
Nollendorfplatz 5.
Tel 217 36 80.

Lumumba Tanzcafé
Steinstraße 12.
Tel 28 38 54 65.

Matrix
Warschauer Platz 18.

Metropol
Nollendorfplatz 5.
Tel 217 36 80.

Ostgut
Mühlenstraße 26–30,
Friedrichshain.

Pfefferbank
Schönhauser Allee 176.
Tel 20 91 49 90.

SchwuZ
Mehringdamm 61
Tel 693 70 25

Sophienclub
Sophienstraße 6.
Tel 282 45 52.

Tränenpalast
Reichstagufer 17.
Map 4 A1.
Tel 20 62 00 11.

Tresor
Leipziger Straße 126a.
Map 1 F5.

SPECTATOR SPORTS

Galopprennbahn Hoppegarten
Goetheallee 1.
Tel (03342) 389 30.

Max-Schmeling-Halle
See Rock, Pop & Jazz.

Olympia-Stadion
See Rock, Pop & Jazz.

Trabrennbahn
Mariendorfer Damm 222,
Tempelhof.
Tel 740 12 12.

CHILDREN'S ACTIVITIES

Berlin Tourismus Marketing GmbH
Am Karlsbad 11.
Tel 25 00 25.
www.btm.de

Berliner Bäderbetriebe
Tel (01803) 10 20 20.

Berliner Grusselkabinett
Schöneberger Straße 23a.
Tel 26 55 55 46.

Circus Cabuwazi
Four locations.
Tel (030) 611 92 75.
www.cabuwazi.de

Deutsches Technikmuseum
Trebbiner Straße 9.
Tel 90 25 40.

Eisstadion Berlin Wilmersdorf
Fritz-Wildung-Straße 9.
Tel 824 10 12.

Ethnologisches Museum
Lansstraße 8.
Tel 20 90 55 66.

FEZ Wuhlheide
An der Wuhlheide,
Köpenick.
Tel 53 07 15 04.

Kinderbauernhof Görlitzer Bauernhof
Wiener Straße 59.
Tel 611 74 24.

Museumsdorf Düppel
Clauertstraße 11.
Tel 802 66 71.

Planetarium am Insulaner
Munsterdamm 90.
Tel 790 09 30.

Puppentheater- museum
Karl-Marx-Straße 135.
Tel 687 81 32.

The Story of Berlin
Kurfürstendamm 207-208.
Tel 88 72 01 00.

Zeiss-Planetarium
Prenzlauer Allee 80.
Tel 42 18 45 12.

Zoologischer Garten
Hardenbergplatz 9,
Charlottenburg.
Tel 25 40 10.

Theatre and Cinema

Berlin can lay many claims to being a centre for artistic greatness, but possibly its most valid claims lie in the areas of theatre and cinema. Berlin has been the capital of German cinema since brothers Emil and Max Skladanowsky showed a series of short films to a spellbound German public in 1896. By 1918 there were already some 251 cinemas in Berlin and by 1925, the number of people involved in the film industry was nearly 50,000. At the same time, Berlin was fast becoming a landmark in European theatre thanks mainly to Reinhardt and Brecht. During the years of Nazi rule, many theatre people were killed or forced to emigrate as the stage became a propaganda machine, but after World War II a revival spread through Berlin's theatres. The popularity of theatre and cinema continues today, perpetuated by the annual Film Festival.

A Berlin International Film Festival poster from 1960

TICKET AND PRICE INFORMATION

Tickets for both cinema and theatre are usually reasonably priced in Berlin, but there are a few tips which are useful to remember if you are planning to visit either.

Students and senior citizens do not always receive a discount at the cinema, but often Tuesday or Wednesday is declared Cinema Day, when some tickets are 1–2 cheaper. It is worth knowing that most ticket offices do not accept credit cards, so take cash.

For theatres, it is usually possible to pre-book tickets two weeks before a performance. You can buy them directly from the box office of the theatre or by telephone. Independent ticket vendors usually charge a commission of between 15 and 22 per cent.

Hekticket Theaterkassen specializes in last-minute tickets, so check with them on the day for special deals.

MAJOR STAGES

The **Deutsches Theater** and its small hall **Kammerspiele** on Schumannstrasse are top-class theatres and offer a varied repertoire of productions. At **Volksbühne** you can see interesting performances of classical plays in modern settings and new plays by young authors.

The **Berliner Ensemble** (or BE for short) was once managed by Bertolt Brecht and Heiner Müller. The spectacles created by these two are still performed today. Other major venues include the **Maxim Gorki Theater**, the **Renaissance-Theater** and the **Schlosspark Theater**.

ALTERNATIVE THEATRE

There are a number of alternative theatres in Berlin. **Theater am Halleschen Ufer** is devoted to avant-garde theatre and considered the city's best

alternative stage. The smaller boulevard theatres like **Theater am Kurfürstendamm**, **Komödie am Kurfürstendamm** or **Berlins Volkstheater Hansa**, offer different, and somewhat lighter programmes.

Other notable venues include **Bat-Studiotheater** and the **Kleines Theater**.

MUSICALS, REVIEWS AND CABARETS

There are three main musical theatres in Berlin, in addition to the many small venues which fit musicals into their more general repertoire. **Friedrichstadtpalast**, in the eastern part of the city, stages many of the new major shows, while the **Theater des Westens** in Charlottenburg tends to be more traditional. The **Musical Theater Berlin am Potsdamer Platz** is a modern theatre established in the newly built Potsdamer Platz in 1999.

As for cabaret, there are probably as many acts in Berlin today as there were in the 1920s. **Distel**, in Friedrichstrasse, continues its success from GDR times, and **Stachelschweine** celebrates its popularity in western Berlin. Other great venues for lively musicals, reviews and cabarets include **Bar jeder Vernunft**, **Chamäleon Variété**, **Dr Seltsam Kabarett**, **Scheinbar**, **Wintergarten Variété** and **Wühlmäuse**.

BIG SCREENS AND BIG FILMS

After the fall of the Berlin Wall, many new multiplex cinemas were built, the biggest being the **CinemaxX Potsdamer Platz** and the **Cinestar Sony Center**.

The retro façade of Friedrichstadtpalast in the east of Berlin

Mainstream Anglo-American movies tend to be dubbed rather than subtitled.

For a breath-taking cinematic experience, try the **IMAX** on Potsdamer Platz – it is Germany's biggest screen.

STUDIO CINEMA

There are plenty of small studio cinemas scattered across town which show a number of new independent films. **Hackesche Höfe Kino** or **Central**, situated near Hackescher Markt, offer a pleasant break from city life and have bars of their own.

The **Arsenal**, on Potsdamer Platz, shows German film classics while, if you are interested in original language films, Berlin has its fair share of options. **Cinéma Paris** in Charlottenburg is the place to go for French films, while the **Odeon** in Schöneberg specializes in English and American films.

OPEN-AIR CINEMA

Open-air cinemas start operating as soon as the weather allows. The biggest is **Waldbühne** – a concert hall with seating for an audience of 20,000. Others can be found in Hasenheide, Künstler Haus Bethanien garden in Friedrichshain or in UFA-Fabrik. The films shown are a mixture of new releases and old classics, and showings tend to start at around 9pm.

DIRECTORY

TICKET AND PRICE INFORMATION

Hekticket Theaterkassen
Hardenbergstraße 29d.
Map 2 B4.
Tel 230 99 30.

MAJOR STAGES

Berliner Ensemble
Bertolt-Brecht-Platz 1.
Map 1 F3.
Tel 28 408 155.
www.berliner-ensemble.de

Deutsches Theater
Schumannstraße 13.
Map 1 F3.
Tel 28 44 12 25.
www.deutsches-theater.berlin.net

Kammerspiele
Schumannstraße 13a.
Map 1 F3.
Tel 28 44 12 22.
www.deutsches-theater.berlin.net

Maxim-Gorki Theater
Am Festungsgraben 2.
Map 4 C2.
Tel 20 22 11 29.

Renaissance-Theater
Hardenbergstraße 6.
Map 2 A3.
Tel 312 42 02.

Schlosspark Theater
Schlossstraße 48.
Tel 700 96 90.

Volksbühne
Rosa-Luxemburg-Platz.
Tel 247 67 72.

ALTERNATIVE THEATRE

Bat-Studiotheater
Belforter Straße 15.
Tel 44 01 89 12.

Berlins Volkstheater Hansa
Alt-Moabit 48.
Tel 39 90 99 09.

Kleines Theater
Südwestkorso 64.
Tel 821 20 21.
www.kleines-theater-de

Komödie am Kurfürstendamm
Kurfürstendamm 206.
Map 2 A5.
Tel 88 59 11 88.

Theater am Halleschen Ufer
Tempelhofer Ufer 10.
Tel 251 31 16.

Theater am Kurfürstendamm
Kurfürstendamm 206.
Map 2 A5.
Tel 88 59 11 88.

MUSICALS, REVIEWS AND CABARETS

Bar jeder Vernunft
Schaperstraße 24.
Map 2 B5.
Tel 883 15 82.

Chamäleon Variété
Rosenthaler Straße 40–41.
Map 5 D4.
Tel 282 71 18.

Distel
Friedrichstraße 101.
Map 1 F3.
Tel 204 47 04.

Dr Seltsam Kabarett
Max & Moritz, Oranienburger Straße 162.
Map 5 D1.
Tel 695 159 11.
www.drseltsam.net

Friedrichstadt-palast
Friedrichstraße 107.
Map 1 F3.
Tel 23 26 23 26.
www.friedrichstadt palast.de

Musical Theater Berlin am Potsdamer Platz
Marlene-Dietrich-Platz 1.
Map 4 A3.
Tel (0180) 544 44.

Scheinbar
Monumentenstraße 9.
Tel 784 55 39.

Stachelschweine
Europa-Center.
Map 2 C4.
Tel 261 47 95.
www.die-stachel schweine.de

Theater des Westens
Kantstraße 12.
Tel (0180) 882 28 88.
www.theater deswestens.de

Wintergarten Variété
Potsdamer Straße 96.
Tel 25 00 88 88.
www.wintergarten-variete.de

Wühlmäuse
Pommernallee 2–4.
Tel 213 70 47.

BIG SCREENS AND BIG FILMS

CinemaxX Potsdamer Platz
Potsdamer Straße 1–19.
Map 4 A3.
Tel (0180) 524 63 62 99.
www.cinemaxx.de

Cinestar Sony Center
Postdamer Straße 4.
Map 4 A3.
Tel 26 06 62 60.

IMAX
Potsdamer Straße 4.
Map 4 A3.
Tel 26 06 64 00.

STUDIO CINEMA

Arsenal
Potsdamer Straße 2.
Map 4 A3.
Tel 26 95 51 00.

Central
Rosenthaler Straße 39.
Map 5 D1.
Tel 28 59 99 73.

Cinéma Paris
Kurfürstendamm 211.
Tel 881 31 19.

Hackescher Höfe Kino
Rosenthaler Straße 40–41.
Map 5 D1.
Tel 283 46 03.

Odeon
Hauptstraße 115.
Tel 78 70 40 19.

OPEN-AIR CINEMA

Waldbühne
Glockenturmstraße 1.
Tel (01805) 33 24 33.

BERLIN STREET FINDER

Map references given for historic buildings, hotels, restaurants, bars, shops and entertainment venues refer to the maps included in this section of the guidebook. The key map below shows the area of Berlin covered by the Street Finder. The maps include all major sightseeing areas, historic attractions, railway stations, bus stations, U-Bahn stations and the suburban stations of the S-Bahn. The names of the streets and squares in the index and maps are given in German. The word Straße (or STRASSE, Str) indicates a street, Allee an avenue, Platz a square, Brücke a bridge and Bahnhof a railway station.

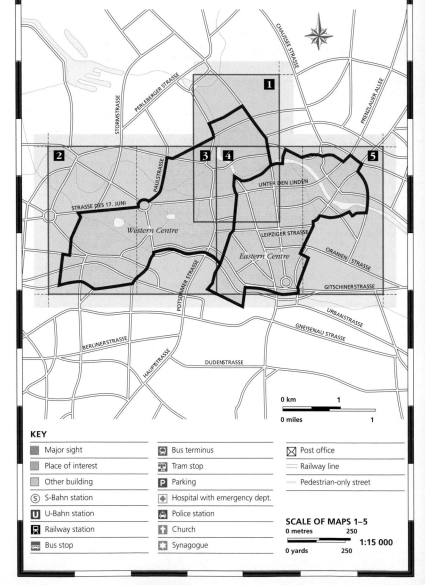

KEY

Major sight	Bus terminus	Post office
Place of interest	Tram stop	Railway line
Other building	Parking	Pedestrian-only street
S-Bahn station	Hospital with emergency dept.	
U-Bahn station	Police station	**SCALE OF MAPS 1–5**
Railway station	Church	0 metres 250
Bus stop	Synagogue	**1:15 000**
		0 yards 250

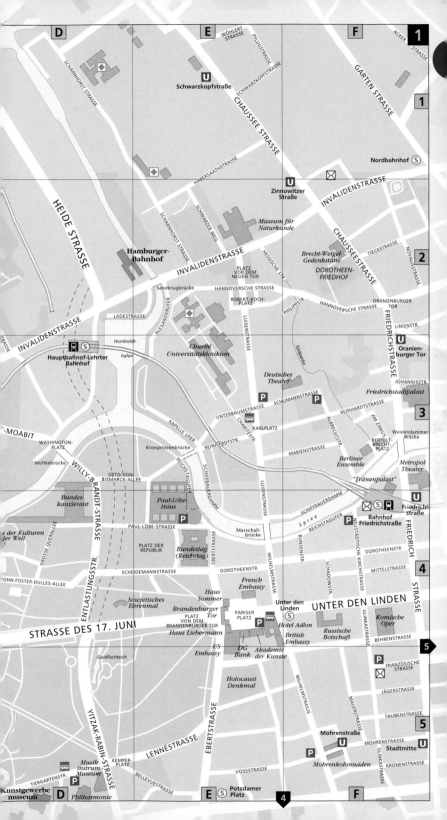

EASTERN GERMANY

Eastern Germany at a Glance

The eastern region of Germany is immensely rich in tourist attractions. The imposing valley of the Elbe River, the beautiful lake district of Lower Brandenburg, attractive trails in the Harz Mountains of Saxony-Anhalt, the Thuringian Forest as well as the Erzgebirge and the Lusatian Mountains in Saxony all invite the visitor with their dramatic scenery and excellent recreational facilities.

Eastern Germany is rich in historic sights, too, ranging from the Baroque residences of Potsdam in Brandenburg to the grand architecture of Dresden and Leipzig in Saxony and the important cultural centre of Weimar in Thuringia. The most rewarding destinations in the region are featured here.

The Magdeburg Reite, *in the market square, is the copy of one of Thuringia's most famous sights. The identity of the rider is not certain.*

Naumburg Dom *is a huge, well preserved Gothic cathedral (see pp150–51), one of Germany's greatest buildings. Splendid statues of its founders, Ekkebart and Uta, adorn the walls of the presbytery.*

Erfurt Dom *dominates the townscape. A massive Gothic structure, the cathedral's three towers were built on the Romanesque foundations of an earlier church.*

SAXONY-ANHALT
(see pp142–5?)

THURINGIA
(see pp180–97)

Weimar, *with its picturesque market square (see pp194-5) and historic buildings, was an important cultural centre for many centuries. Friedrich Schiller, Johann Wolfgang von Goethe and Johann Sebastian Bach all lived here.*

Sanssouci *in Potsdam* (see pp136–7), *the enchanting Baroque summer residence built for Prussia's King Frederick the Great, stands on the site of former gardens and vineyards.*

0 km   20

0 miles   20

LOCATOR MAP

Schloss Wörlitz *is surrounded by a romantic landscaped park* (see pp156–7) *criss-crossed by a network of waterways open to pleasure boats.*

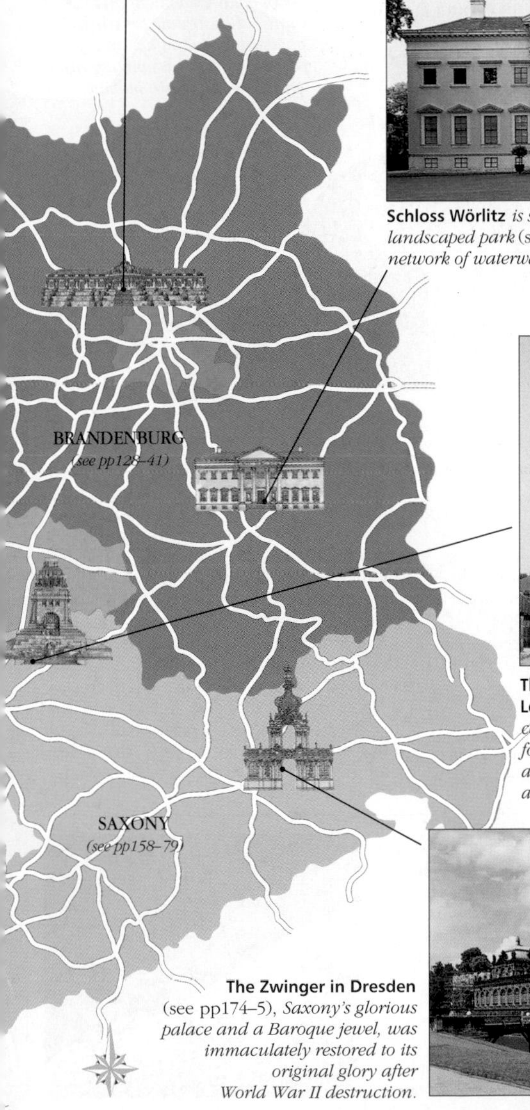

BRANDENBURG
see pp128–41)

SAXONY
(see pp158–79)

The Völkerschlachtdenkmal in Leipzig (see pp162–3) *was erected to celebrate the centenary of the battle fought by Prussia, Austria, Russia and Sweden against Napoleon's army in 1813.*

The Zwinger in Dresden (see pp174–5), *Saxony's glorious palace and a Baroque jewel, was immaculately restored to its original glory after World War II destruction.*

Meissen Porcelain

Until the early 18th century the only porcelain known in Europe was that imported from the Far East, and the Chinese jealously guarded the secrets of its production. Finally, in 1707, Johann Friedrich Böttger and Ehrenfried Walther von Tschirnhaus succeeded in developing a recipe which made it possible to produce genuine porcelain. A factory was set up in Meissen, and from 1713 it began to export its products to the entire European continent. Its first famous designers were Johann Joachim Kändler and Johann Gregor Höroldt.

Figurine by J. J. Kändler

The Porcelain Museum, *opened in 1906, holds exhibitions and demonstrations illustrating the various stages in the manufacture of porcelain. The museum also runs courses on porcelain-making.*

BOTTGER STONEWARE

Johann Friedrich Böttger's first success in recreating Chinese ceramics came in 1707 when, with the assistance of Ehrenfried Walther von Tschirnhaus, he managed to produce stoneware almost identical to that produced in Yi Hsing. The stoneware was dark, varying in colour from red to brown.

These plates and bowls *are typical examples of Böttger stoneware; its plain and simple lines were modelled on Far-Eastern designs.*

The dark colour of the dishes is due to the use of red clays.

The "Yellow Lion" design, *dating from c.1728, was used to decorate the first Meissen service.*

Imari tree

The "Yellow Lion" was in reality a tiger.

FAR-EASTERN MOTIFS

Until the 17th century the only porcelain known in Europe came from the Far East, and the first items made from Saxon hard porcelain were initially strongly influenced by the Asian products. In Meissen, Chinese figurines and dishes were copied, adapting "European" shapes, but using Japanese or Chinese motifs for decoration. Special designs were created to adorn the services intended for the royal court. The oldest among these include the "Yellow Lion" and the "Red Dragon". New designs, inspired by European art, began to appear after 1738, and gradually replaced the Asian patterns.

PRODUCTION PROCESS

The process of porcelain production has not changed significantly over the centuries. The formula for "hard-paste" porcelain contains kaolin, quartz and feldspar. Each product is dried and fired, with glazed products being fired twice. The decoration can be applied before or after the glazing process. Hand-painted and gilded items are the most expensive.

Demonstration of the intricate art of hand-painting porcelain at the Meissen factory

TABLEWARE

In the second half of the 18th and in the 19th centuries, porcelain manufacturers developed their own designs. This proved so popular that some remain in production to this day. The best-known Meißen designs are the "vine-leaves" and the "onion" patterns, first introduced in the 18th century. Customers can thus still replace items in the services which have graced their family tables for generations.

This coffee pot and cup is decorated with the cobalt "onion" pattern, depicting stylized pomegranate fruits.

FINE-ART MOTIFS

A new type of decoration, which became popular in the second half of the 18th century, involved the accurate copying of famous paintings or etchings onto a vase, a pot or a plate. This type of decoration proved particularly popular during the Classicist period.

Decorator copying an etching onto a vessel

Vase decorated with a miniature of a painting by Antoine Watteau

SERVICES AND FIGURINES

Several outstanding sculptors and painters were employed in the Meißsen porcelain manufacture to design unique services and figurines for the royal courts. The most famous among them are the services designed by Johann Joachim Kändler. He also created sets of figurines to adorn dining tables, vases and censers (containers for burning incense) for decorating the home, and large religious compositions for churches.

"Swan" Service Tureen

Figurine of August III

Europa, a figure from the "Four Continents" series, designed by J. J. Kändler

MARKS ON MEISSEN PORCELAIN

All porcelain manufacturers mark their products with their own symbols. The symbols are generally applied under the glaze, at the bottom of the piece. The Meissen factory initially used marks that imitated Japanese or Chinese writing; later, for a short time, letters were used, and from 1724 blue trademarks in the shape of crossed swords became the standard mark. The last three symbols below identify the respective court for which each piece of porcelain was produced.

K.P.F.
Königliche Porzellan-Fabrik, trademark used in 1723

K.P.M.
Königliche Porzellan-Manufaktur, trademark used in 1723–4

Trademarks used from 1724

AR
Augustus Rex, the initials of King August

K.H.K
Königliche Hof-Küche

K.H.C.W.
Königliche Hof-Conditorei Warschau

Luther and the Reformation

Coat of arms

In 1517, on the eve of All Souls' Day (31 October), Martin Luther nailed his 95 "theses" to the doors of the castle church in Wittenberg, condemning the practice of indulgences. His subsequent pronouncements, in which he criticized many aspects of the Church's teaching, made him the "father" of the Reformation movement in Germany and other countries. Luther's teaching gained the support of many of the princes, who in 1531 formed the Schmalkalden Union and started to introduce a new administration to the Church. This led to religious wars which finally ended with the Augsburg Peace Treaty, signed in 1555, which confirmed the religious division of Germany.

The Bible, *translated into German by Luther, was first published in one volume in 1534. One year later an illustrated, two-volume luxury version was published in Augsburg.*

The Schlosskapelle *in Hartenfels Castle, in Torgau (see p164), was built in 1543–4 and consecrated by Martin Luther. It is generally considered to be the first church built specifically for the Lutheran community.*

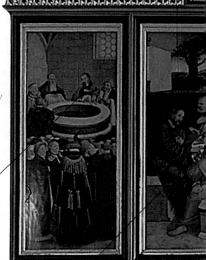

The baptism of a child is performed by Philipp Melanchthon.

The Last Supper, at the centre of the altar, stresses the importance attached by Lutherans to the sacrament of communion. The figures of the Apostles are portraits of the main church reformers.

Martin Luther, *the great theologian and religious reformer, initiator of Church reform and founder of Lutheranism, is depicted in this portrait by Lucas Cranach the Elder (1520).*

This group of faithful, listening to the sermon, includes members of Luther's family.

Luther's Room (Lutherstube), *shown here, is part of Luther's House in Wittenberg* (see p154). *The famous reformer lived here with his wife and family.*

Cup Bearer Serving at the Table is the title of a portrait by Lucas Cranach the Younger.

Philipp Melanchthon, *an associate of Luther's and the co-founder of Lutheranism, initiated a great educational reform. He was also known as* praeceptor Germaniae, *Germany's teacher.*

REFORMATION ALTAR

The main altar of St Mary's Church in Wittenberg *(see pp154–5)* is one of the most important works of art of the Reformation period. The central picture was painted by Lucas Cranach the Elder (c.1539), the wings by his son, Lucas Cranach the Younger, before 1547.

Protestant confession is taken by Johannes Bugenhagen.

Sermon preached by Martin Luther, who points to the figure of the crucified Christ.

Katharina von Bora, *a former nun, became Martin Luther's wife in 1525. She lies buried in the Marienkirche in Torgau (see p164), in a tomb which survives to this day.*

BRANDENBURG

The province of Brandenburg is a lowland region criss-crossed by a dense network of rivers, canals and lakes. Quiet in part, it is also crossed by some of the main tourist routes to Berlin. Its most popular attractions are the historic sights of its capital city, Potsdam, and the Spreewald, where all day can be spent boating on the waterways of the Lusatian forests and villages.

In early medieval times, the area that was to become present-day Brandenburg was the scene of violent conflict between various Germanic tribes. The latter conquered the region, and in 1157 created the margravate of Brandenburg. Its first ruler was Albrecht der Bär (Albert the Bear), from the house of Ascan. From 1415, Brandenburg was ruled by the Hohenzollern dynasty. It was quick to embrace the Reformation, which was officially adopted here as early as 1538. In 1618, Brandenburg merged with the duchy of Prussia through personal union. The region became entangled in the Thirty Years' War and suffered devastating losses; depopulated and plundered, it took Brandenburg many years to rise from the ashes. In 1701, the Great Elector, Frederick III, crowned himself King Frederick I, and the whole region now assumed the name of Prussia.

While Berlin remained the seat of power and a strong industrial and cultural centre, 18th-century Potsdam also played an important role: it was, after all, the favourite haunt of Frederick the Great. Other towns in the region were less significant – Brandenburg was, and still is, a fairly rural region. Reunification in 1990, however, has opened up the newly created land to Berliners and tourists alike.

Travellers in Brandenburg will encounter ancient tree-lined avenues that stretch to the horizon. The Spreewald, Brandenburg's lake district, is an oasis of tranquillity, ideal for boating and cycling. Brandenburg also has grand castles in Oranienburg, Branitz just outside Cottbus and Rheinsberg, Gothic churches and monasteries in Lehnin and Chorin and the towns of Brandenburg/Havel and Potsdam.

Baroque palace in Rheinsberg, on the shores of the Grienericksee

◁ A picturesque corner in the Babelsberg Palace in Potsdam

Exploring Brandenburg

Brandenburg is ideally suited for gentle exploration by bicycle or car, and its proximity to Berlin allows the visitor to make a one-day excursion to the capital. A whole day should be allocated for visiting Potsdam and the castle of Sanssouci, and another day for a boat trip in the Spreewald. A visit to Cottbus can be combined with an excursion to Frankfurt an der Oder. The best time for a visit to Chorin is the summer when concerts are held there in the ruined monastery.

SEE ALSO

- *Where to Stay* pp490–91
- *Where to Eat* pp528–30

Cecilienhof, the summer residence of the
Hohenzollern family in Potsdam

Schloss Branitz in Cottbus

KEY

▬▬	Motorway
▬▬	Major road
----	Minor road
━━━	Main railway
----	Minor railway
▬▬	International border
▬▬	Regional border

For additional map symbols *see back flap*

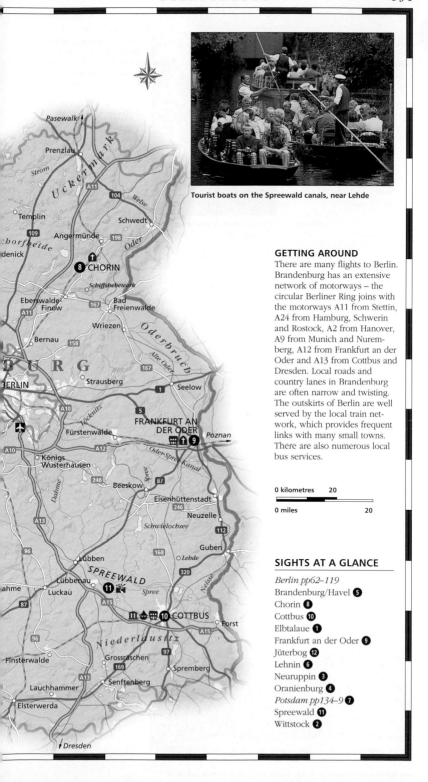

Tourist boats on the Spreewald canals, near Lehde

GETTING AROUND

There are many flights to Berlin. Brandenburg has an extensive network of motorways – the circular Berliner Ring joins with the motorways A11 from Stettin, A24 from Hamburg, Schwerin and Rostock, A2 from Hanover, A9 from Munich and Nuremberg, A12 from Frankfurt an der Oder and A13 from Cottbus and Dresden. Local roads and country lanes in Brandenburg are often narrow and twisting. The outskirts of Berlin are well served by the local train network, which provides frequent links with many small towns. There are also numerous local bus services.

0 kilometres   20

0 miles   20

SIGHTS AT A GLANCE

Berlin pp62–119
Brandenburg/Havel ⑤
Chorin ⑧
Cottbus ⑩
Elbtalaue ①
Frankfurt an der Oder ⑨
Jüterbog ⑫
Lehnin ⑥
Neuruppin ③
Oranienburg ④
Potsdam pp134–9 ⑦
Spreewald ⑪
Wittstock ②

Elbtalaue ●

Road map D2. ⊡ *to Wittenberge or Bad Wilsnack.* ⓘ *Am Markt 5, Bad Wilsnack (038791-26 20).*

The Elbe valley in the western part of Prignitz is an area of gentle rolling hills and unspoiled nature. Storks, increasingly rare in Germany, nest here to this day. When travelling around this parkland it is worth stopping at **Pritzwalk** to admire the late-Gothic Nikolaikirche (St Nicholas church). Another place of interest is **Perleberg** with its picturesque market square featuring an original 1515 timber-frame building, a sandstone statue of the French knight Roland (1546), now standing by the 1850 Town Hall, and the town's star attraction – the 15th-century Gothic Jakobskirche (church of St Jacob).

Bad Wilsnack owes its fame to the discovery of the therapeutic properties of the iron oxide-rich mud found in the surrounding marshes. Already known in medieval times, the town was an important place of pilgrimage. After a church fire, in 1384, three hosts displaying the blood of Christ were found untouched on the altar. The Gothic **Nikolaikirche** (church of St Nicholas), which survives to this day, was built soon after for the pilgrims.

Plattenburg Castle, in a scenic situation on an island, is also worth a visit. Combining late-Gothic and Renaissance architecture, it is used as a venue for concerts.

Chapel of the Holy Sepulchre in Heiligengrabe, near Wittstock

Wittstock ●

Road map E2. ⚇ *13,700.* ⊟ ⓘ *Walter-Shulz-Pl. 1, Wittstock/Dosse (03394-43 34 42).* **www**.wittstock.de.

The small town of Wittstock was first awarded its municipal status in 1284. From the 13th century to the Reformation, Wittstock was the see of the Havelberg bishops. Although much of the town was destroyed, the original city walls remained almost completely intact, with one surviving gate – the **Gröper Tor**. All that remains of the former bishop's castle is the gate tower, which now houses a small museum. The town's star attraction is the Gothic **Marienkirche** with its late-Gothic reredos depicting the crowning of St Mary. It originated in the wood carving workshop of Claus Berg, probably after 1532. Other interesting features include the 1516 sacrarium and the late-Renaissance pulpit.

Environs

Ten km (6 miles) to the west lies **Heiligengrabe**, with its Gothic Cistercian Abbey. One of its many highlights is

the 1512 **Chapel of the Holy Sepulchre** with an intricately sculpted gable and some charming timber-frame cloister buildings.

Neuruppin ●

Road map E2. ⚇ *27,300.* ⊟ ⓘ *Karl-Marx-Str. 1 (03391-454 60).* **www**.neuruppin.de.

The town of Neuruppin, in a scenic location on the shores of a large lake, the Ruppiner See, is mainly Neo-Classical in style, having been rebuilt to the design of Bernhard Matthias Brasch after the great fire of 1787. The only older buildings are the Gothic post-Dominican church and two small hospital chapels. Neuruppin is the birthplace of the architect **Karl Friedrich Schinkel** and the novelist **Theodor Fontane** *(see p27).*

Environs

The beautiful, albeit neglected palace of **Rheinsberg**, 25 km (16 miles) to the north, was converted from 16th-century Renaissance castle in 1734–7. In 1734–40 it was the residence of the Crown Prince, who later became Frederick the Great, King of Prussia. Some 30 km (19 miles) northeast of Rheinsberg is the National Socialist concentration camp **Ravensbrück**, for women and children. It is now a place of remembrance.

Schinkel monument

Oranienburg ●

Road map E3. ⚇ *30,000.* ⊟ ⊟ ⓘ *Bernauer Str. 52 (033 01-70 48 33).* **www**.tourismus-or.de.

The star attraction of the town is **Schloss Oranienburg,** the Baroque residence built for Louisa Henrietta von Nassau-

The Gothic-Renaissance Plattenburg Castle, in the Elbtalaue

Oranien, wife of the Great Elector Friedrich Wilhelm. Designed by Johann Gregor Memhardt and Michael Matthias Smids, it was built in 1651–5 and later extended to reach its present H-shape.

🏛 Schloss Oranienburg
Schlossplatz 1. *Tel (03301) 38 63.*
⏲ *Apr–Oct: 10am–6pm Tue–Sun;*
Nov–Mar: 10am–5pm Sat–Sun.

Early-Renaissance palace in Caputh, north of Lehnin

Environs

Sachsenhausen, which is located northeast of Oranienburg, is now a place of remembrance and a museum. Opened in 1936 by the National Socialists, this concentration camp claimed the lives of 100,000 inmates.

🏛 Sachsenhausen
Tel (03301) 20 00. ⏲ *mid-Mar–mid-Oct: 8:30am–6pm Tue–Sun;*
mid-Oct–mid-Mar: 8:30am–4:30pm
Tue–Sun. www.gedenkstaette-sachsenhausen.dev

Brandenburg/ Havel ❺

Road map E3. 🏘 *87,700.* 🚆 🚌
🛈 *Steinstraße 66–67 (03381-20 87/29).* 🎭 *Havelfestspiele (Jun).* www. städt-brandenburg.de

Brandenburg is the oldest town of the region. It was settled by Slavs as early as the 6th century, and a mission episcopate was established here in 948. Scenically sited on the Havel River, it has preserved historic centres on three islands, despite wartime destruction. The oldest island is the **Dominsel**, with its

Romanesque **Dom St Peter und St Paul**. This cathedral was constructed from 1165 to the mid-13th century. In the 14th century it was raised and given new vaultings. It contains numerous valuable Gothic objects, including the **"Czech" altar** (c.1375), the present main altar (from Lehnin, 1518) and the sacrarium of the same year. The most valuable treasures are on display in the **Dommuseum**.

Other sights worth visiting are the huge, 15th-century **Katharinenkirche** built by Hinrich Brunsberg, the **Gotthardkirche**, in the Altstadt ("old town"), with its Romanesque façade and Gothic interior, the Gothic **Rathaus** (Town Hall), with a statue of Roland from 1474, and the **Stadtmuseum**, a museum of local history.

🏛 Dommuseum
Burghof 9. *Tel (03381) 22 43 90.*
www.brandenburg-dom.de
⏲ *10am–4pm Mon–Fri, 10am–5pm Sat, 11am–5pm Sun.* 📷

🏛 Stadtmuseum
Ritterstr. 96. *Tel (03381) 52 20 48.*
⏲ *9am–5pm Tue–Fri, 10am–5pm Sat & Sun.* 📷

Lehnin ❻

Road map E3. 🏘 *3,100.* 🚌
🛈 *Friedensstraße 3 (03382-730 717).*

Visitors mainly come to see the huge Klosterkirche (abbey) founded for the Cistercian order of Otto I, son of Albert the Bear. The church was built from the late 12th to the late 13th century, originally in Romanesque, then in early-Gothic style. Following the dissolution of the monastery, in 1542, the buildings fell into disrepair, but much of the abbey has survived.

⛪ Klosterkirche
Klosterkirchplatz. *Tel (03382) 76 86 10.* ⏲ *Apr–Oct: 9am–noon, 1–4pm Mon–Fri, 11am–noon, 1–5pm Sat, 1–5pm Sun; Nov–Mar: 10am–4pm Mon–Fri, 1–4pm Sat–Sun.* www.klosterkirche-lehin.de

Environs

Caputh, situated 23 km (14 miles) to the north, has an early-Baroque **Palace** built during the second half of the 17th century, as summer residence for the wives of the Great Electors. The interior has many original features.

The Gothic "Czech" altar in the Dom St Peter und St Paul in Brandenburg

Potsdam ❼

An independent city close to Berlin, Potsdam, with almost 138,000 inhabitants, is also the capital of Brandenburg. The first documented reference to Potsdam dates back to AD 993; it was later granted municipal rights in 1317. The town blossomed during the times of the Great Electors and then again in the 18th century. Potsdam suffered very badly during World War II, particularly on the night of 14–15 April 1945 when Allied planes bombed the town centre.

A sculpture on display in Park Sanssouci

Sightseeing in Potsdam
Potsdam remains one of Germany's most attractive towns. Tourists flock to see the magnificent royal summer residence, Schloss Sanssouci, to stroll around Neuer Garten (new garden) with its Marmorpalais (marble palace) and Cecilienhof, to visit the old city centre and the Russian colony of Alexandrowka, to be entertained in the film studios of Babelsberg and to take a walk around the parks of Schloss Babelsberg.

♠ Cecilienhof
Am Neuen Garten (Neuer Garten).
Tel (0331) 969 42 44. 695.
◻ Apr–Oct: 9am–5pm Tue–Sun; Nov–Mar: 9am–4pm Tue–Sun.
The Cecilienhof residence played a brief but important role in history, when it served as the venue for the 1945 Potsdam Conference (see p139). Built between 1914 and 1917, the palace is the most recent of all Hohenzollern dynasty buildings. Designed by Paul Schultze-Naumburg in the style of an English country manor, Cecilienhof is a sprawling, asymmetrical, timber-frame building with inner courtyards and irregular breaks.

The palace remained a residence of the Hohenzollern family after they had lost the crown – the family stayed in Potsdam until February 1945. Today the palace is a hotel, where visitors interested in history are able to relax amid green shrubs. The large, scenic park remains open to the public even when the rooms used during the Potsdam Conference are closed to visitors.

♠ Marmorpalais
Am Neuen Garten (Neuer Garten).
Tel (0331) 969 42 46. 695.
◻ 15 May–15 Oct: 10am–5pm Tue–Sun; 16 Oct–14 May: 10am–4pm Sat & Sun (only with guide).
This small palace, situated on the edge of the lake, is a beautiful example of early Neo-Classical architecture. The palace is named after the Silesian marble used on its façade. The main part of it was built between 1787 and 1791 by Carl von Gontard to a design and under the direction of Carl Gotthard Langhans, on the initiative of King Friedrich Wilhelm II.

⛲ Alexandrowka
Russische Kolonie Allee/Puschkinallee.
🚊 92, 95. 🚌 604, 609, 638, 639.
A visit to Alexandrowka takes the visitor into the world of Pushkin's fairy tales. Wooden log cabins with intricate carvings, set in their own gardens, create a charming residential estate. They were constructed in 1826 under the direction of the German architect Snethlage, for twelve singers of a Russian choir that was established in 1812.

⛲ Holländisches Viertel
Friedrich-Ebert-Str , Kurfürstenstr., Hebbelstr., Gutenbergstr. 🚌 138, 601–604, 606–612, 614, 631, 632, 650. 🚊 92, 95.
Just as amazing as the Russian colony of Alexandrowka is the Holländisches Viertel (Dutch quarter), part of a Baroque town built in the middle of Germany. Dutch workers arrived in Potsdam in the early 18th century and,

A view of the Baroque Dutch district known as Holländisches Viertel between 1733 and 1742, a settlement was built for them on the orders of Friedrich Wilhelm I to plans by Johann Boumann the Elder. It comprised 134 gabled houses arranged in four groups. The houses were built from small red bricks and finished with stone and plaster details.

🔒 Nikolaikirche

Alter Markt. *Tel* (03381) 280 93. 🚌 601, 603, 692, 694, 🚊 91, 92, 93, 95, 96, 98. ◯ May–Oct: 2pm–5pm Fri–Sun; Nov–Apr: 2–4pm Sat–Sun.
This imposing church built in the late Neo-Classical style, is indisputably the most beautiful church in Potsdam. It was

The Nikolaikirche, with its dome resting on a colonnaded wall

built on the site of an earlier, Baroque church, which burned down in 1795. It was designed during 1828–30 by Karl Friedrich Schinkel and the building work was supervised by Ludwig Persius. The interior decoration and furnishings of the church date from the 1850s, but were mostly based on the earlier designs by Schinkel.

🎠 Marstall

Breitenstr. 1a. *Tel* (0331) 271 81 12. 🖼 🚌 601, 603, 692, 694. 🚊 91, 92, 93, 95, 96, 98. ◯ 10am–6pm daily.
This long Baroque pavilion, once used as royal stables, is the only remaining building of a royal residence. It was constructed in 1714 and currently houses a film museum devoted to the history and work of the nearby Babelsberg Film Studio.

🏛 Bildergalerie

Zur Historischen Mühle. *Tel* (0331) 969 41 81. 🚌 612, 614, 695. ◯ 15 May–15 Oct: 10am–5pm Tue–Sun. 🖼
Baroque paintings once owned by Frederick the Great, including Caravaggio's *Doubting Thomas*, Guido

VISITORS' CHECKLIST

Road map E3. *Tel* (0331) 27 55 80. 🚉 Lange Brücke. ℹ Friedrich-Ebert-Str. 5; Am Alten Markt (0331–27 55 80). *Fax* (0331) 27 55 829. Hofkonzerte (May–Sep); Musikfestspiele Sanssouci (Jun). **www**.potsdam.de

Reni's *Cleopatra's Death*, as well as paintings by Rubens and van Dyck, are on show in the picture gallery situated next to Schloss Sanssouci.

Caravaggio's *Doubting Thomas*, on show in the Bildergalerie

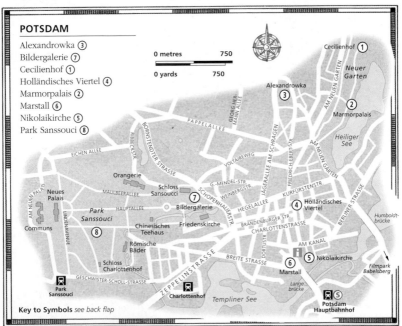

POTSDAM

0 metres 750
0 yards 750

Key to Symbols see back flap

Park Sanssouci

Flower-filled urn, Park Sanssouci

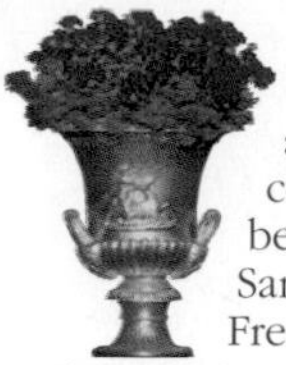

The enormous Park Sanssouci, which occupies an area of 287 hectares (700 acres), is one of the most beautiful palace complexes in Europe. The first building to be constructed on the site was Schloss Sanssouci, built as the summer palace of Frederick the Great. It was erected in 1747, on the site of a former orchard. Over the years, Park Sanssouci was expanded considerably and other palaces and pavilions added. To enjoy the park fully, allow at least a whole day.

Communs
Situated next to a pretty courtyard, this building has an unusually elegant character. It is now used to house palace staff.

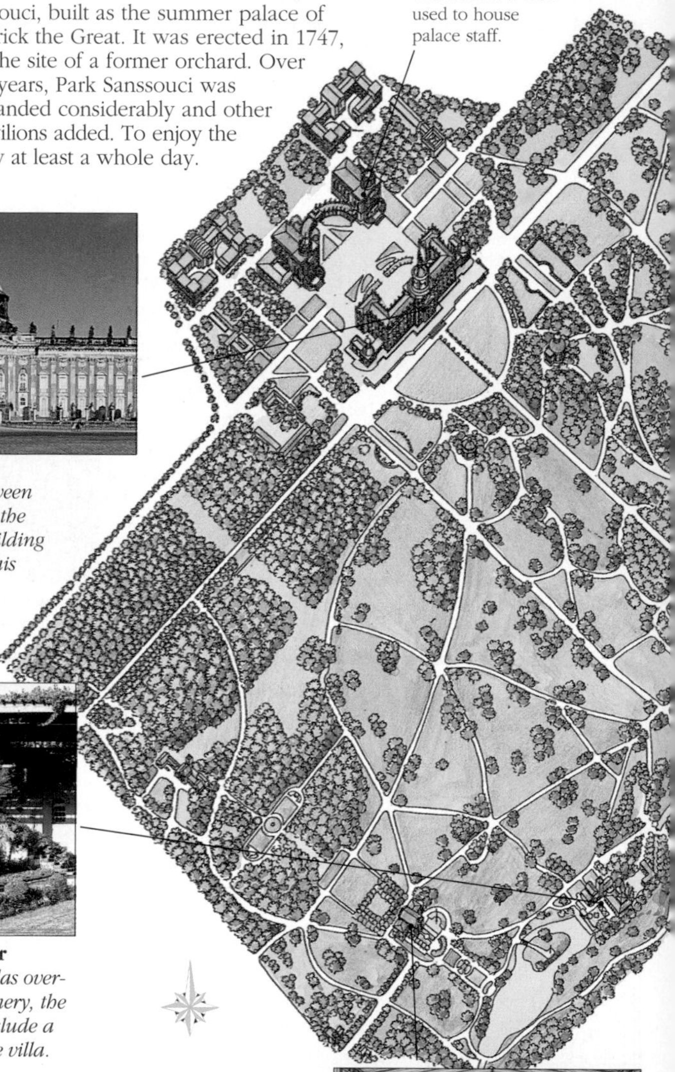

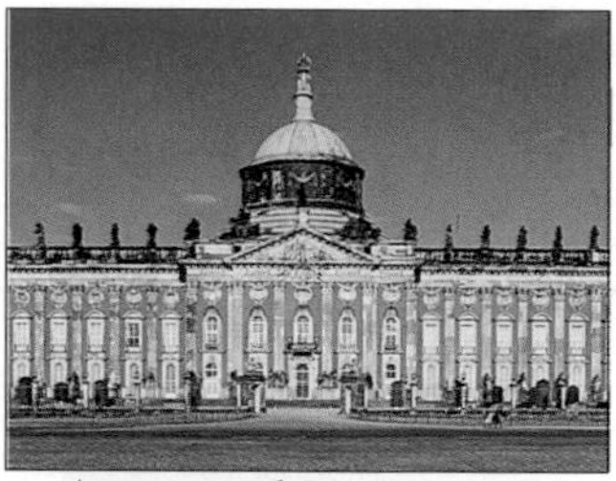

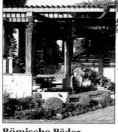

★ Neues Palais
Constructed between 1763 and 1769, the monumental building of the Neues Palais is crowned by a massive dome.

Römische Bäder
Shaded by pergolas overgrown with greenery, the Roman baths include a Renaissance-style villa.

0 metres 200

0 yards 200

Schloss Charlottenhof
This Neo-Classical palace gained its name from Charlotte von Gentzkow, the former owner of the land on which the palace was built.

STAR SIGHTS

- ★ Neues Palais
- ★ Schloss Sanssouci

For hotels and restaurants in this region see pp490–91 and pp528–30

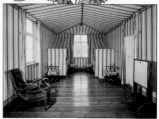

Lustgarten
The extensive park-land is made up of several gardens. The Lustgarten (pleasure garden) is nearest to the Orangerie.

VISITORS' CHECKLIST

An Der Orangerie 1. **Tel** (0331) 969 42 02. 606, 695. Mar–Oct: 9am–5pm; Nov–Feb: 9am–4pm (in winter, visit possible only with guided tour). Fri. (free access to park).

Orangerie
This large Neo-Renaissance palace was built in the mid-19th century to house foreign royalty and other guests.

Neue Kammern
Once the orangerie of the Sanssouci Palace, this Rococo pavilion was later rebuilt as a guest house.

★ Schloss Sanssouci
A beautifully terraced vineyard creates a grand approach to Schloss Sanssouci, the oldest building in the complex.

Bildergalerie
Built between 1755 and 1764, this is Germany's oldest purpose-built museum building. The Baroque pavilion houses an art gallery.

Chinesisches Teehaus
An exhibition of exquisite Oriental porcelain is housed in the small, Rococo-style Chinese Tea House.

Friedenskirche
The Neo-Romanesque Church of Peace is modelled on the Basilica of San Clemente in Rome.

Paintings in the music room, in Schloss Sanssouci

♣ Schloss Sanssouci

Zur Historischen Mühle. **Tel** *(0331) 969 41 90.* ☐ *Apr–Oct: 9am–5pm; Nov–Mar: 9am–4pm Tue–Sun.* **Damenflügel & Schlossküche:** *15 May–15 Oct: 10am–12:30pm & 1–5pm Sat & Sun.*

This Rococo palace was built in 1745–7 by Georg Wenzeslaus von Knobelsdorff to sketches by Frederick the Great. Knobelsdorff and Johann August Nahl designed the interior. *Sanssouci* ("carefree") was the perfect name for the enchanting castle. The Damenflügel, the castle's west wing which was added in 1840 to house ladies and gentlemen of the court, and the Schlossküche (castle kitchen) can also be visited.

♣ Schloss Neue Kammern

Zur Historischen Mühle (Lustgarten). **Tel** *(0331) 969 42 06.* ☐ *1 Apr–14 May 10am–5pm Sat & Sun; 15 May–31 Oct 10am–5pm Tue–Sun.* ✇ *obligatory.*

The Neue Kammern (new chambers) adjoin Schloss Sanssouci in the west, like the Bildergalerie in the east. As part of this ensemble it was originally built in 1747 as an orangery, to a design by Georg Wenzeslaus von Knobelsdorff who gave it its elegant Baroque forms. The building has an attractive roof with sloping ends and sides. In 1777 Frederick the Great ordered the building to be transformed into guest accommodation. The architect, Georg Christian Unger, left the exterior of the orangery largely untouched but converted the interior into

sumptuous suites and four elegant halls. The Rococo décor has been maintained, similar to that of other palaces and pavilions of Sanssouci.

☷ Orangerieschloss

Maulbeerallee. (Nordischer Garten). **Tel** *(0331) 969 42 80.* ☐ *13 May–15 Oct: 10am–5pm Tue–Sun;* **viewing terrace** ☐ *1 Apr–12 May: 10am–5pm Sat & Sun; 13 May–31 Oct 10am–5pm Tue–Sun.*

Above the park towers the Orangerie, designed in Italian Renaissance style and crowned by a colonnade. It was built to house guests, not plants, and served as guest residence for Tsar Nicolas and his wife, King Friedrich Wilhelm IV's sister. The Orangerie was constructed in 1852–60 for the king by Friedrich August Stüler, with the final design partly based on plans by Ludwig Persius. Modelled on the Regia Hall in the Vatican, the rooms were grouped around the Raphael Hall and decorated with replicas of this great Italian master's works. The observation terrace offers a good view over Potsdam.

☷ Chinesisches Teehaus

Ökonomieweg (Rehgarten). **Tel** *(0331) 969 42 22.* ☐ *15 May– 15 Oct: 10am–5pm Tue–Sun.*

The lustrous, gilded pavilion that can be seen glistening between the trees from a

Figure on the roof of Chinesisches Teehaus

distance is the Chinese Teahouse. Chinese art was very popular during the Rococo period – people wore Chinese silk, wallpapered their rooms with Chinese designs, lacquered their furniture, drank tea from Chinese porcelain and built Chinese pavilions in their gardens. The one in Sanssouci was built in 1754–56 to a design by Johann Gottfried Büring. Circular in shape, it has a centrally located main hall surrounded by three studies. Between these are pretty *trompe l'oeil* porticos. The structure is covered with a tent roof and topped with a lantern. Gilded ornaments, columns and Chinese figures surround the pavilion. Originally a tea room and summer dining house, it houses today a collection of 18th-century porcelain.

☷ Römische Bäder

Lenné-Str. (Park Charlottenhof). **Tel** *(0331) 969 42 24.* ☷ *606.* ☷ *94, 96.* ☐ *15 May–15 Oct: 10am–5pm Tue–Sun.*

The Roman baths, situated by the edge of a lake, form a picturesque group of pavilions which served as accommodation for the king's guests. They were designed in 1829–40 by Karl Friedrich Schinkel, with the help of Ludwig Persius. The gardener's house at the front stands next to a low, asymmetrical tower, built in the style of an Italian Renaissance villa. In the background, to the left, extends the former bathing pavilion, which is currently used for temporary exhibitions. The pavilions are grouped around a garden planted with colourful shrubs and vegetables.

♣ Schloss Charlottenhof

Geschwister-Scholl-Str. (Park Charlottenhof). **Tel** *(0331) 969 42 28.* ☷ *94, 96.* ☐ *15 May–15 Oct: 10am–5pm Tue–Sun.* ✇ *obligatory.*

This small Neo-Classical palace stands at the southern end of Park Sanssouci, known as Park Charlottenhof. Built in

1826–9 for the heir to the throne, the future King Friedrich Wilhelm IV, this small, single-storey building was designed by Karl Friedrich Schinkel in the style of a Roman villa. Some of the wall paintings, designed by Schinkel in the so-called Pompeiian style, are still in place. There is also a collection of Italian engravings. The most interesting part of the interior is the Humboldt Room. The palace is surrounded by a landscaped park designed by Peter Joseph Lenné.

♠ Neues Palais

Am Neuen Palais. *Tel (0331) 969 42 55.* ☐ *Apr–Oct 9am–5pm Sat–Thu; Nov–Mar 9am–4pm Sat–Thu.* 📷 ✔ *obligatory.*

One of Germany's most beautiful palaces, this imposing Baroque structure, on the main avenue in Park Sanssouci, was built for Frederick the Great to initial plans by Georg Wenzeslaus von Knobelsdorff in 1750. Its construction, to designs by Johan Gottfried Büring, Jean Laurent Le Geay and Carl von Gontard, was delayed until 1763–9, after the Seven Years' War. The vast, three-wing structure comprises over 200 richly adorned rooms and has many interesting sculptures. The south wing houses the kings' quarters.

The impressive Marble Hall in the Baroque Neues Palais

THE POTSDAM CONFERENCE

Towards the end of World War II, the leaders of the Allies – Winston Churchill, Franklin Roosevelt, and Joseph Stalin – met in Schloss Cecilienhof in Potsdam. The aim of this conference, which lasted from 17 July until 2 August 1945, was to resolve the problems arising at the end of the war. The main participants changed, however, before it was concluded. Churchill was replaced by newly-elected Clement Attlee, and Harry S. Truman took over after President Roosevelt died. The conference set up the occupation zones, the demilitarization and monitoring of Germany, the punishment of war criminals and the reparations. It also revised the German borders. These decisions established the political balance of power in Europe, which continued for 45 years.

Attlee, Truman and Stalin in Potsdam

♠ Schloss Babelsberg

Im Park Babelsberg. *Tel (0331) 969 42 02.* 🚫 *for renovation until 2007.*

Built in 1833–5 for Prince Wilhelm (Kaiser Wilhelm I), by Karl Friedrich Schinkel, this extravagant castle ranks as one of his finest works. An irregular building with many towers and bay windows, built in the spirit of English Neo-Gothic, with allusions to Windsor Castle and Tudor style, it now holds the Museum of Pre-History.

♿ Filmpark Babelsberg

Großbeerenstr. *Tel (0331) 721 27 55.* ☐ *11 Apr–31 Oct 10am–6pm daily.* 📷 **www**.filmpark.de

This amazing film park was laid out on the site where Germany's first films were produced in 1912. From 1917 the studio belonged to Universum-Film-AG (UFA), which produced some of the most famous films of the silent era, including Fritz Lang's *Metropolis* and some films with Greta Garbo. The *Blue Angel*, with Marlene Dietrich, was also shot at Babelsberg, but subsequently, the studios were used to film propaganda for the Nazis. The studio is still operational today, and the public can admire some of the old sets, the creation of special effects and stuntmen in action.

♿ Einsteinturm

Albert-Einstein-Str. ☐ *once every month, by arrangement with the Urania Society (0331-288 23 33).* 🚌 *694.*

This tower, built in 1920–21 by Erich Mendelsohn, is one of the finest examples of German Expressionist architecture. Its fantasy forms were to demonstrate the qualities of reinforced concrete to spectacular effect. However, the cost of formwork, assembled by boat builders, limited the use of the material to the first storey, while the upper floors are plastered brickwork.

Chorin

Road map *E2.* 🏰 *510.* 🚉 *Kloster Chorin, Amt 11A.* **Tel** *(033366) 703 77.* ⭕ *Apr–Oct: 9am–6pm daily; Nov–Mar: 9am–4pm daily.* 🎵 *Choriner Musiksommer.*

On the edge of the vast **Schorfheide** heathland, which has been listed as a World Biosphere Reserve by UNESCO, stands one of Brandenburg's most beautiful Gothic buildings – the Cistercian **Kloster** (abbey) of Chorin. The Cistercians arrived here in 1258, but work on the present Gothic abbey did not start until 1270. The church is a triple-nave, transeptial basilica, with a magnificent façade. Preserved to this day are two wings of the monastic quarters plus several domestic buildings. Following the dissolution of the monastery in 1542, the entire complex fell into disrepair. Today the church, deprived of its traditional furnishings, is used as a venue for classical concerts. The park established by Peter Joseph Lenné is conducive to pleasant strolls.

Environs
For visitors to Niederfinow, the giant **Schiffshebewerk** (bargelift) is a definite must. This wonder of technology was designed for lifting and lowering ships from one canal to another. Commissioned in 1934, it is 60 m (197 ft) tall and capable of lifting barges laden with 1,000 tonnes or more.

Portal of the St Marienkirche in Frankfurt an der Oder

Frankfurt an der Oder

Road map *F3.* 🏰 *87,900.* 🚉 🚌 ℹ️ *Karl-Marx-Str. 1. (0335-32 52 16).* 🎵 *Frankfurter Musikfesttage (Mar); Hansefest (Jul); Kleist-Tage (Oct).*

Frankfurt, on the banks of the river Oder, was granted municipal rights in 1253, prospered in the 13th century and joined the Hanseatic league in 1368. In 1945, the right bank was ceded to Poland and is now known as Słubice.

Viadrin University, founded in 1506, was reopened in 1991 and now educates both German and Polish students. The town's most famous resident was the playwright and writer Heinrich von Kleist who was born here in 1777.

The Gothic **Rathaus** (town hall) in the centre escaped destruction in World War II and now houses an art gallery. The main church, **Marienkirche** (church of St Mary), is a vast, five-nave Gothic church which has stood in ruins since 1945. Some of the Gothic furnishings were rescued and can now be seen in **St Gertraud** (church of St Gertrude) which dates back to 1368. The main altar from 1489 and the huge, 5m- (16ft) -tall candelabrum from 1376 are particularly valuable. Another Gothic church, originally built for the Franciscans in 1270, has been transformed into the **C.P.E. Bach Konzerthalle** (concert hall), named after Carl Philipp Emmanuel Bach, son of Johann Sebastian.

Environs
Neuzelle, 36 km (23 miles) to the south, has a magnificent former Cistercian Abbey, with an impressive Baroque relief façade.

Cottbus

Road map *F3.* 🏰 *121,000.* 🚉 *Bahnhofstr.* 🚌 ℹ️ *Berliner Platz 6. (0355-754 20);* **www**.cottbus.de 🎵 *Karnevalsumzug (Feb); Cottbuser Musik-Herbst (Oct).*

Tourists rarely visit Cottbus, despite the many attractions offered by the town. Its enchanting town square is surrounded by impressive Baroque buildings. The house

The Baroque Schloss Branitz in Cottbus

at No. 24 is the quaint Löwen-apotheke (lion's pharmacy), which now houses a small pharmaceutical museum, the **Brandenburgisches Apothekenmuseum**, with displays of historical interiors. Nearby, the Gothic **Ober-kirche St Nikolai** features an unusual original late-Gothic mesh vaulting. Another interesting Gothic structure, the **Wendenkirche** (Sorbian church), is a former Francis-can church, from the 14th–15th centuries.

Other attractions of the town include the remains of the medieval city walls with three preserved towers. Per-haps the most attractive build-ing in Cottbus is the **Staats-theater** (state theatre) designed in Jugendstil (Art Nouveau style) by Bernhard Sehring and built in 1908.

The **Wendisches Museum** is devoted to the culture of the Sorbs which is experiencing a revival *(see p181)*.

Schloss Branitz is a late-Baroque palace, originally built in the 18th century, at the southeastern edge of town. It became the residence of Prince Hermann von Pückler-Muskau in 1845, who had its interior redesigned by Gottfried Semper. Today, the palace houses the **Fürst-Pückler-Museum**, which exhibits paintings by Karl Blechen, a local artist from Cottbus. The star attraction of the palace is its **Park**, which was designed by Prince Pückler-Muskau himself. This vast landscaped garden includes a lake with an island on which stands a grass-covered mock-Egyptian earth pyramid containing the tomb of the extravagant and eccen-tric Prince.

🏛 **Schloss Branitz and Fürst-Pückler-Museum**
Kastanienalle 11. **Tel** (0355) 751 50.
⬤ Apr–Oct: 10am–6pm daily, Nov–Mar: 11am–5pm; Tue–Sun. 📷

🏛 **Wendisches Museum**
Mühlenstr. 12. **Tel** (0355) 79 49 30.
⬤ 8:30am–6pm Tue–Fri, 2–6pm Sat–Sun and bank holidays.

🏛 **Brandenburgisches Apothekenmuseum**
Altmark 24. **Tel** (0355) 239 97.
⬤ 10am–5pm Tue–Fri; 2 & 3pm Sat–Sun. 📷

Boats and canoes in the Spreewald, near Lübben

Spreewald ⓫

Road map F3. 🚉 Lübben.
ℹ️ Raddusch, Lindenstr. 1 (035433-722 99), Lübbenau, Ehm-Welk-Str. 15 (03542-36 68). 🚉 📷 Spreewaldfest in Lübbenau (Jul) and Lübben (Sep). www.spreewald.de

Designated as one of the World Biosphere Reserves, this marshy region, criss-crossed by hundreds of small rivers and canals, attracts large numbers of tourists each year. An all-day trip by **Kahn** (boat) or canoe, which is best started in **Lübben** or **Lübbenau**, can prove to be an unfor-gettable experience. The splendour of nature, numerous water birds and the endless chain of small restaurants which serve meals straight from the jetty, ensure an exciting day for the visitor. Do not miss the local speciality, pickled gherkins.

Lübben has an original Gothic church and a Baroque palace, rebuilt in the 19th century. Lüb-benau features a small Baroque church and the Neo-Classical house of the von Lynar family. In **Lehde** the small open-air museum and the private collection of the **Bauernhaus- und Gurken-museum** – the only gherkin museum in Germany – are highly recommended.

Statue on Jüterbog town hall

Environs
Luckau, 18 km (11 miles) west of Lübben, has a lovely town square, surrounded by attractive Baroque houses with stucco façades, and the ornamented, 14th-century Gothic Nikolaikirche.

Jüterbog ⓬

Road map E3. 🏰 13,000. 🚉 🚌
ℹ️ Markt 21 (03372-46 31 13).

Jüterbog is a small, pictur-esque town featuring many Gothic structures including some well-preserved sections of three city walls with gates and towers, dating back to the 15th century. It also boasts a beautiful town hall with arcades and three churches. The **Nikolaikirche** (church of St Nicholas), the largest of them, is a magnificent hall church, with a twin-tower façade, built in several stages. The so-called New Sacristy features a set of medieval wall paintings, while the naves contain many Gothic furnishings.

Environs
Five km (3 miles) to the north of Jüterbog stands **Kloster Zinna**, a former Cistercian Abbey with an early-Gothic stone church. It features 16th-century stained-glass windows depicting the saints Bernhard and Benedikt.

The early-Gothic ex-Cistercian Kloster Zinna, near Jüterbog

SAXONY-ANHALT

The scenic Harz mountains, a popular recreation area with fascinating rock formations and pleasant walks, are the best known attraction of Saxony-Anhalt. Yet this state also boasts a number of interesting towns, such as Lutherstadt Wittenberg and Magdeburg, steeped in history and blessed with magnificent historic remains, which range from Romanesque churches and abbeys to medieval castles.

This province consists of the areas of the former Duchy of Anhalt and the Prussian province of Saxony, that part of the Kingdom of Saxony which was incorporated into Prussia after the Congress of Vienna (1815) as punishment for supporting Napoleon.

The landscape in this region is highly varied. Its northern part, the Altmark, is a largely flat area of farmland and heath. The gentle hills of the Harz Mountains in the southwest, although not especially high (their highest peak, the Brocken, rises to only 1142 m/3747 ft), are picturesque and fairly well provided with tourist facilities. The eastern, flat part of the region is more industrialized. It also includes two very important towns: the small town of Wittenberg, where Martin Luther proclaimed his theses in 1517, thus launching the Reformation, and Dessau, the former capital of the Duchy of Anhalt and from 1925 to 1932 the seat of the Bauhaus Art School. The southern part of the province, with its interesting and varied landscape, features one of the land's most impressive historic buildings – the gigantic Naumburg Cathedral.

After World War II Saxony-Anhalt was occupied by the Soviets, and in 1949 it was incorporated into the GDR. It underwent major industrial development, mainly due to lignite mining. The state of Saxony-Anhalt was first created in 1947, only to be abolished five years later. It was finally re-established as a federal state in 1990, with Magdeburg as its capital.

Timber-frame houses in Quedlinburg

◁ Family house near the small town of Halberstadt

Exploring Saxony-Anhalt

Touring Saxony-Anhalt can be an unforgettable experience, especially for admirers of Romanesque art, as this region abounds in churches and abbeys of that period. A visit to Wörlitz provides the opportunity to see one of Germany's most beautiful landscaped gardens. Nature lovers, hill-walkers and, in the winter, cross-country skiers should include a few days in the romantic Harz Mountains in their schedule. An added attraction here is a ride on the narrow-gauge railway drawn by a steam engine which, today as in years gone by, still links some of the most interesting places of the region.

Interior of the Gothic cathedral in Havelberg

Pritzwa

Seeha

Salzwedel

M

Kakerbeck   Bism
Klötze   (Altm

Gardelegen

Colbitz-
Letzinger
Heide

Haldensleben

Wolmirstedt

Hannover

A2

MAGDEBURG ⑩

S A C H S E

Oschersleben   Schöne

Huysburg

Osterwieck

WERNIGERODE ①**HALBERSTADT**

②   Blankenburg   **QUEDLINBURG**

Brocken
△1142m   ④   ⑥   **BERNBU**

Elbingerode   THE HARZ   Aschersleben
MOUNTAIN TRAIL   ③

Hettstedt

Harzgerode   242

Eislebe

Sangerhausen

Göttingen   Helme   A38

QUERFURT ⑧

Zoo-Park in Dessau

KEY

═══	Motorway
───	Major road
·····	Minor road
═ ═	Under construction
───	Scenic route
~~	Main railway
----	Minor railway
───	Regional border
△	Summit

For additional map symbols see back flap

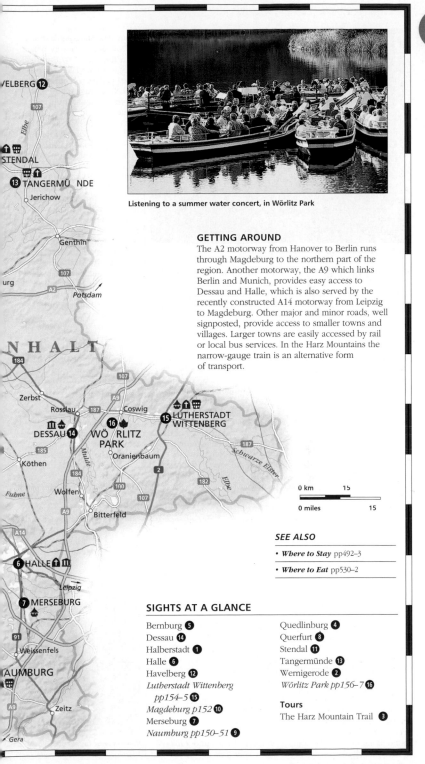

Listening to a summer water concert, in Wörlitz Park

GETTING AROUND

The A2 motorway from Hanover to Berlin runs through Magdeburg to the northern part of the region. Another motorway, the A9 which links Berlin and Munich, provides easy access to Dessau and Halle, which is also served by the recently constructed A14 motorway from Leipzig to Magdeburg. Other major and minor roads, well signposted, provide access to smaller towns and villages. Larger towns are easily accessed by rail or local bus services. In the Harz Mountains the narrow-gauge train is an alternative form of transport.

```
0 km          15
0 miles       15
```

SEE ALSO

SIGHTS AT A GLANCE

Interior of the Gothic Cathedral of Halberstadt

Halberstadt ❶

Road map D3. 🏛 *42,000.* 🚉 🚌
ℹ️ *Hinter dem Rathause 6 (03941-55 18 15).* **www**.halberstadt.de

Halberstadt enjoys a picturesque location in the foothills of the Harz Mountains. Its history goes back to the 9th century, when it became a seat of a mission episcopate. Once an important town, Halberstadt had 80 per cent of its buildings destroyed during World War II. Fortunately, many of its beautiful historic buildings have now been re-stored to their former glory.

The vast **St Stephans Dom** is the fourth successive church built on the same site. Construction began in the 13th century and the church was consecrated in 1491. The two-tower tran-septial basilica ranks as one of the most beautiful pure Gothic forms in Germany. Its oldest part is the 12th-century font. Also notable are the Romanesque Crucifixion group (c.1220), set above the choir screen, and several examples of Gothic sculpture. Stained-glass windows from around 1330 have survived in the Marian Chapel, and 15th-century windows can be found along the cloisters and in the presbytery.

Romanesque Crucifixion group in the Dom, Halberstadt

The adjoining chapter build-ings contain one of Ger-many's richest cathedral treasures – the **Domschatz**, with precious 12th-century tapestries, numerous sculp-tures and liturgical vessels.

Other interesting churches to have survived in the old town district include the Romanesque 12th-century **Liebfrauenkirche** and the Gothic **Marktkirche St. Mar-tini** with a statue of Roland, symbolizing the freedom of the city. Remaining tim-ber-frame houses can be seen in Gröper- and Taubenstrasse.

🏛 Domschatz
Tel 03941 24237.
⭘ *call for times.*
🎫 *obligatory.*

Environs
An original 12th-century Benedictine church stands in Huysburg, 11 km (7 miles) to the northwest.

Wernigerode ❷

Road map D3. 🏛 *36,000.* 🚉 🚌
ℹ️ *Nicolaiplatz 1 (03943-63 30 35).*
🎭 *Rathausfest (Jun); Schlossfestspiele (Jul & Aug).* **www**.wernigerode.de

Wernigerode is attractively situated at a confluence of two rivers. Timber-frame houses lean across its steep, winding streets, and a mas-sive castle rises above the

town. The **Harzquerbahn**, a narrow-gauge railway which links the small towns and villages in the Harz Moun-tains, between Wernigerode and Nordhausen, provides another popular tourist attraction. The Brockenbahn runs between Wernigerode and the Brocken mountain.

Strolling around the Old Town it is well worth step-ping into St John's Church, featuring a Romanesque west tower. It contains some late-Gothic features, including the font and the altar. The variety of ornaments adorning the houses in Wernigerode is truly staggering. Particularly interesting are the houses along **Breite Straße**, the town's main shopping street which is closed to traffic.

⚜ Schloss Wernigerode
Am Schloss 1. **Tel** 03943-55 30 30.
⭘ *May–Oct: 10am–6pm; Nov–Apr: 10am–4pm Tue–Fri; 10am–6pm Sat & Sun.* 🖼
The fairy-tale castle, spiked with towers, was created during the years 1861–83 on the site of an older fortress. Now a museum, it houses the Stolberg-Wernigerode family art collection. The castle ramparts afford a fantastic view of the town and the nearby Harz mountains.

Environs
The small town of **Osterwieck**, 22 km (14 miles) to the north, has over 400 timber-frame buildings, dating mainly from the 16th and 17th centuries.

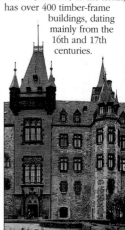

The romantic façade of Schloss Wernigerode, now a museum

The Harz Mountain Trail ❸

The tourist trail across the Harz Mountains leads through charming historic towns and villages, as well as past the other attractions of the region including some fascinating caves and unusual rock formations.

VISITORS' CHECKLIST

Length: *55 km (34 miles)*
Stopping places: *there are many attractive restaurants all along the trail, in every town.*
🎭 *Walpurgisnacht, Thale: 30 Apr.*

The Rübeland Caves ①
Rübeland's main attractions are the Hermannshöhle and Baumannshöhle, two caves with amazing stalactites and stalagmites.

Blankenburg ②
This charming mountain town is overlooked by an 18th-century castle. The Teufelsmauer, a spectacular 4-km (2-mile) long sandstone cliff, attracts many climbers.

Thale ③
Many mountain walks start in Thale, including one to the Hexentanzplatz, a platform suspended above a cliff, from where witches fly to Sabbath celebrations in the Walpurgis Night.

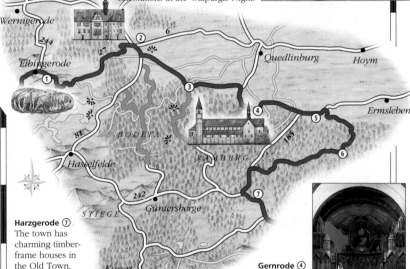

Harzgerode ⑦
The town has charming timber-frame houses in the Old Town, and a 16th-century castle.

Burg Falkenstein ⑥
This huge castle, built in the 12th century and extended many times, is now a museum. From the castle, the visitor can enjoy a splendid view over the surrounding Harz Mountains.

Gernrode ④
The star attraction in this town is the 10th-century church of St Cyriacus. Its interior is devoid of ornaments, yet enchantingly pure in form.

Ballenstedt ⑤
The former home of the von Anhalt-Bemburg family enchants visitors to this day with its imaginative design, including the Baroque castle set in a park.

| 0 km | | 2 |
| 0 miles | | 2 |

KEY

- ▬ Tour route
- ▬ Other road
- ═ Scenic route
- ☀ Viewpoint

The Renaissance portal of Quedlinburg Schloss

Quedlinburg ❹

Road map D3. 🏛 *26,000.* 🚊 🚌
🛈 *Markt 2 (03946-90 56 24 and 90 56 25).*

The rise of the small town of Quedlinburg was closely connected with its convent, established in 936 by Emperor Otto I and his mother, St Mathilde. On the hill above the town stands the vast Romanesque structure of the **Stiftskirche St Servatius** (Collegiate Church of St Servatius), built between 1017 and 1129. Its old crypt, the Huysburg, which belonged to the previous church, features Romanesque wall paintings and contains tombs of the prioresses and of the Emperor Henry and his wife Mathilde.

An exhibition of treasures is shown in the arms of the transept, including the Romanesque reliquary of St Servatius and the remaining fragments of the 12th-century Knüpfteppich (tapestry). The **Quedlinburg Schloss**, a Renaissance palace surrounded by gardens, occupies the other side of the hill.

Both Old and New Town of Quedlinburg have valuable examples of timber-frame architecture. The buildings date from various times – the modest house at **Wordgasse 3**, from around 1400, is the oldest surviving timber-frame building in Germany. Also noteworthy are the numerous churches, including the 10th-century **Norbertinenkirche**, the **Wippertikirche** with its early-Romanesque crypt, and the 15th century, late-Gothic **Marktkirche St Benedicti**.

Bernburg ❺

Road map D4. 🏛 *36,000.* 🚊 🚌
🛈 *Lindenplatz 9 (03471 346 930).*
🎭 *Walpurgisnacht (May).*

Once the capital of one of Anhalt's Duchies, Bernburg enjoys a picturesque location on the banks of the Saale River. It has a **Bergstadt** (upper town) and a **Talstadt** (lower town), and its attractions include the Gothic

parish churches and the town square with its Baroque buildings. The most important historic building is the **Bernburg Schloss**, a castle built on a rock. It owes its present appearance to refurbishments (1540–70), yet many features of this multi-wing structure are much older, including the 12th-century Romanesque chapels and Gothic towers.

Burg Giebichenstein, in Halle, with the Arts and Crafts College

Halle ❻

Road map D4. 🏛 *232,300.* 🚊 🚌
🛈 *Große Ulrichstraße 57 (0345-47 23 30).* 🎭 *Händel-Festspiele (Jun); Hallesche Musiktage (Nov).*

Halle is an old town with a rich history in commerce and trade, its wealth founded on the production and sale of salt. Later, the town was turned into a centre for the

The impressive Bernburg Schloss, built on a rock

Renaissance residence in Merseburg

chemical industry. Halle has preserved most of its historic heritage. On the **Marktplatz** (town square) stands an interesting church, **Unser Lieben Frauen** (Our Dear Lady), whose late-Gothic main body (1530–54) was positioned between two pairs of towers that had remained intact from previous Roman-esque churches. Nearby is the **Roter Turm** (Red Tower), an 84-m (276 ft) tall belfry, built in 1418–1506. The house at Nikolaistraße 5, the birthplace of Georg Friedrich Händel, now houses a small museum, the **Händel-Haus**. In Dom-platz stands the early-Gothic **Dom**, built in 1280–1331 by the Dominicans and restored between 1525 and 1530 in Renaissance style, and ele-vated to the rank of cathedral. Inside there is an interesting pulpit dating from 1525, and the statues of saints situated by Peter Schroh's pillars.

Halle has some other medieval churches, including the late-Gothic **Moritzkirche** built in the latter part of the 14th century. It is also worth visiting the **Staatliche Galerie**, housed in the refurbished Citadel building known as **Moritzburg** and built during 1484-1503. On the outskirts of town stands **Burg Giebichen-stein**, the former castle resi-dence of the Magdeburg bishops. The upper part of the castle remains in ruins, while the lower part houses an Arts & Crafts College.

🏛 **Staatliche Galerie**
Friedemann-Bach-Platz 5. **Tel** (0345) 21 25 90. ☐ 11am–8:30pm Tue, 10am–6pm Wed–Sun & public holidays. 🎟 free last Sun of month.

Merseburg **⑦**

Road map D4. 🏘 40,000. 🚉 🚌
🚶 Burgstr. 5 (03461-21 41 70).

The first sight visitors see as they arrive in Merseburg is the **Domburg** – a vast complex of buildings spiked with towers, consisting of a cathedral and residential premises. The cathedral is not uniform in style; it includes some Romanesque elements (the eastern section and twin towers in the west) erected in the 11th and 12th centuries, and the late-Gothic triple-nave main body, which was built in 1510–17. All that remains of the older, early-Romanesque structure is the crypt, underneath the presby-tery. The cathedral contains remarkable Gothic and Renaissance features, as well as numerous sarcophagi of bishops, such as that of Thilo von Troth (1470). The chapter buildings house a library with precious manuscripts, includ-ing the **Merseburg Bible** (c. 1200). Adjacent to the cathedral is a three-wing Renaissance-style **Schloss**. Magnificent portals and an attractive oriel in the castle's west wing are noteworthy.

Querfurt **⑧**

Road map D4. 🏘 11,000. 🚌
🚶 Markt 14 (034771-237 99).

The narrow streets of Quer-furt are crammed with timber-frame houses, and the giant **Schloss** towers over the town square with its Renaissance town hall. The castle's present form is the result of Renais-sance refurbishments, but it maintains many Romanesque features, such as the 11th-century donjon (keep), known as **Dicker Heinrich** (Fat Henry) and a 12th-century church. Also worth seeing is the burial chapel, the Baroque **Fürstenhaus** (ducal house) and a small museum, situated in the for-mer armoury and granary.

Naumburg **⑨**

Road map D4. 🏘 30,500. 🚉 🚌
🚶 Markt 12 (03445-27 31 12).
www.naumburg-tourismus.de
🎭 Hussiten-Kirsch-Fest (Jun).

The town's star attraction is the **Dom** (cathedral of Saints Peter and Paul *see pp150–51*). There is a late-Gothic **Rathaus** (town hall), restored in Renaissance style, and the main square is surrounded by quaint houses. Further attract-ions include the **Marientor** gate (1455–6) with the puppet theatre, and the Gothic **Stadtkirche St. Wenzel** (Church of St Wenceslas). The latter has two paintings by Lucas Cranach the Elder as well as the 18th-century organ that Johann Sebastian Bach played on. Friedrich Nietz-sche, the philosopher, spent his childhood at No. 18 Wein-garten, now a small museum.

Gothic stone retable of the main altar in Naumburg Dom

Naumburg Dom

The impressive Cathedral of Saints Peter and Paul in Naumburg is one of the finest Gothic structures in Germany. The present cathedral is the second to be built on the same site; only a section of the eastern crypt survived of the earlier Romanesque church. Construction started before 1213, with the earliest parts including the late-Romanesque east choir, the transept and the main body. The early-Gothic west choir was built in the mid-13th century, the newer Gothic east choir c.1330. The northeast towers date from the 15th century, the southwest towers from 1894.

West choir

Stained-glass Windows in the Presbytery
The stained-glass windows depict scenes of the apostles of virtue and sin. Some sections are original 13th-century work, but two were completed in the 19th century.

★ Founders' Statues
The statues of Margrave Ekkebard and his wife, Uta, are true masterpieces – the artist succeeded marvellously in capturing the beauty and sensitivity of his subjects.

★ Portal of the West Reading Room
The Gothic twin portal depicts the Crucifixion, a moving and highly expressive group sculpture by the brilliant "Naumburger Meister" whose identity remains unknown.

STAR FEATURES

★ Founders' Statues

★ Portal of the West Reading Room

★ Main Portal

Pulpit
The richly orna-mented pulpit basket, from 1466, and the adjoining stairs have recently been renovated.

VISITORS' CHECKLIST

Domplatz 16–17. **Tel** (03445) 23 01 10. ☐ Mar–Oct: 9am–6pm Mon–Sat, noon–6pm Sun; Nov–Feb: 10am–4pm Mon–Sat, noon–4pm Sun.

St Mary's Altar
This late-Gothic triptych (c.1510) depicts the Virgin Mary with the Infant, framed by Saints Barbara and Catherine, with the Apostles in the wings.

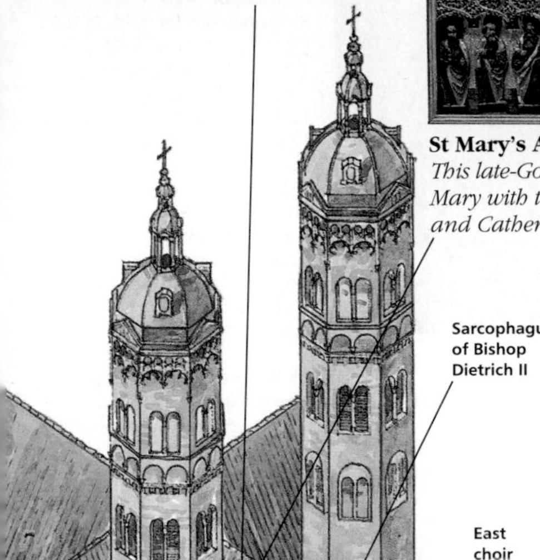

Sarcophagus of Bishop Dietrich II

East choir

East Choir Altar
This Gothic altar features the Virgin Mary with the Infant Jesus, surrounded by the figures of the saints.

The Main Altar, built in the mid-14th-century, is a stone retable depicting the Crucifixion with the saints which was transferred from another altar.

★ **Main Portal**
The late-Romanesque, 13th-century portal is decorated on the left side with eagles. The tympanum features Christ in a mandorla (almond-shaped area) supported by angels.

Interior of the Gothic presbytery in the Magdeburg Dom

Magdeburg ⑩

Road map D3. 🏛 *235,000.* 🚃 🚌
🛈 *Ernst-Reuter-Allee 12 (0391-54 04 903).* 🎷 *Jazzfestival (Jun), Klassik-Open Air (Jul).* **www.** *magdeburg-tourist.de*

The large-scale development of Magdeburg, today the capital of Saxony-Anhalt and a port on the river Elbe, began in the 10th century when Emperor Otto I established his main residence here. In medieval times the town became a political and cultural centre. Following the abolition of the archbishopric and the destruction wrought by the Thirty Years' War, it lost its political importance. About 80 per cent was destroyed during World War II, but it is still worth a visit since many historic buildings have been reconstructed in the Old Town.

🏛 Dom St Mauritius und St Katharina

Domplatz. *Tel (0391) 534 61 59.* ◯ *Mon–Sun.*
The vast Magdeburg cathedral is one of the most important Gothic churches in Germany.

Its construction, which started in 1209 on the site of an earlier Romanesque church, was completed in 1520, although much of it was built by the mid-14th century. The result is a lofty, aisled basilica with transept, cloisters, a ring of chapels surrounding the presbytery and a vast twin-tower façade. The cathedral has several magnificent, original sculptures. Other notable features include the tomb of Emperor Otto I, as well as the 12th-century bronze tomb plaques of archbishops Friedrich von Wettin and Wichmann. The memorial for the dead of World War I is the work of Ernst Barlach, dating from 1929. Visitors to the cathedral may notice several elements that were preserved from ancient structures and have been incorporated into the walls or used as ornaments inside the building.

🏛 Kulturhistorisches Museum

Otto-von-Guericke-Str. 68–73.
Tel (0391) 540 35 01. ◯ *10am–5pm Tue–Sun.* 🗐
This museum contains works of art, archaeological finds and historic documents of the town. Its most valuable exhibit is the Magdeburger Reiter (Magdeburg Rider), a sculpture dating from around 1240 of an unknown ruler on a horse (probably Otto I).

🛐 Kloster Unser Lieben Frauen

Regierungsstr. 4–6.
Kunstmuseum *Tel (0391) 56 50 20.* ◯ *10am–5pm Tue–Sun.* 🗐
This Austere Romanesque church, Magdeburg's oldest building, was built for the Norbertine order during the second half of the 11th and the early 12th centuries. Stripped of all its ornaments, it now serves as a concert hall. The adjacent Romanesque abbey is a museum with medieval and modern sculptures (Barlach, Rodin).

🛐 Halle an der Buttergasse

Alter Markt. Weinkeller Buttergasse.
The basement of a late-Romanesque market hall from c.1200 was rediscovered in 1948, and is used today as a wine cellar.

🏛 Rathaus

Alter Markt.
The present Baroque town hall, built in 1691–8 on the site of an earlier, late-Romanesque town hall, was restored after World War II.

🛐 Pfarrkirche St Johannis

Am Johannisberg 1.
Viewing tower
Tel (0391) 540 21 26. ◯ *Mar–Oct: 10am–6pm Tue–Sun; Nov–Feb: 10–5pm.* 🗐
The ruins of this church, near the market square, are the remains of the Gothic church of St John, which was destroyed during World War II. In 1524 Martin Luther preached here.

Kloster Unser Lieben Frauen in Magdeburg

Stendal ⑪

Road map D3. 39,600.
Kornmarkt 8
(03931-65 11 90).

In medieval times Stendal was one of the richest towns of the Brandenburg margravate, and its most valuable historical remains date from that period. The late-Gothic **St Nikolai** cathedral was built in 1423–67, on the foundations of a Romanesque Augustinian church. Its star attractions are 15th-century stained-glass windows in the presbytery and the transept.

The late-Gothic, 15th-century church **St Marien** (St Mary) has some original Gothic elements, and the oldest parts of the **Rathaus** (town hall) date back to the 14th century. Other attractions include the remains of the town walls, with a beautiful tower, **Uenglinger Torturm**.

Gothic traceries of the cloisters in the Dom, Havelberg

Havelberg ⑫

Road map D3. 7,000.
Uferstr. 1. (039387-79 091).

Havelberg played an important role in the Christianization of this region, with a mission episcopate established here as early as the mid-10th century. The present cathedral – **Dom St Marien** – was built in 1150–70, and although redesigned in the early 14th century, it nevertheless maintained its Romanesque character. Its most interesting features include

Back of the Gothic Rathaus in the market square in Tangermünde

huge stone candelabra taken from the former reading room, dating back to around 1300, and the present reading room, which is decorated with reliefs carved in the workshop of the Parler Family, in Prague, between 1396 and 1411.

Tangermünde ⑬

Road map D3. 10,000.
Kirchstrasse 13 (039322-223 93).

Situated at the confluence of the Tanger and Elbe rivers, this town grew rapidly during medieval times. For centuries it remained the seat of the Brandenburg margraves, and King Charles IV chose it as his second residence. The town joined the Hanseatic League, and grew in status thanks to its trade links.

The present **Rathaus** (town hall) has lovely timber-frame architecture. Today it houses the municipal museum.

The only remains of the old castle are its main tower and the **Kanzlei** (chancellery). In 1377, King Charles IV brought the Augustinian monks to town and had the **St Stephanskirche** (church of St Stephen) built for them. Construction continued until the end of the 15th century. This magnificent, late-Gothic hall church with transept and cloister contains interesting features: a 1624 organ made in the

Hamburg workshop of Hans Scherer the Younger, the 1619 pulpit created by Christopher Dehne and a font dating from 1508, the work of Heinrich Mente.

The east wing of the beautiful Gothic **Rathaus** (town hall) dates back to 1430 and is the work of Heinrich Brunsberg, its richly ornamented spire being typical of his work. The west wing with its arcades was added around 1480, and the external stairs date from the 19th century.

Tangermünde has retained some remains of the city walls, dating from around 1300 and including a magnificent late-Gothic gate, the **Neustädter Tor**, whose tall, cylindrical tower has intricate, lacy ceramic ornaments.

> **Rathaus (Stadtgeschichtliches Museum)**
> Markt. **Tel** (039322) 42 153.
> 15 Feb–Nov 10am–5pm Tue–Sun.

Environs
A Romanesque **Klosterkirche** (abbey) in Jerichow, 10 km (6 miles) north of Tangermünde, is the earliest brick structure of the region. It was built in the 1150s, for Norbertine monks. The west towers were completed during the 15th century. Its austere, triple-nave vaulted interior is impressive. There are also many remains of the former abbey.

Interior of the former Norbertinenkirche, in Jerichow, north of Tangermünde

Dessau ⑭

Road map E3. 🏔 *84,400.* 🚌 🚆
ℹ️ *Zerbster Str. 2c (0340-204 14
42).* 🎭 *Kurt-weill-fest (late
Feb–Mar).* **www**.dessau.de

Dessau, once a magnificent
city and the capital of the
duchy of Anhalt-Dessau, is
less attractive today, yet it has
some excellent historic sights.
In the town centre are some
interesting Baroque churches
and the **Johannbau**, the
remains of a Renaissance
ducal residence.

Dessau is also known for
the **Bauhaus** complex. Built
in 1925 to a design by Walter
Gropius, it is the home of the
famous art school, which
moved here from Weimar.
The **Bauhausmuseum** is
housed in one of its wings.
Nearby, in Friedrich-Ebert-
Allee, five of the so-called
Meisterhäuser – master
houses for the Art College
professors – have survived
World War II. The houses of
Lyonel Feininger and Paul
Klee are open to the public.
Wassily Kandinsky was also a
former resident. The **Kornhaus**, on Elballee, restored in
1996, contains a restaurant,
café and dance hall.

Many splendid residences
set in landscaped gardens
were built in 18th- and 19th-
century Dessau. In the town
centre stands a Neo-Classical
palace, **Schloss Georgium**,
built in 1780 to a design by
Friedrich Wilhelm von Erdmannsdorff. Today it houses a
collection of old masters,
including works by Rubens,
Hals and Cranach.

🏛 **Bauhausmuseum**
Gropiusallee 38. *Tel* (0340) 65 08
250. ◯ 10am–6pm daily. 📷

♣ **Schloss Georgium**
Puschkinallee 100. *Tel* (0340) 61 38
74. ◯ 10am–5pm Tue–Sun. 📷

Environs
Haldeburg, which is situated
on the outskirts of Dessau,
has a Neo-Gothic hunting
lodge built in 1782–3, and
Mosigkau boasts **Schloss
Mosigkau**, Princess Anna
Wilhelmina's Baroque residence, designed by Christian
Friedrich Damm. It contains
some excellent examples of
17th-century painting.

In **Oranienbaum**, 12 km (7
miles) east of Dessau, stands a
late-17th-century, early-Baroque
palace that was built for
Princess Henrietta Katharine
of Orange by the Dutch architect Cornelius Ryckwaert.

♣ **Schloss Mosigkau**
Knobelsdorffallee 2. *Tel* (0340) 52
11 39. ◯ Apr–Oct: 10am–5pm
Tue–Sun; May–Sep: 10am–6pm
Tue–Sun. ● Dec–Mar. 📷 📷

Lutherstadt Wittenberg ⑮

Road map E3. 🏔 *55,000.* 🚌 🚆
ℹ️ *Schlossplatz 2 (03491-41 48 48).*
🎭 *Wittenberger Stadtfest & Luthers
Hochzeit (Jun).*
www.wittenberg.de

This small town, named
after its most famous resident,
Martin Luther, enjoys a scenic
position on the banks of the
Elbe River. Its main
development took place

during the 16th century,
under the Great Elector,
Frederick the Wise. Wittenberg became the capital of
the Reformation thanks to the
work of Martin Luther and
Philipp Melanchthon, and as
such it attracts many visitors.
Another famous resident of
that period was the painter
Lucas Cranach the Elder.

♣ **Schloss Wittenberg**
Schlossplatz. **Museum für
Naturkunde und Völkerkunde**
(Museum of Natural History and
Ethnography) *Tel* (03491) 43 34
920. ◯ 9am–5pm Tue–Sun. 📷
Built for Frederick the Wise
in 1489–1525, the castle was
greatly altered during reconstruction following fire and
wartime damage. A museum
is housed in the west wing.

**The tomb of Frederick the Wise,
in Schlosskirche**

🔒 **Schlosskirche**
Schlossplatz. *Tel* (03491) 40 25 85.
◯ May–Oct: 10am–5pm Mon–Sat,
11:30–5pm Sun; Nov–Apr: 10am–
4pm Mon–Sat, 11:30am–4pm Sun.

Built after 1497, this church
was made famous by Martin
Luther, who allegedly posted
his theses on its door in 1517.
The original door no longer
exists, but the church contains many interesting tombs,
including that of Frederick the
Wise, created in 1527 in the
workshop of Hans Vischer, as
well as modest tombs of Martin Luther and Melanchthon.

Schloss Georgium in Dessau

The market square with Baroque fountain, in Lutherstadt Wittenberg

⚏ Cranachhaus

Markt 4. **Tel** *(03491) 420 19 17.*
◯ *10am–5pm Mon–Sat (from 1pm Sun).* ● *Nov–Apr: Mon.*
This beautiful, early 16th-century Renaissance house once belonged to Lucas Cranach the Elder and was the birthplace of his son, Lucas Cranach the Younger. His studio was located at No. 1 Schlossstraße.

⚏ Rathaus

Markt 26. ● *until further notice.*
The Renaissance town hall was built in 1523–35, and later twice extended in the 16th century. In its forecourt are two 19th-century monuments: to Martin Luther by Gottfried Schadow and to Philipp Melanchthon by Friedrich Drake.

⛪ Marienkirche

Kirchplatz. **Tel** *(3491) 40 44 15.*
◯ *May–Oct: 10am–5pm daily; Nov–Apr: 10am–4pm daily.*
The Gothic church of St Mary with its twin-tower façade was built in stages, between the 13th and 15th centuries. Luther was married to Katharina von Bora in this church where he also preached, and six of their children were baptised. Inside there is a magnificent Reformation altar (constructed in 1547), the work of father and son Cranach, as well as interesting tombs and epitaphs.

⚏ Melanchthonhaus

Collegienstr. 60. **Tel** *(03491) 40 32 79.* ◯ *Apr–Oct: 10am–6pm daily; Nov–Mar: 10am–5pm Tue–Sun.* ▨
This museum is devoted to Luther's closest ally, Philipp Schwarzerd, generally known as Melanchthon.

⚏ Lutherhalle

Collegienstr. 54. **Tel** *(03491) 42 030.*
◯ *same as Melanchthonhaus.* ▨
The museum, which is in the former residence of Martin Luther and his family, also chronicles the work of Lucas Cranach the Elder. It has a large number of documents relating to the Reformation and Luther's translation of the Bible.

LUTHERSTADT WITTENBERG TOWN CENTRE

Cranachhaus ③
Lutherhalle ⑦
Marienkirche ⑤
Melanchthonhaus ⑥

Rathaus ④
Schloss Wittenberg ①
Schlosskirche ②

0 metres   500
0 yards   500

Wörlitz Park ⑯

Wörlitz is a charming, English-style landscaped
garden, the first of its kind in continental Europe.
It was established in stages, commencing in 1764, for
Prince Leopold III, Frederick Franz of Anhalt-Dessau.
Many famous gardeners worked in Wörlitz, including
Johann Friedrich Eyserbeck and Johann Leopold
Ludwig Schoch, as well as the architect Friedrich
Wilhelm von Erdmannsdorff. In its centre stands a
Neo-Classical palace, holding a collection of paintings.
Another interesting collection, including stained-glass
paintings, can be admired
in the Gotisches Haus.

Floratempel
*Modelled on an ancient
temple with columns, this
Neo-Classical temple served
as a music pavilion.*

★ Gotisches Haus
*This country house, built
in stages, is one of the
earliest examples of
German Neo-Gothic
style. It now houses a
collection of stained-
glass paintings.*

Rousseau-Insel,
lined with poplars,
was modelled on
Ermenonville, the
island where the
French philosopher
was first buried.

SCHOCHS GARTEN
Kleines Walloch
Floratempel
Palmenhaus
SCHOCHS GARTEN
Gotisches Haus
Nymph
Wörlitzer See
Rosennsel
Rousseau-Insel
Schloss
SCHLOSS-GARTEN
Kirche
NEUMARKS-GARTEN
Marstall
Friedericken-brücke

Rosen-Insel
*Rose island was created as one
of several artificial islands in the
part of the garden designed by
Johann Christian Neumark.*

**Gondolas
on the Lake**
*Romantic
gondolas wait by
the jetties to take
tourists across the
lake and
to the islands.*

For hotels and restaurants in this region see pp492–3 and pp530–32

VISITORS' CHECKLIST

Förstergasse 26 (0349 05-202 16); www.woerlitz-information.de **Schloss** *Apr–Oct: 10am–5pm Tue–Sun; May–Sep: 10am–6pm Tue–Sun.*

Lake Concert
Classical concerts are held on Wörlitz Lake in the evening during the summer season. The audience is all afloat in boats.

Amalien-Insel
In keeping with the fashion of the day, this artificial island, on Großes Walloch lake, has a grotto, which provides a cool resting place.

The Pantheon, built in 1795–6, houses a collection of antique sculptures.

0 metres	500
0 yards	500

Pantheon

WEIDEN-HEGER

Herderinsel *Großes Walloch* *Amalien-Insel*

NEUE ANLAGEN

agoge

Wörlitzer See
The largest of the three lakes, which are all joined by canals, this is prettiest when the water lilies are in bloom.

Stein, a working artificial volcano modelled on Mount Vesuvius in Italy, is currently being renovated.

Stein

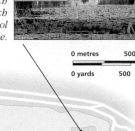

★ **Synagogue**
Built in 1790 and modelled on the Vesta Temple in Rome, the synagogue was gutted by the National Socialists in 1938 and now shows a Jewish history exhibit.

STAR FEATURES

★ Gotisches Haus

★ Synagogue

SAXONY

*S*axony has a long history and is rich in historic sites. Its capital city, Dresden, ranks among the most beautiful and interesting towns in Germany, despite the devastation it suffered during World War II. The region also boasts the enchanting Erzgebirge Mountains and the glorious scenery of "Saxon Switzerland", where the mighty Elbe river runs amid fantastic rock formations.

In the 10th century, Emperor Otto I created an eastern border province (margravate) in the area presently known as Saxony. It quickly grew in size as it expanded into neighbouring territories inhabited by the Polabian Slavs. It was divided and part became the Meissen Margravate, ruled by the powerful house of Wettin from 1089. This dynasty's political power increased when it acquired the Saxon Electorate in 1423; subsequently the entire region under their rule became known as "Saxony".

From 1697 until 1763 Saxony was united with Poland, and the Saxon Great Electors, Frederick Augustus the Strong and his son Frederick Augustus II, were also kings of Poland. During this period Saxony flourished, and Dresden became a major centre of the arts and culture until the Seven Years' War (1756–63) put an end to the region's prosperity. In 1806, Saxony declared itself on the side of Napoleon, and the Great Elector acquired the title of King. But Saxony paid a heavy price for supporting Napoleon – following the Congress of Vienna (1815), the kingdom lost the northern half of its territory to Prussia, and in 1871 it was incorporated into the German Empire.

At the end of World War II Saxony was in the Soviet-occupied zone and became part of the GDR in 1949. Since 1990 it has been a state in the Federal Republic of Germany. Saxony is densely populated and in some parts heavily industrialized, but it also has many interesting and unspoiled towns.

The scenic Bastei rocks in Saxon Switzerland

◁ Kriebstein Castle, overlooking the Zschopau river

Exploring Saxony

When travelling in Saxony, a visit to Dresden is a must. Visitors should set aside several days to explore its historic sights and magnificent museums. Dresden is also a convenient base for excursions to the attractive landscapes of the Sächsische Schweiz ("Saxon Switzerland") and further afield – to Bautzen, Görlitz and Zittau, or to the Erzgebirge Mountains, towards Freiberg and Chemnitz. Another town worth visiting, at least for a day, is Leipzig with its historic sights, cultural events, trade fairs and exhibitions.

The Old Town of Bautzen, situated high above the banks of the Spree River

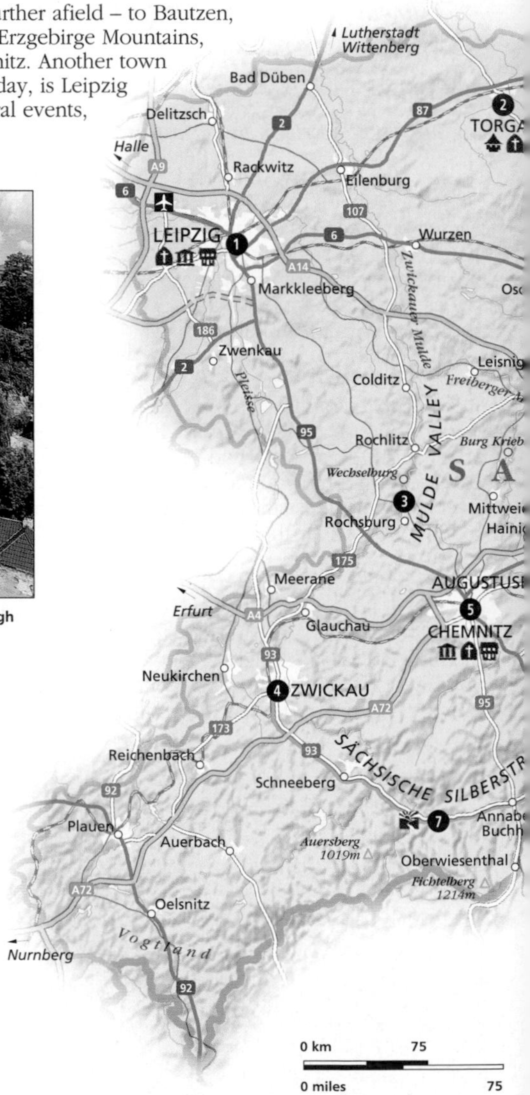

SIGHTS AT A GLANCE

Augustusburg **6**
Bad Muskau **16**
Bautzen **15**
Chemnitz **5**
Dresden
   pp168–77 **11**
Freiberg **8**
Görlitz **17**
Kamenz **14**
Leipzig pp162–3 **1**
Meißen **9**
Moritzburg **10**
Mulde Valley **3**
Pirna **12**
Torgau **2**
Zittau **18**
Zwickau **4**

Tours
Sächsische Schweiz **13**
Sächsische Silberstraße **7**

SEE ALSO

• *Where to Stay* pp493–5

• *Where to Eat* pp532–4

GETTING AROUND

Leipzig and Dresden both have airports, as well as excellent train and road connections with the rest of Germany. The A6 motorway runs west from Görlitz, through Dresden and Chemnitz; the A13 links Dresden with Berlin, and the A14 with Leipzig. Other roads, national and regional, are clearly sign-posted, and all the towns described in this guide can also be reached by local buses.

The giant castle and cathedral complex in Meissen

Saddle horses grazing on paddocks near Kamenz

Young musicians in the Barockgarten, in Großsedlitz, near Dresden

KEY

═══	Motorway
▬▬▬	Major road
═══	Minor road
═ ═	Under construction
▬▬▬	Scenic route
～～～	Main railway
───	Minor railway
▬▬▬	International border
▬▬▬	Country border
△	Summit

Leipzig ❶

Granted town status in 1165, Leipzig is not only one of Germany's leading commercial towns, but also a centre of culture and learning, with a university founded in 1409. An important centre for the German publishing and book trade, it is the home of the Deutsche Bücherei, the German national library established in 1912. During the Leipziger Messe (autumn and spring trade fairs), it receives a great number of visitors, and it has much to offer in terms of entertainment, including concerts by the renowned Gewandhaus symphony orchestra and the Thomanerchor boys' choir, which boasts Johann Sebastian Bach as a past choirmaster.

Lofty interior of the Neo-Classical Nikolaikirche

Exploring Leipzig

Most of the interesting sights can be found in the old town encircled by the Ring road, which includes Europe's biggest railway station, the **Hauptbahnhof**, built in 1902–15 to a design by William Lossow and Max Kühne. The heart of musical Leipzig beats in the eastern part of the old town, around Augustusplatz. Here stands the **Neues Gewandhaus** (built 1977–81) and the **Opernhaus** (built 1959–60). The University Tower nearby is being redesigned.

In Nikolaikirchhof stands the **Nikolaikirche** (church of St Nicholas). The present church was built during the 16th century, although the lower sections of its north tower date from the 12th century. It has Neo-Classical furnishings. The **Alte Handelsbörse** (old stock exchange) in Naschmarkt is

an early-Baroque building, designed by Johann Georg Starcke. Built in 1678–87 and reconstructed almost from the ground after World War II, it is now a concert hall. In front of the building stands a monument (1903) to Goethe showing him as a student.

In the market square, near the beautiful Renaissance town hall, is the **Alte Waage**, the old municipal weigh-house, a Renaissance work by Hieronymus Lotter. It was built in 1555 and reconstructed in 1964 following damage in World War II.

The area to the south of the town square is taken up by a block of trade fair buildings. The most interesting are the beautifully restored **Specks Hof** (Reichestraße/Nikohinstraße), the oldest arcade in Leipzig with three enclosed courts built between 1908 and 1929, and **Mädlerpassage**, built in 1912–14, a Modernist commercial building with a three-tier passageway connecting Grimmaische Straße and Naschmarkt. Beneath it is the **Auerbachs Keller**, magnificent, 16th-century vaults, immortalized by Goethe in *Faust* and featuring a room bearing his name. The **Commerzbank** (Klostergasse/Grimmaische Straße) and the **Riquet Café**, a fine Viennese-style coffee house, are attractive Art Nouveau buildings.

Lovers of Johann Sebastian Bach's music will wish to visit **Thomaskirche**, the magnificent late-Gothic

church of St Thomas, built in 1482–96, where Bach was the choirmaster from 1723. It now contains the composer's tomb. Worth noting are the beautiful Renaissance galleries built by Hieronymus Lotter, in 1570. The famous Thomanerchor choir still sings at services on Friday evenings and Saturday afternoons, and organ concerts are held in the churches of St Thomas and St Nicholas during the summer months. Bach is also commemorated with a monument in front of the church (1908). Nearby, the **Bosehaus**, a Baroque 17th-century building, is the home of the Bachmuseum, devoted to the composer.

🏛 **Grassimuseum**
Johannisplatz 5–11.
◑ *until early 2007.*
Museum für Völkerkunde, Museum für Angewandte Kunst and Musikinstrumentemuseum
Tel (0341) 213 37 19. **www**.
grassimuseum.de ◯ *Library and museum shop with workshops and lectures. Exhibitions 10am–6pm Tue–Sun, 10am–8pm Thu.*
The modernized and renovated Grassimuseum will be one of Germany's greatest museum complexes, housing three fascinating, separate collections: the Museum für Völkerkunde (ethnography) with exhibits from around the world; the Musikinstrumentemuseum (musical instruments) with a magnificent collection, including the world's oldest surviving clavichord, and the Museum für Angewandte (decorative arts) with its stunning gold and ivory ornaments, as well as the valuable town treasury.

The early-Baroque pavilion of the Alte Handelsbörse, the old stock exchange

The Russische Kirche, a pastiche of the churches in Novgorod

🏛 Deutsches Buch- und Schriftmuseum

Deutscher Platz 1. **Tel** *(0341) 227 13 24.* ☐ *9am–4pm Mon–Sat.*
This museum is devoted to the history of German literature. It contains rare manuscripts and old prints.

🏛 Museum der Bildenden Künste

Katharinenstr. 10 (Sachsenplatz). **Tel** *(0341) 216 99 14.* ☐ *10am–6pm Tue & Thu–Sun, noon–8pm Wed.*
The Leipzig fine art museum has an excellent collection of German masters, including

Lucas Cranach the Elder, Martin Schongauer and Caspar David Friedrich, as well as other magnificent European paintings. There are canvases by Jan van Eyck, Rubens, Frans Hals, Tintoretto and sculptures by Balthasar Permoser, Antonio Canova and Auguste Rodin.

🛕 Russische Kirche

Philipp-Rosenthal-Str. 51a. **Tel** *(0341) 878 14 53.* ☐ *10am–5pm daily (to 4pm in winter).*
The Russian Orthodox Church of St Alexius was built in 1912–13 to commemorate the 22,000 Russian soldiers who died in 1813, in the Battle of the Nations. The architect, Vladimir Pokrowski, based his design on the churches of Novgorod in Russia.

🏛 Völkerschlachtdenkmal

Prager Str. **Tel** *(0341) 878 04 71.* ☐ *Apr–Oct: 10am–6pm daily, Nov–Mar: 10am–4pm daily.* 🎟
This giant, Teutonic-style monument is the work of Bruno Schmitz. Completed for the centenary of the 1813 Battle of the Nations, which pitched the combined Prussian, Austrian and Russian armies against Napoleon, it now houses a museum.

🏛 Altes Rathaus

Markt 1. **Tel** *(0341) 261 77 60.* **Museum für Geschichte der Stadt Leipzig** ☐ *10am–6pm Tue–Sun.*
The grand Renaissance town hall, built in 1556 to a design by Hieronymus Lotter, is now the home of the municipal museum. One room is devoted to Felix Mendelssohn-Bartholdy, who conducted the symphony orchestra from 1835 until his death in 1847.

🏛 Bacharchive und Bachmuseum

Thomaskirchhof 15–16. **Tel** *(0341) 913 72 00.* ☐ *10am–5pm daily.*
This museum houses archives and documents relating to the life and works of the composer, J. S. Bach.

LEIPZIG CITY CENTRE

Alte Handelsbörse ④
Altes Rathaus ⑥
Alte Waage ⑤
Gewandhaus ②
Mädlerpassage ⑦
Nikolaikirche ③
Opernhaus ①
Thomaskirche ⑧

0 metres 200
0 yards 200

Key to Symbols *see back flap*

Doorway of Schloss Hartenfels, with its coat of arms, in Torgau

Torgau ❷

Road map E3. 🏛 *23,000.* 🚉 🚌
i *Markt 1 (03421-70 140).* 🎭
Torgauer Auszugsfest (Apr).

This small town, with its
scenic location on the Elbe,
was once the favourite
residence of the Saxon
Electors. Its main square is
surrounded by attractive
houses of various styles, in
particular Renaissance. The
Renaissance **Rathaus** (town
hall), built in 1561–77, has a
lovely semicircular oriel.
Other old town attractions
include the **Marienkirche**, a
late-Gothic church with an
extended Romanesque west
section. The interior has many
original features, including a
painting by Lucas Cranach the
Elder, *The Fourteen Helpers*,
and the tomb of Luther's wife,
Katharina von Bora, who died
in Torgau.
The main historic building
in Torgau is the Renaissance
Schloss Hartenfels, built on
the site of a 10th-century
castle. Its courtyard is surrounded by clusters of residential wings, including the
late-Gothic Albrechtspalast
built in 1470–85, the Johann-
Friedrich-Bau (1533–6) with
its beautiful external spiral
staircase and the early-
Baroque west wing (1616–23).
The **Schlosskapelle** (castle
chapel), which was conse-
crated by Martin Luther in
1544, is considered to be one
of the oldest churches built
for Protestants.

Muldetal ❸

Road map E4.

Several magnificent old
castles nestle in the scenic
hills at the confluence of two
rivers – the Zwickauer Mulde
and the Freiberger Mulde. In
the small town of **Colditz**,
with its timber-frame houses,
lovely Renaissance town hall
and Gothic church of St
Egidien, stands a huge Gothic
castle built in 1578–91 on the
site of an 11th-century castle.
During World War II it was a
famous prisoner-of-war camp
known as Oflag IVC.
In **Rochlitz**, 11 km (7 miles)
south of Colditz, stands
another large castle, built in
stages from the 12th to the
16th centuries. Travelling
further south you will
encounter other castles: the
Wechselburg, a reconstructed
Baroque castle featuring a
late-Romanesque collegiate
church, as well as the Renaissance castle in **Rochsburg**. In
the neighbouring Zschopau
valley stands the magnificent,
oval **Burg Kriebstein**, built in
stages and completed in the
late 14th century. This fortress
houses a small
museum and con-
cert hall, and
medieval music
concerts are held
here during the
summer.

Zwickau ❹

Road map E4. 🏛
120,000. 🚉 🚌
i *Hauptstr. 6 (0375-
27 13 240).* 🎭 *Robert-
Schumann-Tage (Jun);
TrabiTreffen (Jun).*

An old com-
mercial town,
Zwickau flourished
in the 15th and
16th centuries.
Today it is known
for the Trabant cars
that were produced
here during the
GDR era. Almost all
the town's attrac-
tions can be found
in the old town, on
the banks of the

Zwickauer Mulde river and
encircled by the Ring road.
The most important historic
building in the town is the
Dom St Marien (cathedral of
St Mary), a magnificent late-
Gothic hall-church built
1453–1537. Preserved to this
day are its original main altar
dating from 1479, the work of
Michael Wolgemut, the grand
architectural Holy Tomb of
Michael Heuffner, dating from
1507, as well as a Renaissance
font and a pulpit of 1538,
both by Paul Speck.
Also worth visiting in the
old town are the **Old Pharmacy**, the **Schumann-Haus**,
the composer's birthplace
(1810), and the Renaissance
Gewandhaus (cloth house),
once the seat of the Drapers'
Guild and now a theatre.

Chemnitz ❺

Road map E4. 🏛 *260,000.* 🚉
Georgstr. 🚌 *Markt.* **i** *Markt 1
(0371-19 433).*

After World War II, when
90 per cent of its buildings
had been reduced to rubble,
the town was rebuilt in the

Gate of the Renaissance pulpit in the Dom St Marien, in Zwickau

Lew Kerbel's monument to Karl Marx at the Stadthalle in Chemnitz

Socialist-Realist style and renamed Karl-Marx-Stadt. Only a handful of historic buildings escaped destruction. The most interesting among these is the **Schlosskirche**, the former Benedictine abbey church St Maria, on the edge of a lake, built at the turn of the 15th and 16th centuries.

Sights in the town centre include the reconstructed **Altes Rathaus** (old town hall), the Gothic **Roter Turm** (red tower) and remains of fortifications. In the main square is the reconstructed Baroque **Siegertsches Haus**, originally built in 1737–41 to a design by Johann Christoph Naumann. The new town centre is dominated by the vast **Stadthalle** (city hall) with Lew Kerbel's 1971 monument to Karl Marx. The **König-Albert-Kunstsammlungen** has a museum of natural history and a fine arts collection, including works by Karl Schmidt-Rottluff.

🏛 **König-Albert-Kunstsammlungen**
Theaterplatz 1. *Tel (0371) 488 44 24.* ◯ noon–7pm Tue–Fri, 10am–7pm Sat, Sun. 🅰

Augustusburg ❻

Road map E4. 🏠 5,000. 🚆 🛈 Marienberger Str. 24 (037291-395 50). **Schloss** ◯ Apr–Oct: 9:30am–6pm daily, Nov–Mar: 10am–5pm daily.

The small town is insignificant compared with the vast palace complex bearing

the same name. The best way to get there is by cable car, from Erdmannsdorf. This Renaissance hunting palace was built for the Great Elector, Augustus, in 1567–72, on the site of the former Schloss Schellenberg, which had been destroyed by fire. Constructed under Hieronymus Lotter and Erhard van der Meer, it is a symmetrical, square building with towered pavilions at each corner, joined by galleries, gates and a chapel to the east, with an altar by Lucas Cranach the Younger. Today the palace houses several museums devoted to motorcycles, coaches and hunting.

Sächsische Silberstraße ❼

See pp166–7.

Freiberg ❽

Road map E4. 🏠 45,000. 🚆 🚌 🛈 Burgstr. 1 (03731-236 02). 🎪 Bergstadtfest (Jun).

Development of this mining town was due to the discovery of silver deposits, and Freiberg was granted town status in 1186. It escaped World War II with remarkably little damage.

Today its attractions include the reconstructed old town and many historic buildings, the gem among them being the **Dom St Marien** (cathedral). This late-Gothic hall-church, erected at the end of the 15th century, features a

magnificent main portal, the Goldene Pforte, dating from 1225–30. Inside are many original items, such as a tulip-shaped pulpit (1505), two Baroque organs by Gottfried Silbermann and many sculptures and epitaphs.

When visiting nearby Untermarkt, it is worth going to the **Stadt-und Bergbaumuseum** (municipal and mining museum) which explains the history of mining in the area, as well as the collection of minerals at the **Mineralien-und Lagerstätten-sammlung der Bergakademie**. A stroll along the winding streets will take the visitor to **Obermarkt**, where the 15th-century Gothic town hall, a fountain with the statue of the town's founder and attractive houses can be seen.

Otto of Meissen, founder of Freiberg

🏛 **Dom St Marien**
Untermarkt 1. **Goldene Pforte** *Tel (03731) 225 98.* 🅰 May–Oct: 10 & 11am, 2, 3 & 4pm daily; Nov–Apr 11am, 2 & 3pm daily. **Organ presentation** 11:30am Sun.

🏛 **Stadt-und Bergbau-museum**
Am Dom 1. *Tel (03731) 202 50.* ◯ 10am–5pm Tue–Sun. 🅰

🏛 **Mineralien-und Lagerstättensammlung der Bergakademie**
Brennhausgasse 14. *Tel (03731) 39 22 64.* ◯ 9am–noon & 1–4pm Wed–Fri, 9am–4pm Sat

Façade of the Renaissance Schloss Augustusburg

Sächsische Silberstraße ●

The Saxon silver route, through the Erzgebirge (mineral ore mountains), takes the visitor to some of the most interesting and scenic places of the region. Silver was mined here from the 12th century, and mining traditions have been preserved to this day. Small towns entice visitors with their interesting parish churches, former mining settlements, museums and disused mines.

Schneeberg ①
A small mining town, which to this day cultivates its art and crafts traditions, Schneeberg is also famous for the St Wolfgangkirche, with an altar masterpiece by Lucas Cranach the Elder.

Annaberg-Buchholz ③
Although the town enjoyed only a brief spell of prosperity in the 16th century, its church from that period, St Annen, ranks among the most beautiful examples of late-Gothic architecture in Saxony.

Oberwiesenthal ②
This important wintersports resort, close to the Czech border and at the foot of the Fichtelberg, offers a ski-jump, downhill ski runs and toboggan runs.

```
0 km        5
0 miles     5
```

Wolkenstein

Ehrenfrie-dersdorf

Obernhau

Aue

Lauter

Schwarzenberg

171

174

101

95

174

Marienberg ⑥
This small town, with its wonderful Renaissance town hall, is known mainly for the production of furniture.

KEY

▬▬ Suggested route

═══ Other road

▭▭ Scenic route

--- State boundary

⚹ Viewpoint

Greifensteine ⑤
Fantastic, craggy rock formations in the north of the region, shaped like an amphitheatre, attract rock-climbers and hill-walkers.

Frohnau ④
The biggest attraction of this town is its old forge, featuring the Frohnauer Hammer, a huge original hammer that remained in use until 1904.

TIPS FOR DRIVERS

Length of the route: 55 km (34 miles).
Stopping points: inns and restaurants in every town.

Meissen

Road map 4E. 🏙 36,000. 🚌 🚉
ℹ️ *Markt 3 (03521-419 40).*
🎭 *Stadt- und Weinfest (Sep).*
www.stadt-meissen.de

Meissen is famous for its porcelain manufacture. Its history began in 929, when Henry I made it the bridgehead for his expansion to the east, into Slav territories. In 966 Meissen became the capital of the newly established Meissen Margravate, and in 968 a bishopric.

This town has retained much of its charm. In the town square is the late-Gothic **Rathaus** (town hall), built in 1472–8, some beautiful Renaissance houses and the **Frauenkirche**, a late-Gothic, 15th-century church boasting the world's oldest porcelain carillon, which was hung here in 1929. It is also worth taking a stroll to St Afra's church, built in the 13th century for the Augustian monks.

🏰 Albrechtsburg
Domplatz 1. **Tel** *(03521) 47 070.*
🕙 *Mar–Oct: 10am–6pm daily,
Nov–Feb: 10am–5pm daily.*
⬤ *10–31 Jan.* 📷
The Albrechtsburg is a vast, fortified hilltop complex with a cathedral and an Elector's palace. The latter was built in 1471–89 for the Wettin brothers, Ernst and Albrecht. Designed by Arnold von Westfalen, its special feature is the magnificent external spiral staircase. From 1710 the palace was used as a porcelain factory. It was restored to its

The Baroque hunting lodge in Moritzburg

former glory in 1864. Huge wall paintings of this period, showing historical scenes, are the work of Wilhelm Römann. The cathedral church of St John the Evangelist and St Donat, built from the mid-13th century to the early 15th century, has some splendid early-Gothic sculptures, an altar by Lucas Cranach the Elder in the Georgskapelle and ducal tombs in the Fürstenkapelle.

🏛 Staatliche Porzellan-Manufaktur
Talstraße 9. **Tel** *(03521) 46 87 00.*
🕙 *May–Oct: 9am–6pm daily;
Nov–Apr: 9am–5pm daily.*
The first porcelain factory in Europe was set up in 1710 in the castle and moved to its present premises in 1865. Documents relating to the history of the factory and many interesting examples of its products are on display in the exhibition rooms. Guided tours and demonstrations take the visitor through all the stages of the porcelain manufacturing process.

Moritzburg ⑩

Road map 4E. 🚌 ℹ️ *Schlossallee 3b
(035207-85 40).* 🎭 *Kammermusikfestival (Aug); Fischzug (Oct).*

The first hunting lodge in this marshy region was built in the mid-16th century, for Moritz of Saxony. The present **Schloss Moritzburg** is the result of extensive alterations ordered by Augustus the Strong, directed by Matthäus Daniel Pöppelmann, and carried out in 1723–26. The result is a square building, with four cylindrical corner towers. Much of the interior has survived, including period furnishings and hunting trophies.

Also open to visitors is the 17th-century castle chapel decorated with splendid stucco ornaments. Augustus the Strong ordered the marshes to be drained, and the newly available land to be transformed into landscaped gardens and lakes. The **Fasanenschlösschen** (little pheasant castle) in the eastern part of the gardens features several interesting Rococo interiors, and also houses a zoological exhibition.

At the end of World War II, the German artist Käthe Kollwitz spent the last years of her life in Moritzburg. The house in which she lived and worked is now the **Käthe-Kollwitz-Gedenkstätte**.

🏰 Schloss Moritzburg
Tel *(035207) 8730.* 🕙 *Apr–Oct: 10am–5pm daily; Nov–Mar: 10am–4pm Tue–Sun.* 📷

🏰 Fasanenschlösschen
⬤ *Closed for renovation until 2007.*

The late-Gothic Rathaus in Meissen

For hotels and restaurants in this region see pp493–5 and pp532–4

Dresden ⑪

One of Germany's most beautiful cities, Dresden first gained its pre-eminence in the year 1485, when the Albertine Wettins decided to establish their residence here. The town blossomed during the 18th century when it became a cultural centre and acquired many magnificent buildings. Almost all of these, however, were completely destroyed during the night of 13/14 February 1945, when British and American air forces mounted a vast carpet-bombing raid on the city. Today, meticulous restoration work is in progress to return the historic city centre to its former glory, now with renewed effort because of the damage caused by flooding in 2002.

Newly renovated Frauenkirche

Statue of the Saxon King Johann, in front of the Sächsische Staatsoper

🎭 Sächsische Staatsoper

Theaterplatz 2. *Tel (0351) 49 110.*
Tours *Tel (0351) 491 14 96.*
The imposing, Neo-Renaissance building of the Saxon state opera is one of Dresden's landmarks. It is also known as Semperoper after its creator, the famous architect Gottfried Semper, who designed it twice: the first building, erected in 1838–41, burned down in 1869, the second one was completed in 1878. Reconstruction after World War II dragged on until 1985. The opera house was the venue for many world premieres, including *Tannhäuser* and *The Flying Dutchman* by Richard Wagner, as well as many works by Richard Strauss.

In front of the opera, in Theaterplatz, is a monument to the Saxon King Johann, by Johannes Schilling.

🎭 Schinkelwache

Theaterplatz. **Box office** 🛈 *Tel (0351) 491 17 05.* ⬚ *10am–6pm Mon–Fri, 10am–1pm Sat.*
This small Neo-Classical building, with its sophisticated lines and its immaculate

proportions, is the work of the famous Berlin architect, Karl Friedrich Schinkel. It was built between 1830 and 1832.

⛪ Hofkirche

Theaterplatz. (Entrance on Schlossplatz). ⬚ *daily.*
This monumental Baroque royal church has served as the Catholic Dom (cathedral church) of the Dresden-Meißen Diocese since 1980. The presence of this Catholic church in staunchly Protestant Saxony was dictated by political necessity: in his struggle for the Polish crown, the Elector, Augustus Strong, was forced to convert to Catholicism. The church was designed by an Italian architect, Gaetano Chiaveri, and built in 1738–51.

The church's interior has two-tier passageways which run from the main nave to the side naves. Rebuilt after World War II, it features a magnificent Rococo pulpit by Balthasar Permoser, a painting by Anton Raphael Mengus entitled *Assumption* in the main altar, and the vast organ – the last work of Gottfried Silbermann.

⛪ Frauenkirche

An der Frauenkirche. *Tel (0351) 65 60 656.* ⬚ *10am–noon, 1pm–6pm daily.*
This giant church, designed by Georg Bähr and built in 1726–43, has been largely restored to its former glory. Once again, the shining, giant dome dominates the city's skyline. Completely destroyed in 1945 by Allied bombing, its shell survived intact, only to collapse later. Reconstruction started in 1993 and the crypt opened in 1996. Work continues and should be finished in 2006.

🎭 Residenzschloss

Taschenberg 2. **Temporary exhibitions** *Tel (0351) 49 14 619.* ⬚ *10am–6pm Wed–Mon.* **Hausmannsturm** ⬚ *Apr–Oct: 10am–6pm Tue–Sun.*
This former residence of the

Façade of a wing of the Residenzschloss, with sgraffito decoration

Wetting family was built in stages from the late 15th to the 17th centuries. It is now restored and houses some of the most beautiful art collections in East Germany, including the world famous Grünes Gewölbe (Green Vaults), a vast collection of royal jewels, gems and table decorations. The Hausmannsturm, which is a tall tower, affords a great view of the Dresden skyline.

⚜ Fürstenzug

Augustusstr.

Langer Gang (long walk) is a long building, erected in 1586–91, which connects the castle with the Johanneum. The elegant façade facing the courtyard is decorated with *sgraffito* and has shady arcades supported by slim columns. It provided an excellent backdrop for tournaments and parades. The wall facing the street features the so-called Fürstenzug (procession of dukes) – a magnificent, 102 m (111 yd)-long frieze depicting the procession of many Saxon rulers. The frieze was originally created by Wilhelm Walther in 1872–6 using the *sgraffito* technique, but it was replaced in 1907 by 24,000 Meissen porcelain tiles.

VISITORS' CHECKLIST

Road map E4. 480,000. Dresden-Klotzsche 15 km (9 miles) from centre. Hauptbahnhof, Wiener Platz (0351-461 37 10). Prager Str. 10–11 (0351-49 19 20); Schinkelwache, Theaterplatz. **www**.dresden.de Sächsische Dampfschiffahrt, Radebeul, Hertha-Lindner-Str. 10. (0351) 86 60 90. Flottenparade der Sächs. Dampfschiffahrt (May); Elbhangfest (Jun); Stadtfest (Aug); Weihnachtsmarkt (Nov–Dec).

🏛 Verkehrsmuseum (Johanneum)

Augustusstr. 1. **Tel** (0351) 86 440. 10am–5pm Tue–Sun.

This late 16th-century Renaissance building, originally designed as royal stables by Paul Buchner, was refurbished in the mid-18th century and housed first a gallery of paintings, later an armoury and a porcelain collection. Since 1956 it has been a museum of transport, with old trams, locomotives, a collection of vintage cars and models of famous German ships.

Fragment of the Fürstenzug, outside Langer Gang

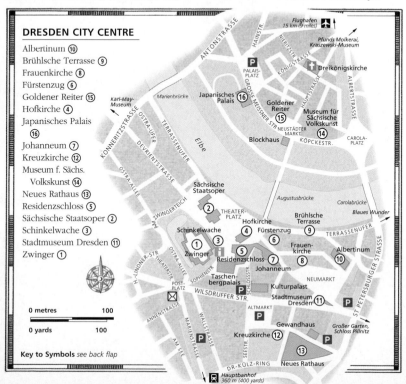

DRESDEN CITY CENTRE

Albertinum ⑩
Brühlsche Terrasse ⑨
Frauenkirche ⑧
Fürstenzug ⑥
Goldener Reiter ⑮
Hofkirche ④
Japanisches Palais ⑯
Johanneum ⑦
Kreuzkirche ⑫
Museum f. Sächs. Volkskunst ⑭
Neues Rathaus ⑬
Residenzschloss ⑤
Sächsische Staatsoper ②
Schinkelwache ③
Stadtmuseum Dresden ⑪
Zwinger ①

0 metres 100
0 yards 100

Key to Symbols see back flap

🏛 Brühlsche Terrasse

Brühlsche Terrasse.

Once part of the town's fortifications, this attractive terrace
subsequently lost its military
importance and was trans-
formed into magnificent gardens by Heinrich von Brühl
after whom it is named.
Offering splendid views over
the River Elbe, it was known
as "the balcony of Europe".
There are several great buildings on the terraces – the first
one, seen from Schlossplatz, is
the Neo-Renaissance **Landtag**
(parliament building); next to
it is a small Neo-Baroque building, the **Secundogenitur**
library built for the second
generation of Brühls, now a
popular café; this is followed
by the **Kunstakademie** (art
academy), known as Zitronen-
presse (lemon squeezer)
because of its ribbed glass
dome. Among the statues and
monuments on the terrace are
works by the sculptor Ernst
Rietschel, the architect Gottfried Semper and the painter
Caspar David Friedrich.

🏛 Albertinum

Brühlsche Terrasse. *Tel (0351) 491
45 90. Galerie Neue Meister.* 📷
closed for renovation until 2009.

Originally a royal arsenal, the
Albertinum was rebuilt in its
current Neo-Renaissance style
in the 1880s by Carl Adolf
Canzler. Forty years earlier,
Bernhard von Lindenau had
donated his considerable
fortune to the city to set up a
collection of contemporary
art, which was then housed in
the Albertinum. Today, the
building houses a number of
magnificent collections. That
of the **Galerie Neue Meister**,
which was established in the
mid-19th century, contains
paintings from the 19th
and 20th centuries, including

Two Women on Tahiti, Paul Gauguin, 1892, in the Albertinum

works by the German
Impressionists Lovis Corinth
and Max Liebermann, land-
scapes by Caspar David
Friedrich, canvases by the
Nazarine group of painters
and works by European
masters such as Edgar Degas,
Paul Gauguin, Vincent van
Gogh, Édouard Manet and
Claude Monet. The **Skulp-
turensammlung** (on display
at the Zwinger *(see p174–5)*
throughout the renovation
work) is a small collection
of sculptures, including
remarkable works by
Balthasar
Permoser. The
most famous of
the collections
is the Grünes
Gewölbe
(green
vaults), a vast
collection of royal
jewels and other precious
items. The Albertinum is closed
for renovation until 2009.

🔒 Kreuzkirche

An der Kreuzkirche.
Tel (0351) 439 39 20. 🕐 *Summer:
10am–6pm Mon–Fri; winter:
10am– 4pm Mon–Fri.* **Tower**
🕐 *10am–5pm daily.*

The present
Baroque/Neo-
Classical church was
built in 1764–92 to a
design by Johann
Georg Schmidt. To
commemorate the
shelling in World
War II, the interior
has not been fully
restored. The Cross
of Nails from the

ruins of Coventry Cathedral in
England creates a powerful
symbolic link between the
two countries.

🏛 Goldener Reiter

Neustädter Markt.

The **Neustadt** (new town),
on the right bank of the Elbe,
lost much of its former glory
through destruction in World
War II. Visitors may
therefore be sur-
prised to come
across this
glistening,
gilded eques-
trian statue of
Augustus the
Strong in the
middle of a
square, at the end
of the plane tree-
lined Hauptstraße.
The monument,
which is the work
of Jean Joseph Vinache, was
erected in 1736.

**The Goldener Reiter
in the new town**

🏛 Neues Rathaus

Dr.-Külz-Ring.

The giant Neo-Renaissance
new town hall, in the southwest of the old town, was
erected in 1905–1910. Its
round tower (70 m/230 ft),
crowned with a gilded statue
of Hercules, offers the best
view of the old city centre. In
the foyer is a large model of
the city as planned for 2015.

🏛 Museum für Sächsische Volkskunst (Jägerhof)

Köpckestr. 1. *Tel (0351) 803 08 17.*
🕐 *10am–6pm Tue–Sun.*

This Renaissance hunting
lodge on the north bank of

Secundogenitur library on Brühlsche Terrasse

◁ **Schloss Moritzburg, near Dresden**

the Elbe was built between 1568 and 1613. Its west wing – the only part that escaped destruction – now houses a museum of ethnography with collections of Saxon culture and traditions, especially from the Erzgebirge Mountains.

🏛 Japanisches Palais

Palaisplatz. *Tel (0351) 81 44 50.* **Museum für Völkerkunde** (Museum of Ethnography) ◯ *10am–6pm Tue–Sun.* **Landesmuseum für Vorgeschichte** (State Museum of Prehistory) ◯ *10am–6pm daily.* **Staatliche Naturhistorische Satitilingen Dresden** ◯ *10am–6pm Tue–Sun.*

Originally the Dutch Palais, this three-wing structure was built in 1715. It was extended in 1729–31, by Zacharias Longuelune, for Augustus the Strong's Japanese porcelain collection, at which time the palace changed its name. The porcelain was never actually housed here, however, and for years the palace served as a library.

🏛 Pfunds Molkerei

Bautzner Str. 79. *Tel (0351) 80 80 80.* ◯ *10am–6pm Mon–Sat, 10am–3pm Sun.*

In the 19th-century part of the Neustadt, with its many bars, galleries, pubs and fringe theatres, stands this old dairy founded by Paul Pfund. Its interior is lined with dazzling, multi-coloured tiles, showing Neo-Renaissance motifs relating to the dairy's products. Today there is a shop which offers hundreds of dairy products, as well as a small bar, where visitors can sample the specialities.

🏛 Kraszewski-Museum

Nordstr. 28. *Tel (0351) 804 44 50.* ◯ *10am–6pm Wed–Sun.*

This small museum is devoted to the life of the Polish writer

The Baroque Schloss Pillnitz, Augustus the Strong's summer residence

Józef Ignacy Kraszewski who, having escaped arrest in Warsaw, settled in Dresden in 1853. Inspired by the town's history, several of his novels (for example *Hrabina Cosel, Brühl*) are set during the time of Augustus the Strong.

🌿 Großer Garten

City centre.

The history of this great garden goes back to the 17th century, although it has been redesigned several times since. At the park's centre stands an early Baroque palace built in 1678–83 to a design by Johann Georg Starcke. A miniature railway takes visitors to Carolasee, a boating lake. It also stops at the botanical gardens in the northwest section of the park, and at the zoo. The Mosaikbrunnen (mosaic fountain) nearby was designed by Hans Poelzig and built in 1926.

🏛 Blaues Wunder

Loschwitz/Blasewitzer Brücke.

The suspension bridge which spans the River Elbe in the eastern part of the town is painted blue and nicknamed "blue wonder". Built in 1891–3, its main span is 141.5 m (464 ft) long. The bridge leads to Loschwitz, a neighbourhood in a picturesque location amidst hills, which has many attractive villas and small palaces built in the 19th century.

🏛 Schloss Pillnitz

Tel (0351) 261 30. **Kunstgewerbemuseum Bergpalais** ◯ *May–Oct: 10am–6pm Tue–Sun.* **Wasserpalais** ◯ *May–Oct: 10am–6pm Wed–Mon.*

This charming summer residence, on the banks of the Elbe, was built in 1720–23 by Augustus the Strong and designed by Matthäus Daniel Pöppelmann. There are two parallel palaces: the Bergpalais (mountain palace) and the Wasserpalais (water palace); the latter can be reached by stairs directly from the river jetty. Between 1818 and 1826 the two palaces were joined by a third one, the Neues Palais. Today the Bergpalais houses a fascinating crafts museum. The main attraction, however, is the large park, laid out in English and Chinese styles, with an orangery and pavilions.

🏛 Karl-May-Museum

Radebeul. Karl-May-Str. 5. *Tel (0351) 837 30 10.* ◯ *Mar–Oct: 9am–6pm; Nov–Feb: 10am–4pm Tue–Sun.* ◉ *24, 25, 31 Dec, 1 Jan.*

Radebeul, 5 km (3 miles) northwest of Dresden, is much visited by the fans of Winnteou, a fictional Indian chief, and his friend Old Shatterhand. A museum is devoted to the life and work of the author, Karl May, who lived and died in Radebeul. It also displays May's large collection of Native American costumes and other items.

The suspension bridge across the Elbe River, nicknamed "Blaues Wunder"

The Zwinger

The most famous building in Dresden is the Zwinger, a beautiful Baroque structure. Its name means 'intermural', and it was built in the space between the former town fortifications. Commissioned by Augustus the Strong, it was constructed in 1709–32 to a design by Matthäus Daniel Pöppelmann, with the help of the sculptor Balthasar Permoser. Its spacious courtyard, once used to stage tournaments, festivals and firework displays, is completely surrounded by galleries into which are set pavilions and gates. Today it houses several art collections.

Mathematisch-Physikalischer Salon

A valuable collection of scientific instruments from different ages, this also features clocks, sextants and globes, including a priceless 13th-century Arabic globe of the sky.

Kronentor

This gate owes its name (crown gate) to the crown positioned on top of its dome.

Main entrance

Allegorical figures crown the balustrades.

★ Porzellansammlung

The porcelain collection holds Japanese and Chinese pieces but its centrepiece is a collection of Meissen porcelain, including parts of the stunning Swan Service made for Heinrich Brühl, to a design by Joachim Kaendler.

Glockenspielpavillon

Once known as Stadtpavillon (town pavilion), the name of this building was changed to carillon pavilion when it acquired a carillon with Meissen porcelain bells, in 1924–36.

Wallpavillon

A stunning marriage of architecture and sculpture, this Baroque masterpiece is crowned by a statue of Hercules, symbolizing the Elector, Augustus the Strong.

VISITORS' CHECKLIST

Sophienstraße/Ostra-Allee/Theater-platz. **Porzellansammlung** *Tel* (0351) 491 42000. ⬜ 10am–6pm Tue–Sun. **Mathematisch-Physikalischer Salon** *Tel* 491 42000. ⬜ 10am–6pm Tue–Sun. **Rüstkammer** *Tel* 491 42000. ⬜ 10am–6pm Tue–Sun. 🏛

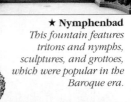

★ Nymphenbad
This fountain features tritons and nymphs, sculptures, and grottoes, which were popular in the Baroque era.

Courtyard

Galerie Alte Meister
This gallery of old masters occupies the wing which was added by Gottfried Semper (see pp176–7).

★ Rüstkammer
Exhibited in the armoury are magnificent arms, with the best examples dating from the 16th century, including a suit of armour made for Erik XIV by Eliseus Libaerts in 1562–4.

STAR FEATURES

★ Nymphenbad

★ Porzellansammlung

★ Rüstkammer

Gemäldegalerie Alte Meister

The Dresden gallery of old masters contains what is considered to be one of Europe's finest art collections. Its core consists of the canvases collected by the Wettin family from the 16th century, but the majority of exhibits were purchased at the order of King Augustus II the Strong and his son Augustus III. It was during that time that the gallery was moved to its own premises – first to the Johanneum and later to its present home in the Zwinger, built by Gottfried Semper in 1847–55.

2nd floor

1st floor

Feast of Love (c.1717)
The so-called fête galante is one of many splendid paintings by Antoine Watteau, depicting a flirtatious group in a park.

Madonna and Infant Triptych (1437)
This superb small triptych depicting the Virgin Mary with the Holy Infant, St Catherine and the Archangel St Michael, is one of very few works signed by its creator, Jan van Eyck.

Ground floor

Girl Reading a Letter
(c.1659) This exquisite painting, of a lone woman by the window reading a letter, is among the finest works by Jan Vermeer van Delft.

Main entrance

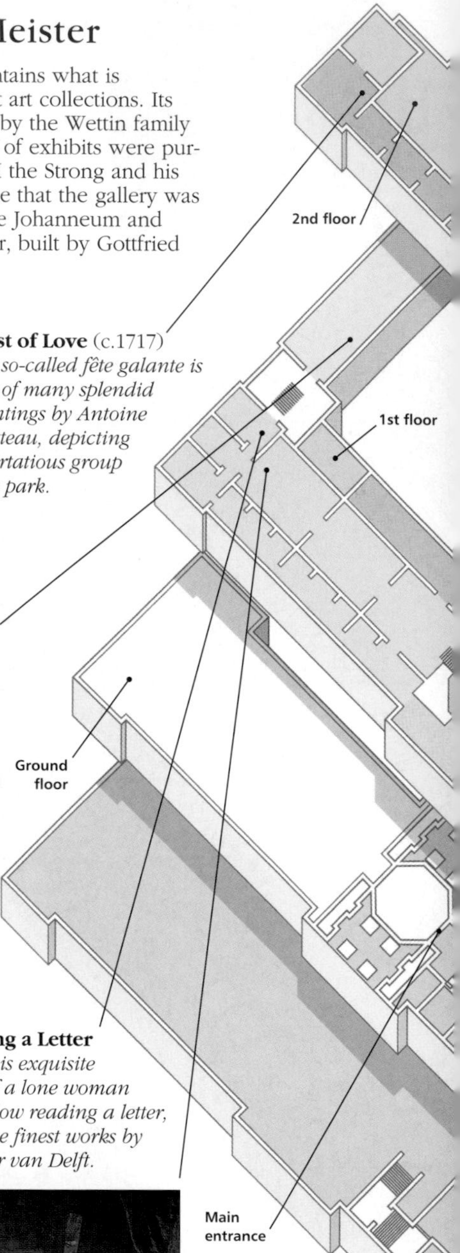

GALLERY GUIDE

The ground floor has works by Canaletto; the 1st floor has German paintings and 15th to 18th-century European works, and the 2nd floor has 18th-century and Spanish pastels, paintings and miniatures.

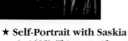

★ **Self-Portrait with Saskia**
(c.1635) This magnificent painting depicting Rembrandt with his wife, Saskia, is considered by some to be a representation of the Prodigal Son of the Bible.

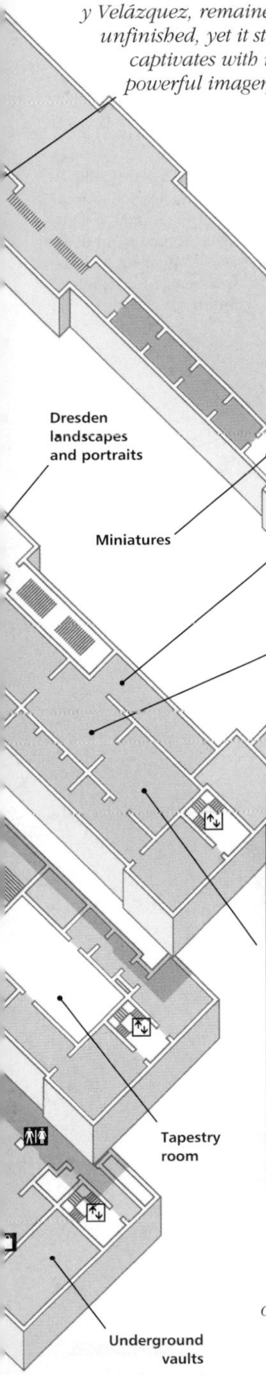

Portrait of a Man (c.1633)
This highly expressive portrait, by Diego Rodríguez de Silva y Velázquez, remained unfinished, yet it still captivates with its powerful imagery.

VISITORS' CHECKLIST

Theaterplatz 1. **Tel** *(0351) 491 42000.* ☐ *10am–6pm Tue–Sun.*

Tribute Money (c.1516)
Titian depicts the theme of this popular New Testament parable in an unusual way, zooming in on the figures of Christ and a Pharisee who shows Him a coin.

Dresden landscapes and portraits

Miniatures

Sleeping Venus (c.1508–10)
This famous nude was probably painted by Giorgione, but when he died of the plague in 1510, his friend, Titian, completed the work.

KEY

- ☐ 15th–17th-century Italian painting
- ☐ 15th–16th-century German painting
- ☐ Canaletto and scenes of Dresden
- ☐ 17th-century Dutch and Flemish painting
- ☐ 17th-century French painting
- ☐ Spanish painting
- ☐ 18th-century Italian and French painting
- ☐ German, Czech, Austrian, English and Swiss painting
- ☐ Non-exhibition space

Tapestry room

Underground vaults

★ **Sistine Madonna** (1512/13)
This enchanting picture of the Madonna and Child by Raphael owes its name to St Sixtus's church in Piacenza, for which Pope Julius II had commissioned it.

STAR EXHIBITS

★ Self-Portrait with Saskia

★ Sistine Madonna

Market square with Renaissance Rathaus (town hall) in Pirna

Pirna ⑫

Road map F4. 🏛 *38,000.* 🚉 🚌
ℹ️ *Am Markt 7 (03501-465 70).*
www.pirna.de
🎭 *Stadtfest (Jun).*

In the old town, on the banks of the River Elbe, Pirna has preserved an amazingly regular, chequerboard pattern of streets. Time has been kind to the many historic buildings in this town. Its greatest attraction is the **Marienkirche**, a late-Gothic hall-church with fanciful vaulting designed by Peter Ulrich von Pirna and painted by Jobst Dorndorff, in 1545–6. Inside, an original late-Gothic font and a Renaissance main altar can be seen.

Other interesting buildings are the mid-16th century **Rathaus** (town hall) with its Gothic portals, the beautiful houses in the town square and the ex-Dominican, Gothic church of St Heinrich. **Schloss Sonnenstein**, extended during the 17th and 18th centuries, towers above the old town.

Environs
10 km (6 miles) southwest of Pirna is the picturesque **Schloss Weesenstein**, much altered from its Gothic origins until the 19th century. It houses a small museum with an interesting collection of wallpapers.

⛪ **Museum Schloss Weesenstein**
Müglitztal, Am Schlossberg 1.
Tel *(035027) 54 26.* ⬜ *Apr–Oct: 9am–6pm; Nov–Mar: 9am–5pm.*

Sächsische Schweiz ⑬

Saxon switzerland, the wonderfully wild region around the gorge cut into the Lusatian mountains by the River Elbe, features stunningly bizarre rock formations and several formidable castles. The best way to explore the area is on foot as many places are inaccessible to cars. Alternatively you can admire the spectacular scenery from a boat, on the Elbe.

Großsedlitz ①
This vast Baroque park, established after 1719 to a design by Johann Christoph Knöffel, continues to delight visitors to this day with its flower beds and numerous sculptures.

Stolpen ⑦
The 35-year old Countess Cosel, one of Augustus II the Strong's mistresses, was imprisoned in this castle, built on rock.

Bastei ⑥
The "bastion" comprises so-called inselbergs – bizarre, tall rock formations that rise abruptly. Connected by foot-bridges, they offer splendid views.

Weissig
Heidenau
Pirna
Elba
Gottlenba
Teplice

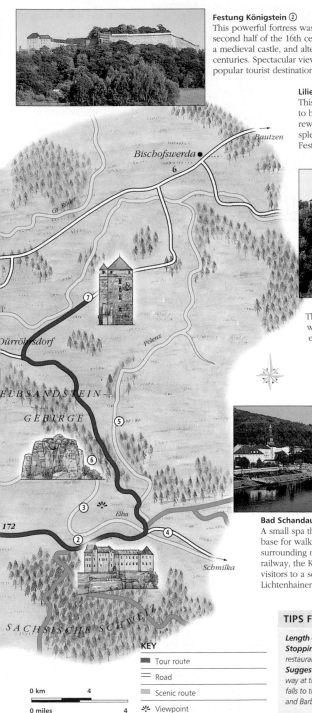

Festung Königstein ②
This powerful fortress was built in the second half of the 16th century on the site of a medieval castle, and altered in subsequent centuries. Spectacular views have made it a popular tourist destination.

Lilienstein ③
This tall rock, which has to be climbed on foot, rewards the visitor with splendid views of Festung Königstein.

Burg Hohnstein ④
The castle, which holds within its walls a medieval building, is now a museum and one of Germany's largest youth hostels.

Bad Schandau ⑤
A small spa that is popular as a base for walking tours into the surrounding mountains. A small railway, the Kirnitzschtalbahn, takes visitors to a scenic waterfall, the Lichtenhainer Wasserfall.

Bautzen

Bischofswerda ●

6

Gr. Röder

7

Polenz

Dürröhrsdorf

ELBSANDSTEIN-GEBIRGE

⑤

⑥

③

Elba

172

②

④

Schmilka

SÄCHSISCHE SCHWEIZ

TIPS FOR VISITORS

Length of tour: 41 km (25 miles).
Stopping places: inns and restaurants in every town.
Suggestions: walk from the railway at the Lichtenhainer Waterfalls to the Kuhstall (cow stable) and Barbarine needle rocks.

KEY

■ Tour route
= Road
■ Scenic route
☀ Viewpoint

0 km   4
0 miles   4

For additional map symbols *see back flap*

Gothic altar from 1513 in St Annen church, in Kamenz

Kamenz ⑭

Road map F4. ⚒ 16,800. 🚉 🚌
ℹ Pulsnitzer Str. 11 (03578 379 205).
🎭 Hutbergfest (May).

The best time for a visit to Kamenz is the end of May or June, when the rhododendrons that cover the Hutberg (294 m/965 ft high) are in flower. The poet, Gotthold Ephraim Lessing, was born in Kamenz in 1729. Although his house no longer exists, the **Lessingmuseum**, founded in 1929, is devoted to his work.

A great fire destroyed much of the town in 1842, but it spared the late-Gothic **St Marien** church, a four-nave 15th-century structure with Gothic altars and other interesting features. Equally noteworthy for their furnishings are the Gothic ex-Franciscan **St Annen** church and the unusual hall-church **Katechismuskirche**. Originally part of the town's fortification system, it has a row of loopholes on its upper storey. The old cemetery and the Gothic funereal church **Begräbniskirche St Just** are also worth a visit. As is the new **Museum der Westlausitz**, a museum of the local region.

🏛 Lessingmuseum
Lessingplatz 1–3. **Tel** (03578) 380 50. 🕐 9am–5pm Tue–Fri, 1pm–5pm Sat–Sun.

Bautzen ⑮

Road map F4. ⚒ 44,000. 🚉 🚌
ℹ Hauptmarkt 1 (03591-4 20 16).
🎭 Vogelhochzeit (Jan); Internationales Folklorefestival (Jun).

This town is scenically situated on a high rock overhanging the Spree River valley. Known mainly for its top-security jail for political prisoners during the GDR era, today it enchants visitors with its beautifully reconstructed old town. Many signs are bilingual, German and Sorbian, reflecting the fact that Bautzen is the cultural capital of the Sorbs. The winding streets with their original houses, the city walls, the curiously crooked **Reichenturm** tower and the Baroque town hall in the town square form a very attractive complex. It is also worth climbing the

Impressive Baroque entrance to the Domstift in Bautzen

15th-century **Alte Wasserkunst**, a tower that pumped Spree water up to the town. It is the symbol of Bautzen and offers splendid views.

The cathedral **Dom St Peter** is now used jointly by Catholics (choir) and Protestants (nave). The late-Gothic **Schloss Ortenburg** houses the **Sorbisches Museum**, devoted to Sorbian history and culture.

🏛 Sorbisches Museum
Ortenburg 3. **Tel** (03591) 42 403. 🕐 Apr–Oct: 10am–5pm Mon–Fri, 10am–6pm Sat & Sun; Nov–Mar: 10am–4pm Mon–Fri, 10am–5pm Sat & Sun.

Doorway of the Neo-Renaissance palace in Bad Muskau

Bad Muskau ⑯

Road map F4. ⚒ 4,170. 🚌
ℹ Schlossstr. 6 (035771-504 92).

Bad Muskau, a small town and spa, boasts one of Saxony's most beautiful parks, which has been included in the UNESCO Cultural Heritage list. It was created in 1815–45 by the writer Prince Hermann von Pückler-Muskau. The Neo-Renaissance palace at its centre was destroyed in World War II and is currently closed for reconstruction, but the English-style landscaped park surrounding it, a nature reserve since 1952, is well worth visiting. Its main part, on the northern shores of the Lusatian Neisse River, is in Poland. A joint Polish-German programme, aimed at revitalizing the park, has opened the entire area to visitors from both sides of the border.

For hotels and restaurants in this region see pp493–5 and pp532–4

Baroque Neptune fountain in Untermarkt, in Görlitz

Görlitz ⑰

Road map F4. 🏛 66,000. 🚇 🚌
ℹ *Brüderstraße 1 (03581-475 70 & 194 33).* 🎭 *Kultursommer (May–Sep); Sommertheater (Jul); Straßentheaterfestival (Aug).*

This border town, whose eastern part, Zgorzelec, has belonged to Poland since 1945, boasts a long history. Its oldest records date back to 1071. Founded in 1210–20, the town flourished in the 15th and 16th centuries. In 1990 an extensive restoration plan was begun, and now visitors can see its historic buildings in their former glory.

The charming houses in **Obermarkt** (upper market), the Renaissance portals and decorations on houses in Brüderstraße and the fascinating **Untermarkt** (lower market), with its vast town hall complex, enchant everyone. The older wing of the town hall, the work of Wendel Roskopf, has an amazing external staircase with Renaissance ornaments, and winds around the statue of Justice.

One of the most remarkable churches is the imposing five-nave, 15th-century **Hauptstadtpfarrkirche St Peter und St Paul** whose Baroque furnishings are among the finest in Saxony. Also noteworthy is the **Oberkirche**, with an original Gothic main altar and 15th-century wall paintings in the side nave. One of Görlitz's curiosities is the **Heiliges Grab** (Holy tomb), built in 1481–1504, a group of three chapels that are replicas of churches in Jerusalem. Görlitz still has remains of its medieval town fortifications with original towers and gates, including the **Kaisertrutz**, a 15th-century barbican, extended in the 19th century and now home to the town's art collection.

Environs
The small town of **Ostritz**, 16 km (10 miles) to the south, has a charming original Cistercian abbey, St Marienthal (1230). Its red-and-white buildings are to this day inhabited by nuns, who show visitors around and serve food and home-brewed beer.

Zittau ⑱

Road map F4. 🏛 28,000. 🚇 🚌
ℹ *Markt 1 (03583-75 21 37).* 🎭 *Klosterfest (Ascension) (May); Fest am Dreiländereck (Jun).*

Zittau is an excellent starting point for excursions into the Zittau Mountains, a paradise for rock-climbers, walkers and nature lovers. The town itself has a splendidly preserved old town, with many historic buildings, such as the beautiful, Baroque **Noacksches Haus** (Markt 2). The Neo-Renaissance **Rathaus** (town hall) was built in 1840–45, to a design by Carl Augustus Schramm. The **Johanniskirche**, designed by Karl Friedrich Schinkel, combines elements of Neo-Classical and Neo-Gothic styles and is an excellent example of Historicist architecture.

Environs
The charming spa town of **Oybrin**, 9 km (6 miles) south of Zittau, can be reached by narrow-gauge railway. Its attractions include the hilltop ruins of a Gothic abbey, immortalized by Caspar David Friedrich. It is worth timing your visit for a Saturday evening in summer, when you can witness the procession of torch-bearing monks or listen to a concert.

Fountain with a statue of Roland, the French knight, in Zittau

THE SORBS

The Sorbs, also known as the Lusatians or Wends, are an indigenous Slav minority who live in the eastern regions of Saxony and Brandenburg. Their ancestors, the Lusatian Slavs, were conquered by Germans in the 10th century. Although condemned to extermination by the National Socialists, today they enjoy complete cultural autonomy. The revival of their language and traditions is apparent in the bilingual signs in towns.

THURINGIA

Thuringia is a beautiful state, with much to entice the visitor. The Thuringian Forest, in the south, is a highland area densely covered with spruce, beech and oak forests, inviting visitors to ramble along its enchanted trails, while the area's medieval abbeys, castles and charming small towns are popular destinations with those who are interested in art and history.

The Kingdom of Thuring, as it was known in the 5th century, was conquered by the Franks in the following century. The demise of the Thuringian landgraves, who had ruled here for hundreds of years, resulted in the outbreak of the Thuringian War of Secession. It ended in 1264, with most of Thuringia falling into the hands of the Wettin dynasty.

Split into several smaller principalities, the region lost its political might, but driven by the ambitions of many of its rulers, magnificent castles, churches and abbeys were built everywhere. Thanks to enlightened royal sponsors many towns became important cultural centres, such as 18th-century Weimar, whose residents at one time included Johann Wolfgang von Goethe, Friedrich Schiller, Johann Gottfried Herder and Christoph Martin Wieland.

After World War II, Thuringia was initially occupied by the US Army, but it soon passed into the Soviet sphere of influence, and in 1949 it became part of the GDR. In 1952 Thuringia lost its status as a federal state, but this was later restored in the reunited Federal Republic of Germany, in 1990.

The majority of tourist attractions can be found in the southern part of the state. The Thuringian Forest has many popular health resorts and wintersport centres, such as Oberhof. This highland area, cut with deep river gullies, is littered with medieval castles built on steep crags. Many of these are now no more than picturesque ruins, but others, such as the Wartburg, have been completely restored to their former glory, and today delight visitors with their magnificent interiors.

Schloss Belvedere, the royal summer residence in Weimar

◁ A path through the beautiful Thüringer Wald (Thuringian Forest)

Exploring Thuringia

A visit to Thuringia is most enjoyable in late summer, when the magnificent forests of the Thuringian Mountains are set ablaze with all the hues of red and yellow as the leaves turn colour, or in spring when verdant green cloaks the trees. Allow at least one day to explore Erfurt, the state's capital city, with a further two days in Weimar. Eisenach, with its magnificent Wartburg castle, is also a must.

Street vendor selling hand-painted Easter eggs in Erfurt

SIGHTS AT A GLANCE

Altenburg **⑭**
Eisenach-Wartburg
  pp186–7 **①**
Erfurt pp192–3 **⑧**
Gera **⑬**
Gotha **⑥**
Heiligenstadt **②**
Jena **⑩**
Kyffhäuser Mountains **⑤**
Mühlhausen **③**
Rudolstadt **⑪**
Saalfeld **⑫**
Sondershausen **④**
Weimar pp194–5 **⑨**

Walks

Thüringer Wald
  (Thuringian Forest) **⑦**

Petersburg fortress in Erfurt

The fields near Meiningen, in the Thuringian Forest

GETTING AROUND

Erfurt has an airport. The A4 motorway running through Thuringia links Gera with Jena, Weimar, Erfurt, Gotha and Eisenach. Other towns can be reached by local roads, which are clearly signposted. When touring the Thuringian Forest it is well worth following one of the marked tourist routes, such as Klassikerstraße (the route of the classics) or Porzellanstraße (porcelain street).

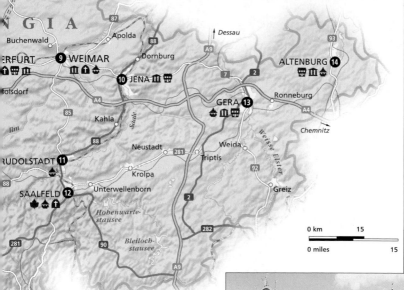

KEY

▬	Motorway
▬	Major road
═══	Minor road
═ ═	Under construction
∿∿∿	Main railway
—	Minor railway
▬	Regional border

The Renaissance town hall in Gotha

Eisenach – Wartburg ❶

The mighty fortress towering above the town is the
legendary castle which was probably founded by
Ludwig the Jumper, in the late 11th century. Reputedly,
it was the setting for the singing contest immortalized
by Wagner in his opera *Tannhäuser*. Between 1211
and 1228 the castle was the home of Saint Elizabeth of
Thuringia, and from 4 May 1521 until March 1522
Martin Luther found refuge here while he translated the New Testament into German. Major
reconstruction in the 19th century gave the
castle its old-time romantic character.

Festsaal
*The impressive and ornate Festival Hall
extends over the entire length and width
of the Romanesque Palas. Today, it is
the venue for a number of events.*

★ Elisabethkemenate
*The mosaics adorning the
walls of St Elizabeth's
rooms illustrate the story of
the saint's life. They were
designed by August Oetken
and placed in 1902–06.*

Landgrafenzimmer
*In 1854 the landgraves'
chambers in the oldest part
of the castle, the Palas, were
decorated with paintings
depicting the castle's history,
by Moritz von Schwind.*

Bergfried
*This vast, square tower
crowned with a cross is the
work of 19th-century restorers.*

STAR FEATURES

★ Elisabethkemenate

★ Lutherstube

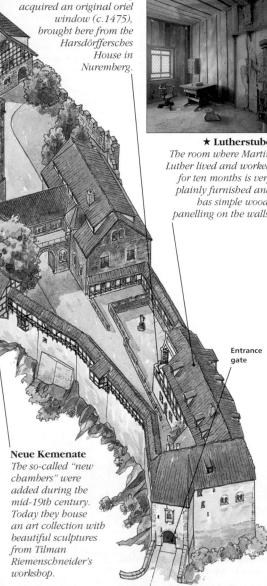

Vogtei
In 1872 this building acquired an original oriel window (c.1475), brought here from the Harsdörffersches House in Nuremberg.

★ Lutherstube
The room where Martin Luther lived and worked for ten months is very plainly furnished and has simple wood-panelling on the walls.

Entrance gate

Neue Kemenate
The so-called "new chambers" were added during the mid-19th century. Today they house an art collection with beautiful sculptures from Tilman Riemenschneider's workshop.

VISITORS' CHECKLIST

Road map C/D4. 🏯 44,000. 🚂
🚌 🛈 Markt 9 (03691-79 23-0).
🎭 Thüringer Bachwochen (Mar–Apr). Wartburg Tel (03691) 25
00; www.wartburg-eisenach.de 🗓
guided tours Mar–Oct: 8:30am–5pm daily (gate closes 8pm); Nov–Feb: 9am–3:30pm daily (gate closes 5pm). 🖼 🗓 🚻 🍴 🖼

Exploring Eisenach

The town, at the foot of the castle hill, was founded in the middle of the 12th century and played an important political role in medieval times. There are interesting remains of fortifications, dating from the late 12th century, which include a Romanesque gate, the Nikolaitor. The Nikolai-kirche nearby, also Romanesque in style, once belonged to the Benedictine Sisters. In the market square is a 16th-century town hall, and in Lutherplatz stands the house where Martin Luther once lived; it is now a small museum of his work.

🛐 Predigerkirche
Predigerplatz 4.
Tel (03691) 78 46 78. 🗓 noon–5pm Tue–Sun. 🖼
This church, built in honour of Elisabeth von Thüringen shortly after she had been canonized, is part of the Thüringer Museum and has been used for changing exhibitions since 1899. It also houses a permanent exhibition, "Medieval Art in Thuringia".

🏛 Automobile Welt Eisenach
F. Naumanstr. 10. Tel (03691) 77 21 2. 🗓 11am–5pm Tue–Sun.
This car museum celebrates the local car manufacturing industry in Eisenach. Its collection includes old BMWs and Wartburgs.

🏛 Bachhaus
Frauenplan 21. Tel (03691) 7 93 40. 🗓 10am–6pm daily. 🖼
www.bachaus.de
Johann Sebastian Bach, the famous composer, was born in Eisenach in 1685. His birthplace is now demolished, but this small museum nearby is devoted to his life and work.

The Bachhaus and museum, surrounded by a garden

Heiligenstadt ❷

Road map C4. 🏚 *17,500.* 🚆 🚌
ℹ *Wilhelmstr. 50 (03606-67 71 41).*

This pleasant spa and health resort, well placed for visiting the landscaped gardens of Eichsfeld, is worth an extended stop. Heiligenstadt is the birthplace of Tilman Riemenschneider, an outstanding sculptor of the Gothic era; it is also the place where the poet and writer Heinrich Heine was baptized in 1825, at the age of 28.

Heiligenstadt has several churches worth visiting, including the Gothic **Pfarrkirche St Marien** with its original wall paintings dating from around 1500. Not far from the church stands the **Friedhofskapelle St Annen**, an octagonal Gothic cemetery chapel. The town's most interesting church, however, is the **Stiftskirche St Martin**, dating back to the 14th–15th centuries. It has a well-preserved Romanesque crypt and an amusing Gothic pulpit, made in the shape of a book-holding chorister.

Mühlhausen ❸

Road map D4. 🏚 *38,000.* 🚆 🚌
ℹ *Ratsstr. 20 (03601-40 47 70).*
🎭 *Mühlhauser Stadtkirmes (Aug).*
www.muehlhausen.de

Mühlhausen is one of Thuringia's oldest towns, with its earliest records dating back to AD 967. In medieval times it enjoyed the status of an imperial free town, which could explain why it became the centre of political activities during the 1525 Peasants'

Part of the well-preserved town walls surrounding Mühlhausen

War, led by Thomas Müntzer, a local clergyman. In 1975, on the 450th anniversary of the revolt, the town underwent restoration, and it delights visitors to this day with its beautifully preserved old town surrounded by **city walls**, including gates and towers, which have survived almost intact.

Mühlhausen's streets are lined with charming timber-frame houses. It is also worth stepping into one of the six Gothic churches in this area. The **Pfarrkirche Divi Blasii**, built for the Teutonic Knights, has 14th-century stained-glass windows in the presbytery. The ex-Franciscan **Barfüßerklosterkirche** (on the Kornmarkt) houses a museum devoted to the Peasants' War. The huge five-nave 14th-century **Marienkirche**, a hall-church, is one of Thuringia's largest sacral buildings. It has a magnificent main portal and late-Gothic altars. Another interesting historic structure is the **Rathaus** (town hall), in a narrow street between the old and the new town. This vast complex was enlarged several times, from medieval times until the 18th century.

Sondershausen ❹

Road map D4. 🏚 *23,000.* 🚌
ℹ *Markt 9 (03632-78 81 11).*
🎭 *Residenzfest (Jun).*
www.sondershausen.de

Sondershausen was the capital city of the small principality of Schwarzburg-Sondershausen. The town's main attraction is the **Schloss** (ducal palace), a sprawling building, almost triangular in shape, built in stages from the 16th to the 19th century. The palace features some interesting original interiors. Particularly noteworthy are the **Am Wendelstein** rooms, decorated with 17th-century stucco ornaments, as well as the Neo-Classical Liebhabertheater (connoisseurs' theatre, c.1835) and the Baroque Riesensaal (giants' hall), a ballroom with 16 enormous statues of ancient gods. When strolling around the palace gardens it is worth looking at the **Karussell**, an octagonal building dating from 1700.

The most interesting Neo-Classical building complex in town can be found around **Marktplatz** (market square).

Environs
In the **Hainleite** hills, 4.5 km (3 miles) south of Sonder-shausen, stands the Jagdschloss Zum Possen, once an 18th-century hunting lodge, now an inn. The timber-frame observation tower nearby, dating from 1781, affords beautiful views of the district. **Nordhausen**, situated 20 km (12 miles) to the north, is worth visiting for its attractive timber-frame houses and its 14th-century cathedral, Dom zum Heiligen Kreuz, with a Romanesque crypt.

The extensive façade of the ducal palace in Sondershausen

For hotels and restaurants in this region see pp495–7 and pp534–6

Monument to Wilhelm I in the Kyffhäuser Mountains

Kyffhäuser Mountains **⑤**

Road map D4. **ℹ** *Bad Franken-hausen, Anger 14 (034671-71 7).*

This small mountain range, which runs along the border between Thuringia and Saxony-Anhalt, is not only picturesque but also shrouded in legends and associated with important historic events.

According to one legend, the Emperor Frederick I Barbarossa found his final resting place in one of the caves. Allegedly, he did not drown during the Crusades, as historic records would have us believe, but is waiting here, in the company of six knights. As soon as his beard is long enough to wind three times around the table, it is said, he will return to save Germany from oppression. On the site of the former imperial palace now stands a giant monument with a figure of Barbarossa and an equestrian statue of Emperor Wilhelm I – the work of Bruno Schmitz, erected in 1891–6.

A small health resort, **Bad Frankenhausen**, nestles at the foot of the mountains. It has a number of Gothic churches and a Renaissance palace, now home to a small museum. Nearby, on the **Schlachtberg** (slaughter mountain), the decisive battle in the Peasants' War took place. Today there is a circular pavilion with a vast panoramic picture of the battle, painted in 1971–5.

Gotha **⑥**

Road map D4. **🏠** *48,000.* **🚊 🚌**
ℹ *Hauptmarkt 2 (03621-22 21 38).*
www.gotha.de

From 1640 the old commercial town of Gotha was the capital of Saxe-Gotha and later of Saxe-Coburg-Gotha Duchy, the dynasty from which Prince Albert, Queen Victoria's husband, descended. The vast ducal palace, **Schloss Friedenstein**, built in 1643–55, towers above the city. This mighty rectangular structure was the first Baroque building in Thuringia. Particularly noteworthy are the ballroom, the palace chapel with the ducal sarcophagi in the crypt and the court theatre, built in 1683. The palace museum houses an art collection including works by famous artists such as Peter Paul Rubens, Anton van Dyck, Frans Hals and Jan van Goyen. The palace garden is also worth a visit. To the south of the palace stands a Neo-Renaissance building, which was purpose-built for the ducal art collection. Now it houses the **Museum der Natur**, a natural history museum. The Renaissance town hall (1567–77) in the old town is surrounded by a number of interesting houses.

Gotha played an important role in the German workers' movement: the Socialist Workers' Party (today's SPD), was founded here in 1875. The conference hall has been reconstructed and now houses the **Gedenkstätte der Deutschen Arbeiterbewegung** (memorial to the German workers' movement).

⚓ Schloss Friedenstein
Tel *03621-82 340.* ☐ *May–Oct: 10am–5pm Tue–Sun; Nov–Apr: 10am–4pm Tue–Sun.*

🏛 Gedenkstätte der Deutschen Arbeiterbewegung
Am Tivoli 3. ***Tel*** *(03621) 70 41 27.* ☐ *only by prior arrangement.*

Doorway of the Renaissance town hall on the Hauptmarkt, in Gotha

Thüringer Wald (Thuringian Forest) ❼

Narrow, winding roads lead through the mountains, which are densely covered with spruce forests. Small towns, charming spas and wintersports resorts nestle in the valleys, while the ruins of once fearsome castles occupy the hilltops. This is prime walking country, and Gotha is the best starting point for a walking holiday. For a longer hike, stop in Ilmenau, and from there follow the upward trail marked G, to a hunters' shelter and a foresters' lodge.

Friedrichroda ①
The Neo-Gothic Reinhardsbrunn castle in Friedrichroda was the place where Queen Victoria met her fiancé, Prince Albert von Sachsen-Coburg-Gotha, in 1840.

Drei Gleichen ⑨
This name, meaning "three of the same", refers to three castles – Mühlburg and Burg Gleichen have stood in ruins for centuries, but the third castle, Wachsenburg, has survived and now serves as a hotel.

Arnstadt ⑧
This picturesque town, once the home of Johann Sebastian Bach, features a town hall in the Mannerist style, dating from the late 16th century. Other places of interest are an early-Gothic church and a Baroque palace which is now home to a wax museum.

TIPS FOR WALKERS

Length: 150 km (90 miles).
Stopping places: inns and restaurants in every town.
Suggestions: walk along the Goethe-Wanderweg trail, from Ilmenau. Train journey by Waftbahn, from Gotha via Friedrichroda to Tabarz.

Trusetal ②
The magnificent waterfall in Trusetal, the work of human hands, was built in the mid-19th century. Another site worth visiting is the nearby Marienglashöhle in Friedrichroda, an unusual crystal grotto.

Schmalkalden ③
This charming little town, packed with timber-frame houses, attracts visitors to the Wilhelmsburg, its Renaissance palace, and to Neue Hütte, an interesting old smelting plant dating from 1835.

| 0 km | 75 |
| 0 miles | 75 |

Oberhof ④
This is a popular winter-sports resort, with excellent ski-jumps. In the summer it is worth visiting the Rennsteiggarten, the town's botanical gardens with a vast collection of alpine plants.

Suhl ⑤
Famous from the 16th century as a centre of arms manufacture, Suhl's history can today be gleaned in the local Waffen-museum (armaments museum).

Ilmenau ⑥
This small university town, teeming with life, is the starting point of the so-called Goethe-Wanderweg, a walking trail leading to all the places where the famous poet once stayed.

Paulinzelle ⑦
The 12th-century Romanesque abbey, now in ruins, was once a home for Benedictine monks, but it was later abandoned during the Reformation.

KEY

▬▬	Suggested route
═	Other road
▬	Scenic route
☼	Viewpoint

Erfurt ⓼

The Thuringian capital, Erfurt, is also the oldest town in the region – its earliest historic records date from AD729, and in AD742 a bishopric was founded here. As an important trading post between east and west, the town grew quickly. Erfurt University was founded in 1392; it became a stronghold for radical thought, and Martin Luther was one of its distinguished pupils. Until the 17th century, Erfurt was famous for its red dyes extracted from the madder root; in the 18th century the town became a horticultural centre, and to this day it hosts important horticultural exhibitions.

Picturesque half-timbered houses, lining the Krämerbrücke

Exploring Erfurt

The town, on the banks of the river Gera, is dominated by two hills. On the higher one, **Petersberg**, stands a huge fortress surrounding a Romanesque church, while the lower **Domberg** has two churches, the **Dom St Marien** and the **St Severi-kirche**. From the Domplatz, at the foot of the hill, a row of narrow streets leads to Fisch-markt. If you cross the river here, you will get to Erfurt's old commercial district and its market square, the Anger.

⛪ Dom St Marien

Domberg. *Tel* (0361) 646 12 65.
◯ May–Oct: 9am–5pm Mon–Sat, noon–5pm Sun; Nov–Apr: 10am–4pm Mon–Sat, noon–4pm Sun. **Maria Gloriosa** ◯ closed for renovation work until 2007. 📷
The wide stairs leading from Domplatz to the main entrance of the cathedral provide a good view over the 14th-century Gothic presbytery, which is supported by a massive vaulted substructure, known as the Kavaten. The main body of the cathedral dates from the 15th century, but its huge towers are the

remains of an earlier Romanesque building. **Maria Gloriosa**, a huge bell 2.5 m (8 ft) in diameter, hangs in the centre tower. Cast by Gerhard Wou in 1497, it is one of the largest bells in the world. The church interior has well preserved Gothic decorations and rich furnishings. Particularly valuable are the 14th- and 15th-century stained-glass windows, the Gothic stalls

Rich furnishings in the Gothic interior of Dom St Marien

(c.1370) and Wolfram, a Romanesque bronze candelabra, (c.1160), shaped like a man.

⛪ St Severi-Kirche

Domberg. *Tel* (0361) 57 69 60.
◯ Nov–Feb: 1pm–4pm Tue–Thu, 10am–3pm Mon, Fri–Sat; Mar–Oct: 10am–4pm, 1pm–4pm Sun.
This five-nave Gothic hall-church, next to the cathedral, dates from the late 13th and early 14th century. Inside it has the Gothic sarcophagus of St Severus, from about 1365, a huge font of 1467 and interesting Gothic altars.

⊞ Fischmarkt

This small market square, with its Neo-Gothic town hall (1870–74), is surrounded by houses dating from various periods, including the 16th-century Renaissance buildings **Zum Breiten Herd** (No. 13, To the Wide Hearth) and **Zum Roten Ochsen** (No. 7, To the Red Ox). On the streets off the market square are three Gothic churches: Michaeliskirche, opposite the ruins of the late-Gothic university buildings, the twin-nave Allerheiligenkirche (late 13th to early 14th century), and the ex-Dominican Predigerkirche.

⊞ Krämerbrücke

The "merchant bridge" which spans the River Gera is one of Erfurt's most interesting structures. The present stone bridge was built around 1325. It is lined by 32 houses with shops, dating mainly from the 17th to 19th centuries, which replaced its 60 original medieval houses. On its eastern viaduct stands Ägidienkirche, a 14th-century Gothic church.

⛪ Augustinerkloster–Augustinerkirche

Augustinerstr. 10. *Tel* (0361) 576 60 10. 📷 Apr–Oct: 10am–noon, 2–4pm Mon–Sat; Nov–Mar: 10am–noon, 2–3pm Mon–Sat. 📷 Sun after mass. 📷
This early Gothic church was built for Augustinian monks at the end of the 13th century. Particularly noteworthy are its original Gothic stained-glass windows. In the neighbouring monastery, the reconstructed cell where Martin Luther lived as a monk can be admired.

Fischmarkt, surrounded by houses from various periods

🏛 Stadtmuseum

Johannesstr. 169. **Tel** *(0361) 655 56
50.* ◯ *10am–6pm Tue–Sun.*
Erfurt's history museum is
housed in a beautiful, late-
Renaissance building called
Zum Stockfisch (To the Dried
Cod), built in 1607.

🏯 Anger

Now pedestrianized, this is a
market square and Erfurt's
main shopping street, lined
with attractive 19th-century
mansions and commercial
premises. There are two
Gothic churches: **Kaufmanns-
kirche** and **Reglerkirche**,
with a huge Gothic altar
dating from around 1470. At
Nos. 37 and 38 there is the
Dacherödensches Haus, a
complex of beautiful Renaissance buildings.

🏛 Angermuseum

Anger 18. **Tel** *(0361) 55 45 611.*
◯ *10am–6pm Tue–Sun.*
Barfüßerkirche Barfüßerstr. 20
Tel *(0361) 64 64 010.* ◯ *Apr–Oct:
10am–1pm & 2–6pm Tue–Sun.* 🖾
The museum, housed in a
Baroque building, has a
collection of decorative and
sacred arts including paintings
by Lucas Cranach the Elder,
and 19th- and 20th-century
German works. One of its
rooms is decorated with
Expressionist murals (1923–4)
by Erich Heckel. The
medieval section is in the
presbytery of the **Barfüßerkirche**, a former Franciscan

church that was destroyed
during World War II.

🏛 EGA and Gartenbaumuseum

Cyriaksburg, Gothaer Str. 38. **Tel**
(0361) 223 22 0. ◯ *9am–5pm daily
(to 8pm May–Oct).* **Museum Tel**
(0361) 22 39 90. ◯ *10am–6pm
Tue–Sun.* ◉ *Jan & Feb.* 🖾
On the hill around Erfurt's
ruined castle (c.1480) are the
grounds of the International
Garden Show (*Erfurter
Gartenausstellung International*). As well as exhibition
halls, show gardens and palm
houses, there is a museum of
horticulture and beekeeping.

Environs

Molsdorf, 10 km (6 miles) to
the southeast, has a lovely
16th-century Baroque palace
set in landscaped parkland,
with a museum.

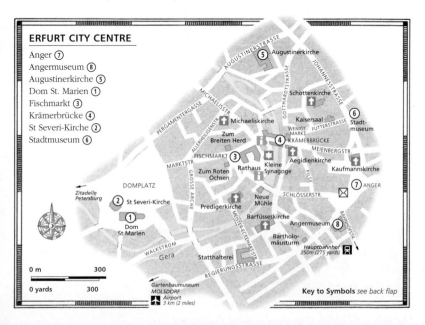

ERFURT CITY CENTRE

Anger ⑦
Angermuseum ⑧
Augustinerkirche ⑤
Dom St. Marien ①
Fischmarkt ③
Krämerbrücke ④
St Severi-Kirche ②
Stadtmuseum ⑥

0 m   300
0 yards   300

Key to Symbols *see back flap*

Weimar ❾

Had it not been for the enlightened sponsorship of its rulers, Weimar would have become just another residential town in Thuringia. The town flourished, particularly under Duke Carl Augustus and his wife Anna Amalia, when Goethe, Schiller and Herder lived here. Famous 19th- and 20th-century residents included Franz Liszt, Richard Strauss, Friedrich Nietzsche and many distinguished writers and artists associated with the Bauhaus School, which was founded here in 1919. It also gave its name to the Weimar Republic, the democratic German State, lasting from World War I to 1933.

Exploring Weimar

Weimar is relatively small and most of its tourist attractions are near the town centre, on the left bank of the Ilm River. In the north of the centre are the Neues Museum and the Stadtmuseum (municipal museum). Many interesting buildings can be found around Theaterplatz, from where you proceed towards the Markt to visit the ducal palace. In the south of the centre are the former homes of Goethe and Liszt.

🏛 Neues Museum

Weimarplatz 5. *Tel (03643) 54 59 63.* ⬜ *Apr–Oct: 11am–6pm Tue–Sun; Nov–Mar: 11am–4pm Tue–Sun.*
This Neo-Renaissance building, once the Landesmuseum (regional museum), was transformed into a gallery in 1999. It displays modern art, with its central collection made up of works by Paul Maenz.

🏛 Stadtmuseum

Karl-Liebknecht-Str. 5–9. *Tel (03643) 90 38 68.* ⬛ *currently closed for renovation.*
This museum is devoted to the history of Weimar, but it also holds an interesting natural history collection. It is housed in a Neo-Classical house, which was built in the late 18th century for the publisher Justin Bertuch.

St Peter und St Paul, also known as the Herderkirche

🎭 Deutsches Nationaltheater

Theaterplatz 2. *Tel (03643) 75 53 01.*
The present Neo-Classical building, built in 1906–7 to a design by Heilmann & Littmann, is the third theatre to stand on this site. Famous conductors who worked here include Franz Liszt and Richard Strauss, and it was also the venue for the world premiere of Wagner's *Lohengrin.* In 1919 the National Congress sat in the Nationaltheater and passed the new constitution for the Weimar Republic. In front of the theatre is a monument to Goethe (who founded the theatre) and Schiller, by the sculptor Ernst Rietschel (1857).

🏛 Bauhaus-Museum

Theaterplatz.
Tel (03643) 54 59 61. ⬜ *10am–6pm daily.* 🖼
This museum is devoted to the famous art school, which was founded in Weimar in 1919, moved to Dessau in 1925 *(see p154)* and later, in 1933, to Berlin *(see p88).*

🏛 Wittumspalais

Theaterplatz.
Tel (03643) 54 53 77. ⬜ *Apr–Sep: 10am–6pm Tue–Sun; Oct–Mar: 10am–4pm Tue–Sun.* 🖼
The Dowager Duchess Anna Amalia lived in this Baroque palace, designed by Johann Gottfried Schlegel and built in 1767–9. Visitors can admire fine interiors and mementos of the Enlightenment figure Christoph-Martin Wieland.

🏛 Schillerhaus

Schillerstr. 12.
Tel (03643) 54 53 50. ⬜ *Apr–Oct: 9am–6pm Wed–Mon; Nov–Mar: 9am–4pm Wed–Mon.* 🖼
The museum is in the house where Friedrich Schiller wrote *Wilhelm Tell* (1804) and spent the last years of his life.

⛪ St Peter und St Paul

Herderplatz. *Tel (03643) 85 15 18.* ⬜ *Apr–Oct: 10am–noon, 2–4pm daily; Nov–Mar: 10am–noon, 2–3pm daily.*
This late-Gothic hall-church has Baroque furnishings and an original altar painted by the Cranachs. It is also known as the Herderkirche, after the poet who preached here.

🏛 Kirms-Krackow-Haus

Jakobstr. 10. *Tel (03643) 54 53 83.* ⬜ *May–Oct: 10am–1pm, 2–6pm Tue–Sun.* ⬛ *Nov–Apr.* 🖼
This Renaissance house, which was extended in the late 18th century, is now the Herder-Museum and a literary centre.

♟ Schloss

Burgplatz 4. **Schlossmuseum**
Tel (03643) 54 59 60. ⬜ *Apr–Oct: 10am–6pm Tue–Sun; Nov–Mar: 10am–4pm Tue–Sun.* 🖼
This vast ducal castle was rebuilt in the Neo-Classical style for Duke Carl Augustus. It has original interiors and fine paintings by the Cranachs and Peter Paul Rubens.

The Schloss in Burgplatz, with its tall Renaissance tower

For hotels and restaurants in this region see pp495–7 and pp534–6

Picturesque Baroque summer residence known as Schloss Belvedere

VISITORS' CHECKLIST

Road map D4. 🏠 *62,000.* 🚉
Schopenhauerstr. 🚌 *Washing-tonstr.* 🛈 *Markt 10 (03643-74 50).* **www.**weimar.de
🎭 *Bach-Tage (Mar), Spiegelzelt (May/Jun), Kunstfest (Aug/Sep), Fest an Goethes Geburtstag 28 Aug), Liszt-Tage (Oct), Zwiebelmarkt (Oct).*

♣ Herzogin-Anna-Amalia Bibliothek

Platz der Demokratie 4. **Tel** *(03643) 54 52 00.* ◐ *closed for renovation until Oct 2007.*

This former Mannerist palace, also known as Grünes Schloss (green castle), became the duchess' library, in 1761–6. Its oval Rococo interior is one of the finest of its type in Europe.

♣ Schloss Belvedere

Tel *(03643) 54 54 00.* ◐ *Apr–mid-Oct: 10am–6pm Tue–Sun; mid-Oct–Nov; 10am–4pm Tue–Sun.* 🖾

This ducal summer residence, which was built 1724–32 in Belvedere Park, has a fine collection of decorative art from the Rococo period, and a collection of vintage vehicles.

🏛 Goethe-Museum

Frauenplan 1. **Tel** *(03643) 54 53 00.* ◐ *as Wittumspalais opposite.* 🖾

This house was presented to Goethe by the Duke Carl Augustus. It was here that the writer studied and wrote his most famous work, *Faust.* Today the museum shows items associated with Goethe and other Enlightenment poets from Weimar.

♣ Goethes Gartenhaus

Park an der Ilm. ◐ *as Wittumspalais opposite.* 🖾

Goethe's first home in Weimar, and later his summer house, this small villa stands in the pleasant park alongside the River Ilm which Goethe helped design.

♬ Liszt-Haus

Marienstr. 17. **Tel** *(03643) 54 54 01.* ◐ *Apr–Sep: 10am–4pm daily.* ◐ *Oct–Mar: 10am–6pm daily.* 🖾

Franz Liszt lived here in 1869–86, while he composed the *Hungarian Rhapsody.* His apartment and the room in which he worked have been preserved to this day.

Environs

Buchenwald, 8 km (5 miles) north of Weimar, was the site of a concentration camp set up by the Nazis. During the period 1937 to 1945, over 54,000 people were killed here. It is now a place of remembrance, a museum and a documentation centre.

🏛 Buchenwald

Tel *(03643) 43 02 00.* ◐ *Apr–Nov: 10am–6pm Tue–Sun; Nov–Mar: 10am–4pm Tue–Sun.*

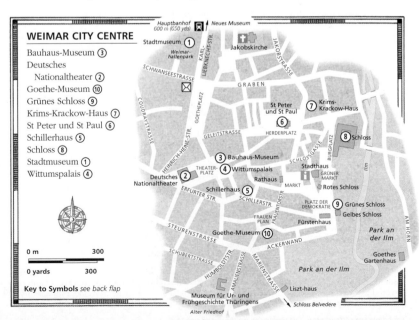

WEIMAR CITY CENTRE

Bauhaus-Museum ③
Deutsches Nationaltheater ②
Goethe-Museum ⑩
Grünes Schloss ⑨
Krims-Krackow-Haus ⑦
St Peter und St Paul ⑥
Schillerhaus ⑤
Schloss ⑧
Stadtmuseum ①
Wittumspalais ④

0 m   300
0 yards 300

Key to Symbols *see back flap*

The modest Gothic town hall on Marktplatz, in Jena

Jena ⑩

Road map D4. 🏚 100,000. 🚆 🚍
ℹ *Johannisstr. 23 (03641-49 80 50).*
www.jena.de

Jena is famous for the world-renowned Carl-Zeiss–Jena Optical Works and its university, founded in 1558. One of the most important schools in Germany, its former tutors included Schiller, Fichte and Hegel. The oldest university building is the **Collegium Jenense**. The main building was built by Theodor Fischer in 1905–8. The complex includes a 120-m (394-ft) cylindrical tower block, completed in 1972 and known as the "phallus Jenensis".

In the town's main square, Marktplatz, stands the late-Gothic **Rathaus** (town hall), dating from the early 15th century. Once every hour, a figure known as the Schnapp-hans tries to catch a ball, a symbol of the human soul. The Gothic church of **St. Michael** nearby was built in the 15th and the 16th centuries. The **Stadtmusem Alte Göhre** has an interesting collection of regional history. In Unterer Markt the **Roman-tikerhaus** is worth a visit; formerly the home of Johann Gottlieb Fichte, it now houses a museum devoted to the Romantic period.

Also worth visiting are the fascinating **Optisches Museum** on the history of the Carl Zeiss Works and the **Zeiss-Planetarium**, the world's oldest of its type. In the north is the **Goethe-Gedenkstätte**, a museum devoted to Goethe's work as poet, politician and scientist.

🏛 **Stadtmuseum Göhre**
Markt 7. **Tel** *(03641) 359 80.*
◯ *10am–5pm Fri–Wed,
2–10pm Thu, 11am–6pm Sat–Sun.*

🏛 **Romantikerhaus**
Unterer Markt 12A. **Tel** *(03641) 44 32 63.* ◯ *10am–5pm Tue–Sun.*

🏛 **Optisches Museum**
Carl-Zeiss-Platz 12. **Tel** *(03641) 44 31 65.* ◯ *10am–4:30pm Tue–Fri, 11am–5pm Sat.*
Historical Zeiss-Workshop 📷
11:30am Sat.

Environs
Dornburg, 12 km (8 miles) to the northeast, has three palaces: the Altes Schloss, a Gothic castle transformed in the Renaissance; the Renaissanceschloss (1539–47) and the charming Rokoko-schloss (1736–41).

Rudolstadt ⑪

Road map D4. 🏚 28,000. 🚆 🚍
ℹ *Marktstr. 57 (03672-42 45 43).*
🎭 *Tanz-und Folk Fest (Jul).*

Although Rudolstadt has the Gothic-Renaissance St Andreas church, a fascinating 16th-century town hall and some historic houses in the old town, tourists come here mainly to see majestic **Schloss Heidecksburg**, a vast palace perched on a hill. Its present form is mainly the result of reconstruction work carried out in the mid-18th century by Johann Christoph Knöffel and Gottfried Heinrich Krone. Inside are some beautifully

Baroque Schloss Heidecksburg towering over Rudolstadt

arranged Rococo state rooms. The museum also holds a splendid porcelain collection, a gallery of paintings and the so-called Schiller's Room. From the castle there are fantastic views of the Schwarza valley.

♣ **Schloss Heidecksburg**
Schlossbezirk 1. **Tel** *(03672) 42 90 22.*
◯ *Apr–Oct: 10am–6pm Tue–Sun; Nov–Mar: 10am–5pm Tue–Sun.*

Entrance gate to the 11th-century Schloss Ranis, near Saalfeld

Saalfeld ⑫

Road map D4. 🏚 34,000. 🚆 🚍
ℹ *Am Markt 6 (03671-339 50).*

Saalfeld flourished in the 14th–16th centuries. From 1680 it was the seat of the Duchy of Sachsen–Saalfeld, and the magnificent Baroque **Schloss**, built between 1676 and 1720, dates from this period. The former palace chapel, now used as a concert hall, is particularly noteworthy. Also worth visiting is the **Johanniskirche**, a late-Gothic hall-church with interesting furnishings, a valuable Gothic Holy Tomb and the sculpted life-size figure of John the Baptist, carved by Hans Gottwalt, a student of Tilman Riemenschneider.

Another interesting building in Saalfeld is the early-Renaissance **Rathaus** (town hall), built in 1529–37. The town also has remarkably well preserved medieval town fortifications with gates and towers. In the southern part of the town stands the **Hoher Schwarm**, ruins of a Gothic castle from the 13th century. In Garnsdorf, on the outskirts of Saalfeld, are the **Feen-grotten**, grottoes created by both natural and human activity. From the mid-16th century until 1846 alum slate was mined in this cave, called "Jeremiasglück" (Jeremiah's good fortune). It was finally closed due to humidity, but the dripping water has created some astonishingly colourful stalagmites and stalactites.

♣ Feengrotten
Feengrottenweg 2. *Tel (03671) 550 40.* ☐ Mar–Oct: 9am–5pm daily; Nov: 10am–3:30pm Sat–Sun; Dec–Feb: 10am–3:30pm daily.

Environs
From Saalfeld it is worth taking a trip to the Hohenwarte-Talsperre, an artificial lake and paradise for watersports enthusiasts. **Schloss Ranis**, a scenic hill-top castle, was probably built in the 11th century for an emperor. Later it became the seat of the Thuringian landgraves, Meißen margraves and the counts of Schwarzburg. Now it houses a museum of the region's natural history.

Gera ⑬

Road map D4. 🏠 *121,000.* 🚃 🚌 🛈 *Heinrich Str. 35 (0365-830 44 80).* 🎭 *Geraer Höhlerfest (Sep).*

The second largest town in Thuringia, Gera is not very impressive at first sight, although it has many attractions, including a picturesque **Rathaus** (town hall) whose oldest, Renaissance part dates from 1573–6. The Geraer Elleblon, on the right-hand side of the entrance, is a unit of measurement equal to 57 cm (22 in). A short distance from the market square, in Nikolaiberg, you will find the **Salvatorkirche**. This Baroque church received its Secession-style interior in 1903, after a fire. The theatre (1900–02) was designed in the same style, by

Picturesque Altenburg Castle complex

Heinrich Seeling. The Küchengarten (kitchen garden) surrounds the ruins of **Schloss Osterstein** of which only the Baroque orangerie remains. It now houses the **Kunstsammlung**, with paintings by Lucas Cranach the Elder, Max Liebermann and others.

Otto Dix, a leading artist of the *Neue Sachlichkeit*, was born in Gera, and his birthplace has been turned into the **Otto-Dix-Haus**.

♣ Kunstsammlung
Küchengartenallee 4. *Tel (0365) 832 21 47.* ☐ 1–8pm Tue, 10am–5pm Wed–Fri, 11am–6pm Sat & Sun.

🏛 Otto-Dix-Haus
Mohrenplatz 4. *Tel (0365) 832 49 27.* ☐ 1–8pm Tue, 10am–5pm Wed–Fri, 11am–6pm Sat & Sun.

The multi-coloured Renaissance doorway of the Rathaus in Gera

Altenburg ⑭

Road map E4. 🏠 *45,000.* 🚃 🚌 🛈 *Moritzstr. 21 (03447-51 28 00).* 🎭 *Musikfestival (Aug/Sep); Prinzenraubfest (Jul).*

In Germany, Altenburg is known as "Skatstadt", the town of skat, a traditional and very popular card game. Altenburg also has some fascinating historic remains. The **Schloss** (ducal castle), which towers over the old town, has a 10th-century tower, reconstructed mainly in the Baroque style. Today the castle houses the **Spielkartenmuseum** (museum of playing cards). The late-Gothic castle church is also worth seeing. It has rich Baroque furnishings and an organ which was played by the composer Bach. Next to the castle gardens is the **Lindenau-Museum**, with Augustus von Lindenau's collection of 16th–20th century paintings and sculptures, including works by Simone Martini, Fra Angelico, Auguste Rodin, Ernst Barlach and Max Liebermann. The old town, at the foot of the hill, has a beautiful Renaissance town hall with an enormous octagonal tower. In Brühl Platz is a fountain and the figures of skat players, as well as the Baroque **Seckendorffsche Palais** and the Renaissance chancellery.

🏛 Schloss und Spielkartenmuseum
Schloss 2–4. *Tel (03447) 31 51 93.* ☐ 10am–5pm Tue–Sun.

🏛 Lindenau-Museum
Gabelentzstraße 5. *TEL (03447) 895 53.* ☐ noon–6pm Tue–Fri, 10am–6pm Sat, Sun.

SOUTHERN GERMANY

Southern Germany at a Glance

The southern regions of Germany, with their wealth of natural beauty, historic sights and folk culture, are particularly attractive to tourists. This part of the country includes two *Länder*: Bavaria, famous for its Alps, beer and the fairytale castle of Ludwig II at Neuschwanstein, and Baden-Württemberg, whose highlights include the Bodensee lake, Heidelberg and taking a trip on the scenic Schwarzwaldbahn railway line between Offenburg and Villingen.

LOCATOR MAP

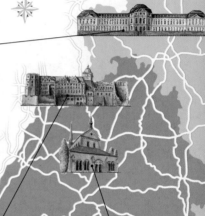

Würzburg Residenz
Set in a magnificent park on the eastern outskirts of the town, this imposing bishop's palace was built between 1720 and 1744, to a design by Balthasar Neumann. The palace is constructed in a U-shape, with a central pavilion flanked by four two-storey courts.

BADEN-
WÜRTTEMBERG
(see pp288–327)

Heidelberg Castle *is one of Germany's finest examples of a Gothic-Renaissance fortress. Its origins go back to the 13th century, but new buildings sprang up around the inner courtyard during the 16th century as the castle gained importance as a royal residence.*

Maulbronn Abbey,
founded in the heart of the Stromberg region in 1147, is one of the best-preserved abbeys in Europe. It was established by Cistercian monks with the bequest of a knight named Walter von Lomersheim and provides a graphic account of the austere life led by the monks.

Vierzehnheiligen Church, *built in 1743–72 to a design by Balthasar Neumann, is one of the most famous examples of South German Rococo. The monumental "Altar of Mercy" (Gnadenaltar) includes statues of the Fourteen Saints of the Intercession, to whom the church is dedicated.*

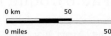

0 km   50

0 miles   50

BAVARIA
(See pp238–87)

Nördlingen Town Hall *was built in the 14th century, but its present form dates from the early 17th century. Prisoners used to be held in a space beneath the external stone stairway. By the wooden entrance is a wall carving of a medieval fool bearing a German inscription that translates as "Now there are two of us."*

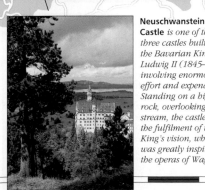

Neuschwanstein Castle *is one of the three castles built for the Bavarian King Ludwig II (1845–86), involving enormous effort and expenditure. Standing on a high rock, overlooking a stream, the castle was the fulfilment of the King's vision, which was greatly inspired by the operas of Wagner.*

The Frauenkirche *in Munich was completed in 1488 and features two 99-m (325-ft) high towers crowned with copper domes. The church is one of the largest in southern Germany.*

The Baroque in Southern Germany

Because of religious conflicts and the Thirty Years' War (1618–48), the Baroque style did not flourish in Germany until the 18th century. Then it did so most lavishly in the southern, Catholic regions of the country. Here, influenced by Italian architecture, the Baroque reached new heights of flamboyance: the impressive spaciousness of religious buildings provided the setting for dynamic compositions in sculpture, fine stuccowork and vividly coloured *trompe l'oeil* paintings. Southern Germany's major artists of the 18th century included Balthasar Neumann, François Cuvilliés and the Asam brothers.

The main altar in Rohr, *which was created by Egid Quirin Asam in 1723, is in the form of a proscenium (stage) with wings. The sculptural group depicts the Assumption of the Virgin Mary into Heaven.*

Ceiling frescos *were a basic element of the Baroque interior. This example by Johann Baptist Zimmermann in the Wieskirche in Steingaden, presents a glowing vision of the afterlife.*

Galleries with curved balustrades add vitality to the interior.

Light plays a vital role in enlivening the interior decoration.

Figures of saints *clad in flowing, dynamic robes and standing in curving, asymmetrical poses, complement the rich iconography and complex composition of the altars.*

18th-century *monasteries in southern Germany, like this one in Ottobeuren with its imposing stairway, are reminiscent of royal residences.*

Late Baroque church *façades, such as that of the Theatinerkirche in Munich, have a "rippled" design that creates an unusual effect of light and shadow.*

Vaults with fine painting and exquisite stuccowork round off the architectural elements.

The monstrance in Passau *is a fine example of the art of 18th-century goldsmiths, who created these receptacles for the consecrated Host.*

The pulpit and other furnishings are designed to blend harmoniously with the decoration.

Stuccowork *fills every interior space that is not decorated with paintings. Sometimes gilded, sometimes white, it may depict complex scenes or, in some cases, be adorned with ornamental designs.*

BAROQUE INTERIORS

Although they may seem over-elaborate, the late Baroque interiors of southern German churches are carefully-planned compositions intended to have a powerful effect. Their magnificent combination of architecture, sculpture and painting, and often organ music, resulted in *"Gesamtkunstwerk"* – a homogenous work that combines all the arts.

BAROQUE RESIDENCES

South German Baroque was not limited solely to religious architecture. As well as the magnificent monasteries and pilgrimage churches, it was also the inspiration for the impressive residences that were built by abbots as well as by bishops. As in the rest of Europe, these were modelled on the French royal palace in Versailles with its imposing grandeur, striking interiors and breathtaking gardens.

The Baroque vestibule *in the Neues Schloss in Schleissheim* (see pp264–5) *is decorated with exquisite stuccowork and frescos.*

Schloss Nymphenburg *was a summer residence of the rulers of Bavaria. It has a grand driveway and a park* (see pp224–5).

Schloss Favorite *is a small palace that forms part of a huge Baroque-style residence in Ludwigsburg* (see pp306–7).

The German Alps

Part of Germany extends into a fairly moderate section of the Alps, Europe's highest mountain range. They stretch from the Bodensee (Lake Constance) to Berchtesgaden. A section of the northern calcareous Alps belonging to the Eastern Alps of Allgäu, Bavaria and Salzburg falls within Germany. The mountains are a holidaymaker's paradise all year round. In the summer mountain walks can be enjoyed, with well-marked trails, as well as climbing, hang-gliding and paragliding; in the winter skiing is possible in superbly equipped resorts.

Alpine Chough

Alpine meadows *are rich pasture lands, providing premium quality hay. They are also home to a rich variety of wildflowers.*

Mountain streams *have, over the years, cut a path through the rocks to create picturesque ravines. One of the most beautiful is this one at Wimbachklamm.*

Mountain peaks with their breathtaking jagged rocks.

Local architecture blends happily into the landscape.

THE ALPINE LAKES

A melting glacier created many lakes in Bavaria. Their clear, unpolluted waters attract all kinds of watersports enthusiasts, while the picturesque surroundings are equally popular with other recreational users.

The Königssee, with its crystal-clear waters, is located high in the Berchtesgaden National Park.

The Watzmann is Germany's second highest peak.

Schwarzeck

Steinplatte

Reit im Winkl

Schliersee

Oberaudorf

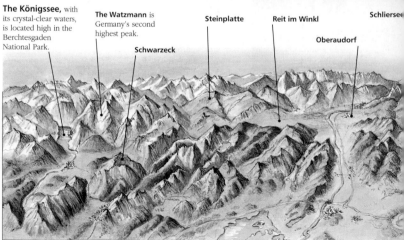

The Zugspitze, *at 2,963m (9,700 ft), is the highest peak in all of Germany.*

ALPINE FLORA AND FAUNA

Alpine vegetation varies according to height above sea level. On the lower slopes are mixed deciduous forests. Higher up are Alpine forests, generally coniferous. Above the tree line, dwarf mountain pine grow and higher still are stretches of high-altitude meadows. Beyond this is bare rock. Wild goats are found above the tree line and chamois in the foothills.

The Alpine ibex *lives only in the Italian and Swiss Alps. This wild goat with long, backward-curving horns is a rare sight.*

The mouflon *is a wild sheep with large horns. It is also found in Corsica and Sardinia.*

Alpine rock jasmine *forms carpets of colour on the mountain slopes.*

The Alpine pasqueflower *is a white variant of the species that tolerates the harsh soil and climatic conditions of its Alpine habitat.*

The peacock butterfly *is a common Eurasian species that has adapted successfully to the harsh Alpine environment.*

Alpine thrift, *with its round heads of pink and purple flowers, is a delightful sight.*

Tegernsee

Kochelsee is overlooked by one of the largest hydroelectric power stations in Germany.

Garmisch-Partenkirchen is one of the venues of the annual Four Ski Jumps competition.

Walchensee

Alpspitze

The Zugspitze is the highest peak in Germany.

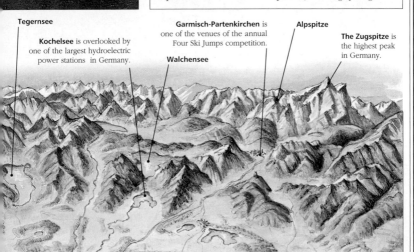

MUNICH

The capital of Bavaria, Munich is sometimes called "Germany's secret capital". Lying right at the heart of Europe, the city rapidly overshadowed once powerful neighbours, such as Ingolstadt, Augsburg and Nuremberg, to become southern Germany's main metropolis. With its vibrant cosmopolitan atmosphere, fine buildings, museums and shops, it is one of the country's most popular tourist destinations.

The citizens of Munich have been known for centuries for their love of the arts. The masterpieces that were created here during the Baroque and Rococo periods were equal to Italian and French works.

In the 19th century, the town's development continued along Neo-Classical lines, gaining for it the name of "Athens on Isar". Just how appropriate the name is can be seen when strolling along Ludwigstrasse or Königsplatz or visiting the Glyptothek, which houses Ludwig I's collection of Greek and Roman sculptures.

In the late 19th century the Munich Academy of Fine Arts was amongst Europe's best art schools. Not many cities have as great a choice of world-class theatres, operas and museums as can be found here in Munich.

But it is not only art that gives Munich its unique charm. The country's biggest folk festival, the Oktoberfest, is held each year in Theresienwiese, where visitors to the town can join in the revelries or just sit and watch, ordering a plate of sauerkraut with sausages and washing it down with some of the excellent Bavarian beer.

When planning a shopping trip to Munich visitors can be sure that its shops are equal to those of Paris and Milan, not only in the breadth of their range but also in terms of their prices.

The town is also one of Germany's main centres of high-tech and media industries. Many TV stations and film studios, as well as over 300 book and newspaper publishers, have their main offices in Munich.

The Neo-Gothic Rathaus in Marienplatz, Munich's central square

◁ Interior of the Baroque Asamkirche, built between 1733 and 1746 by the Asam brothers

Exploring Munich

Munich, the capital of Bavaria, is exceptionally rich
in interesting museums, churches and historic
sights. This urban conurbation of about 1.2
million inhabitants increasingly swallows
up the neighbouring areas. Many tourist
attractions are located outside the town
centre but, thanks to excellent public
transport, it is easy to visit them. It is
worth taking a trip to Nymphenburg
to visit the famous palace and gardens
there. Another interesting excursion
is a stroll along Leopoldstraße or
Theresienwiese, where the huge,
annual Oktoberfest is held.

GETTING THERE

Munich is an important railway junction
and has its own international airport. It
also has motorway connections with all
the major towns and cities in Germany.

The distinctive towers of Munich's skyline

STAR SIGHTS

Churches

Asamkirche ⑥
Bürgersaal ❶
Dreifaltigkeitskirche ❸
Frauenkirche ❹
Ludwigskirche ㉑
Michaelskirche ❷
Theatinerkirche (St Cajetan) ⑮

Buildings

Altes Rathaus ❾
Bayerische Staatsbibliothek ⑳
Feldherrnhalle ⑭
Neues Rathaus ❿
Propyläen ㉗
Residenz (pp216–17) ⑬
*Schloss Nymphenburg
  (pp224–5)* ㉙
Villa Stuck ㉝

Museums and Galleries

Alte Pinakothek (pp222–3) ㉓
Archäologische
  Staatssammlung ⑲

Bayerisches National-
  museum ⑰
Deutsches Jagd- und
  Fischereimuseum ❺
*Deutsches Museum
  (pp228–9)* ㉜
Glyptothek ㉕
Haus der Kunst ⑯
Lenbachhaus ㉘
Neue Pinakothek ㉒
Pinakothek der Moderne ㉔
Schack-Galerie ⑱
Staatliche Antiken-
  sammlungen ㉖
Stadtmuseum ❼
Völkerkundemuseum ⑪

Other Attractions

Bavaria-Filmstadt ㉞
Englischer Garten ㉛
Hofbräuhaus ⑫
Olympiapark ㉚
Theresienwiese ㉟
Viktualienmarkt ❽

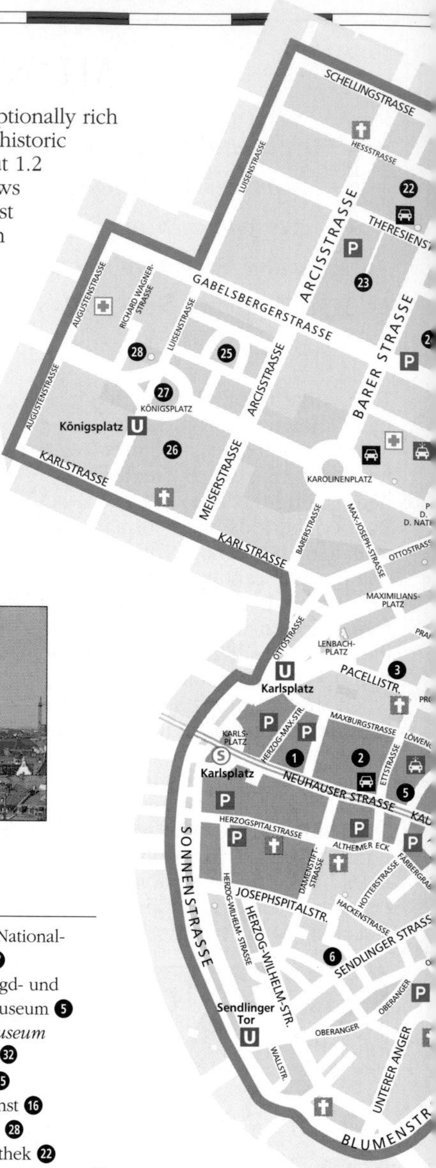

KEY

▪	Street-by-Street map *pp210–11*
P	Parking
🛈	Tourist information
⊠	Post office
🚕	Taxi-rank
✝	Church, cathedral, chapel
Ⓢ	S-Bahn
U	U-Bahn

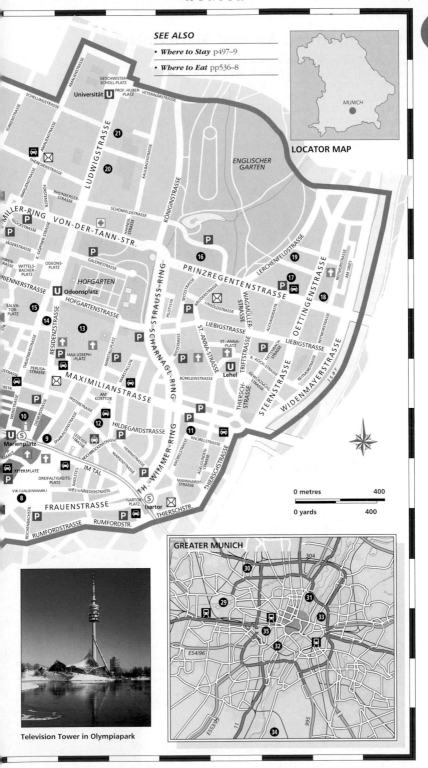

SEE ALSO

- *Where to Stay* p497–9

- *Where to Eat* pp536–8

LOCATOR MAP

ENGLISCHER GARTEN

MUNICH

GREATER MUNICH

0 metres 400

0 yards 400

Television Tower in Olympiapark

Street-by-Street: Around Marienplatz

In medieval times, Marienplatz was Munich's salt- and corn-market. The origins of Munich itself lie with a handful of monks who built their abbey here, giving the place its name (from the word for 'monks') and its heraldic arms. In 1158 Welf Henry the Lion bestowed town status on Munich and 30 years later the town was allocated to the Wittelsbachs, who soon established a residence here. During the Reformation, Munich became a bastion of Catholicism and an important centre of the Counter-Reformation. Its magnificent churches, the Altes Rathaus (old town hall) and the Residenz all bear witness to that era.

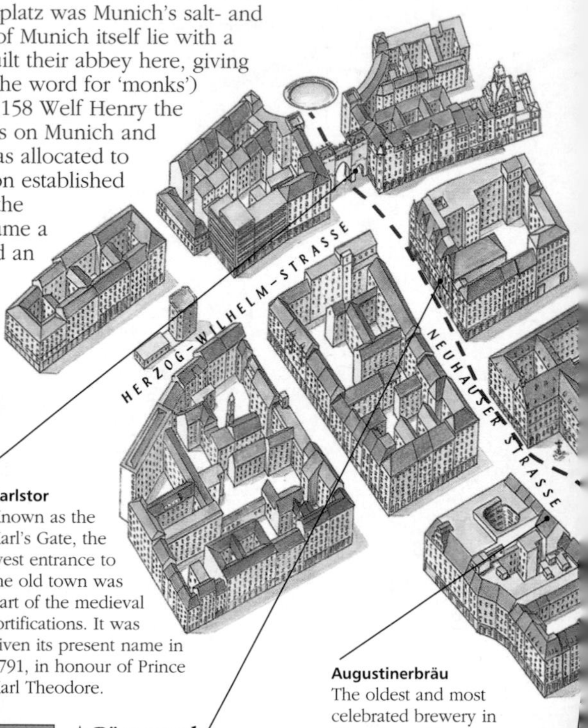

Karlstor
Known as the Karl's Gate, the west entrance to the old town was part of the medieval fortifications. It was given its present name in 1791, in honour of Prince Karl Theodore.

Augustinerbräu
The oldest and most celebrated brewery in Munich was founded by Augustinian monks in 1328. It currently occupies two 19th-century houses with picturesque façades.

★ Bürgersaal
Bürgersaal was built in 1709–10 for a Marian congregation (followers of the Virgin Mary), as a place of meeting and worship. It includes an upper and lower church. Rupert Mayer, an opponent of Nazism, is buried in the crypt. He was beatified in 1987 ❶

| 0 metres | 50 |
| 0 yards | 50 |

Michaelskirche
The interior of St Michael's Church is surprisingly large. The massive barrel vaulting over the nave is the second largest after St Peter's Basilica in Rome ❷

STAR SIGHTS

★ Altes Rathaus

★ Bürgersaal

★ Frauenkirche

★ Neues Rathaus

KEY

 ▬ ▬ ▬ Suggested route

Deutsches Jagd- und Fischereimuseum
A huge collection of hunting and fishing exhibits is housed in the Augustinerkloster. The deconsecrated church, which has an ornate Rococo interior, once belonged to the Augustinian order ❺

LOCATOR MAP

★ **Frauenkirche**
Partially demolished in 1944–45, this imposing church, with its landmark dome-topped towers, has been rebuilt along Gothic lines ❹

★ **Neues Rathaus**
The ornate façade of the new town hall includes figures from Bavarian legend and history. The bronze statue at the top is the "Münchner Kindl" – a character that features in the city's heraldic arms ❿

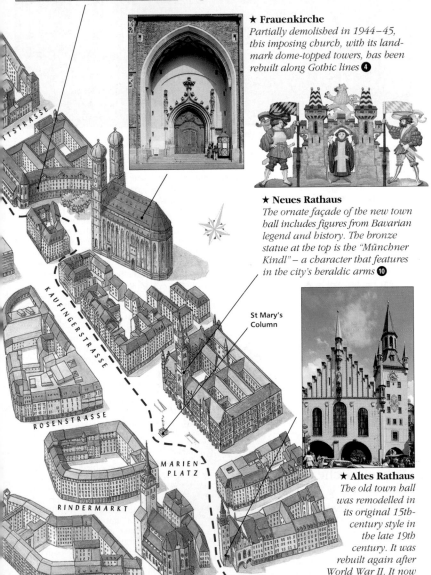

St Mary's Column

★ **Altes Rathaus**
The old town hall was remodelled in its original 15th-century style in the late 19th century. It was rebuilt again after World War II. It now houses a collection of historic toys ❾

Interior of the Bürgersaal, featuring original 19th-century frescoes

Bürgersaal ❶

Neuhauser Straße 14. **Map** 1 F4.
U or **S** Karlsplatz. 🚋 18, 19, 20,
21, 27. **Lower church hall** ◯
8am–7pm daily. **Upper church hall**
◯ Apr–Oct: 9am–5pm daily;
Nov–Mar: 10am–4pm daily.

This church belonging to the
Marian congregation was
designed by Giovanni
Antonio Viscardi and built by
Johann Georg Ettenhofer in
1709–10. (The Marian congregation, founded in 1563, is
linked to the Jesuit order.)
    The church was damaged
during World War II, but still
features original frescos. In
the oratory is a figure of the
Guardian Angel by Ignaz
Günther (1770), a fine example
of south-Bavarian Rococo.
Rupert Mayer, parish priest
during World War II and
Munich's leading opponent of
Nazism, is buried in the crypt.

Michaelskirche ❷

St Michael's Church

Neuhauser Straße 52. **Map** 2 A4. **U**
or **S** Karlsplatz. 🚋 18, 19, 20, 21,
27. ◯ 8:30am–7pm Mon–Wed, Sat,
8:30am–9pm Thu, 10am–7pm Fri,
7am–10pm Sun.

The monumental St Michael's
Church was built by Duke
Wilhelm V for the Jesuits who

arrived here in 1559. The
foundation stone was laid in
1585 and initial building work
on the first church, which was
smaller than the present one,
commenced in 1588. How-
ever, the tower in front of
the presbytery collapsed,
demolishing a large part of
the building. A transept and
new presbytery were added
to the remaining part of the
building and the church –
which was the first Jesuit
church in northern Europe –
was consecrated in 1597. The

**Statue of St Michael at the
entrance to Michaelskirche**

interior of Michaelskirche is
awe-inspiring, with its wide,
well-proportioned nave, three
pairs of shallow chapels on
either side, a short transept
and an elongated presbytery.
It is not certain who was the
architect of the project, but it
is believed that Wolfgang
Müller created the main body
of the church and Wendel
Dietrich the Mannerist façade.
Later extensions are thought
to be the work of a Dutch
architect, Friedrich Sustris.
    In the church crypt, which
is open to the public, are the
tombs of many members of the
Wittelsbach dynasty, including
King Ludwig II.

Dreifaltigkeits-
kirche ❸

Holy Trinity Church

Pacellistraße 6. **Map** 2 A3. 🚋 19.
◯ 8am–4pm daily.

The Baroque church of the
Holy Trinity is one of the few
historic buildings in the city
to have avoided bomb
damage during World War II.
The church was built as a
votive gift from the city's
burghers, aristocracy and
clergy in the hope of averting
the dangers threatened by the
War of the Spanish Succession
(1702–14). The foundation
stone was laid in 1711 and

For hotels and restaurants in this region see pp497–9 and pp536–8

the church was consecrated seven years later. The royal architect, Giovanni Antonio Viscardi, assisted by Enrico Zucalli and Georg Ettenhofer, created a building that is one of the most beautiful examples of Italian Baroque in Munich. The church's original features include the dome fresco by Cosmas Damian Asam, *The Adoration of the Trinity*.

Frauenkirche ❹

Frauenplatz 1. **Map** 2 B4. **U** or **S** Karlsplatz & Marienplatz. 🚊 19. **Church** 🕐 7am–7pm Sat–Thu, 7am–6pm Fri. **Tower** 🕐 Apr–Oct: 10am–5pm Mon–Sat. ⏺ Sun & holidays.

The site of the Frauenkirche was originally occupied by a Marian chapel, which was built in the 13th century. Some two hundred years later, Prince Sigismund ordered a new, much bigger church to be built on the site. Its architects were Jörg von Halspach and Lukas Rottaler. The Frauenkirche was completed in 1488, though the distinctive copper onion-domes were not added to its towers until 1525. The church is one of southern Germany's biggest Gothic structures, which can accommodate a congregation of about 2,000.

A triple-nave hall with no transept features rows of side chapels, a gallery surrounding the choir and a monumental western tower. The whole huge structure measures over 100 m (330 ft) in length and almost 40 m (130 ft) wide.

The church treasures that escaped destruction during World War II include a Marian painting, dating from around 1500, by Jan Polak; the altar of St Andrew in St Sebastian's chapel, with statues by Meister von Rabenden and paintings by Jan Polak, dating from 1510; and the monumental tomb of Emperor Ludwig IV of Bavaria, the work of Hans Krumpper (1619–22).

Deutsches Jagd- und Fischerei- museum ❺

German Museum of Hunting and Fishing

Neuhauser Straße 2. **Map** 2 A4. **Tel** (089) 22 05 22. **U** or **S** Marienplatz. 🚊 18, 19, 20, 21, 27. 🕐 9:30am–5pm Mon–Wed, Fri–Sun, 9:30am–9pm Thu. 📷

Immediately adjacent to St Michael's Church is the Augustinerkloster, the former Augustinian church, which now houses the Museum of Hunting and Fishing. The original building dates from around 1300 (the first Augustinian monks arrived here in 1294). It was rebuilt in the mid-15th century and then remodelled in the Baroque style in 1620–21. The church was decon-secrated in 1803. Since 1966, the building's ornate Rococo interior has housed a very interesting museum, with a collection of weapons dating from the Renais-sance, Baroque and Rococo periods, as well as hunting trophies and related paintings, prints and

Carving on main Frauenkirche portal

dioramas. Artists represented in the museum's collection include several great names such as Rubens, Snyders and Antonio Pisanello.

Asamkirche ❻

Asams' Church

Sendlinger Straße 32. **Map** 2 A5. **U** Sendlinger Tor. 🚊 16, 17, 18, 27. 🚌 52, 152. 🕐 8am–6pm daily. ✝ 5pm Mon, Tue, Thu, 8:30am Wed, 6pm Fri, Sat, 10am Sun. 📷 noon Sat.

Officially known as St Johann-Nepomuk, this gem of Rococo architecture stands in Sendlingerstrasse and is part of a complex built by the Asam brothers in the mid-18th century. In 1729–30, the sculptor and stuccoist Egid Quirin Asam acquired two properties that he intended to convert into a family home for himself. He subsequently acquired a plot adjacent to these properties, where he wished to build a church devoted to the newly canonized St Nepomuk, a Bohemian monk who had drowned in the Danube. Above the entrance to the church is a statue of the saint.

At the same time, Cosmas Damian, the brother of Egid Quirin Asam, bought a plot on which he built the presby-tery. The church building adjoins the residential house of Egid Quirin. The two buildings were joined by a corridor and from one of his bedroom windows the artist could see the main altar.

In this small but unique church, the Asam brothers achieved a rare and striking unity of style. In the church's dimly lit interior, with its rich, dynamically shaped single nave, no surface is left unembellished. Irresistibly, the eye is drawn to the altar, which features a sculpted group of the Holy Trinity.

Pulpit in the Rococo-style Asamkirche

A painting by Wilhelm von Kaulbach (1847) from the Stadtmuseum collection

Stadtmuseum ❼
Town Museum

St Jakobsplatz 1. **Map** 2 A5.
Tel *(089) 23 32 23 70.* Ⓤ *or*
Ⓢ *Marienplatz.* Ⓤ *Sendlinger Tor.*
⬜ *10am–6pm Tue–Sun.* 📷 💻

A few steps away from the Viktualienmarkt, on St Jakobsplatz, stands the Town Museum. Its rich collection has been housed since 1880 in the former arsenal building, which was built in 1491–93 by Lucas Rottaler. It is one of Munich's most fascinating museums, where everyone will find something to their taste, with exhibits illustrating the everyday lives of Munich's citizens of all classes throughout the centuries.

The museum's greatest treasures are the famous set of dancing Moors by Erasmus Grasser (1480). Originally this was a group of eighteen lime-wood carvings of dancing figures in highly expressive postures, surrounding the figure of a woman. Only ten of the figures, which were created originally to decorate the ballroom of the Altes Rathaus, have survived. Also on the ground floor, in the Waffenhalle, is a splendid collection of arms. Other

displays include furniture (with pieces in styles ranging from Baroque to Art Deco), photographs, film, brewing equipment and musical instruments. There is also a fascinating doll collection, which is one of the largest in the world. It includes paper dolls from India and China, European mechanical dolls and a variety of original puppets. Also worth seeing is the museum's collection of paintings and prints, particularly the posters. As well as its permanent displays about the history of the city, the museum regularly stages special exhibitions.

The museum also houses a cinema, the *Filmmuseum*, which puts on nightly showings of English-language films.

Viktualienmarkt ❽

Peterplatz-Frauenstraße. **Map** 2 B5.
Ⓤ *or* Ⓢ *Marienplatz.* 🚌 *52.*

Right at the heart of the city is the Viktualienmarkt, a large square that has been the city's main marketplace for the last two hundred years. The locals say that a tourist who fails to visit this "rustic heart" of Munich can never boast that he has seen the Bavarian capital. Apart from stalls selling vegetables and fruit brought in daily from suburban orchards or

Colourfully laden market stalls in Munich's Viktualienmarkt

village gardens, the local beer garden provides a welcome retreat for a beer or snack.

One of the features of the square is a statue of a famous Munich actor and comedian, Karl Valentin (1882–1948).

An impressive view over the market and nearby Marienplatz can be enjoyed from the tower of Peterskirche (St Peter's Church), which stands alongside the square.

Signs of the Zodiac adorning the clock face on the Altes Rathaus

Altes Rathaus ❾
Old Town Hall

Marienplatz 15. **Map** 2 B4. Ⓤ *or*
Ⓢ *Marienplatz.* ⬤ *to visitors.*
Spielzeugmuseum *Tel* *(089) 29
40 01.* ⬜ *10am–5:30pm daily.* 📷
www.toymuseum.de

Munich's old town hall stands in the eastern part of Marienplatz, immediately next to the new town hall. The original building, which has been remodelled several times over the centuries, was built in 1470–75 by Jörg von Halspach, who also designed the Marian church.

The building's present Neo-Gothic look is the result of remodelling work carried out between 1877 and 1934, when the nearby dual carriageway ring road was being built.

The interior of the building, which was restored following World War II bomb damage, features the Dance Hall with a wooden cradle vault. It is adorned with an old frieze featuring 87 (originally 99) heraldic arms painted by Ulrich Fuetrer in 1478, and a further seven carved by Erasmus Grasser in 1477. The figures standing by the walls are copies of the famous dancing Moors, whose originals by Erasmus Grasser (1480) are kept in the Town Museum (Stadtmuseum).

The lofty tower rising above the old city gate (Talbrucktor) was remade in 1975 based on pictures dating from 1493. Since 1983, the tower has housed the toy collection of the Spielzeugmuseum.

Neues Rathaus ⑩
New Town Hall

Marienplatz. **Map** 2 B4. **Tel** (089) 23 32 31 91. Ⓤ or Ⓢ *Marienplatz.* ⬜ **Town Hall and Tower:** *May–Oct: 9am–7pm Mon–Fri, 10am–7pm Sat & Sun; Nov–Apr: 9am–4pm Mon–Thu, 9am–1pm Fri.* ⬤ *Sat, Sun.* ⬛ ⬜ **Carillons:** *Apr–Oct: 11am, noon, 5pm daily; Nov–Mar: 11am, noon.*

The Neo-Gothic new town hall standing in Marienplatz was built by Georg Hauberrisser in 1867–1909. Its 100-m (330-ft) high façade features a fascinating set of statues depicting Bavarian dukes, kings and electors, saints, mythical and allegorical figures as well as a variety of gargoyles inspired by medieval bestiaries. The central façade features an 80-m (260-ft) high clock tower, known as Glockenspiele. Each day, at 11am and 5pm, the bells ring out a carillon, while mechanical knights fight a tournament and a crowd dances. The latter is a reenactment of the first coopers' dance, which was held in 1517 to boost the morale of citizens when the town was beset by the plague. Other mechanical figures appear in the windows on the seventh floor in the evenings (9:30pm in summer, 7:30pm in winter). These are flanked by figures of the town guardsman carrying a lantern and the Guardian Angel blessing a Munich child, the *"Münchner Kindl"*.

Richly decorated entrance to the Völkerkundemuseum

Statue on façade of Neues Rathaus

Völkerkunde-museum ⑪
State Museum of Ethnography

Maximilianstraße 42. **Map** 2 D4. **Tel** (089) 210 136 100. ⬜ *9:30am–5:15pm, Tue–Sun.* 🚇 *19.* ⬜

On the opposite side of the ring road from the Maximilianeum (the Upper Bavaria Government building) is the State Museum of Ethnography. Built in 1858–65, to a design by E. Riedel, its façade is decorated with eight figures personifying the virtues of the Bavarian people: patriotism, diligence, magnanimity, piety, loyalty, justice, courage and wisdom. Originally intended to house the Bavarian National Museum (now in Prinzregentenstraße), the building has been home to the State Museum of Ethnography since 1925. It is the second largest (after Berlin) ethnographic museum in Germany.

The origins of the museum's collection go back to 1782, when curios taken from the treasures of various Bavarian rulers were exhibited in a gallery in the gardens of the residence. Attention began to focus on ethnography after expansion of the collection in 1868. The museum currently houses some 300,000 exhibits depicting the art and culture of non-European nations, with a particular emphasis on the Far East (China and Japan), South America and Eastern and Central Africa. The collection is presented in a series of changing exhibitions.

Hofbräuhaus ⑫

Platzl 9. **Map** 2 C4. **Tel** (089) 22 16 76. Ⓤ or Ⓢ *Marienplatz.* ⬜ *9am–11:30pm daily.*

The Hofbräuhaus is the most popular beer hall in Munich and a great tourist attraction. Established as a court brewery in 1589 by Wilhelm V, it was originally housed in Alter Hof, but moved to Platzl in 1654. In 1830 permission was granted to build an inn where beer could be sold to the public.

The Neo-Renaissance form of the building dates from 1896. The Schwemme, on the ground floor, is a large hall with painted ceiling and room for about 1,000 guests. The Festsaal, on the first floor, has a barrel-shaped vault and can accommodate 1,300 guests.

In a courtyard, surrounded by chestnut trees, is the beer garden, which is always very popular during the summer.

Guests enjoying a drink in the beer garden of the Hofbräuhaus

Residenz ⑬

Necklace dating from 1557

This former residence of Bavarian kings has housed a museum since 1920. Over the years, the original Wittelsbachs' castle, which had stood on the site since the 14th century, was gradually extended. Major work in the 17th century included new surroundings for the Brunnenhof and the construction of buildings around the imperial courtyard, Hofkapelle and Reiche Kapelle. Königsbau and Festsaalbau were added in the first half of the 19th century. The Renaissance façade includes two magnificent portals and features a statue of the Holy Virgin as Patroness of Bavaria (Patrona Boiariae).

Hofkapelle
This imposing chapel, dating from the early 17th century, was modelled on St Michael's Church. Vault decorations date from 1614.

Reiche Kapelle
This was the private chapel of Maximilian I. Though smaller than the Residenz's other chapel, it is richly furnished.

Grottenhof
In the eastern section of this courtyard is this grotto lined with crystal, coloured shells and tufa.

★ Nibelungensäle
Built by Leo von Klenze, Königsbau features five Halls of the Nibelungs. The rooms owe their name to the wall paintings, which depict scenes from the famous German medieval epic Nibelungenlied.

★ **Cuvilliés-Theater**
Built in 1751–53, this masterpiece of theatre architecture was designed by François Cuvilliés, and is considered to be Europe's finest surviving Rococo theatre. The world premiere of Mozart's Idomeneo was staged in the theatre on 29 January 1781.

VISITORS' CHECKLIST

Residenzmuseum Max-Joseph-Platz 3. **Map** 2 C3. **Tel** (089) 29 06 71. **U** Odeonsplatz. ☐ 1 Apr–Oct: 9am–6pm daily; Nov–31 Mar: 10am–4pm daily. ☑
Staatliche Sammlung Ägyptischer Kunst Max-Joseph-Platz 3. **Tel** (089) 29 85 46. **U** Odeonsplatz. ☐ 9am–5pm Tue–Fri, 7–9pm Tue (additional), 10am–5pm Sat, Sun. ☑
Cuvilliés-Theater Residenzstrasse 1. **Tel** (089) 29 06 71. ☐ closed until 2008.

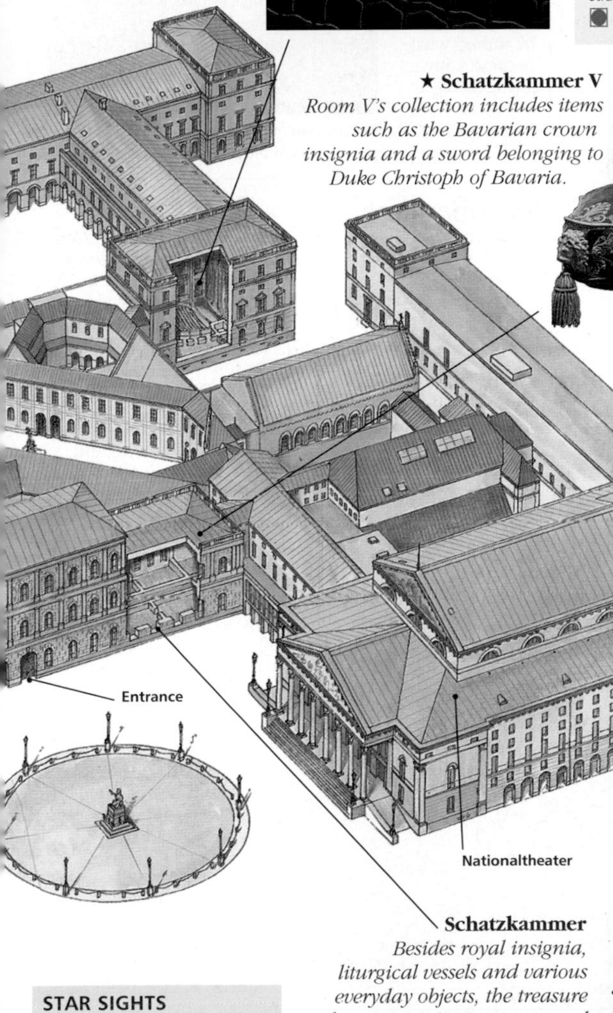

★ **Schatzkammer V**
Room V's collection includes items such as the Bavarian crown insignia and a sword belonging to Duke Christoph of Bavaria.

Entrance

Nationaltheater

Schatzkammer
Besides royal insignia, liturgical vessels and various everyday objects, the treasure house contains some unusual gold and jewellery items. The star attraction of Room III is this small equestrian statue of St George, the work (1586–97) of Friedrich Sustris.

STAR SIGHTS

★ Cuvilliés-Theater

★ Nibelungensäle

★ Schatzkammer V

Feldherrnhalle ⑭

Odeonsplatz. **Map** 2 B3.
Ⓤ *Odeonsplatz.* 🚋 *19.* 🚌 *53.*
⬤ *to the public.*

Until 1816, the site of this
monumental building was
occupied by a Gothic town
gate – Schwabinger Tor. In
the early 19th century, however, when Kings Maximilian
I Joseph and Ludwig I
decided to expand Munich
northwards and westwards,
their chief architect, Leo von
Klenze, ordered the gate to
be pulled down, as it stood in
the way of the prestigious
thoroughfare (Ludwigstrasse)
that he intended to build.

Built in 1841–44, the Feldherrnhalle was designed by
Friedrich von Gärtner, who
modelled it on the Loggia dei
Lanzi in Florence. Intended as
a monument to the heroes of
Bavaria, the interior contains
statues of two great military
leaders, Johann Tilly and
Karl Philipp von Wrede by
Ludwig Schwanthaler.

The central carved
composition devoted to
the heroes of the 1870–71
Franco-Prussian War is
much newer, dating from
1882. It was designed by
Ferdinand von Miller.

The Feldherrnhalle
was the scene of Hitler's
unsuccessful "Beer-hall
Putsch". This resulted
in the building
acquiring a certain
cult status in Nazi
propaganda, and
is no longer
open to the
public.

Pediment on the gable of Theatinerkirche, with copper dome behind

---

HITLER AND THE FELDHERRNHALLE

On the evening of 8 November 1923, Adolf Hitler
announced the start of the "people's revolution" in the
Bürgerbräukeller and ordered the takeover of the central
districts of Munich. On 9 November a march of some 2,000
people acting on his orders was stopped by a police
cordon outside the Feldherrnhalle in Residenzstraße. Four
policemen and 16 of Hitler's supporters were shot. The
marchers were dispersed, and Hitler fled to Uffing am
Starnberger See,
but was arrested
and imprisoned.
When Hitler
finally came to
power in 1933,
he turned what
became known
as the Hitler-
Putsch into a
central element
of the Nazi cult.

**The accused in the trial against the
participants in the Hitler-Putsch of 1923**

Theatinerkirche (St Cajetan) ⑮
St Cajetan's Church

Theatinerstraße 22. **Map** 2 B3. Ⓤ
or Ⓢ *Marienplatz.* 🚋 *19.* ⬜ *7am–
6pm daily.*

In Odeonsplatz, next to Feldherrnhalle, stands one of the
most magnificent churches
in Munich, St Cajetan's
Church. When Henrietta
Adelaide of Savoy
presented the Elector
Ferdinand with his long-
awaited heir, Maximilian,
the happy parents vowed
to build an abbey in
commemoration.
The project was
given to an
Italian architect,
Agostino Baralli,

who based his design on St
Andrea della Valle, in Rome.

Although construction work
on the church ended in 1690,
the façade – designed by
François de Cuvilliés – was
not completed until 1765–68.
The interior of the church is
adorned with stuccos by
Giovanni Antonio Viscardi
and furnished in rich Baroque
style. Its twin towers and
copper dome are dominant
features on the Munich skyline.

Haus der Kunst ⑯
Arts House

Prinzregentenstraße 1. **Map** 3 D2.
Tel (089) 21 12 71 13. 🚌 *53, 55.*
⬜ *10am–8pm daily, 10am–10pm
Thu.* 🎫 *(free on Sundays and
national holidays).*

Built between 1933 and 1937,
the Neo-Classical building is
the work of a Nazi architect,
Paul Ludwig Trost. It opened
its doors in 1937 with a display
of propaganda art, which was
proclaimed by the Nazis as
"truly German". This was
followed by "The Exhibition
of Degenerate Art", in which
several masterpieces of modern
art were ridiculed.

Since 1945 the building has
become a dynamic centre of
modern art that is famous for
its temporary exhibitions.

Its central hall, the Ehrenhalle
(Hall of Honour), which was
subdivided into smaller
spaces, is currently being

reopened in stages, each stage accompanied by a special exhibition. This process will continue into 2005, when the hall will once again become the centre of the building. It will house new visitor facilities, as well as a permanent exhibition documenting the history of the Haus der Kunst.

Bayerisches Nationalmuseum **⓱**
Bavarian National Museum

Prinzregentenstraße 3. **Map** 3 E3.
Tel (089) 211 24 01. 🚋 17. 🚌 100.
🕐 10am–5pm Tue–Wed, Fri–Sun, 10am–8pm Thu. 🌑 Mon.

The Bavarian National Museum was founded in 1855 by King Maximilian II. Between 1894 and 1900 it acquired a new building in Prinzregentenstrasse, which was designed by Gabriel von Seidel; this building alone is worth a closer look. The complex structure consists of wings representing various architectural styles, while the ground floor features halls that are built in styles that are appropriate to their exhibits. Romanesque and Gothic art can thus be seen in Neo-Romanesque and Neo-Gothic rooms, Renaissance art in Neo-Renaissance rooms and Baroque in Neo-Baroque rooms. The individual rooms have been arranged in subject groups, with paintings and sculptures supplemented by superb collections of decorative art and everyday objects. The exhibits include a beautiful sculpture of the Madonna by Tilman Riemenschneider.

Conrad Meit's *Judith* (1515), Bavarian National Museum

The first-floor collections are arranged thematically and include German porcelain, clocks, glass paintings, ivory carvings, textiles and gold items. Particularly interesting is a collection of small oil sketches, painted by artists when designing some large-scale compositions, such as an altar or a ceiling painting.

In the basement rooms is a collection of folk art. This includes the popular Christmas cribs. These multi-figure compositions are the works of Bavarian and Italian artists.

Poster advertising an exhibition at the Schack-Galerie

Schack-Galerie **⓲**

Prinzregentenstraße 9. **Map** 3 E3.
Tel (089) 23 80 52 24. 🕐 10am–5pm Wed–Sun. 🚌 100. 🚋 17.

The magnificent collection of German paintings on display in this gallery come from the private collection of Adolf Friedrich von Schack. They are housed in this elegant building built in 1907 by Max Littmann for use by the Prussian Legation.

As Schack's main interest was in 19th-century painting, the gallery features works that represent the Romantic period, including Leo von Klenze and Carl Spitzweg, as well as witty, fairy-tale works by Moritz von Schwind. Particularly notable are his *Morning, In the Woods* and *Rübezahl* – in which the mythical Guardian of the Riesengebirge Mountains wanders through an enchanted forest. Late 19th-century painters are represented by Franz von Lenbach, Anselm Feuerbach and, above all, by Arnold Bocklin. Bocklin's Romantic works, which are full of symbolism, include *Villa on the Coast* and *Man Scaring a Deer*. The gallery has a large collection of landscapes, including interesting sun-soaked Italian scenes by German masters, as well as a valuable collection of paintings devoted to historic themes.

Archäologische Staatssammlung **⓳**
Prehistory Museum

Lerchenfeldstraße 2. **Map** 3 E2.
Tel (089) 211 24 02. 🚋 17. 🚌 100. 🕐 9am–4:30pm Tue–Sun. 🎟 admission free Sun and national holidays. ♿

Immediately adjacent to the Bavarian National Museum is the Prehistory Museum, which was founded in 1885 by King Ludwig II. Since 1976, this spacious building has housed a rich collection of artifacts excavated in various parts of Bavaria. The oldest items in the collection date from the Palaeolithic era while later exhibits illustrate the region's early history. The collection includes Bronze Age, Roman and early Medieval treasures.

A 3rd-century mosaic floor from a Roman villa, on display in the Prehistory Museum

Bayerische Staatsbibliothek ⑳
Bavarian National Library

Ludwigstraße 16. **Map** 2 C1, C2.
Tel (089) 286 38 23 22. **U** *Odeon,
Universität.* ◯ *9am–9pm Mon–Fri,
10am–5pm Sat–Sun.*   *(telephone
bookings required).*

The monumental Bavarian
national library was
designed by Friedrich von
Gärtner, who took over, in
1827, from Leo von Klenze
as the main architect on the
prestigious Ludwigstrasse
project – commissioned by
King Ludwig I. Gärtner was
also responsible for the
Feldherrnhalle, Siegestor,
St Ludwig's Church, and the
University building.

This massive structure, in a
style reminiscent of the Italian
Renaissance, was erected
between 1832 and 1843. Its
external staircase is adorned
with the seated figures of
Thucydides, Hippocrates,
Homer and Aristotle, by
Ludwig von Schwanthaler.

Equally impressive are the
stairs leading to the main
rooms, which are modelled
on the Scala dei Gianti of the
Doge Palace in Venice. With
its collection of 5 million
volumes, the library is on a
par with the Berlin Staatsbibliothek *(see p68)* as the
biggest in Germany.

**A statue of Hippocrates at the
Bavarian National Library**

**The imposing twin-tower façade
of Munich's Ludwigskirche**

Ludwigskirche ㉑
St Ludwig's Church

Ludwigstraße 20. **Map** 2 C1.
U *Universität.* ◯ *7am–8pm daily.*

Inspired by the Romanesque
churches of Lombardy,
Friedrich von Gärtner built
this monumental triple-nave
basilica with transept and
twin-tower façade between
1829 and 1844.

The building's vast interior
features magnificent original
frescos that were designed
by the main exponent of the
Nazarene style, Peter von
Cornelius, and painted by
his associates. Von Cornelius
himself painted the massive
choir fresco, *The Last Judgement.* One of the biggest
frescos in the world, it rivals
in size Michelangelo's *Last
Judgement,* which hangs in
the Sistine Chapel, Rome.

Neue Pinakothek ㉒
The New Pinakothek

Barerstraße 29. **Map** 2 A1. *Tel (089)
23 80 51 95.* **U** *Theresienstraße.*
🚊 *2.* 🚌 *27.* ◯ *10am–5pm
Thu–Mon, 10am–8pm Wed.* 🎧

The Bavarian collection of
modern European paintings
and sculptures is housed in a
building built by Alexander
von Brancas between 1975
and 1981. It holds a

representative collection of
German works, from Neo-
Classicism through Romantic-
ism, the "Nazarenes", German
and Austrian Biedermeier,
Realism, Historicism,
Impressionism, Pointillism
and Secession paintings.

The collection also includes
works by renowned French
Realists, Impressionists, Post-
Impressionists and Symbolists,
purchased in 1909–11, when
the gallery's director was the
art historian Hugo von Tschudi.

The collection includes
Ferdinand Georg Waldmüller's
*Young Peasant Woman with
Three Children Standing at
the Window* (1840), Friedrich
Overbeck's *Italia and
Germania* (1828), Edouard
Manet's *Breakfast in the Studio*
(1868), Honoré Daumier's
Don Quijote (1868), Edgar
Degas' *Ironing Woman* (1869),
Paul Gauguin's *Birth of Christ*
(1869), Walter Crane's
Neptune's Horses (1892),
Gustav Klimt's *Music* (1895)
and Lovis Corinth's *Portrait of
Count Eduard von Keyserling*
(1900). The gallery ends with
a small selection of Symbolist
and Art Nouveau paintings.

The space between the Old
and New Pinakothek has been
turned into a sculpture park
that features, among others, a
work by Henry Moore.

**Goya's *Die Marquesa de Caballero*
in the Neue Pinakothek**

Alte Pinakothek ㉓
The Old Pinakothek

See pp222–3.

Façade of the Glyptothek, with its central column portico

Pinakothek der Moderne ㉔

Barer Straße 40. **Map** 2 A2.
Tel (089) 23 80 53 60. **U** Königs-
platz. 🚋 53. 🚏 27. ◯ 10am–5pm
Tue–Wed Sat–Sun, 10am–8pm
Thu–Fri. 🌐 except Sun. ♿ 🖥
www.pinakothek-der-moderne.de

Designed by the German architect Stephan Braunfels, this gallery was built to complement the collections in the Alte and Neue Pinakotheks nearby. The modern building brings together the worlds of art, design, graphics, jewellery and architecture under one roof.

Highlights of the collection include Cubist works by Picasso and Georges Braque, and paintings by Matisse, Giorgio De Chirico and Max Beckmann. Pop Art, Minimal Art and Photorealism are also represented. The design exhibition is outstanding.

Glyptothek ㉕
Glyptotheca

Königsplatz 3. **Map** 1 F2.
Tel (089) 28 61 00. **U** Königsplatz.
◯ 10am–5pm Tue–Sun, 10am–8pm
Thu.

The Königsplatz complex, including Glyptothek and Propylaeum, was the work of Leo von Klenze. It was built in 1816–34 to house Ludwig I's collection of Greek and Roman sculptures and was the first public museum to be devoted to a single art discipline.

The most famous pieces in the museum's collection are the ancient statue of a young man, *Apollo of Terentia* (560 BC), the tomb stele of Mnesareta (380 BC) and sculptures from the front of the Aphaia temple of Aegina.

Staatliche Antiken-sammlungen ㉖
The National Collection of Antiquities

Königsplatz 1. **Map** 1 F2. **Tel** (089) 59 98 88 30. **U** Königsplatz. ◯ 10am–5pm Tue–Sun, 10am–8pm Wed. 🌐

Built in 1838–48 by Georg Friedrich Ziebland, this building is on the south side of the Königsplatz. Since 1967, it has housed one of the world's finest collections of antique vases from the 5th and 6th centuries BC. There are also many other master-pieces of Greek, Roman and Etruscan ornamental art, jewellery and small statues. Among the famous exhibits is a golden Greek necklace from the 4th century BC.

Propyläen ㉗

Königsplatz. **Map** 1 F2.
U Königsplatz.

Derived from the Propylaea to the Athenian Acropolis, this magnificent Neo-Classical structure stands at the end of Brienner Strasse and is visible from as far as Karolinenplatz. Built by Leo von Klenze in 1846–62, its austere form, featuring Doric porticos, provides an excellent final touch to the composition of Königsplatz by linking together the National Collection of Antiquities and the Glyptotheca.

The Propyläen is also a symbolic gateway to the new parts of the city. It was funded by the private foundation of King Ludwig I, although built after his abdication.

The carved decorations depict scenes from the Greek War of Liberation against Turkey (1821–29), led by King Otto I, son of Ludwig I.

Lenbachhaus ㉘

Luisenstraße 33. **Map** 1 F2. **Tel** (089) 23 33 20 00. **U** Königsplatz. ◯ 10am–6pm Tue–Sun. 🌐

This Italian-style villa was built between 1887 and 1891 by Gabriel von Seidl for Franz von Lenbach, a painter who was very popular with the establishment.

Since 1929, the villa has housed the Municipal Art Gallery. Apart from master-pieces such as *Portrait of a Man*, by Jan Polak (c.1500) and *Friends from the Young Days* by Carl Spitzweg (1855), it also has the world's biggest collection of works by a group known as *Der Blaue Reiter* (The Blue Rider) artists. The Russian painter Wassily Kandinsky was a leading proponent of this movement.

Fountain in the beautiful front garden of the Lenbachhaus

Alte Pinakothek ㉓

Construction work on the Alte Pinakothek, one of the world's most famous art galleries, began in 1826 and was completed 10 years later. Leo von Klenze designed the Italian-Renaissance-style building. The history of princely collections goes back to the Renaissance period, when Wilhelm IV the Steadfast (ruled 1508–50) decided to adorn his residence with historic paintings. His successors were equally keen art collectors and, by the 18th century, an outstanding collection of 14th- to 18th-century paintings had been amassed.

St Luke Painting the Madonna (c.1440)
This is one of the most frequently copied masterpieces by the Dutch painter Roger van der Weyden.

★ Four Apostles (1526)
These two panels were painted by Albrecht Dürer, a founding figure of the German school of art. They were acquired in 1627 by Maximilian I from the town of Nuremberg.

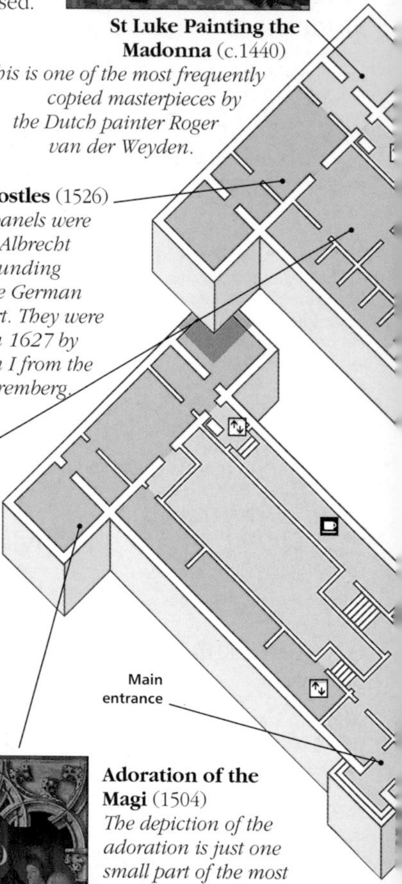

Emperor Charles V (1548)
This portrait was painted by the Venetian artist Titian during the Emperor's visit to the Reich's Parliament in Augsburg.

Main entrance

Adoration of the Magi (1504)
The depiction of the adoration is just one small part of the most important altarpiece by Hans Holbein the Elder.

KEY

☐ Flemish and Dutch paintings

☐ German paintings

☐ Italian paintings

☐ French paintings

☐ Spanish paintings

☐ 16th–17th-century paintings

STAR EXHIBITS

★ Descent from the Cross

★ Four Apostles

★ Land of Cockaigne

Rape of the Daughters of Leukippos (1618)
A highlight of the museum is the Rubens collection, which includes his depiction of the abduction of Hilaeria and Phoibe by Castor and Pollux.

VISITORS' CHECKLIST

Barer Straße 27. **Road map** 2
A1. *Tel* (089) 23 80 52 16.
Ⓤ Königsplatz. 🚌 53. 🚊 27.
🕐 10am–5pm Wed–Sun,
10am–8pm Tue. 💳 (admission
free to children up to age 8.)
♿ 🚻 🔲 📷

GALLERY GUIDE
The ground-floor rooms of the gallery are devoted to the works of German old masters dating from the 16th and 17th centuries. On the first floor are works by Dutch, Flemish, French, German, Italian and Spanish artists.

First floor

★ Descent from the Cross (1633)
Rembrandt's dramatic vision of the Saviour's sacrifice emotively depicts Christ's passion.

Disrobing of Christ (c.1583–84)
The gallery's small but interesting collection of Spanish paintings includes this work by El Greco, one of his three most important compositions.

Ground floor

★ Land of Cockaigne (1566)
In this vividly detailed painting by Pieter Brueghel the Elder, the Flemish artist depicts the mythical land of plenty. The work is an ironic condemnation of gluttony and laziness, themes that are depicted in its many humorous scenes.

Schloss Nymphenburg ㉙

One of Europe's most beautiful palaces, Schloss Nymphenburg grew up around an Italianate villa built in 1663–64 for the Electress Henriette-Adelaide to a design by Agostino Barelli. The palace was dedicated to the pastoral goddess Flora and her nymphs, hence the name. Several additions were made over the years, including four pavilions. These were designed by Joseph Effner and Enrico Zuccalli who directed works from 1715. Built to the side of the original villa, these were connected by arcaded passageways.

Porcelain parrot in front of the factory

★ Gallery of Beauties
Portraits of royal favourites include this one of Helene Sedlmayr, a 17-year-old girl from Munich.

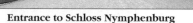

Entrance to Schloss Nymphenburg
Seen in this view are the original Italianate villa and two of the side pavilions that were added later.

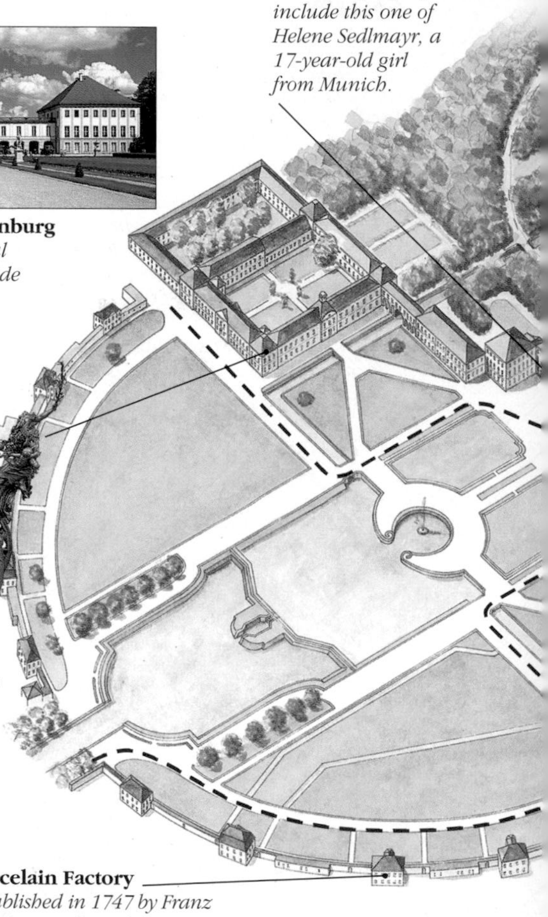

Marstallmuseum
The former stables house a collection of carriages that once belonged to Bavarian rulers. They include the magnificent carriages of Ludwig II.

Porcelain Factory
Established in 1747 by Franz Anton Bustelli and transferred to Nymphenburg in 1761, this is one of the oldest porcelain factories in Europe.

KEY

━ ━ ━ Suggested route

STAR SIGHTS

★ Amalienburg

★ Festsaal

★ Gallery of Beauties

★ Amalienburg
The interior of this hunting lodge in the Schlosspark is a superb example of Rococo style by François Cuvilliés.

VISITORS' CHECKLIST

Tel (089) 17 90 80.
Ⓤ Rotkreuzplatz. 🚋 12.
🕐 Apr–15 Oct: 9am–6pm daily; 16 Oct–Mar: 10am–4pm daily.

Magdalenenklause
After a lifetime of revels, Maximilian Emanuel commissioned a hermitage where he could pray and meditate. It was completed in 1725.

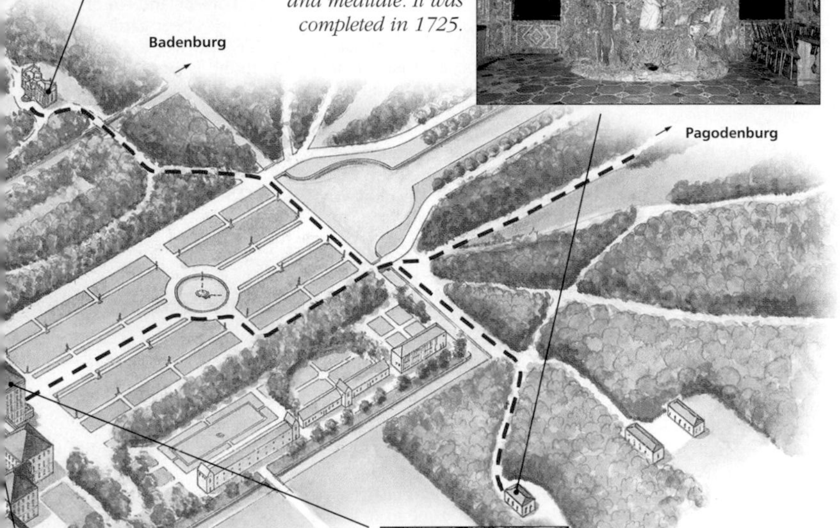

Badenburg

Pagodenburg

Museum Mensch und Natur
This museum is devoted to geology and human biology.

Lackkabinett
This small 17th-century cabinet owes its name to its panels of black and red Chinese lacquer.

Botanical Garden
A collection of botanical specimens, including many rare plants, is featured in this fascinating garden.

★ Festsaal
Featuring decorations devoted to the goddess Flora, this vast Rococo ballroom is the work of father and son – Johann Baptist and Franz Zimmermann.

View from the platform of the television tower in Olympiapark

Olympiapark ③⓪

Tel (089) 30 67 24 14. **U** Olympia-zentrum. 🚋 20, 25, 27. **Television tower** ◯ 9am–midnight daily. 🖼️

Built for the 1972 Olympic Games, this vast sports stadium can be spotted from almost anywhere in Munich, as it is the site of a 290-m (950-ft) high television tower, the Olympiaturm. The entire complex was designed by Germany's leading architects, Behnisch and Partners.

The stadium has three main facilities: the Olympic Stadium, which seats 62,000 spectators, the Olympic Hall and the Swimming Hall. In what is one of the most original constructions of 20th-century German architecture, all three are covered by a vast trans-parent canopy, stretched between a series of tall masts to form an irregular tent.

The stadium includes many other facilities, such as an indoor skating rink, a cycle racing track and tennis courts.

The sports complex is located beside the park's artificial lake. Opposite it is a hill that was constructed from rubble removed from the city after war destruction.

Apart from sporting events, the Olympiapark hosts many popular events, including fire-works displays and regular open-air rock and pop concerts in the summer months.

Englischer Garten ③①

U Giselastraße. 🚌 54.

The idea of creating this garden, which would be open to all the inhabitants of Munich and not only to its aristocracy, came from Count von Rumford, an American-born chemist and physicist who lived in Bavaria from 1784. As the region's Minister of War, he was responsible for reorganizing the Bavarian army. His idea of creating a garden of this size – the garden covers an area of 5 sq km (1,235 acres) – right in the centre of a large city, was quite unique in Germany. In 1789, taking advantage of his influential position, he persuaded Karl Theodor to put his plans into action.

The project leader was Friedrich Ludwig von Sckell. He was brought to Munich from Schwetzingen by the Elector to create the garden on an area of former marshland.

Chinese Tower in the Englischer Garten

Opened in 1808, the Karl-Theodor-Park is today known simply as the Englischer Garten (English Garden). It is a popular place for long walks, jogging or just lying on the grass in the cool shade of a spreading old tree.

There are some interesting old buildings in the park, such as the Monopteros, a Neo-Classical temple by Leo von Klenze (1837), and the Chinese Tower (1789–90), which is similar to the pagoda in London's Kew Gardens. The Tower stands in one of the park's beer gardens.

It is also worth dropping in to the Japanese Teahouse, where the gentle art of tea brewing is demonstrated.

Deutsches Museum ③②

See pp228–9.

Franz von Stuck's *Die Sünde*, on display in the Villa Stuck

Villa Stuck ③③

Prinzregentenstraße 60. **Tel** (089) 45 55 51 0. 🚋 18. 🚌 51, 55. ◯ 11am–6pm Wed–Sun. 🖼️

This villa was the home of the famous painter Franz von Stuck, the co-founder of the Munich Secession school of painting. As well as numerous portraits, nudes and sculptures, Von Stuck was the creator of many mythological and allegorical scenes, all painted in dark colours and full of

Submarine used in the film *Das Boot*, displayed in Bavaria-Filmstadt

Theresienwiese ㉟

Theresienhöhe. **U** *Theresienwiese.*
Oktoberfest (Sep–Oct).

For most of the year this is simply a vast oval meadow encircled by the Bavariaring. Theresienwiese comes into its own once a year, however, during the Oktoberfest. Then it turns into a gigantic, boisterous beer-drinking venue, with stalls, marquees, funfair and loud music.

Towering above the meadow is a monumental 18-m (59-ft) high statue, symbol of the state of Bavaria. Made in 1844–50, the statue is the work of Ludwig Schwanthaler. It incorporates an internal staircase leading to the figure's head, where there is a viewing platform.

Just behind the statue is the Ruhmeshalle, a Neo-Classical building surrounded by a colonnade. Designed by Leo von Klenze and built in 1843–53, the building contains numerous busts of eminent Bavarians.

Bavaria statue in Theresienwiese

eroticism. These include eight variations (1893) on the theme of sin. His *Amazon* (1897) stands in front of the villa.

Franz von Stuck built the villa in 1897–98, to his own design, decorating it with his own paintings and sculptures. Since 1968, it has housed a museum. A permanent exhibition of Stuck's work is displayed in the magnificent music room on the ground floor, while the second-floor rooms are used for temporary exhibitions devoted mainly to early 20th-century art.

Bavaria-Filmstadt ㉞

Bavariafilmplatz 7. **Tel** (089) 64 99
20 00. 25. ☐ Mar–Oct: 9am–4pm
daily; Nov–Feb: 10am–3pm daily.

Commonly known as Hollywood on Isar, this vast site in the southern suburb of Geiselgasteig covers an area of over 3.5 sq km (865 acres).

Since 1919 the world's greatest cinema stars have worked here, including Orson Welles and Billy Wilder. The British film director Alfred Hitchcock made his first films here (*The Pleasure Garden*, 1925 and *The Mountain Eagle*, 1926). Elizabeth Taylor, Gina Lollobrigida and Romy Schneider have all stood in front of the cameras here.

Strolling visitors to the site will often come across some well-known characters who have appeared in films such as *E.T.* or *The Neverending Story*, which were filmed here. The sets of other films made here, including *Enemy Mine* and *Cabaret*, can also

be seen. You can also peep into the submarine that was reconstructed for Wolfgang Petersen's classic film *Das Boot* (1981) – the film follows the voyage of one such boat during World War II.

VIP tours of the Filmstadt include stuntmen shows and fascinating demonstrations of many technical film-making tricks and techniques. A special attraction is the cinema called Showscan, whose seats move according to the story on the screen, giving visitors the sensation of a trip through the universe or of flying through the tunnels of an old silver mine.

While taking a look behind film sets you may even catch a glimpse of a movie star or a celebrity, as the studio is also used for recording TV shows.

OKTOBERFEST

Munich's Oktoberfest is one of the biggest folk fairs in Europe. In 1810 the site on which it is held was the venue for a horse race, held to celebrate the marriage of Ludwig (later King of Bavaria) and Thérèse von Saxe-Hildburghausen. A few years later it became the venue for an autumn fair that has grown into an enormous event over the years. Chief amongst the attractions is beer, drunk in vast quantities, in marquees erected by the breweries. The festival starts in late

Revellers at the annual Oktoberfest in Theresienwiese

September with a huge procession through the town and the ceremonial opening of the first barrel of beer. It finishes, 16 days later, on the first Sunday of October.

Deutsches Museum ㉜

The Deutsches Museum, one of the oldest and largest museum of technology and engineering in the world, draws over 1.4 million visitors each year. It was founded in 1903 by Oskar von Miller, an engineer. The building in which it is housed, located on the Museum Island, was designed by Gabriel von Seidl in 1925. The collections cover most aspects of technology, from its history to its greatest achievements. The museum also houses one of the world's largest libraries of technology.

Exterior of the Museum
The building combines Neo-Baroque, Neo-Classical and modern elements.

Decorative Arts
This plate with the portrait of a lady from Ludwig I's "gallery of beauty" is an example of reproduction techniques applied to porcelain. The ceramics section illustrates the development of faience, stoneware and porcelain.

Second floor

First floor

★ Physics
Galileo's workshop features a large collection of the scientific equipment used by the famous astronomer and physicist to establish the basic laws of mechanics.

★ Pharmaceutics
Among the exhibits in this recently created section is a model of a human cell magnified 350,000 times and graphically illustrating how it functions.

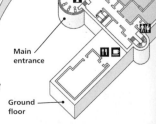

Main entrance

Ground floor

MUSEUM GUIDE
The museum's 18,000 exhibits are displayed over seven floors. While those on the lower floors include heavy vehicles and sections on chemistry, physics, scientific instruments and aeronautics, those on the middle floors relate to the decorative arts. The upper floors are devoted to astronomy, computers and microelectronics.

Sixth floor

Fifth floor

Fourth floor

Third floor

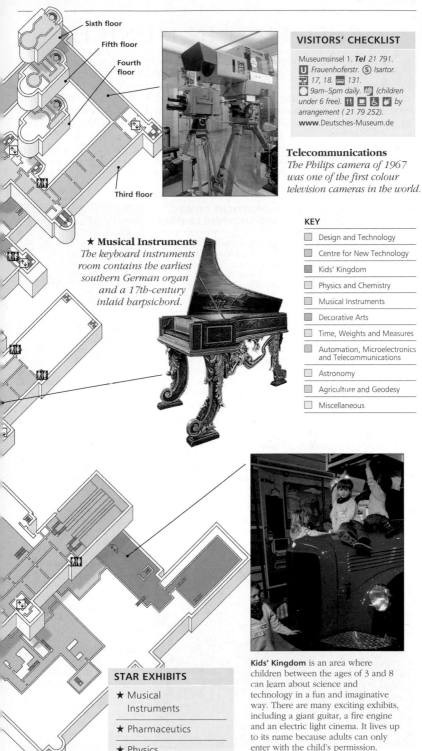

VISITORS' CHECKLIST

Museumsinsel 1. *Tel 21 791*. U *Frauenhoferstr.* S *Isartor.* 17, 18. 131. 9am–5pm daily. (children under 6 free). by arrangement (21 79 252). www.Deutsches-Museum.de

Telecommunications
The Philips camera of 1967 was one of the first colour television cameras in the world.

★ Musical Instruments
The keyboard instruments room contains the earliest southern German organ and a 17th-century inlaid harpsichord.

KEY

- Design and Technology
- Centre for New Technology
- Kids' Kingdom
- Physics and Chemistry
- Musical Instruments
- Decorative Arts
- Time, Weights and Measures
- Automation, Microelectronics and Telecommunications
- Astronomy
- Agriculture and Geodesy
- Miscellaneous

Kids' Kingdom is an area where children between the ages of 3 and 8 can learn about science and technology in a fun and imaginative way. There are many exciting exhibits, including a giant guitar, a fire engine and an electric light cinema. It lives up to its name because adults can only enter with the child's permission.

STAR EXHIBITS

- ★ Musical Instruments
- ★ Pharmaceutics
- ★ Physics

For hotels and restaurants in this region see pp497–9 and pp536–8

SHOPPING IN MUNICH

Munich often claims to be Germany's richest and most sophisticated city, and so when it comes to shopping you are sure not to be disappointed. The key shopping areas are dotted around the centre of the city. You can conveniently walk around the pedestrianized central area, with numerous options for taking a break for lunch or a coffee. Not to be missed is the visual and gourmet treat of the Viktualienmarkt food market, the classic department store Ludwig Beck and some of the smaller speciality stores tucked away in side streets. In the less commercial shopping streets, stores tend to open late morning or in the afternoon only.

Accessories from Slips

MAIN SHOPPING AREAS

Munich's key luxury shopping street is Maximilianstraße and those streets connected to it, Theatinerstraße, Brienner-straße and Residenzstraße. Here you will find all the top international brands and jewellery stores. For more affordable shops head to the central pedestrianized area between Kaufingerstraße, Neuhauserstraße and Marienplatz. Here you will find family stores, large chains, mid-market fashion, souvenirs and department stores. For less conventional areas with small specialist boutiques and local designers seek out the Glockenbach-viertel around Hans-Sachs Straße, or streets radiating out from Gärtnerplatz, home to the Art Nouveau State Theatre and relaxed cafés. Schwabing is the young Bohemian area with a variety of casualwear and jeanswear stores, plus fashion boutiques and plenty of laid-back bistros and coffee bars.

DEPARTMENT STORES AND SHOPPING CENTRES

The most famous department store in Munich is **Ludwig Beck**, which has a particularly impressive Christmas decorations department in December. **Galeria Kaufhof** is another large national department store chain offering several floors of goods. Shopping Centres (*Einkaufspassagen*) are also aplenty. **Fünf Höfe** ("the five courtyards") is central and upmarket. It sits between Theatiner, Maffei, Kardinal-Faulhaber and Salvator streets and mixes shopping, art and culture with cafés including a great restaurant/café attached to the Kunsthalle art museum. Munich has three other large shopping malls. **Olympia-Einkaufszentrum** (OEZ) is vast with over 140 stores on two levels. **Perlacher** shopping mall (PEP) has over 110 stores. The **Riem Arcaden** is home to the largest branch of H&M, a huge Lego store, C&A and Ludwig Beck Fashion.

Pedestrianized shopping area in central Munich

FASHION

Munich has a wide variety of shops for clothes and accessories. Try the following boutiques to find Munich-style chic. **Theresa** has the best choice of designer fashion and accessories, while **Slips** in Gärtnerplatz boasts the pick of top brands and **Off & Co** in Schwabing has fashion items for both men and women. Hohenzollern-straße in Schwabing is a good place to shop for youth-styled street fashion and trainers. For traditional Bavarian Loden costumes take a look in **Loden-Frey**.

CHILDREN'S SHOPS

Munich is a stylish and expensive city and parents love to dress their children accordingly. This means there are some good shopping opportunities for kids' clothing and toys, mainly in the department stores and C&A. A large central store for

The exclusive shopping centre, Fünf Höfe

One of the city's regularly held flea markets

mother, baby and toys is **Schlichting**, as well as **Thierchen Kindermode** for original handmade clothing. **Noemi & Friends** is a kids' beauty salon cum accessories shop, a haven for little and big girls. **Die Puppenstube** is also good for old-fashioned toys and gifts.

FLEA MARKETS

Flea markets are popular, especially at the weekends. Most take place on Saturday, some every two weeks and most only from spring to late autumn. The key ones around Munich are **Zenith Flohmarkt** at Lilienthalallee, **Air Antik**

fleamarket at the airport between the terminals, every second Sunday in the month, and **Flohmarkt Riem**, the largest in Bavaria, at the trade show grounds.

FOOD SHOPPING

Viktualienmarkt *(see p214)* is a huge produce market, selling fruit, vegetables, spices, meat, poultry, fish, preserves and flowers. It is a feast for all the senses and a permanent fixture – open daily. *Bio* is the German word for organic and Germans have always been enthusiastic about organic produce. **Basic Bio** is a good organic supermarket in the city centre. For a selection of gourmet

treats head to **Dallmayr** or **Käfer**, the city's top delicatessens, while butchers' shops sell the famous Bavarian white sausages.

CHRISTMAS MARKET

Munich holds a traditional Christmas market *(Christkindlmarkt)* from the first week of Advent until Christmas Eve. The market is a great tourist attraction and special trips are organized from all over Europe. Wooden stalls sell a huge variety of handcrafted decorations, in particular wooden mangers and tree decorations, all delicately carved, in addition to candles, ornaments, food and mulled wine.

***Christkindlmarkt**, Munich's Christmas market*

DIRECTORY

DEPARTMENT STORES AND SHOPPING CENTRES

Galeria Kaufhof
Kaufingerstraße 1–5. **Map** 2 B4. **Tel** (089) 231851.
www.galeria-kaufhof.de

Ludwig Beck
Marienplatz 11.
Map 2 B4.
Tel (089) 7236910.
www.ludwigbeck.de

Fünf Höfe
Theatinerstraße. **Map** 2 B4.
www.fuenfhoefe.de

Olympia Einkaufszentrum
Hanauerstraße 68.
www.olympia-einkaufszentrum.de

Perlacher Einkaufspassage
Thomas Dehler Straße 12.
www.einkaufscenter-neuperlach.de

Riem Arcaden
Willy-Brandt-Platz 5.
www.riem-arcaden.de

FASHION

Loden-Frey
Maffeistraße 7.
Map 2 B4.
www.loden-frey.com

Off & Co
Belgradstraße 5.
www.offandco.com

Slips
Am Gärtnerplatz 2.
www.slipsfashion.de

Theresa
Maffeistraße 3. **Map** 2 B4.
www.mytheresa.com

CHILDREN'S SHOPS

Die Puppenstube
Luisenstraße 68.
Tel (089) 2723267.

Noemi & Friends
Marktstraße 13,
Schwabing.
www.noemiandfriends.de

Schlichting
Weinstraße 8. **Map** 2 B4.
www.schlichting.de

Thierchen Kindermode
Hans-Sachs-Straße 15.

FLEA MARKETS

Air Antik
Munich Airport Center.
Tel (08441) 871254.
www.airantik.de

Flohmarkt Riem
Am Messeturm.
Tel (089) 960 51632.
www.flohmarkt-riem.com

Zenith Flohmarkt
Lilienthalallee. **Tel** (089) 30765512. www.flohmarkt-freimann.de

FOOD SHOPPING

Basic Bio
Westenriederstraße 35.
Map 2 B4. **Tel** (089) 242 0890. www.basic-ag.de

Dallmayr
Dienerstraße 14–15. **Map** 2 B4. www.dallmayr.de

Käfer
Prinzregentenstraße 73.
www.feinkost-kaefer.de

Viktualienmarkt
Peteplatz-Frauenstraße.
Map 2 B4.

ENTERTAINMENT IN MUNICH

Munich is best known for the Oktoberfest, the Olympic grounds and Hofbräuhaus, but it also has an international reputation as a city of culture. There are 56 theatres, three large orchestras and one opera house. Munich has the rich and the powerful of its past to thank for creating and preserving

Bird from
Munich Zoo

its many splendid venues. This cultured metropolis on the Isar caters to all tastes, from traditional to modern, whether in theatre, music or film. There are several festivals during the year, as well as various sporting events, when the city comes alive, attracting visitors from all over the world.

ENTERTAINMENT GUIDES AND TICKETS

Munich Found is the best events magazine and the **Tourist Board** has comprehensive listings of events happening all over Munich. Also, check the Thursday edition of *Süddeutsche Zeitung* and the daily *Münchner Merkur*.

You can book tickets direct from box offices by phone or in person. There are also two **Zentraler Kartenverkauf** ticket kiosks in Marienplatz underground concourse, or use the **Abendzeitung Schalterhalle** (kiosk).

THEATRE, OPERA AND CLASSICAL MUSIC

State theatres are subsidized and so tickets are very reasonably priced. The Bavarian State Orchestra, Opera and Ballet all perform at the **Nationaltheater**. The **Deutsches Theater** offers musicals and shows, while the **Prinzregententheater** has the Bavarian State Opera and a concert hall. The Art

Nouveau **Staatstheater am Gärtnerplatz** presents opera, ballet, operetta, musicals and the Symphony Orchestra. **Gasteig Culture Center** is a world-class concert hall, home to the Munich Philharmonic Orchestra. The city also hosts an opera festival in July.

MUSIC AND DANCE

The **Pasinger Fabrik** offers a good programme of jazz, chansons and café theatre. There are numerous dance events and dance clubs. Big name artists, such as James Blunt, Massive Attack and The Rolling Stones, tend to perform at the **Circus Krone Bau**, **Zenith Kulturhalle**, **Olympiahalle** and the **Olympic Stadium**.

FILM

As the centre of the German film industry Munich offers 76 cinemas, the **Bavarian Film Studios** and a college for film and television. Try the English tour of the studios daily at 1pm. The **Munich Film Festival**

in July boasts over 200 films on 15 screens, almost all of them German, European or world premieres.

FESTIVALS

Munich's most famous festival is the **Oktoberfest**. For the whole of September it takes over a dedicated fairground, Theresienwiese, with beer

Munich's world-famous Oktoberfest

tents, traditional Bavarian brass bands, people dressed in traditional Bavarian costume (*Trachten*), fairground rides and the famous iced gingerbread hearts, *Lebkuchen*. There is also the **Tollwood Festival** in July and December, which has music, food, a circus, performances in tents, family fun and a craft fair. Munich also celebrates the *Dult* on three occasions throughout the year. *Dult* is the old word for street fair or market and there are traditional stalls and merry-go-rounds. Carnival or *Fasching* is celebrated throughout Munich with parties, processions and dressing up, but it is not as important here as in other cities.

The imposing Nationaltheater on Max-Joseph-Platz

Munich's ultra-modern Allianz Arena

SPORT

Most Münchners love the outdoors. Many make regular trips to the not too distant Alps. Running, skiing, rollerblading, cycling, Nordic walking and football are all very popular. The English Garden in the city centre is a huge park where people rollerblade, cycle, run or just meet up with friends.

Munich has two football teams: FC Bayern and TSV 1860 München, also known as "the Lions" because they are sponsored by the Löwenbräu Munich brewery with a lion as its coat of arms. The **Allianz Arena** is the fantastic stadium built for the 2006 World Cup. It is an architectural marvel which lights up in various colours. For Bayern Munich merchandise head to the **FC Bayern Shop** in the Arena. The shop website gives details of other stores located at Central Station and the Hofbräuhaus.

Other key sporting events are the Bavarian International Tennis Championships (ATP tournament), the BMW International Golf Open and Munich Blade Night, Monday evenings from April to September, when rollerbladers take over the streets. Runners will enjoy the Media Marathon and also the Münchner Stadtlauf (city run). A sport unique to Munich is surfing on the River Isar at the weirs.

KIDS' ENTERTAINMENT

Children will love Kids' Kingdom – **Kinderreich** – in the Deutsches Museum. The area is designated for children and has giant interactive games and water games, plus a real fire engine. Adults can only enter with their kids. Several playgrounds can be found along the River Isar in the city centre, but the best is **Westpark Spielzone Ost Untersendling** which can be reached by the underground. The new **Sea Life Olympia-park** centre is also an excellent outing, as is the zoo at **Tierpark Hellabrunn**.

Sea life exhibit at Olympiapark Munich

DIRECTORY

MUNICH STREET FINDER

Map references given in this chapter for sights (and in the Munich hotel and restaurant listings at the back of the book) refer to the maps here. The key map below shows the area of Munich covered by the *Street*

Finder. The maps include the major sightseeing areas, historic attractions, railway stations, bus stations, U-Bahn and S-Bahn stations and train stations. The word Straße (Str.) indicates a street, Platz a square, Brücke a bridge and Bahnhof a railway station.

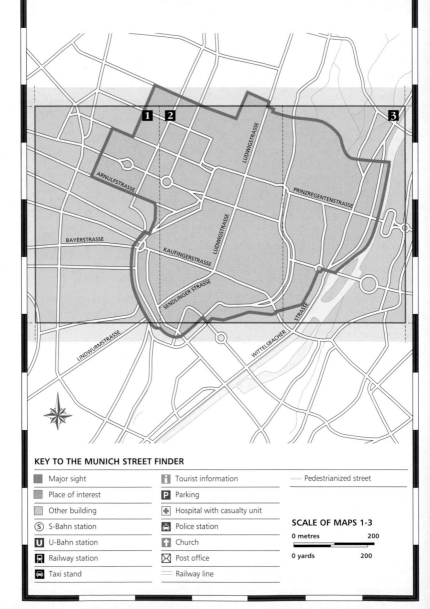

KEY TO THE MUNICH STREET FINDER

■ Major sight	ℹ Tourist information	— Pedestrianized street
■ Place of interest	🅿 Parking	
■ Other building	✚ Hospital with casualty unit	
Ⓢ S-Bahn station	🚓 Police station	**SCALE OF MAPS 1-3**
Ⓤ U-Bahn station	✝ Church	0 metres 200
🚆 Railway station	⊠ Post office	0 yards 200
🚖 Taxi stand	══ Railway line	

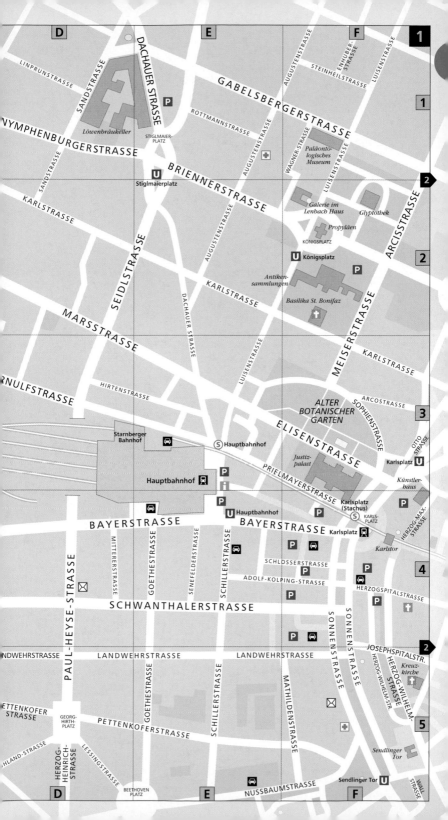

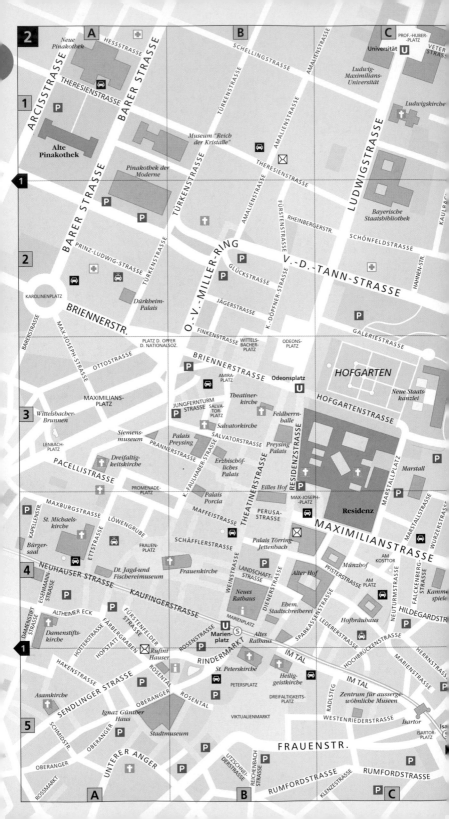

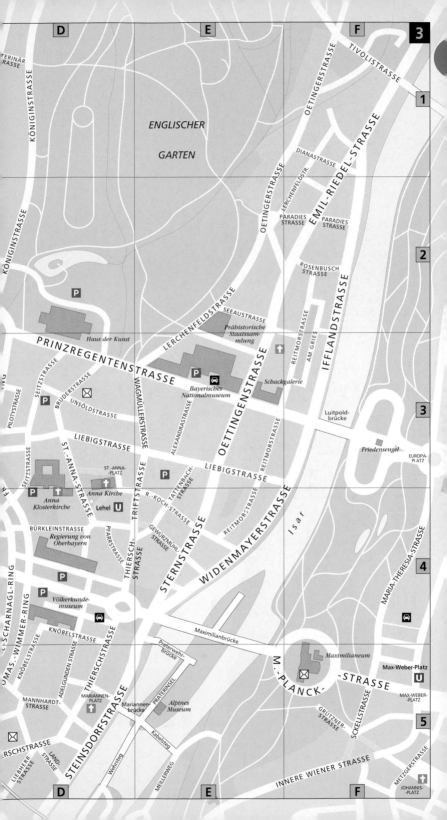

BAVARIA

Bavaria is the biggest federal state in the Federal Republic of Germany. It is made up of regions that, in the past, were either independent secular territories or bishoprics. It includes former free towns of the Holy Roman Empire, such as Nördlingen, Rothenburg ob der Tauber, Dinkelsbühl, Nuremberg and Augsburg, which lost their independence to Bavaria only in the early 19th century.

The area that is now known as Bavaria was inhabited in early times by Celts and Romans. The German Baiovarii, which gave the territory its name, arrived here during the 5th and 6th centuries. In the second half of the 6th century, the area was conquered by the Franks then, from 1180 until 1918, Bavaria was ruled by the Wittelsbach dynasty. During Medieval times, this split into the Upper Bavarian line (Straubing, Ingolstadt and Munich) and the Lower Bavarian line (Landshut). In 1505, separate provinces were once again combined into a single country. During the 16th and 17th centuries the duchy of Bavaria was the bulwark of Roman Catholicism within the Holy Roman Empire and during the reign of Maximilian I, Bavaria fought against the Protestant Union in the Thirty Years' War. For his loyalty to Rome, Maximilian I was rewarded in 1623 with the title of Elector, which meant that he could vote in elections for the Emperor. Following the fall of the Holy Roman Empire, Bavaria became a kingdom and remained as such until 1918.

Bavaria's turbulent history has left behind a rich architectural and cultural heritage. In addition to Roman antiquities, Baroque fortresses and fairy-tale castles, the region also has more than its share of glorious Alpine scenery, beer halls and colourful festivals, all of which make this one of the most popular parts of Germany for tourists. The capital, Munich, is a lively cosmopolitan city of wide boulevards and leafy squares with a wide choice of shops, restaurants, cinemas and theatres.

Girls dressed in national costume celebrating St Leonard's Festival

◁ Interior of the Abbey library, in Metten

Exploring Bavaria

Bavaria is a paradise for tourists. Its beautiful lakes
attract lovers of water sports, while the
mountainous regions of the Bavarian Forest
offer the unspoiled charms of nature.
The Alps, with their charming
mountain hostels and num-
erous ski-lifts, provide endless
possibilities for enjoyment.
Towns and villages feature
magnificent historic sights and
the capital, Munich, combines the
advantages of a lively metropolis
with a peaceful atmosphere that
is not often found in large cities.

The façade and central rotunda of Bayreuth's Eremitage

SIGHTS AT A GLANCE

Fulda ↑ | Erfurt ↑

Bad Neustadt
an der Saale
279
Schweinfurt
Hammelburg
Werneck
Frankfurt
ASCHAFFENBURG **1**
Karlstadt
BAMBER
POMMERSFELDE
WÜRZBURG **6**
Kitzingen
Neustadt an
der Aisch
ROTHENBUR
OB DER TAU **17**
13
ANSBACH
Heilbronn →   Gunzenhausen
11
DINKELSBÜHL
NÖRDLIN **12**
Donauwört
Dillinger
der Don
Günzburg
Ulm   Neus
Neu-Ulm   AUGSBUR
300
LANDS
AM
Memmingen
45 OTTOBEURE
Scho
Marktoberdorf
KEMPTEN **41**
LINDAU
42
FÜSSEN **44**
Bodensee   HOHENSCHWANGAU **40**
SCHL
Feldkirch   **43**   NEU
OBERSTDORF   WANS

0 km   30
0 miles   30

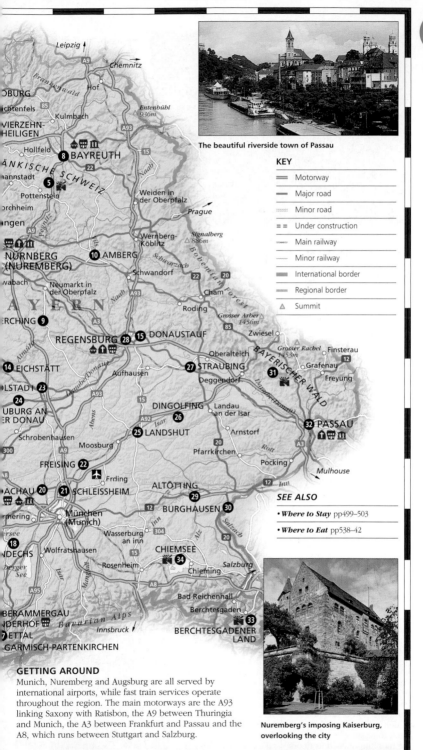

Leipzig
Chemnitz
Hof
Entenbühl 936m
OBURG
ichtenfels 85
Kulmbach
VIERZEHN-
HEILIGEN
Hollfeld
8 BAYREUTH
ÄNKISCHE SCHWEIZ
annstadt
5
Pottenstein
Weiden in
der Oberpfalz
orchheim
Prague
ingen
Wernberg-
Köblitz
Signalberg
△886m
NÜRNBERG
(NUREMBERG)
10 AMBERG
wabach
Schwandoff
Neumarkt in
der Oberpfalz
B A Y E R N
22 20
Cham
RCHING 9
Roding
Grosser Arber
1456m
REGENSBURG 28 15 DONAUSTAUF
Zwiesel
Grosser Rachel
1453m Finsterau
14 EICHSTÄTT
Oberaltech
BAYERISCHER WALD
27 STRAUBING
31
12
Grafenau
Freyung
Aufhausen
Deggendorf
LSTADT 23
24
UBURG AN
ER DONAU
DINGOLFING
Landau
an der Isar
26
32 PASSAU
Schrobenhausen
Moosburg
25 LANDSHUT
Arnstorf
FREISING 22
Pfarrkirchen
Pocking
ACHAU 20
Frding
21 SCHLEISSHEIM
ALTÖTTING
Mulhouse
mering
München
(Munich)
29
BURGHAUSEN 30
18
Wasserburg
an inn
NDECHS
Wolfratshausen
CHIEMSEE
34
Rosenheim
Chieming
Salzburg
Bad Reichenhall
Berchtesgaden
BERAMMERGAU
Bavarian Alps
NDERHOF
ETTAL
Innsbruck
33
BERCHTESGADENER
LAND
GARMISCH-PARTENKIRCHEN

The beautiful riverside town of Passau

KEY

▬	Motorway
▬	Major road
▦	Minor road
= =	Under construction
▬	Main railway
▬	Minor railway
▬	International border
▬	Regional border
△	Summit

SEE ALSO

- *Where to Stay* pp499–503
- *Where to Eat* pp538–42

GETTING AROUND

Munich, Nuremberg and Augsburg are all served by
international airports, while fast train services operate
throughout the region. The main motorways are the A93
linking Saxony with Ratisbon, the A9 between Thuringia
and Munich, the A3 between Frankfurt and Passau and the
A8, which runs between Stuttgart and Salzburg.

Nuremberg's imposing Kaiserburg,
overlooking the city

Red sandstone exterior of Schloss Johannisburg, Aschaffenburg

created by Maximilian von Welsch in 1715, in what was the then fashionable, geometric French style. It is now laid out in English-garden style.

♠ Schloss Weissenstein
Tel (09548) 98180.
☐ Apr–Oct: 10am–5pm daily.
every hour. (Short tour: 11:30am and 4:30pm.)

Coburg ❸

Road map D5. 👥 44,000. 🚉
🛈 Herrngasse 4 (09561-741 80).

Former residence of the Wettin family, Coburg is situated on the bank of the river Itz. It is dominated by a massive fortress, the **Veste Coburg**, which is one of the largest in Germany. Coburg's origins go back to the 11th century, but its present-day appearance is mainly the result of remodelling that was carried out in the 16th and the 17th centuries.

The fortress consists of a number of buildings clustered around several courtyards and surrounded by a triple line of walls. The complex is now a museum, housing various collections, including prints and drawings, arms and armour.

In 1530, the fortress provided refuge to Martin Luther who, as an outlaw, hid here from April until October. The room in which he hid is

Aschaffenburg ❶

Road map C5. 👥 67 000. 🚉
🛈 Schlossplatz 1 (06021-39 58 00).

Situated in Lower Franconia, Aschaffenburg enjoys a scenic position on the hilly right bank of the river Main. The town became the second seat of the Mainz bishops in the 13th century, the first being Mainz.

The northwest part of the old town features a majestic, red sandstone riverside castle, **Schloss Johannisburg**, which was once occupied by the Mainz bishops-electors.

The castle gallery holds a fine collection of European paintings, dating from the 15th to the 18th century. It includes works by Hans Baldung Grien and the most important collection of Lucas Cranach canvases in Europe. In the castle library are valuable medieval codices, such as the 10th-century *Book of Gospel Readings (Evangelarium)* from Fulda.

Occupying a scenic position above a vineyard a short distance to the northwest of the castle is Pompejanum. The Bavarian king Ludwig I was so fascinated with the discovery of Pompeii that he ordered a replica of the Castor and Pollux villa (*Casa di Castore e Polluce*) to be built. This he filled with his rich collection of antiquities. After undergoing restoration work to repair war damage, the museum opened its doors to the public again in 1994.

♠ Schloss Johannisburg
Schlossplatz 4. *Tel* (06021) 38 65 70. ☐ Apr–Sep: 9am–6pm Tue–Sun; Oct–Mar: 10am–4pm Tue–Sun.

Pommersfelden ❷

Road map D5. 🛈 Hauptstraße 11 (09548-922 00).

On the edge of the Steiger-wald – a popular hiking area – is the small village of Pommersfelden, which is dominated by its magnificent Baroque palace, **Schloss Weissenstein**. The palace was commissioned by the Mainz Archbishop and Elector and the Prince-Bishop of Bamberg, Lothar Franz von Schönborn. It was built, in only five years (1711–16), to a design by the famous architect, Johann Dientzenhofer.

This masterpiece of secular Baroque architecture is worth visiting for several reasons. Particularly interesting is the three-storey-high ornamental ceiling by Johann Rudolf Byss. The most spectacular room is the Marble Hall, which features paintings by Michael Rottmayr. The well-preserved interior of the palace houses a gallery, a library, and a valuable collection of furniture. After visiting the palace, you can take a stroll around its gardens, which were

Ornate entrance to Coburg's Stadthaus

furnished with antique
furniture and features
a portrait of Luther,
painted by Lucas
Cranach the Younger.

Among the most
important buildings in
the old town are the
late-Gothic church of
St Maurice and a
beautiful Renaissance
college building that
was founded by Prince
Johann Casimir in
1605. On the opposite
side of the market

**Interior of the monumental, Baroque
Vierzehnheiligen church**

square is the town
hall, originally built in
1577–79 and remodelled in
the 18th century.

Further along is the town
castle, **Schloss Ehrenburg**,
which was built in the 16th
century on the site of a dissolved Franciscan monastery.
The castle burned down in
1693 and was subsequently
rebuilt. The façade facing the
square was remodelled by
Karl Friedrich Schinkel in
Neo-Gothic style.

The castle has some fine
interiors, including the
Baroque Riesensaal and
Weisser Saal and a chapel
with rich stucco decorations.

♠ **Veste Coburg**
Tel (09561) 87 979. ⬜ Apr–Oct:
10am–5pm daily; Nov–Mar: 1–4pm
Tue–Sun. 🅿

♠ **Schloss Ehrenburg**
Schlossplatz 1. *Tel* (09561) 808
832. ⬜ Apr–Sep: 9am–5pm
Tue–Sun; Oct–Mar: 10am–3pm
Tue–Sun. 🎫 every hour. 🅿

Vierzehnheiligen ❹

Staffelstein. **Road map** D5.
Tel (09571) 950 80. ⬜ Apr–Oct:
7am–7pm; Nov–Mar: 8am–5pm.

High above the river Main
is Banz Abbey, a Benedictine
monastery built in 1695 by
Johann Leonhard and
Leonhard Dientzenhofer.
Directly opposite stands the
pilgrimage church of the
Fourteen Saints of Intercession.
The first chapel, erected on
this site in the 16th century,
proved to be too small to
accommodate the growing
numbers of pilgrims so, in
1741, the foundation stone

was laid for the monumental
new church, designed by
Balthasar Neumann. Built in
1741–72, this is one of the
most famous masterpieces of
South German Baroque, with
magnificent Rococo
furnishings. The building is
a cross-shaped basilica,
with a monumental twin-
tower façade.

The interior has
an exceptionally
dynamic style,
achieved by
combining the
longitudinal and
central planes: the
three ovals laid along
the main axis join with
the two circles of the
transept. The centrepiece
of the nave is the "Altar
of Mercy", which stands
at the spot where,
according to a 1519
legend, a shepherd
had visions of Christ
with the fourteen
Saints of Intercession.
The altar features statues
of the fourteen saints, and
are the work of F X
Feuchtmayr and J G Üblher
(1763). The rich stucco
decorations and frescoes
are the work of Giuseppe
Appiani.

**Madonna from
Marienkapelle in
Ebermannstadt**

Fränkische Schweiz ❺

Road map D5.

The area popularly known as
Franconian Switzerland
(*Fränkische Schweiz*) covers
the area between Nuremberg,
Bamberg and Bayreuth. One
of Germany's most beautiful
tourist regions, it offers its
visitors picturesque green
meadows, magnificent high-
lands covered with cornfields,
imposing castles perched on
top of high rocks, fabulous
dolomite rocks and deep
caves with stalactites. Its
towns and villages, with their
charming inns and timber-
frame houses, look like a
setting for *Snow White and
Seven Dwarfs*. The main
routes across the area
run alongside its
rivers – the Wiesent,
Leinleiter, Püttlach
and Trubach. The
Wiesent, which is
ideal for canoeing,
cuts across the
region from east to
west, joining the river
Regnitz near the town
of Forchheim. The
town features many
timber-frame houses,
including the old town
hall dating from the
14th to the 16th
century. Near
Forchheim, in
Ebermannstadt, is
a Marian church with
a fine Madonna. The
federal route B470
leads to the picturesque
village of Tüchersfeld, which
is built into the rocks. A good
base for exploring this area is
the village of Pottenstein. St
Elizabeth of Thuringia is said
to have stayed here
in 1227. To the
east of the castle
is a cave with
impressive
stalactites.

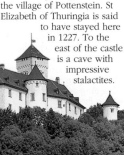

Schloss Greifenstein in Heiligenstadt, in Fränkische Schweiz

Würzburg ❻

The bombing raid on Würzburg on 16 March 1945 lasted for about 20 minutes and destroyed over 80 percent of the town's buildings. It seemed that Würzburg, which occupies a picturesque position on the banks of the river Main, had been erased from the face of the earth. Like Dresden, however, the town rose from the ashes and once again it enchants visitors with its rich heritage of historic sights. As well as being a popular tourist destination, Würzburg is also an important commercial and cultural centre for Lower Franconia and home of the excellent Franconian wine.

View over Würzburg, with Dom St Kilian in the foreground

🚇 Residenz
See pp246–7.

⛪ Dom St Kilian
Domplatz. *Tel* (0931) 321 18 30.
◯ 10am–5pm Mon– Sat, 1–6pm Sun and holidays.

Next to the great cathedral churches of Mainz, Speyer and Worms, this is Germany's fourth largest Romanesque church. It was built in 1045–1188, its patron saint an Irish monk who came to Würzburg in AD 686.

The church is a three-nave basilica with a transept and a twin-tower façade. Inside, the Romanesque main nave with its flat roof contrasts sharply with the Baroque stucco embellishments of the choir.

In the north nave is an interesting group of bishops' tombs, including two that are the work of Tilman Riemenschneider. At the end of the north transept is a chapel, which was built by Balthasar Neumann for the bishops of the House of Schönborn.

⛪ Neumünster-Kirche
St-Kilians-Platz.

Just north of the cathedral, the Neumünster-Kirche was built in the 11th century at the burial site of St Kilian and his fellow Irish martyrs, St Kolonat and St Totnan.

The church's imposing Baroque dome and its red sandstone façade date from the 18th century. Featured in

The beautiful red sandstone façade of Neumünster-Kirche

the interior are numerous works of art, including a late 15th-century Madonna and the *Man of Sorrow* by the 15th-century German sculptor Tilman Riemenschneider. The north door leads to a lovely small courtyard; the remains of the cloister date from the Hohenstauf period. Under a lime tree is the resting place of a famous medieval minstrel Walther von der Vogelweide.

A procession is held each year on St Kilian's day (8 July) when theological students carry the skulls of the martyrs, contained in a transparent box, from the west crypt to the cathedral where they are put on public display.

⊞ Bürgerspital
Theaterstraße.

The Bürgerspital was founded in 1319 by Johann von Steren. Hospitals like this originally provided charitable care for the old as well as the infirm, and today this institution provides care for over one hundred elderly residents of Würzburg. It operates as a self-financing foundation, its main source of income being from vine-growing. Residents are given a quarter of a litre (½ pint) of an excellent home-produced wine each day, with double the ration on Sundays. Visitors can also sample various vintages.

⊞ Juliusspital
Juliuspromenade.

Just a short distance away from Bürgerspital is another hospital. Founded in 1576 by Julius Echter, Juliusspital was remodelled in the 17th and the 18th centuries. The Rococo pharmacy (1760–65) in the hospital arcades has survived intact and is well worth a visit.

🚇 Rathaus
Rueckermainstraße.

Würzburg's picturesque town hall was built in several stages. Begun in the 13th century, it was subsequently extended in the 15th and 16th centuries. Particularly noteworthy are the beautiful 16th-century paintings on the façade and the late-Renaissance tower, Roter Turm, which dates from around 1660.

An old crane near Alte Mainbrücke over the river Main

🏛 Alte Mainbrücke

Connecting the old town and Festung Marienberg, this beautiful bridge was built in 1473–1543. It is the oldest bridge over the Main.

⛪ Festung Marienberg

Fürstenbau-Museum
Tel (0931) 355 170. ⬜ Apr–Oct: 9am–6pm Tue–Sun. ⬤ Nov–Mar. 🗝
Mainfränkisches Museum
Tel (0931) 205 940. ⬜ Apr–Oct: 10am–5pm Tue–Sun; Nov–Mar: 10am–4pm Tue–Sun. 🗝
Burgführungen 🎫 Apr–Oct: 11am, 2pm, 3pm Tue–Fri; 10am, 11am, 1pm, 2pm, 3pm, 4pm Sat–Sun.

Built on the site of an old Celtic stronghold, the Marienberg Fortress towers above the town. In AD 707 a church was built here and, in 1201, work commenced on a fortress that served as the residence of the prince-bishops until 1719. Within its fortifications stands the first original donjon church dating from the 13th century, and the Renaissance-Baroque palace. The museum exhibits illustrate the 1,200-year history of the town. The former arsenal now houses the Franconian Museum with its valuable collection of sculptures by Tilman Riemenschneider.

VISITORS' CHECKLIST

Road map C5. 🏘 128,000. ✈ 7 km (4½ miles) west. 🚉 Haupt-bahnhof. 🛈 Falkenhaus am Markt (0931-37 23 35). 🎪 Afrikafestival (May), Würzburger Weindorf (May/ Jun), Mozartfest (Jun), Kilianifest (Jul), Bachtage (Nov–Dec).

⛪ Käppele

Mergentheimer Strasse.
Standing at the top of a hill at the southwestern end of the city, this twin-towered Baroque chapel is the work of Balthasar Neumann (1747–50). Its interior is lavishly decorated with beautiful wall paintings by Matthias Günther.

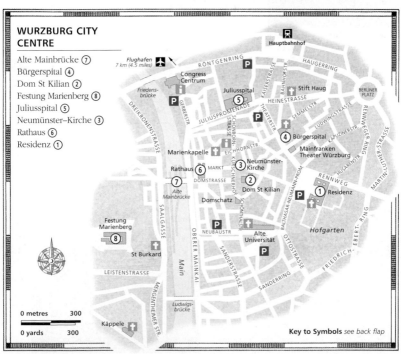

Festung Marienberg, built on a hill overlooking the river Main

WURZBURG CITY CENTRE

Hauptbahnhof

Flughafen 7 km (4.5 miles)

Congress Centrum

Friedens-brücke

RÖNTGENRING
HAUGERRING
BERLINER PLATZ

Juliusspital ⑤
Stift Haug
HEINESTRASSE

GERBERSTR
DREIKRONENSTRASSE
JULIUSPROMENADE
KAISERSTRASSE
BAHNHOFSTR
THEATERSTR
SEMMELSTR
LUDWIGSTRASSE
RENNWEGER RING

④ Bürgerspital
KAPUZINERSTR

Marienkapelle
EICHHORNSTR
Mainfranken Theater Würzburg
HUSARENSTR
MARTIN-LUTHER-STRASSE

Rathaus ⑥ MARKT
DOMSTRASSE
③ Neumünster-Kirche
KIRCHHOF
② Dom St Kilian
RENNWEG

⑦ Alte Mainbrücke
SCHÖNBORNSTRASSE
① Residenz
EBERT-RING

Domschatz
SCHÖNTALSTR
BALTHASAR-NEUMANN-PROM.
Hofgarten
OTTOSTRASSE

Festung Marienberg ⑧
SAALGASSE
NEUBAUSTR
Alte Universität
SANDERSTRASSE
FRIEDRICH-

St Burkard
OBERER MAINKAI
Main
SANDERRING

LEISTENSTRASSE
MERGENTHEIMER STR
Ludwigs-brücke

| 0 metres | 300 |
| 0 yards | 300 |

Käppele

Key to Symbols see back flap

Residenz in Würzburg

Sculpture from Residenz garden

This vast complex on the eastern edge of the town was commissioned by two prince-bishops, the brothers Johann Philipp Franz and Friedrich Karl von Schönborn. Its construction between 1720 and 1744 was supervised by several architects, including Johann Lukas von Hildebrandt and Maximilian von Welsch. However, the Residenz is mainly associated with the architect Balthasar Neumann, who was responsible for the overall design.

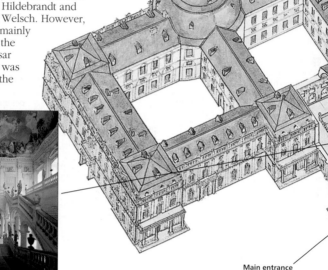

Napoleon's bedroom

Main entrance

Martin-von-Wagner-Museum entrance

★ Treppenhaus
The work of the Venetian artist Giovanni Battista Tiepolo, the largest fresco in the world adorns the vault of the staircase.

Frankonia-Brunnen
This fountain, designed by Ferdinand von Miller, was constructed in the parade square in front of the Residenz. It was funded by donations from the inhabitants of Würzburg.

The Coat of Arms of the Patron
The richly carved coat of arms are by Johann Wolfgang von der Auwery and are the personal arms of Friedrich Karl von Schönborn, Prince-Bishop of Bamberg and Würzburg.

★ Kaisersaal
The centrepiece of the palace, the sumptuous emperor's chamber, testifies to the close relationship between Würzburg and the Holy Roman Empire.

VISITORS' CHECKLIST

Residenzplatz 2. **Tel** (0931) 35 51 70. ☐ Apr–Oct: 9am–6pm daily; Nov–Mar: 10am–4pm daily. ● 1 Jan, 24, 25, 31 Dec. 🚫

Garden Hall
This vast, low hall has Rococo stucco works by Antonio Bossi, dating from 1749. There is also a painting on the vaulting by Johan Zick dating from 1750, depicting The Feast of the Gods *and* Diana Resting.

Venetian Room
This room is named after three tapestries depicting the Venetian carnival. Further ornaments include decorative panels with paintings by Johann Thalhofer, a pupil of Rudolph Byss.

★ Hofkirche
The church interior is richly decorated with paintings, sculptures and stucco ornaments. The side altars were designed by Johann Lukas von Hildebrandt and feature paintings by Giovanni Battista Tiepolo.

STAR SIGHTS

★ Hofkirche

★ Kaisersaal

★ Treppenhaus

Bamberg ⓐ

Situated on seven hills like ancient Rome, Bamberg features a splendidly preserved old town, encircled by the branches of the river Regnitz. The town is famous not only for its exceptional artistic heritage but also for its excellent beer, produced by one of the nine breweries that operate here. Its long history goes back to AD 902, when the Babenberg family established their residence here. The town grew and prospered in the wake of the Thirty Years' War. In 1993, Bamberg became a UNESCO World Heritage Site.

Beautiful rose garden at the rear of the Neue Residenz

Exploring Bamberg

A good place to start sightseeing is the Domplatz, one of Germany's loveliest squares, with its magnificent cathedral church and the old bishop's palace. After visiting the Neue Residenz you can go down to the river, where you will find the water palace, Concordia. The old town is reached by crossing one of two bridges – Untere or Obere Brücke.

⛨ Dom

See pp250–51.

⛨ Alte Hofhaltung

Historisches Museum
Domplatz 7. **Tel** (0951) 519 07 46.
◯ 9am–5pm Tue–Sun.
On the west side of Domplatz stands a magnificent portal, featuring statues of the imperial couple Heinrich II and Kunigunde. This is the gate to the former bishop's residence, built at the turn of the 15th and 16th centuries in place of an old fortress of Heinrich II. Within the wings of the building is a pleasant courtyard. The museum that is housed here focuses on the history of the region.

⛨ Neue Residenz und Staatsgalerie

Domplatz 8. **Tel** (0951) 519 390.
◯ Apr–Sep: 9am–6pm daily;
Oct–Mar: 10–4pm daily.
www.schloesser-bayern.de
The Neue Residenz, with its richly decorated apartments and the Emperor's Room, was built in 1695–1704 and is the work of Johann Leonhard Dietzenhofer. Its walls are adorned with magnificent frescos painted by the Tyrolean artist Melchior Steidl. The walls and pillars feature the Habsburg family tree, while 16 statues represent Emperors of the Holy Roman Empire. The Neue Residenz houses a collection of old German masters, including *The Flood* by Hans Baldung Grien and three canvases by Lucas Cranach the Elder.

⛨ Karmelitenkloster

Kreuzgang ◯ 8:30–11.30 am, 2:30–5:30pm daily.
The hospital-abbey complex of St Theodore was founded in the late 12th century by Bishop Eberhard. Since 1589 the church and abbey have belonged to the Carmelite order. The south tower and Romanesque portal are the remains of the massive 12th-century basilica. The interior of the church was redesigned in the late 17th and early 18th centuries so the altar is now situated at its western end, while the entrance is on the site of the previous presbytery. The layout of the cloisters on the south side of the church is typical of Cistercian designs.

⛨ Wasserschloss Concordia

Concordiastrasse. ◯ to the public.
This magnificent Baroque palace, which enjoys a scenic position on the water's edge, was built for Counsellor Böttinger between 1716 and 1722, to a design by Johann Dientzenhofer. The building now houses a science institute.

⛨ Altes Rathaus

The Baroque lower bridge, Untere Brücke, provides a magnificent view over the upper bridge, Obere Brücke,

The Baroque palace Concordia on the bank of the river Regnitz

Picturesque fishermen's cottages in Klein-Venedig

VISITORS' CHECKLIST

Road map D5. 71,000.
8 km (5 miles) to the southeast.
Geyerswörthstraße 3 (0951-
297 62 00). Calderon-
Festspiele (June), Sandkirchweih
(August). **www**.bamberg.info

with its fabulous town hall.
This originally Gothic seat of
the municipal authorities was
remodelled in 1744–56 by
Jakob Michael Küchel. The
half-timbered structure of the
Rottmeisterhaus, which seems
to be gliding over the waves
of the river Regnitz, was
added in 1688.

🏛 Klein-Venedig
"Little Venice" is a district of
fishermen's cottages, their
picturesque façades adorned
with pots of geraniums.
Visitors come here for a glass
of Rauchbier – a local beer
with a smoky flavour – while
they enjoy the view.

🏛 Grünermarkt
With its historic houses and
adjacent Maximilianplatz,
Grünermarkt lies at the heart
of the old town. Here you
will find the magnificent

Baroque St Martin's Church,
built in 1686–91 by the
Dientzenhofer brothers. Also
notable are the late-Baroque
buildings of the St Catherine
Hospital and Seminary, built
by Balthasar Neumann, which
now serves as the town hall.

🔒 Kirche St Michael
Michaelsberg.
Fränkisches Brauereimuseum
Apr–Oct: 1–5pm Wed–Sun.
The Benedictine abbey that
stood on this site was founded
in 1015. The surviving church
was built after 1121 and later
remodelled in the 16th and
17th centuries. On the ceiling
of the church, nicknamed
the "Botanical Gardens", are
paintings depicting almost
600 species of medicinal
plants. The abbey's Baroque
buildings date from the 17th
and 18th centuries and are
the work of Johann Dientzen-

hofer and Balthasar Neumann.
The domestic quarters include
the abbey's brewery, which
now houses a museum.

🏛 Schloss Seehof
Memmelsdorf. Apr–Oct: 9am–6pm
Tue–Sun. Nov–Mar.
Built and designed by Antonio
Petrini in 1686, this was origi-
nally the summer residence of
the prince-bishops of Bamberg.
The nine magnificent state
rooms have been restored
and are open to the public.

Façade of Schloss Seehof in
Memmelsdorf

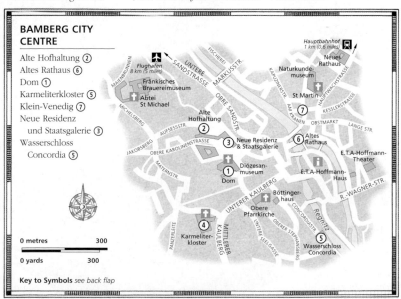

BAMBERG CITY CENTRE

Alte Hofhaltung ②
Altes Rathaus ⑥
Dom ①
Karmeliterkloster ④
Klein-Venedig ⑦
Neue Residenz
 und Staatsgalerie ③
Wasserschloss
 Concordia ⑤

0 metres 300
0 yards 300

Key to Symbols see back flap

Bamberg Cathedral

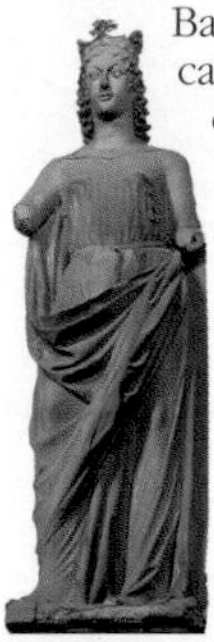

Bamberg's skyline is dominated by the cathedral of St Peter and St George, which combines the late Romanesque and early French-Gothic styles. Its construction started about 1211 and the church was consecrated in 1237. This is a triple-nave basilica with two choirs, whose apses are flanked by two pairs of towers. The cloisters were built between 1399 and 1457, while the monumental sculptures adorning the portals date from the 13th century. The western choir of the cathedral holds the only papal grave in Germany, that of Pope Clement II, who had been the local bishop.

Sculpted figure of Ecclesia

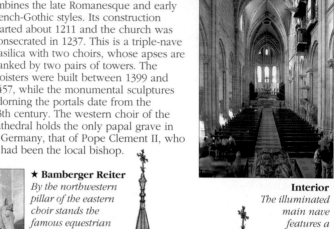

Interior
The illuminated main nave features a graceful, early Gothic, cross-ribbed vault.

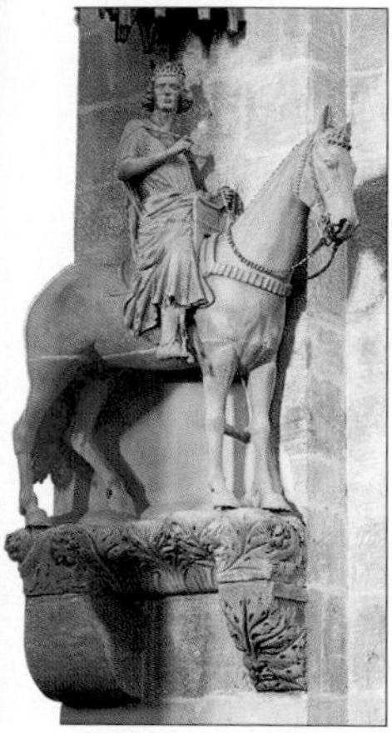

St George's Choir

★ **Bamberger Reiter**
By the northwestern pillar of the eastern choir stands the famous equestrian statue of the "Bamberg Rider", dating from about 1230. Many scholars have puzzled over the identity of the rider, but the riddle remains unsolved.

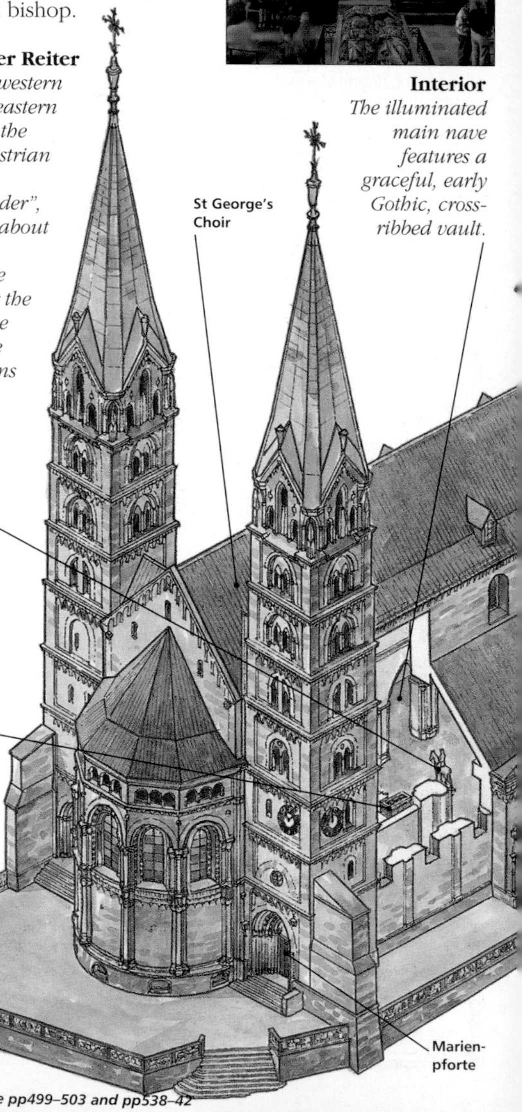

★ **Tomb of Heinrich II and Kunigunde**
This beautiful sarcophagus of the imperial couple is the work of Tilman Riemenschneider, completed in 1513.

Marien-pforte

St Peter's Choir

Emperor's Cloak
*The Diocesan Museum
houses an exhibition
of sacral art. It also
features a collection
of imperial vestments,
including Heinrich II's
blue cloak of stars.*

Hochaltar des Peterschores
*The main altar of
the west choir is
adorned with
sculptures
depicting the
Crucifixion
(1648–49) by
Justus Glesker.*

★ Marian Altar by Veit Stoß
*Veit Stoß was commissioned to create
this altar by his son, Andrew Stoß,
who was a Carmelite prior in
Nürnberg at the time. After
the victory of the Reformation in
Nürnberg, however, he moved
to Bamberg in 1543.*

STAR SIGHTS

★ Bamberger Reiter

★ Marian Altar by Veit Stoß

★ Tomb of Heinrich II and Kunigunde

Marienpforte
*This magnificent
stonework adorns the
main entrance. The
tympanum features
reliefs depicting scenes
from the Last Judgement.*

Bayreuth ❽

Lovers of German music associate this town with the composer Richard Wagner (1813–83), who took up residence here in 1872. Established in 1231, Bayreuth originally belonged to the family of Count von Andechs-Meran; in 1248 it passed to the Margraves of Nuremberg (von Zollern) and, since 1806, Franconian Bayreuth has belonged to Bavaria. The town flourished during the 17th and 18th centuries when it was the residence of the Margraves, particularly during the time of Margravine Wilhelmine, sister of the Prussian King Frederick the Great and wife of Margrave Frederick.

Extraordinary Baroque interior of the Markgräfliches Opernhaus

🎭 Markgräfliches Opernhaus

Opernstraße 14. *Tel (0921) 759 69 22.* ⏰ *Apr–Sep: 9am–6pm daily; Oct–Mar: 10am–4pm daily.* 📷

One of the finest theatres in Europe, the Markgräfliches Opera House was built in the 1740s by Joseph Saint-Pierre. Its ornate Baroque interior was designed by Giuseppe Galli Bibiena and his son Carlo, who came from a famous Bolognese family of theatre architects.

♣ Neues Schloss

Ludwigstraße 21. *Tel (0921) 759 21.* ⏰ *Apr–Sep: 9am–6pm daily; Oct–Mar: 10am–4pm daily.* 📷

The Neues Schloss (New Castle) was commissioned by Margravine Wilhelmine and built by Joseph Saint-Pierre. The elongated, three-storey structure combines classical lines with a rustic ground floor. The Italian wing was added in 1759. To this day nearly all the rooms have retained their original Baroque and Rococo decor. The park is arranged in a typically English style.

🏛 Villa Wahnfried

Richard-Wagner-Museum. Richard-Wagner-Straße 48. *Tel (0921) 75 72 816.* ⏰ *Apr–Oct: 9am–5pm daily (to 8pm Tue & Thu); Nov–Mar: 10am–5pm daily.* 📷 ● *Easter Sunday.*

On the northeast side of the castle garden is Villa Wahnfried. Built for Wagner by Carl Wölfel, the villa was destroyed during World War II but was restored in the 1970s. In the garden is Wagner's tomb and that of his wife Cosima, the daughter of Franz Liszt.

🏛 Franz-Liszt-Museum

Wahnfriedstraße 9. *Tel (0921) 516 64 88.* ⏰ *Sep–Jun: 10am–noon, 2–5pm daily; Jul-Aug: 10am–5pm daily.* 📷

A short distance from Villa Wahnfried, at the junction of Wahnfriedstrasse and Liszt-strasse, stands the house in which Hungarian composer Franz Liszt died in 1886. It now houses a museum dedicated to the composer.

🏛 Eremitage

4 km (2.5 miles) northeast of town. *Tel (0921) 759 69 37.* ⏰ *Apr–Sep: 9am–6pm daily, 1 Oct–15 Oct: 10am–4pm.* ● *15 Oct–Mar.*

In 1715–18, following the example of the French king Louis XIV and the fashion among the nobility for playing at ascetism, Margrave Georg Wilhelm ordered the building of the Eremitage complex as a retreat. With its horseshoe-shaped orangery, the hermitage (or Altes Schloss) was given to Margravine Wilhelmine as a birthday present. She then set about transforming it into a pleasure palace.

Tomb of Wagner and his wife in the garden of Villa Wahnfried

RICHARD WAGNER (1813–1883)

The German composer is inseparably linked with Bayreuth, where he enjoyed his greatest artistic triumphs. His career, which did not run smoothly in early days, began in Magdeburg, Königsberg and Riga. From there he had to flee, via London to Paris, from his pursuing creditors. His reputation was firmly established by successful performances of his romantic operas *The Flying Dutchman* (1843) and *Tannhäuser* (1845) in Dresden. Wagner's long-time sponsor was the eccentric Bavarian king, Ludwig II. From 1872 Wagner lived in Bayreuth, where Festspielhaus was built specifically for the operas.

Bust of Wagner by Arno Breker (1939)

Festspielhaus, specially designed venue for the annual Wagner Festival

VISITORS' CHECKLIST

Road map D5. 75,000. 10 km (6 miles) to northeast. Hauptbahnhof. Luitpoldplatz 9 (0921-885 88). Musica Bayreuth (May), Fränkische Festwoche (May), Richard-Wagner-Festspiele (Jul–Aug), Bayreuther Barock (Sep).

Festspielhaus

Festspielhügel. **Tel** (0921) 787 80. 10am, 10:45am, 2:15pm, 3pm, Tue–Sun (mornings only during the Festival). Apr–Jul (for rehearsals), Nov.
Each July and August, Wagner festivals are held in this theatre, which was built in 1872–75 to a design by Gottfried Semper. The world premiere of *The Ring of the Nibelung* was performed here in 1876.

Environs

Approximately 20 km (12 miles) to the northwest of Bayreuth is the town of **Kulmbach**. Famous for its countless breweries, the town hosts a big beer festival each year, in July and August. Its town hall has a beautiful, Rococo façade dating from 1752. From here you can walk to the castle hill to visit the Plassenburg Fortress, which has belonged to the Hohenzollern family since 1340. Until 1604, this was the seat of the von Brandenburg-Kulmbach Margraves. This vast structure was built in 1560-70. The gem in its crown is the Renaissance courtyard with arcades (Schöner Hof). The castle houses a vast collection of tin figurines, with some 30,000

items. In **Ködnitz**, to the southeast of Kulmbach, is the Upper Franconian Village School Museum. Based on the original school furnishings and various old photographs, the exhibition illustrates the teaching methods that were used in this region more than a hundred years ago.

Some 25 km (16 miles) from Bayreuth, in Sanspareil Park near Hollfeld, is the **Felsentheater** – an unusual 80-seat theatre set in a natural grotto.

Felsentheater, in a natural grotto in Sanspareil Park near Bayreuth

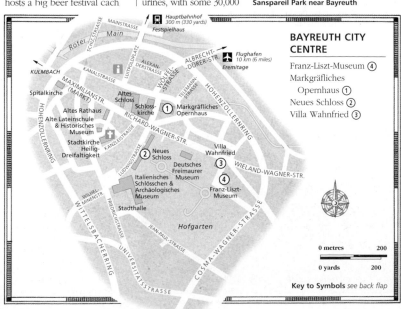

BAYREUTH CITY CENTRE

Franz-Liszt-Museum ④
Markgräfliches
  Opernhaus ①
Neues Schloss ②
Villa Wahnfried ③

Berching

Map D6. 🏛 *7,500.* ℹ️ *Petten-koferplatz 12 (08462-205 13).*

This charming little town, situated in the valley of the river Sulz, boasts a history that stretches back to the 9th century. To this day it retains the complete enclosure of its medieval city walls, including towers and gates with old oak doors. The most beautiful of the towers is the *Chinesische Turm* (the Chinese Tower).

The regional museum is well worth visiting, as are some of the local churches. These include an early Gothic church, Mariae Himmelfahrt, remodelled after 1756 by M Seybold and featuring some beautiful Rococo stucco ornaments. The Baroque St Lorenz, with its 13th century tower and original late-Gothic altar, is also noteworthy.

Amberg

Map D5. 🏛 *43,000.* ℹ️ *Zeüghaüsstr. 1a (09621-102 39).*

Situated at the edge of the Franconian Jura, on the banks of the river Vils, Amberg owes its development to local iron ore deposits and the steel industry. The well-preserved, oval-shaped old town is still encircled by medieval walls. At the centre is an enchanting market square with the vast 15th-century late-Gothic hall-church, Pfarrkirche St Martin, and Gothic town hall (1356), both still with their original interiors.

Amberg was once the residential town of the Rhine palatines, whose Renaissance palace and chancellery have survived to the present day.

The symbol of Amberg is the Stadtbrille, the bridge spanning the river Vils, whose arches reflected in the river resemble a pair of spectacles – hence its nickname "the town's spectacles".

The late-Gothic main altar in St George's Church, Dinkelsbühl

Dinkelsbühl

Map D6. 🏛 *11,000.* 🚉 ℹ️ *Marktplatz (09851-902 40).* 🎭 *Kinderzeche (mid-Jul).*

This old Franconian town is one of the best-preserved medieval urban complexes in Germany. The walls surrounding the city include four towers – Wörnitzer, Nördlinger, Seringer and Rothenburger Tor – which are all almost intact. The residential district of the town consists mainly of timber-framed houses. The finest example of these is the Deutsches Haus, which stands opposite St George's Church. Dating from the late 15th to the early 16th century, the house once belonged to the Drechsel-Deufstetten family and is now a hotel-restaurant.

The late-Gothic Church of St George is a triple-nave hall-church with no transept. Together with the presbytery, it forms one large interior crowned with magnificent network vaults. The most valuable items of the interior furnishings include the pulpit, the font – which dates from around 1500 – and the Crucifixion in the main altar, which is attributed to Michael Wolgemut. A fine view of the town can be obtained from the church tower.

In Turmgasse stands the Baroque palace of the Teutonic Order, built in 1760–64 by Mathias Binder.

Nördlingen

Map D6. 🏛 *20,000.* 🚉 ℹ️ *Marktplatz 2 (09081-842 16).* 🎭 *Stabenfest (May), Nördlinger Pfingstmesse Scharlachrennen (Jun–Jul), Sommerfestspiele (Jul), Historisches Stadtmauernfest (every third year in Sep; next in 2007).*

The town is situated in the Ries Basin, which is an immense and well-preserved crater that was formed millions of years ago by a meteor strike.

During the Middle Ages Nördlingen was a free town of the Holy Roman Empire and an important trade centre. The fortification walls which surround the city, including fifteen towers (dating from the 14th to the 15th centuries) have survived almost intact to this day.

The late-Gothic church of St George was built by Nikolaus Eseler, who also built the St George Church in Dinkelsbühl. The church is a triple-nave hall-church with round pillars and network vaults. Its imposing west tower, known as the Daniel Tower, offers a magnificent

The symbol of Amberg is the bridge named "the town spectacles"

panoramic view of the town and its environs.

The St Salvator's Church features original Gothic altars and a portal that has the scene of the *Last Judgement* in the tympanum.

The former hospital of the Holy Spirit is now home to an interesting **Stadtmuseum**. The 14th-century town hall features a striking external stone stairway (1618).

Statue from the Tanzhaus façade

🏛 **Stadtmuseum**
Vordere Gerbergasse 1.
Tel (09081-273 82 30).
⏰ Mar–Oct: 1:30–4:30pm Tue–Sun.
📷 Nov–Feb: open only to guided tours (reserve a place in advance by telephone). 🎟

Ansbach ⓭

Map D6. 🚶 *40,000*. 🚉
ℹ *Johann-Sebastian-Bach-Platz 1 (0981-512 43 or 194 33.* 📷
Ansbacher Frülingsfest (May), Bach-Woche (every two years in Jul: the next one is in 2007), Ansbacher Rokokospiele (Jul), Heimatfest (Jul).

The town, situated west of Nuremberg, began its history in AD 748 with the foundation of a Benedictine Abbey by a man named Gumbert. A settlement called Onoldsbach, which sprang up nearby, is now called Ansbach. From 1460 until 1791 Ansbach was the home of the von Brandenburg-Ansbach Margraves and in 1791 it was incorporated into Prussia; after 1806 it passed into Bavaria. The Markgräfliche residence is

situated in the north-eastern part of the Old Town. Remodelled several times it is now a Baroque neo-Classical structure. Its 27 original state apartments include the Mirror Room, Mirror Gallery, Dining Room and Audience Room. It now houses the Museum of Faience and Porcelain. The nearby Hofgarten has a 102-metre (335-ft) long Orangery. It also houses a Kaspar Hauser Collection.

🏛 **Markgrafenmuseum**
Kaspar-Hauser-Platz 1.
Tel (0981) 977 50 56. ⏰
May–Sep: 10am–5pm daily;
Oct–Apr: 10am–5pm Tue–Sun. 🎟

🏛 **Markgräfliche Residenz "Ansbacher Fayence und Porzellan"**
Promenade 27. *Tel* (0981) 953 83 90. ⏰ Apr–Sep: 9am–6pm Tue–Sun; Oct–Mar: 10am–4pm Tue–Sun. 📷 hourly. ♿

Eichstätt ⓮

Map D6. 🚶 *15,000*. 🚉
ℹ *Domplatz 8 (08421-988 00).*

Willibald, a close companion and compatriot of the Anglo-Saxon missionary Boniface, established a missionary-abbey (Eihstat) here. Soon afterwards Eichstätt became an episcopal town. In 1634 a fire ripped through the town, destroying four-fifths of its houses and four churches; after this the town was rebuilt in Baroque style.

Eichstätt is home to the country's only Catholic university, established in 1980. On the outskirts of town, on

Majestic Walhalla near Donaustauf

a hill overlooking the River Altmühl, stands the picturesque Willibald Castle, which until the 18th century was the residence of prince-bishops. Now it houses an interesting museum of artifacts from the Jurassic era, where visitors can see a very well preserved skeleton of *archaeopteryx*.

A new bishop's residence was built nearby from 1702 until 1768. Its west wing features a magnificent staircase and the Mirror Room, in which the works of Mauritio Pedetti, Johann Jakob Berg and Michael Franz are displayed.

Donaustauf ⓯

Walhalla. *Tel* (09403) 96 16 80.
⏰ Apr–Sep: 9am–5:45pm; Oct: 9am–4:45pm; Nov–Mar: 10am–11:45am & 1–3:45pm. 🎟

In 1830-41 Leo von Klenze built the Walhalla *(see above)*. This monument to the national glory occupies a scenic location on the River Danube. The building stands on a raised terrace and has the form of a Neo-Classical columned temple (similar to the Parthenon in Athens). It is adorned with 121 marble busts of artists and scientists.

Orangery of the Markgräfliche residence, in Ansbach

Nürnberg (Nuremberg) ⑯

Situated on the river Pegnitz, Nuremberg is not only a paradise for lovers of its famous gingerbread and sausages but is also the symbol of Germany's history. The earliest records of the town, the second largest in Bavaria, date from 1050 when it was a trading settlement. From 1219 Nuremberg, a free town of the Holy Roman Empire, was an important centre of craft and commerce. Its most rapid development took place in the 15th and 16th centuries, when many prominent artists, craftsmen and intellectuals worked here, making Nuremberg one of the cultural centres of Europe.

Picturesque alley near Frauentor

Exploring Lorenzer Seite

The southern part of the old town, known as Lorenzer Seite, is separated from the northern part by the river Pegnitz and encircled to the south by the city walls. Many of the area's historic treasures were carefully reconstructed following severe bomb damage during World War II.

⛩ Frauentor

Frauentorgraben.
Frauentor is one of the most attractive gates into the old town. It is installed in the massive city walls that were constructed during the 15th and 16th centuries. The vast tower, Dicker Turm, was erected nearby in the 15th century. Königstor, a magnificent gate that once stood to the right of Dicker Turm, was dismantled in the 19th century. Beyond Frauentor are a number of alleys with half-timbered houses, shops and cafés, built after the war.

⛪ Marthakirche

Königstraße 74–78.
Dating from the 14th century, the small hospital church of St Martha is tucked between the surrounding houses. Though its interior is virtually devoid of furnishing, it features some magnificent Gothic stained-glass windows, which date from around 1390.

⛩ Mauthalle

Hallplatz 2.
The massive structure that dominates Königstrasse is a Gothic granary built in 1498–1502 by Hans Beheim the Elder. It originally housed the town's municipal scales and the customs office. In the 19th century, the building was converted into a department store and continues in that role today, following post-war reconstruction.

🏛 Germanisches Nationalmuseum

See pp260–61.

⛪ St Lorenz-Kirche

Lorenzer Platz.
The most important building in Nuremberg is the Gothic church of St Lorenz, whose basilica-style main body was built around 1270–1350. The vast hall presbytery was added much later, in 1439–77. On entering the church it is worth taking a look at the magnificent main

```
0 metres        300
0 yards         300
```

Key to Symbols see back flap

SIGHTS AT A GLANCE

Panoramic view over the rooftops of Nuremberg

Impressive Mauthalle dominating Königstraße

portal, which is adorned with sculptures. In the main nave of the church, suspended from the ceiling above the altar, is a superb group sculpture, *Annunciation*, the work of Veit Stoß (1519). He was also the creator of the crucifix within the main altar and the magnificent statue of the Archangel Michael standing by the second pillar

the 1350 Gothic original. Diagonally across the square is the Nassauer Haus, a Gothic mansion whose lower storeys were built in the 14th century. The upper floors were added in the 15th century.

A short distance from the square, in Karolinenstraße, is a fine sculpture by Henry Moore.

✚ Heilig-Geist-Spital

In the centre of town, on the banks of the river Pegnitz, stands the Hospital of the Holy Spirit. Founded in 1332, this is one of the largest hospitals built in the Middle Ages and features a lovely inner courtyard with wooden galleries. The wing that spans the river was built during extension works in 1488–1527. Lepers were kept at some distance from the other patients, in a separate half-timbered building that was specially erected for the purpose. From 1424 until 1796, the insignia of the Holy Roman Empire were kept here rather than in the castle.

The Heilig-Geist-Spital now houses an old-folks' home and a restaurant. The entrance to the building is on the northern side of the river.

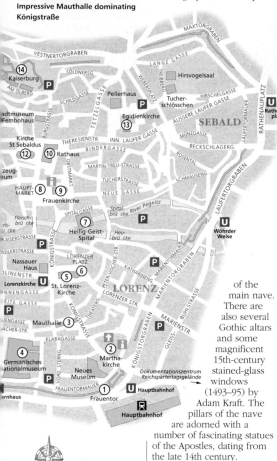

of the main nave. There are also several Gothic altars and some magnificent 15th-century stained-glass windows (1493–95) by Adam Kraft. The pillars of the nave are adorned with a number of fascinating statues of the Apostles, dating from the late 14th century.

🏛 Lorenzer Platz

Overlooked by the church of St Lorenz, Lorenzer Platz is a popular meeting place for the citizens of Nuremberg and visitors alike. Outside the church is the Fountain of the Virtues, *Tugendbrunnen* (1589), with water cascading from the breasts of its seven Virtues. Nearby is a statue of St Lorenz, which is a copy of

Heilig-Geist-Spital reflected in the waters of the river Pegnitz

Exploring Nürnberg (Nuremberg)

Nuremberg was once an important publishing centre. Schedel's *Liber Cronicarum* was published here in 1493 and, in 1543 – following the town's official adoption of the Reformation in 1525 – *The Revolutions of the Celestial Spheres* by Copernicus was published. The Thirty Years' War ended the town's development but, during the 19th century, it became the focus for the Pan-German movement. In 1945–49 the town was the scene of the trials for war crimes of Nazi leaders.

Detail of *Schöner Brunnen*, in Hauptmarkt

🏯 Hauptmarkt

Each year the Hauptmarkt provides a picturesque setting for the town's famous Christkindlesmarkt, which goes on throughout Advent. At this famous market you can buy gingerbread, enjoy the taste of German sausages, warm yourself with a glass of red wine spiced with cloves and buy locally made souvenirs.

Nuremberg's star attraction is the Gothic *Schöner Brunnen* (Beautiful Fountain), which was probably erected around 1385 but replaced in the early 20th century with a replica. It consists of a 19-metre (62-ft) high, finely carved spire

standing at the centre of an octagonal pool. The pool is surrounded by a Renaissance grille that includes the famous golden ring: the local tradition is that if you turn the ring three times, your wishes will come true. The pool is adorned with the statues of philosophers, evangelists and church fathers, while the spire is decorated with the statues of Electors and of Jewish and Christian heroes. Features and details of the original fountain are kept in the **Germanisches National-museum** *(see pp260–61).*

🏯 Frauenkirche

Hauptmarkt. ⏱ 9am–6pm Mon–Sat, 12:30pm–6:30pm Sun, 9am–5pm Fri. Commissioned by Emperor Charles IV, this Gothic hall-church dates from 1352–58. Over its richly decorated vestibule is the oriel of the west choir. Its gable contains a clock from Männleinlaufen, installed in 1509. Each day at noon the clock displays a procession of Electors paying homage to the Emperor. Also noteworthy is the Gothic altar *(Tucher Altar)*, which dates from 1445.

🏯 Rathaus

Rathausplatz.
The present town hall consists of several sections. Facing the Hauptmarkt is the oldest, Gothic part, built in 1332–40 and remodelled in the early 15th century. Behind, facing Rathausplatz, the Renaissance part, built in 1616–22 by Jakob Wolff. Its magnificent portals are decorated with heraldic motifs. The courtyard features a fountain dating from 1557.

🏛 Spielzeugmuseum

Karlstraße 13–15. *Tel* (0911) 231 31 64. ⏱ 10am–5pm Tue–Fri, 10am–6pm Sat–Sun. 🚫 Good Friday, 24, 25, 26, 31 Dec. 🅿
This enchanting toy museum, established in 1971, houses a magnificent collection of tin soldiers and a huge collection of dolls and puppets. Its greatest attraction, however, is a collection of antique dolls' houses, filled with miniature furniture and equipment.

🏯 Kirche St Sebald

Winklerstraße 26. ⏱ *year-round:* 11am–6pm Sun; Jan/Feb: 9:30am–4pm Mon–Sat; Mar–May & Oct–Dec: 9:30am–6pm Mon–Sat; Jun–Sep: 9:30am–8pm Mon–Sat.
The oldest of Nuremberg's churches, Kirche St Sebaldus was built in 1230–73 as a Romanesque, two-choir basilica. During remodelling in the 14th century, it was given two side naves and a soaring western hall-choir. The Gothic towers were completed in the late 15th century. At the centre of the presbytery is the magnificent tomb of St Sebald. This cast bronze structure was made by Peter Vischer the Elder. It houses a silver coffin (1397) containing relics of the saint. The church features some splendid carvings by Veit Stoß, including a magnificent statue of St Andrew (1505), which stands in the ambulatory around the presbytery, the Volckamersche Passion (1499) and the Crucifixion scene in the main altar (1520). Also noteworthy is the magnificent Gothic font and the Tucher family epitaph by Hans von Kulmbach (1513).

Heraldic arms adorning the tympanum of the town hall portal

For hotels and restaurants in this region see pp499–503 and pp538–42

The timber-frame building of the Dürerhaus

⛪ Egidienkirche

Egidienplatz.

Egidienkirche is the only surviving Baroque church in Nuremberg. Its façade, built after the fire of 1696, hides a building containing elements of the previous Romanesque-Gothic Benedictine church. The older chapels, including the Euchariuskapelle, Tetzel-kapellethe and Wolfgang-kapelle, survive to this day.

⛪ Kaiserburg

Kaiserburg-Museum. Innerer Burghof. **Tel** (0911) 200 95 40. ☐ Apr–Sep: 9am–6pm daily; Oct–Mar: 10am–4pm daily. 🖼

The three castles that tower over Nuremberg include the central burgraves' castle, with the Free Reich's buildings to the east, and the Imperial castle (whose origins go back to the 12th century) to the west. When climbing up the Burgstrasse you will first reach the Fünfeckturm (Pentagonal Tower), which dates from 1040. The oldest building in town, it is an architectural relic of the von Zollern burgraves' castle. At its foot are the Kaiserstallung (Emperor's stables), which now houses a youth hostel. A continued climb will bring you, on the left, to the court-yard of the imperial palace, which features a round tower (*Sinwellturm*) dating from the 12th century, and a deep well – the *Tiefe Brunnen*. Passing through the inner gate of the castle you will finally reach its heart, the residential building.

🏠 Albrecht-Dürer-Haus

Albrecht-Dürer-Straße 39. **Tel** (0911) 231 25 68. ☐ Jul–Sep & during Christkindlesmarkt: 10am–5pm daily, 10am–8pm Thu; Oct–Jun: 10am–5pm Tue–Sun, 10am–8pm Thu. 🖼 🗡

Born in 1471 in a house on the corner of Burgerstrasse and Obere Schmiedgasse, the renowned artist and engraver Albrecht Dürer lived in this house from 1509 until his death in 1528. On the three-hundredth anniversary of his death, the building was bought by the town and many rooms have since been reconstructed. The ground-floor room now contains a printing press dating from Dürer's time. Copies of his pictures provide a useful insight into the work of this famous Nuremberg citizen.

🏛 St-Johannis-Friedhof

Am Johannisfriedhof.

The St John's Cemetery is one of the best preserved and most important in Europe. Since it was established in 1518, it has provided a resting place for many famous people, including Albrecht Dürer (No. 649), the sculptor Veit Stoß (No. 268), the goldsmith Wenzel Jamnitzer (No. 664) and the painter Anselm Feuerbach (No. 715).

The cemetery also contains a rich array of tombs from the 16th, 17th and 18th centuries.

🏛 Dokumentationszentrum Reichsparteitagsgelände

Bayernstr. 110. **Tel** (0911) 231 56 66. ☐ 9am–6pm Mon–Fri, 10am 6pm Sat–Sun.

The vast, unfinished building complex in the southern part of town dates from the Nazi era. Its construction began in 1933 and it was intended to be a venue for National Party gatherings. The building now houses a historical exhibition and archive.

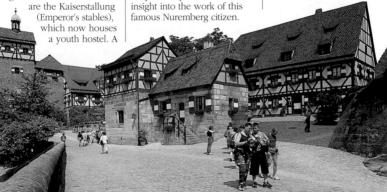

The buildings of the Kaiserburg, towering over the town

Nuremberg: Germanisches Nationalmuseum

This museum, which was officially opened in 1852, was founded by a Franconian aristocrat named Hans von Aufsess. It houses a unique collection of antiquities from the German-speaking world. In 1945, towards the end of World War II, the buildings that had originally housed the museum were bombed. The modern architecture of the new building, which was completed in 1993, cleverly incorporates the remaining fragments of a former Carthusian abbey. Among the most valuable items in the museum's collection are works by Tilman Riemenschneider, Konrad Witz, Lucas Cranach the Elder, Albrecht Altdorfer, Albrecht Dürer and Hans Baldung Grien.

Madonna with Child Crowned by Angels
This picture was painted by Hans Holbein the Elder (c.1465–1524) who created many festive altarpieces using warm colours.

★ Archangel (1516)
This enchanting wood-carving of the archangel Raphaël is one of many works produced by Veit Stoss after his return from Cracow.

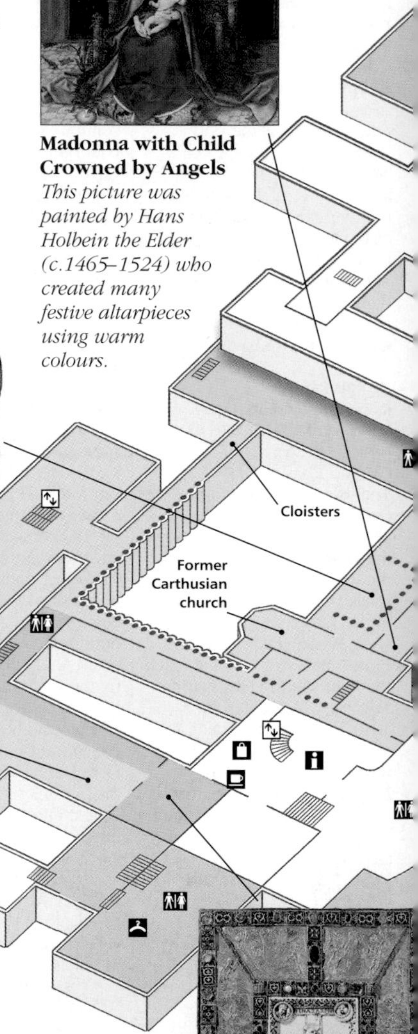

Cloisters

Former Carthusian church

Brooch from Domagnano
This Ostrogothic buckle from the 5th century AD, shaped like an eagle, was discovered in the late 19th century in Domagnano, in San Marino. It probably belonged to a rich Ostrogothic aristocrat.

Ground floor

★ Cover of the Codex Aureus
The richly ornamented cover of the Codex Aureus, *also known as the Golden Gospel Book of Echternach, was produced in Trier in the 10th century.*

GALLERY GUIDE

The exhibits have been arranged in sections, ranging from prehistory to the Middle Ages, and are located on the ground and first floors. Twentieth-century art is on the second floor and the toy collection is housed separately.

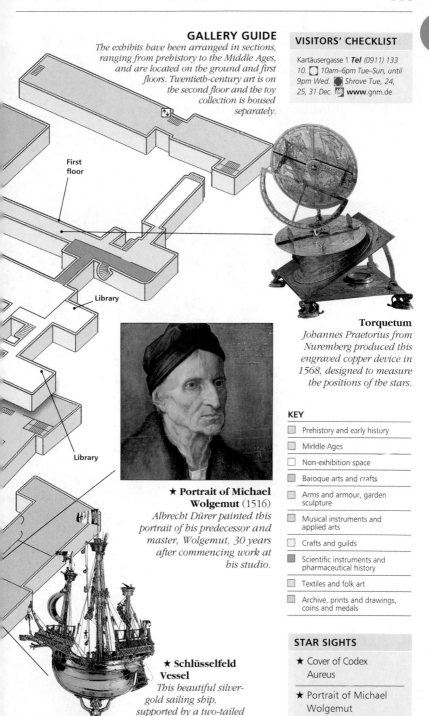

First floor

Library

Library

VISITORS' CHECKLIST

Kartäusergasse 1 **Tel** *(0911) 133 10*. ☐ *10am–6pm Tue–Sun, until 9pm Wed.* ● *Shrove Tue, 24, 25, 31 Dec.* ☑ www.*gnm.de*

Torquetum
Johannes Praetorius from Nuremberg produced this engraved copper device in 1568, designed to measure the positions of the stars.

KEY

- ☐ Prehistory and early history
- ☐ Middle Ages
- ☐ Non-exhibition space
- ☐ Baroque arts and crafts
- ☐ Arms and armour, garden sculpture
- ☐ Musical instruments and applied arts
- ☐ Crafts and guilds
- ☐ Scientific instruments and pharmaceutical history
- ☐ Textiles and folk art
- ☐ Archive, prints and drawings, coins and medals

★ Portrait of Michael Wolgemut (1516)
Albrecht Dürer painted this portrait of his predecessor and master, Wolgemut, 30 years after commencing work at his studio.

STAR SIGHTS

- ★ Cover of Codex Aureus
- ★ Portrait of Michael Wolgemut
- ★ Schlüsselfeld Vessel
- ★ Archangel

★ Schlüsselfeld Vessel
This beautiful silver-gold sailing ship, supported by a two-tailed mermaid, is an ornamental table vessel made in 1503 by an unidentified goldsmith from Nuremberg.

Street-by-Street: Rothenburg ob der Tauber ⑰

Eagle crest from the town hall

If you want to sample the atmosphere of the Middle Ages, visit Rothenburg on the river Tauber, whose origins go back to the 12th century. Rothenburg was granted the status of a free town within the Holy Roman Empire in 1274 but its major growth took place in the 15th century. During the Thirty Years' War (1618–48) the town, which fought on the Protestant side, was captured by the Emperor's army. Little has changed since that time and the city walls still surround Gothic cathedrals and an array of gabled houses.

Reichsstadtmuseum
The former Dominican abbey now houses a museum devoted to the town's history. The abbey kitchen – the oldest surviving kitchen in Germany – is also open to visitors.

Franziskanerkirche
In this Gothic church is a retable depicting The Stigmatization of St Francis, *believed to be an early work by Tilman Riemenschneider.*

★ St Jakobs Kirche
In the Gothic church of St Jakob (built between 1373 and 1464) is the superb Zwölfbotenaltar by Friedrich Herlin.

★ Mittelalterliches Kriminalmuseum
Many blood-curdling exhibits are on display at this museum, which houses a collection of instruments of torture and punishment.

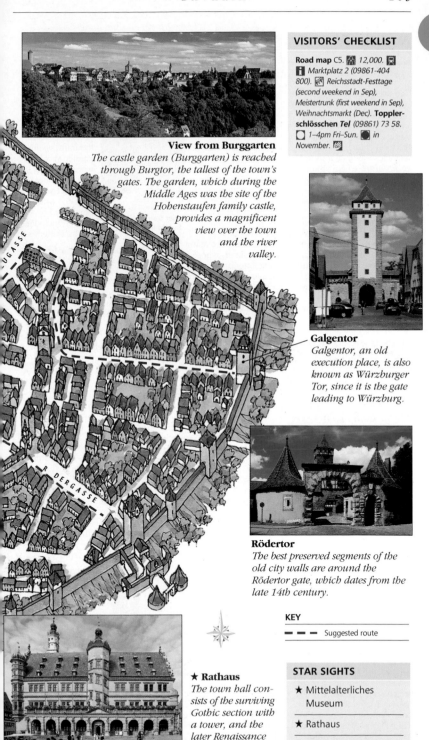

View from Burggarten
The castle garden (Burggarten) is reached through Burgtor, the tallest of the town's gates. The garden, which during the Middle Ages was the site of the Hohenstaufen family castle, provides a magnificent view over the town and the river valley.

VISITORS' CHECKLIST

Road map C5. 🚶 12,000. 🚌
ℹ️ Marktplatz 2 (09861-404 800). 🎭 Reichsstadt-Festtage (second weekend in Sep), Meistertrunk (first weekend in Sep), Weihnachtsmarkt (Dec). **Topplerschlösschen Tel** (09861) 73 58. ◻ 1–4pm Fri–Sun. 🔴 in November. 🎫

Galgentor
Galgentor, an old execution place, is also known as Würzburger Tor, since it is the gate leading to Würzburg.

Rödertor
The best preserved segments of the old city walls are around the Rödertor gate, which dates from the late 14th century.

KEY

– – – Suggested route

★ Rathaus
The town hall consists of the surviving Gothic section with a tower, and the later Renaissance structure with Baroque arcades.

STAR SIGHTS

★ Mittelalterliches Museum

★ Rathaus

★ St Jakobs Kirche

Andechs

Road map D7. 🛈 *Andechserstraße 16 (08152-932 50).*

The village of Andechs, at the summit of the 700-m (2,300-ft) high Holy Mountain of the same name, is not only the destination of pilgrimages to the local church, but also of many less spiritual trips to the *Braüstüberl*, where visitors can refresh themselves with a glass or two of the excellent beer brewed by local monks.

The present triple-nave Gothic hall-church was built in 1420–25. Its Rococo interior dates from 1755. The lower tier of the main altar contains the famous *Miraculous Statue of the Mother of God* (1468), while the upper tier features the *Immaculata* by Hans Degler (1609). On selected feast days, holy relics are displayed on the altar gallery.

Lake near the Holy Mountain of Andechs

Landsberg am Lech ⑲

Road map D7. 🚶 *24,000.* 🚉
🛈 *Hauptplatz 152 (08191-12 82 46).*

The history of Landsberg goes back to 1160 when Henry the Lion built his castle here, on the right bank of the river Lech. During the 13th century, the surrounding settlement grew into a town, which soon became a major trading centre. Religious conflicts, culminating in the Thirty Years' War, put an end to the town's development but, in the late 17th century, the town once again became

an important commercial and cultural centre. Adolf Hitler wrote *Mein Kampf* here, while serving a prison term for his unsuccessful coup attempt in Munich.

At the heart of Landsberg is the Hauptplatz with its Baroque town hall and the intricately carved 14th-century tower, Schmalztor.

In Ludwigstrasse is the late-Gothic parish church, Stadtpfarrkirche Mariä Himmelfahrt, whose Baroque-style interior features a statue of the *Madonna and Child* by Hans Multscher. Bayertor, the original town gate, is in the eastern part of the old town.

The town's **Neues Stadt-museum** is a useful source of information on local history.

🏛 **Neues Stadtmuseum**
Von-Helfenstein-Gasse 426.
Tel *(08191) 94 23 26.* ◯ *2–5pm Tue–Sun.* ♿

Dachau ⑳

Road map D6. 🚶 *35,000.* 🚉
🛈 *Konrad-Adenauer-Straße 1 (08131-75286 or 75287).*

For most people the name Dachau is inextricably linked with the concentration camp that was built here by the Nazis in 1933. Since 1965, the whole site has been designated as a memorial, **KZ-Gedenkstätte Dachau**, to the 32,000 prisoners who died there, with a permanent exhibition in the former domestic quarters of the camp.

Dachau is a beautiful town with many historic buildings. On the southwestern edge of the old town stands **Schloss Dachau**, summer residence of the Wittelsbachs. The palace that stands here today was created in the 18th century from the western wing of an earlier castle, the work of Joseph Effner.

In the early 19th century the castle housed a colony

Relief from the church façade in Landsberg

of artists who had tired of city life. They were known as *Gruppe Neu Dachau*. Even earlier, however, the beauty of the surrounding countryside had been discovered by the impressionist painter Max Liebermann (1847–1935). The **Dachauer Gemäldegalerie** contains works of art inspired by local scenery, including one by Liebermann.

🏛 **Dachauer Gemäldegalerie**
Konrad-Adenauer-Straße 3.
Tel *(08131) 56 75 16.* ◯ *11am–5pm Wed–Fri, 1–5pm Sat–Sun.* ♿

♣ **Schloss Dachau**
Schlossstraße 2. **Tel** *(08131) 879 23.* ◯ *Apr–Sep: 9am–6pm Tue–Sun; Oct–Mar: 10am–4pm Tue–Sun.* ♿

⚰ **KZ-Gedenkstätte Dachau**
Alte Römerstraße 75. **Tel** *(08131) 66 99 70.* ◯ *9am–5pm Tue–Sun.* ♿

Schleissheim ㉑

Road map D6. Oberschleißheim.

Schleissheim is situated barely 14 km (9 miles) from Munich, making it within easy reach for an afternoon visit to its Baroque palace and park.

Surrounded by canals and now somewhat neglected, the park was established in the 17th and 18th centuries and includes three palaces. The modest **Altes Schloss** was

Baroque façade of the Wittelsbach palace, Schloss Dachau

built in 1623 for Prince Wilhelm V. Now it houses an exhibition of religious folk art.

Schloss Lustheim is a small, Baroque, hermitage-type palace, built in 1684-87 by Enrico Zucalli for the Elector Max Emanuel. As well as its beautiful interiors and stunning frescoes, it boasts a magnificent collection of Meissen porcelain, which is displayed in the **Museum Meißener Porzellan**.

The newest building is the **Neues Schloss**, designed by Enrico Zucalli. Work began in 1701 but was not completed until the second half of the 18th century. Despite wartime damage, it retains many original features. It now houses exhibits belonging to the Bavarian State Museum.

The imposing bulk of the Neues Schloss in Ingolstadt

♣ **Altes Schloss**
Tel (089) 315 52 72. ◻ *10am–5pm Tue–Sun.*

♣ **Neues Schloss**
Tel (089) 315 87 20. ◻ *Apr–Sep: 9am–6pm Tue–Sun; Oct–Mar: 10am– 4pm Tue–Sun.* ● *Mon.*

♣ **Schloss Lustheim**
Tel (089) 31 58 72 0. ◻ *Apr–Sep: 9am–6pm Tue–Sun; Oct–Mar: 10am–4pm Tue–Sun.*

Museum Meißener Porzellan
◻ *Apr–Sep: 9am–6pm Tue–Sun; Oct–Mar: 10am–4pm Tue–Sun.*

Freising ㉒

Road map D6. ⌂ *40,000.* ▯ ◻ *Marienplatz 7 (08161-541 22).*

Situated on the banks of the river Isar is the old town of Freising. Its history is closely connected with St Korbinian, who founded the bishopric here in the early 8th century. Korbinian died around AD 725 and his remains still lie in the crypt of the Dom – the Cathedral Church of the Birth of the Virgin Mary and St Korbinian (1159–1205). This is a five-nave basilica, without transept, with an elongated choir and a massive twin-tower western façade. Its interior was remodelled in

Baroque style by the Asam brothers, in 1724–25. The four-nave Romanesque crypt features a famous column, which is decorated with carvings of fantastic animals *(Bestien-säule)*. Nearby is the **Diözesan-museum,** whose vast ecclesiastical collection includes two paintings by Rubens.

Detail from Neues Schloss in Schleissheim

At the south-western end of the old town stands a former monastery, Weihenstephan, which is home to the world's longest-established brewery.

🏛 **Diözesanmuseum**
Domberg 21. *Tel (08161) 487 90.* ◻ *10am–5pm Tue–Sun.*

Ingolstadt ㉓

Road map D6. ⌂ *115, 000.* ▯ ◻ *Rathausplatz 2 (0841-305 30 30).*

Lying on the river Danube, this former seat of the Wittelsbach family features many important historic buildings dating from the

Middle Ages and the Renaissance and Baroque periods. Among the most outstanding is the Church of the Virgin Mary, a triple-nave hall structure with circular pillars, chapels and choir with an ambulatory. Inside is the original Gothic-Renaissance main altar dating from 1572.

Another notable building is the Neues Schloss, built between the 15th and 18th centuries, with its stately rooms and Gothic chapel. It now houses the **Bayerisches Armeemuseum**.

A true gem of Bavarian architecture is the **Church of St Maria Victoria**, the work of Cosmas Damian Asam.

The **Deutsches Medizin-historisches Museum** exhibits medical instruments and has a garden with medicinal plants.

🏛 **Bayerisches Armeemuseum**
Neues Schloss, Paradeplatz 4. *Tel (0841) 937 70.* ◻ *8:45am–4:30pm Tue–Sun.*

🏛 **Deutsches Medizin-historisches Museum**
Anatomiestraße 18–20. *Tel (0841) 305 18 60.* ◻ *10am–noon, 2–5pm Tue–Sun.*

Striking Baroque interior of the Church of St Maria Victoria, Ingolstadt

Arcaded courtyard of Neuburg Castle

Neuburg
an der Donau ㉔

Road map D6. 🏙 *25,000.* 🚉
ℹ *Ottheinrichplatz A118 (08431-552 40).*

Perched on a promontory overlooking the river Danube, Neuburg is one of Bavaria's loveliest towns. During the Middle Ages, it changed hands frequently but was eventually ruled by Ottheinrich the Magnanimous, under whom the town grew and prospered on an unprecedented scale. He was the founder of the castle, built between 1534 and 1665, whose massive round towers still dominate the town. Its earliest part is the east wing. The courtyard, which is surrounded by arcades, features beautiful frescos by Hans Schroer. In the tower is a staircase adorned with paintings. The castle chapel, completed in 1543, is one of the oldest, purpose-built Protestant churches in Germany.

In Amalienstrasse, leading down towards the town, stands the former Jesuits' College and the Court Church (Hofkirche). Work on the church began in the late 16th century and was completed in 1627. It was intended to be a Protestant church, but the ruling family converted back to Catholicism during its construction and it was taken over by the Jesuits who turned it into a counter-reformation

Heraldic crest on Neuberg Castle

Marian church. The triple-nave hall-structure has an exquisite interior decorated in gold, white and grey.

Among many old buildings that survive in the town centre are the Graf-Veri-Haus and the Baron-von-Hartman-Haus in Herrenstrasse. To the east of town stands the Grünau Castle (Jagdschloss), built for Ottheinrich in 1530–55.

Environs
18 km (11 miles) to the south, Schrobenhausen is the birthplace of the painter Franz von Lenbach, who was born in 1836. A museum in Ulrich-Peisser-Gasse is devoted to his life and work. While there, it is worth visiting St Jacob's Church, to see the fine 15th-century wall painting there.

🏛 **Schlossmuseum Neuburg**
Residenzstraße 2. *Tel* (08431) 88 97. ☐ *Apr–Sep: 9am–6pm Tue–Sun; Oct–Mar: 10am–4pm Tue–Sun.* 📷

Landshut ㉕

Road map E6. 🏙 *57,000.* 🚉
ℹ *Altstadt 315 (0871-92 20 50).*
🎭 *Fürstenhochzeit (every 4 years, next in 2009), Hofmusiktage (every 2 years, next in 2008), Frühjahrsdult (Apr–May), Bartlmädult (end Aug), Haferlmarkt (Sep).*

The earliest records of Landshut date from 1150. One hundred years later this was already a town and the main

centre of power of the Dukes of Lower Bavaria. In 1475 the town was the scene of a lavish medieval wedding, when Duke Georg of the House of Wittelsbach married the Polish Princess Jadwiga. Since 1903 the town has held regular re-enactments of the wedding feast (Landshuter Fürstenhochzeit).

Landshut has preserved its medieval urban layout, with two wide parallel streets, Altstadt and Neustadt, with clusters of historic 15th–16th century buildings. Opposite the town hall in Alstadt is the **Stadtresidenz**, a town house modelled on the Palazzo del Tè in Mantua. Sometimes known as the "Italian House", this was the first Renaissance palace to be built in Germany.

The vast brick church of St Martin (1385–1500) is a triple-nave, narrow hall-church featuring a presbytery, network vaults (1459) and the tallest church tower in Bavaria.

Landshut is dominated by the fortified 13th–16th century **Burg Trausnitz**, featuring a medieval tower, a Renaissance palace (1568–78) and the **Kunst- und Wunderkammer** ("room of arts and wonder"), a branch of the Bayerisches Nationalmuseum *(see p219).*

Environs
From Landshut, it is worth taking a trip to Moosburg, situated 14 km (9 miles) to

Stained-glass window in Landshut depicting Duke Georg and Jadwiga

the west. Its early 13th-century Church of St Castulus features a 14-m (46-ft) high Marian altar by Hans Leinberger (1514).

♣ Burg Trausnitz & Kunst- und Wunderkammer
Tel (0871) 92 41 10. ⬜ *Apr–Sep:* 9am–6pm daily; Oct–Mar: 10am–4pm. ▦

♣ Stadtresidenz
Altstadt 79. *Tel* (0871) 92 41 10. ⬜ Apr–Sep: 9am–6pm Tue–Sun; Oct–Mar: 10am–4pm Tue–Sun. ▦ obligatory. ▦ ⬤ Mon.

Interior of St George's Chapel in Landshut

Dingolfing ㉖

Road map E6. 🏛 15,400. 🚏 Dr-Josef-Hastreiter-Straße 2 (08731-50 11 28).

The main tourist attraction in this small town on the banks of the river Isar is its Gothic castle. Built in the 15th century by the Bavarian dukes, this vast edifice now houses the Regional Museum. It is also worth taking a stroll past the Pfarrkirche St Johannes, a late-Gothic brick building dating from the late 15th century. Although what remains of its furnishings are merely the poor remnants of its former glory, nevertheless the church is still considered one of the most beautiful Gothic buildings in Bavaria.

Environs
In Landau an der Isar, situated 13 km (8 miles) to the east of Dingolfing, stands the picturesque Baroque church of Mariä Himmelfahrt, dating from the first half of the 18th century.

There is also an interesting small church, the Steinfelskirche (c.1700) inside a natural rock cave. In Arnstorf, 30 km (19 miles) to the east, is one of the few remaining Bavarian castles on water. Known as the Oberes Schlofl, the castle was probably built in the 15th century and remodelled during the 17th and 18th centuries.

Straubing ㉗

Road map E6. 🏛 44,500. 🚏 🚏 Theresienplatz 20 (09421-94 43 07). 🎭 Gäubodenvolksfest (August), Agnes-Bernauer-Festspiel (July, every four years, next in 2007).

This market town enjoys a picturesque setting on the river Danube. The 60-m (200-ft) long Strassenmarkt, which consists of two squares, Theresienplatz and Ludwigplatz, is a part of the former trade route that led to Prague. The area is lined with historic buildings in Baroque, Neo-Classical and Secession styles.

At the centre of Strassen-markt stands the 14th-century municipal tower, which offers a splendid view over the towns of the Bavarian Forest. At Ludwigplatz 11 is the "Lion's Pharmacy", where the famous Biedermeier painter, Karl Spitzweg, worked as an apprentice in 1828–30.

Turning from Theresienplatz into Seminargasse or Jakobs-gasse, you will reach the monumental brick structure of the parish church of St Jakob (1400–1590). This triple-nave hall-church, crowned with a network vault, retains many original features, including stained-glass windows in the chapels of Maria-Hilf-Kapelle (1420) and St Bartholomew. The so-called Moses' Window in the Chapel of St Joseph was made in 1490 in Nuremberg, based on a sketch provided by Wilhelm Playdenwurff. In the Cobbler's Chapel (Schusterkapelle) hangs a painting of *Madonna and Child*, by Hans Holbein

(c.1500). Overlooking the Danube is a 14th–15th century castle, part of which is now used as a museum, **Museum im Herzogschloss**. The **Gäubodenmuseum** has a magnificent collection of Roman artifacts.

Environs
In the tiny village of Aufhausen, 21 km (12 miles) to the west, is the beautiful late-Baroque pilgrimage church of Maria Schnee. Built by Johann Michael Fischer in 1736–51, it includes magnificent wall paintings by the Asam brothers and a statue of the Madonna. Commissioned by Duke Wilhelm V of Bavaria, the Gnadenmadonna is believed to pardon sins.

In Oberalteich, some 10 km (6 miles) to the east, is the beautiful church of St Peter and St Paul built in the early 17th century for the Benedictine order. Inside, an unusual hanging staircase leads to the galleries, while the vestibule is decorated with stucco ornaments, depicting bird motifs.

In Windberg, 22 km (14 miles) east of Oberalteich, is a Romanesque Marian church whose main portal (c.1220) features an image of the Madonna in the tympanum.

🏛 Gäubodenmuseum
Fraunhoferstraße. *Tel* (09421) 818 11. ⬜ 10am–4pm Tue–Sun. ▦

🏛 Museum im Herzogschloss
Tel (09421) 211 14. ⬜ Apr–Jan: 10am–4pm Thu–Sun. ▦

Main altar in Ursulinenkirche, Straubing

Regensburg (Ratisbon) ㉘

The area of Regensburg was once a Celtic settlement and later a campsite of the Roman legions. The outline of the Roman camp is still visible around St Peter's Cathedral. In the early 6th century, Regensburg was the seat of the Agilolfa ruling family and, in AD 739, a monk named Boniface established a bishopric here. From AD 843, Regensburg was the seat of the Eastern Frankish ruler, Ludwig the German. From 1245 it was a free town of the Holy Roman Empire and throughout the Middle Ages remained South Germany's fastest growing commercial and cultural centre.

Picturesque Steinere Brücke leading to the old town of Regensburg

🏛 Steinerne Brücke

An outstanding example of medieval engineering, this 310-m (1,000-ft) long bridge over the Danube was built in 1135–46. It provides the best panoramic view of Regensburg. Near the bridge gate, Brückentor, stands an enormous salt warehouse topped with a vast five-storey roof.

🏛 Wurstküche (Wurstkuchel)

Thundorferstraße. ◻ 8am–7pm daily.

Immediately behind the salt warehouse is the famous *Wurstküche* (sausage kitchen), which has probably occupied this site since as early as the 12th century and may have served as a canteen for the builders of the bridge. Its Regensburger sausages are definitely worth trying.

🏛 Altes Rathaus

Rathausplatz. ▨ May–Sep: 3:15pm Mon–Sat. **Reichstagsmuseum**.
Tel (0941) 507 34 40.
▨ (every 30 or 60 mins) Apr–Oct: 9:30am–noon 2–4pm Mon–Sat, 10am–noon 2–4pm Sun; Nov–Mar: 9:30am–noon, 2pm– 4pm Mon–Sat, 10am–noon Sun. ▨

In Rathausplatz stands an old 15th-century town hall with a 13th-century tower. It contains a splendid, richly decorated hall – *Reichssaal* – where the Perpetual Imperial Diet (the first parliament of the Holy Roman Empire) sat between 1663 and 1806. Benches in the chamber were coloured to indicate who could sit where: for example, red benches for Electors. The adjoining new town hall dates from the late 17th–early 18th century.

Late-Gothic oriel on the side elevation of the Altes Rathaus

🔒 Dom St Peter

Domschatzmuseum

Krautermarkt 3.
Tel (0941) 576 45. ◻ Apr–Oct: 10am–5pm Tue–Sat, noon–5pm Sun; Dec–Mar: 10am–4pm Fri–Sat, noon–4pm Sun. ◕ Nov. ▨

Towering above the city, on the site of the former Roman military camp, is the massive brick structure of St Peter's Cathedral. Built between 1250 and 1525, its imposing western towers were added only in 1859–69. The master architect, Ludwig, modelled his design for the building on French examples (the Rayonnant style). The stained-glass

SIGHTS AT A GLANCE

Alte Kapelle ⑤
Altes Rathaus ③
Dom St Peter ④
Schloss Thurn und Taxis ⑥
Steinerne Brücke ①
St Jakob Kirche ⑦
Wurstküche ②

19th-century spires on the Gothic St Peter's Cathedral

windows of the choir date from the early 14th century. The **Domschatzmuseum** has a collection of ecclesiastical vestments.

⚜ Alte Kapelle
Alter Kornmarkt.
The Old Chapel is really a Marian collegiate church. It stands on the foundations of an older, early Romanesque chapel dating from the Carolingian period. The building has been remodelled several times and contains some beautiful Rococo stuccoes by Anton Landes.

⛪ Schloss Thurn und Taxis
Emmeramsplatz 5. *Tel* (0941) 504 81 33. ◯ daily. ◪ Apr–Oct: 11am, 2pm, 3pm, 4pm (also 10am Sat–Sun); Nov–Mar: 10am, 11am, 2pm, 3pm Sat–Sun. ▨
In the south end of the town you will find the buildings and churches of the former St Emmeram Abbey, which have been

Enchanting Rococo interior of Alte Kapelle

the burial chapel. In 1998, the Bavarian State Museum opened a branch here, the Schatzkammer, which has valuable collections of decorative art.

⚜ Baumburger Turm
Watmarkt.
Regensburg has many unique ancestral palaces dating from the 14th–15th centuries, with high towers modelled on Northern Italian architecture. Some 20 of the original 60 towers have survived. One of the most beautiful is the residential tower, Baumburger Turm. Nearby, at Watmarkt 5, stands the equally beautiful Goliathhaus, where Oskar Schindler lived for a time in 1945. A commemorative plaque has been placed at the rear of the building.

Key to Symbols *see back flap*

tastefully incorporated into the palace complex of the ducal family von Thurn und Taxis. These include a Gothic cloister dating from the 12th–14th centuries, a library with magnificent frescos by Cosmas Damian Asam and

Gothic portals of St Emmeram Abbey in Schloss Thurn und Taxis

Winter view of Gnadenkapelle complex, from Altötting

Altötting ㉙

Road map E6. 🕍 *11,000.* ℹ️
Kapellplatz 2a (08671-50 62 19). 🚉
🎪 *pilgrimages to Altötting (Whitsun).*

Altötting is renowned as the
earliest destination of
pilgrimages to the "Miraculous
Statue" of the Virgin Mary
(1330). The statue stands in
the Wallfahrtskapelle St Maria,
which consists of two parts.
The central, octagonal chapel,
Gnadenkapelle (c.AD 750)
was once the baptistery. The
external chapel was built in
1494 and the ambulatory in
1517. As well as the Miraculous
Statue, it houses the so-called
"Silver Prince", representing
the miraculously cured son of
the Prince-Elector, Karl
Albrecht. Many Bavarian
kings and princes wished to
be buried here, including
King Ludwig II, who requested
that his heart be placed here
after his death.

Nearby is the interesting
Romanesque-Gothic church
of St Philip and St Jacob
(1228–30 and 1499–1520). Its
Neo-Classical interior contains
many tombstones, while a
separate chapel, Tillykapelle,
is the burial place of Johann
Tserclaes von Tilly, a hero of
the Thirty Years' War and the
Emperor's general.

The **Schatzkammer**
(Treasury) is housed in the
former sacristy. Its collection
includes an exquisite example
of French enamel and gold
artwork, the *Goldenes Rössl*
(Golden Steed), which dates
from around 1400. Despite its
name, the theme of this work,
by a celebrated Parisian
goldsmith, is the Adoration of

the Magi. It was commission-
ed by Isobel of Bavaria as a
New Year gift for her husband,
Charles VI of France.

🏛 **Schatzkammer**
Kapellplatz 21. **Tel** (08671) 51 66.
☐ Apr–Oct:10am–noon, 2–4pm
Tue–Sun. 📷

Walkway around Gnadenkapelle, in
Altötting, filled with offerings

Burghausen ㉚

Road map E6. 🕍 *17,000.* ℹ️
Stadtplatz 112 (08677-88 71 40). 🚉

The very picturesque town of
Burghausen is situated on the
river Salzach. Towering over
the town, the river and the
lake is Burghausen Castle, a
large castle complex built on
a high ridge stretching for

1,100 m (1,200 yds). Work on
the castle started in 1253, but
most of the buildings were
erected during the reign of
King George the Rich and
therefore have magnificent,
late-Gothic forms. The king's
wife, Jadwiga Jagiellon,
whom he married in grand
style in Landshut *(see p266),*
was later rejected by him and
she spent her final days in the
fortress of Burghausen.

The **Burg** consists of two
main parts: the main castle,
with tower, the residential
quarters, the courtyard and
domestic buildings; and the
castle approach (Vorburg).
The residential building has
some fine 15th- and 16th-
century paintings. A special
door links the Prince's
quarters with the "internal"
Chapel of St Elizabeth. Next
to the chapel is the mid-13th-
century Dürnitz, which served
originally served as a ballroom
and banqueting hall .

The castle approach consists
of five courtyards (Vorhof). In
the fourth courtyard is the
"external" Chapel of St
Jadwiga (Aussere Burgkapelle
St Hedwig) – the work of
Wolfgang Wiesinger, a native
of Salzburg (1489). This has
numerous original buildings,
including the town hall, which
was created by combining
three burgher houses dating
from the 14th–15th centuries
The parish church of St Jakob
(1353-1513) in Burghausen is
a three-nave basilica.

⛪ **Burg**
Tel (08677) 4659.
🏛 **Staatliche Sammlung**
☐ Apr–Sep: 9am–6pm daily;
Oct–Mar: 10am–4pm daily.

Panoramic view of Burghausen, with its vast castle complex on the hill

Bayerischer Wald ③⑤

The Bavarian forest stretches north to the rive Danube, between Regensburg and Passau. It is part of Central Europe's largest woodland and provides idyllic grounds for a variety of outdoor pursuits. The local rocks contain large quantities of quartz, which contributed to the early development of the glass industry here. To this day, the region produces some fine, blown-glass artifacts. The region also hosts a number of popular festivals throughout the year.

Spiegelau ③
Spiegelau is one of the most popular starting points for tourists planning hiking trips into the mountains.

Zwiesel ①
In the old glassworks, which survive to this day, you can watch workers using blow irons to produce vases, jugs and other objects made of glass.

Grafenau ④
The main attractions of this small town are its snuff and furniture museums and the old town hall.

Frauenau ②
Along with Zwiesel, this is the oldest centre of glass production in the area. The local museum illustrates the town's history.

NATIONALPARK
BAYERISCHER
WALD

CHAM
Regen
DEGGENDORF
HENGERSBERG
STRAKONITZ
PASSAU

Finsterau ⑥
Situated close to a vast artificial lake, Finsterau has an interesting open-air museum that displays examples of the local building trade.

Freyung ⑤
The main attraction of the town is the Schloss (Castle) Wolfstein, which now houses a museum of hunting and fishing.

KEY

▬	Suggested route
═	Other road
▬	Scenic route
☀	Viewpoint

0 km   8
0 miles   8

TIPS FOR WALKERS

Starting point: Zwiesel.
Distance: 82 km (51 miles)
Getting there: train to Frauenau, on the Zwiesel-Granau line; or Bodenmais, terminus of another branch line from Zwiesel.

Entrance to the port of Lindau ▷

Street-by-Street: Passau ❷

Passau, whose long history goes back to Roman times, lies on a peninsula between the rivers Danube and Inn, near the Austrian border. During the second half of the 5th century, St Severinus established a monastery in Passau as well as several more nearby. In 739, an Irish monk called Boniface, known as "Germany's Apostle", founded a bishopric here and for many years this was the largest diocese of the Holy Roman Empire. Large parts of the town were destroyed by fires in 1662 and 1680. Reconstruction was carried out by Italian artists, who gave the town its Baroque, Rococo and Neo-Classical façades. However Passau retains a medieval feel in its narrow alleys and archways.

Passauer Glasmuseum
Opposite the old town hall is the beautiful patrician Hotel Wilder Mann, which now houses the Glasmuseum. The museum's vast collection includes valuable examples of Bohemian, Austrian and Bavarian glasswork.

★ Dom St Stephan
St Stephan's Cathedral is a true masterpiece of Italian Baroque, built by Italian architect Carlo Lurago to replace the original Gothic structure, which was largely destroyed by fire in the 17th century.

★ Altes Rathaus
Dating from the 14th–15th century, the old town hall was created by combining eight patrician houses. The structure features a Neo-Gothic tower.

Deggendorf

Passau-Hauptbahnhof

University

DOMPLATZ

ANGER STRA

GROSSE MESSER

INNKAI

MARIEN–BRÜCKE

Neue Bischofsresidenz
Built by Domenico d'Angeli and Antonio Beduzzi in 1713–30, the Neue Residenz has a pilaster façade with protruding balconies and roof balustrade.

For hotels and restaurants in this region see pp499–503 and pp538–42

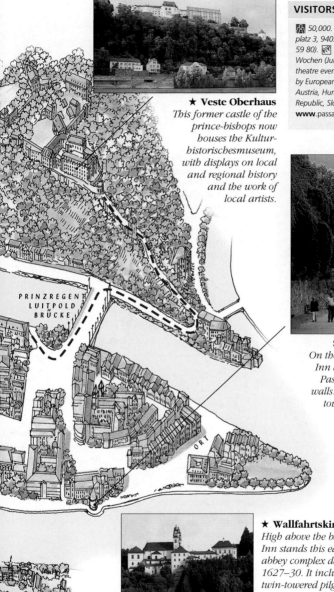

★ **Veste Oberhaus**
This former castle of the prince-bishops now houses the Kultur-historischesmuseum, with displays on local and regional history and the work of local artists.

VISITORS' CHECKLIST

🏠 50,000. 🚉 🛈 *Rathaus-platz 3, 94032 Passau (0851 95 59 80).* 🎭 *Festival Europäische Wochen (Jun-Jul) music and theatre events, plus exhibitions by European artists (mainly from Austria, Hungary, the Czech Republic, Slovakia and Poland).* www.passau.de

Schaiblingsturm
On the bank of the river Inn are the remains of Passau's Gothic town walls. They include this tower, built in 1481.

PRINZREGENT
LUITPOLD
BRÜCKE

O R T

★ **Wallfahrtskirche Mariahilf**
High above the banks of the river Inn stands this early-Baroque abbey complex dating from 1627–30. It includes a pretty twin-towered pilgrimage church.

STAR SIGHTS

★ Altes Rathaus

★ Dom St Stephan

★ Veste Oberhaus

★ Wallfahrtskirche Mariahilf

| 0 metres | 100 |
| 0 yards | 100 |

KEY

 — — — Suggested route

Berchtesgadener Land ❸

Berchtesgadener Land is one of the most beautiful regions, not just in Germany, but in the whole of Europe. It occupies the area of the Berchtesgadener Alps whose boundaries are defined by the river Saalach to the west, the river Salzach to the east, the "Stony Sea" *(Steinernes Meer)* to the south and, to the north, Untersberg, which is 1,972 m (7,500 ft) above sea level. To the south of Berchtesgaden village lies the National Park (Nationalpark Berchtesgaden).

★ **Ramsau an der Ache**
Set in an enchanting location in the Ramsau Valley, this village is a popular base for visitors to the area. Spectacular views of the mountains can be enjoyed from the small parish church.

Hintersee
This scenic lake has given its name to a picturesque hamlet nearby. A walk around the lake takes about one hour.

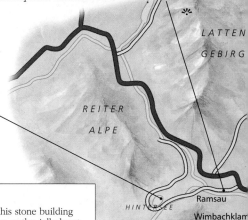

LATTEN
GEBIRG

REITER
ALPE

HINTERSEE

Ramsau
Wimbachklam

NATIONAL-
PARK
BERCHTESGADEN

KEHLSTEINHAUS

Standing on the summit of Kehlstein, this stone building resembling a mountain shelter is known as the Adlerhorst (Eagle's Nest). It was given to Hitler as a birthday present· in 1939 by one of his closest allies, Martin Bormann, and it became one of the Führer's favourite residences. The approach to the building is a true engineering masterpiece: the initial section, the Kehlsteinstrasse, is a scenic mountain road, which passes through

five tunnels and offers some breathtaking views. The final ascent is via a lift. The whole project took 13 months to complete. After the war, the Eagle's Nest fell into the hands of the Americans, then, in 1960, it passed into private hands. The building now houses a restaurant that is very popular with tourists, not only because of its history but also for the spectacular views that it provides over part of the Alps.

Nationalpark Berchtesgaden
This magnificent national park, which is home to many rare species of plants and animals, can be visited by joining organized tours between May and October.

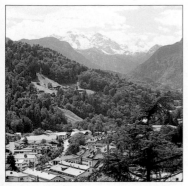

Berchtesgaden
The capital of the region features many historic buildings. The Schloss, originally an Augustinian priory, now houses the art treasures collected by Crown Prince Ruprecht. The local salt mine has been a source of wealth since the 16th century.

VISITORS' CHECKLIST

Road map E7. *8,500.* *Berchtesgaden.* *Bahnhofplatz 4, 83471 Berchtesgaden (08652-65 65 00).*

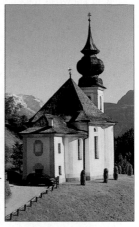

Wallfahrtskirche Maria Gern
One of the loveliest Baroque buildings in the region, the pilgrimage church of Maria Gern was built in 1709 in this idyllic location.

0 km 5
0 miles 5
UNTERS-BERG
Winkl
Maria Gern
Bischofs-wiesen
Hallein
Berchtes-gaden
Schönau am Königssee
Königssee
KÖNIGSSEE
OBERSEE

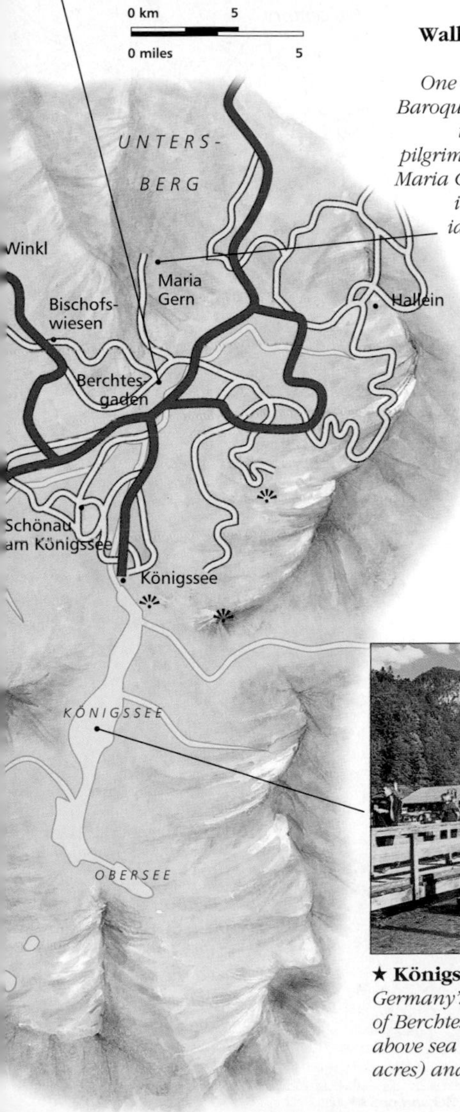

KEY

- Major road
- Minor road
- River
- Viewpoint

STAR SIGHTS

★ Königssee

★ Ramsau an der Ache

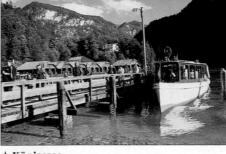

★ Königssee
Germany's highest lake, Königssee is the focal point of Berchtesgadener Land. Lying 600 m (2,000 ft) above sea level, it covers an area of 5.5 sq km (1,360 acres) and reaches a depth of 188 m (616 ft).

Touring Chiemsee ㉞

Bavaria's largest lake, Chiemsee is a real paradise for watersports enthusiasts, with sailors, water-skiers, swimmers and divers all enjoying the opportunities it offers. The lake is set amidst magnificent Alpine scenery in the region known as the Chiemgau, which stretches eastwards from Rosenheim to the border with Austria along the river Salzach. Chiemsee is surrounded by numerous small towns and villages and dotted with islands, some of which feature fascinating historic buildings. Excellent land, water and rail transport facilities ensure trouble-free travel to all destinations in the area.

Fraueninsel
Like its neighbour Herreninsel, this island is rich in art treasures. Its abbey (Klosterkirche) was founded in 766 and taken over by Benedictine nuns in the mid-9th century.

Obing
Hinzing
Halfing
HARTSEE
Eggstätt
Bad Endorf
LANGBÜRGNER SEE
SIMSSEE
Stock
Prien
Harras
Urschalling
Bernau

Stock
The harbour town of Stock is connected by narrow-gauge steam railway to the Chiemsee's main resort of Prien. The railway, the Chiemsee-bahn, is over one hundred years old.

Urschalling
The 12th-century church of St Jakobus features magnificent wall paintings dating from the 13th and 14th centuries.

Herrenchiemsee Palace
In 1873, King Ludwig II bought Herreninsel, with the intention of building a replica of the Palace of Versailles here. Funds ran out and the project was not completed, but the magnificent central section and park are well worth visiting.

KEY

- Motorway
- Major road
- Minor road
- River
- Viewpoint

For hotels and restaurants in this region see pp499–503 and pp538–42

Seeon Abbey

This post-Benedictine abbey, surrounded by the waters of Klostersee, was built in stages during the 11th and 12th centuries. It was remodelled in 1438–43 by Konrad Pürkel, a master-builder from Burghausen.

VISITORS' CHECKLIST

Road map E7.
🛈 *Tourismusverband Chiemsee, Alte Rathausstraße 11, 83209 Prien am Chiemsee (08051-690 50).* **www**.mychiemsee.de

Castle in the Rock

One of the most interesting curiosities of this region is the "Höhlenburg" – a castle carved into a rock on the bank of the river Traun, some 30 m (98 ft) above water level. Visits are allowed only with a guide.

Chieming

Chieming lies on the eastern shore of the lake. Its 6-km (4-mile) long beach is an ideal place for sunbathing and swimming in the waters of the lake.

Chiemsee

Lying at an altitude of 518 m (1,700 ft), the lake covers an area of 80 sq km (20,000 acres) with a depth of 70 m (230 ft). Its size makes it popular with sailing enthusiasts.

Colourful Alpine inn, dating from 1612, in Oberammergau

Garmisch-Partenkirchen ③⑤

Road map D7. 27,000.
Richard-Strauss-Platz 2 (08821-18 07 00). Neujahrs-Springen (1 Jan); Hornschlitten-Rennen (6 Jan); Ski World Cup Races; Richard Strauss Tage (Jun).

Lying in the valley of the river Loisach, Garmisch-Partenkirchen is the best-known resort in the Bavarian Alps. To say that it offers ideal skiing conditions would be to state the obvious. In 1936, it hosted the Winter Olympic Games and, in 1978, the World Skiing Championships. From Garmisch-Partenkirchen, Germany's highest peak, Zugspitze (2964 m/9,720 ft), can be reached by taking the narrow-gauge railway to Zugspitzblatt and from there a cable car, which reaches the summit in a few minutes. Garmisch-Partenkirchen's parish church of St Martin (Alte Pfarrkirche St Martin) is worth a visit. It was built in the 13th century and extended in the 15th century and features some well-preserved Gothic wall paintings and a wooden-beam ceiling. The **Werdenfelser Museum** shows how people in this region lived in the past, with a collection of furniture, clothing and room reconstructions.

Oriel window in Garmisch-Partenkirchen

🏛 **Werdenfelser Museum**
Ludwigstraße 47. **Tel** (08821) 21 34.
◯ Dec–Oct: 10am–1pm, 3–6pm, Tue–Fri, 10am–1pm Sat–Sun.

Oberammergau ③⑥

Road map D7. 4,700. Eugen-Papst-Straße 9A (08822-923 10). Oberammergauer Passionsspiele May–Oct, every ten years: next 2010); König-Ludwig-Lauf (Feb); König-Ludwig-Feiern (24 Aug).

Situated some 20 km (12 miles) north of Garmisch-Partenkirchen, and standing on the site of a 9th-century Welfs' fort, Oberammergau is world famous for its folk art and passion plays. The Thirty Years' War (1618–48) and the plague of 1632 came close to wiping out the entire population of the village. Its surviving inhabitants pledged that if they were saved from extinction they would stage for ever more a play about Christ's Passion. No further deaths occurred and, to this day, the villagers have kept their pledge. Every ten years (the next is in 2010), some 2,000 people take part in the six-hour-long spectacle, in which they transform themselves from Bavarians into Jews and Romans from the time of Christ. About one hundred performances are staged between mid-May and mid-October in the huge Passionsspielhaus.

Some of the buildings that are worth seeing in Oberammergau include the Rococo church of Saint Peter and Saint Paul (1735–40) and the famous *Pilatushaus*, with its illusionist painting of Christ before Pilate on the façade. The **Heimatmuseum** has a notable collection of carved wooden cribs.

🏛 **Heimatmuseum**
Dorfstraße 8. **Tel** (08822) 941 36. ◯ Apr–Jan: 10am–5pm Tue–Sun.

Ettal ③⑦

Road map D7. 974.

About 4 km (2.5 miles) from Oberammergau is the tiny resort of Ettal, which is best known for its Benedictine abbey, founded by Emperor Ludwig IV of Bavaria. The abbey's foundation stone was laid in 1330, while the Church of the Virgin Mary and the convent were consecrated in 1370. The church building is a Gothic structure but, in 1710–52, Josef Enrico Zuccalli and Franz Schmuzer carried out major remodelling work in the Baroque style. The church interior is decorated with rich Rococo stuccowork by Johann Baptist and Johann Georg Ubelhör, and wall paintings by Martin Knoller.

The monastery produces some fine fruit liqueurs, flavoured brandies and beer.

The Baroque Benedictine abbey in Ettal

Linderhof ⓧ

In the early 1850s, Linderhof was bought by the
Bavarian King Maximilian II. This remote mountain
district had great appeal to the heir to the throne,
Ludwig, later to become the eccentric King Ludwig II.
In 1874, work started on remodelling the existing
Königshäuschen (royal cottage) in the Neo-Rococo
style. The palace is surrounded by a delightful garden,
which is dotted with romantic little buildings, including
Schwanenweiher (Swan Lake), *Venusgrotte* (Venus grotto)
and the *Marokkanisches Haus* (Moroccan house).

VISITORS' CHECKLIST

Road map D7. **Schloss
Linderhof**. *Tel* (08822) 920 30.
◻ *Apr–Sep: 9am–6pm daily;
Oct–Mar: 10am–4pm daily.* 🌊

Tapestry Room
The walls of this room are
painted in a style that is reminiscent of tapestry work, with
depictions of pastoral scenes.

Reception Room
Although the palace was
intended as a private
residence, King Ludwig II
insisted on the provision
of a suitably ornate and
regal reception room.

Dining Room
Designed by Christian Jank,
the dining room was
completed in 1872. It features
gilded panelling by Phillip
Perron and stuccowork by
Theobald Behler.

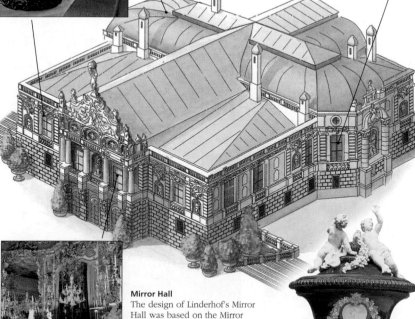

Mirror Hall
The design of Linderhof's Mirror
Hall was based on the Mirror
Room of the royal residence in
Munich *(pp216–17)*.

Terraces
Terraces in front of the palace
are adorned with sculptures and
include a pool with a fountain.

Schloss Neuschwanstein ⊛

Set amidst magnificent mountain scenery on
the shores of the Schwansee (Swan Lake),
this fairy-tale castle was built in 1869–86 for
the eccentric Bavarian King Ludwig II, to a
design by the theatre designer Christian Jank.
When deciding to build this imposing residence, the king was undoubtedly inspired
by Wartburg Castle in Thuringia *(see pp186–7)*,
which he visited in 1867. The pale grey
limestone castle, which draws on a variety of
historical styles, is a steep 30-minute walk
from the nearby village of Hohenschwangau
and offers spectacular views of the
surrounding scenery.

★ **Singers' Hall**
*The Sängersaal was
modelled on the
singing room of the
Wartburg castle
in Eisenach.*

Study

Vestibule
*The walls of the vestibule
and of other rooms in the
castle are lavishly covered
with paintings depicting
scenes from old German
myths and legends.*

★ **Throne Room**
*The gilded interior of the
throne room reminds one
of Byzantine temples and the
palace church of All Saints
in the Residenz (see pp216–17)
in Munich.*

Dining Room
*Like other rooms in
the palace, the dining
room includes fabulous
pictures, intricately
carved panels and
beautifully decorated
furniture, all bearing
witness to the skill and
artistry of the 19th-
century craftsmen.*

★ Castle Building
Schloss Neuschwanstein is the archetypal fairy-tale castle and has provided the inspiration for countless toy models, book illustrations and film sets.

Two-storey arcades
surround the castle courtyard.

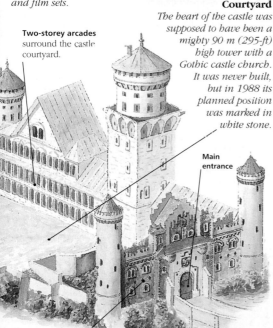

Main entrance

Gatehouse
During construction, temporary accommodation was built for the king on the second floor of the gatehouse, completed in 1872.

VISITORS' CHECKLIST

Road map D7. Neuschwanstein-strasse 20. **Tel** *(08362) 93 98 80.* ☐ *Oct–Mar: 10am–4pm daily; Apr–Sep: 9am–6pm daily.* 🎟️ ✔️ ♿ *(limited access).* 🍴 🛍️ 📷 ℹ️

Courtyard
The heart of the castle was supposed to have been a mighty 90 m (295-ft) high tower with a Gothic castle church. It was never built, but in 1988 its planned position was marked in white stone.

STAR FEATURES

★ Castle Building

★ Singers' Hall

★ Throne Room

Hohen-schwangau ㊵

Road map D7. 🚇 *Schwangau 3,818.* ℹ️ *Schwangau 08362-819 80. Ticket service: Hohenschwangau Alpseestr. 12 (08362-930 830 80).*

The skyline of Schwangau is dominated by two castles, Schloss Neuschwanstein (left) and the majestic **Schloss Hohenschwangau**. The fortified castle that occupied this site in the Middle Ages was remodelled in 1538–47 and, in 1567, it passed into the hands of the Wittelsbach family. The property was destroyed during the course of the Tyrolean War but in 1832 the heir to the throne (later Maximilian II) ordered the ruins to be rebuilt in Neo-Gothic style. The plans were prepared by the painter Domenico Quaglio; after his death, work on the castle was continued by the architects Georg Friedrich Ziebland and Joseph Daniel Ohlmüller.

This four-storey building, standing on medieval foundations, is flanked by angular towers. The wall paintings that decorate the rooms of the castle date from 1835–36. Their iconographic content, which is based on old Germanic sagas, is the work of Moritz von Schwind. A walk around the castle provides an excellent opportunity to study the Wittelsbach family history and to see the mid-19th century furnishings. There are magnificent views of the surroundings from the castle's lovely terraced gardens.

🏰 **Schloss Hohenschwangau**
Tel *(08362) 930 830.* ☐ *Apr–Sep: 9am–6pm Mon–Wed & Fri–Sun, 9am–8pm Thu; Oct–Mar: 10am–4pm.* ⬤ *24 Dec.* 🎟️

Neo-Gothic castle of Maximilian II in Hohenschwangau

The Rococo Throne Room in the Kempten Residenz.

Kempten ⓐ

Road map C7. 🏘 68,000. 🚉
🛈 Rathausplatz 24 (0831-252 52
37). 🎭 Allgäuer Festwochen (Aug).

Kempten lies at the centre of one of Germany's most attractive tourist regions, the Allgäu, which stretches from Bodensee lake to the west and the river Lech to the east. The town, which boasts a history of over 2,000 years, was first mentioned by the Greek geographer and historian Strabon as a Celtic settlement, Kambodounon. Later, the Romans established Cambodunum on the right bank of the river Iller. Along with Augusta Vindelicorum (Augsburg) and Castra Regina (Regensburg), this was one of the most important towns in the Roman province of Raetia.

Medieval Kempten grew around a Benedictine Abbey, founded in 752. In the north-western part of town, near the former abbots' residence, is the church of St Lorenz. A triple-nave, galleried basilica with an octagonal cupola and a twin-tower façade, this is the work of Michael Beer and Johann Serro. The town's parish church of St Mang dates from the 15th century. In the Rathausplatz is an attractive town hall dating from 1474 and other historic buildings, including the Londoner Hof with its Rococo façade (1764). The **Allgäu-Museum** details the history of Kempten and the surrounding area. On the right bank of the river Iller, is the **Archäologischer Park**, with excavated remains of Roman Cambodunum.

🏛 **Allgäu-Museum**
Kornhaus, Grober Kornhausplatz 1.
Tel (0831) 540 21 20. ◘
10am–4pm Tue–Sun. 🎫

🏛 **Archäologischer Park
Cambodunum**
Cambodunumweg 3. **Tel** (0831)
797 31. ◘ May–Oct: 10am–5pm
Tue–Sun; Nov–Apr:10am–4:30pm
Tue–Sun. ● Dec–Mar.

Lindau ⓑ

Road map C7. 🏘 24,000. 🚉 🛈
Ludwigstraße 68 (08382-26 00 30 or
19 433). 🎭 Lindauer Kinderfest (Jul).

In Roman times Lindau was a fishing settlement, which used to lie over three islands. The first historic records of the town date from 882. On the south side of the old-town island lies the harbour with its 13th-century lighthouse (Mangturm). The new lighthouse (Neuer Leuchtturm), built in 1856, stands on the neighbouring pier and offers a splendid view over the lake and the Alps. The marble Lion of Bavaria opposite is the symbol of Lindau.

The old town features many historic buildings, such as the Gothic-Renaissance town hall in Reichsplatz, which was built in 1422–36 and later remodelled in 1578. The picturesque Maximilianstrasse is lined with the houses of rich patricians; their shady arcades (Brodlauben) are typical of Lindau architecture.

In Schrannenplatz, in the northwest area of the town, stands the church of St Peter. Since 1928 this has been the war memorial chapel for World War I victims. Its eastern section dates from the mid-12th century while the bigger, western section was built between 1425 and 1480. The interior contains many wall paintings, including some by Hans Holbein the Elder dating from 1485–90. Nearby stands the Diebsturm (Thief's Tower) of 1380. The **Stadtmuseum** (town museum) is housed in Haus zum Cavazzen (1729) in Markt-platz, which also features a lovely Neptune fountain.

On the south side of the Market Square stands the Protestant Church of St Stephen, which dates from the 12th century and was remodelled in Baroque style in 1782. The Catholic Church of St Mary, built in 1748–52, has a lovely Rococo interior.

🏛 **Stadtmuseum Lindau**
Marktplatz 6. **Tel** (08382) 94 40 73.
◘ Apr–Oct: 11am–5pm Tue–Fri,
Sun, 2pm–5pm Sat. ● Nov–Mar.

Epitaph of the family of Andreas Bertsch, in the Stadtmuseum Lindau

For hotels and restaurants in this region see pp499–503 and pp538–42

Oberstdorf 43

Road map C7. 🏔 11,000. 🚆 ℹ️
Verkehrsamt, Marktplatz 7 (08322-70 00).

Oberstdorf lies in the valley of the River Iller. The ideal skiing conditions and the mild all-year-round climate make this one of the most popular health resorts and winter sports centres in Germany. Nearby is the skiing stadium (Schattenberg-Skistadion) with its famous ski-jump, where the annual "four ski-jump" tournament starts each year.

Although the fire of 1865 destroyed large sections of the settlement here, some of the most important historic buildings escaped. These include Seelenkapelle, whose façade is decorated with a 16th-century wall painting typical of the region, and two chapels, Lorettokapelle and Josephskapelle, which were joined together in 1707. Just to the east of Oberstdorf is the 2,224-m (7,300-ft) Mount Nebelhorn, whose summit can be reached in a few minutes by cable car. This offers a spectacular view over the majestic Allgäuer Alps as well as providing an excellent starting point for mountain hiking.

Madonna in the Church of St Mang, in Füssen

Füssen 44

Road map D7. 🏔 16,000. 🚆 ℹ️
Kurverwaltung, Kaiser-Maximilian-Platz 1 (08362-938 50).

Situated conveniently on an important trade route, Füssen experienced its most rapid growth in the late Middle Ages, as witnessed by many of the buildings in Reichen-strasse and the remains of the town fortifications, which include Sebastiantor and sections of the walls with five turrets. Perched on a rock, high above the town, stands the palace of the Augsburg prince-bishops. Started in 1291 by the Bavarian Prince Ludwig II the Severe, construction was continued in 1490-1503 by the Augsburg bishops. The residential buildings of the palace range around a courtyard whose walls are decorated with trompe l'oeil door and window frames.

At the foot of the castle stands the former Benedictine Abbey (Kloster St Mang), which was erected in the 9th century at the burial site of St Magnus, the "Apostle of the Allgäu". The only surviving part of the abbey is the late 10th-century crypt with the remains of wall paintings.

Late-Baroque interior of the Abbey Library, in Ottobeuren

Ottobeuren 45

Road map D7. 🏔 7,500. ℹ️
Marktplatz 14 (08332-92 19 50).

Situated 8 km (5 miles) from Memmingen, the small health resort of Ottobeuren is the site of one of Germany's most famous Benedictine abbeys. Founded in 764, the abbey is still a place of prayer and work for the monks who live here, having withstood even the radical secularization of 1803. In the 18th century the abbey was remodelled by the Abbot Rupert II. The foundation stone for the building complex was laid in 1717 and work began under the direction of Simpert Kraemer. The new buildings were completed in 1731. The richly decorated interiors, with stuccoes by Andrea Maini, still survive. A new abbey church was built between 1737 and 1766 with construction super-vised initially by Simpert Kramer. In 1748, this was taken over by Johann Michael Fischer, who was responsible for its final appearance.

The interior of the church has a magnificent unity of style: Rococo stuccoes by Johann Michael Feuchtmayr are in perfect harmony with the vault frescos by Johann Jakob Zeiller as well as the splendid altars and stalls by Martin Hörmann and Johann Zeiller's brother Franz Anton Zeiller. The abbey's three organs, which are particularly beautiful, can be heard at regularly held recitals.

Ski-jump complex in Oberstdorf

Augsburg 46

Situated at the confluence of the Lech and
Wertach rivers, Augsburg is the third largest
town in Bavaria and one of the oldest in
Germany. As early as 15 BC this was the
site of a Roman camp, which later became
a town known as Augusta Vindelicorum.
Until the end of the 13th century, the town
was ruled by powerful bishops. From 1316,
as a Free Imperial City of the Holy Roman
Empire, Augsburg grew to become one of
the richest and most powerful cities in
Germany. The Thirty Years' War (1618–48),
however, put an end to the town's prosperity.

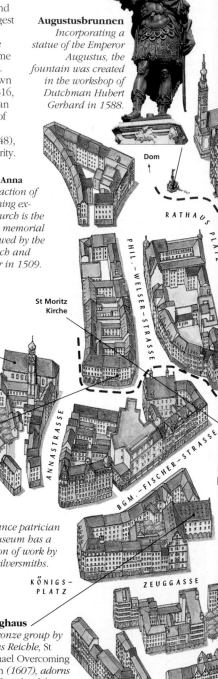

Augustusbrunnen
*Incorporating a
statue of the Emperor
Augustus, the
fountain was created
in the workshop of
Dutchman Hubert
Gerhard in 1588.*

Dom

RATHAUS PLATZ

PHIL.-WELSER-STRASSE

Church of St Anna
*The star attraction of
this unassuming ex-
Carmelite church is the
Renaissance memorial
chapel endowed by the
brothers Ulrich and
Jacob Fugger in 1509.*

St Moritz
Kirche

ANNASTRASSE

BGM.-FISCHER-STRASSE

**Maximilian-
museum**
*Set in a Renaissance patrician
mansion, the museum has a
splendid collection of work by
local gold- and silversmiths.*

KÖNIGS-
PLATZ

ZEUGGASSE

Zeughaus
*A bronze group by
Hans Reichle,* St
Michael Overcoming
Satan *(1607), adorns
the façade of the
former arsenal
building.*

For hotels and restaurants in this region see pp499–503 and pp538–42

VISITORS' CHECKLIST

Road map D6. ![] 265,000. ![]
5 km (3 miles) to the north. ![]
![] Schiessgrabenstr. 14 (0821-
50 20 70). ![] Frühjahrsplärrer
(week following Easter), Herbst-
plärrer (Aug/Sep), Friedenfest
(8 Aug), Mozartsommer
(Aug/Sep). **www**.augsburg.de

★ Rathaus

The magnificent town hall,
built by Elias Holl in 1615–20,
is generally regarded as
Germany's finest example
of Mannerist architecture.

View of the monumental Gothic
Dom of the Holy Virgin

🔒 Dom of the Holy Virgin (Mariä Heimsuchung)

Frauenstraße 1. ☐ 9am–5:30pm.
Originally a Romanesque
twin-choir, pillared basilica
with crypt, western transept
and two towers, dating from
994–1065, the structure was
remodelled between 1331 and
1431 along Gothic lines. The
church was given two further
side aisles, a choir with an
ambulatory and a French-style
ring of chapels. Original
features include the richly
carved portals and the famous
Romanesque bronze door
with 35 panels depicting
allegorical figures. There are
some unique stained-glass
windows, dating from 1140.

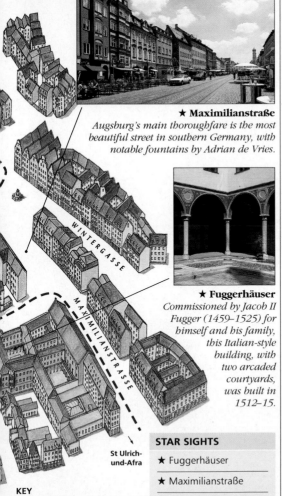

★ Maximilianstraße

Augsburg's main thoroughfare is the most
beautiful street in southern Germany, with
notable fountains by Adrian de Vries.

★ Fuggerhäuser

Commissioned by Jacob II
Fugger (1459–1525) for
himself and his family,
this Italian-style
building, with
two arcaded
courtyards,
was built in
1512–15.

🏛 Fuggerei

Fuggerei-Museum, Mittlere Gasse 13.
Tel (0821) 319 88 10. ☐ May–Oct:
9am–8pm daily; Nov–Apr: 9am–6pm
daily. ● 24 Dec–28 Feb. ![]
The Fuggerei, in Augsburg's
Jakobervorstadt (Jacob's
Suburb), is Europe's oldest
social housing estate. It was
founded in 1516 by Jacob
Fugger, a member of what
was then the richest family in
Europe. The intention was to
provide homes for the town's
poorest citizens, particularly
families with children. Today,
however, it has evolved into a
home for retired citizens.

The 52 houses in Fuggerei
were built in 1516–25 and line
six streets. They are surrounded by gardens. One of the
buildings is the **Fuggerei-
Museum**, which is devoted to
the history of the estate and
has a fascinating shop, the
Himmlisches Fuggereilädle.

WINTERGASSE

MAXIMILIANSTRASSE

St Ulrich-
und-Afra

STAR SIGHTS

★ Fuggerhäuser

★ Maximilianstraße

★ Rathaus

KEY

- - - Suggested route

BADEN-WURTTEMBERG

This German state, which includes territories of the former Grand Duchy of Baden, is one of the country's most popular tourist destinations. Its charming old university towns, such as Tübingen and Heidelberg, historic castles, luxurious resorts and the magnificent recreation areas of the Schwarzwald (Black Forest) and Bodensee (Lake Constance) guarantee enjoyable and memorable holidays.

This region's turbulent history, which has been ruled over the years by Palatinate electors, counts and finally kings of Wurttemberg, as well as by margraves and Grand Dukes of Baden, has given the province its cultural and religious diversity.

This southwestern area of Germany was the cradle of two great dynasties that played a significant part in German and European history and culture. The Hohenstaufen family – which originated from Swabia – produced kings and emperors who ruled during the most magnificent period of the German Middle Ages (1138–1254). These included Frederick I Barbarossa and Frederick II. The Hohenzollern family, also from Swabia, produced Brandenburg dukes, Prussian kings including Frederick the Great and German emperors from 1871–1918.

In Heidelberg the enlightened elector Ruprecht I founded the first university in Germany in 1386 and shortly after this epoch-making event, further universities were established in Tübingen and Freiburg im Breisgau. Many towns and villages in the region can boast a history going back to Roman times. The Romans used to grow vines in the area of Baden-Wurttemberg and now wines from the region are renowned worldwide for their high quality.

Baden-Wurttemberg, however, does not only represent an illustrious past, but also an impressive present. Unemployment figures for the region are the lowest in Germany, and many companies that are known and respected throughout the world – such as Bosch, DaimlerChrysler, Porsche and the software company SAP – have their production plants here.

Magnificent French-style garden in front of the palace in Ludwigsburg

◁ **Bodensee (Lake Constance), in the foothills of the Alps**

Baden-Wurttemberg

With its magnificent castles, luxurious resorts and the beautiful recreation areas of the Black Forest, Baden-Wurttemberg is one of Germany's most popular tourist destinations. In addition, the region's long and turbulent history has given it a rich cultural and religious diversity. The southwest region of Germany was the cradle of two dynasties that played important roles in German and European history and culture – the Hohenstaufen and Hohenzollern families. The great number of urban centres in the state is due to the influence of these two families. Baden-Wurttemberg also has more universities than any other state in Germany, the oldest being located at Heidelberg, Tübingen and Freiburg im Breisgau.

The picturesque castle in Sigmaringen, in the region of Schwäbische Alb

KEY

═══	Motorway
──	Major road
⋯⋯	Minor road
⋯⋯	Main railway
──	Minor railway
──	International border
──	County border
△	Summit

Weinheim
A67
MANNH 6
CHWETZINGEN 7
9
HEIDELBERG
36
A5
9
BRUCHSAL 8
35
MAULBRO
KARLSRUHE 10
Ettlingen
36
Rastatt
Pforzheim
BADEN-BADEN 11
Gaggenau
462
294
A5
Hornisgrinde 1164m
BADEN
Strasbourg
28
Offenburg
28
Freudenstadt
36
33
Kinzig
Lahr
294
Neckar
A81
3
Gutach
294
Emmendingen
Elz
S C H W A R Z W A L D
Kandel 1242m
33
Villingen-Schwenningen
ROTTWEIL 23
Lemberg 1015m
FREIBURG IM BREISGAU 29
30
Furtwangen
Trossin
Tuttlinge
Feldberg 1493m
Donaueschingen
Bad Krozingen
31
A5
315
Müllheim
Blumberg
317
Todtmoos
3
Schopfheim
St Blasien
Lörrach
314
34
Waldshut-Tiengen
Basel

The Gothic town hall in Ulm

SEE ALSO

• **Where to Stay** pp503–6

• **Where to Eat** pp542–5

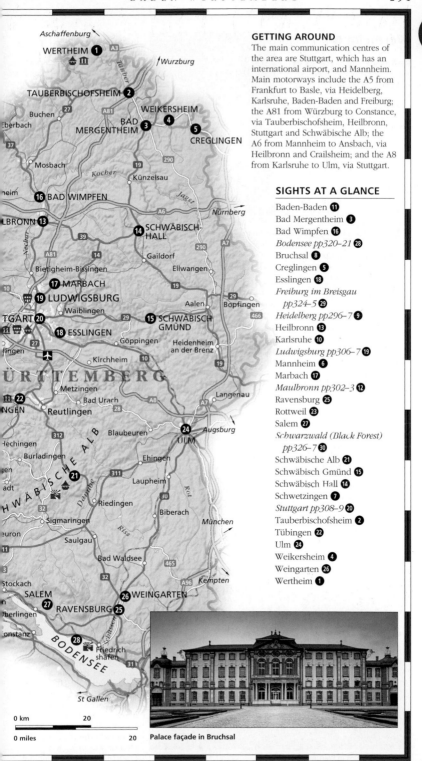

Aschaffenburg
Wurzburg
WERTHEIM ❶
A3
Tauber
TAUBERBISCHOFSHEIM ❷
Buchen
27
A81
WEIKERSHEIM
berbach
BAD
MERGENTHEIM ❸ ❹
37
CREGLINGEN ❺
Mosbach
Kocher
19
290
Künzelsau
heim
❶❻ BAD WIMPFEN
Jagst
Nürnberg
LBRONN ❶❸
A6
39
❶❹ SCHWÄBISCH-
HALL
290
A7
14
Gaildorf
A81
Bietigheim-Bissingen
Ellwangen
10
❶❼ MARBACH
19
❶❾ LUDWIGSBURG
Aalen
Bopfingen
Waiblingen
29
❶❺ SCHWÄBISCH
GMÜND
466
TGART ❷⓿
❶❽ ESSLINGEN
Göppingen
Heidenheim
an der Brenz
fingen
27
Kirchheim
10
19
URTTEMBERG
Metzingen
Langenau
❷❷
Bad Urach
A8
A7
NGEN
Reutlingen
28
Augsburg
312
Blaubeuren
❷❹
Hechingen
ULM
Burladingen
Ehingen
en
311
Laupheim
adt
S❷❶
C
H
W
Ä
B
I
S
Riedingen
Biberach
München
32
Donau
Sigmaringen
Riss
euron
Saulgau
11
Bad Waldsee
3
465
Stockach
32
A96
Kempten
SALEM
❷❻ WEINGARTEN
❷❼ RAVENSBURG ❷❺
berlingen
onstanz
❷❽
BODENSEE
Friedrich
shafen
31
St Gallen
0 km   20
0 miles   20

GETTING AROUND

The main communication centres of the area are Stuttgart, which has an international airport, and Mannheim. Main motorways include the A5 from Frankfurt to Basle, via Heidelberg, Karlsruhe, Baden-Baden and Freiburg; the A81 from Würzburg to Constance, via Tauberbischofsheim, Heilbronn, Stuttgart and Schwäbische Alb; the A6 from Mannheim to Ansbach, via Heilbronn and Crailsheim; and the A8 from Karlsruhe to Ulm, via Stuttgart.

SIGHTS AT A GLANCE

Palace façade in Bruchsal

Wertheim ●

Road map C5. ⚐ *24,500.* 🚂 ℹ️
Am Spitzen Turm (09342-1066). 🎭
Altstadtfest (Jul), Burgweinfest (Aug).

Standing at the point where
the rivers Tauber and Main
meet is the town of Wertheim,
whose earliest historic records
date from 1183. A gunpowder
explosion in 1619 plus the
destruction caused by the
Thirty Years' War turned the
Wertheimer Burg, the von
Wertheim family castle, into a
romantic ruin. Its tall watchtower offers panoramic views.

Wertheim's market square is
lined with half-timbered houses, while the Baroque Protestant church nearby, dating from
the 15th–18th centuries, has
tombs of members of the von
Wertheim family. The most
spectacular is the tomb of
Count Ludwig II von Löwen-
stein-Wertheim and his wife,
Anna von Stolberg. This is the
work of Michael Kern (1618).
Also worth visiting are the
Glasmuseum and the **Grafschaftsmuseum Wertheim**,
with collections of Frankish
costumes, paintings and coins
and displays on wine-making.

🏛 **Glasmuseum**
Mühlenstraße 24. **Tel** *(09342) 68
66.* ⭕ *Apr–Oct & 1st Advent Sun–6
Jan: 10am–noon & 2–5pm Tue–Thu,
1–7pm Fri–Sat, 1–5pm Sun;
May–Aug: 3pm–5pm Mon.*

🏛 **Grafschaftsmuseum
Wertheim**
Rathausgasse 6–10. **Tel** *(09342) 30
15 11.* ⭕ *10am–noon, 2:30pm–
4:30pm Tue–Fri, 2:30pm–4:30pm
Sat, 2pm–5pm Sun.* 🎭

**Half-timbered houses and tower by
Schloss Tauberbischofsheim**

Tauberbischofs-
heim ●

Road map C5. ⚐ *13,000.* 🚂
ℹ️ *Marktplatz 8 (09341-803 33).*

Boniface, the Anglo-Saxon
missionary to the German
tribes, established Germany's
first nunnery in AD 735. Its
first prioress, Lioba, who
was related to
Boniface, gave
her name to the
Baroque church
that stands in
Tauberbischofs-
heim's market
square.

The town, which
enjoys a picturesque
location in the
valley of the river
Tauber, still has a group of
original half-timbered houses.
On the market square the
Baroque Rehhof (1702) and
the old "Star Pharmacy" in a

**Heraldic crest from the
castle in Bad
Mergentheim**

house once occupied by
Georg Michael Franck, grand-
father of the Romantic poets
Clemens and Bettina Brentano.

In the eastern section of
Hauptstraße stands Haus
Mackert – a Baroque mansion
built in 1744 for a wealthy
wine merchant. In Schlossplatz is the Kurmainzisches
Schloss, an imposing edifice
built in the 15th–16th centuries, that now houses the
Landschaftsmuseum.

🏛 **Landschaftsmuseum
Kurmainzisches Schloss**
Tel *(09341) 37 60.* ⭕ *Palm
Sunday–Oct: 2:30–4:30pm Tue–Sat,
10am–noon & 2–4:30pm Sun.* 🎭

Bad Mergentheim ●

Road map C5. ⚐ *25,000.* 🚂
ℹ️ *Marktplatz 3 (07931-5 71 31).*
🎭 *Markelsheimer Weinfest (after
Whitsun).*

Lying in a charming spot
on the river Tauber, Bad
Mergentheim was, from
1525 until 1809, the
seat of the Grand
Masters of the
religious order
of the "House of
the Hospitallers
of Saint Mary of
the Teutons in
Jerusalem", more
commonly known
as the Teutonic
Knights. When
three Hohenlohe brothers
entered the Order in 1220,
they contributed to it their
share of their father's estate.
This laid the foundations for
one of the most powerful
Teutonic commands at the
heart of the Holy Roman
Empire. From 1244 until 1250
Heinrich von Hohenlohe held
the office of Grand Master.

The former Hohenlohe's
castle, built in the 12th–13th
centuries, was remodelled in
Renaissance style in 1565–74
by Michael Bronner and
Blasius Berwart. They gave
the castle its winding stairs
and the opulent ornamental
decor of the staircase. The
Baroque-Rococo Schlosskirche
dominates the complex. Its
interior was designed by
François Cuvilliés, while the

Scenic castle ruins in Wertheim

ceiling fresco *(The Victorious Cross)* is the work of Nicolaus Stuber. The castle is now the home of a very interesting museum of the Order, the **Deutschordensmuseum**.

Many of the town's historic buildings survive to this day, including the 13th-century Church of the Knights of St John of Jerusalem and the Dominican church containing the epitaph of the Grand Master Walther von Cronberg. The **Pfarrkirche** (Parish church) in the Stuppach district contains a masterpiece by Grünewald (1519), known as the *Madonna of Stuppach.*

🛈 Pfarrkirche in Stuppach
Kapellenpflege. *Tel (7931) 26 05.* ◻ Mar–Apr: 10am–5pm daily; May–Oct: 9:30am–5:30pm daily; Nov: 11am–4pm daily. ● Dec–Feb. 🖼

🏛 Deutschordensmuseum
Schloss. *Tel (07931) 522 12.* ◻ Apr–Oct: 10:30am–5pm Tue–Sun; Nov–Mar: 2–5pm Tue–Sat, 10:30am–5pm Sun. 🖼

Weikersheim ❹

Road map C5. 🏘 8,000. 🚻 *Am Marktplatz 7 (07934-102 45).*

Eleven kilometres (7 miles) east of Bad Mergentheim is the picturesque little town of Weikersheim. A Rococo fountain from 1768 stands at the centre of its market square while, on the north side, stands the late-Gothic parish church. The latter is a triple-nave hall-church with a single-tower western façade and two towers by the choir. Inside are many tombs of the von Hohenlohe family. Also on the market square stands the **Tauberländer Dorfmuseum**, which charts the history of rural life in Franconia. In the western part of town stands the very well preserved **Schloss Weikersheim**,

ure of drummer Weikersheim's Hofgarten

the palace complex of the Counts von Hohenlohe, which dates from the 16th–18th centuries. Its highlight is undoubtedly the vast Rittersaal, a sumptuous banqueting hall that measures 35 m (115 ft) long × 12 m (39 ft) wide × 9 m (29 ft) high. The counts and their aristocratic guests used to enter this room on horseback. Its very rare, original furnishings include paintings and reliefs depicting hunting scenes.

A true rarity is the original Baroque Hofgarten (palace garden), designed by Daniel Matthieu and built in 1709.

♟ Schloss Weikersheim
Tel (07934) 99 29 50. ◻ Apr–Oct: 9am–6pm daily; mid-Nov–Mar: 10am–noon & 1pm–5pm daily. 🖼

🏛 Tauberländer Dorfmuseum
Marktplatz. *Tel (07934) 12 09.* ◻ Apr–Oct:2–5pm Wed, Fri, Sat, Sun. 🖼

Creglingen ❺

Road map C5. 🏘 5,000. 🚉 🚻 *Romantische Straße 14 (07933-6 31).*

Upstream from Weikersheim, on the Bavarian border, is the small town of Creglingen. Here, sometime in the distant past, a ploughman found a luminous holy wafer in a clod of earth and within a few years, the **Herrgottskirche** was built, where the host was put on display for visiting pilgrims. Between 1502 and 1506 Tilman Riemenschneider

Altar by Tilman Riemenschneider, in Creglingen's Herrgottskirche

carved an altar for the church. The main theme of the polyptych is the *Assumption of the Virgin Mary*, considered to be the artist's masterpiece.

The town is also home to the esoteric collection of the famous **Fingerhutmuseum** (Thimble Museum).

🛈 Herrgottskirche
Kohlersmühle. *Tel (07933) 338 or 508.* ◻ Apr–Oct: 9:15am–5:30pm daily; Nov–Mar: 10am–noon & 1–4pm Tue–Sun. ● 24, 25, 31 Dec, 7 31 Jan.

🏛 Fingerhutmuseum
Kohlersmühle. *Tel (07933) 370.* ◻ Apr–Oct: 10am–12:30pm 2 5pm Tue–Sun; Nov–Dec, Feb–Mar: 1–4pm Tue–Sun. ● Jan. 🖼

TEUTONIC ORDER

The Order of the Hospital of St Mary of the German House in Jerusalem was officially founded in Acre (Akkon) in 1190. Its aim was to care for sick pilgrims or Crusaders wounded in fights with the Saracens. In 1231–83, the Teutonic Knights took over all of Prussia and, in 1308–09 all Eastern Pomerania around Danzig, and they moved their headquarters from Venice to Marienburg on the river Nogat. In 1525 the Grand Master, Albrecht von Hohenzollern-Ansbach, converted to Lutheranism and secularized Teutonic Prussia. However, the Order remained in existence in the Holy Roman Empire: its German Master, Walter von Cronberg, who had his residence in Mergentheim, became *de facto* Grand Master. Napoleon abolished the Order in 1809, but it still exists today, with its headquarters based in Vienna since 1809.

The Wasserturm (Water Tower) in Friedrichsplatz, Mannheim

Mannheim ❻

Road map B5. 🏛 *326,000.* 🚉 🛈
Willy-Brandt-Platz 3 (0621-10 10 11).
🎬 *Mannheim-Heidelberger Filmfestival (mid-October).*

Mannheim existed as a small fishing hamlet as far back as 766. In 1606, Elector Frederick IV the Righteous ordered a fortress to be built on the site, at the junction of the rivers Rhine and Neckar. A trading settlement sprang up nearby, which was soon granted town status. Having been repeatedly destroyed through the years, the town was finally rebuilt in Baroque style during the reign of the Elector Johann Wilhelm.

The town-centre layout follows the regular Baroque pattern of the early 18th century, when the town was divided into 136 regular squares. In 1720, when Elector Charles III Philip decided to move his residence from Heidelberg to Mannheim, the foundation stone for a Baroque palace was laid in the grounds of a former citadel.

With over 400 rooms, this became one of the largest and most opulent of all German palaces. Like many other residences built by European rulers at that time, the palace was modelled on Versailles. The main palace is built to a horseshoe layout, and its symmetry is emphasized by a central projecting entrance. Building work was carried out by Johann Clemens Froimont, Alessandro Galli da Bibiena, Guillaume d'Hauberat and Nicolas de Pigage.

The second largest town of the region, Mannheim boasts many other historic buildings, including the post-Jesuit Church of St Ignatius and St Francis Xavier, designed by Alessandro Galli da Bibiena and built in 1733–60. Original wall-paintings by Egid Quirin Asam no longer exist, but the altars have survived to this day. These include J I Saler's *Silver Madonna in Radiant Glory* (1747). Also worth visiting are the Baroque Altes Rathaus (1701–23) and Secessionist buildings in Friedrichsplatz such as the Kunsthalle and Wasserturm – the symbol of Mannheim.

The town has several interesting museums: the **Städtische Kunsthalle** has a large collection of 19th- and 20th-century art, including Francis Bacon's *Study After Velasquez's Portrait of Pope Innocent X.* The museum is renowned for its major temporary exhibitions. The **Reiss-Engelhorn-Museen** has a fine collection of 18th-century Dutch paintings and sections devoted to early history and ethnography. Another big attraction is the **Landesmuseum für Technik und Arbeit** (Museum of Technology and Labour). Opened in 1990, this houses a collection of historic machinery. Mann-

Statue of Elector Karl Theodor in Mannheim's Jesuitenkirche

heim saw the first official demonstration of many inventions that have now become part of everyday life. In 1817, Baron Karl Friedrich von Sauerbronn demonstrated his first bicycle here and, in 1886, Carl Friedrich Benz unveiled his first automobile, produced at the nearby factory.

🏛 **Städtische Kunsthalle**
Moltkestraße 9. *Tel (0621) 293 64 13.* ◯ *11am–6pm Tue–Sun.* ● *during Carnival, 1 May, 24, 31 Dec.* 🎫

🏛 **Landesmuseum für Technik und Arbeit**
Museumsstraße 1. *Tel (0621) 429 89.* ◯ *9am–5pm Tue, Thu & Fri, 9am–8pm Wed, 10am–6pm Sat–Sun.* ● *Good Friday, 24, 25, 31 Dec.* 🎫

🏛 **Reiss-Engelhorn-Museen**
Quadrat D5 and C5. **www.** mannheim.de/reiss_museum.de *Tel (0621) 293 31 51.* ◯ *11am–6pm Tue–Sun.* 🎫

Paul Cézanne's *Pipe Smoker* (c.1890), in the Städtische Kunsthalle, Mannheim

Schwetzingen ❼

Road map B5. 🏛 *21,500.* 🛈
Dreikönigstr. 3 (06202-94 58 75).
🎬 *Schwetzinger Festspiele (May), Mozartkonzerte (Sept).*

Schwetzingen's Baroque-Renaissance palace was built during the reign of the Electors Johann Wilhelm, Charles II Philip and Karl Theodor as their summer residence. Erected on the site of a medieval castle that was later converted into a hunting lodge, it is one of the best known palace complexes of

Baroque Schwetzingen Palace, set amid beautiful gardens

18th-century Europe. The conversion of the 16th-century hunting lodge was carried out by J A Breuning and the side wings were built by Alessandro Galli da Bibiena. The magnificent Rococo theatre, designed by Nicolas de Pigage, was built in 1752, while the palace garden is the work of Johann Ludwig Petri, who designed it in the French style. The garden includes a mosque with two minarets and a bathhouse. In 1776 Friedrich Ludwig von Sckell converted it into an English-style garden.

Heraldic insignia from Bruchsal Palace

Speyer to Bruchsal. He not only initiated the town's development but, most importantly, ordered a palace to be built for himself and his court. The foundation stone of **Schloss Bruchsal** was laid in 1720 and the building works were carried out by Maximilian von Welsch, who was responsible for the right wing, and Michael Rohrer, who built the left wing between 1723 and 1728. The main body, preceded by a ceremonial courtyard, was designed by Baron Anselm von Grünstein. The central part of the palace is occupied by a magnificent staircase built by the great Balthasar Neumann, with stuccowork by Johann Michael Feuchtmayer and paintings by Johann and Januarius Zick. The palace suffered severe bomb damage in 1945, but its major part was reconstructed between 1952 and 1977.

St Peter's church was built in 1740–49 by Michael Rohrer to Balthasar Neumann's 1736 design. The church features magnificent Baroque tombs of Schönborn and his successor Cardinal Franz Christoph von Hutten. The palace garden was designed in the French style by Johann Scheer.

This former residence of prince-bishops now houses a section of the Karlsruhe Museum, which features the largest collection of Flemish and French tapestries in Germany. It is also home to the **Deutsches Musik-automaten Museum**, which includes 200 mechanical musical instruments. Short demonstrations are given on these throughout the day.

⚜ **Schloss Bruchsal**
Tel (07251) 74 26 61. ⬜ *9:30am–5pm Tue–Sun.* ⬜ *hourly.* ● *25, 31 Dec.* ⬜
Deutsches Musikautomaten Museum ⬜ *10am–5pm Tue–Sun.* ⬜ *11am, 2pm, 3:30pm.* ● *Shrove Tuesday, 24, 25, 31 Dec.* ⬜

⚜ **Schloss Schwetzingen**
Tel (06202) 12 88 28.
Schloss ⬜ *Apr–Oct: 10am–4pm Tue–Sun; Nov–Mar: 11am–2pm Fri, 1am–3pm Sat–Sun.* ⬜ *obligatory, every hour.*
Garden ⬜ *Apr–Sep: 8am–8pm daily; Oct & Mar: 9am–6pm daily; Nov–Feb: 9am–5pm daily.*

Bruchsal ❽

Road map B6. 🏠 *40,000.* 🚉 ℹ *Am Alten Schloss 2 (07251-505 94 60).*

Bruchsal belonged to the Bishops of Speyer from 1056 until 1806, since when it has been part of Baden. The town rose to prominence in the 17th century, when the Prince-Bishop of Speyer, Damian Hugo von Schönborn moved his residence from

Central façade of the Baroque Schloss Bruchsal

Street-by-Street: Heidelberg **⑨**

Situated on the banks of the river Neckar, Heidelberg is one of Germany's most beautiful towns. For centuries it was a centre of political power, with a lively and influential cultural life. In 1386, Germany's first university was established here by the Elector Ruprecht I. Building of the palace began during his reign, continuing until the mid-17th century. However, in the late-17th century, French incursions totally destroyed medieval Heidelberg, including the castle. The town was subsequently rebuilt in the early 18th-century in Baroque style.

Marktplatz
Now adorned with the Neptune Fountain, the market square was, in the past, the site of executions and the burning of witches and heretics.

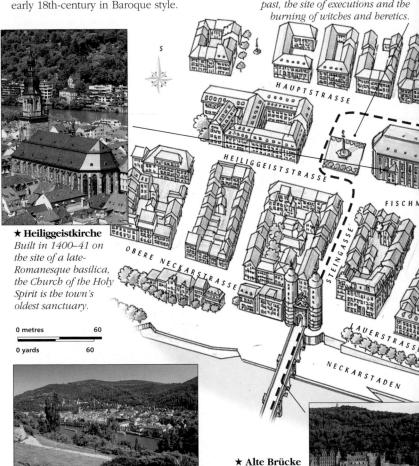

★ Heiliggeistkirche
Built in 1400–41 on the site of a late-Romanesque basilica, the Church of the Holy Spirit is the town's oldest sanctuary.

HAUPTSTRASSE

HEILIGGEISTSTRASSE

FISCHM

OBERE NECKARSTRASSE

STEINGASSE

LAUERSTRASSE

NECKARSTADEN

| 0 metres | 60 |
| 0 yards | 60 |

Philosophenweg
Built in 1817 on the slopes of Heiligenberg, at an altitude of 200 m (650 ft), the "Philosophers' Walk" offers magnificent views of Heidelberg and its castle.

★ Alte Brücke
This imposing, nine-span bridge over the river Neckar was built in 1786–88 by Mathias Maier. In the background is the Heidelberger Schloss.

For hotels and restaurants in this region see pp503–6 and pp542–5

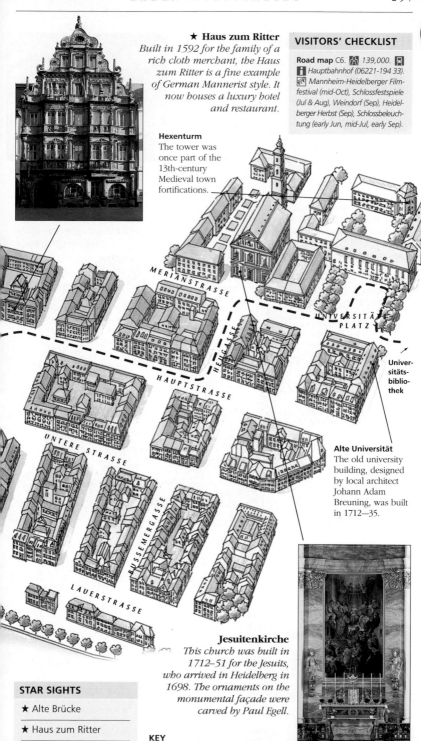

★ Haus zum Ritter
Built in 1592 for the family of a rich cloth merchant, the Haus zum Ritter is a fine example of German Mannerist style. It now houses a luxury hotel and restaurant.

VISITORS' CHECKLIST

Road map C6. 👥 *139,000.* 🚉
ℹ️ *Hauptbahnhof (06221-194 33).*
🎦 *Mannheim-Heidelberger Film-festival (mid-Oct), Schlossfestspiele (Jul & Aug), Weindorf (Sep), Heidel-berger Herbst (Sep), Schlossbeleuch-tung (early Jun, mid-Jul, early Sep).*

Hexenturm
The tower was once part of the 13th-century Medieval town fortifications.

MERIANSTRASSE

UNIVERSITÄTS PLATZ

Univer-sitäts-biblio-thek

HEILIGGASSE

HAUPTSTRASSE

UNTERE STRASSE

BUSSEMERGASSE

LAUERSTRASSE

Alte Universität
The old university building, designed by local architect Johann Adam Breuning, was built in 1712—35.

Jesuitenkirche
This church was built in 1712–51 for the Jesuits, who arrived in Heidelberg in 1698. The ornaments on the monumental façade were carved by Paul Egell.

STAR SIGHTS

★ Alte Brücke

★ Haus zum Ritter

★ Heiliggeistkirche

KEY

— — — Suggested route

Heidelberg Castle

Detail from Ruprechtsbau

Towering over the town, the majestic castle is really a vast residential complex that was built and repeatedly extended between the 13th and 17th centuries. Originally a supremely well-fortified Gothic castle, but now mostly in ruins, this was the seat of the House of Wittelsbach palatines. After remodelling in the 16th century, the castle became one of Germany's most beautiful Renaissance residences. However, its splendour was extinguished by the Thirty Years' War and the 1689 war with France, during which most of the structure was destroyed.

★ Ottheinrichsbau
The Deutsches Apotheken-museum is housed within the shell of this Renaissance building. It features Baroque and Rococo workshops and a travelling pharmacy.

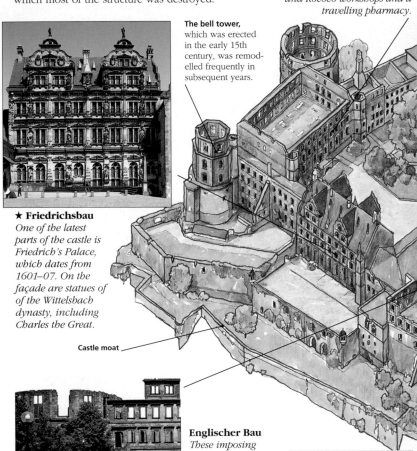

The bell tower, which was erected in the early 15th century, was remodelled frequently in subsequent years.

★ Friedrichsbau
One of the latest parts of the castle is Friedrich's Palace, which dates from 1601–07. On the façade are statues of of the Wittelsbach dynasty, including Charles the Great.

Castle moat

Englischer Bau
These imposing ruins in the castle complex are the remains of a 17th-century building that Friedrich V built for his wife Elizabeth Stuart.

STAR SIGHTS

★ Friedrichsbau

★ Ottheinrichsbau

★ Ruprechtsbau

Pulverturm

*Built during the reign of the
Elector Ruprecht, this 14th-
century tower once formed
part of the castle defences.*

Brunnenhalle
This Gothic loggia features early-
Romanesque columns taken from the
palace of Charles the Great in Ingelheim.

Torturm

**Main
entrance**

★ Ruprechtsbau
*Built around 1400 by a
master builder from
Frankfurt, this is the oldest
surviving part of the castle.*

🏛 Alte Universität
Grabengasse 1. **Tel** (06221) 54 21
52. **Universitätsmuseum** ◯
*Apr–Sep: 10am–4pm Tue–Sun; Oct:
10am–4pm Tue–Sun; Nov–Mar:
10am–4pm Tue–Sat.* 🖼
Designed by Mainz architect
Johann Adam Breuning, the
university was built in
1712–35. On the north wall
and ceiling are allegorical
paintings by Ferdinand Keller.
In front of the building is a
fountain crowned by a
sculpture in the form of the
heraldic Palatinate lion.

🏛 Universitätsbibliothek
Plöck 107–109. **Tel** (06221) 54 23
80. **Ausstellungsraum** ◯
10am–7pm Mon–Sat.
The monumental building of
the university library, designed
by Joseph Durm of Karlsruhe,
was erected in 1901–05 near
the church of St Peter. The
Heidelberg library, with over
2 million volumes, is one of
the largest in Germany. The
exhibition rooms hold many
precious manuscripts and old
prints, including the famous
Codex Manesse, illustrated
with 137 beautiful miniatures.

🏛 Kurpfälzisches Museum
Hauptstraße 97. **Tel** (06221) 58 34
020. ◯ *10am–6pm Tue–Sun.* 🖼
The French Count Charles de
Graimberg spent the bulk of
his considerable fortune on
building up an extensive
collection of fine drawings,
paintings, arms and various
curios associated with the
history of the Palatinate and
the castle of Heidelberg. In
1879, his collection became
the property of the town and
forms the core of this very
interesting museum, which
also includes a fascinating
archaeology section.

🔒 Heiliggeistkirche
Hauptstraße.
This collegiate church, whose
Baroque dome is one of the
city's landmarks, was built in
1400–41. The canons of the
college were also university
scholars and therefore the
church aisle features special
galleries for the extensive
collections of library books –
Bibliotheca Palatina. The
choir features a tombstone of
Ruprecht III and his wife,
Elisabeth von Hohenzollern.

Karlsruhe ⑩

Road map B6. 🌇 269,000.
🚂 🚌 *Bahnhofsplatz 6 (0721)
194 33;* www.karlsruhe.de
🎭 *Internationales Trachten-und-
Folklorefest (Jun).*

Karlsruhe, which is one of the "youngest" towns in Germany, flourished during the 19th century as a centre for science and art. In 1945, it lost its status as a regional capital, but is now the seat of the Bundesverfassungsgericht – the highest courts of the Federal Republic.

The town originated in 1715 when the margrave of Baden, Karl Wilhelm von Baden-Durlach, ordered a lodge to be built in the middle of his favourite hunting grounds. Karl liked the area and the lodge so much that he decided to move his residence here and live the remainder of his days in peace – hence the town's name, meaning "Karl's rest". The original Baroque-style design was expanded during the reign of his successor, Karl Friedrich.

The palace, which forms the hub of 32 streets, was designed by Leopoldo Retti, Mauritio Pedetti, Balthasar Neumann, Philippe de la Gaupière and others, and built in 1749–81. The town is based on a fan-like plan, spreading from a base formed by the open-sided wings of the palace. The rest of the circle, whose centre is marked by the octagonal palace tower (1715), is filled with green areas, including the palace garden.

A pyramid containing the tomb of Karl Wilhelm von Baden-Durlach in Karlsruhe

In the early 19th century, the town was remodelled along Neo-Classical lines. The main architect of this large-scale project was Friedrich Weinbrenner, who created this masterpiece of urban design. The equilateral market square is positioned along the palace axis. It is filled with similar but not identical buildings and features a central pyramid containing Karl Wilhelm's tomb. South of Marktplatz is the circular Rondellplatz. Weinbrenner's other works include the monumental town hall (1811–25), the Protestant town church and the Catholic parish church of St Stephen.

Karlsruhe has some very interesting museums. The Badisches Landesmuseum in the castle features a large collection of antiquities, decorative arts, sculpture, porcelain and furniture, from the Middle Ages to the present day. In a Neo-Renaissance building (1843–46) is the **Staatliche Kunsthalle**, with its large collection of mainly German and Dutch paintings from the 16th–19th centuries. These include the famous *Crucifixion* by Grünewald (1523).

Entirely different in character are the collections of the Zentrum für Kunst und Medientechnologie (ZKM) – an establishment that has combined the role of art college and museum since 1997. It occupies a former ammunitions factory in the western part of the town. Its core is the **Museum für Neue Kunst**, featuring installations, computer art and videos and other work by contemporary artists. The **Stadtmuseum im Prinz-Max-Palais**, based in a mansion named after the last chancellor of the Kaiserreich, contains the local history museum.

🏛 **Staatliche Kunsthalle**
Hans-Thoma-Straße 2–6. *Tel (0721)
9 26 33 59.* ⏲ *10am–5pm Tue–Fri,
10am–6pm Sat–Sun.* 🎫

🏛 **Museum für Neue Kunst**
Lorenzstraße 9. *Tel (0721) 81 000.*
⏲ *10am–6pm Wed–Fri, 11am–6pm
Sat–Sun.* 🎫

🏛 **Stadtmuseum im Prinz-Max-Palais**
Karlstraße 10. *Tel (0721) 1 33 42 31.*
⏲ *10am–6pm Tue, Fri & Sun,
10am–7pm Thu, 2–6pm Sat.*

The Baroque residence of the Dukes of Baden in Karlsruhe

For hotels and restaurants in this region see pp503–6 and pp542–5

Baden–Baden ⓫

Road map B6. 🏛 *50,000.*
✈ *Baden Airport (5 km/3 miles
northwest of town).* 🚃 🛈
*Schwarzwaldstraße 52 & i-Punkt in
der Trinkhalle (07221-27 52 00).*

Known as the "summer
capital of Europe", this
elegant spa resort is one of
the oldest towns in Germany
and was once the favourite
destination of European
aristocracy from Russia to
Portugal. Even before the
Romans built their camp here
around AD 80, the site was
occupied by a Celtic settlement of the Latenian period.

In the early years of the
modern era, *Civitas Aurelia
Aquensis* – known simply as
Aquae – was already known
in Italy for the therapeutic
properties of its waters. In the
3rd century AD, Aquae was
conquered by the Germanic
tribe of Alamains and in the
6th century AD by the Francs,
who built a fortress in the
town. The Margrave Hermann
II, known as "Marchio de
Baduon", was the first
important ruler of Baden.

During the horrific Black
Death, the qualities of the
local waters were once again
recognized as being beneficial
to health. During the
Palatinate War of Succession,
Baden-Baden was almost
totally destroyed but, by the
end of the 18th century, it
had become one of Europe's
most fashionable
resorts.

The old town of
Baden-Baden lies at
the foot of the Schloss-
berg (castle hill). The
oldest surviving
building in the town is
the Gothic collegiate
church, built during
the 13th–15th centuries
and then remodelled
in the 18th century.
It contains several
valuable epitaphs. To
the south of the
church is the bathing
hall – Friedrichsbad –
which was built in
Neo-Renaissance style
in 1877. Nearby stands
the magnificent New
Palace, which was the

Baden-Baden's casino, set in the elegant Kurhaus

residence of margraves from
the 15th century onwards. It
was remodelled along
German Renaissance lines in
the 16th century by Kaspar
Weinhart. The interiors are
decorated with paintings by
Tobias Stimmer.

Most of the spa buildings
are the work of Friedrich
Weinbrenner. His elegant
Kurhaus in Werderstraße has
been used as a casino since
1838. The most famous
gamester at the casino was
Fyodor Dostoevsky, who was
not always lucky at roulette.
His novel *The Gambler* (1866)
is supposedly set in Baden-
Baden. Nearby is the Trinkhalle (pump room), with its
mineral water fountains. Built
in 1839–42, it is decorated
with wall paintings illustrating
Black Forest legends.

Rising behind the spa area
is the last project completed
by Leo von Klenze before his
death – the Orthodox burial

**The Neo-Renaissance Trinkhalle (pump
room) in Baden-Baden**

chapel of a Romanian aristocratic family, the Stourdza
Mausoleum. In Schillerstraße
is the villa built in 1867 for the
Russian writer, Ivan Turgenev,
who lived here until 1872.

🏛 Brahmshaus
Maximilianstraße 85. **Tel** *(07221) 7
11 72.* ⏰ *3–5pm Mon, Wed, Fri,
10am–1pm Sun.* 📷
The exhibition displayed in
this house is devoted to the
life and works of the German
composer Johannes Brahms
who lived here from 1865
until 1874.

🔒 Kloster Lichtental
Hauptstraße 40.
Tel *(07221) 50 49 10.* ⏰ *3pm
Tue–Sun.* 📷 *Group tours (minimum
7 persons), advance telephone
booking required.* ⬤ *every first Sun
of the month.* 📷
This Cistercian nuns' abbey,
situated on the outskirts of
town, has a church dating
from the 14th–15th centuries.
Its ducal chapel contains
many epitaphs of the Baden
margraves. The abbey also
has an interesting museum.

🏛 Staatliche Kunsthalle Baden-Baden
Lichtentaler Allee 8a. **Tel** *(07221)
300 763.* ⏰ *10am–6pm Tue–Sun,
11am–8pm Wed*
The Staatliche Kunsthalle
Baden-Baden is an exhibition
venue that specializes in
modern and contemporary art.

🏛 Stadtmuseum
Lichtentaler Allee 10. **Tel** *(07221) 93
22 72.* ⏰ *11am–6pm Tue–Sun,
11am–8pm Wed.*
The Stadtmuseum includes
sections on glass, porcelain
and paintings, as well as some
old gambling equipment.

Maulbronn ⑫

Situated on the edge of the Stromberg region, Maulbronn grew up around a Cistercian monastery, which was founded in 1147 in the valley of the river Salzach by monks who came here from Alsace. The church, built in 1147–78, is an elongated, triple-nave basilica with a transept and a chancel. The early Gothic porch in front of the church was added in 1220. Outside the enclosure are domestic buildings, such as a former mill, a forge, a bakery and a guest house. Defence walls with turrets and a gate tower encircle the entire complex, which was designated a UNESCO World Heritage Site in 1993.

★ Chapter House
The monks assembled in this Gothic hall to discuss their private and public affairs. The hall has two naves, supported by three pillars.

★ Brunnenkapelle
Built opposite the entrance to the refectory, the Well Chapel, with its intricate Gothic forms, is where the monks used to wash their hands before meals.

Inner Courtyard
Once a garden, the monastery's inner courtyard is surrounded by cloisters. It is a place that inspires contemplation.

Cloisters

STAR FEATURES

- ★ Brunnenkapelle
- ★ Chapter House
- ★ Mourning
- ★ Stalls

The Porch
The porch, also known as "Paradise", was built onto the church façade in the early 13th century.

For hotels and restaurants in this region see pp503–6 and pp542–5

Cloisters

In the Middle Ages, monks meditated as they walked around the cloisters, which gave them protection from the vagaries of the weather. Talking was strictly forbidden.

VISITORS' CHECKLIST

Road map C6. 6,400.
Stadtverwaltung Maulbronn, Klosterhof 31 (07043-10 30).
www.maulbronn.de
Info-Zentrum Klosterhof.
Tel (07043) 92 66 10.
Mar–Oct: 9am–5:30pm daily; Nov–Feb: 9:30am–5pm Tue–Sun.
11:15am, 3pm.

Church Interior

Originally the church had a wooden ceiling. In 1424 it was replaced with a network vault, which stands in stark contrast to the plain walls.

★ Mourning

This Gothic relief, made in around 1390 in the Parler family workshop, was part of an altar, which no longer exists. Today, it can be seen on the altar in the monastery's choir.

★ Stalls

Richly decorated with carved ornaments, the late-Gothic stalls date from around 1450.

Heilbronn ⑬

Road map C6. 🏙 119,000. 🚊
ℹ️ *Kaiserstraße 17 (07131-
56 22 70).* 🎭 *Pferdemarkt (Feb),
Neckarfest (Jun), Stadtfest (Jun),
Heilbronner Herbst (Sep).*

Heilbronn's earliest records
date from the 8th century,
when the town was known as
"Helibrunna". By the late 19th
century, Heilbronn had
become Wurttemberg's main
industrial centre, with a large
port on the river Neckar.

Having suffered major destruction during World War II,
the town's surviving buildings
include the church of St Kilian,
a Gothic basilica from the
second half of the 13th century, with a triple-nave hall-
choir flanked by two towers.
The western tower was built
in 1508–29. The magnificent
altarpiece is an original late-
Gothic polyptych, the work of
Hans Seyffer (1498).

Near the 15th–16th-century
Rathaus (town hall) is a house
reputed to have been the
home of Käthchen, a char-
acter in Heinrich von Kleist's
play *Das Käthchen von Heilbronn.* Near the rebuilt
church of St Peter and St Paul
(originally the church of the
Teutonic Order) stands the
former Teutonic convent –
the Deutschhof.

**Isaak Habrecht's astronomical
clock on Heilbronn town hall**

**Half-timbered houses on the bank of the river
Kocher, in Schwäbisch Hall**

Schwäbisch Hall ⑭

Road map C6. 🏙 35,000. 🚊
ℹ️ *Am Markt 9 (0791-75 12 46).*
🎭 *Kuchen-und Brunnenfest der
Haller Salzsieder (Whitsun).*

Archaeological exca-
vations in 1939 proved
the existence of a
Celtic settlement on this
site as early as 500 BC.
The town features a
great number of
historic buildings from
various periods,
including many half-
timbered 15th–16th-
century houses,
Baroque town houses,
and a Rococo town
hall and town palace
(Keckenburg). The
most interesting
building is the hall-
church of St Michael,
whose Gothic main
body was built in
1427–56. The Romanesque
tower on the western façade,
however, dates from the 12th
century. The late-Gothic hall-
choir (1495–1527) is famous
for its decorative network
vaults. Original furnishings
include the main altar, the
stalls and the Holy Sepulchre.

Schwäbisch Gmünd ⑮

Road map C6. 🏙 63,400. 🚊
ℹ️ *Marktplatz 37/1 (07171-60 34
250).* 🎭 *Internationales Schatten-
theater Festival (Jun), European
Church Music (Jul).*

This town – the birthplace of
the architect Peter Parler and
painters Hans Baldung Grien

and Jörg Ratgeb –
was once renowned
throughout Europe
for the magnificent
goods produced by
its goldsmiths. It
has many great
historic buildings,
mainly churches,
such as the late-
Romanesque
church of St John,
which dates from
around 1220, but
was subsequently
remodelled. The
church of St Cross
is famous not only for being
the first Gothic hall-church in
southern Germany, but also
the first major work of the
famous family of architects –
the Parlers. This triple-nave
hall with a hall-choir,
featuring an ambulatory
and a ring of side
chapels, was built in
several stages, between
1320 and 1521. Its
western façade has a
high triangular
top with blind
windows.

Inside the church
are many valuable
historic relics, such as
the Holy Sepulchre
(1400), the stalls,
which date from
around 1550, and the
organ gallery
(1688). Other
interesting structures
in the town include
the town

**Madonna with Child,
in Marktplatz,
Schwäbisch Gmünd**

fortifications and several half-
timbered houses.

Bad Wimpfen ⑯

Road map C6. 🏙 6,676. 🚊 ℹ️
Carl-Ulrich-Straße 1 (07063-9 72 00).
🎭 *Talmarkt (Jun/Jul), Zunftmarkt
(Aug), Weihnachtsmarkt (Dec).*

The town of Bad Wimpfen
was created out of two
settlements, Bad Wimpfen am
Berg and Bad Wimpfen im
Tal, which remain distinct to
this day. The settlement on
top of the hill grew around
the Hohenstauf family palace,
whose chapel and well-
preserved arcade windows,
resting on pairs of decorated
columns, can still be seen.

Built at the order of Frederick I Barbarossa in 1165–75, this was the main and the biggest imperial palace (Kaiserpfalz) of the Holy Roman Empire. One of the surviving towers offers a spectacular view over the Neckar valley.

Set in a picturesque location, Bad Wimpfen features many half-timbered houses dating from the 16th–18th centuries.

Bad Wimpfen im Tal is built around the former collegiate church of St Peter and St Paul. This is a triple-nave basilica with transept, two eastern towers and cloister, dating from the 13th–15th centuries. The south façade of the transept and the portal are richly decorated with carvings, which are probably the work of Erwin von Steinbach, one of the builders of Strasbourg Cathedral. The church interior features many original carved statues and stalls.

Marbach ⑰

Road map C6. 🏠 1,450. 🚉
ℹ️ *Marktstraße 23 (07144-10 20).*

This small town would probably never merit an entry in any guidebook were it not for the fact that the great writer Friedrich Schiller was born here in 1759. The modest, half-timbered house, in which the famous poet spent his childhood, has survived to this day and is now a small museum – the **Schiller-Geburtshaus**. The town also possesses a vast museum of literature (**Schiller-Nationalmuseum**), which is housed in a Neo-Baroque palace. Its collection is not limited to the life and work of Schiller, but also includes many documents relating to German literature.

Other attractions in Marbach include some of the original half-timbered houses and the remains of the town walls and town gates in the old town. The late-Gothic Alexanderkirche is also worth a visit. Built in the second half of the 12th century by Aberlin Jörg, it features interesting network vaulting covered with ornamental paintings.

Friedrich Schiller statue in Marbach

🏛 **Schiller-Geburtshaus**
Niklastorstraße 31. **Tel** (07144) 175 67. ⏲ 9am–5pm daily. ⬤ 24–31 Dec. 📷

🏛 **Schiller-Nationalmuseum**
Schillerhöhe 8–10. **Tel** (07144) 84 80 10. ⏲ 10am–6pm Thu–Sun, 10am–8pm Wed. ⬤ 24–31 Dec. 📷

Esslingen ⑱

Road map C6. 🏠 92,000.
ℹ️ *Marktplatz 2 (0711-39 69 39 69).*

Set among vineyards on the banks of the river Neckar, the beautiful town of Esslingen is famous for its sparkling wines. The town's historic buildings were fortunate in surviving intact the ravages of World War II. A walk through the winding streets and narrow alleys of the old centre will yield many interesting sights, while a climb to the top of the hill affords a splendid view of the town and the Neckar valley, as well as the amazing **Innere Brücke**, a 14th-century bridge. From there visitors can descend towards the market square, stopping on the way to visit Frauenkirche, a Gothic hall-church dating from the 14th century. Its front tower, the work of Ulrich and Matthäus von Ensingen, was added later. In the market square is the Stadtkirche St Dionysius, the oldest church in town, built in the 13th century on the site of an earlier, 8th-century building. Inside are magnificent early-Gothic stained-glass windows and late-15th-century Gothic furnishings, including the choir partition, the sacrarium and the font. The nearby church of St Paul, built in the mid-13th century for the Dominicans, is the oldest surviving Dominican church in Germany. In neighbouring Rathausplatz stands the half-timbered old town hall, Altes Rathaus, with its beautiful Renaissance façade, and the Baroque new town hall. Designed as a palace for Gottlieb von Palm by Gottlieb David Kandlers, the Neues Rathaus was built between 1748 and 1751.

The picturesque houses and chapel of Esslingen's 14th-century Innere Brücke

Ludwigsburg ⑲

Palace crest

Situated near Stuttgart and known as the "Versailles of Swabia", Ludwigsburg was founded in 1704 on the initiative of Eberhard Ludwig, Duke of Wurttemberg. At the heart of the town is the vast palace complex, which the Duke ordered to be built for his mistress, Countess Wilhelmina von Graevenitz. The construction of the palace, which was carried out between 1704 and 1733, involved many outstanding architects and interior decorators, including Philipp Jenisch, Johann Nette, Donato Frisoni and Diego Carlone.

Northern Garden
This magnificent Baroque park is the venue for a flower show ("Blooming Baroque") that is held here during the summer.

★ Western Gallery
The gallery features opulent stucco ornaments by Ricardo Retti and Diego Carlone (1712–15).

★ Marble Hall
This vast hall in the new wing of the palace was remodelled in 1816, but still retains some of its Baroque interior decor.

★ Queen's Library
The library is housed in the east wing of the palace, in the apartments arranged for Queen Charlotte Mathilde.

The new wing of the palace houses a museum devoted to court art of the Neo-Classical period.

★ Schloss Favorite
The "Favorite" hunting lodge was built between 1716 and 1723, but its interior has been remodelled in Neo-Classical style.

The old wing
contains the palace's oldest apartments.

Märchengarten
The landscaped section of the park includes the "Fairy-tale Garden", which contains figures and models from German fairy-tales.

The upper fruit garden attracts visitors with its picturesque paths, which are lined with apple trees and grapevines.

Restaurant and café

Emichsburg
This romantic castle, built in 1798–1802, was named after the founder of the Wurttemberg dynasty.

STAR SIGHTS

★ Marble Hall

★ Queen's Library

★ Schloss Favorite

★ Western Gallery

Stuttgart ⑳

The capital of Baden-Wurttemberg, Stuttgart is one of the largest and most important towns of the Federal Republic. It grew from a 10th-century stud farm, known as Stutengarten, to become the ducal (1321) and later the royal (1806) capital of Wurttemberg. Beautifully situated among picturesque hills, the town is a major industrial centre with many important manufacturing plants. It is also a well-known publishing and cultural centre, with a world-famous ballet company, chamber orchestra and splendid art collections.

Exploring Stuttgart

Start your tour of Stuttgart at Schlossplatz, continuing along Königstraße towards the Palace Gardens, with their many interesting buildings, and stopping to pay a visit to the Staatsgalerie, whose extension was designed by the British architect James Stirling. From there you can return via Konrad-Adenauer-Strasse, heading towards Karlsplatz, then to Schillerplatz and Marktplatz with its magnificent town hall, finally ending the walk at Hegelhaus museum.

🏛 Schlossplatz

At the centre of the square stands the **Jubiläumssäule** – a column erected in 1842–46 to celebrate the 25-year reign of Wilhelm I. The square also features sculptures by many famous artists, including Alexander Calder and Alfred Hrdlicka. The east side of the square features a huge palace complex, **Neues Schloss**, built in 1746–1807, while on the opposite side stands **Königs-bau**, a Neo-Classical structure erected in 1856–60.

Neo-Classical façade of Stuttgart's Staatstheater

🏛 Kunstmuseum Stuttgart

Kleiner Schlossplatz 1. *Tel (0711) 216 21 88.* ◯ *10am–6pm Tue–Sun, 10am–9pm Wed & Fri.* **www.** kunstmuseum-stuttgart.de 🖼 🔢 🚹

The spectacular glass cube of the Kunstmuseum Stuttgart was designed by the Berlin architects Hascher & Jehle. It houses the Municipal Art Collection, which includes works by such artists as Adolf Hölzel, Joseph Kosuth, Dieter Krieg, Dieter Roth, the Swabian Impressionists and has an outstanding collection of Otto Dix's work.

🍂 Schlossgarten

The magnificent gardens stretching north of the Neues Schloss were established in the early 19th century. They have maintained, to this day, much of their original charm, with neat avenues and inter-esting sculptures. The attrac-tions include the **Carl-Zeiss-Planetarium**, which runs an excellent science programme, using equipment made by the famous optics company.

On the edge of the park stands a vast Neo-Classical theatre building, the **Württem-bergisches Staatstheater**, built in 1909–12 by Max Littmann. In 1982–3 it was given a new, dome-covered wing, the Theaterpavilion, designed by Gottfried Böhm.

🏛 Staatsgalerie

See pp312–13.

♣ Altes Schloss

Württembergisches Landes-museum Schillerplatz 6. *Tel (0711) 27 93 498.* ◯ *10am–5pm Tue–Sun.* 🖼

When Wurttemberg castle burned down in 1311, it was decided to move the family seat to Stuttgart. In 1325, the existing small castle was extended, creating Dütnitzbau. This wing has survived and can be seen from Karlsplatz. A large-scale Renaissance remodelling project, designed by Aberlin Tresch and carried out in 1553–78, gave the castle its square layout, with three-storey arcaded cloisters encircling the inner courtyard. The southwestern wing contains the Schlosskapelle (chapel), the first sacral build-ing in Stuttgart built especially for the Protestants. The castle now houses the **Württember-gisches Landesmuseum**,

The façade of Stuttgart's Neues Schloss, combining Baroque and Neo-Classical elements

Cloistered courtyard of the Renaissance Altes Schloss

which includes vast collections of decorative art, including those displaying the ducal and royal insignia of Wurttemberg. The prehistory section includes jewellery from the Frankish period and the preserved tomb of a Celtic nobleman from Hochdorf.

✠ Schillerplatz
This is undoubtedly one of Stuttgart's most beautiful areas. It is here that the stud farm that gave Stuttgart its name is said to have stood. Today, a pensive statue of Friedrich Schiller, the work of the Danish sculptor Bertel Thorwaldsen (1839), occupies the centre of the square.

Schillerplatz is surrounded by historic buildings: the **Old Chancellery**, built in 1542–44 and extended upwards in 1566,

now houses a restaurant, the Prinzenbau (1605–78), and the Stiftsfruchtkasten, an attractive gabled granary (1578), now home to a museum of musical instruments.

✠ Stiftskirche (Hl. Kreuz)
Stiftstraße 12.
From the south side of Schillerplatz there is a view of the presbytery of the collegiate church of the Holy Cross. This Gothic church, the work of Hänslin and Aberlin Jörg, was built in the 15th century and incorporated the walls of the previous, early-Gothic church. Despite World War II damage, this newly renovated church still has the original stone gallery of the dukes of Wurttemberg, built in 1576–84 by Simon Schlör to a design by Johann Steiner, as well as Gothic furnishings.

Figures of saints adorning the façade of the Stiftskirche

VISITORS' CHECKLIST
Road map C6. 🕎 586,000. ✈ south of town. 🚌 🛈 Königstraße 1A (0711-22 28 240). 🎭 Frühlingsfest (Apr/May), Stuttgarter Weindorf (Aug/Sep, Oct/Nov), Fellbacher Herbst (Oct), Weihnachtsmarkt (Dec). **www**.stuttgart-tourist.de

⚏ Hegelhaus
Eberhardstraße 53. **Tel** (0711) 216 67 33. ☐ 10am–5:30pm Mon–Fri, 10am–6:30pm Thu, 10am–4pm Sat.
Georg Wilhelm Friedrich Hegel – the creator of one of the most important modern philosophical systems – was born in this house on 27 August 1770. The house is now a museum, which houses an exhibition devoted to the life and work of the famous philosopher.

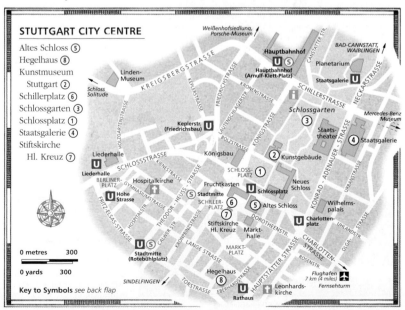

STUTTGART CITY CENTRE

Altes Schloss ⑤
Hegelhaus ⑧
Kunstmuseum Stuttgart ②
Schillerplatz ⑥
Schlossgarten ③
Schlossplatz ①
Staatsgalerie ④
Stiftskirche Hl. Kreuz ⑦

🏛 Linden-Museum/ Staatl. Museum für Völkerkunde

Hegelplatz 1. **Tel** *(0711) 2 02 23.*
⭕ *10am–5pm Tue, Thu–Sun,
10am–8pm Wed.* 🈳

The Linden Museum is one of Germany's finest ethnology museums. It was founded by Count Karl von Linden, who was also its director from 1889 until 1910. The museum contains many fascinating exhibits from all over the world, including figures from the Indonesian theatre of shadows, a Tibetan sand mandala, a 6th–8th-century mask from Peru in South America and a full-size reproduction of an Islamic bazaar.

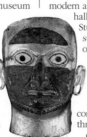

Peruvian mask in the Linden-Museum

🚇 Weißenhofsiedlung

Am Weißenhof 20. **Exhibition rooms**
Tel *(0711) 2 57 91 87.* ⭕ *10am–2pm
Tue–Sat, 10–3pm Sun.* 🅿 *from Am
Weißenhof 15, 11am Sat.* **Architektur-Galerie Tel** *(0711) 257 14 34.*
⭕ *2–6pm Tue–Sat, noon–5pm Sun.*

A building exhibition held in 1927 in Stuttgart had housing as its main theme. It left behind a complete housing estate that still exists today, although it was badly bombed during World War II. Most of the houses represent functionalism, which was being promoted at the time by the Bauhaus. The estate, which was to serve as an example to other towns and estates, has some interesting houses,

including works by Mies van der Rohe (Am Weißenhof 14–29), Le Corbusier (Rathenaustraße 1–3), Peter Behrens (Hölzelweg 3–5) and Hans Scharoun (Hölzelweg 1).

🎭 Liederhalle

Berliner Platz 1.

A must for all lovers of modern architecture, Liederhalle, in the centre of Stuttgart, is a successful synthesis of tradition and modernism. Built in 1955–56 by Adolf Abel and Rolf Gutbrod, this fine cultural and congress centre, with three concert halls clustered around an irregular hall, is still impressive today.

🏛 Mercedes-Benz-Museum

Mercedesstraße 137. **Tel** *(0711)
172 25 78.* ⭕ *9am–5pm Tue–Sun.*
🌑 *public holidays.*

To the east of the town centre, in the Obertürkheim district, is the famous Mercedes-Benz-Museum. Its splendid collection illustrates the development of motorcar production, from the earliest models to today's state-of-the-art, computerized products. Set up to celebrate the centenary of their inventions, the museum features over 70 historic vehicles, all in immaculate condition. The collection includes the world's two oldest automobiles, Gottlieb Daimler's horseless carriage and Carl Benz's three-

Some of the models on display in the Mercedes-Benz-Museum

wheeled automobile from 1886. Also on display is a hand-made limousine that was built in the 1930s for the Emperor of Japan and the first "Popemobile", which was built for Pope Paul VI.

Another interesting exhibit is the famous 1950s racing car, *Silberpfeil* (Silver Arrow), as well as models that were built for attempts on world speed records. Also on display are scores of the latest models that have been produced by the company.

The visitor can also learn the history of Daimler-Benz AG, which was created by the merger in 1926 of Daimler-Motoren-Gesellschaft and Benz & Cie., Rhein. The company's subsequent 1999 merger with Chrysler created one of the world's largest car manufacturing concerns, DaimlerChrysler.

🎭 Fernsehturm

⭕ *9am–10pm daily.*

Built between 1954 and 1956 this television tower was the world's first to be built entirely from ferro-concrete. It is 217 m (712 ft) high and stands on top of a wooded hill, Hoher Bopser. Its observation platform provides splendid views over Schwäbische Alb, Schwarzwald and, on a clear day, even the Alps.

🏛 Porsche-Museum

Porschestr. 42. **Tel** *(0711) 9 11 25
685.* ⭕ *9am–4pm Mon–Fri,
9am–5pm Sat, Sun, public holidays.*

Stuttgart's other famous car manufacturer also has its own museum, which includes

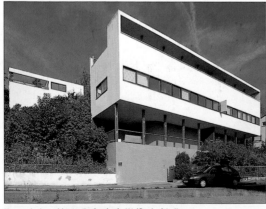

House designed by Le Corbusier in Weißenhofsiedlung

around 50 examples of these fast and expensive vehicles, some of which are built to order. The history of the company is documented in a film shown in the museum's cinema. Free guided tours of the factory production lines are available. These are very popular and it is advisable to book well in advance.

🏢 Markthalle

Dorotheenstraße 4. ⏱ *7am–6:30pm Mon–Fri, 7am–4pm Sat.*

Stuttgart's market hall, built in 1912–14 in Art Nouveau style on the site of an earlier vegetable market, is one of the finest in Europe. Built as a food exchange, it has magnificent frescos. Today it still sells fresh fruit and vegetables to the general public, and it now also houses a small restaurant and café.

♣ Schloss Solitude

Solitude 1. *Tel (0711) 69 66 99.* ⏱ *Apr–Oct: 9am–noon, 1:30–5pm Tue–Sun; Nov–Mar: 10am–noon, 1:30–4pm Tue–Sun.*

This exquisite small palace, standing on the slopes of a hill, was built for Prince Karl Eugene between 1763 and 1767. The Prince not only commissioned the project, but also took an active part in the design of the residence, which is the work of Pierre Louis Philippe de la Guêpière, who was responsible for introducing the Louis XVI-style to Germany. Many consider this palace to be his masterpiece.

Following its full restoration in 1990, and the provision of 45 residential studio apartments, the palace now serves art students on scholarships from all over the world. A 15-km (9-mile) long, straight road connects Schloss Solitude with Ludwigsburg.

JOHANNES KEPLER (1571–1630)

This outstanding astronomer and mathematician was born in Weil der Stadt. He studied theology in Tübingen, where he encountered the work of Nicolaus Copernicus, becoming a fervent advocate of his theory. Forced to flee in 1600, Kepler went to Prague where he worked with Tycho Brahe. Many years of research led him to formulate three laws of planetary motion. Kepler is also the inventor of the twin-lens telescope.

🏢 Bad Cannstatt

Once an independent health resort, Bad Cannstatt is now a district of Stuttgart. Set in a beautiful park, it has a late-Gothic parish hall-church, a Neo-Classical town hall and a Kursaal (spa-house), built in 1825–42. One of its attractions is the Neo-Classical Schloss Rosenstein, built in 1824–29 at the request of King Wilhelm I, based on amended designs by John Papworth. The King was also the initiator of the beautiful "Wilhelm's complex". This includes a Moorish-style villa located in a symmetrically laid-out park, with many Oriental-style pavilions and other decorative elements. Completed in the 1840s, its main designer was Karl Ludwig Wilhelm von Zanth. The park has now been transformed into a botanical-zoological garden.

Environs

Stuttgart provides a convenient base for exploring the surroundings. In **Sindelfingen**, 15 km (9 miles) southwest, it is worth visiting the Romanesque Church of St Martin Canons, which was founded in 1083. While you are there, take a stroll along Lange Straße to the old town hall, which dates from 1478 and is joined with the Salt House (1592). The two buildings, both half-timbered in their upper sections, now house the town museum.

A little further to the west, **Weil der Stadt** is the birthplace of the astronomer Johannes Kepler and the reformer Johannes Brenz. The town's late-Gothic church of St Peter and St Paul was completed in 1492 by Aberlin Jörg. Inside is a beautiful Renaissance sacrarium, dating from 1611. The Marktplatz, with a statue of Kepler at its centre, has a Renaissance town hall (1582). Nearby, at Keplergasse 2, stands the house in which the famous astronomer was born and which now houses a small museum, the Kepler-Museum.

Another place worthy of a visit is **Waiblingen**, 10 km (6 miles) to the northeast of Stuttgart. It features a Romanesque church, the vaults of which are decorated with some splendid wall paintings dating from 1515.

The façade of the Schloss Solitude, in the hills to the west of Stuttgart's centre

Staatsgalerie

The Staatsgalerie grew from the museum of fine arts founded in 1843 by King Wilhelm I and containing the king's private collection. Now it ranks among the finest of German galleries. As well as its own magnificent collection of old masters and modern artists, the gallery has an extensive collection of graphics. In 1984 the art gallery acquired an extension designed by James Stirling.

★ The Mourning of Christ (c.1490)
This subtle depiction of Christ is the work of the Venetian artist Giovanni Bellini.

Bathsheba at her Toilet (c.1485)
In this painting, which is a fragment of a lost triptych illustrating Justice, Hans Memling uses the Old Testament story of Bathsheba to exemplify the abuse of power, intervention by God and the reformation of a sinner.

★ St Paul in Prison (1627)
In this, one of his earliest works, Rembrandt depicted the Apostle Paul awaiting death in a humble cell.

Entrance to Alte Staatsgalerie

Entrance to Neue Staatsgalerie

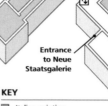

Crossing of the Rhine near Rhenen (1642)
The Dutch painter Jan von Goyen became famous for his evocative landscapes, which were often executed in uniform tones of lead-grey or brown-green.

STAR EXHIBITS

★ Iphigenie

★ St Paul in Prison

★ The Mourning of Christ

KEY

■	Italian painting
☐	German painting
☐	Dutch painting
☐	19th-century painting
☐	20th-century painting
☐	Sculpture Garden
☐	Graphic arts
☐	Non-exhibition rooms

★ Iphigenie (1871)
Anselm Feuerbach's painting was inspired by a play by Goethe, Iphigenie on Tauris.

GALLERY GUIDE
Permanent exhibitions are located over the first floor of the two buildings. In the Alte Staatsgalerie are works by the old masters and from the 19th-century. The Neue Staatsgalerie holds 20th-century art. The ground floors are currently closed until 2007.

VISITORS' CHECKLIST

Konrad-Adenauer-Straße 30–32.
Tel *(0711) 47 04 00.*
⬚ *10am–6pm Tue, Wed, Fri–Sun, 10am–9pm Thu.* ▨ *(Wed free).* www.staatsgalerie.de

Spring Fields (1887)
One of the leading members of the French Impressionist movement, Claude Monet was unsurpassed in his rendition of iridescent light.

Mother and Child (1905)
This painting by Pablo Picasso represents his "pink period", which preceded the famous Cubist experiments of this great Spanish artist.

First floor

Female Nude Reclining on a White Pillow (1917)
Amadeo Modigliani became famous for his idiosyncratic portraits and female nudes.

Ground floor

Schwäbische Alb 21

The mountain range of Schwäbische Alb (the Swabian Jura) extends like an arc, 220 km (137 miles) long and 40 km (25 miles) wide, from the Upper Rhine around Schaffhausen, in Switzerland, to Nördlinger Ries, at the border between the federal counties of Baden-Wurttemberg and Bavaria. The highest peak in the range is Lemberg (1,015 m/3,330 ft). Beech woods and scented juniper shrubs dominate the mellow landscape, whose whole system of interconnected stalagmitic caves was carved from the sedimentary limestone rocks.

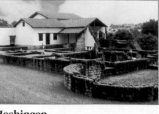

Hechingen
On the outskirts of Hechingen, the remains of a 1st–3rd-century AD Roman villa are open to the public.

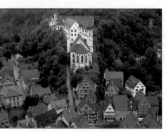

Haigerloch
In the vaults of this castle is a vast bunker that was used as an atomic research laboratory towards the end of World War II.

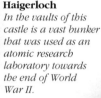

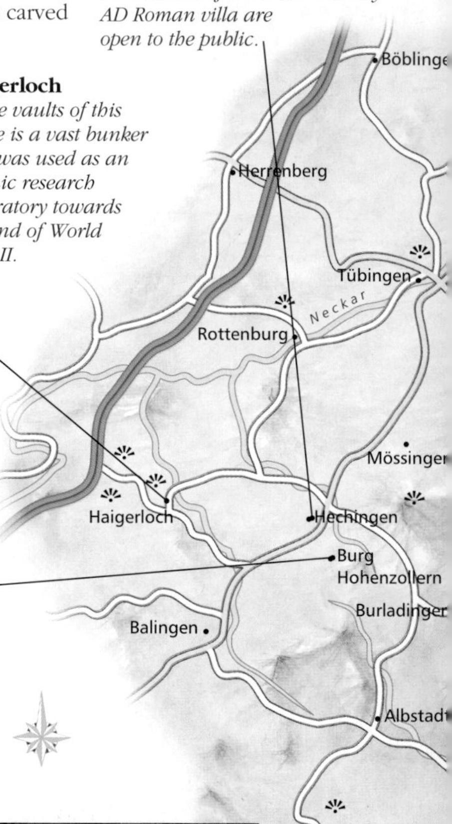

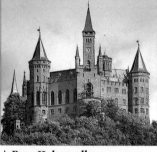

★ Burg Hohenzollern
The ancestral seat of the Hohenzollern family was remodelled in 1850-67. Only the 15th-century St Michaelkapelle survives from the original fortress.

★ Beuron
Beuron's magnificent Benedictine Abbey was founded in the 11th century. Its subsequent remodelling resulted in a Baroque structure, which survives to this day.

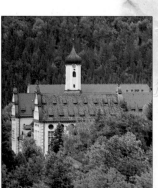

STAR SIGHTS

- ★ Burg Hohenzollern
- ★ Sigmaringen
- ★ Beuron

For hotels and restaurants in this region see pp503–6 and pp542–5

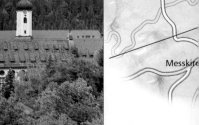

Swabian Jura Landscape
The gentle hills and enchanting villages attract hikers and tourists from all over the world.

VISITORS' CHECKLIST

ℹ Schwäbische Alb
Tourismusverband, Marktplatz 1,
Bad Urach (07125-94 81 06).
www.schwaebischealb.de

Hohenneuffen
A massive castle dominates the tiny town of Neuffen. It is the most impressive ruin in the Swabian Jura.

KEY

▭	Motorway
—	Main road
—	Secondary road
—	River
☼	Viewpoint

Wendlingen

Kirchheim

Nürtingen

Beuren
Hohenneuffen

Reutlingen
Bad Urach

Lichtenstein
Burg Lichtenstein

Münsingen

SCHWÄBISCHE ALB

Riedlingen

Sigmaringen

Lichtenstein
This romantic castle was immortalized in a novel by Wilhelm Hauff.

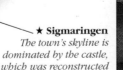

★ Sigmaringen
The town's skyline is dominated by the castle, which was reconstructed following a fire in 1893. Only the towers of the medieval fortress remain.

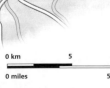

0 km   5

0 miles   5

Tübingen ❷

Road map C6. 👥 *85,000.* 🚆 ℹ
*An der Neckarbrücke 1 (07071-913
60).* 🛍 *Mon, Wed, Fri.*

Along with Heidelberg and
Freiburg im Breisgau,
Tübingen is the home of one
of southern Germany's three
most famous universities. It
was founded in 1477 by
Count Eberhard the Bearded.

The first records of the
fortress that later gave rise to
a settlement on this site date
from 1078. By around 1231,
the settlement had become
a town. In 1342, Tübingen
passed into the hands of the
counts of Wurttemberg,
having previously belonged
to the counts Palatinate.

Schloss Hohentübingen,
which towers over the town,
has a magnificent gateway
(Unteres Tor). Built in 1606,
it is richly adorned with the
coat of arms of the House of
Wurttemberg. The walled
castle complex, with its central
courtyard and long approach,
was built in stages during
1507–15, 1534–42 and 1606.

A walk along the Burgsteige
will bring you to the picturesque old town. Here, at the
centre of Marktplatz, is the
Neptune Fountain, the work
of Heinrich Schickhard, dating
from 1617. In the western
corner of the square is a
lovely Renaissance town hall,
built in 1435 and
extended in the

Tübingen's Gothic-Renaissance town hall

16th century. It features an
astronomical clock, which
dates from 1511. *Sgraffiti* on
the western façade dates from
1876; those on the elevations
facing Haaggasse date from
the 16th century.

The collegiate church of
St George (**Stiftskirche St
Georg**), built in 1440–1529, is
a triple-nave hall with rows of
side chapels, galleries and a
single tower. Of particular
note are the ducal tombs, the
late-Gothic reading-room and
the stained-glass windows of
the choir, dating from 1475.
Magnificent stalls, adorned
with carved figures of the
Prophets, date from the late
15th century.

The bookstore in Holzmarkt
(Buchhandlung Heckenbauer)
is where Hermann
Hesse

once served as an
apprentice bookseller.
On the banks of the
Neckar stands the
Hölderlinturm, in
which the German
poet Hölderlin lived
from 1807 until his
death. Not far from
here stands the large
building of the Alte
Burse, which was built
in 1478–80 and later
remodelled in 1803-
1805. The building
was once used to
accommodate students
and as a lecture hall.
Martin Luther's close
associate, Philipp
Melanchthon, lectured here
between 1514 and 1518.

The Protestant seminary in
Neckarhalde was founded by
Prince Ulrich in 1536. Its
graduates include the poets
Hölderlin, Mörike and Schiller
and the philosophers Hegel
and Schelling.

The **Kunsthalle** is famous
throughout Germany not only
for its temporary exhibitions,
but also for its fine collection
of modern art. Other popular
attractions in Tübingen include
the **Stadtmuseum**, which is
devoted to the town's history,
and the **Auto-und Spielzeugmuseum**.

🏛 **Museum Schloss
Hohentübingen**
Burgsteige 11. **Tel** *(07071) 297 73 84.*
⏰ *May–Sep: 10am–6pm Wed–Sun,
Oct–Apr: 10am–5pm Wed–Sun.* 🖼

🔐 **Stiftskirche St Georg**
Tel *(07071) 525 83.* ⏰ *Apr–Sep:
9am–5pm daily, Oct–Mar:
9am–4pm daily.* 🖼

🚍 **Hölderlinturm**
Bursagasse 6. **Tel** *(07071) 220 40.*
⏰ *10am–noon, 3–5pm Tue–Fri,
2–5pm Sat, Sun, public holidays.* 🖼

🏛 **Kunsthalle**
Philosophenweg 76. **Tel** *(07071)
969 10.* ⏰ *10am–6pm Wed–Sun,
10am–8pm Tue (during exhibitions).*

🏛 **Statdtmuseum**
Kornhausstraße 10. **Tel** *(07071)
204 17 11 or 94 54 60.*
⏰ *11am–5pm Tue–Sun.* 🖼

🏛 **Auto- und Spielzeug-
museum**
Brunnenstraße 18. **Tel** *(07071) 92
900.* ⏰ *Apr–Oct: 10am–noon,
2–5pm Wed–Sun; Nov–Mar: 10am–
noon, 2–5pm Sun and public
holidays only.* 🖼

Unteres Tor leading to Schloss Hohentübingen

For hotels and restaurants in this region see pp503–6 and pp542–5

Rottweil ㉓

Road map C7. 🏛 *24,000.* 🚆 🛈
Hauptstraße 21–23 (0741-49 42 80).
🎭 *Fasnet (last Mon of Carnival),
Jazzfest (May), Klassikfestival (Jun),
Ferienzauber (Aug).*

Situated on the banks of the
river Neckar, Rottweil is one
of the oldest towns in Baden-
Wurttemberg. It grew from a
Roman settlement that was
established on a hilltop here
in AD 73. In 1234 Rottweil
was granted town status and,
by 1401, it had become a free
town of the Holy Roman
Empire. Between 1463 and
1802 it belonged to the Swiss
Confederation, which was
founded in 1291 by the
cantons of Uri, Schwyz and
Unterwalden. In 1802, the
town passed into the rule of
the dukes of Wurttemberg.

Rottweil has many historic
remains, including sections of
the fortified city walls, with
several well-preserved turrets.

The parish church of St
Cross (Heilig-Kreuz-Münster),
built in 1230–1534, has a
triple-nave basilica with stellar
and network vaults. Late-
Gothic altars, including St
Bartholomew's, by Michael
Wolgemut and a crucifix
attributed to Veit Stoss, are
among its features.

To the south of the church
stands the late-Gothic town
hall (1521). On the opposite
side of the street, at Hauptstraße 20, the **Stadtmuseum**
has an outstanding collection

Fountain and "Black Gate" in Rottweil's main street, Hauptstraße

of prehistoric remains. The
Dominikanermuseum has an
interesting exhibition of
Roman relics. These include
the famous Orpheus
mosaic, dating from the
2nd century AD, and an
outstanding collection of
late-Gothic sculpture,
including the statue of St
Barbara by Multscher
(c.1450).

The Hauptstraße is
lined with burghers'
houses, displaying
characteristic oriel
windows. One of the
most beautiful historic
buildings in Rottweil is the
Kapellenkirche, built in
1330–1478. Its 70-metre (230-
ft) tower and three portals are
adorned with carved
ornaments reminiscent of the
French Gothic style. The
Baroque interior features
frescos by Josef Fiertmayer,
who was a pupil of renowned
painter and architect Cosmas
Damian Asam. The Gothic
Dominican church, built in
1266–82 and remodelled in
the 18th century, has some
frescos by Joseph Wannen-

macher (1755). Roman baths
dating from the 2nd century
AD have been excavated at
the corner of what is now
the cemetery.

Rottweil is famous for
its carnival processions
(Fasnet), a tradition that
goes back to the Middle
Ages. A collection of
carnival costumes can be
seen in the Stadtmuseum.

The **Puppen- und
Spielzeugmuseum** has a
fine collection of historic
dolls and toys which is
perfect for keeping the
children entertained.

Kapellenturm,
Rottweil

🏛 **Stadtmuseum**
Hauptstraße 20. **Tel** *(0741) 494
330.* ⬜ *10am– noon, Tue–Sun.*
⬛ *Mon.* 🈲

🏛 **Dominikanermuseum**
Am Kriegsdamm. **Tel** *(0741) 78 62.*
⬜ *2–5pm Tue–Sun.* ⬛ *public
holidays.* 🈲

🏛 **Puppen- und
Spielzeugmuseum**
Hochbrücktorstraße 9.
Tel *(0741) 942 21 77.*
⬜ *10am–12:30pm, 2pm–5:30pm
Wed–Fri, 2pm–5pm Sat, 11am–5pm
Sun.* 🈲

Crucifixion **attributed to Veit Stoss
in Heilig-Kreuz-Münster, Rottweil**

Ulm ㉔

Road map B6. 🏠 *115,000.* 🚉
ℹ️ *Münsterplatz 50 (0731-161 28 30.*
📷 *Fischerstechen (every fourth year in Jul: 2005, 2009 etc.), Schwörmontag (3rd Mon in Jul), Stadtfest (Jun).*

Lying on the river Danube, Ulm dates back to 854. It became a town in 1165 then, in 1274, a free town of the Holy Roman Empire. During the 15th century Ulm was one of the richest towns in Europe but the Thirty Years' War put an end to its rapid development. In 1810 Ulm came under the rule of the Wurttemberg kings. The town is renowned as the birthplace of Albert Einstein. During World War II, most of the old town was destroyed during bombing raids.

The Münster is a true masterpiece of European Gothic architecture. A vast, five-nave basilica, its 161-m (530-ft) high west tower is the highest church tower in the world. The cathedral's construction, from 1377 until 1545, was overseen by the greatest builders of the German Gothic – Heinrich and Michael Parler, Urlich von Ensingen, Hans Kun and Matthäus Böblinger. The unfinished cathedral was extended in 1844–90, based on the original medieval design. The interior contains many outstanding features,

Gothic font in Ulm Cathedral

including the altar by Hans Multscher (1443), the famous stalls with figures of philosophers, poets, prophets and apostles carved by Jörg Syrlin the Elder, 15th-century stainedglass windows, and the font, by Jörg Syrlin the Younger.

The town has many fine historic buildings, including the GothicRenaissance town hall, which is decorated with brightly coloured frescos and features an astronomical clock. Other features of Marktplatz include the Gothic fountain *Fischkasten* (Fish Crate), dating from 1482, and the Reichenauer Hof, which dates from 1370–1535.

The **Ulmer Museum**, which is housed in a number of historic 16th- and 17th-century buildings, has a collection of art spanning a period from the Middle Ages to the present day. The collection includes the work of local artists, such as Hans Multscher. The **Deutsches Brotmuseum** specializes in artifacts related to bread and bread-making, including items depicting bread in art and graphic designs.

🏛 **Ulmer Museum**
Marktplatz 9. **Tel** *(0731) 161 43 30.*
🕐 *11am–5pm Tue–Sun, 11am–8pm Thu (during exhibitions).* 📷

🏛 **Museum der Brotkultur**
Salzstadelgasse 10. **Tel** *(0731) 699 55.* 🕐 *10am–5pm Tue, Thu–Mon, 10am–8:30pm Wed.* 📷

Ravensburg ㉕

Road map C7. 🏠 *45,000.* 🚉
ℹ️ *Kirchstraße 16 (0751-823 24).*
📷 *Fasnet (Feb), Rutenfest (Jul).*

The first historic records of the "Ravespurc" fortress date from 1088, when it was one of the seats of the Welf family. It is believed to be the

Main altar by Hans Multscher in Ravensburg's Liebfrauenkirche

birthplace of Henry the Lion, the powerful Duke of Saxony and Bavaria, born in 1129. The settlement that sprang up at the foot of the castle was granted town status in 1251. From 1395, paper was produced here and, during the 15th century, the town became one of the richest in Germany from its involvement in the linen trade.

Standing in Kirchstraße is the 14th-century parish church of Liebfrauenkirche, which retains original 15th-century features, including the main altar and some fine stainedglass windows.

In Marienplatz stands the late-Gothic town hall (14th–15th century), with its lovely Renaissance bay window. Also in Marienplatz is the Waaghaus (1498), which housed the weigh-house and mint on the ground floor, with a trading hall upstairs, when Ravensburg was engaged in coin production. The watchtower *(Blaserturm)* is crowned by a Renaissance octagon that has become the symbol of the town. Another attractive building here is the Lederhaus, which dates from 1513–14. Near the town hall is the old 14th–15th century granary *(Kornhaus)*.

Marktstraße features many old burgher houses. No. 59, the oldest house in town, dates from 1179. The neighbouring house was built in 1446. The tall white cylindrical tower that can be seen from here is known as the "sack of flour" *(Mehlsack)*. It was erected in the 16th century. A mgnificent view of the town can be obtained from Veitsburg, which occupies the site of the original Welf castle.

Astronomical clock on Ulm's Gothic-Renaissance town hall

Former Cistercian abbey complex in Salem, now a secular building

Weingarten 26

Road map C7. 22,500.
Münsterplatz 1 (0751-40 51 25).
Blutritt (day after Ascension).

Count Henry of the House of Welf founded a Benedictine abbey in Weingarten in 1056. During the Romanesque period, around 1190, the monks of the abbey produced a chronicle of the House of Welfs, known as the *Welfenchronik*.

Ambitious plans, drawn up in the 18th century at the initiative of Abbot Sebastian Hyller, provided for an extension of the abbey and the construction of another vast complex of buildings. Two side courtyards and four external courtyards, encircled with curved galleries with smaller pavilions, were planned to be grouped around the church. These were designed by Casper Moosbrugger, Franz Beer, Enrico Zucalli and others, and built in 1715–24.

The church is reminiscent of the Basilica of St Peter's in Rome. Although it is half the size of the latter, it is nevertheless an immense structure. Inside are some magnificent ceiling frescos by Cosmas Damian Asam, while the carved and inlaid choir stalls are the work of Joseph Anton Feuchtmayer. Also of note is the organ by Josef Gabler. In an ingenious design, the organ pipes are concealed within a series of towers to avoid obscuring the windows of the façade.

The **Alamannenmuseum** has a fascinating exhibition of relicts that have been found in graves dating from the Merovingian period.

🏛 **Alamannenmuseum**
Karlstr. 28. **Tel** (0751) 405 125.
3–5pm Tue–Sun, 3–6pm Thu.

Salem 27

Road map C7. 8,500.

The first Cistercian monks arrived in Salmansweiler (now known as Salem) in 1134. Between 1299 and 1414 they built a church according to the rules of their order, which espoused poverty and banned any decoration of the monastic buildings.

The abbey is a triple-nave basilica with transept and straight-end choir. Its austere façade is relieved by blind windows, some of which have attractive traceries. In later years the restraints of poverty were relaxed to the extent that the abbey now has an interesting tabernacle (1500), stalls (1594) and early-Renaissance altars (dating from the 18th century).

The new abbey buildings were built between 1700 and 1710 and constitute **Schloss Salem**. The buildings include some richly decorated abbot's apartments and the extremely impressive Emperor's room (*Kaisersaal*), which was built between 1708 and 1710.

Since its secularization in 1802, the abbey has been the private property of the Baden margraves who keep some of their art collection here. The west wing houses a private boarding school founded by Kurt Hahn, who also founded Gordonstoun in Scotland.

⚓ **Schloss Salem**
Tel (07553) 814 37. Apr–Oct: 9:30am–6pm Mon–Sat, 10:30am–6pm Sun.

Ceiling fresco in Weingarten's abbey

The Bodensee 28

Sometimes known as Lake Constance, the Bodensee lies on the border of Germany, Switzerland and Austria. The area surrounding the lake is one of the most attractive in Germany, in terms of both natural beauty and cultural heritage. Towns and villages around the shores feature countless reminders of past times and cultures. The best time for a visit is summer, when local fishermen stage colourful fairs and water sports are possible.

The Bodensee
The lake is 15 km (9 miles) across at its widest point and 74 km (46 miles) long. It lies at an altitude of 395 m (1,295 ft) and reaches 252 m (826 ft) in depth.

Reichenau
The greatest attraction of this island is the Bene-dictine abbey, which was famed during the era of Otto the Great (10th century) for its illumi-nated manuscripts. It has a beautiful Romanesque-Gothic church and an intoxicating herb garden.

Stockach

Ludwigshafen

ÜBERLINGER SEE

Überlingen

Singen

Radolfzell

Gottmadingen

ZELLERSEE

Reichenau

Mainau

Konstanz

UNTERSEE

Kreuzlingen

★ Mainau
Mainau is known as the "Island of Flowers". The most beautiful displays are in the park surrounding the Baroque palace, which was built in 1739–46. It is currently owned by the Lennart Bernadotte family.

STAR SIGHTS

★ Konstanz

★ Mainau

★ Wasserburg

★ Konstanz (Constance)
The largest town in the region, its main attraction is the magnificent 11th-century Romanesque cathedral. The vaults over the central aisle were built between 1679 and 1683.

Meersburg

The exquisite Baroque town of Meersburg has two residences – the Baroque Neues Schloss and the Altes Schloss. The latter is a 16th-century structure built on top of a hill. It contains within its walls an old Carolingian palace.

VISITORS' CHECKLIST

Map 7 C. 🏠 *Bahnhofplatz 13, Konstanz (07531-13 30 32).* **www.**konstanz.de **Sea Life Centre** *Hafenstr. 9, Konstanz (07531-12 82 70).* 🕐 *Jul–11 Sep: 10am–7pm daily; Mar–Jun & 12 Sep–Oct: 10am–6pm daily. Nov– Apr: 10am–5pm Mon–Fri, 10am– 6pm Sat & Sun.* 🏢 **Heimat- museum Reichenau** *Ergat 1.* **Tel** *(07534) 920 70.* 🕐 *Apr–Oct: 2:30–5:30pm Tue–Sun.* 🏢

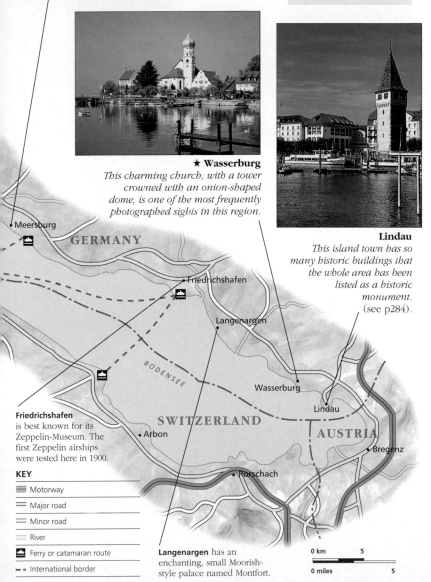

★ **Wasserburg**
This charming church, with a tower crowned with an onion-shaped dome, is one of the most frequently photographed sights in this region.

Lindau
This island town has so many historic buildings that the whole area has been listed as a historic monument. (see p284).

GERMANY

• Meersburg

• Friedrichshafen

Langenargen

BODENSEE

Wasserburg

Lindau

SWITZERLAND

• Arbon

AUSTRIA

• Bregenz

Friedrichshafen
is best known for its Zeppelin-Museum. The first Zeppelin airships were tested here in 1900.

• Rorschach

KEY

▬	Motorway
▭	Major road
▭	Minor road
	River
⛴	Ferry or catamaran route
– –	International border

Langenargen has an enchanting, small Moorish-style palace named Montfort.

0 km		5
0 miles		5

Freiburg im Breisgau ㉙

The counts von Zähringen first established Freiburg in 1120. The town, which later belonged to the counts von Urach, became so rich over the years that, in 1368, it bought its freedom and voluntarily placed itself under the protection of the Habsburgs. Marshal Vauban fortified the town in the 17th century, when Freiburg briefly belonged to France. Since 1805 it has been part of Baden. Situated between Kaiserstuhl and Feldberg, it is a natural gateway to the southern Black Forest.

Freiburg University
Freiburg University occupies a Baroque post-Jesuit complex. In the main entrance stands this statue of the pensive Aristotle.

This former Jesuit church belongs to the university complex.

Tourist information

RATHAUS-PLATZ

RATHAUSGASSE

Railway station

BERTOLDSTRASSE

Fischerau
Fischerau and, parallel to it, Gerberau are picturesque streets in the old town, running along the Gewerbebach stream.

Bertholdsbrunnen
(Berthold's fountain) stands at the intersection of Bertholdstraße and Kaiser-Joseph-Straße, known as "Kajo".

0 metres	50
0 yards	50

Martinstor
St Martin's Gate was part of the 13th-century town fortifications. Its present appearance is the result of work carried out in 1900.

STAR SIGHTS

★ Bächle

★ Münster – the Main Altar

★ Kaufhaus

KEY

--- Suggested route

◁ Picturesque scene with fruit trees in blossom in the Schwarzwald (Black Forest)

Haus zum Walfisch
The façade of the Whale House in Franziskanergasse, with its lovely bay window, is a magnificent example of late-Gothic style.

VISITORS' CHECKLIST

Road map B7. 🏘 197,000. 🚉
🛈 Rotteckring 14 (0761-388 18 80). 🎭 Fasnet (end of carnival), Frühlingsmesse (May), Internationales Zeltmusikfest (Jun), Weintage (Jun), Weinkost (Jun), Herbstmesse (Oct), Umwelt-Film-Festival (Oct). www.freiburg.de

Münsterplatz
The picturesque square at the foot of the cathedral, lined by houses of various periods, from Gothic to Rococo, is still used for markets.

★ Bächle
From the Middle Ages, fast-flowing canals have been running along the streets, draining excess surface waters, and providing the water needed to extinguish the frequent fires.

★ Münster – the Main Altar
The cathedral, which started in c.1200 as a Romanesque basilica, was completed by 1513 in the French Gothic style. Inside is the original main altar by Hans Baldung Grien.

★ Kaufhaus
Completed in 1520, with ground-floor arcades and richly adorned gables, the Kaufhaus (literally buying house) was used by local merchants for meetings, conferences and lively festivities.

For hotels and restaurants in this region see pp503–6 and pp542–5

Schwarzwald (Black Forest) ㉚

Covered with tall fir trees and spruces, the Schwarzwald is one of Germany's most picturesque regions. The area is famous not just for its cuckoo clocks, *Kirschwasser* (schnaps) and *Schwarzwälder Kirschtorte* (Black Forest Gâteau); in the past, Celts and later the Romans came to appreciate the therapeutic qualities of the local spring waters. (The sources of the rivers Donau and Neckar are here.) The area is also a paradise for skiers, climbers, ramblers, hang-glider pilots and sailors.

★ Staufen im Breisgau

The town is also known as Faust-stadt: Dr Faustus, who had resided here, died in 1539 – he is variously reputed to have blown himself up, to have been strangled or to have had his neck broken.

Todtnau

Todtnau is not only a sports centre and a base for hikers and cyclists: it also has a fanstastic annual festival devoted entirely to Schwarzwälder Kirschtorte *(Black Forest Gateau).*

Todtmoos

The heart of this resort is the Baroque pilgrimage church, which dates from the 17th–18th centuries. Popular dog-sleigh races are held annually in the town.

VISITORS' CHECKLIST

Road map 7 B, C. 🛈 *Wehratal-
str. 19, Todtmoos (07674-906 00;
www.todtmoos.de).* 🚇 *Offen-
burger Weinmarkt, Weihnachtsmarkt.* 🎭 *Schlosskonzerte in
Rastatt (July), Dog-sleigh races in
Todtmoos (Jan) and Bernau (Feb).*

Gutach

*In the open-air museum near
the small town of Gutach
visitors can see the Schwarzwald's oldest house – the
Vogtsbauernhof – which
dates from the 16th century.*

★ Furtwangen

*The main attraction
of Furtwangen is its
clock museum
(Uhrenmuseum),
which houses a
collection of more
than 8,000 varied
chronometers.*

| 0 km | 10 |
| 0 miles | 10 |

Hangloch-Wasserfall

*This magnificent
mountain waterfall near
Todtnau is one of the
most beautiful in the
Black Forest.*

★ St Blasien

*In the beautiful health
resort of St Blasien is a
Benedictine Abbey,
founded in the 9th
century. Crowned with a
vast dome, its church
(1783) is an excellent
example of early
Neo-Classical style.*

KEY

▬	Motorway
▬	Main road
▬	Secondary road
▬	River
✲	Viewpoint

STAR SIGHTS

★ Furtwangen

★ St Blasien

★ Staufen im Breisgau

WESTERN GERMANY

Western Germany at a Glance

Famed for its excellent wines and the festivities of
Cologne's annual carnival, Western Germany is the
country's wealthiest and most heavily industrialized
region. The Ruhr district still harbours enormous
industrial potential, while Frankfurt am Main is
Germany's largest financial centre. The region is
also rich in tourist attractions – visitors are drawn to
the romantic castles which line the Rhine and Mosel
valleys, to Cologne with its majestic twin-towered
cathedral, the spa town of Aachen, the museums of
Frankfurt and Kassel and the imposing
Romanesque cathedrals of Speyer,
Worms and Mainz.

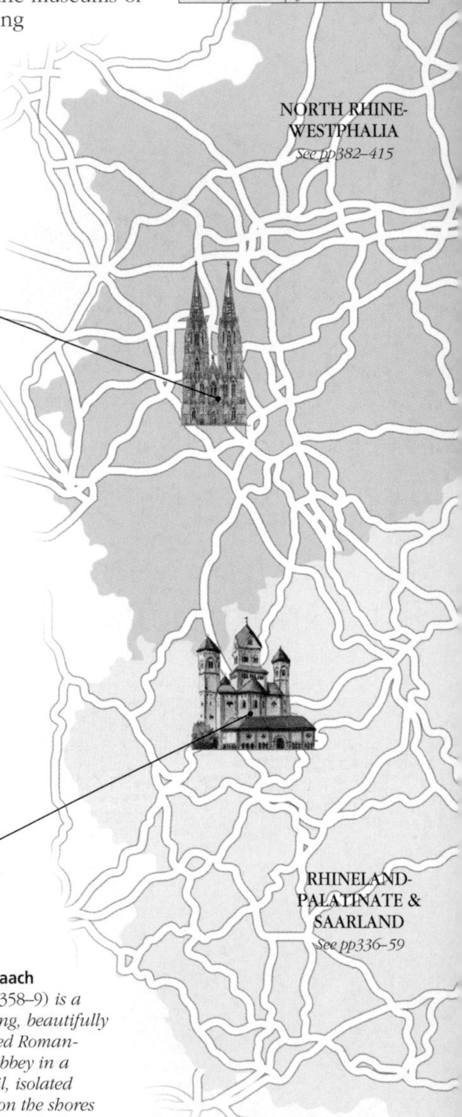

**NORTH RHINE-
WESTPHALIA**
See pp382–415

Cologne Cathedral (see pp402–3),
*which was not completed until the
19th century, is generally considered
one of the most outstanding Gothic
buildings in Germany.*

```
0 kilometres        100

0 miles             100
```

**RHINELAND-
PALATINATE &
SAARLAND**
See pp336–59

Maria Laach
(see pp358–9) *is a
charming, beautifully
preserved Roman-
esque abbey in a
tranquil, isolated
setting on the shores
of the Laacher See.*

◁ Burg Katz, St Goarhausen, Rhineland Palatinate

Detmold *is best known for its magnificent castle (see p415) – one of the most beautiful examples of the "Weser Renaissance" style of architecture.*

The Museum Fridericianum in Kassel (see pp364–5), *originally built to house Friederich II's art collection, has hosted the* documenta, *an exhibition of contemporary art that has achieved international acclaim, every four to five years since 1955.*

HESSE
See pp360–81

Fulda Cathedral (see p368) *is one of the finest Baroque churches in Hesse. It was built on the site of the previous Romanesque church and follows the original layout.*

The old town in Frankfurt am Main (see p375) *is centred around the Römerberg – a square surrounded by attractive half-timbered houses, with the Fountain of Justice as a focal point.*

Wine in Western Germany

Of the great European vineyards, Germany's are the farthest north. There are 13 wine-growing regions in Germany, but the most famous German vineyards are those in the western part of the country, especially the Rheingau, Pfalz, Rheinhessen and Mosel-Saar-Ruwer regions. The most widely drunk alcoholic beverage in Germany is beer – unlike in France, Italy or Spain – and therefore the wines produced here are mainly high-quality wines of named vineyards, with a relatively low production of table wine.

Vineyards in Edenkoben, in the southern part of the Weinstraße (*see p347*), in the Palatinate

The Mosel-Saar-Ruwer *region produces superb white wines from the Riesling grape. The highest quality wines are those marked with the letters QmP.*

IMPORTANT FACTS ABOUT GERMAN WINE

Region and climate

Gentle, rocky hills stretching along the river bends – perfect for Rieslings – are typical of the Mosel-Saar-Ruwer and Rheingau regions. Clay and limestone soil, appropriate for the Müller-Thurgau variety, are found in Hesse on the Rhine. The German climate is considerably more severe than that of southern countries, which gives the wines a slightly sharp, refreshing taste.

Typical grape varieties

The red grape is not cultivated in great quantities. The most popular red variety is the Spätburgunder, known in France as Pinot Noir, which produces a heavy wine with a strong flavour. White grapes are much more popular, especially the famous Rieslings, from which the best white wines are produced, the Müller-Thurgau, which gives a light wine with a fruity bouquet, the Grauburgunder (Pinot Grigio) and the Weißburgunder (Pinot Blanc). Less well-known are: Silvaner, Gewürztraminer, Grüner Veltliner and Gutedel. Rosé wines are produced from the Portugieser variety, cultivated in the Rhineland–Palatinate (Pfalz) and Rheinhessen.

Famous wine producers

Mosel-Saar-Ruwer: Fritz Haag, Heymann-Löwenstein, Karthäuserhof, Dr. Loosen, Egon Müller, J.J. Prüm, C. von Schubert, Willi Schaefer; Rheingau: Georg Breuer, Robert Weil; Rheinhessen: Gunderloch, Keller; Pfalz: Müller-Catoir, Georg Mosbacher, Dr. Bürklin-Wolf, Reichsrat von Buhl.

The Nahe *is famous for its white wines, produced from Silvaner as well as Riesling and Müller-Thurgau grapes.*

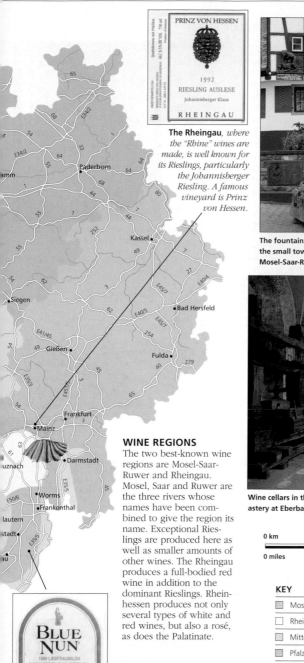

The Rheingau, *where the "Rhine" wines are made, is well known for its Rieslings, particularly the Johannisberger Riesling. A famous vineyard is Prinz von Hessen.*

The fountain of the "Wine Witch" in the small town of Winningen, in the Mosel-Saar-Ruwer region

Wine cellars in the former Cistercian monastery at Eberbach in the Rheingau region

WINE REGIONS

The two best-known wine regions are Mosel-Saar-Ruwer and Rheingau. Mosel, Saar and Ruwer are the three rivers whose names have been combined to give the region its name. Exceptional Rieslings are produced here as well as smaller amounts of other wines. The Rheingau produces a full-bodied red wine in addition to the dominant Rieslings. Rheinhessen produces not only several types of white and red wines, but also a rosé, as does the Palatinate.

Liebfraumilch *has been produced in the Rheinhessen region for over 40 years. Mainly designed for export, it is a sweetish, medium-class of wine, a blend of several grape varieties.*

| 0 km | 70 |
| 0 miles | 70 |

KEY

- Mosel–Saar–Ruwer
- Rheinhessen
- Mittelrhein
- Pfalz
- Nahe
- Rheingau
- Ahr
- Hessische Bergstraße

Romanesque Architecture

Western Germany boasts some of the most interesting examples of Romanesque architecture in the whole of Europe. Charlemagne's famous chapel in Aachen was erected as early as the Carolingian period. The cathedral in Trier and the church of St Maria im Kapitol in Cologne are among the most outstanding creations of early-Romanesque architecture of the Frankish dynasty. In the 12th century, the most important German centres of art were Cologne and the towns of the central Rhineland, with three magnificent cathedrals in Speyer, Mainz and Worms, and the monastery in Maria Laach, preserved to this day.

The choir of St Martin in the Dom in Mainz *is an example of the spaciousness that is typical of the late-Romanesque style.*

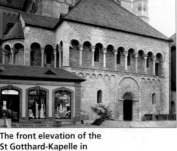

The front elevation of the St Gotthard-Kapelle in Mainz *has upper galleries with arcades decorated with friezes – a common feature of Romanesque architecture.*

Twin western towers

Gallery above the vestibule

Lavishly decorated main portal

The northern portal of the Dom in Worms *is framed by an offset architrave and flanked by pairs of columns, as are the portals of many other Romanesque cathedrals.*

The monastery in Maria Laach *has many capitals with intricate decorations, such as these carvings with human faces.*

Cross-vaulting (or cross-ribbed vaulting)

Tower at the intersection of the nave and transept

The system of vaults also acts as support.

Twin eastern towers

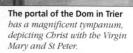

The portal of the Dom in Trier *has a magnificent tympanum, depicting Christ with the Virgin Mary and St Peter.*

ROMANESQUE CATHEDRALS

Cathedrals of the type shown here were built with a basilica-type internal arrangement, including a transept and presbytery, and a double choir usually ending in a semicircular apse. The Dom in Speyer has a massive twin-towered west front, as shown here. The other pair of towers rises above the presbytery, and the intersection of the nave and transept has a lower, broad fifth tower.

ROMANESQUE CAPITALS

Romanesque churches in the Rhine Valley feature exquisite stone sculptures. The capitals, with their extraordinary variety of form, ranging from simple blocks to fine figurative or animal-decorated compositions, are of particular interest.

Water-leaf capital of a bonded column

Simplified Corinthian capital

Cushion (or block or cube) capital

Zoömorphic (animal-decorated) capital

The St Gotthard-Kapelle in Mainz, *next to the Dom, was the archbishop's personal chapel for private prayer. It is comparable to similar private buildings in secular palaces.*

RHINELAND–PALATINATE AND SAARLAND

The Rhineland-Palatinate is one of Germany's most romantic regions, attracting visitors with its vineyards, gentle hills and fairy-tale castles along the Rhine and Mosel valleys. Several towns, such as Trier, have kept reminders of their Roman heritage.

These two states, which border France in the west, did not emerge in their present form until after World War II. The Rhineland-Palatinate was created from the previously independent Bavarian Palatinate and the southern part of the Central Rhineland, making it a true jigsaw-puzzle of territories without a coherent history. The Saarland was under French rule until 1956. Today, it forms a bridge between France and Germany, the two driving forces of European unity.

The turbulent history of the region has left many traces. The picturesque Mosel Valley is lined with grand Medieval fortresses, such as Burg Eltz, while Worms on the Rhine is the setting for most of the Nibelungen legend as well as the residence of the mythical king of Burgundy, Gunther.

The Nibelung treasure is still said to lie at the bottom of the Rhine. The impressive cathedral in Worms, along with the Romanesque cathedrals of Speyer and Mainz, is a fascinating example of Medieval sacral architecture.

The "Deutsches Eck" in Koblenz is the strategic spot where the Mosel flows into the Rhine, and Koblenz also marks the beginning of the romantic Rhine Valley. A boat trip upriver, justifiably popular with visitors, will pass some spectacular rocky scenery, including the famous Lorelei Rock and countless castles set among vineyards on either side of the gorge.

The famous ironworks complex in Völklingen is a reminder of a bygone era, when most of the Saarland's inhabitants were active in mining, steelworks and other heavy industries.

Panorama of Saarbrücken, with the Saar river in the foreground

◁ The snow-covered Medieval fortress of Burg Eltz, in the Mosel Valley

Exploring Rhineland-Palatinate and Saarland

White wine enthusiasts come here, attracted by the beautiful, picturesque valleys of the Rhine and Mosel rivers, with their Medieval castles and small towns. Travelling along the Deutsche Weinstraße (German wine route), Germany's oldest tourist route, visitors can see fascinating historic buildings and taste the different types of wine made by the numerous small vineyards scattered throughout the entire region. Speyer and Mainz have monumental Romanesque cathedrals, while Trier boasts many interesting Roman relics. The huge ironworks in Völklingen is a surprising sight, transporting visitors back to a time when heavy industry ruled much of the region.

SEE ALSO

- **Where to Stay** pp506–8
- **Where to Eat** pp545–6

The imposing red-sandstone building of the Dom in Mainz

The proud complex of Schloss Stolzenfels near Koblenz, designed by Karl Friedrich Schinkel

Bonn

Cologne (Köln)

Adenau
Hobe A
△ 747m

Liège
Schneifel

Prüm
Eifel

Gerolstein

Daun

MOSELTAL

3

RHEINLAN

Bitburg

Wittlich

Bernkastel Kues

Schweich
Morbach

TRIER 1

Hunsrück
Erbeskopf
818m

Birkenfeld

Nohfelden

Mettlach
Sankt Wendel

SAARLAND

Ottweiler

Dillingen
2
SAARLAND

Saarlouis
Neunkirche

Völklingen

Saarbrücken
Man

Metz

0 km   20

0 miles   20

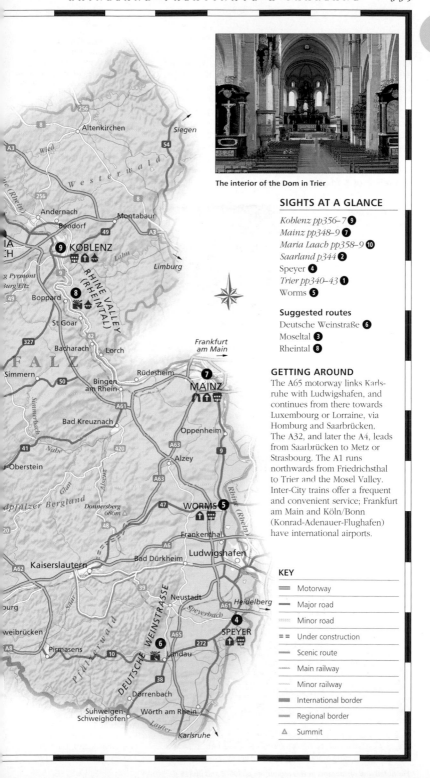

The interior of the Dom in Trier

SIGHTS AT A GLANCE

Koblenz pp356–7 **9**
Mainz pp348–9 **7**
Maria Laach pp358–9 **10**
Saarland p344 **2**
Speyer **4**
Trier pp340–43 **1**
Worms **5**

Suggested routes

Deutsche Weinstraße **6**
Moseltal **3**
Rheintal **8**

GETTING AROUND

The A65 motorway links Karlsruhe with Ludwigshafen, and
continues from there towards
Luxembourg or Lorraine, via
Homburg and Saarbrücken.
The A32, and later the A4, leads
from Saarbrücken to Metz or
Strasbourg. The A1 runs
northwards from Friedrichsthal
to Trier and the Mosel Valley.
Inter-City trains offer a frequent
and convenient service; Frankfurt
am Main and Köln/Bonn
(Konrad-Adenauer-Flughafen)
have international airports.

KEY

▬▬	Motorway
▬	Major road
┈┈	Minor road
▬ ▬	Under construction
▬	Scenic route
~~	Main railway
─	Minor railway
▬▬	International border
▬	Regional border
△	Summit

Trier ❶

One of Germany's oldest towns, Trier was founded in 16 BC as *Augusta Treverorum*, supposedly by the Emperor Augustus himself. In the 3rd and 4th centuries it was an imperial seat and the capital of the *Belgica prima* province. In the 5th century the town, which now numbered 70,000 inhabitants, was conquered and destroyed by Germanic tribes. Trier never returned to its former importance – in the 17th century it had a mere 3,600 inhabitants, and 100 years later they still numbered fewer than 4,000. The town, which is also the birthplace of Karl Marx, has a rich architectural heritage.

🚪 Porta Nigra

Tel (0651) 754 24. ◯ *1 Apr–30 Sep: 9am–6pm daily; Oct–Mar: 9am–5pm daily; Nov–Feb: 9am–4pm daily.* 📷

This town gate, named *Porta Nigra* (black gate) in the Middle Ages because of the colour of its weathered stone, was erected in the 2nd century (a similar gate would have stood at the town's southern entrance). The oldest German defensive structure, it still impresses with its colossal size: 36 m (118 ft) long, 21.5 m (70.5 ft) wide and 30 m (27 ft) high. Two gateways lead onto a small inner courtyard, and there are two tiers of defence galleries with large open windows. It is flanked by two towers – the four-storey western tower and the three-storey unfinished eastern tower, made of huge blocks of sandstone.

In the 12th century, the building was transformed into the two-storey church of St Simeon and served as such until the early 19th century.

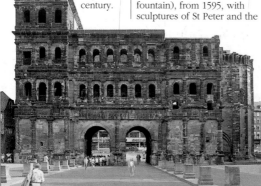

The magnificent *Porta Nigra*, gigantic Roman gateway into Trier

Petrusbrunnen (fountain of St Peter) in Hauptmarkt

🚪 Hauptmarkt

Trier's main market square, undoubtedly one of the most attractive in Germany, dates back to the 10th century. The Marktkreuz (market cross) erected around the same time symbolized the town's right to hold markets. Today there is a copy of the original cross mounted on a granite Roman column, with a relief of the Lamb of God. On the southeastern side of the square is the Petrusbrunnen (St Peter's fountain), from 1595, with sculptures of St Peter and the Four Virtues. On the southwestern side stands the 15th-century Steipe, with a steep gabled roof. Originally it was used by the town councillors as guesthouse and banqueting hall. The Baroque Rotes Haus (red house) next door dates from 1683. Löwenapotheke, in a 17th-century building on the southeastern side of the square, is Germany's oldest pharmacy, its records dating back to the 13th century.

🏛 Bischöfliches Dom- und Diözesanmuseum

Windstraße 6–8. *Tel* (0651) 710 52 55. ◯ *Apr–Oct: 9am–5pm Mon–Sat; Nov–Mar: 9am–5pm Tue–Sat, 1–5pm Sun.* ● *1 Jan, 24 & 25 Dec.* 📷

A 19th-century building near the cathedral, once a Prussian prison, now houses the art collection of the Diocese, including early Christian works of art. Its pride of possession is a 3rd-century ceiling painting from the imperial palace which once stood on the site of the cathedral. The fresco was rediscovered in 1945, and some 70,000 pieces were painstakingly reassembled over the following decades. Another exhibit is the reconstructed crypt of the Benedictine church of St Maximin, which has 9th-century Carolingian wall paintings.

⛪ Dom St Peter

Tel (0651) 979 07 90.
◯ *Apr–Oct: 6:30am–6pm daily; Nov–Mar: 6:30am–5:30pm daily.* 📷

The present cathedral incorporates the remains of an older 4th-century church. The oldest cathedral in Germany, it was constructed in stages – in the early 11th century, late 12th century, mid-13th century and 14th century. It is a triple-nave, two-choir basilica with transept and six towers, and its furnishings include several outstanding objects, such as the tomb of the papl envoy Ivo (1144).

⛪ Liebfrauenkirche

An der Meerkatz 4. *Tel* (0651) 979 07 90. ◯ *Apr–Oct: 7:30am–6pm daily; Nov–Mar: 7:30am–5:30pm daily.* 📷

Adjoining the cathedral is the Liebfrauenkirche (Church of Our Dear Lady), built in 1235–60. Along with the

The Liebfrauenkirche – one of the country's earliest Gothic churches

cathedral in Marburg, this is one of the earliest examples of German Gothic architecture. Its ground plan is based on the Greek cross, and the tower above the dome accentuates the intersection of the naves. Its western portal is richly decorated with carved ornaments and iconographic symbols. The interior features many outstanding relics, including 15th-century wall paintings on twelve columns, which symbolize the 12 apostles. There are also some impotant tombs, including that of a local nobleman, Karl von Metternich (1636), which is found in the northeast chapel.

⊞ Aula Palatina (Konstantin-Basilika)

Konstantinplatz. **Tel** *(0651) 42 570.*
◯ *Apr–Oct: 10am–6pm Mon–Sat, noon–6pm Sun; Nov–Mar: 11am–noon & 3–4pm Tue–Sat, noon–1pm Sun.*
The *Aula Palatina* (Palatinate hall) dates from AD 310. An elongated, rectangular brick building 67 m (220 ft) long, 27.5 m (90 ft) wide and 30 m (98 ft) high with a vast semi-circular apse, it served as the throne hall of the Roman emperor or his representative. Following the town's sacking by Germanic tribes, the building was reduced to rubble. In the 12th century the apse was converted into a tower, to

VISITORS' CHECKLIST

Road map A5. 🏠 *99,000.*
🚉 *An der Porta Nigra.*
ℹ *Simeonstraße 60 (0651-97 80 80).* **www**.trier.de

accommodate the archbishop. In the 17th century, the *Aula Palatina* was integrated into the newly-built palace and its eastern wall partly demolished. During Napoleonic and Prussian times, the hall served as army barracks. The Prussian king Friedrich Wilhelm IV eventually ordered its reconstruction. From 1856 it has served as the Protestant church of St Saviour. Restored after bombing in 1944, its giant size still seems remarkable.

The monumental, austere exterior of the Aula Palatina

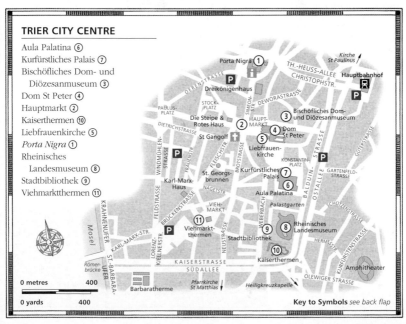

TRIER CITY CENTRE

Aula Palatina ⑥
Kurfürstliches Palais ⑦
Bischöfliches Dom- und
   Diözesanmuseum ③
Dom St Peter ④
Hauptmarkt ②
Kaiserthermen ⑩
Liebfrauenkirche ⑤
Porta Nigra ①
Rheinisches
   Landesmuseum ⑧
Stadtbibliothek ⑨
Viehmarktthermen ⑪

0 metres 400
0 yards 400

Key to Symbols *see back flap*

Portal of the Kurfürstliches Palais

♦ Kurfürstliches Palais

Konstantinplatz. *Tel (0651) 949 42 02.* ◯ *the Palais is an administrative building and so visits that are not part of a public function are possible only by appointment.*

The Kurfürstliches Palais is considered to be one of the most beautiful Rococo palaces in the world. It has undergone several transformations over the centuries and remains of the earlier buildings can still be seen. The present building was designed by Johannes Seiz and built in 1756–62 for Archbishop Johann Philipp von Walderdorff. The sculptures were created by Ferdinand Tietz. The central tympanum shows Pomona, Venus, Apollo and a group of angels. The stairs, which lead from the garden to the inner staircase, were designed in the 18th century, but not built until 1981. They have beautiful handrails with typical Rococo motifs. The gardens are equally beautiful and include a miniature garden, a landscape garden and a mother-and-child area.

🏛 Rheinisches Landesmuseum

Weimarer Allee 1. *Tel (0651) 977 40.* ◯ 9:30am–5pm Tue–Fri, 10:30am–5pm Sat & Sun; May–Oct: 9:30am–5pm Mon–Fri, 10:30am–5pm Sat & Sun. ● 1 Jan, 24, 25 & 26 Dec. (free 1st Mon of the month).

Only a few steps separate the electoral palace from the

Rhine regional museum founded in 1877. Its collections are grouped into four sections: pre-historic, Roman, Franconian-Merovingian, and medieval to contemporary. The largest space is devoted to Roman relics. Star exhibits include a magnificent mosaic depicting Bacchus, from the dining room of a Roman villa, and the lovely statuette of a nymph, undoubtedly the work of a major artist. Equally impressive is a stone carving showing a ship loaded with four giant barrels, sailing on the Mosel River. Dating from AD 220, it decorated the tomb of a local wine-merchant.

⛲ Stadtbibliothek

Weberbach 25.

The municipal library contains a number of important collections that were assembled here in the early 19th century, when many monastic libraries closed down. Among its treasures the library holds 74 full-page miniatures of the famous Trier Apocalypse (c.800), as well as one of the few surviving copies of the first Bible printed by Gutenberg.

�† m Kaiserthermen

Weimarer Allee/Kaiserstr. *Tel (0651) 442 62.* ◯ Apr–Sep: 9am–6pm; Oct & Mar: 9am–5pm; Nov–Feb: 9am–4pm daily.

Not far from the Rheinisches Landesmuseum are the

remains of the vast imperial baths. Built in the early 4th century, during the reign of Constantine, they were the third largest bathing complex in the Roman world. The remaining sections of the walls and foundations indicate the former layout. Best preserved are the walls of the *caldarium*, the room with the hot water pool. Next to it is the round *tepidarium*, the warm baths. The spacious *frigidarium* was used for cold baths. Considerable room was given to the *palaestra*, an outdoor exercise area.

♦ Viehmarktthermen

Viehmarktplatz. *Tel (0651) 994 10 57.* ◯ 9am–5pm Tue–Sun.

Following excavations completed in 1994, the remains of these Roman baths, along with those of medieval refuse pits and the cellars of a Capucin monastery, are now on display to the pubic under a large glass canopy.

⛲ Jesuitenkolleg

Jesuitenstr. 13. ◯ 7am–6pm daily.

The Gothic Church of the Holy Trinity was built for Franciscan monks, who settled in Trier before 1238. The surviving church, from the late 13th century, went to the Jesuits in 1570. The college (1610–14) was transferred to the university following the dissolution of the Jesuit Order. It now houses a theological seminary. In the church, the tomb of Friedrich von Spee (1591–1635) is worth a visit.

Nymph in Rheinisches Landesmuseum

Vast complex of the Kaiserthermen (imperial baths)

🏛 Amphitheater

Petrisberg. *Tel* (0651) 730 10. ⬜
Apr–Sep: 9am–6pm; Oct & Mar: 9am–5pm; Nov–Feb: 9am–4pm daily. 🖼

Near the imperial baths are the ruins of the Roman amphitheatre, dating from the 1st century AD. This was the scene of gladiatorial fights and animal contests. The entire structure, consisting of an elliptical arena and a stepped auditorium, was surrounded by a high wall, divided into individual storeys by colonnaded arcades. The complex was designed to seat up to 20,000 people. In the 5th century the inhabitants of Trier used the amphitheatre as a place of refuge from the increasingly frequent raids by Germanic tribes.

🏛 Heiligkreuzkapelle

Arnulfstraße/Rotbachstraße.

The Chapel of the Holy Cross, in a secluded spot, is one of Trier's more interesting historic buildings. Built in the Romanesque style in the second half of the 11th century, at the initiative of the parson of Arnulfa Cathedral, it is a small building with a ground plan in the shape of the Greek cross and an octagonal tower set within the cross. Although it suffered serious damage during World War II, it was meticulously restored to its original state in the years 1957–8.

🏛 Pfarrkirche St Matthias

Matthiasstraße. 85. *Tel* (0651) 310 79. ⬜ *8am–7pm daily.*

This church's history dates back to the 5th century, when it became the burial place of St Eucharius, the first bishop of Trier. From the 8th century, the church was run by Benedictine monks. In the 10th–11th centuries a new church was erected as burial site of the relics of the apostle, St Matthew. It was twice remodelled at the turn of the 15th to 16th centuries, when it acquired its rich Gothic vaults. The present abbey dates from the 16th century. The shrine holding the apostle's relics ensured that the church became one of the most important destinations for pilgrims in the region.

The ruins of Barbaratherme, ancient Roman baths

🏛 Barbaratherme

Südallee. *Tel* (0651) 994 10 57.
⬤ *closed until further notice (dilapidated).* 🖼

Not far from the Roman bridge across the Mosel River are the ruins of the Barbara baths, dating from the 2nd century AD. Although above ground not much has been preserved, the extensive system of underground heating channels, the *hypocaustum*, clearly demonstrates the original size of this public bath complex. In the Middle Ages, Patrician and aristocratic families transformed the baths into their residences. In the 17th century Jesuit monks dismantled the remaining structures, and used the recovered building materials to construct their own college.

🏛 Kirche St Maximin

Maximinstraße. *Tel* (0651) 710 52 55. ◩ *obligatory.*

In the Middle Ages there were as many as four abbeys in Trier. St. Maximin Abbey was founded on the burial site of its patron saint, who died in AD 325. The surviving church was built in the 13th century, on the foundations of the previous buildings. Its Romanesque–Gothic forms were partly obscured by the remodelling work carried out in 1580–1698. The church's most valuable historic remains were the Carolingian wall paintings, which originally adorned the crypt. These are now displayed in the Rheinisches Landesmuseum.

🏛 Kirche St Paulin

Thebäerstraße. *Tel* (0651) 270 850.
⬜ *Mar–Sep: 9am–6pm Mon, Wed–Sat, 11am–6pm Tue, 10am–6pm Sun; Oct–Feb: 9am–5pm Mon, Wed–Sat, 11am–5pm Tue, 10am–5pm Sun.*

This church was built in the 12th century, on the foundations of an older Christian chapel. In 1674 it was blown up by the French army. St Paulin, its patron saint and bishop in Trier, was one of the few to voice his opposition to the Aryan credo of Emperor Constantine II, in which he rejected the divinity of Christ and proclaimed himself alone to be made in God's image. Paulin did not meet with a martyr's death, but was exiled to Phrygia (now Turkey), where he died in 358. The present church, a true gem of Rococo architecture, was designed by Balthasar Neumann, who also created the main altar.

Baroque ceiling paintings in the Rococo Kirche St Paulinus

Saarland ❷

This German state, bordered by Luxembourg and France, was long disputed between France and Germany, but has now been firmly integrated into the Federal Republic. Almost forgotten are its coal and steel industries, which declined in the 1960s and 70s. The region has seen a turbulent history – it was ruled in turn by Celts, Romans and Franks. In the 17th century, on the order of Louis XIV, Vauban built the town-fortress of Saarlouis. Saarbrücken, an 18th-century town, is famous for its Baroque architecture, mostly created by Friedrich Joachim Stengel.

Von Nassau-Saarbrücken family tombs in Saarbrücken

Saarbrücken

Road map B6. 🏠 190,000. 🚉 ℹ️
Saargalerie, Reichsstr. 1 (0681-194 33 or 93 80 90). 🎬 *Max Ophüls-Preis (Jan), Perspectives du Théâtre (May), Saar Spektakel (Aug).*

The capital of Saarland, Saarbrücken was first built as the Franconian fortress of *Sarabrucca*. The town, situated on the banks of the Saar River, flourished in the 17th and 18th century, under the rule of Duke Wilhelm Heinrich von Nassau-Saarbrücken.

The churches and other prestigious buildings are largely the work of Friedrich Joachim Stengel, court architect to the von Nassau-Saarbrücken family. He designed the Catholic **Basilika St Johann** (1754–8) in the market square, as well as the monumental **Schloss**, the palace on the opposite bank of the Saar (1739–48). Its original, modern façade, created in 1989 after damage in World War II, is the work of the architect Gottfried Böhm.

Opposite the Schloss stands the **Altes Rathaus** (old town hall), dating from 1748–50, which today houses an interesting museum of ethnography. The Protestant **Ludwigskirche** (1762–75) is

one of the last works completed by Stengel. A true architectural gem, it is laid out in the shape of a Greek cross. The **Stiftskirche St Arnual**, in the southwestern part of the town, contains the splendid Gothic and Renaissance tombs of the von Nassau-Saarbrücken family. Since 1960 it has also featured a "German–French Garden". One of the garden's entrances leads to Gulliver-Miniwelt (miniature world of Gulliver), where small versions of the world's most famous buildings are exhibited.

Völklinger Hütte, the historic steelworks in Völklingen

Völklingen

Road map B6. 🏠 43,500.
ℹ️ *Rathausstr. 57 (06898-132 800).*

About 10 km (6 miles) west of Saarbrücken lies the small industrial town of Völklingen, which was granted town status in 1937. In 1881, Carl Röchling, a native of Saarbrücken, bought a small steel mill, the **Völklinger Hütte**, which he soon developed as the heart of his family's industrial empire. The steel mill still exists, and in 1994 it became a UNESCO World Heritage Site, listed as a historical object of international importance. Another attraction is an original, early 20th-century housing estate.

Homburg

Road map B6. 🏠 42,000. ℹ️ *Rathaus, Am Forum 5 (06 841-10 11 66).*

This town grew up around the Hohenburg castle, which now is just a picturesque ruin. In the Schlossberg nearby were unearthed the remains of a fortress, which was built in 1680–92 by Sébastien Le Preste Vauban on the orders of the French King Louis XIV. The greatest attraction of Homburg, however, is its Schlossberg caves, the largest man-made caves in Europe, cut into the red sandstone.

Ottweiler

Road map B5. 🏠 16,000.
ℹ️ *Schlosshof 5 (06 824-35 11).*

The small picturesque town of Ottweiler has a beautifully preserved old town. The Alter Turm (old tower), which in the 15th century formed part of the town's fortifications, now serves as a belfry to the parish church, whose origins go back to the 15th century. Its present Baroque form was the work of Friedrich Joachim Stengel from 1756–7.

Rathausplatz is a beautifully proportioned complex of historic houses, mostly the homes of wealthy citizens, dating from the 17th and 18th centuries. Many have half-timbered upper halves. The Altes Rathaus (old town hall, 1714) combines two different building methods – the base is stone, the top half-timbered. In Schlossplatz is the Renaissance Hesse Haus (c.1590).

Moseltal ❸

The Mosel river, 545 km (338 miles) long, is one of the longest tributaries of the Rhine. The Mosel valley between Trier and Koblenz, where the Mosel flows into the Rhine, is one of the most beautiful parts of Germany. On both sides of the river, romantic castles tower over endless vineyards, where excellent white grapes are grown – both are typical features of the charming landscape.

Burg Thurant ②
Near the town of Alken stands Thurant castle, which was built in the 13th century. It is the only twin-towered castle along the Mosel.

Matthias-Kapelle ①
This late-Romanesque chapel was once used to house the remains of the Apostle Matthew. These were later transferred to the Matthiaskirche in Trier.

Burg Pyrmont ⑤
Pyrmont's grim 13th-century medieval castle was remodelled and extended several times during the Baroque era.

Cochem ⑥
The castle in Cochem, originally built in the 11th century, was completely destroyed by French soldiers in 1689. The present castle was rebuilt in the 19th century.

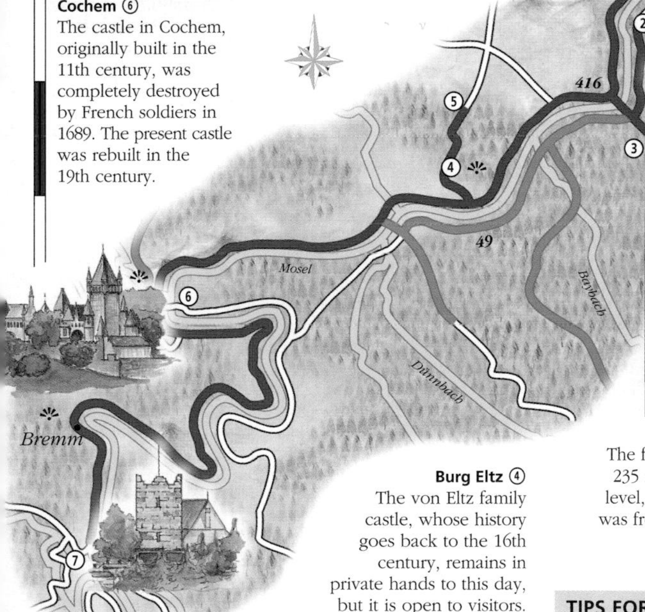

Ehrenburg ③
The first fortress, rising to 235 m (771 ft) above sea level, was built in 1120. It was frequently remodelled in later years.

Burg Eltz ④
The von Eltz family castle, whose history goes back to the 16th century, remains in private hands to this day, but it is open to visitors.

Burg Arras ⑦
This fortress was built around 900–950 as part of the fortifications against frequent pillaging raids by Normans.

0 km 5

0 miles 5

KEY

- Suggested route
- Scenic route
- Other road
- River, lake
- Viewpoint

TIPS FOR DRIVERS

Length of the route: *about 75 km (46 miles).*
Stopping-off points: *there are numerous restaurants and cafes in Cochem; small pubs can be found along the entire route.*
Additional attractions: *a boat trip on the Mosel River, from Koblenz to Cochem or Trier.*

Altar in the Dreifaltigkeitskirche, in Speyer

Speyer ⓪

Road map B6. 🏛 *47,000.* 🚉 🛈
Maximilianstraße 13 (06232-14 23 92).
🎭 *Brezelfest (Jul), Kaisertafel (Aug), Altstadtfest (Sep), Bauernmarkt (Sep).*

In the 7th century, Speyer was the seat of a diocese. As a free city of the Holy Roman Empire from 1294 until 1779, 50 sessions of the imperial parliament took place here. The most famous session was in 1529, when the Protestant states of the Holy Roman Empire lodged a protest (hence "Protestant") against the decisions of the Catholic majority.

The most important historic building in Speyer is the Romanesque **Kaiserdom** (St Maria und St Stephan), a World Heritage Site. For a time, before being superseded by the gigantic abbey of Cluny in Burgundy, this was the largest monumental Romanesque building in Europe. The Dom, built in 1025–61 on the initiative of Conrad II, is a triple-nave, cross-vaulted basilica with transept, vestibule, choir, apse and several towers. Its magnificent triple-nave crypt, the burial place of Salian emperors, has stunning stone carvings, some worked by Lombard stonemasons. **St Afra's**, dating from around 1100, has some interesting sculptures, including *Christ Bearing His Cross* and *Annunciation* (c.1470). The Domnapf, a vast stone bowl seen at the forecourt of the cathedral, dates from 1490. It was used during enthroning ceremonies, when the newly

anointed bishop would order it to be filled with wine right to the brim in order to win the hearts of his flock.

Another 11th-century interesting building is the **Mikwe** in Judenbadgasse, a ritual Jewish bath for women, and the remains of a synagogue nearby. To the west of the Dom stand the remains of the medieval fortifications including the **Altpörtel**, a 14th- to 16th-century town gate. The late-Baroque **Dreifaltigkeitskirche** (church of the Holy Trinity), built in 1701–17, is an architectural masterpiece with marvellous interiors.

Worms ⑤

Road map B5. 🏛 *83,000.* 🚉
🛈 *Neumarkt 14 (06241-250 45).*

Worms is one of the oldest towns in Germany. In the Middle Ages it was the home of the Reich's Parliament, hosting more than 100 sessions. The **Dom St Peter** is one of the largest late-Romanesque cathedrals in Germany, along with the cathedrals in Mainz and Speyer. It was built in 1171–1230 as a two-choir basilica, with eastern transept, four towers and two domes. Its northern nave includes five beautiful sandstone reliefs from a Gothic cloister, which no longer exists. The interior furnishings date mainly from modern times. Particularly noteworthy is the high altar designed in the 18th century by Balthasar Neumann, and the stalls dating from 1760.

Tombstones in the Heiliger Sand Jewish cemetery in Worms

A short distance from the cathedral is the Marktplatz (market square), with the interesting **Dreifaltigkeitskirche** church of the Holy Trinity (1709–25). Northeast of the square stands the **Stiftskirche St Paul** (church of St Paul), built in the 11th–12th centuries and completed in the 18th century, with original 13th century wall paintings. Nearby is the only surviving Renaissance residential building in Worms, the **Rotes Haus** (red house).

In the western part of the old town is the **Heiliger Sand** (holy sands), the oldest Jewish cemetery in Europe, where the earliest tombstones date from the 11th and 12th centuries. Also worth a visit is the 14th-century **Liebfrauenkirche** (Church of Our Dear Lady). The most noteworthy feature of the **Magnuskirche** (11th–12th centuries) is its crypt, from around AD 800, while the **Stiftskirche St Martin** (late 11th century) has some interesting portals.

A relief from 1488, in the Dom in Worms

The vast Romanesque Dom St. Peter in Worms

Deutsche Weinstraße ⑥

The "German Wine Route" starts in Bockenheim and ends in Schweigen, near the Alsatian town of Weißenburg. The tour suggested here includes the most interesting sections of this route. This is one of the most beautiful parts of Germany, where visitors will encounter aspects of German and European historical and cultural heritage at every step, set among the picturesque scenery of the endless vineyards covering the sun-drenched slopes of the Pfälzer Wald.

Bad Dürkheim ⑧
This famous resort is best known for its annual Wurstmarkt, held in September. Despite its name, it celebrates the wine harvest, and sausages take second place.

St Martin ⑥
Not much remains of the Romanesque church of St Martin, but the 16–18th-century buildings surviving in the town continue to enchant visitors.

Hambacher Schloss ⑦
Only a romantic ruin remains of this vast hill-top fortress, whose fame is based on the Hambacher Fest when, on 27 May 1832, students protested against the fragmentation of Germany.

Landau ⑤
This little town has the remains of the fortress built by Vauban, and an extraordinarily beautiful post-Augustinian church.

Trifels ④
This grim, ruined castle once served as a prison for many important people, including the King of England, Richard the Lionheart.

NATURPARK
PFÄLZER
WALD

0 km   5

0 miles   5

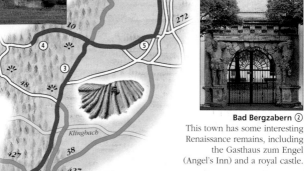

Leinsweiler ③
Hilltop Hof Neukastel was once the home of the German impressionist artist Max Slevogt, and to this day, wall paintings by the artist can be seen here.

Klingbach

Bad Bergzabern ②
This town has some interesting Renaissance remains, including the Gasthaus zum Engel (Angel's Inn) and a royal castle.

Dörrenbach ①
The star attractions in this small town are the half-timbered town hall and the Gothic church surrounded by fortifications.

KEY

▬	Suggested route
▬	Scenic route
═	Other road
═	River, lake
⚡	Viewpoint

TIPS FOR DRIVERS

Length: 83 km (51 miles).
Stopping-off points: Landau has many cafés and restaurants. The spa town of Bad Dürkheim, with its cafés and wine bars, is also a good place to stop.
Signs: Look for signposts showing a bunch of grapes or a wine jug.

Mainz ❼

The town, which grew out of the Roman military camp *Moguntiacum* established in 39 BC, is today the capital of the Rhineland-Palatinate. Mainz is the home of an important German television station (ZDF). It is also the main centre of trade for the popular Rhine wines. Its splendid late-Romanesque cathedral symbolizes the power of the Kurfürsten, the prince-electors, who used to crown German kings. Indisputably the town's most famous son is Johannes Gutenberg – the inventor of printing.

🏛 Kurfürstliches Schloss
Peter-Altmeier-Allee.
Römisch-Germanisches Zentralmuseum
Tel (06131) 91 240.
⏱ 10am–6pm Tue–Sun.
Construction of the Baroque electoral palace, began in 1627 during the rule of Archbishop Georg von Greifenclau, was completed more than a century later, in 1775–6, under Johann Friedrich Carl Joseph von Erthal. Today the palace houses the fascinating museum of Roman and Germanic history.

Statue of Gutenberg in Gutenbergplatz

🏛 Gutenberg-Museum
Liebfrauenplatz 5. *Tel* (06131) 12 26 40. ⏱ 9am–5pm Tue–Sat, 11am–3pm Sun. ◐ public holidays.
Johannes Gensfleisch zum Gutenberg became famous as the inventor of the printing process using movable metal type. The letters were cast in a special apparatus and set in

columns. Gutenberg himself prepared the Bible for printing and publication in 1454–5. From the original 200 copies, only 46 have survived to this day.

The museum, which opened in 1900, shows a reconstruction of the master's workshop from 1450. The collection comprises priceless early books, including the Gutenberg Bible and the Psalter published in 1457 by Fust & Schöffer, Gutenberg's erstwhile partners and latterday creditors. The Psalter was the first work to be printed using three different colours of inks.

🏛 Kaiserdom
See pp350–51.

🏛 Gutenbergplatz
A short distance from the Protestant parish church of St John is Gutenbergplatz, a pleasant square with a statue of the inventor. Set in its

paving stones is a line marking the 50th parallel. The Staatstheater (state theatre) in the square is an interesting late Neo-Classical building from 1829–33.

Historic half-timbered houses in Kirschgarten

🏛 Kirschgarten
Near the Baroque hospital of St Roch, built in 1721 and now an old people's home, runs a street called Kirschgarten (cherry orchard). This is one of the loveliest parts of old Mainz, which suffered serious damage in World War II. The well-preserved complex of historic half-timbered houses, dating from the 16th–18th centuries, makes this district worth visiting and a pleasant place for a stroll.

⛪ Kirche St Stephan
Kleine Weißgasse 12. *Tel* (05131) 23 16 40. ⏱ 10am–noon 2–5pm Mon–Sat, 2–5pm Sun.
A short distance from Kirschgarten stands the Gothic parish church of St Stephen. It was built in stages, on the site of an older building dating from the 10th century. Construction began in the mid-13th century and continued until the end of the 15th century. The resulting church is a triple-nave hall with eastern transept and a single-nave choir. The adjacent late-15th century cloisters are a true gem of late-Gothic design. The original stained-glass windows in the presbytery, destroyed during World War II, were replaced by six new ones in 1978–81, designed and partly made by Marc

The Baroque Kurfürstliches Schloss and museum

For hotels and restaurants in this region see pp506–8 and pp545–6

Landing stage for boats on the Rhine

VISITORS' CHECKLIST

Road map B5. 🏙 190,000. 🚉
🛈 *Im Brückenturm am Rathaus
(06131-28 62 10).* 🎭 *Mainzer
Fastnacht (Jan/Feb), Johannis-
nacht (Jun), OpenOhr Festival
(Whitsun), Mainzer Zeltfestival
(end of Jun/early Jul) Weinforum
Rheinhessen (last weekend in
Oct).* **www**.mainz.de

Chagall. Set against a beautiful blue background, they depict biblical scenes, including Abraham with the three travellers, the Patriarch pleading to God to spare the righteous in Sodom and Go-morrah, Jacob's dream, and Moses with the Tablets of the Ten Commandments.

The church interior contains many other interesting orig-inal features. The four large brass candelabra were cast in Mainz in 1509. The small polyptych depicting the Cruci-fixion dates from around 1400, while its movable wings were made some 100 years later. The niche below the tower contains the Holy Tomb (c.1450).

🏛 Römersteine
Southeast of the University campus are the impressive remains of the Roman aque-duct, dating from the 1st century AD. The Zahlbach valley was a vantage point for the southwestern flank of the Roman camp, *Castrum Moguntiacum*, but it presen-ted a major technical problem of supplying the camp with drinking water. The aqueduct was built by Roman engin-eers. Although some of its pillars were 23 m (75 ft) high, the present remains only reach up to 10 m (32 ft).

Environs
It is also worth making an excursion to **Oppenheim**, a centre of the wine trade 20 km (12 miles) to the south. The pride of this town is its Gothic Katharinenkirche, a church built of red sandstone in the 13th–14th centuries. The neighbouring hill and the ruins of Landskron castle provide the most spectacular view over the Rhine valley. The Weinbau-museum, museum of viti-culture, is also worth visiting.

MAINZ CITY CENTRE

Gutenberg-Museum ②
Gutenbergplatz ④
Kaiserdom ③
Kirche St Stephan ⑥
Kirschgarten ⑤
Kurfürstliches Schloss ①

Hauptbahnhof
200m (220 yards)

Flughafen
25 km (15 miles)

0 metres 250

0 yards 250

Key to Symbols *see back flap*

Römersteine

Kaiserdom

Crucifix in the St Gotthard-Kapelle

The greatest attraction of Mainz is its superb cathedral, gleaming red in the sunshine. Together with those of Speyer and Worms it is one of the only three Romanesque imperial cathedrals to have survived almost intact to this day. Its basic framework was laid out in 1081–1137 and 1183–1239, but its oldest parts date from the early 11th century, with the rows of Gothic side chapels added during the 13th and 14th centuries. Although neither the Gothic altars nor the magnificent choir screen have survived to this day, it is still possible to see the large group of bishops' monuments from the 13th to the 19th century.

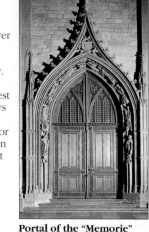

Portal of the "Memorie" Burial Chapel
The late-Gothic portal, leading to the Romanesque burial chapel of the cathedral canons, was made by Madern Gerthener, after 1425.

Two large and two small towers are symmetrically positioned on the ends of the cathedral.

Pulpit
This Neo-Gothic pulpit was made in 1834 by Joseph Scholl.

St Stephen's Choir
The Romanesque eastern choir, one of the first parts to be built, is simpler in style than other parts of the cathedral.

Round staircase towers are from the previous building, built in the early 11th century.

★ Monument of Heinrich Ferdinand von der Leyen

This Baroque monument of the Dom rector, the work of Johann Mauritz Gröninger, was erected during his lifetime, in 1706.

VISITORS' CHECKLIST

Bischöfliches Dom- und
Diözesanmuseum Domstr. 3.
Tel (06131) 25 33 44.
◻ 10am–5pm Tue–Sun.
www.dommuseum-mainz.de

St Martin's Choir
The late-Romanesque western choir with its trefoil closing is an early 13th-century addition.

★ Stalls

These superb Rococo oak stalls encircle almost the entire presbytery. They were created by Franz Anton Hermann, who completed them in 1767.

Main entrance

Tomb of Jakob von Liebenstein

The late-Gothic tomb of the archbishop von Liebenstein, who died in 1508, is the work of an unknown artist. It depicts the deceased in draped robes, lying under an ornate canopy.

STAR SIGHTS

★ Monument of Heinrich Ferdinand von der Leyen

★ Stalls

Rhine Valley (Rheintal) ⑧

The Celts called it *Renos*, the Romans *Rhenus*, while to Germanic tribes it was the Rhein, or *Vater Rhein* ("Father Rhine"), as it is known today. The source of this mighty, 1320-km (825-mile) long river is in Switzerland, from where it flows through Liechtenstein, Germany, Luxembourg and Holland, yet the Germans regard it as "their" river. The Rhine is steeped in many legends – it was into this river that Hagen von Tronje, faithful follower of King Gunther and slayer of Siegfried, threw the treasure of the Nibelungs, and Lohengrin's swan is said to appear near the town of Kleve *(see p388)* to this day.

Bonn
Bendorf
Rhein
Siegen
Koble
Trier
Saarbrücken
①

Stolzenfels ①

The existing castle complex has little in common with the original 13th-century fortress, which burned down in 1688. In the early 19th century, the ruins were bought by the future king Friedrich Wilhelm IV. The castle, designed by the famous Prussian architect Karl Friedrich Schinkel, was built in 1833–45.

②

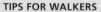

0 kilometres   5

0 miles   5

Saarbrücken

Boppard ②

Boppard's most famous sights are the remains of the Roman military camp of Bodobrica, the church of St Severus (12th–13th centuries), famous for its wall paintings, and the Medieval market square, built on the site of Roman hot baths. Michael Thonet, the creator of famous chairs made from bent wood, was born here in 1796.

TIPS FOR WALKERS

Length of the route: about 125 km (78 miles).
Stopping-off points: the best places to stop are Boppard or Bacharach, offering the widest choice of bars and restaurants.
Further attractions: a boat trip on the Rhine river, from Koblenz to Mainz.

St Goar ③

The town takes its name from Goar, an Aquitanian hermit who settled here in the mid-6th century. His burial place is in the magnificent 11th-century crypt of the Stiftskirche (the parish church, which today is a Protestant church).

◁ The Mosel River near Trittenheim at Rhineland-Palatinate

Marksburg ⑧

From 1117 this castle, which towers over the Rhine and the small town of Braubach, has been owned at different times by the von Braubachs and the powerful Epstein family. The Marksburg is the only castle along this stretch of the Rhine which has never been damaged.

Loreley ⑦

The Loreley Rock, onto which many boats have been smashed by the strong currents, has been a source of inspiration for many poets. A 19th-century legend tells of a beautiful blonde combing her hair and luring unlucky sailors to their deaths with her song.

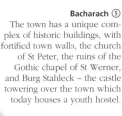

Pfalzgrafenstein ④

In the middle of the Rhine River stands the proud and mighty fortress of Pfalzgrafenstein – one of the most beautifully situated castles in the Rhineland. Its origins date back to 1326, but its present shape is the result of Baroque refurbishments in the 17th–18th centuries.

Bacharach ⑤

The town has a unique complex of historic buildings, with fortified town walls, the church of St Peter, the ruins of the Gothic chapel of St Werner, and Burg Stahleck – the castle towering over the town which today houses a youth hostel.

Burg Sooneck ⑥

In the 13th century, Sooneck castle was the home of various robber knights. The fortress fell into ruin in the late 17th century, due to frequent raids by the French. In the 19th century it was bought by the Hohenzollerns, who rebuilt the castle in its original form.

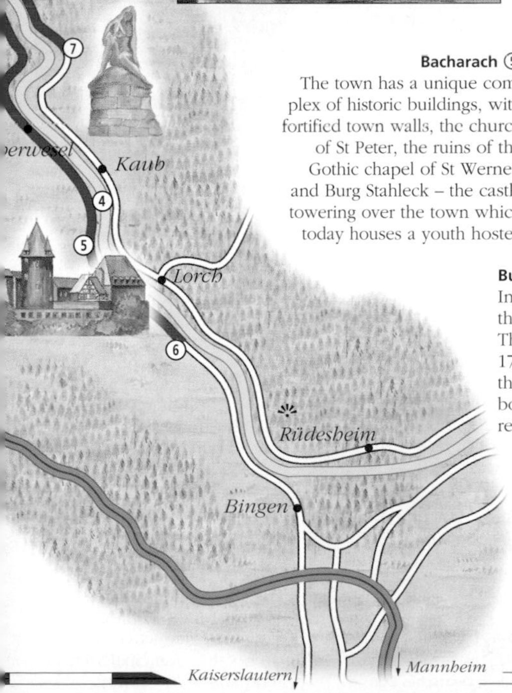

KEY

▬	Motorway
▬	Key text
▬	Scenic route
═	River
❉	Viewpoint

Limburg

Ems

Ems

verwesel *Kaub*

Lorch

Rüdesheim

Bingen

Kaiserslautern | *Mannheim*

For hotels and restaurants in this region see pp506–8 and pp545–6

Koblenz ⑨

The name which the Romans gave to their camp in 9 BC – *castrum ad confluentas,* meaning the "camp at the confluence" – reflects the town's strategic importance, for it is here that the Mosel flows into the Rhine. From the Middle Ages until the 19th century, Koblenz was the seat of the powerful archbishop–electors of Trier. It was also the birthplace of Prince von Metternich, the 19th-century Austrian statesman. Today it is a modern metropolis which attracts many visitors, and is the main centre of the region's cultural life.

Romanesque twin-tower façade of the Basilika St Castor

▦ Deutsches Eck

Ludwig-Museum im Deutsch-herrenhaus. Danziger Freiheit 1. *Tel (0261) 30 40 40.* ☐ *10:30am–5pm Tue–Sat, 11am–6pm Sun & public hols.*

The "German corner" is the place where the Mosel flows into the Rhine. Here stands the enormous equestrian statue of Emperor Wilhelm I. Designed by Bruno Schmitz, it was erected in 1897, destroyed in World War II and replaced with a copy in 1993. The name refers to the complex of buildings known as Deutschherrenhaus belonging to the Order of Teutonic Knights. Only part of the three-wing residence of the Order's Commander, built in the early 14th century, has survived to this day. Following its refurbishment in 1992 the building now houses the Ludwig-Museum, with a collection of modern art (mainly German and French post-1945 artists) donated by Peter and Irene Ludwig.

🔒 Basilika St Castor

Kastorstraße 7.

The collegial church of St Castor was built in 817–36 on the initiative of the archbishop of Trier, on a site previously occupied by an early Christian church. The treaty of Verdun, which divided the Carolingian Empire between the three sons of Ludwig I the Pious, was signed here in 843. The present appearance of the church is the result of extensions from the 11th–13th centuries. Inside are beautiful wall epitaphs of the Trier archbishops Kuno von Falkenstein (1388) and Werner von Königstein (1418). Also noteworthy is the pulpit dating from 1625.

▦ Florinsmarkt

Mittelrhein-Museum Florinsmarkt 15–17. *Tel (0261) 129 25 20.* ☐ *10:30am–5pm Tue–Sat, 11am–6pm Sun.*

This square takes its name from the Romanesque-Gothic church of St Florin, dating from the 12th and 14th centuries. The Mittelrheinisches Museum with its collection of archaeology and medieval art of the Central Rhine region occupies three historic buildings. The Kaufhaus, in the centre, dates from 1419–25 and 1724. The image of a horse-rider shows the robber baron Johann von Kobem, beheaded in 1536, who now sticks his tongue out at passers-by every half hour. To its right stands the late-Gothic Schöffenhaus, and to its left is the Baroque Bürresheimer Hof, from 1659–60.

The Renaissance Alte Burg, now housing archives and a library

♟ Alte Burg

Burgstraße 1.

In the Middle Ages, the powerful von Arken family had a fortified residence built for themselves in the north-western section of the Roman fortifications. In 1277 it was taken over by Heinrich von Finstingen, the archbishop of Trier, who ordered its extension. The fortress was to protect him from the citizens of Koblenz who were striving for independence. Successive archbishops continued with the conversion of the building, which acquired its final shape in the 17th century. The eastern Renaissance façade of the complex is particularly attractive. Today it houses the municipal archives and parts of the library.

The spur between the Mosel and the Rhine, called Deutsches Eck

For hotels and restaurants in this region see pp506–8 and pp545–6

🔒 Liebfrauenkirche

Florinspfaffengasse 14.
Tel (0261) 315 50.
🕐 8am–6pm Mon–Sat,
9am–12:30pm Sun.

At the highest point
in the old town
stands the
Romanesque church
of Our Dear Lady. Its
history dates back to
early Christian times,
but its present form
is the result of
remodelling work
carried out in
1182–1250. A triple-
nave basilica with galleries,
it has a twin-tower western
façade. The beautiful, elongated Gothic choir was added
in 1404–30.

**Statue of the
Madonna in
Liebfrauenkirche**

♟ Kurfürstliches Schloss

Neustadt.
Not far from the bridge across
the Rhine stands the electoral
palace, an example of the
Rhineland's early Neo-Classical architecture. It was built,
and for a short time occupied,
by Clemens Wenzeslaus von
Sachsen, the last of Trier's
electors. Construction of the
castle began in 1777, to a
design prepared by Michael
d'Ixnard, and continued until

1786, oversen by
Antoine François
Peyère the Younger.

🏛 Festung Ehrenbreitstein

Landesmuseum Koblenz
Tel (0261) 66 75 40 00.
🕐 15 Mar–end Nov:
9:30am–5pm daily.

On the opposite side
of the Rhine stands the
mighty fortress of
Ehrenbreitstein, one
of the largest in the
world. A smaller fort-
ress was erected on
this site in 1000, and extended in subsequent years by
the archbishops and electors
of Trier, who lived in this
indomitable fortress from 1648
to 1786. Trier's holiest relic,
the Rock Christi (vestments
of Christ) was kept here. The
appearance of the fortress has
not changed much since Prus-

VISITORS' CHECKLIST

Road map B5. 🏙 109,300. 🚉
🛈 Bahnhofplatz 17 (0261-313
04); Jesuitenplatz (0261-13 09 20).
🎭 Internationale Musiktage (Mar/
Apr), Altstadtfest mit dem Fest
der Stadtteile (Jun/Jul), Koblenzer
Gauklerfest (Jul), Rhein in Flammen
(Aug), Schängelmarkt (Sep),
Koblenzer Mendelssohn-Tage
(autumn). www.koblenz.de

sian days. It offers splendid
views over Koblenz, the
Rhine and the Mosel. Today,
it is home to the **Landesmuseum Koblenz** (regional
museum) with an interesting
collection on the development of technology, and
to the **Rhein-Museum** with
hydrological collections. At
Wambachstraße 204, in the
same district, is the house
of Beethoven's mother.

The Classical façade of the Kurfürstliches Schloss

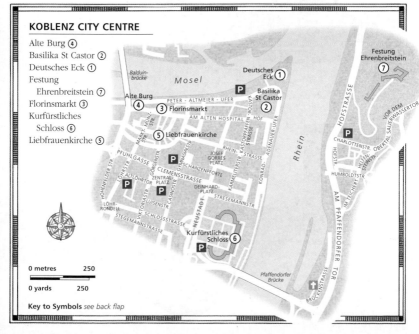

KOBLENZ CITY CENTRE

Alte Burg ④
Basilika St Castor ②
Deutsches Eck ①
Festung
 Ehrenbreitstein ⑦
Florinsmarkt ③
Kurfürstliches
 Schloss ⑥
Liebfrauenkirche ⑤

0 metres 250
0 yards 250

Key to Symbols see back flap

Maria Laach

Capital of a vestibule column

A true masterpiece of German and European Romanesque architecture, the Maria Laach Abbey stands next to the Laacher See, a lake formed in the crater of an extinct volcano. Its construction started in 1093 at the behest of Heinrich II, who also lies buried here. Building continued from 1093 until 1220. Until secularization in 1802, the Abbey was the home of the Benedictines. Since 1892 the church has once again been resounding with Gregorian chants, which are sung here several times a day.

View from the West
The monumental western façade of the abbey consists of a semicircular apse, a massive, square 43-m (141-ft) tall central tower, and two slim 35-m (115-ft) tall flanking towers.

★ Tomb of Heinrich II
The tomb of the Count Palatine Heinrich II, who died in 1095, dates from about 1280. His effigy has been reproduced in a magnificent walnut wood block, which to this day has kept its original colours.

Löwenbrunnen
The lion fountain, which adorns the atrium, was made in 1928. It was modelled on the famous Alhambra fountain in Granada, Spain.

Main entrance

The "Paradise", the courtyard, is meant to symbolize the Garden of Eden.

Church entrance

Detail from a Column Capital
The western entrance is surrounded by columns with interesting capitals. Carved figures can be seen, including that of a devil recording the sins of each entrant and others which are pulling each other's hair out.

Mosaics
The interior is decorated with paintings and mosaics created over centuries by artists of the Beuronese School. In the main eastern apse is a mosaic of Christ the Ruler dating from 1911.

The church towers have arcaded galleries, typical of Romanesque style.

VISITORS' CHECKLIST

Road map B5. 🚌 6032 from Niedermendig or Mayen, 6031 from Andernach.
Tel (02652) 590.
⬜ 5:30am–8pm daily.
Crypt – information by video show. 🍴 🅿 ♿
www.maria-laach.de

Stained-glass Windows
Three vast stained-glass windows in the main eastern apse were made by a contemporary artist, W. Rupprecht, in 1956.

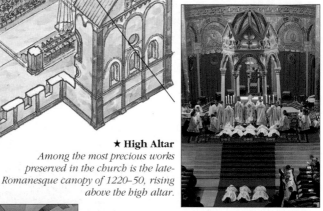

★ **High Altar**
Among the most precious works preserved in the church is the late-Romanesque canopy of 1220–50, rising above the high altar.

★ **Crypt**
The vaults of the exquisite early-Romanesque crypt are supported by austere square capitals. This is also the resting-place of Gilbert, the first abbot at Maria Laach.

STAR SIGHTS

★ Tomb of Heinrich II

★ High Altar

★ Crypt

HESSE

esse lies in the very heart of present-day Germany. Scattered over the region are reminders of its former glory: Roman camps, Carolingian buildings, Romanesque churches and Gothic cathedrals with lofty spires. Territorial partitions, so typical of the former German Reich, brought about the blossoming of art and architecture during the Renaissance and the Baroque eras.

A post-World War II creation, the borders of this federal state roughly approximate those of its 13th-century forerunner. For most of its history, Hesse was divided between Hesse-Darmstadt and Hesse-Kassel.

Today, when admiring the distinctive panorama of Frankfurt am Main – its towering banks and skyscrapers more reminiscent of New York's Manhattan than of a European metropolis – it is hard to believe that this was the birthplace of Goethe. The importance of this city extends far beyond Hesse: it is the financial centre of the European Union, and its annual Book Fair is the largest event of its kind in the world.

Darmstadt became famous as a centre for Jugendstil (Art Nouveau) early in the 20th century. Wiesbaden is the seat of Hesse's state government, and Marburg is one of the best-known university towns. In the 16th century, at the times of fierce religious feuds, the first Protestant university was built here. The Church of St Elizabeth is one of the earliest examples of Gothic architecture in the region. Lovers of modern art will know of Kassel – every five years it hosts the *documenta*, an exciting exhibition of artistic developments.

Hesse has much more to offer. The Waldecker Land, near Kassel, boasts the Eder lake and attractive health resorts. Eberbach in the picturesque Rheingau, the wine-growing area around Eltville, has a well-preserved former Cistercian abbey, which has been used as a film setting.

Park and Baroque Orangery of the palace complex in Fulda

◁ Frankfurt's skyscraper district, nicknamed "Mainhattan"

Exploring Hesse

Eltville, situated in the Rheingau, one of Germany's most important wine-producing regions, is famous for its Riesling wine. Frankfurt am Main, known around the world as a great financial and commercial centre, also has fantastic museums, drawing visitors with their out-standing art collections, while the International Book Fair is a true paradise for readers and bookworms. In the 19th century, wealthy socialites chose Bad Homburg as their favourite spa, while the romantic town of Marburg still has the lively atmosphere of a university town.

The Dom in Limburg, overlooking the Lahn river

The giant Niederwalddenkmal near Rüdesheim

SIGHTS AT A GLANCE

SEE ALSO
- *Where to Stay* pp508–10.
- *Where to Eat* pp547–8.

The Messeturm in the Frankfurt fairgrounds, designed by Helmut Jahn

GETTING AROUND

The A7 motorway, cutting across Hesse in a north–south direction, provides a fast transport link. Starting from Hannover, it runs through Göttingen, Kassel and Fulda to Würzburg in Bavaria. The A4 runs from Dresden, via Weimar, to Bad Hersfeld. From there visitors can take the A7 or the A5, towards Gießen, Bad Homburg, Frankfurt am Main and onwards to Darmstadt and Heidelberg. The fast ICE railway connects Kassel and Frankfurt am Main with Basel (in Switzerland), Stuttgart, Berlin and Munich. Frankfurt am Main has one of Europe's largest airports.

KEY

	Motorway
	Main road
	Minor road
	Under construction
	Main railway
	Minor railway
	International border
△	Summit

Statue of the Brothers Grimm in Hanau

Kassel ①

The cultural, scientific and commercial centre of northern Hesse, Kassel suffered severe damage during World War II due to the armaments industries based here, and much of the town has been rebuilt in functional 1950s style. Today, Kassel has become synonymous with one of the most important shows of contemporary art – *documenta* – held here every five years (the 12th documenta is scheduled for 2007). The town is equally famous for its outstanding collection of European art, housed in the splendid Schloss Wilhelmshöhe, as well as for its parks and gardens, especially the large forest-park adjoining the castle.

17th-century cameo-decorated tureen in the Landesmuseum

🏛 Hessisches Landes-museum

Brüder-Grimm-Platz 5. *Tel (0561) 316 80 300.* ◯ 10am–5pm Tue–Sun. ● 1 May, 24, 31 Dec. 🖾 *(free Fri.)*

Outstanding items in the Neo-Baroque Hesse Regional Museum, built in 1910–13, are the astronomical instruments, originally installed in 1560 in a landgrave's castle, which no longer exists. The ethnographic section has displays of Hessian folk costumes and regional craft items.

The Landesmuseum also houses one of Europe's most unusual museums: the fascinating Tapetenmuseum

(wallpaper museum). Established in 1923, the museum presents the history of wallpaper and the methods of its production around the world. The collection includes examples of leather wall coverings (cordovans) and wallpapers representing Secession and Art-Deco styles as well as the "world's literature on wallpaper". *Vues de Suisse* (views of Switzerland), dating from 1802, is one of the earliest examples of scenic wallpaper. It was printed using 95 different inks and 1,024 wooden blocks. Equally famous is the panoramic *Rénaud et Armide*, from the workshop of Joseph Dufours, printed in 1828 using 2,386 wooden blocks.

🏛 Neue Galerie

Schöne Aussicht 1. *Tel (0561) 316 80 400.* ◯ 10am–5pm Tue–Sun. ● 24, 25 & 26 Dec. 🖾 *(free Fri.)*

The New Gallery, founded in 1976 and devoted to 19th- and 20th-century art, occupies a Neo-Classicist building from 1871–4. The main emphasis of the gallery's collection is on Romantic and Impressionist paintings. It includes canvases by artists such as Carl Schuch, Max Slevogt and Lovis Corinth.

The splendid collection of 20th-century paintings focuses on German Expressionism. An entire room is also devoted to the installations of the controversial sculptor and performance artist Joseph Beuys.

Wallpaper (1670–80), in the Tapetenmuseum

🏛 Brüder-Grimm-Museum

Schöne Aussicht 2. *Tel (0561) 787 20 33.* ◯ 10am–5pm daily (until 8pm Wed). ● 1 Jan, Good Friday, 24, 25, 31 Dec. 🖾

Next to the New Gallery is the small Schloss Bellevue, built in 1714 by Paul du Ry. Although brothers Jacob and Wilhelm Grimm were born in Hanau, they lived in Kassel from 1798 until 1830, and in 1960 a museum devoted to the lives and work of the famous fairy-tale tellers and philologers was opened, containing many first editions.

An illustration for Cinderella, one of the Grimm fairy-tales

🏛 Kunsthalle Fridericianum

Friedrichsplatz 18. *Tel (0561) 707 27 20.* ◯ 11am–6pm Wed–Sun. ● Mon–Tue. 🖾

Königsplatz and Friedrichsplatz were designed by the court architect, Simon Louis du Ry. The northwestern side of the latter is occupied by the Neo-Classical Fridericianum, built by du Ry in 1769–76. Its founder, Landgrave Friedrich II, had always intended it to be a museum, and it became the second public museum (after the British Museum in London) to be built in Europe, and the first one on the European mainland. Since 1955, the Fridricianum has been the main venue for Kassel's multimedia contemporary art show – the *documenta*, which every five years takes over the entire city. An additional exhibition hall, the Documentahalle, was opened in 1992, in the nearby Staatstheater.

The Ottoneum, home of the first permanent theatre in Germany

🏛 Ottoneum

Steinweg 2. **Naturkundemuseum**
Tel (0561) 787 40 14. ⬜ 10am–
5pm Tue–Sun (until 8pm Wed). 🈂
The Ottoneum (1604–5), built
for Landgrave Maurice the
Learned, was Germany's first
permanent theatre. Designed
by Wilhelm Vernukken and
remodelled in the late 17th
century by Paul du Ry, it was
converted into a natural history
museum in 1885.

🌿 Orangerie

An der Karlsaue 20c. **Tel** (0561) 316 80
500. **Museum für Astronomie und
Technikgeschichte** ⬜ 10am–5pm
Tue–Sun. ⬛ 24, 25, 31 Dec.
Zeiss-Planetarium 🎟 2pm Tue,
Sat, 2 & 8pm Thu, 3pm Wed, Fri, Sun.
🈂 (free Fri.)
The southern part of Kassel is

home to Karlsaue, a vast
palace and garden complex
named after its founder, Landgrave Karl. The site was
earlier occupied by a small
Renaissance Schloss (1568),
surrounded by a garden. In
1702–10 Pierre-Etienne Monnot built the large Orangery,
which now houses a museum
of astronomy and technology.
Monnot is also the creator of
Marmorbad, a bath pavilion
from 1722, while the kitchen
pavilion was designed by
Simon Louis du Ry in 1765.

🏰 Wilhelmshöhe

Gemäldegalerie Alter Meister.
Schloss Wilhelmshöhe. **Tel** (0561) 31
68 00. ⬜ 10am–5pm Tue–Sun.
⬛ 1 May, 24, 25, 31 Dec. 🈂
At the top of Wilhelmshöher
Allee, designed in 1781, stands
Wilhelmshöhe, a magnificent
palace and park. The palace
is situated along the axis of
the avenue that runs up the
hill, through a long forest
glade. The original intention
was to fill it with a series of
cascades, but only a few of
these were ever built. At the
top of the hill is the Octogon,
crowned with the statue of
Hercules, the symbol of the
town. The palace was designed by Simon Louis du Ry and

Heinrich Christoph Jussow
and built in 1793–1801 for the
Elector Wilhelm. Now it
houses the Gemäldegalerie
Alte Meister with its outstanding collection of European
masters including paintings
by Rubens, Titian, Rembrandt,
Dürer and Poussin. There is a
large and attractive park.

Cascades, with Octogon and
Hercules statue, in Wilhelmshöhe

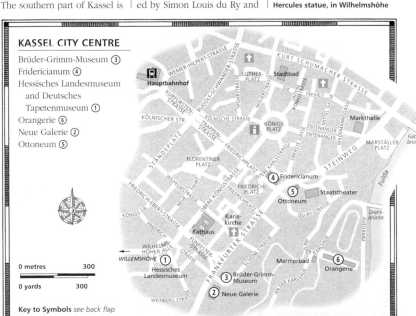

KASSEL CITY CENTRE

0 metres   300
0 yards   300

Key to Symbols see back flap

Fritzlar ❷

Road map C4. 🏠 15,500. 🚌 🚃
Kasseler Straße. 🛈 *Rathaus,*
Zwischen den Krämen 5 (05622-98
86 43). 📷 *Pferdemarkt (Jul),*
Stadtfest (Aug).

The beautiful town of Fritzlar
has preserved its original,
nearly complete ring of medieval walls with watchtowers,
bastions and over 450 half-
timbered houses from various
periods. In the early 8th century, St Boniface, the apostle
of Germany, had the holy oak
of the Germanic god Donar,
which grew here, cut down to
build a Christian chapel. In
724 he founded the Benedictine **Dom** (abbey of St Peter).
In 1118 the original church
was replaced by a cruciform,
vaulted basilica with a triple-
nave crypt, and this was remodelled in the 13th and 14th
centuries. Adjacent to the
church is a lovely 14th-cen-
tury ambulatory. The church
interior is rich in historic
treasures. The east wall of the
transept is decorated with
wall paintings from c.1320,
and the south nave includes a
Pietà (1300). The 14th-century
parish church of the Franciscan Order nearby has a lovely
painting of the Madonna, on
the northern wall of the choir.
In Fritzlar's picturesque old
town stands the **Rathaus**
(town hall), whose lower
floors date from the 12th
century, while the upper ones
were added in the 15th century. The exquisite **Hochzeitshaus** (wedding house), in the
street of the same name, is a
Renaissance half-timbered
house, built in 1580–90,
which now houses a
museum. Another interesting
sight is the **Alte Brücke**, a
13th-century stone bridge
spanning the Eder River.

Relief of St Martin, on the walls of
the Rathaus in Fritzlar

Waldecker Land ❸

The Waldecker land, situated west of Kassel, was
once an independent county and later, until 1929,
a free state within the German Reich. Today this
region, with its Eder-Stausee (reservoir), is one
of the most attractive tourist regions in Germany. The wooded hills provide a perfect
setting for long rambles, the roads and tracks
are ideally suited for cycling tours and the
rivers and lakes permit visitors to practise
a wide variety of watersports.

Korbach ②
Korbach is a beautiful
old town with many
half-timbered houses.
Worth seeing are the
Gothic church of St
Kilian with its inter-
esting 14th-century
pulpit, and the
church of St Nicho-
las, with the
Baroque tomb of
Georg Friedrich
von Waldeck
(1692).

Frankenberg ⑤
This small town is brimming
with half-timbered houses.
The town hall (1509), also
half-timbered, has humorous
polychrome wood-carvings.
The Gothic Marienkirche with
its 15th-century wall paintings
is also worth visiting.

KEY

🟫	Motorway
🟥	Suggested route
⬜	Scenic road
=	Other road
=	River, lake
☆	Viewpoint

0 km	10
0 miles	10

Bad Arolsen ①
Both the sculptor Christian Daniel
Rauch and the painter Wilhelm von
Kaulbach were born in this spa
town, and they are commemorated
in two museums. The star attraction,
however, is the Baroque castle
(1713–28) of the von Waldeck family,
designed by Julius Ludwig Rothweil.

Waldeck ③
The old fortress of Waldeck is now a
hotel. It offers superb views over the
Eder-Stausee reservoir and the small
town of Waldeck with its 18th-century
half-timbered houses. The Gothic
town church has a high altar (c.1500),
devoted to the Virgin Mary.

TIPS FOR VISITORS

Length of route: 110 km (68 miles).

Stopping-off points: There are many good cafés and restaurants in every town along the route.

Further attractions: Cruises and ferries run on the Edersee. A viewing platform on top of the Peterskopf hill, near Hemfurth, can be reached by electric train.

Bad Wildungen ④
This popular spa town has many
charming half-timbered houses.
The church has a priceless altar
painted with scenes of the Passion
by Konrad von Soest (1403).

Projecting gate of the Baroque Stadtschloss in Fulda

Fulda ❹

Road map C5. 🏙 60,000. 🚊 🏢
Bonifatiusplatz 1 (0661-1 02 18 14).

Fulda's history began in March 744, when Sturmius, a pupil of St Boniface, laid the foundation stone for the Benedictine abbey. Ten years later the body of St Boniface, who had been murdered by Frisian pagans, was laid to rest here. The town, which grew around the abbey, experienced its heyday during the Baroque period, and a new Baroque building, designed by Johann Dientzenhofer, was built in 1704–12 on the foundations of the old abbey. The **Dom St Salvator und Bonifatius** is a triple-nave basilica with a dome above the nave intersection, a monumental eastern façade and a shrine with the saint's relics under the high altar, in the western section.

Opposite the cathedral stands the **Stadtschloss** (former episcopal palace), a shoe-shaped edifice, built by Johann Dientzenhofer and Andreas Gallasini, with richly decorated Baroque and Rococo interiors. Particularly noteworthy are the Kaisersaal (imperial hall) on the ground floor, the magnificent Mondsaal (moon chamber, formerly the ballroom) and the charming Rococo-style Spiegelsaal (chamber of mirrors) on the first floor. Today, some of the palace chambers hold an impressive collection of porcelain. The palace complex includes a large landscaped garden and an orangery, which houses a café.

THE BROTHERS GRIMM

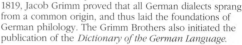

The two brothers are known around the world as collectors of German folk-tales, which were first published in 1812 and subsequently translated into most languages. Fairy-tales such as *Hänsel and Gretel*, *Cinderella* and *Little Red Riding Hood* have been favourites for generations of children. Above all, however, the brothers were scholars. In his *German Grammar*, published in 1819, Jacob Grimm proved that all German dialects sprang from a common origin, and thus laid the foundations of German philology. The Grimm Brothers also initiated the publication of the *Dictionary of the German Language*.

To the north of the Dom stands the round **Michaelskirche**, a Carolingian chapel dating from 822, one of the oldest church buildings in Germany. Inside the church has a ring of eight columns and a crypt supported by a single column. The circular gallery, the long side nave and the western tower are 11th-century additions.

Other interesting sights in Fulda are the Baroque **Heilig-Geist-Kirche** (church of the Holy Spirit), built in 1729–33 by Andreas Gallasini, and the late-18th century parish church of St Blasius. In the 8th century, five abbeys were established on the four hills surrounding the town. On Petersberg stands the former Benedictine **Peterskirche**, from the 9th–15th centuries, with a Carolingian crypt.

Inside the church is one of Germany's oldest wall paintings, dating from 836–47.

Alsfeld ❺

Road map C4. 🏙 18,000. 🚊 🏢
Am Markt 12 (06631-9 11 02 43).
🎭 *Pfingstfest (Whitsun), Akademischer Marktfrühschoppen (May), Stadt- und Heimatfest (Aug), Historischer Markt (Sep).*

The first historic records of Alsfeld date from the late 9th century. Today the town attracts visitors with its pretty old town with numerous 16th–17th century half-timbered houses. On the eastern side of the town square stands a grand late-Gothic **Rathaus** (town hall), built in 1512–16, and one of the finest examples of half-timbered structures

Half-timbered houses in Alsfeld

For hotels and restaurants in this region see pp508–10 and pp547–8

anywhere in Germany. Other interesting features in the market square are the stone **Weinhaus**, with its distinctive stepped gable (1538), and the Renaissance **Hochzeitshaus** (wedding house), dating from 1565. Opposite the town hall stands the **Stumpfhaus** (1609), its façade beautifully decorated with wood carvings and paintings. From the town hall runs the picturesque Fulder Gasse, with the Gothic parish church **Walpurgiskirche** (13th–15th centuries), which has 15th-century wall paintings. In Rossmarkt stands the former Augustian **Dreifaltigkeitskirche** (church of the Holy Trinity), from the 13th–15th centuries. It was from here that in 1522 the monk Tilemann Schnabel began to spread the Reformation in Alsfeld. The 18th-century **castle** in Altenburg, 2km (1 mile) from Alsfeld, enjoys a hilltop position.

Detail on the Rathaus, in Marburg

Marburg ❻

Road map C4. 🏚 80,000. 🚉
ℹ️ Pilgrimstein 26 (06421-991 20).
🎪 Maieinsingen (30 Apr),
3-Tage Marburg (Jul), Elisabethmarkt (Oct), Weihnachtsmarkt (Dec).

When in 1248 the county of Hesse broke away from Thuringia, Marburg became one of the most important seats of the landgraves. The first landgrave, Heinrich II, lived in the castle that towers over the town. The town's history is inseparably linked with the 13th-century figure of Elisabeth of Thuringia, wife of Ludwig IV, who devoted her life to the poor and died here. In 1527, Philipp the Magnanimous founded the first Protestant university in the Reich at Marburg. He also instigated the first Marburg Colloquy in 1529, to unify the Protestant faith. The "articles" presented by Martin Luther to Melanchthon and Zwingli later formed the basis for the Augsburg

Creed. Today, Marburg is a picturesque university town. A tour of the town should start from the **Elisabethkirche**, at the bottom of the hill. Built in 1235–83, it is (after Trier) Germany's second purely Gothic church. There is a large set of Gothic altars from the early 16th century, including the altars of St Elisabeth (1513) and of the Holy Family (1511). Next to the north choir entrance stands the statue of St Elisabeth with a model of the church (1480). The choir contains the tomb of the Saint, positioned under the baldachin (c.1280). The vestry houses the greatest treasure, the reliquary of St Elisabeth (1235–49). In the south choir is an interesting group of monuments to the Hessian landgraves, from the 13th–16th centuries.

The **Universitätsmuseum für Bildende Kunst** holds a collection of paintings produced after 1500, with a predominance of 19th- and 20th-century German artists. Around the market square stands a group of historic, half-timbered houses from the 14th–17th centuries. Particularly pretty are the Sonne (sun, No. 14), the Stiefel (boot, No. 17) and the house at No. 19. The Steinhaus (stone house, No. 18), built in 1318, is the oldest in Marburg, along with that at No. 13 Hirschgasse. At No. 16 Markt is the Renaissance Künstlerhaus (artists' house). High

The Gothic portal of the Elisabethkirche in Marburg

above the town (287 m/942 ft above the sea) towers the **Landgrafenschloss**, the landgraves' castle dating from the 10th–16th centuries. The two-storey Fürstenbau (dukes' building) has a large ducal chamber, dating from 1330. The Wilhelmsbau was built in 1492–8. It houses a museum of sacral art with mementoes of the debate between Luther, Zwingli and Melanchthon.

🔒 **Elisabethkirche**
Elisabethstraße. **Tel** (06421) 655 73. 🕐 Apr–Sep: 9am–6pm; Oct: 10am–5pm; Nov–Mar: 10am–4pm.

🏛 **Universitätsmuseum für Bildende Kunst**
Biegenstraße 11. **Tel** (06421) 282 23 45. 🕐 11am–1pm & 2–5pm Tue–Sun.

⚜ **Landgrafenschloss und Universitätsmuseum für Kulturgeschichte im Wilhelmsbau**
Schloss 1. **Tel** (06421) 282 23 45.
🕐 Apr–Oct: 10am–6pm Tue–Sun; Nov–Mar: 10am–4pm Tue–Sun.

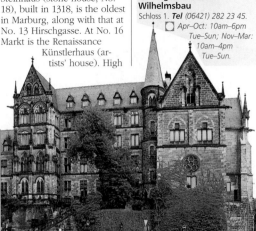

The Alte Universität (old university) in Marburg

Gießen ❼

Road map C4. 👥 72,000. 🚆 ℹ️
Berliner Platz 2 (0641-194 33).

Giessen was granted town
status in 1248, and in 1607
it acquired its university. In
Brandplatz stands the partially
reconstructed **Altes Schloss**
(old palace), dating from the
14th–15th centuries. Now the
home of the Oberhessisches
Museum, it holds a large collection of art dating from the
Gothic period to today.

The **Botanischer Garten** is
one of Germany's oldest botanical gardens, established in
1609 for the purposes of
scientific research. To the
north of it stands the **Neues
Schloss** (new palace), built in
1533–9 for Landgrave Philipp
the Magnanimous. It miraculously escaped damage when
the town was bombed in
1944. The Wallenfelssches
Haus nearby houses inter-
esting ethnological collections. The only remaining part
of the Gothic **Pfarrkirche St
Pankratius**, which was almost
completely destroyed in 1944,
is its tower, dating from 1500.

At No. 2 Georg-Schlosser-
Straße is the **Burgmannen-
haus**, an attractive half-timbered mansion
dating from
the 14th
century.

Portal of the Altes Schloss in Gießen

Along with the old stable
block in Dammstraße, it is the
only half-timbered building
that has survived to this day.

Wetzlar ❽

Road map C5. 👥 54,000. 🚆
ℹ️ *Domplatz 8 (06441-997 750).*

Occupying a picturesque
spot on the banks of the
Lahn river, Wetzlar is overlooked by the ruins of the
12th-century **Kalsmunt** fortress. It was built for the
Emperor Friedrich I Barbarossa (1122–90). Only parts of
the tower remain intact. The
Dom (Collegiate Church of St
Mary) was begun in 897 but
by the late 15th century had
only been partly completed.
The splendid western double
portal has remained unusable
for the last 500 years –
although the iconography of
the tympanum was finished,
the stairs leading to the
entrance were never built. If
they had been built, they
would have led not to the
church's nave, but to a courtyard. Wetzlar's Dom is a rare,
perhaps even unique surviving example of the typical appearance of most European
churches in the mid-15th century. Inside the church are
several interesting historic
artifacts, including the statue
of the *Madonna on the Moon
Crescent* (mid-15th century)
and a late-Renaissance
Crucifixion.

In 1772, the young
Johann Wolfgang
von Goethe spent
three months in
Wetzlar working as
an apprentice at
the court of appeal.
During this time
he fell in love with
Charlotte Buff, called
Lotte, who was
engaged to one of
Goethe's friends.
The **Lottehaus**, her
former home, has a
collection of items
relating to Goethe
and Lotte. It was
the suicide of a
friend, Karl Wil-
helm Jerusalem,
who lived in the

18th-century **Jerusalemhaus**
at No. 5 Schillerplatz, that
inspired Goethe to write his
tragic novel, *The Sorrows of
Young Werther* (1774). Jerusalem had suffered unrequited
love, just like Goethe. The
novel, which was published
two years later, made Goethe
famous around Europe, but it
also unwittingly led many
young men to commit suicide.

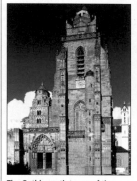

**The Gothic south tower of the
Dom in Wetzlar**

Weilburg ❾

Road map B5. 👥 13,500. 🚆
ℹ️ *Mauerstraße 6 (06471-76 71).*

Weilburg enjoys a parti-
cularly scenic location in
a bend of the Lahn River. The
town is dominated by the
majestic Renaissance–Baroque
Schloss of the Nassau-Weil-
burg family. The monumental
castle complex was created in
stages. Its main section dates
from the Renaissance era; the
east wing was built in 1533–9;
the south and west wings in
1540–48 and the west tower
in 1567. The northern part of
the palace was completed in
1570–73. In the late-17th
century, various Baroque
additions were made, mainly
to the interior of the castle.
The 16th-century furnishings
show the rich ornamentation
typical of the German Renaissance. The **Obere Orangerie**
(upper orangery), built in
1703–5 and today used for
temporary exhibitions, and
the **Hofkirche** (castle church),
dating from 1707–13, are the
work of Ludwig Rothweil.
Terraces lead from the castle

to the Lahn river, which is crossed by an 18th-century stone bridge. In Frankfurt-straße stands the **Heiliggrab-kapelle** (Chapel of the Holy Sepulchre), dating from 1505.

Limburg ⑩

Road map B5. 🏔 *31,000.* 🚉
ℹ️ *Hospitalstraße 2 (06431-61 66).*

Limburg's history dates back to the 8th century. In 1821, the town became the see of a newly created diocese.

The **Dom** (collegiate cathedral church of St George) towers high above the Lahn river. This monumental building, whose style combines late-Romanesque and early French-Gothic, was erected in 1190–1250. Its well-proportioned interior contains a rich variety of historic artifacts, including some 13th-century wall paintings in the presbytery and the transept, a font dating from the same period and the tombstone of Konrad Kurzbold, who founded the first church on this site.

To the south of the Dom stands the **Burg** (castle), an irregular structure built in the 13th–16th centuries. It houses the interesting **Diözesan-museum** (Diocese museum).

Limburg has many original examples of beautiful half-timbered buildings. The houses at No. 1 Römerstraße, No. 6 Kolpingstraße, No. 4 Kleine Rütsche and No. 11

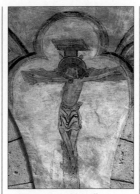

Romanesque–Gothic wall paintings in the Dom in Limburg

Kornmarkt date from the last decade of the 13th century. Near the 14th-century **Alte Lahnbrücke** (old Lahn bridge), with its defensive towers, stands a mansion belonging to the Cistercians of Eberbach. The post-Franciscan Sebastiankirche (church of St Sebastian) dates from the 14th and 18th centuries.

Bad Homburg ⑪

Road map C5. 🏔 *52,000.* 🚉
ℹ️ *Kurhaus, Louisenstraße 58 (06172-17 81 10).* 🎭 *Fugato (Sep every two years – the next is in 2007), Laternenfest (Sep yearly).*

Bad Homburg grew up around a fortress whose earliest records date back to 1180. Friedrich II von Hessen-Homburg initiated the con-

version of the medieval castle into the **Schloss**, a Baroque palace built in 1678–86. It features a magnificent Festsaal (ballroom) and Spiegelkabinett (hall of mirrors). The only part of the former complex remaining today is the 14th-century Weißer Turm (white tower). Following the annexation of Hesse-Homburg by Prussia in 1866, the palace became the favourite summer residence of the royal then (from 1871) imperial family.

Along with Baden-Baden and Wiesbaden, Homburg was one of Germany's most fashionable spas, and today the town reflects its former splendour. The **Kurpark**, a landscaped park established in 1854–67, was designed by Peter Joseph Lenné.

The **Spielbank** (1838), in Brunnenallee claims to be the oldest casino in the world. Built in 1887–90, the **Kaiser-Wilhelm-Bad** is still used as the main bath complex for therapeutic treatments. An Orthodox chapel, designed by Leonti Nikolayevich Benois for the Russian Orthodox nobility, was finished in 1899.

Environs
Saalburg, 7 km (4 miles) to the northwest, has a Roman fortress, which was completely reconstructed in 1898–1901. The fortress formed part of the *limes*, the fortified border that separated the Roman Empire from its Germanic neighbours in the 1st to 3rd century AD.

The grand edifice of the Kaiser-Wilhelm-Bad in the Kurpark, Bad Homburg

Eltville

Road map B5. 🚗 17,000. 🚉 ℹ️
Rheingauerstr. 28 (06123-90 98 0).
🎭 *Biedermeier- und Sektfest (Jul).*

In the 2nd century, the area
that is now the old town was
a Roman *latifundium,* a large
agricultural estate. In 1332,
Eltville was granted town
status. Part of the Mainz
diocese, it is today known for
its excellent sparkling wine.

In 1337–45 the **Burg**
(castle) was extended at the
request of Archbishop Heinrich von Virneburg. The east
wing of the castle was added
in 1682–3 by Giovanni Angelo
Barell. The only part of it
remaining today is the five-
storey residential tower; the
rest of the building is a picturesque ruin. In the tower
are original 14th-century wall
paintings and friezes.

The twin-naved **Pfarrkirche
St Peter und St Paul** (parish
church) was built in
1350–1430. The vestibule has
well-preserved wall
paintings (1405)
showing scenes
from the Last
Judgement. The
town boasts
several attractive
mansions,
including Hof
Langenwerth
von Simmern
(1773), Stock-
heimer Hof (1550) and
Gräflich-Eltzscher Hof
(16th–17th century).

**Crest of the Hessische Staats-
weingüter-Vinothek, in Eltville**

Wiesbaden 🔟

Road map C5. 🚗 270,000. 🚉
ℹ️ *Markstr. 6 (0611-172 97 80).*
🎭 *Internationale Maifestspiele (May),
Theatrium (Jun).*

Wiesbaden is the modern
capital of Hesse. Highly
valued as a spa by the
Romans, who exploited the
healing properties of its
waters, the town grew from
a small settlement known as
aquae mattiacorum after the
Germanic tribe of the Mattiacs.
In 1774 the Nassau-Usingen
family chose Wiesbaden as
their residence. This, as well
as the subsequent rapid

**The Baroque Biebrich Palace,
south of Wiesbaden**

growth of the town as a spa
resort in the 19th century, laid
the foundations for its lasting
prosperity. Today, the town is
still dominated by large-scale
developments carried out in
the spirit and style of Classicism and Historicism.

The **Stadtschloss** (municipal
castle), today the seat of the
state parliament, was built in
1835–41. In Schlossplatz the
Neo-Renaissance **Markt-
kirche,** built in 1853–62, soars
above the town's other
buildings.

In front of the
church stands a
statue of Wilhelm
I the Great von
Nassau-Oranien.
The oldest
building in the
town is the
Altes Rathaus
(old town hall),
dating from 1610. In Wilhelmstraße is the imposing Neo-
Renaissance and Neo-Baroque
Hessisches Staatstheater
(state theatre). It was built in
1892–4 for Kaiser Wilhelm II
to the designs of the theatre

architects Fellner and Helmer.
Adjacent to the Marktkirche is
the attractive Kurhauskolon-
nade (spa house colonnade).
It was erected in 1825 and is
the longest colonnade in
Europe. The early 20th-century
Kurhaus (spa house) itself,
with its grand façade and
portico, is the work of Friedrich Thiersch. Inside is the
original **Spielbank** (casino),
where Fyodor Dostoyevsky
and Richard Wagner tried
their luck at the tables.

To the south of the town
centre stands **Schloss Biebrich**, where the counts von
Nassau-Usingen resided until
the early 19th century, when
they moved to the newly built
palace in the town centre.
The Schloss was built in
stages during the 18th century. The north pavilion was
built first, in 1700, followed
nine years later by the south
pavilion. The wings, which
join the two pavilions, and
the central rotunda were
added during the first two
decades of the 18th century.
Finally, the two external
wings were added in 1734–44,
creating an overall horseshoe
layout. The interior is richly
furnished, predominantly in
Baroque-Rococo style.

On the northern outskirts of
the town is a large hill, the
Neroberg, whose summit can
be reached by funicular railway. At the top is the so-
called **Griechische Kapelle**
(Greek chapel). Built in 1847–
55 by Philipp Hoffmann, it
served as a mausoleum for
Princess Elisabeth von Nassau,
the niece of Alexander I Tsar of
Russia, who died young.

The attractive façade of Hessisches Staatstheater in Wiesbaden

The ornate Gothic portal of Pfarrkirche St Valentin, in Kiedrich

Kiedrich ⑭

Road map B5. 🏠 *3,400.* 🚉
ℹ️ *Markstr. 27 (06123-90 50 11).*

The earliest recorded mention of Kiedrich was in the mid-10th century, in a document produced by the Archbishop Friedrich of Mainz. One of the town's main attractions is the **Pfarrkirche St Valentin**, a gem of Gothic architecture. The church was built in stages, beginning with the main hall (1380–90). The west tower was added in the early 15th century and the light, lofty choir in 1451–81. Some time later the central nave was raised to the level of the choir, creating a row of galleries above the aisles, and at the same time the magnificent star vaults were created. The whole project was financed from donations made by countless pilgrims who came to pray to the relics of St Valentine, kept here since 1454. A statue of the saint adorns the western portal. The early 15th-century tympanum depicts the *Annunciation* (on the left) and the *Coronation of the Virgin Mary* (on the right); above is an image of *God the Father giving His Blessing,* with two archangels playing musical instruments. Inside, the church harbours an incredible wealth of ancient art treasures. The high altar and St Catherine's altar in the south aisle date from the late-Renaissance period. The magnificent Gothic stalls were created in 1510, while the church organ is one of the oldest in Germany, with pipes made in 1310. Next to the parish church stands a late-Gothic, two-storey funeral chapel built in 1445.

Kiedrich has several interesting old mansion houses, such as the Schwalbacher Hof (1732). The **Rathaus** (town hall) is evocative of the late-Gothic style, although it was built much later (1585–6).

Environs

Five km (3 miles) west of Kiedrich, in Oestrich, is **Kloster Eberbach**, a former Cistercian abbey. This vast complex, built between the 12th and 14th centuries, was once home to nearly 300 monks and is one of the best-preserved medieval monasteries in Germany. The church interior provided the setting for some of the scenes in the film *The Name of the Rose*, based on the novel by Umberto Eco. The Cistercians used to have their own vineyards here, and today the abbey buildings are used by the Hessian Wine Co-operative to press, ferment, store and sell Eberbacher Steinberg, a famous white Rheingau wine.

A short way to the west, in **Winkel**, stands the Baroque castle of Reichardshausen, which in the early 19th century was the home of Princess Luise von Nassau.

🏰 **Kloster Eberbach** *Tel* (06723) 91 78 11. 🕐 *Apr–Oct: 10am–6pm daily; Nov–Mar: 11am–5pm daily.* 🚫 *24, 25, 31 December, Carnival Mon.* 🅿️

Rüdesheim ⑮

Road map B5. 🏠 *10,000.* 🚉
ℹ️ *Geisenheimerstr. 22 (06722-194 33).* 🎆 *Fireworks (Jul), Weinfest (Aug).*

Rüdesheim, enjoying a picturesque location on the banks of the Rhine, has a long history going back to Roman times. The town is famous for its main street, the **Drosselgasse**, which is lined with countless wine bars and shops. There are also the remains of three castles: the **Boosenburg**, the **Vorderburg** and the 12th-century **Brömserburg**, which also houses a wine museum.

Rüdesheim also has several historic mansions, including the half-timbered Brömserhof (1559) with a collection of musical instruments, and the early 16th-century Klunkhardshof. Above the town towers the **Niederwalddenkmal**, a statue of Germania, 10.5 m (34 ft) high, built to commemorate victory in the Franco-Prussian War of 1870–71, which resulted in German unification. The monument affords excellent views of Bingen and the Rhine valley.

Gabled and half-timbered houses in Drosselgasse, in Rüdesheim

Frankfurt am Main ⑯

Frankfurt, nicknamed "Mainhattan" and "Chicago am Main" because of its skyscrapers, is one of the main economic and cultural centres of both Germany and Europe. The headquarters of many major banks and newspaper publishers are based here, including those of the *Frankfurter Allgemeine Zeitung*, one of Europe's most influential newspapers. The city's International Book Fair is the world's largest event of its kind. Goethe was born in Frankfurt, and the Johann-Wolfgang-Goethe-Universität is one of Germany's most famous universities. The city also boasts magnificent art collections.

The Neo-Renaissance façade of the Alte Oper

🎭 Alte Oper

Opernplatz 8. *Tel* (069) 134 04 00.
The monumental old opera house stands near the Stock Exchange. Built in 1872–80, it was completely burned down during World War II. Subsequently rebuilt, it is today used as a conference centre. Its façade and decorations are a fine imitation of the Italian Renaissance style.

🏛 Eschenheimer Turm

Große Eschenheimer Straße
The Eschenheimer Turm, at the corner of Hochstraße, presents a silhouette typical of old Frankfurt. A relic of the medieval town's fortifications, it was designed by Klaus Mengoz; construction began in 1400 and was completed in 1428 by Madern Gerthener. The façade of the tower features many attractive bay windows; it also has two reliefs depicting eagles, the symbol of the German empire and the city of Frankfurt.

Putti with model ship, at the front of the Börse

🏛 Börse

Börsenplatz.
According to historical records, local merchants founded the town's first Stock Exchange in 1558. The new building, designed by Heinrich Burnitz and Oskar Sommer, was erected in 1864–79. It has been used again by stockbrokers since 1957, and is open to the public. Like the old opera house, the stock exchange is designed in Neo-Renaissance style.

🏛 Hauptwache

An der Hauptwache.
Built in 1730, the Hauptwache was originally a guardhouse. Later it was turned into a prison. Dismantled stone by stone during the construction of the town's underground system, it was reassembled in its original form following the completion of the project. Since 1904 the Hauptwache has been a chic café and a popular meeting place.

🏛 Goethehaus

Großer Hirschgraben 23.
Tel (069) 13 88 00. ◻ 10am–6pm Mon–Sat, 10am–5:30pm Sun. 🎫
www.goethehaus-frankfurt.de
Southwest of the Hauptwache is Johann Wolfgang Goethe's family home. The great German poet, novelist and dramatist was born here on 28 August 1749. The house, along with many other buildings in Frankfurt, was totally destroyed in World War II, but later lovingly restored. Its interior was reconstructed to represent the style typical of the mid- to late- 18th century. Goethe lived in this house until 1775, when he moved to Weimar. The desk at which he wrote his early works, including the first versions of *Götz von Berlichingen* (1771) and *Egmont* (1774), has been preserved.

The adjacent building now houses the Goethemuseum. Opened in 1997, the museum recreates the atmosphere of the 1750–1830 period, and holds a collection of items related to the writer. There is an excellent library, which contains some of his writings.

The distinctive Neo-Classical rotunda of the Paulskirche

Portal of the Goethehaus, with the ancestral family crest

🏛 Paulskirche

Paulsplatz. **Tel** (069) 21 23 85 89.
⬜ 10am–5pm daily.

The distinctive Neo-Classical rotunda of the church was begun in 1786 but not completed until 1833, due to continuous hostilities with France. Today, however, this building is no longer thought of, or indeed used as, a church. After the first, albeit ill-fated, German National Assembly met here following the revolutionary upheavals of 1848–9, the church became a symbol of republican and liberal Germany. The Paulskirche now serves as a venue for many important events. Each year the awards ceremony for the prestigious German Publishers' Peace Prize takes place here.

🏛 Römerberg

Located in the centre of Frankfurt's old town, this square contains the Gerechtigkeitsbrunnen (fountain of justice). Its highlight, however, is the **Römer** (literally the Roman). So-called after the remains of ancient settlements, it is a complex of 15th- to 18th-century houses, including the Altes Rathaus (old town hall), which were rebuilt after World War II. Opposite is a group of half-timbered houses, commonly referred to as Ostzeile. The Steinernes Haus

VISITORS' CHECKLIST

Road map C5. 🏘 660,000. ℹ️ *Hauptbahnhof (069-21 23 88 00); Römerberg 27 (069-21 23 88 00).* 🎭 *Dippemesse (spring, autumn), Wäldchestag (Whitsun), Kunsthandwerk Heute (May/Jun), Mainfest (Aug), Book Fair (Oct), Christkindlmarkt (Dec).* **www**.frankfurt.de

(stone house) was originally built in 1464 for a Cologne silk merchant. Recently reconstructed, it is now the home of the Frankfurter Kunstverein (artists' league).

The Ostzeile on the Römerberg, one of the symbols of Frankfurt

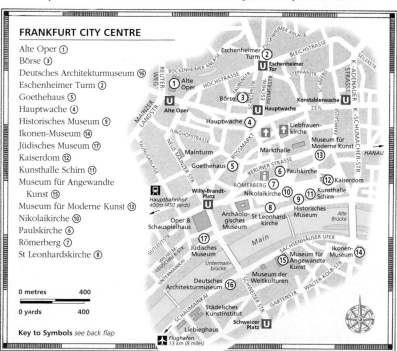

FRANKFURT CITY CENTRE

0 metres 400
0 yards 400

Key to Symbols see back flap

🏛 Jüdisches Museum

Untermainkai 14–15. *Tel* (069) 21 23 50 00. ⬜ 10am–5pm Tue–Sun, 10am–8pm Wed. 🖼

The Jewish community of Frankfurt was the second largest in Germany, after that of Berlin. This museum, in the former Rothschild Palace, documents the rich cultural heritage of Frankfurt's Jews.

⛪ St Leonhardskirche

Alte Mainzer Gasse.

Close to the banks of the Main stands the church of St Leonhard, a fine example of Gothic and Romanesque architecture. A five-naved hall-church with an elongated choir, it was built in stages in the 13th and 15th centuries. Inside are many treasures, including at the front of the main nave a copy of Leonardo da Vinci's *Last Supper* by Hans Holbein the Elder, from 1501. Next to it is St Mary's altar, created by master craftsmen from Antwerp in 1515–20. On the north wall of the choir visitors can see a fresco depicting the *Tree of Life and the Apostles* (1536) by Hans Dietz.

🏛 Historisches Museum

Saalgasse 19. *Tel* (069) 21 23 55 99. ⬜ 10am–5pm Tue, Thu–Sun, 10am–8pm Wed. 🖼

The new building housing the history museum was finished in 1972. The museum has an interesting display of items relating to Frankfurt's history, including a fascinating model of the medieval town, a collection of local prehistoric finds and several decorative

The early-Gothic Alte Nikolaikirche, in Frankfurt's Römerberg

architectural fragments from buildings that were destroyed during World War II.

The adjacent building is the Saalhof, which dates back to the time of the Emperor Friedrich I Barbarossa (1122–90). In 1333, the building passed into private hands and from then on it frequently changed its appearance.

⛪ Alte Nikolaikirche

Römerberg.

The twin-naved church of St Nicholas, also known as Alte Nikolaikirche, was consecrated in 1290. Used as a court church until the late 15th century, it now serves a Lutheran congregation. Popular attractions are its many statues of St Nicholas (Santa Claus) and the 40-bell carillon, which twice a day plays German folk songs.

🏛 Kunsthalle Schirn

Römerberg 6. *Tel* (069) 299 88 211. ⬜ 10am–7pm Fri–Sun & Tue, 10am–10pm Wed & Thu. 🖼

One of Europe's most prestigious exhibition buildings, the Kunsthalle opened in 1986. It hosts temporary art exhibitions featuring archaeological themes and the work of old masters and contemporary artists.

⛪ Kaiserdom

Domplatz 14. *Tel* (069) 297 03 20. ⬜ 9am–noon, 2:30–6pm Mon–Fri. **Dommuseum** *Tel* (069) 13 37 61 86. ⬜ 10am–5pm Tue–Fri, 11am–5pm Sat & Sun.

Near the archaeological park, where the ruins of a Carolingian fortress have been unearthed, stands the imperial cathedral, used for the coronation of German kings from 1356, and of Holy Roman Emperors from 1562. The cathedral, dedicated to St Bartholomew and Charlemagne, was built during the 13th, 14th and 15th centuries, on the site of a Carolingian chapel. It has several priceless masterpieces of Gothic art, including the magnificent 15th-century Maria-Schlaf-Altar and a high altar dating from the second half of the 15th century. The choir has original 14th-century stalls; above these there is a fresco painted in 1427 which depicts scenes from the life of the cathedral's patron saint, Bartholomew.

The Dom's huge tower affords some magnificent views of the town. While in the cloisters is the Dommuseum which has an interesting collection of liturgical objects, sacred art and precious artifacts.

🏛 Museum für Moderne Kunst

Domstraße 10. *Tel* (069) 21 23 04 47. ⬜ 10am–5pm Tue & Thu–Sun, 10am–8pm Wed. 🖼

The modern art museum occupies a building that looks like a slice of cake. It was designed by Hans Hollein in 1989–92. The museum's collection represents all the major artistic trends from the 1960s until the present day, and includes works by Roy Lichtenstein, Andy Warhol

The magnificent late-Gothic high altar in the Kaiserdom

For hotels and restaurants in this region see pp508–10 and pp547–8

Hollein's modern design, housing the Museum für Moderne Kunst

and Claes Oldenburg. Temporary exhibitions held here focus on multi-media shows, incorporating photography and video art.

⛪ Ikonen-Museum

Brückenstraße 3–7. **Tel** (069) 21 23 62 62. ◯ 10am–5pm Tue–Sun, 10am–8pm Wed. 🖼

The museum of icons holds an extensive collection of Russian-Orthodox icons from the 16th–19th centuries. It is housed in the Deutschordenshaus, originally built in 1709–15 by Maximilian von Welsch for the Order of the Teutonic Knights. The present building is a faithful copy of the earlier Baroque three-wing structure destroyed in World War II. Inside is the 14th-century Teutonic Church of St Mary, with original altars and 14th- to 17th-century wall paintings.

🏛 Museum für Angewandte Kunst

Schaumainkai 17. **Tel** (069) 21 23 40 37. ◯ 10am–5pm Tue–Sun, 10am–9pm Wed.

The Museum of Applied Arts was opened in 1983, in a building designed by Richard Meier. He used a Biedermeier house, the Villa Metzler, and added a modern wing. The museum has a collection of some 30,000 objects of applied art from Europe and Asia.

Nearby, in a villa with a large garden in Schaumainkai, is the small but fascinating Museum der Weltkulturen (ethnography museum), which is well worth a visit.

🏛 Deutsches Architekturmuseum

Schaumainkai 43. **Tel** (069) 21 23 88 44. ◯ 11am–6pm Tue–Sun, 11am–8pm Wed. 🖼

One of the most interesting museums in the Schaumainkai complex is undoubtedly the museum of architecture, opened in 1984 in an avant-garde building designed by Oswald Mathias Ungers. The museum has a permanent collection as well as temporary exhibitions concentrating mainly on developments in 20th-century architecture.

Nearby, at No 41 Schaumainkai, is the Deutsches Filmmuseum, which holds documents and objects relating to the art of film-making and the development of film technology. The museum has its own cinema, which shows old and often long-forgotten films.

⛪ Liebieghaus

Schaumainkai 71. **Tel** (069) 21 23 86 15. ◯ 10am–5pm Tue & Thu–Sun, 10am–8pm Wed. 🖼

The Liebieghaus was built in 1896 for the Czech industrialist Baron Heinrich Liebieg. Today it houses a museum of sculpture, with works ranging from antiquity through to Mannerism, Baroque and Rococo. The museum also has superb examples of ancient Egyptian and Far Eastern art, as well as works from the Middle Ages and the Renaissance. Its highlights are the works of Neo-Classical masters such as Antonio Canova, Bertel Thorwaldsen and Johann Heinrich Dannecker.

The Liebieghaus, home of the museum of sculpture

🏛 Naturmuseum Senckenberg

Senckenberganlage 25. **Tel** (069) 754 20. ◯ 9am–5pm Mon, Tue, Thu & Fri, 9am–8pm Wed, 9am–6pm Sat & Sun. 🖼

This museum, near the university, is one of the best natural history museums in Germany. Besides a vast collection of plants and animals, including dinosaur skeletons, it contains human and animal mummies from Egypt.

Environs

Hanau, 30 km (19 miles) east of Frankfurt, is the birthplace of the brothers Wilhelm and Jakob Grimm. An exhibition devoted to their lives and work is held at the local history museum, in Philippsruhe, a Baroque palace.

The Deutsches Architekturmuseum, in Schaumainkai

Frankfurt – Städelsches Kunstinstitut

The founder of this excellent museum, the banker Johann Friedrich Städel, bequeathed his art collection to the town in 1815. Since then, the museum has grown through acquisitions and donations, and now contains many masterpieces from seven centuries of European art. It moved to a Neo-Renaissance building in 1878, on the picturesque "museum embankment" by the Main. In the 1920s it acquired the Hohenzollern collection from Sigmaringen. The building gained a new wing in 1990 (designer Gustav Peichl), and was renovated in 1995–9.

Ideal Portrait of a Woman (c.1480)
Simonetta Vespucci, mistress of Giuliano Medici, is the subject of this painting by Sandro Botticelli. Her pendant belonged at the time to the Medici collection.

Ecce Homo
Members of the family who commissioned this painting from Hieronymus Bosch also originally figured in it, but they were later painted over and now only a few figures are partially visible.

First floor

★ Lucca Madonna
This small painting by Jan van Eyck, which evokes an intimate and intensely private atmosphere, takes its name from its former owner, Charles Ludwig de Bourbon, Duke of Lucca.

KEY

- 19th-century paintings
- 20th-century paintings
- German, Dutch and Flemish 17th- and 18th-century paintings
- Italian, French and Spanish 17th- and 18th-century paintings
- German and Dutch 14th–16th-century paintings
- Italian 14th–16th-century paintings

Around 100,000 prints and drawings, dating from the 14th century to the present day and making up one of Germany's most valuable collections, are exhibited in this exhibition hall.

Main entrance

Library

★ **The Geographer** (1669)
Although the signature on the painting is not genuine, there is no doubt that this picture, depicting a scholar at work, is the work of Jan Vermeer van Delft.

VISITORS' CHECKLIST

Schaumainkai 63.
Tel (069) 605 09 80.
www.staedelmuseum.de
⬜ 10am–7pm Tue–Sun, 10am–9pm Wed & Thu. 🎟 (free Tue.) ♿ 🏪 📷 ✏

Second floor

★ **Blinding of Samson** (1636)
Rembrandt's dramatic painting depicts the violent blinding of Samson by the Philistines after Delilah cut off his hair.

GALLERY GUIDE
The ground floor of the building is used for changing exhibitions of prints and drawings, as well as a book store and a museum shop. The first floor is devoted to 19th- and 20th-century art and the second floor to the Old Masters.

Pilgrimage to the Isle of Cythera (c.1710)
Jean-Antoine Watteau painted three pictures on this theme, inspired by Dancourt's play The Three Sisters. The museum holds the earliest of the three, which shows a Flemish influence.

Ground floor

Orchestra Players (1870–74)
Edgar Degas, not completely satisfied with his painting, retrieved it from its owner. In 1874, he cropped it on three sides, added a bit at the top and repainted the entire painting.

STAR EXHIBITS

★ Lucca Madonna

★ Blinding of Samson

★ The Geographer

Darmstadt ⑰

Road map C5. 🏰 *138,000.* 🚉
🛈 *Luisencenter, Luisenplatz 5
(06151-951 50 13); for tickets only
(06151-27 99 995).* 🎪 *Frühlingfest
(Mar/Apr), Schlossgrabenfest (May),
Heinerfest (early Jul), Herbstfest (Oct).*

The earliest historical records
of Darmstadt, which was
probably named after Dari-
mund, a Frankonian settler,
date from the 12th century.
Until 1479, the castle and the
town belonged to the Counts
von Katzenelnbogen, and
later to Hessian landgraves. In
1567, the Landgraves von
Hessen-Darmstadt chose
Darmstadt as their residence,
and they continued to live
here until 1918.

To the north of the old
town stands the **Residenzschloss**, initially a ducal
palace, and from 1806 residence of the Landgraves von
Hessen-Darmstadt. The Re-
naissance-Baroque complex is
centred around three courtyards. The earlier medieval
castle, which stood on the
same site, burned down in
1546. The present palace was
created in stages, with its
earliest parts, the Renaissance
wings, dating from 1567–97.
The Glockenbau has a 35-bell
carillon which can be heard
every half hour; it was completed after the Thirty Years'
War, in 1663. Further modifications, planned in 1715–30,
were never completed. Two

Baroque wings, the so-called
Neubau or Neuschloss (new
castle), surround older buildings to the south and west.
The Schloss was bombed in
World War II and subsequently rebuilt. Today it houses the
provincial and university
library, while the Glockenbau
is home to the fascinating
Schlossmuseum (castle
museum). As well as a
splendid collection of
coaches and furniture,
it contains the famous
Darmstädter Madonna
(1526), by Holbein.
Also worth seeing,
the late-Renaissance
Rathaus (town hall),
built in 1588–90, sur-
vived World War II.
The 15th-century choir
of the **Stadtkirche** has
an enormous monu-
ment (1587) to Magda-
lena zur Lippe, first
wife of Landgrave
Georg I the Pious. To
the southwest of the
Stadtkirche stands the
Altes Pädagog, built
in 1629 as an educa-
tional establishment.

To the north of the Schloss
is the **Hessisches Landesmuseum** (regional museum of
Hesse), erected in 1892–
1905. Its collection includes
artifacts dating from the Roman era to the 20th century.
The museum also has an
excellent natural history section, whose exhibits include
the impressive skeleton of a

mammoth as well as birds of
every species native to
southern Hesse. Set in the park
behind the museum is the
Baroque Prinz-Georg-Palais
(1710), which houses the
**Großherzoglich-Hessische
Porzellansammlung**, an
extensive porcelain collection.

The last Grand Duke of
Hesse, Ernst Ludwig, was
an important patron of the
Jugendstil, the German
Art Nouveau movement.
He initiated the build-
ing of an exhibition
and residential com-
plex, the **Mathilden-
höhe**, which was
established in 1901 in
the grounds of the
former ducal park, to
serve the existing
artists' colony led by
Joseph Maria Olbrich.
Olbrich designed the
Ernst-Ludwig-Haus,
which now houses
the **Museum Künst-
lerkolonie**, an exhi-
bition space for the
colony's artists, as
well as the famous
Hochzeitsturm
(wedding tower), erected in
1907–8 to celebrate the Grand
Duke's wedding. The
Behrens-Haus, designed by
the Hamburg architect Peter
Behrens, is sober in contrast.
The Orthodox church of **St
Mary Magdalene** was built in
1897–9 by the Russian architect Leonti Nikolayevich
Benois, in honour of Alice,
wife of the last tsar of Russia
and sister of Ernst Ludwig.

**Statue on the door
of the Behrens-
Haus in Darmstadt**

🏛 **Schlossmuseum**
Residenzschloss, Marktplatz 15.
Tel (06151) 240 35. 🕐 10am–1pm
& 2–5pm Mon–Thu, 10am–1pm Sat
& Sun.

🏛 **Hessisches
Landesmuseum**
Friedensplatz 1. **Tel** (06151) 16 57
03. 🕐 10am–5pm Tue & Thu–Sat,
10am–8pm Wed, 11am–5pm Sun. 🏷

🏛 **Museum
Künstlerkolonie**
Olbrichweg/Bauhausweg. **Tel** (06151)
13 33 85. 🕐 10am–6pm Tue–Sun. 🏷

🏛 **Großherzoglich-
Hessische Porzellan-
sammlung**
Schlossgartenstr. 10. **Tel** (06151) 71
32 33. 🕐 10am–1pm & 2–5pm
Mon–Thu, 10am–1pm Sat & Sun.

Hochzeitsturm and Orthodox Church in Mathildenhöhe, Darmstadt

The Carolingian Torhalle (gate-house) of the Kloster (abbey) in Lorsch

Lorsch ⑱

Road map B5. 🏛 *10,700.* ℹ
Nibelungenstr. 41 (06251-707 99 16).

This small town is mainly known for the **Kloster**, a Benedictine abbey first founded in 764 by Chrodegang of Metz and one of the most important cultural and intellectual centres in Europe in the Carolingian era. It reached the peak of its power in the 8th–13th centuries, before being sold to the Archbishop of Mainz in 1232. The Benedictines were forced to leave, and in their place the Cistercians arrived. The monastery was dissolved during the Reformation, and in 1621 the Spanish Army destroyed and plundered the greater part of the complex.

Fragments of the 13th-century nave, the towers and the gate-house, dating from c.790, are all that has survived. The original 8th-century church, a basilica without transept, burned down in 1090 and was rebuilt in the 12th century. The original crypt is the burial place of Ludwig II the German, the first ruler of the Eastern Franks. The **Torhalle** (gate-house) is one of the most important architectural remains of the Carolingian period, and it was listed as a UNESCO World Heritage Site in 1991. Its lower section is made up of three arcades, equal in height and width, modelled on Roman triumphal arches. The first-floor quarters above were probably used as a guest room or courtroom, and from the 14th century they served as a chapel. Remains of the original wall paintings are still visible here. The façade is decorated with red and white stone mosaics, which were inspired by Franco-Merovingian art. The vertical divides, created by pilasters and entablature, are copies of ancient designs – an architectural feature typical of the Carolingian Renaissance. The chapel's high roof and vaults date from the 14th century.

Michelstadt ⑲

Road map B5. 🏛 *16,000.*
ℹ *Marktplatz 1 (06061-194 33).*
🎪 *Bienenmarkt (Whitsun).*

Michelstadt, set among the hills of the Odenwald, is first mentioned in historical records in 741. From the 13th century the town belonged to the von Erbach family (the future Counts von Erbach).

The town has preserved many historic half-timbered houses and presents a typical image of medieval Germany. The 16th-century **Kellerei** is built around the remains of an earlier castle dating from 970. It now houses a regional museum. The sight most popular with photographers is the half-timbered **Rathaus** (town hall), dating from 1484, with its three towers and an open ground-floor gallery. Nearby stands the late-Gothic, 15th-century **Pfarrkirche St Michael** (parish church of St Michael). Inside are some interesting epitaphs including the double tombstone of Philipp I and Georg I, dating from the late 15th century. A true rarity is the 18th-century **synagogue**, which escaped being burned by the National Socialists in 1938.

In the Steinbach district of Michelstadt stands the **Einhardsbasilika**, a church dating from around 821. The first church built on this site, at the initiative of Einhard, a courtier of Charlemagne, was a small, pillared and vaulted basilica with a short choir ending with a rounded apse. Under the eastern section is a crypt. The parts which remain to this day include the main nave, the north aisle with an apse and the crypt which holds precious religious relics.

Environs
In **Fürstenau**, situated about 1 km (0.6 mile) northwest of Michelstadt, is a beautiful complex including the Altschloss (old palace), remodelled from a medieval castle, the Neuschloss (new palace), dating from 1810, the park and its garden pavilions.

Erbach, 5 km (3miles) south of Michelstadt, became famous as a centre for the art of ivory carving. In No. 1 Otto-Glenz-Straße is the Deutsches Elfenbeinmuseum (German ivory museum), which is devoted to this craft. Other attractions in this town include the overbearing Baroque Schloss (castle) and its interesting art collection.

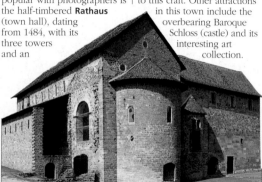

The Carolingian Einhardsbasilika in Michelstadt-Steinbach

NORTH RHINE–WESTPHALIA

*O*riginally consisting of two distinct provinces with somewhat diverging histories, the region of North Rhine-Westphalia today has its own strong identity. It encompasses the vast valley of the Ruhr river, rich in mineral deposits, where over the past 200 years huge conurbations have developed, comprising dozens of industrial cities that are gradually merging into one another.

As a province, the North Rhineland, situated along the lower Rhine valley, goes back to Roman times. In the Middle Ages most of this area was ruled by the Bishops of Köln. The North Rhineland cities grew and prospered thanks to their trade links, and in the 19th century they became major centres of mining and heavy industry.

Westphalia forms the eastern part of the land. Once a Saxon territory, its history was often intertwined with that of the Rhineland. Only its western end has been heavily industrialized.

North Rhine-Westphalia is not the largest of the German regions, but with a population of nearly 18 million it is the most heavily populated one. It is often thought that the region, and in particular the heavily industrialized Ruhr valley, has little to offer to its visitors, but this is a mistaken belief. Its splendid past has left many priceless historic monuments and more recently, thanks to great investment, its industrial cities have transformed themselves into attractive cultural centres.

The history of towns such as Bonn, Aachen, Cologne (Köln) and Xanten goes back to Roman times, and they have preserved much of their ancient heritage to this day. Evidence of Romanesque art, which flourished in the Rhineland, is today apparent in numerous impressive abbeys dotted throughout the region and in the churches of Cologne, which also boasts the colossal Gothic Dom.

Much of North Rhine-Westphalia is rural, and the region offers thousands of kilometres of tracks for walking in the Teutoburg Forest and in the Northern Eifel mountains, as well as splendid conditions for watersports and fishing in the Sauerland. It also has surprisingly good ski slopes, such as in the Rothaar Mountains.

A typical lowland landscape near Xanten, in the Rhineland

◁ The imposing Gothic Kölner Dom (Cologne cathedral), lit up at night

Exploring North Rhine-Westphalia

Despite being heavily industrialized, the land of North Rhine-Westphalia has many attractions for visitors. At least two days should be set aside to admire the historic treasures in Cologne, while those who prefer museums – or shopping – might allocate more time for Düsseldorf. The towns of Bonn, Aachen and Münster should also feature on every visitor's schedule. The best areas for rest and relaxation are the mountain ranges of the Eifel and the Teutoburg Forest, ideally suited for walking and cycling holidays.

SEE ALSO

- *Where to Stay* p510–12
- *Where to Eat* pp549–51

Burg Altena in the Sauerland

SIGHTS AT A GLANCE

Aachen pp394–5 **15**
Altenberg **13**
Bielefeld **28**
Bonn pp408–9 **18**
Brühl **17**
Cologne (Köln) pp398–405 **14**
Dormagen **11**
Dortmund **5**
Duisburg **7**
Düsseldorf pp392–3 **9**
Essen **6**
Hagen **21**
Höxter **25**
Kleve **3**
Königswinter **19**
Lemgo **26**
Minden **29**
Münster pp386–7 **1**
Neuss **10**
Northern Eifel **16**
Paderborn **24**
Sauerland **22**
Siegen **20**
Soest **23**
Solingen **12**
Teutoburger Wald (Teutoburg Forest) **27**
Wuppertal **8**
Xanten **4**

Tours

Münsterland **2**

GETTING AROUND

There are international airports at Düsseldorf, Köln–Bonn (Konrad-Adenauer-Flughafen) and at Münster–Osnabrück. North Rhine-Westphalia has the highest density of motorways anywhere in Germany, making it easy to travel between cities, and providing links with other German regions, Belgium and the Netherlands.

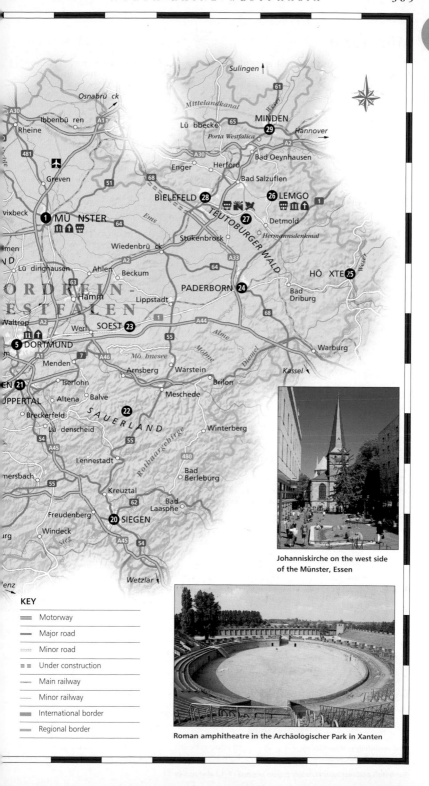

Johanniskirche on the west side
of the Münster, Essen

Roman amphitheatre in the Archäologischer Park in Xanten

KEY

▬▬ Motorway

▬ Major road

▭▭▭ Minor road

= = Under construction

⊶⊶⊶ Main railway

— Minor railway

▬▬ International border

▬ Regional border

Münster ❶

Münster and its surroundings were already inhabited in Roman times, but its history proper started in the 9th century, with the establishment of a bishopric. Town status was granted in 1137, and in the 13th century Münster joined the Hanseatic League. In 1648 the Westphalian Peace Treaty was signed here, ending the Thirty Years' War. Münster's Westfälische Wilhelms-Universität (1773) is one of Germany's largest universities. World War II saw 90 percent of the old town laid to ruins, but most of it has now been rebuilt.

⚅ Erbdrostenhof
Salzstraße 38. ◐ *Closed to the public.*
This beautiful mansion was skilfully positioned diagonally across a corner site. Designed by Johann Conrad Schlaun, it was built in 1753–7, and despite destruction in World War II it still enchants with its "wavy", late-Baroque façade.

⚅ Rathaus
Prinzipalmarkt. **Friedenssaal**
Tel (0251) 492 27 24.
◯ *10am–5pm Tue–Fri, 10am–4pm Sat & Sun.* ◐ *25 Dec.* 🎟
The imposing Gothic town hall, the pride of Münster, was almost completely destroyed during World War II. After its splendid reconstruction, it is again a major draw for visitors. The only parts that had escaped destruction were the furnishings of the main council chamber, which have been returned to their rightful place after the rebuilding work. It

Houses on Prinzipalmarkt, reconstructed in the medieval style

was here that on 15 May 1648 part of the Westphalian Treaty was signed, ending the Thirty Years' War.

⛪ Lambertikirche
Prinzipalmarkt.
St Lamberti is an excellent example of the hall-churches characteristic of Westphalia. It was built in 1375–1450, but the openwork finial of the tower dates from 1887. The cages hanging on the tower held the bodies of the leading Anabaptists, following the crushing of their commune in 1536. It is also worth taking a look at the relief depicting the *Tree of Jesse*, above the southwest entrance, and the figures of the apostles (c.1600) by Johann Koess.

⚅ Dom St Paulus
Domplatz. **Domkammer**
◯ *11am–4pm Tue–Sun.* 🎟
The most precious historic relic in Münster is undeniably

The beautifully restored façade of the late-Gothic Rathaus

its massive St Paulus' cathedral, built in 1225–65 and representing a transitional style between late-Romanesque and early-Gothic. The vast basilica has two transepts, two choirs and a couple of massive towers at the western end. The northern cloister was added in the 14th century, and in the 16th–17th centuries the passage that runs around the presbytery acquired a ring of chapels. In the vestibule stands a group of 13th-century sculptures. Especially worth seeing are the two altars by Gerhard Gröninger (1st half of the 17th century), the early 16th-century stained-glass windows brought here from Marienfeld, the Gothic candelabra and monuments of many bishops. The cathedral's best-known treasure is the astronomical clock (1540), with paintings by Ludger tom Ring the Elder and sculptures by Johann Brabender. At noon, moving figures show the Magi paying tribute to the infant Jesus to the sounds of the carillon.

🏛 Westfälisches Landesmuseum für Kunst und Kulturgeschichte
Domplatz 10. **Tel** (0251) 590 701.
◯ *10am–6pm Tue–Sun.*
The Westphalian regional museum specializes mainly in Gothic art, with a large collection of sculptures and altars rescued in World War II. Its most noteworthy exhibits include the works by Heinrich and Johann Brabender. The upstairs galleries show works by Conrad von Soest and the tom Ring family. Contemporary art is represented by, among others, August Macke's work.

Figure of a saint in Dom St Paulus

⛪ Überwasserkirche
Überwasserkirchplatz.
The Liebfrauenkirche (Church of Our Lady) is popularly named Überwasserkirche (church above the water), after the district on the banks

The Baroque-Classical Schloss, residence of Münster's prince-bishops

of the tiny Aa river. This Gothic edifice was built in c.1340–46, on the site of a Romanesque Benedictine church. Inside are 16th-century votive paintings by Ludger and Hermann tom Ring.

♣ Residenzschloss
Schlossplatz 2.
This beautiful Baroque residence was built in 1767–87, by Prince-Bishop Maximilian Friedrich. It was designed by Johann Conrad Schlaun, a local master of Baroque architecture. Maximilian Friedrich started the redevelopment of Münster in the northern Baroque style. On his initiative the town acquired a large park, part of which was transformed into a botanical garden in 1803. After World War II, the castle was rebuilt and became the headquarters of Münster university.

🏛 Museum für Lackkunst
Windthorststraße 26. **Tel** *(0251) 41 85 10.* ☐ *noon–8pm Tue, noon–6pm Wed–Sun & public holidays.* 🖼
This unique museum, devoted to lacquer ware, has a good collection with items from around the world and from different periods, making a visit to the museum a treat for those interested in this craft.

Watermill in the open-air museum in Mühlenhof

♙ Mühlenhof
Theo-Breider-Weg 1. **Tel** *(0251) 98 12 00.* ☐ *16 Mar–Oct: 10am–6pm daily; Nov–15 Mar: 1–4:30pm Mon–Sat, 11am–4:30pm Sun.* 🖼
This small but interesting open-air museum is situated on the banks of the picturesque Aasee, Münster's lake and main recreation area. Displayed are a number of rural dwellings with authentic furnishings and two mills (17th and 18th centuries).

♣ Drostenhof
Wolbeck, Am Steintor 5.
Southeast of the town, in Wolbeck (now part of the city), is an original Renaissance mansion from the mid-16th century. Its exquisite gatehouse leads into the courtyard of the mansion, which has original fireplaces, doors and ceiling paintings.

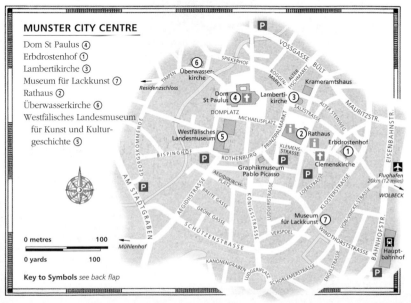

MUNSTER CITY CENTRE

Dom St Paulus ④
Erbdrostenhof ①
Lambertikirche ③
Museum für Lackkunst ⑦
Rathaus ②
Überwasserkirche ⑥
Westfälisches Landesmuseum für Kunst und Kulturgeschichte ⑤

0 metres   100
0 yards   100

Key to Symbols *see back flap*

Münsterland ❷

The region stretching in a narrow strip to the north of Münster is the land of horses and Wasserburgen (moated castles). The castles were surrounded by moats or built on islands to give their owners protection in the surrounding lowlands. Almost 50 Wasserburgen have survived, some converted into residences. Not all are open to visitors as most remain to this day in the hands of the family of the original owners. The best way to tour the flat Münsterland region is by car or bicycle.

Vischering ②
The magnificent Burg Vischering is one of the oldest and best-preserved castles in Westphalia. Founded in 1270, it was extended in the 16th and 17th centuries.

Schloss Raesfeld ⑤
The beautiful 17th-century castle has some original 14th-century elements. Particularly worth seeing is the castle chapel with its Baroque altar.

Havixbeck ①
Two interesting castles are near this small town: the Renaissance Haus Havixbeck and the Renaissance-Baroque Burg Hülshoff, birthplace of and museum to the 19th-century writer Annette von Droste-Hülshoff.

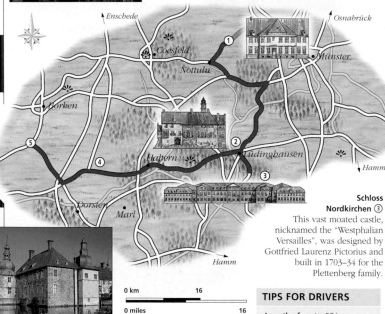

Enschede
Osnabrück
Coesfeld
Nottuln
Münster
Borken
Haltern
Lüdinghausen
Hamm
Dorsten
Marl
Hamm

Schloss Nordkirchen ③
This vast moated castle, nicknamed the "Westphalian Versailles", was designed by Gottfried Laurenz Pictorius and built in 1703–34 for the Plettenberg family.

Schloss Lembeck ④
In its present shape, the Lembeck castle complex is the result of Baroque remodelling, under the direction of Johann Conrad Schlaun. Nearby is a nature reserve.

0 km   16

0 miles   16

KEY

■ Suggested route

  Scenic route

═ Other road

═ River, lake

☀ Viewpoint

TIPS FOR DRIVERS

Length of route: 97 km (58 miles).

Stopping-off points: Every town has inns, and there is a hotel in Schloss Lembeck.

Suggestions: All castles are open to visitors Tuesday to Sunday, with the exception of Nordkirchen, which opens only at weekends.

Kleve (Cleves) ❸

Road map A3. 🏛 *50,000.* 🚆 ⛟
ℹ *Werftstr. 1 (02821-89 50 90).*

The town of Kleve is named after the high cliff, on which a castle was built in the 10th century. Around it a settlement developed, which became a town in 1242. It was ruled by the dukes of Kleve, whose ambitions were far greater than the size of their dominions and reached their peak in 1539, when Anne of Cleves married the English King Henry VIII.

During World War II Kleve lost most of its historic buildings. One that has survived to this day is the imposing Gothic church of the Assumption of the Virgin Mary, **St Mariä Himmelfahrt** (1341–1426). It has remains of the high altar, dating from 1510–13, with reliefs by Henrik Douvermann and Jakob Dericks, as well as beautiful monuments and epitaphs to the von Kleve dukes. Equally worth seeing is the former Franciscan **St Mariä Empfängnis**, a Gothic twin-nave hall-church from the first half of the 15th century. Its noteworthy features include the Gothic stalls (1474) and a magnificent Baroque pulpit (1698). The well-preserved ducal castle of **Schwanen-burg** was remodelled twice: in Gothic style in the late 15th century, and in Baroque style in 1636–66. Testifying to former splendour are the parks established in the mid-17th century by Johann Moritz von Nassau. The most beautiful of these is the **Tiergarten** (animal garden). **Haus Koek-koek**, located nearby, once belonged to the Romantic painter, Barend Cornalis Koekkoek, after whom it was named.

🏰 Schwanenburg
Am Schlossberg. **Tel** *(02821) 22 884.* ☐ *Apr–Oct: 11am–5pm daily; Nov–Apr: 11am–5pm Sat & Sun.* 📷

Environs
The suspension bridge across the Rhine – at 1,228 m (4,028 ft) the longest such structure in Germany – connects Kleve with **Emmerich**. Here it is worth visiting the Martinskirche, which is home to the exquisite, late-10th-century shrine of St Willibrod.

Twelve km (7 miles) to the southeast of Kleve lies the charming town of **Kalkar** which, in around 1500, was home to the famous Kalkar School specializing in wood-carving. The church of St Nicolai has superb furnishings dating from the same period.

Six km (4 miles) southeast stands **Moyland**, a moated castle. It houses a modern art collection, which belongs to the brothers von der Grinten and includes over 4,000 works by the artist Joseph Beuys.

Xanten ❹

Road map B4. 🏛 *19,500.* 🚆 ⛟
ℹ *Kurfürstenstr. 9 (02801-983 00).*

The history of Xanten goes back to the Romans, who founded the settlement of *Colonia Ulpia Traiana* near the local garrison. The present town, however, did not rise out of the ruins of the Roman town. It was established nearby, around the memorial church built on top of the grave

The Hafentempel in the Archäolo-gischer Park in Xanten

of the martyr St Viktor. It was named *ad sanctos* (by the saints), soon to be shortened to Xanten. A powerful town in the Middle Ages, Xanten also features in the Nibelung myth, and was said to be the birthplace of Siegfried.

Undoubtedly the most important historic building in the town is the **Dom St Viktor**, built on the graves of St Viktor and members of the Thebian Legion. The surviving Gothic cathedral dates from 1263–1517. It is worth taking a look at the Gothic sculptures standing by the pillars of the main nave, the shrine of St Victor (1129), the early-Gothic stalls (c.1240) and, above all, the exquisite Marienaltar by Henrik Douvermann. Equally fascinating are the collegial buildings and the cloister holding the tombs and epitaphs of the canons.

Xanten also has many pretty old houses, mainly clustered around the central market square. Another sight worth visiting is the **Klever Tor**, a magnificent double town-gate, dating from the late 4th century, in the northwest of the town. The **Archä-ologischer Park**, established in 1974 on the site of the Roman town, displays many reconstructed Roman public buildings including the impressive Hafentempel (harbour temple).

🪦 Archäologischer Park
Wardter Str. **Tel** *(02801) 29 99.* ☐ *Mar–Oct: 9am–6pm daily; Nov: 9am–5pm daily; Dec–Feb: 10am–4pm daily.* 📷

The Gothic Dom St Victor in Xanten

For hotels and restaurants in this region see pp510–12 and pp549–51

The Young Horses by Emil Nolde, in the Museum am Ostwall

Dortmund ❺

Road map B4. 🏠 600,000. 🚉 🚌
ℹ️ *Königswall 18A (0231-14 03 41).*
🎭 *Dortmund aller art (Aug), Dortmund à la carte (Jun), Hansetage (Nov).*

The large city of Dortmund is famous not only for its excellent beer and highly developed industry, but also for its more than 1,000 years of history. In the Middle Ages, the town grew rich through trade and joined the Hanseatic League; after a period of decline it flourished again in the 19th century.

A walk through the small old town will take visitors to the **Museum für Kunst-und Kulturgeschichte** (museum for art and cultural history) with displays of interiors from various periods, including Secessionist designs by Joseph Maria Olbrich. A short distance from here is the **Petrikirche**, a Gothic 14th-century hall-church, whose greatest attraction is its high altar (1521), the work of Gilles, a master from Antwerp. Also noteworthy is the former Dominican **Propsteikirche**, with its exquisite late-Gothic main altar. A shortcut across the market square and along Ostenhellweg takes the visitor to two more churches: the **Reinoldikirche** and the **Marienkirche**. The former,

Statue on Alter Markt, in Dortmund

dedicated to St Reinold, the patron saint of Dortmund, has an early-Gothic 13th-century main body and a late-Gothic, 15th-century presbytery. It includes many Gothic sculptures and furnishings. The second one, the church of St Mary, is a 12th-century Romanesque structure. It has a magnificent main altar, by Conrad von Soest (1415–20) and a statue of the Madonna (c.1230). The **Museum am Ostwall** has an excellent modern art collection.

🏛 **Museum für Kunst-und Kulturgeschichte**
Hansastr. 3. *Tel (0231) 502 55 22.* ⏰ *10am–5pm Tue, Wed, Fri, Sun, 10am–8pm Thu, noon–5pm Sat.* 🎟

🏛 **Museum am Ostwall**
Ostwall 7. *Tel (0231) 502 32 47.* ⏰ *as above.* 🎟

Environs
10 km (6 miles) northwest, in Waltrop, on the Dortmund-Ems Canal, is the Schiffshebewerk Henrichenburg, a hoist built in 1899 to lift ships.

Essen ❻

Road map B4. 🏠 600,000. 🚉
🚌 ℹ️ *Im Handelshof (am Hauptbahnhof 2) (0201-194 33).*
🎭 *Essen Original (Aug).*

It is hard to believe that this vast industrial metropolis has grown from a monastery, established in 852. The town owes its growth and promi-

nence to the Krupp family, who, over several generations from the mid-19th century, created the powerful German steel and arms industry.

The most important historic building in the town is the **Münster**, the former collegiate church of the canonesses. This unusual edifice consists of the 15th-century Gothic church of St John, an 11th-century atrium and the main church, which in turn has a Romanesque 11th-century frontage and a Gothic 14th– century main body. Without doubt the most precious object held by the church is the *Goldene Madonna*, a statue of the Virgin Mary with the Infant, made from sheet gold, probably c.980. The treasury has an outstanding collection of gold items from the Ottonian period.

Another important sight in Essen is the **Synagogue** built by Edmund Körner in 1911–13. The largest synagogue in Germany, it managed to outlast the Third Reich and is now a place of commemoration.

Visitors who are interested in 20th-century architecture should see the church of **St Engelbert** in Fischerstraße, designed by Dominikus Metzendorf (1934–6), the town-garden in **Margarethenhöhe** built from 1909 to a design by Georg Metzendorf, and the opera house designed by the Finnish architect, Alvar Aalto.

Essen has much to offer to modern art enthusiasts. The **Museum Folkwang** boasts an excellent collection of 20th-century paintings, mainly German Expressionists. It also has a graphic arts section.

The **Grugapark** is a large green area with botanical gardens, zoo and the Gruga-halle, where major concerts are held. To the south of the centre, on the banks of the Baldeneysee, stands **Villa Hügel**, which belonged to the Krupp family until 1945. Today interesting art exhibitions are frequently hosted here. Further south, in **Werden**, is the former Benedictine church of St Ludger, consisting of a 13th-century body preceded by a 10th-century imperial frontage. The treasury holds many precious

The grand Villa Hügel, former home of the Krupp family in Essen

objects including a bronze crucifix from around 1060.

⛫ Museum Folkwang

Goethestr. 41. **Tel** (0201) 884 53 14. ○ 10am–6pm Tue–Thu, Sat & Sun, 10am–midnight Fri. ● 1 Jan, Easter, 1 May, 24 & 31 Dec. ⬛

Environs

Visitors interested in technology should visit **Bochum**, which is also the seat of the excellent Ruhr-Universität. There are two excellent museums: the **Deutsches Bergbau-Museum** devoted to mining, and the **Eisenbahn-museum** (railway museum) in Dahlhausen. Both have world-class exhibits.

Duisburg ❼

Road map B4. 🏙 540,000. 🚉 🚋 ℹ Königstr. 86 (0203-285 44 11).

Duisburg, on the edge of the Ruhr region, underwent a period of rapid development in the 19th and 20th centuries. Once a small town, it became the world's largest inland harbour thanks to its location at the spot where the Ruhr flows into the Rhine.

The small old town was almost totally destroyed in World War II, but the 15th–century Gothic **Salvatorkirche** (church of St Saviour) has been rebuilt. Some of the town's greatest attractions are its museums. The **Wilhelm-Lehmbruck-Museum** focuses on the work of the sculptor Lehmbruck, who was born in Duisburg. The museum has an interesting collection of 20th–century sculptures, including works

by famous artists such as Salvador Dali, Henry Moore, Max Ernst, Emil Nolde and Joseph Beuys. Also worth visiting is the **Museum der Deutschen Binnenschifffahrt** with its collection of barges and inland waterway vessels. In the 16th century, Duisburg was the home of the famous geographer and cartographer Gerhard Mercator, whose collection of globes, maps and charts can now be seen in the **Kulture- und Stadthistorisches Museum**.

⛫ Wilhelm-Lehmbruck-Museum

Friedrich-Wilhelm-Str. 40. **Tel** (0203) 283 26 30. ○ 11am–5pm Tue–Sat, 10am–6pm Sun. ⬛

Environs

CentrO in **Oberhausen**, 14 km (9 miles) north of Duisburg, is the largest shopping and leisure complex in Europe.

Krefeld, 6 km (4 miles) southwest of Duisburg, has been a centre of silk fabric production from the 17th century, and the Deutsches Textilmuseum has over 20,000 exhibits, ranging from antiquity to the present day.

Wuppertal ❽

Road map B4. 🏙 380,000. 🚉 ℹ Elberfeld, Informationszentrum am Döppersberg (0202-194 33); Rathaus (0202-563 66 88).

Wuppertal, capital of the Bergisches Land area, was created in 1929 by combining six towns strung along a 20-km (12-mile) stretch of the Wupper river. The towns are joined by the **Schwebe-bahn**, a monorail constructed in 1900. Carriages are suspended from a single rail, which rests on tall pillars.

The most interesting of the former towns is Elberfeld, with a museum of clocks, and the **Von-der-Heydt–Museum** of 19th- and 20th-century German art. The museum in the Friedrich-Engels-Haus in Barmen (Engelsstr. 10) is worth seeing, and Neviges has a Baroque pilgrimage church, with a much-visited miraculous picture of the Virgin Mary.

⛫ Von-der-Heydt-Museum

Elberfeld, Turmhof 8. **Tel** (0202) 563 62 31. ○ 11am–6pm Tue, Wed, Fri–Sun, 11am–8pm Thu. ⬛ 🗄 🖼

The unusual monorail, linking Wuppertal's six constituent towns

Düsseldorf ❾

Düsseldorf, the administrative capital of North Rhine-Westphalia, received its municipal rights in 1288. From the late 14th century it was the capital of the Duchy of Berg, and from 1614 that of the Palatine. The town owes much to Duke Johann Wilhelm (called Jan Wellem), who lived here in 1690–1716. One of the most important industrial and cultural centres in the Rhine Valley, this European metropolis has a renowned university, superb museums and theatres and, as the German capital of fashion, many excellent shops.

Museum Kunst Palast

Ehrenhof 4–5. ***Tel*** *(0211) 892 42 42.* *11am–6pm Tue–Sun.*

This art museum is one of the most interesting in Germany, with a collection of paintings dating from the 16th to the 20th centuries, including works by Rubens, Cranach and Dutch masters of the 17th century. It also holds a large collection of paintings by the Düsseldorf Academy, active in the first half of the 19th century, whose best known artists were Peter von Cornelius and Friedrich Wilhelm Schadow.

Altstadt

The small old town area suffered severe damage during World War II. Among the surviving monuments it is worth seeing some of the beautiful town houses and the late-Gothic **Rathaus** (town hall), built in the years 1570–73. In front of it stands a famous equestrian statue of the Elector Jan Wellem, built in 1703–11 by Gabriel Grupello. The Düsseldorf castle, burned down in 1872, only has the **Schlossturm** (castle tower) remaining, which now houses a museum of navigation. Another building worth visiting is the Baroque, post-Jesuit **Pfarrkirche St Andreas** (parish church of St Andrew), from the years 1622–9. It has a central ducal mausoleum complex situated behind the presbytery, where the remains of Jan Wellem and others are kept. The **Lambertuskirche**, the former collegiate church of St Lambertus, is a Gothic hall-church with a tall front tower, built in 1288–1394. Some valuable furnishings have survived, including the Gothic sacramentarium and important Gothic ducal tombs, such as that of Duke Wilhelm V, from 1595–9.

Detail from the façade of the Lambertuskirche

Interior of the Pfarrkirche St Andreas

Kunstsammlung Nordrhein-Westfalen

K20: Grabbeplatz 5. ***Tel*** *(0211) 838 11 30.* *10am– 8pm Mon–Fri, 10am–12pm 1st Wed of the month.* **K21:** Ständehausstr. 1. ***Tel*** *(0211) 838 16 00.* *10am–6pm Tue–Fri, 11am–6pm Sat, Sun. 10am–12pm 1st Wed of the month.* *24,25 & 31 Dec.*

The art collection of the state of North Rhine-Westphalia is enormous, featuring mainly the work of 20th-century artists. Particularly valuable are 88 paintings by Paul Klee, which were acquired in 1960. There are also works by Wassily Kandinsky, Marcel Duchamp, Piet Mondrian and Pablo Picasso. The gallery at Grabbeplatz is known as K20, and a second building at Städehaüsstr. 1, where contemporary art is exhibited, is known as K21. Temporary exhibitions are held nearby, at No. 4 Grabbeplatz.

Hetjens-Museum

Schulstraße 4. ***Tel*** *(0211) 899 42 10.* *11am–5pm Tue & Thu–Sun, 11am– 9pm Wed.*

This museum, in the Nesselrode Palace, is the oldest German museum devoted to ceramics. Visitors can learn about techniques for producing faïence and porcelain, and see global exhibits from prehistory to the present day.

Königsallee

The "kings' avenue", often just referred to as Kö, was laid out at the beginning of the 19th century, along the edge of the old city moat. The Kö is lined with expensive shops. Luxurious galleries, exclusive boutiques, department stores, fashion houses and shopping malls are interspersed with bars and restaurants. Particularly noteworthy is the Art Nouveau Warenhaus Tietz (now housing the Kaufhof-Galleria department store), which was built in 1907–9, to a design by Joseph Maria Olbrich.

Hofgarten

Schloss Jägerhof. **Goethemuseum:** Jacobistraße 2. ***Tel*** *(0211) 899 62 62.* *11am–5pm Tue–Fri & Sun, 1–5pm Sat.*

This charming park, originally laid out in 1769 for Elector Karl Theodor, was recreated in the English style at the beginning of the 19th century. The park is a marvellous setting for Schloss Jägerhof, a Baroque hunting lodge dating from the years 1752–63 and built according to a design by

For hotels and restaurants in this region see pp510–12 and pp549–51

The late-Baroque Schloss Benrath

VISITORS' CHECKLIST

Road map B4. 🏛 *600,000*. 🚉 *Konrad-Adenauer-Platz.* ✈ *north of the centre (0211-42 10).* ℹ️ *Immermannstr. 65B, Berliner Allee 33 (0211-17 20 20); Burgplatz 2.* 🎭 *Bootsausstellung (Jan), Rosenmontagszumzug (Carnival Mon), Größte Kirmes am Rhein (end Jul).* **www**.duesseldorf.de

Johann Josef Couven and Nicolas de Pigage. The castle was rebuilt after World War II. It now houses the Goethe-Museum, holding memorabilia and documents related to the writer's life, and a collection of 18th-century art, funded by Ernst Schneider.

🏛 Heinrich-Heine-Institut

Bilker Str. 12–14. **Tel** (0211) 899 55 71. ⬜ *11am–5pm Tue–Fri & Sun, 1–5pm Sat.* 🖼

The celebrated German poet Heinrich Heine was born in Düsseldorf in 1797. This institute was established to preserve his legacy, to conduct research into his work and to organize exhibitions. Düsseldorf's university and a number of streets have also been named after Heine.

⚜ Schloss Benrath

Benrather Schlossallee. **Tel** (0211) 899 72 71. ⬜ *16 Apr–Oct: 10am–6pm Tue–Sun; Nov–15 Apr: 11am–5pm Tue–Sun. Wed until 8pm.* 🖼 🖼

Benrath, part of Düsseldorf since 1929, is home to this beautiful Neo-Classical hunting palace, built for the electors of the Palatine in 1755–73 by Nicolas de Pigage. Decor, beautiful furnishings and an extensive park have survived.

The former city moat which runs alongside Königsallee

Kaiserswerth

Today a part of Düsseldorf, this area prides itself on a history dating back to the 8th century. Its Pfarrkirche St Suitbertus, a Romanesque basilica from the 12th century, has the magnificent 13th-century golden relic of its patron saint. There are also the ruins of a palace, built in the 12th century for Friedrich I Barbarossa.

Environs

The "Neanderthal" part of the Düssel valley was originally named after the poet Joachim Neander. It became famous in 1856, when the remains of apelike creatures were uncovered in a cave. A museum dedicated to these "Neanderthal Men" is located in Mettman, 17 km (11 miles) east of Düsseldorf.

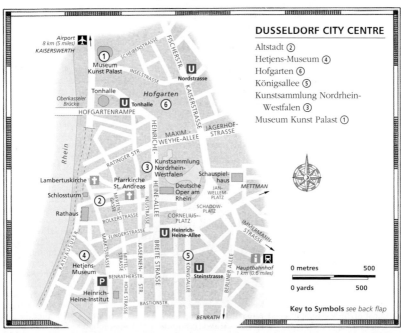

DUSSELDORF CITY CENTRE

Airport
8 km (5 miles)
KAISERSWERTH

Museum Kunst Palast ①
SCHEIBENSTRASSE
INSELSTRASSE
FISCHERSTR.
Nordstrasse
Tonhalle
Oberkasseler Brücke
Hofgarten
Tonhalle ⑥
HOFGARTENRAMPE
KAISERSTRASSE
HEINRICH-WEYHE-ALLEE
MAXIM.-WEYHE-ALLEE
JÄGERHOFSTRASSE
Rhein
RATINGER STR.
Kunstsammlung ③
Nordrhein-Westfalen
Schauspielhaus
Lambertuskirche
Pfarrkirche St. Andreas
Deutsche Oper am Rhein
JAN-WELLEM-PLATZ
METTMAN
Schlossturm
Rathaus ②
NEUSSTRASSE
SCHADOW-PLATZ
CORNELIUS-PLATZ
BOLKERSTRASSE
MARKTSTRASSE
FLINGERSTRASSE
Heinrich-Heine-Allee
IMMERMANN-STRASSE
RATHAUSUFER
Hetjens-Museum ④
MITTELSTRASSE
KASERNEN STR.
BENRATHSTR.
BREITE STRASSE
KÖNIGSALLEE
Steinstrasse
BERLINER ALLEE
Hauptbahnhof
1 km (0.6 miles)
Heinrich-Heine-Institut
HOHE STRASSE
BASTIONSTR.
BENRATH

0 metres   500
0 yards   500

Key to Symbols *see back flap*

Neuss ⑩

Road map B4. 👥 *150,000.* 🚋 🚌
ℹ️ *Büchel 6 (02131-403 77 95).*

The history of Neuss goes
back to Roman days. The
town developed around a
Bernhardine monastery, which
became a girls' boarding
school in the 12th century.
The most famous building is
the magnificent 13th-century
Romanesque **Münster St
Quirinus**. After a fire in 1741,
a Baroque dome with a statue
of St Quirin, the patron saint,
was added to the eastern
tower of the church. Also
worth seeing is the Obertor
(upper gate), built in 1200,
one of the mightiest gates in
the Rhineland.

Dormagen ⑪

Road map B4. 👥 *62,000.* 🚋 🚌
ℹ️ *Dormagen, Schlossstraße 2–4
(02133-25 76 84).* 🎭 *Freilichtspiele
in Zons (Jun–Sep).*

This medium-sized town,
which principally relies on its
chemical industry, would not
be found in a guide book
were it not for two remarkable historic monuments
within the city limits. On the
banks of the Rhine lies the
fortified customs town of
Zons, established around
1373–1400 at the instigation
of archbishop Friedrich von
Saarwerden. This small regular, four-sided fortress has
survived in excellent condition. The buildings in the
settlement are mainly from a
later date, but the walls and
gates, as well as the ruined
castle **Schloss Friedestrom** are
among the most fascinating
examples of Medieval for-
tifications in the Rhine Valley.
Equally interesting is an excursion to **Knechtsteden**,
west of Dormagen, where an
amazing monastery was built
for the Norbertines in the
12th century. Set amid woods
and orchards, the vast twin-
choired basilica has mighty
towers in the eastern section.
There are impressive murals,
including a 12th-century mural
of Christ in the western apsis,
as well as attractive cloisters.

The Gothic post-Cistercian Bergischer Dom in Altenberg

Solingen ⑫

Road map B4. 👥 *165,000.* 🚋 🚌 ℹ️
*Clemens-Galerien Mummstr. 10 (0212-
290 36 01).* 🎭 *Frühjahrskirmes (Mar).*

Solingen is almost synonymous with its famous factory,
where quality scissors and
knives are produced. The
main attraction in town is the
Klingenmuseum, which
shows cutting tools from the
Stone Age to the present day.

Environs
Remscheid, 7 km (4 miles) east
of Solingen has the Röntgen-
museum, dedicated to the
German Nobel Prize winner
Alfred Röntgen, who was born
here and discovered the X-ray.

**Baroque façade of the local
Heimatmuseum in Remscheid**

One of the most beautiful
buildings is the Heimatmuseum
with displays of typical
regional interiors.
Schloss Burg, on the Wupper river, is the 12th-century
fortress of the von Berg family. Many times rebuilt, it now
houses a museum.

Altenberg ⑬

Road map B4. 👥 *5,745.* 🚋 🚌
ℹ️ *Bergisch-Gladbacher-Str. 2, 51519
Odenthal (02202-71 01 31).*

Altenberg near Odenthal has
preserved its **Bergischer
Dom**, a former Cistercian
cathedral and one of the most
important destinations for pilgrims. Built in 1259–1379, it is
also one of the most beautiful
Gothic buildings in Germany.
In accordance with their
rules, the Cistercians built the
church without a tower. The
interior is furnished with
Gothic works of art and has
stunningly beautiful stained-
glass windows, the altar of
the *Coronation of the Blessed
Virgin Mary* from the late
15th century, a beautiful 14th-
century *Annunciation* and a
sacrarium (1490). After the
dissolution of the Order in

1803, the cathedral suffered a turbulent history. It now serves as a church for both Catholics and Protestants.

Children also enjoy a visit to Altenberg because of its **Märchenwald** (fairy-tale wood), an enchanted forest, with interactive scenes and statues representing all the most popular fairy tales.

Köln (Cologne) ⓮

See pp398–9.

Aachen ⓯

Road map A4. ⓘ *254,000.* ⓘ ⓘ
ⓘ *Elisenbrunnen (0241-180 29 60).*
ⓘ *Frühjahrsbend (Apr), horse-riding competitions CHIO (Jun), Europamarkt des Kunsthandwerks (Sep).*

Aachen owes its fame to its hot springs, whose healing powers were already highly rated by the Romans when they established baths here in the 1st–2nd centuries AD. The name of the town, *aquae grani* or Aquisgrani, also relates to the source.

The settlement grew mainly in the 8th century, when Charlemagne chose it as his principal residence in 768. He built a huge palace complex with chapel, cloistered courtyard and hall for himself.

When Charlemagne was crowned emperor in 800, Aachen became the capital of the Holy Roman Empire. Although the town soon lost this title, it remained an important destination for pilgrims because of the valuable relics brought here by Charlemagne. From the 10th to the 14th centuries, all German kings were crowned in the palace chapel.

Subsequently, in the 18th and 19th centuries, Aachen gained great importance as a spa. Many magnificent buildings dating from this splendid era have long since vanished. A further wave of destruction was inflicted by World War II, yet some particularly

magnificent historic monuments have survived. The most important of these, in the centre of the old town, is the **Pfalz** *(see pp396–7)*, a complex of buildings belonging to Charlemagne's former palace. They include a cathedral with a palace chapel and a hall which was rebuilt as the **Rathaus**.

In the old town, not far from the cathedral complex, it is worth visiting the church of St Folian, where a Gothic Madonna dating from 1411 has survived. A short distance south from here stands the Elisenbrunnen (fountain of St Elizabeth), an exceptionally beautiful building where mineral water can be taken. It was built in 1822–7 according to designs by Johann Peter Cremer and Karl Friedrich Schinkel.

After admiring the attractive houses around the central market square visitors can enjoy the **Couven-Museum**. Based in an historic middle-class town house, it has an interesting collection dedicated to the life of the bourgeoisie in the 18th and 19th centuries. There is also a collection of ceramic tiles from the 17th–19th centuries.

The house where Israel Berr Josaphat Reuter established the first-ever news agency in

Statue of David Hansemann

1850 (transferred to London a year later) now houses the **Internationales Zeitungs-museum**, devoted to the history of the press, with over 100,000 newspapers from the 17th century to today.

It is also worth visiting the **Suermondt-Ludwig-Museum**, a short distance beyond the compact town centre, which has a great collection of art from the Middle Ages until the present day, including some beautiful sculptures and paintings from the 17th century.

To the northeast of the old town extends the spa district of Aachen. Here, visitors can stroll through the spa park at their leisure or spend an evening at the casino.

Aachen also has much to offer lovers of modern art: the Ludwig-Forum für Internationale Kunst hosts interesting exhibitions, performances and concerts.

ⓘ **Internationales Zeitungsmuseum**
Pontstr. 13. **Tel** *(0241) 432 45 08.*
ⓘ *9:30am–1pm Tue–Fri.*

ⓘ **Suermondt-Ludwig-Museum**
Wilhelmstr. 18. **Tel** *(0241) 47 98 00.*
ⓘ *noon–6pm Tue–Sun, noon–9pm Wed.*

ⓘ **Couven-Museum**
Hühnermarkt 17. **Tel** *(0241) 432 44 21.* ⓘ *10am–5pm Tue–Sun.*
ⓘ *public holidays.* ⓘ

Environs
Kornelimünster, 6 km (4 miles) southeast of the centre, is a beautiful place with a well-preserved old town and churches. The most important of these is the Pfarrkirche St Kornelius, a former Benedictine monastery which dates from the early 9th century. The surviving building is a 14th-century Gothic basilica, extended by the early 16th century to an imposing five-nave structure. In the 18th century the octagonal chapel of St Kornelius was added to this at the axis of the presbytery.

The Neo-Classical building which houses the casino in Aachen's spa park

The Pfalz in Aachen

The original palace of Charlemagne in Aachen did not survive; of his vast construction only the Pfalzkapelle (palatine chapel) remains. Modelled on the church of San Vitale in Ravenna, Italy, it was built by Odo von Metz in 786–800. In the mid-14th century a front tower was added, and in the years 1355–1414 a new presbytery was built. Side chapels were added later, and in the 17th century the central section was covered by a dome.

Charlemagne, effigy on his shrine

Antique Columns
The arcaded ambulatory is divided by beautiful columns, made from red marble and porphyry which had been brought from Ravenna and Rome.

Hubertus- and Karls- kapelle

Charlemagne's Throne
This modest throne, fashioned from marbled tiles, served as the coronation throne for successive German leaders.

Candelabra
This copper candelabra, a masterpiece of Roman-esque craftsmanship, was a gift from Emperor Friedrich I Barbarossa.

Main entrance

Ungarn- kapelle

STAR SIGHTS

★ The Shrine of Charlemagne

★ Lotharkreuz

★ Pala d'Oro

Bronze doors
The doors, dating from the time of Charlemagne, are the oldest historic monument of their kind in Germany.

★ **Lotharkreuz**
This magnificent cross (c.1000), decorated with a cameo showing a portrait of Emperor Augustus, is one of the most valuable exhibits in the Schatzkammer.

The Gothic presbytery
was modelled on Sainte-Chapelle in Paris.

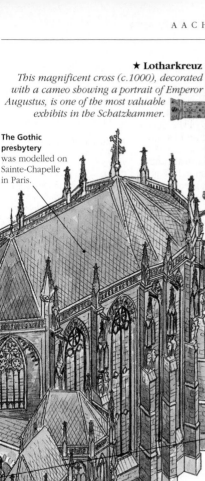

★ **The Shrine of Charlemagne**
The Emperor Charlemagne was canonized as a saint in 1165 and shortly after, probably at the beginning of the 13th century, a golden shrine was made to keep his bones in. It is now on display in the presbytery.

★ **Pala d'Oro**
The front of the main altar is adorned with valuable gold sheets from c.1020, which were funded by Heinrich II.

Matthiaskapelle

Annakapelle

Ambo
The ambo, a pulpit fashioned from gold-plated copper and inlaid with precious stones and ivories, was donated by Heinrich II in 1014.

Proserpina's Sarcophagus
This sarcophagus, in the Schatzkammer (treasury), is a beautiful example of early 3rd-century Roman sculpture. It is thought that the body of Charlemagne rested in this coffin until he was canonized.

Köln (Cologne) ⑭

Originally founded by the Romans as *Colonia Agrippina,* Köln is one of the oldest towns in Germany. The Franks ruled the town from the end of the 5th century, and Charlemagne raised its status to that of an archbishopric. Köln has remained a powerful ecclesiastical centre – it boasts 12 Romanesque churches as well as the famous Gothic cathedral. In the Middle Ages the city also played a significant role in the Hanseatic League, and from 1388 it had a university.

Detail on the Rathaus

🔒 St Andreas
Komödienstraße 4–8.
This late-Romanesque basilica was founded c.1200, with a presbytery added in 1414–20. The saint Albertus Magnus lies buried in the crypt. Particularly noteworthy are the beautiful capitals, which link the pillars between the naves, and the stalls (c.1420–30).

🔒 Pfarrkirche St Mariä Himmelfahrt
Marzellenstraße 32–40.
The parish church of the Assumption of Mary is one of the few Baroque buildings in Köln. It was built for the Jesuit Order in 1618–89, under the direction of Christoph Wamser. It is easy to discover numerous Romanesque and Gothic elements, although these are not surviving parts of an earlier building, but the result of a consciously created link with earlier styles.

Picturesque houses on Fischmarkt

🔒 Dom St Peter und Santa Maria
See pp402–3.

🏛 Römisch-Germanisches Museum
Roncalliplatz 4. *Tel* (0221) 22 12 45 90. ◷ 10am–5pm Tue–Sun.
This modern, glazed building houses archaeological finds dating from the Roman and pre-Roman eras that have been uncovered in Köln and the Rhine Valley. On display are weapons, many items of everyday use, ornamental and artistic objects as well as the superb Dionysus mosaic and the monument to Poblicius.

🏛 Museum Ludwig
Bischofsgartenstraße 1.
Tel (0221) 22 12 61 65.
◷ 10am–6pm Tue–Sun,
10am–11pm first Fri of month. 📷
This museum, combining the private collection of the Ludwig family with the 20th-century works originally held by the Wallraf-Richartz-Museum, has one of Europe's best collections of modern art. There are paintings by Picasso, German Expressionists, Surrealists, American Pop Artists and the Russian Avantgarde as well as many sculptures.

🔒 Groß St Martin
An Groß St Martin 9. *Tel* (0221) 16 42 56 50. ◷ 10:15am–6pm Mon–Fri, 10am–12:30pm & 1:30–6pm Sat, 2–4pm Sun.
This church, with its attractive triangular presbytery and vast tower dominating Fischmarkt, was founded for the Benedictine Order in the late 12th century. The Romans built a sports arena on this site with a swimming pool, remains of which have been uncovered under the crypt. The houses in the surrounding Martinsviertel are post-World War II, however they were built to historic designs and with a medieval street lay-out, making this an intimate and romantic area to explore.

Panorama with the Rathaus, Groß St Martin and the Dom, with the Rhine in the foreground

For hotels and restaurants in this region see pp510–12 and pp549–51

A detail of the Gothic section of
the Rathaus façade

🏛 Wallraf-Richartz-Museum
– Fondation Corboud
See pp404–5.

🏛 Rathaus
Alter Markt. ℹ️ *(0221) 22 10.* ◻️
10am–5pm Mon–Fri, 10am–noon Sat.
Jewish Baths ◻️ *8am–4:45pm Mon–
Thu, 8am–noon Fri, 10am– 4pm Sat,
11am–1pm Sun.* **Praetorium** *Kleine
Budengasse.* ◻️ *10am–5pm Tue–Sun.*
The town hall is an irregular
shape created by successive
modifications. In the first
phase, around 1330, a wing
with a Hanseatic Hall was
built, decorated with Gothic

sculptures of heroes and
prophets. In 1407–14 a vast
Gothic tower was added, and
in the 16th century the arcaded Renaissance Lions Courtyard and a magnificent front
lodge were built. In front of
the town hall, under a glass
pyramid, are the remains of
12th-century ritual Jewish
baths, that were destroyed
after the expulsion of the
Jews in 1424. From Kleine
Budengasse an entrance leads
to the *Praetorium*, the remains
of a Roman town hall.

🏛 Gürzenich
Gürzenichstraße
This Gothic building has a
huge celebration hall (1437–
44). which occupies the entire
first floor. Next to it are the
ruins of the Romanesque
church Alt St Alban. It has a
copy of the sculpture *Parents*
by Käthe Kollwitz.

🔶 Minoritenkirche Mariä
Empfängnis
Minoritenstraße
This modest Gothic Franciscan
church was established in the
13th–14th centuries. It is an
elegant three-naved basilica

VISITORS' CHECKLIST

Road map B4. 👥 *1,005,000.*
🚉 *Hauptbahnhof.* 🚌 *ZOB
Breslauer Platz.* ✈️ *Konrad-
Adenauer Flughafen (02203-
400).* ℹ️ *Unter Fettenhennen 19
(0221-22 13 04 00).* 🛒 *Markt
bei der Apostelkirche 7am–noon
Tue & Fri.* 🎭 *Rosenmontagsumzug (Carnival Rose Mon, Jan/Feb),
Bierbörse (Aug/Sep).*
www.*koelntourismus.de*

without a tower, modelled
on the Elisabethkirche in
Marburg. There are historic
furnishings and a 14th-
century shrine with the
remains of Johannes Duns
Scotus, a Scottish Minorite.

**Place of remembrance, in Alt St
Alban, near the Gürzenich**

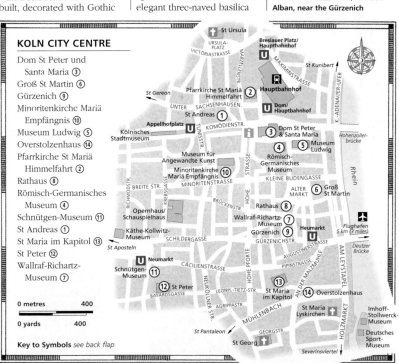

0 metres   400

0 yards   400

Key to Symbols *see back flap*

Exploring Köln (Cologne)

Present-day Köln is a metropolis, known primarily for its trade fairs. It is also an important centre of art and culture, its reputation forged by several excellent museums, numerous historic buildings and superb art galleries. Book and newspaper publishers have their head offices here, as do radio and television stations. The highest number of visitors, however, come to Köln for the five days preceding Ash Wednesday, to join in the fun and watch the grand carnival processions.

🏛 Schnütgen-Museum

Cäcilienstraße 29. **Tel** (0221) 22 12 23 10. ⬜ 10am–5pm Tue–Fri, 11am–5pm Sat & Sun. 📷

The Romanesque church of St Cecilia, built in 1130–60 as a nunnery, was taken over in 1479 by the Augustinian Sisters; today it houses the Schnütgen-Museum. Destroyed during World War II and subsequently rebuilt, this museum specializes in religious art, mainly from the Middle Ages. Its collection includes magnificent sculptures, gold and ivory items and sacral objects.

The Romanesque church of St Gereon, with its vast dome

🏛 St Peter

Leonhard-Tietz-Straße 6.

The late-Gothic church of St Peter is a galleried basilica, built in 1515–39. Following its destruction in World War II, the former vaulting was replaced by a ceiling. The church's greatest attractions include its Renaissance stained-glass windows (1528–30) and the magnificent *Crucifixion of St Peter*, painted after 1637 by Peter Paul Rubens, who spent his childhood here and whose father lies buried in the church.

🏛 St Maria im Kapitol

Marienplatz 19.

Originally built in the early part of the 11th century, as a convent, the church's extension and remodelling took until the early 13th century. Noteworthy among the furnishings are its extensive crypt and the mid-11th-century wooden door in the west closure, richly carved with reliefs depicting scenes from the life of Christ. It also has a superb Renaissance rood screen, and is the only church in Köln with cloisters.

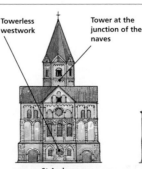

Detail from Stadtmuseum

🏛 Overstolzenhaus

Rheingasse 8.

World War II deprived Köln of many of its historic residential buildings, but this one has been lovingly restored. Built for a prosperous patrician family in the second quarter of the 13th century, it is regarded as one of the town's finest Gothic houses.

🏛 St Maria Lyskirchen

An Lyskirchen 12.

This, the smallest Romanesque church in Köln, was built around 1220 and slightly remodelled in the 17th century. Its greatest attractions are magnificent frescos depicting scenes from the Bible and the lives of the saints, which adorn the vaults (c.1250), as well as the *Schöne Madonna*, a huge statue of the Virgin with the Infant Christ (c.1420).

🏛 Imhoff-Stollwerck-Museum

Rheinauhafen 1a. **Tel** (0221) 931 88 80. ⬜ 10am–6pm Tue–Fri, 11am–7pm Sat & Sun. 📷

This fantastic museum of chocolate explains the history of cocoa bean cultivation as well as the cultural significance, use and marketing of chocolate. It also shows the production process, and lets visitors sample the product.

🏛 St Georg

Georgsplatz 17.

This church was built around the middle of the 11th century, originally as a transept basilica with two choirs. In

ROMANESQUE CHURCHES

Köln has 12 surviving Romanesque churches, bearing testimony to the importance of the Church in the town's development. Built on the graves of martyrs and early bishops of Köln, the forms of the churches influenced the development of Romanesque architecture well beyond the Rhineland. Almost all the churches were damaged in World War II. Some, such as the church of St Kolumba, have not been restored, but most were returned to their former glory.

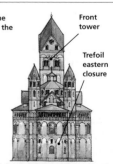

Towerless westwork

Tower at the junction of the naves

Front tower

Trefoil eastern closure

St Andreas

St Aposteln

The attractive Romanesque church of St Kunibert, seen from the Rhine

the mid-12th century the west choir was replaced by a massive frontage (westwork), but the towers were never added.

St Pantaleon
Am Pantaleonsberg 2.

A little way from the centre is this exquisite church, a former Benedictine monastery founded c.950 by Archbishop Bruno, brother of Emperor Otto I. The archbishop and the Empress Theophanu, who completed the building, are both buried here. The church has a superb late-Gothic choir screen with richly carved ornamentation. From the crypt, the remains of a Roman villa are accessible.

Severinsviertel
The Severin Quarter, a district on the southern edge of the old town, owes its name to the 13th-century Romanesque church of St Severinus. The church, largely remodelled in the Gothic style in the 15th and 16th centuries, features rich original furnishings and has a mid-10th-century crypt.

St Aposteln
Neumarkt 30.

This enormous 12th-century church of the Apostles, which towers over Neumarkt, a central square in Köln, is one of the most interesting Romanesque churches in the Rhineland. The original basilica has a trefoil eastern closure, a low tower at the junction of the naves and a tall front tower. It was given two further slim turrets flanking the apse of the presbytery.

From Neumarkt, Hahnenstrasse leads to Rudolfplatz and the Hahnentor, perhaps the most beautiful of all surviving medieval gates.

St Gereon
Gereonsdriesch 2–4.

This church must be the most unusual edifice not only in the Rhineland, but in all of Germany. Its oldest part, an oval building surrounded by small conchas, was built in the late 4th century on the graves of martyrs and – according to legend – founded by St Helen. The Romanesque

presbytery is an 11th-century addition and, in 1219–27, the oval was encircled with a ten-sided, four-storey structure in early-Gothic style. This is topped with a massive dome, 48 m (157 ft) in diameter, with ribbed vault.

St Ursula
Ursulaplatz 24.

This church was built in the 12th century, on the site of an earlier church probably dating from c.400. In the late 13th century the presbytery was rebuilt in Gothic style. The Baroque golden chamber at the southern end, added in the 17th century, is lined with many shrines. According to legend, these hold the remains of St Ursula and 11,000 virgins, all of whom were reputedly killed at the hands of the Huns. The town insignia of Köln also testify to the veneration of the virgins.

St Kunibert
Kunibertskloster 2.

Bishop Kunibert was buried in a church on this site in 663. The present Romanesque church (1215–47) has precious Romanesque stained-glass windows (c.1220–30).

The medieval Hahnentor, exit from Köln towards Aachen

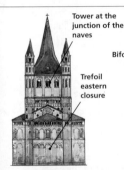

Groß St Martin

Tower at the junction of the naves

Biforium

Trefoil eastern closure

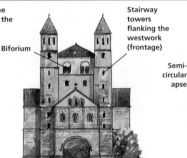

St Pantaleon

Stairway towers flanking the westwork (frontage)

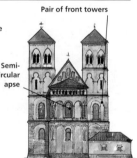

St Kunibert

Pair of front towers

Semi-circular apse

Cologne Cathedral (Kölner Dom)

10th-century Gero Cross

The most famous Gothic structure in Germany, the Kölner Dom is also unusually complex, whether in terms of its splendour, its size or even simply the date of its construction. The foundation stone was laid on 15th August 1248, the presbytery consecrated in 1322. The cathedral was built gradually until c.1520. It then remained unfinished until the 19th century, when Romanticists revived interest in it. The building was finally completed in 1842–80, according to the rediscovered, original Gothic designs.

Pinnacles
Elaborately decorated pinnacles top the supporting pillars.

Cathedral Interior
The presbytery, the ambulatory and the chapels retain a large number of Gothic, mainly early-14th-century, stained-glass windows.

Engelbert Reliquary (c.1630)
The cathedral treasury is famous for its large collection of golden objects, vestments and the fine ornamentation of its liturgical books.

Main entrance

Petrusportal, or the portal of St Peter, the only one built in the second half of the 14th century, has five Gothic figures.

STAR SIGHTS

★ Gothic Stalls

★ Shrine of the Three Kings

★ Altar of the Magi

★ **Gothic Stalls**
The massive oak stalls, built in 1308–11, were the largest that have ever been made in Germany.

Semicircular arches transfer the thrust of the vaults onto the buttresses.

Buttresses support the entire bulk of the cathedral.

VISITORS' CHECKLIST

Cathedral ☐ 6am–7:30pm daily. **Treasury** Domkloster 4. **Tel** (0221) 17 94 05 55. ☐ 10am–6pm daily. ☑ ☑ **Viewing platform** ☐ Jan/Feb & Nov/Dec: 9am–4pm; Mar/Apr & Oct: 9am–5pm; May–Sep: 9am–6pm. ☑ **Organ recitals** Jun–Aug: 8pm Tue. **Exhibition of Rubens tapestries** Whit Sunday until Corpus Christi.

High Altar
The Gothic altar slab, which dates back to the consecration of the presbytery, depicts the Coronation of the Virgin Mary, flanked by the twelve apostles.

★ **Shrine of the Three Kings**
This huge Romanesque reliquary was made by Nikolaus von Verdun in 1190–1220, to hold the relics of the Three Kings. These relics were brought to Köln in 1164 for Emperor Friedrich I Barbarossa.

★ **Altar of the Magi**
This splendid altar (c.1445), the work of Stephan Lochner, is dedicated to the Three Kings, the patrons of Köln.

Mailänder Madonna
This fine early-Gothic carving of the Milan Madonna and Child dates from around 1290. It is currently displayed in the Marienkapelle.

Wallraf-Richartz-Museum – Fondation Corboud

This museum was named after Ferdinand Franz Wallraf, who bequeathed his art collection to the city in 1824, and Johann Heinrich Richartz, who funded the first building. Medieval and early modern paintings (1250 to 1550) form the core of the collection. There are also works by Rubens and Rembrandt, as well as examples from Impressionism, Realism and Symbolism. In 2001 the Wallraf-Richartz-Museum moved to a brand-new building, incorporting many new works from the collection of Gérard Corboud.

Bleaching the Linen (1882)
Max Liebermann created this painting in the early stages of his career, when his work was largely concerned with Realism.

★ **Stigmatization of St Francis** (c.1616)
This dark and mysterious painting, originally created by Peter Paul Rubens for the Capuchin church in Köln, is untypical of the artist's work.

Third floor

Reclining Girl (1751)
This young nude, arranged on her bed in a provocative pose, is an example of the light-hearted works of so-called "boudoir art" that François Boucher specialized in.

Ground floor

★ **Fifer and Drummer** (1502–4)
This subtle painting, the wing of an altarpiece, is the work of Albrecht Dürer, who included himself in the scene – the drummer is a self-portrait of Dürer himself.

Main entrance

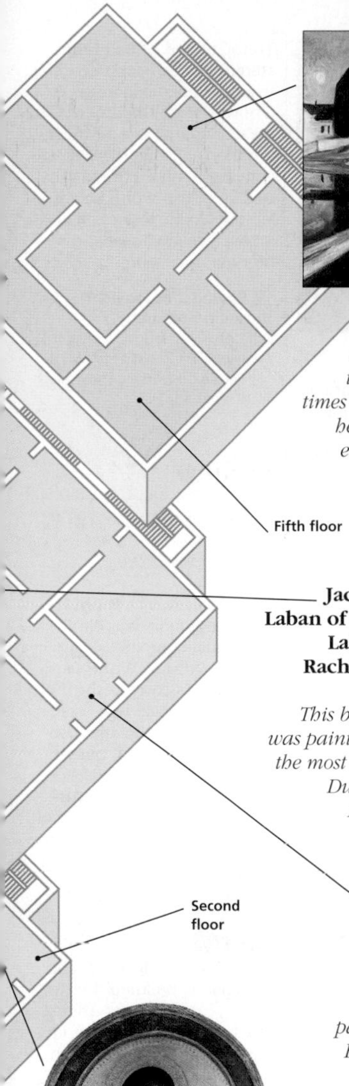

Girls on a Bridge
(1905)
Edvard Munch covered the same subject several times (see p437). The version held in Köln is one of the earliest, and features an urbanized landscape.

Fifth floor

VISITORS' CHECKLIST

Wallraf-Richartz-Museum – Fondation Corboud
Obenmarspforten. *Tel* (0221) 22 12 11 19. ☐ 10am–8pm Tue, 10am–6pm Wed–Fri, 11am–6pm Sat & Sun. ⚓ 🏥 🅿 🎨 📷

GALLERY GUIDE

Each floor in the museum displays paintings belonging to one era. On the second floor, the exhibition begins with the collection of 13th-century art; the third floor holds 16th–18th century art, and on the fifth floor works of art from the 19th century are displayed, organized by the schools of art they represent.

Jacob accuses Laban of giving him Lai instead of Rachel as a wife
(1628)
This biblical scene was painted by one of the most outstanding Dutch masters, Hendrick ter Brugghen.

Second floor

Old Woman and Boy
(c.1650–60)
This scene was painted by Bartolome Esteban Murillo. The artist excelled not only as the master of charmingly senti- mental depictions of the Madonna, but was also an excellent observer of every- day life in 17th- century Spain.

Madonna and Child
(1325–30)
This central panel of a polyptych by Simone Martini is thought to have originated from the San Agostino church in San Giminiano.

KEY

- ☐ Medieval paintings
- ☐ 17th- and 18th-century paintings
- ☐ 19th-century paintings
- ☐ Non-exhibition space

STAR EXHIBITS

★ Fifer and Drummer

★ Stigmatization of St Francis

One of the artificial reservoirs in the northern Eifel

Northern Eifel ⑯

Road map A4. 🚩 *Kalvarienbergstr.
1, 54595 Prüm (0180) 500 22 83.*
🎭 *Bad Münstereifel: Burg in
Flammen (Jul).*

Barely 20 percent of the
Eifel mountain range is in
North Rhine-Westphalia. Low,
forested mountains line the
valley of the Rur river, which
has been dammed in several
places. The resulting artificial
lakes provide a perfect opportunity for relaxation and
sporting activities. There are
also many attractive towns
and fascinating monuments.

Blankenheim is famed for
its picturesque half-timbered
houses, the late-Gothic church
and the frequently modified
12th-century castle of the
counts von Manderscheid-
Blankenheim, which today is
a youth hostel. The source of
the Ahr river can also be seen
here – a house was built over
the top of it in 1726.

In **Schleiden**, the castle,
built in the 12th century and
frequently rebuilt up until the
18th century, is worth visiting.
There is also a late-Gothic
church with valuable stained-
glass windows and an impressive organ dating from 1770.

Probably the most beautiful
town in this region is **Monschau**, which until 1919 was
called Montjoie. It is known
also for the Montjoier Düt-
tchen (croissants) and an excellent mustard. The ruin of a
13th-century castle towers on
a hill. At its foot, the Rur river
runs through a narrow valley,
with attractive small towns,
narrow, steep streets and
timber-frame houses from
various eras. In Hasenfeld

visitors can see a dam dating
from 1904, and an amazing
hydro-electric building, decorated in a way that reflects its
purpose. One of the most
interesting monuments of this
region is the Steinfeld monastery, with a history dating from
the 10th century. In 1121 the
Augustinians settled here, and
in 1126 they accepted the rule
of St Norbert of Xanten, and
this became the first monastery on German territory. A
beautiful Romanesque basilica
was built in the second half
of the 12th century. It has
retained wall paintings from
the 12th and 14th centuries,
and vaulted ceilings from the
16th century. The
**Rheinisches
Freilichtmuseum
Kommern** is an
open-air museum
with examples of
the building styles
typical of the
Northern Eifel. It
is also worth visit-
ing the town of **Euskirchen**,
which has an attractive Gothic
church with superb furnishings, and the moated castle of
Veynau (14–15th centuries).

Picturesque half-timbered
houses in Monschau

The spa town of **Bad Münstereifel** dates back to 830,
when a Benedictine monas-
tery was established here. The
present church is a 12th-cen-
tury Romanesque basilica
with impressive 11th-century
frontage. Also worth seeing
are the Gothic town hall and
a Romanesque house, now
housing a museum.

🏛 **Rheinisches Freilicht-
museum Kommern**
*Auf dem Kahlenbusch. Mechernich-
Kommern. Tel (02443) 998 00.*
⏰ *Apr–Oct: 9am–6pm; Nov–Mar:
10am–4pm.* 🎫

Brühl ⑰

Road map B4. 🏘 *42,000.* 🚉 🚌
🚩 *Uhlstr. 1 (02232-793 45).*
🎭 *Hubertusmarkt (Oct).*

The small town of Brühl has
one of the most beautiful
residential complexes, since
1984 a UNESCO World Heri-
tage Site. As early as the 13th
century, a palace was established here for the archbishops of nearby Köln, but this
was destroyed in 1689. A
Baroque palace, **Augustusburg**, was built on
its foundations in
1725–8, according
to a design by
Johann Conrad
Schlaun. It was
named after the
instigator of the
building, Elector
Klemens August.

Merry-go-round at the
Phantasialand in Brühl

The building was almost immediately refurbished, with a
new façade and furnishings,
the work of François Cuvilliés, and in the 1940s a new
staircase was completed to a
design by Balthasar Neu-
mann. After devastation in
World War II, the palace was
carefully restored, and the
magnificently furnished late-
Baroque and Rococo interior,
especially a stunning dining
room designed by Cuvilliés,
can now be seen again. A
path leads from the orangery
to a Gothic church built for
the Franciscans in the 15th
century. The *Annunciation*
on the high altar is the work
of Johann Wolfgang van der
Auwer, while the magnificent

Phantasialand, the largest theme park in Germany, near Brühl

canopy above was designed by Balthasar Neumann. The castle is surrounded by a Baroque park, designed by Dominique Girard.

About 2 km (1 mile) east of the main residence is another castle, **Falkenlust**, built in 1729–40, to a design by Cuvilliés. Its captivating interior includes a lacquered and a mirror cabinet. Nearby stands an octagonal chapel, its interior decoration modelled on a secluded grotto.

It is also worth visiting the small villa near Augustusburg where the great Surrealist artist Max Ernst was born. It now houses a small display commemorating his work.

Another attraction, which draws a large number of visitors is **Phantasialand**, Germany's largest theme park. Visitors will need several days to see all the attractions of this vast fairground with its roller-coaster, water-rides and numerous merry-go-rounds.

♣ Augustusburg
Tel *(02232) 440 00.* ⬜ *Feb–Nov: 9am–noon & 1:30–4pm Tue–Fri, 10am–5pm Sat & Sun.*

⬜ Falkenlust
Tel *(02232) 440 00.* ⬜ *Feb–Nov: 9am–12:30pm & 1:30–4pm Tue–Fri, 10am–5pm Sat & Sun.*

⬜ Phantasialand
Berggeiststr. 31–41. ***Tel*** *(02232) 362 00.* ⬜ *Apr–Oct: 9am–6pm daily, later in summer.* 🎡

Environs
Two moated houses await the visitor at **Kerpen**, 27 km (17 miles) to the north: the small 16th-century castle of Lörsfeld, and the Baroque palace of Türnich, built in 1756–66.

In **Pulheim-Brauweiler**, 30 km (19 miles) to the north, is an extremely beautiful Benedictine monastery, founded in 1024. Building began in 1048, funded by Rycheza, the wife of the Polish King Boleslav Chrobry.

From here it is worth travelling another 23 km (14 miles) west to **Bedburg**, where the

moated castle is worth seeing. This is a vast brick structure with four wings, which was established in stages over 300 years, starting in around 1300.

Bonn ⓲

See p408.

Königswinter ⓳

Road map B4. 🏃 *35,000.* 🚉 🚌
ℹ️ *Drachenfelsstr. 11 (02223-91 77 11).*

Königswinter lies in the centre of the Siebengebirge, an attractive range of small, wooded mountains (the "seven mountains"), excellently suited for walking. The most popular mountain is the Drachenfels (dragon's rock). The oldest mountain railway in Germany, built in 1883, takes visitors to the top (321 m/1,053 ft). During the ascent visitors can see the Neo-Gothic Drachenburg, a palace dating from 1879–84, and on the top are the ruins of the Gothic Drachenburg, dating from the 12th century. The "dragon" in the name relates to the myth of the Nibelungs – the dragon slain by Siegfried was supposed to have lived here.

The little town of Königswinter, at the foot of the mountains, has picturesque 17th-century half-timbered houses, town houses and late 19th-century hotels.

Environs
Bad Honnef, 6 km (4 miles) to the south, is a charming spa town known as "Nice on the Rhine", where the former chancellor Konrad Adenauer lived until his death. A museum commemorates this great politician.

Situated 15 km (9 miles) to the north is **Siegburg**, where a Benedictine monastery (1064) is worth visiting. The walls of the crypt are from the 11th century, but the present church is a 17th-century building, rebuilt after World War II. The Anno-Schrein is a magnificent Romanesque reliquary box dating from 1183.

The Baroque Schloss Augustusburg in Brühl

Bonn ⑱

Bonn was founded by the Romans in 11 BC, and flourished thanks to the archbishops of Cologne. It gained fame because of Ludwig van Beethoven, who was born here in 1770, and Robert Schumann, who spent the final years of his life here. The world heard of Bonn when, on 10 May 1949, it was elevated to the status of capital of the Federal Republic of Germany. When parliament decided in 1991 to make Berlin the capital of the newly unified country, Bonn was deprived of its role, although seven ministries stayed on.

The Baroque portal of the Beethovenhaus in Bonn

🏛 Beethovenhaus

Bonngasse 20. **Tel** *(0228) 981 75 25.* ☐ *Apr–Oct: 10am–6pm Mon–Sat, 11am–4pm Sun; Nov–Mar: 10am–5pm Mon–Sat, 11am–5pm Sun.* 🖼
The museum is housed in the Baroque 18th-century house where the composer Ludwig van Beethoven was born and lived until the age of 22. He never returned to his home town, but there is a large and impressive collection of memorabilia from his entire life.

🏛 Markt

The central market square in Bonn, shaped like a triangle, owes its present appearance to a mixture of modern and Baroque architecture. Its most outstanding feature is the late-Baroque **Rathaus** (town hall), built in 1737–8, to a design by Michel Leveilly. The centre of the market square is decorated with the Marktbrunnen, a fountain in the shape of an obelisk, erected in 1777 in honour of the Elector Maximilian Friedrich.

Not far from the Markt are some churches worth seeing. The first is the Gothic **Remigius-kirche**, built for the Franciscans in the years 1274–1317, and the second is the Baroque **Namen-Jesu-Kirche** built for the Jesuits according to a design by Jacob de Candreal in the years 1686–1717.

🏛 Rheinufer

The Rhine embankment, which changes its name several times along its course, runs along the western bank of the Rhine. Many of Bonn's attractions are grouped along this street. To the north of Kennedybrücke (Kennedy bridge) lies the Beethovenhalle, a vast concert and congress hall, and to the south of the bridge is the Bonn opera house.

Next to the opera is the Alter Zoll, the former customs house, which is based in one of the bastions that was part of the 17th-century city defences.

🏛 Universität

Am Hofgarten.
Founded in 1818, Bonn University is based in what is probably the most beautiful home for an educational institution anywhere in Germany. The stunningly attractive Baroque castle was built for the Elector Joseph Klemens in 1607–1705, to a design by Enrico Zuccalle, and extended after 1715 by Robert de Cotte.

🏛 Münster St Martin

Münsterplatz.
Bonn's cathedral is a magnificent example of Romanesque architecture in the Rhine Valley. The church was built in around 1150–1230, on the site of an earlier 11th-century cathedral, of which a three-naved crypt has survived. South of it, the romantic 12th-century Romanesque cloister is also worth seeing.

Gold clasps in the Rheinisches Landesmuseum

🏛 Rheinisches Landesmuseum

Colmantstraße 14–16. **Tel** *(0228) 20 700.* ☐ *10am–6pm Tue–Sun, 10am–9pm Wed.*
www.rlmb.de
This interesting regional museum has a vast collection of excavated items dating back to Roman times, as well as medieval and modern art. The skull of a Neanderthal Man is also exhibited here.

The Baroque Elector's palace, housing Bonn University

🏛 Regierungsviertel

Until recently this was the central authority of one of the most powerful countries in Europe. Now it creates a somewhat desolate impression. Some ministries and offices have remained in Bonn, and the transfer to Berlin is taking time, but the town is definitely changing.

The former Bundestag building, in the Regierungsviertel

🏛 Haus der Geschichte der BR Deutschland

Willy-Brandt-Allee 14. **Tel** *(0228) 916 50.* ⬜ *9am–7pm Tue–Sun.* 🏛
This excellent new museum details the history of Germany after World War II, with fascinating multi-media displays. It is one of the architecturally impressive buildings which form Bonn's "Museums Mile".

🏛 Kunstmuseum Bonn

Friedrich-Ebert-Allee 2. **Tel** *(0228) 77 62 60.* ⬜ *11am–6pm Tue–Sun, 11am–9pm Wed.* ⬛ *24, 25 & 31 Dec; Sat, Sun & Mon in carnival.*
This superb museum of 20th-century art, in an interesting building designed by Axel Schultes, has a great collection of Expressionist paintings, including many works by August Macke. Next to the museum is the Kunst- und Ausstellungshalle, which opened in 1992 as a venue for temporary exhibitions.

🏛 Bad Godesberg

The small spa town of Bad Godesberg was incorporated into Bonn as recently as 1969. An elegant neighbourhood, its villas line the spa park. On top of the hill is the Godesburg, a ruined castle dating from the 13th century.

♣ Poppelsdorf

In this leafy southwestern suburb, the Baroque Schloss Clemensruhe (1715–18) is well worth visiting. Both the castle and its extensive park with an attractive botanical garden belong to the university. It is also worth making a detour to the Baroque pilgrimage church on the Kreuzberg, a low hill. The church houses the chapel of the Holy Steps, attributed to Balthasar Neumann.

The Baroque Schloss Clemensruhe, in Poppelsdorf

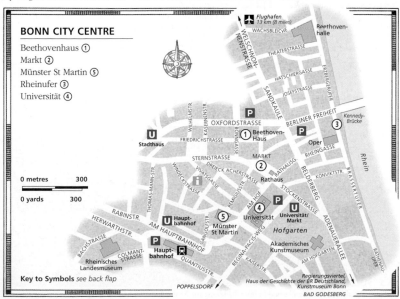

BONN CITY CENTRE

Beethovenhaus ①
Markt ②
Münster St Martin ⑤
Rheinufer ③
Universität ④

0 metres 300
0 yards 300

Key to Symbols *see back flap*

The medieval Oberes Schloss in Siegen

Siegen ⑳

Road map B4. 🏛 *100,000.* 🚌 🚆
ℹ️ *Markt 2 (0271-404 13 16).*
🎭 *Kultur Pur (May/Jun), Rubensfest (Jun/Jul), Weihnachtsmarkt (Dec).*

Beautifully located amidst the hills on the high banks of the Sieg river, Siegen is the largest town in the Siegerland region. For centuries the city was the residence of the dukes of Nassau. Religious divisions in the family resulted in two castles being built in Siegen. The **Oberes Schloss** (upper castle) is a medieval building, frequently refurbished in the 16th, 17th and 18th centuries. The museum, which has been opened inside the castle, has some paintings by Peter Paul Rubens, who was born in Siegen. The lower **Unteres Schloss** is a Baroque palace, which replaced an earlier building. In the centre of Siegen it is also worth visiting the **Nicolaikirche**, a 13th-century hexagonal church with a presbytery and tower, which served as the ducal family mausoleum.

Environs
In **Freudenberg**, 10 km (6 miles) northwest of Siegen, is the small settlement of Alter Flecken, which is reproduced in virtually all German guidebooks. Founded in 1666 at the instigation of Duke Johann Moritz von Nassau, the village consists of identical half-timbered houses.

Hagen ㉑

Road map B4. 🏛 *210,950.* 🚌 🚆
ℹ️ *Rathausstr. 13 (02331-207 58 94).* 🎭 *Marktschreiertage (Jan).*

Hagen would probably not feature in the guidebooks, were it not for Karl Ernst Osthaus, who created an artists' colony here at the beginning of the 20th century, inviting Art Nouveau designers such as Peter Behrens and Henry van der Velde. The magnificent **Hohenhof**, Osthaus' home, was created by van der Velde. It houses the **Karl-Ernst-Osthaus-Museum**, with a collection of modern art. Behrens designed the crematorium in the suburb of Delstern and the beautiful villas **Haus Como** (Hafleyer Str. 35) and **Haus Goedeke** (Amselgasse). In the south of the town is the Westfälisches Freilichtmuseum, a popular open-air museum, which displays many historic workshops and factories with reconstructed equipment.

Sauerland ㉒

Road map B4. ℹ️ *Sauerland-Touristik, Johannes-Hummel-Weg 1, 57392 Schmallenberg (02974-96 980).*

The Sauerland is the region to the south and east of the Ruhr coalfields, making an obvious holiday destination for the inhabitants of this large, industrialized conurbation. Embracing the northern part of the Rhenish slate massif, its densely wooded mountains are not high – the highest peak is Hegekopf at 843 m (2,766 ft). Crossed by rivers teeming with fish and full of artificial lakes, the area is perfect for walking, cycling and fishing.

Enjoyable days can be had on an excursion to one of the caves such as **Attahöhle, Dechenhöhle** and **Heinrichshöhle** near Iserlohn. There are charming towns, too, and in **Breckerfeld**, the Gothic parish church has preserved a superb altar, from around 1520. The main attraction in **Altena** is the superb, gigantic Burg (castle), built in the 12th century and restored in the early 20th century. In 1910 the world's first youth hostel for tourists

One of the charming villages, nestling in the hilly landscape of the Sauerland

For hotels and restaurants in this region see pp510–12 and pp549–51

Timber-frame house, typical of the Sauerland landscape

was created here. The 14th-century Schloss Wocklum in **Balve** was rebuilt in the 18th century. One of the greatest tourist draws in the Sauerland is the **Möhnesee**, a lake with a huge dam, built in 1908–12 and bombed by Allied "dambusters" in 1943 with catastrophic consequences. **Arnsberg** has a regional museum and the lovely Neo-Gothic moated castle Herdringen with assorted furnishings from other castles.

In the south extend the Rothaargebirge (red-haired mountains). Their most beautiful town is the spa resort of Bad Berleburg, while the Kahler Asten mountain and the town of Winterberg are popular winter sports areas.

Soest ㉓

Road map B4. 👥 50,000. 🚉 🚌 ℹ️ Teichsmühlengasse 3 (02921-66 35 00 50). 🎉 Bördetag (May), Gauklertag (Sep), Jahrmarkt Allerheiligenkirmes (Nov).

The Westphalian town of Soest made its mark in history when, in about 1100, the town's civic rights were formulated and subsequently adopted by 65 other towns. Today the town captivates visitors with its well-preserved old town, its historic churches, and the almost completely intact walls which surround the town. The focus of the old town is the Romanesque **Propsteikirche St Patrokli**, founded in 965 by Bruno, archbishop of Cologne, and built in stages until the 13th century. Further historic buildings are grouped around the church: the 18th-century,

Baroque **Rathaus** (town hall), the 12th-century Romanesque **Petrikirche** with its Gothic presbytery, and the 12th-century **Nicolaikapelle**, a chapel with 13th-century wall paintings and an altar painted by Konrad von Soest.

In the northern part of the old town, two churches are worth seeing: the **Hohnekirche** with beautiful early Gothic and early Baroque furnishings, and the **Wiesenkirche** with a magnificent group of stained-glass windows from the 14th and 15th centuries. The window above the northern portal shows the so-called Westphalian Last Supper, depicting a table laden with plentiful Westphalian smoked ham and local pumpernickel bread.

An ornate window in the Dom in Paderborn

Environ

In **Lippstadt**, 23 km (14 miles) east of Soest, it is worth visiting the Gothic Marienkirche. In the suburb of Bökenförde is the 18th-century Baroque moated palace Schwarzenraben, and there is an early-Baroque castle in Overhagen.

Paderborn ㉔

Road map C3. 👥 140,000. 🚉 🚌 ℹ️ Marienplatz 2 (05251-88 29 80). 🎉 Puppenfestspiele (Feb), Schützenfest (Jul), Liborifest (Jul–Aug), Liborikirmes (Oct).

Paderborn has featured on the historical map for over 1,000 years. In the 8th century Charlemagne built a palace here, and in about AD 800, a bishopric was established. The town's most important monument is the beautiful **Dom St Maria, St Kilian und St Liborius**, a Romanesque-Gothic cathedral. This enormous hall-church with two transepts and tall front tower suffered greatly during World War II, but it continues to captivate visitors with its magnificent decor on the richly carved portal, the great Romanesque

crypt, interesting plaques and richly decorated bishops' tombs and epitaphs. The diocesan museum holds the Imad-Madonna, funded by Bishop Imad, an outstanding figure of the Madonna and Child dating from 1051–8. On the northern side of the cathedral a section of the foundations of the emperor's palace can be seen, together with the **Bartholomäuskapelle** (chapel of St Bartholomew), the oldest hall-church in Germany, completed in 1017. To the south of the cathedral complex, on Rathausplatz, is the exceptionally beautiful **Rathaus** (town hall) dating from 1613–20. An example of the Weser-Renaissance style, it is crowned with richly ornamented gables. The **Heinz-Nixdorf-Museumsforum** provides a pleasant break from the past – this museum is dedicated to the history of computers.

Environs

Near **Stukenbrock**, 15 km (9 miles) north of Paderborn, is the theme park Hollywood-Park and the fascinating Safariland, where more than 500 African animals roam freely.

Tower of the Romanesque-Gothic Dom in Paderborn

Front of the early-Romanesque Abtei Corvey in Höxter

Höxter ㉕

Road map C3. 🏠 35,000. 🚊 🚌
🛈 Weserstraße 11 (05271-194 33).
🎫 Corveyer Musikwochen (May–Jun), Huxorimarkt (Sep), Kirchenmusiktage (Nov–Dec).

In a picturesque spot on the Weser river, Höxter can pride itself on its beautiful old town with many timber-frame houses, fragments of the city walls, a Renaissance **Rathaus** (town hall) from 1610, and important churches. The history of **Kilianikirche**, in the centre of the old town, goes back to the late 8th century, although in its present form it is a Romanesque building from the 11th–12th centuries. Also in

the centre of Höxter is a Gothic church built for the Franciscans in 1248–1320.

The city's greatest attraction, however, is the magnificent **Abtei Corvey**, a monastery founded in 822. It was originally built as the church of St Stephen and St Vitus, but only the grandiose two-storey frontage completed in 885 survived. It became the model for several other churches built in Westphalia, while the main body of the church was rebuilt in the 17th century.

Lemgo ㉖

Road map C3. 🏠 42,000. 🚊 🚌
🛈 Kramerstr 1. (05261-988 70).

This exceptionally pretty town was founded in 1190 by Bernhard II von Lippe. It was a member of the Hanseatic League, and had its heyday during the witch hunts of the 17th century. Today, Lemgo has numerous Renaissance monuments – it was spared during World War II, and the Gothic Nicolaikirche and Marienkirche, with Gothic wall paintings and a Renaissance organ by Georg Slegel, have survived. The pearl of the city is the beautiful **Rathaus** (town hall), built in the 15th–17th centuries. It contains an original pharmacy that is still in use. Many timber-frame houses have also survived, the best ones in Papen-, Mittel- and Echternstraße. The most beautiful house in

Façade of a Renaissance pharmacy inside the Rathaus in Lemgo

Lemgo is the **Hexenbürgermeisterhaus**. This "witches' mayor's house" (1571), an excellent example of Weser Renaissance, belonged to the mayor, Hermann Cothmann, who started the witch hunt. It now houses a town museum. Also worth visiting are the **Junkerhaus** (1891), the architect's home, and **Schloss Brake** (13th-16th centuries), a castle which now houses the **Weserrenaissance-Museum**.

🏛 **Weserrenaissance-Museum**
Schloss Brake. *Tel* (05261) 945 00. ⬚ 10am–6pm Tue–Sun.

Teutoburger Wald (Teutoburg Forest) ㉗

Road map C3. 🛈 Detmold, Rathaus Am Markt 5 (05231-97 73 28).
🎫 Andreas-Messe in Detmold (Nov).

A range of low mountains extending from Osnabrück through Bielefeld right up to Paderborn, the Teutoburg Forest is one of the most attractive tourist regions in Westphalia. The best base for walking and cycling holidays is **Detmold**, which has a very attractive old town with well-preserved timber-frame buildings from various periods, and the elegant Residenzschloss, the castle of the zur Lippe family. Originally medieval, the palace was rebuilt in the 16th century in the Weser-

The picturesque Renaissance Rathaus in Höxter

◁ **Königsallee in Autumn, Düsseldorf**

Renaissance style. The interior is composed of 17th and 19th century furnishings. The star feature is a set of eight gobelins crafted in a Brussels workshop around 1670, showing scenes of Alexander the Great's triumphs. Furnishings from the 19th century include designs by Charles Le Brun.

Three km (2 miles) south of Detmold is the spot where in the year AD 9 Cherusko Arminius, known as Hermann, leader of the Germanic tribes, triumphed against the Roman army led by Varus. At the top of the mountain, the **Hermannsdenkmal**, a huge monument designed by Ernst von Bandel, was erected in 1838–75. It was supposed to symbolize the German struggle for unification.

Two fascinating attractions near Detmold are the **Adlerwarte Berlebeck**, an ornithological research station, where eagles and many other birds of prey can be observed, and the **Vogelpark Heiligenkirchen**, a bird park with over 2,000 varieties of birds in all shapes and sizes from around the world.

Bielefeld 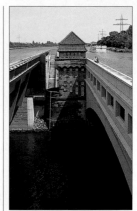㉘

Road map C3. 🏛 *325,000.* 🚉 🚌 ℹ️ *Niederwall 23 (0521-51 69 99).* 🎉 *Hermannslauf (Apr), Leinenweber-Markt (May), Bielefelder Kultur-Sommer (May–Sep), Sparrenburgfest (Jul), Weinmarkt (Sep), Weihnachtsmarkt (Dec).*

On the edge of the Teutoburg Forest, Bielefeld owes its evolution to the production of and trading in linen. The old town is dominated by the **Sparrenburg** castle, built in the 13th century for the von Ravensberg family. In the 16th century the castle was surrounded by new fortifications including new bastions, and in the 19th century the residential part of the city was greatly extended.

The central feature of the old town is Alter Markt (old

market), on which stands the **Nicolaikirche**. This Gothic church suffered heavily in World War II, although the marvellous Antwerp altar (c.1520) was preserved. Nearby, on Obernstraße, stands the **Crüwell-Haus**, an interesting late-Gothic town house from the early 16th century. The street leads to **St Jodokus-Kirche**, a late-Gothic church, whose greatest treasure is the amazing figure of the Black Madonna (c.1220). Further south is the **Kunsthalle**, a modern building with a significant collection of 20th-century art. It is also worth visiting the **Marienkirche** in the new town. Built in 1280–1330, this Gothic church holds the tomb of one of the von Ravensberg dukes (c.1320) and a high altar (c.1400) with a central Gothic section.

Environs
Picturesque **Herford**, 17 km (11 miles) north of Bielefeld, has a lovely old town with timber-frame houses and beautiful Gothic churches.

In **Enger**, 21 km (13 miles) to the north, in the former church of the canons, a tomb dating from 1100 holds the remains of the Saxon Duke Widukind, buried in 807.

The spa town of **Bad Salzuflen** with its pretty old town and spa park is the ideal place for those seeking relaxation.

An observation tower in the Sparrenburg complex in Bielefeld

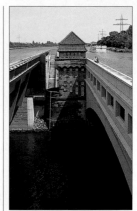

The Wasserstraßenkreuzung (waterway junction) in Minden

Minden ㉙

Road map C3. 🏛 *85,000.* 🚉 🚌 ℹ️ *Domstraße 2 (0571-829 06 59).* 🎉 *Klassik-Open-Air (Jul/Aug).*

Charlemagne created a bishopric here as early as 798. The town evolved thanks to its strategic location on the Weser river. The city's most important monument is the cathedral, **Dompfarrkirche St Petrus und St Gorgonius**. It has a Romanesque presbytery, transept and monumental frontage built in the 11th–12th centuries, although the body of the church is an example of early-Gothic style from the 13th century. It is worth visiting the church treasury with its 11th-century crucifix.

The **Rathaus** (town hall), with 13th-century lower sections, is worth seeing, as are Minden's many charming houses around the market square. A great attraction is the **Wasserstraßenkreuz** (waterway junction), where a 375-m (1,230-ft) long bridge takes the Mittellandkanal across the Weser river.

Environs
On top of a hill in **Porta Westfalica**, 6 km (4 miles) south of Minden, is a giant monument to Kaiser Wilhelm (1892–6) by Bruno Schmitz.

The **Westfälische Mühlenstraße**, (Westphalian mill route), signposted around Minden, takes visitors past 42 different mills and windmills.

Hermannsdenkmal, near Detmold

NORTHERN GERMANY

Northern Germany at a Glance

Northern Germany has very varied landscapes, ranging from the sandy beaches on the Baltic and North Sea coasts to the moraine hills of Schleswig-Holstein and the moorlands of the Lüneburger Heide. Nature-lovers are enchanted by the countless lakes in Mecklenburg and the Harz mountains, while those interested in history or architecture enjoy the Renaissance castles along the Weser River and the Gothic brick architecture in former Hanseatic towns. Historic buildings in Goslar and Hildesheim testify to the importance of these two towns.

Helgoland *is a popular tourist destination. Red cliffs as high as skyscrapers, a picturesque town and the sea aquarium are the star attractions of this island.*

SCHLESWIG-
HOLSTEIN
(see pp454–65)

LOWER SAXONY,
HAMBURG AND
BREMEN
(see pp424–53)

Oldenburg, *symbolized by its heraldic shield, is famous for its large collection of paintings and interiors in its Kunstmuseum (art museum).*

Bremen, *a historic harbour town, draws visitors with its many historic buildings and monuments, including a Renaissance-Gothic town hall.*

Fehmarn, *one of the largest of the German islands, is linked with the German mainland by a railway bridge constructed in 1963.*

Rügen *enchants visitors with its chalky white cliffs, which contrast starkly with the deep blues and greens of the surrounding Baltic Sea.*

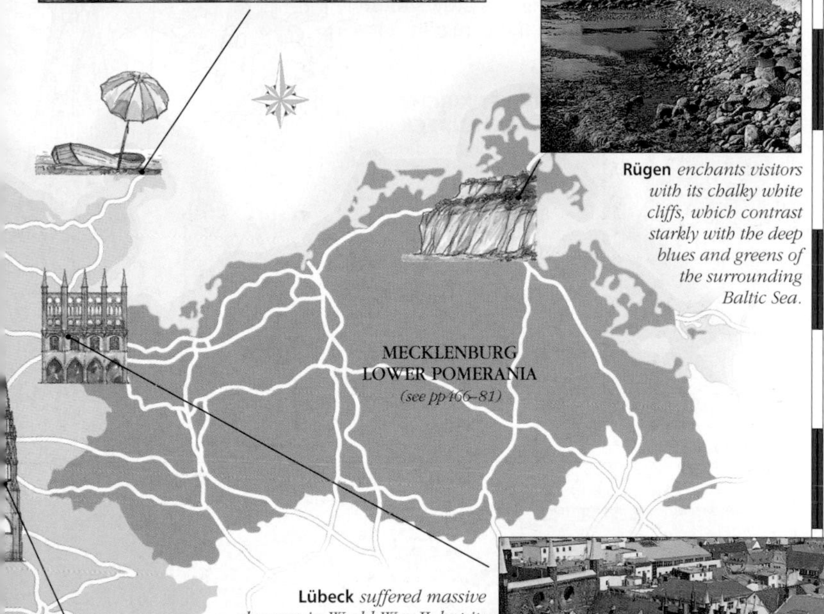

MECKLENBURG
LOWER POMERANIA
(see pp466–81)

Lübeck *suffered massive damage in World War II, but its Gothic town hall survived the attacks and the city's beautiful old town has been rebuilt.*

| 0 km | 50 | |
| 0 miles | | 50 |

Hamburg *not only has attractive museums and valuable monuments, but also such lively and bustling places as the Fischmarkt, a huge market held every Sunday morning where it is possible to purchase virtually anything.*

Gothic Brick Architecture

Terracotta decoration

Brick was used as a building material in many parts of medieval Europe, but in Northern Germany it gave rise to the distinctive style of *Backsteingotik* (brick Gothic). Brick technology was introduced in the mid-12th century by Norbertine monks arriving from Lombardy. The style is characterized by a rich variety of vaults, the use of buttresses instead of supporting arches, and colourful designs achieved by using glazed bricks. Through trade and the activities of religious orders these forms spread throughout the Baltic region.

The storeys are divided by friezes.

MARIENKIRCHE IN LUBECK
Considered the crowning achievement of Backsteingotik, this church, built from around 1260, became the model for countless others, including the cathedral in Schwerin. It is a triple-naved basilica, with a twin-towered façade, braced with buttresses.

The eastern façade *of many churches, such as the Marienkirche in Prenzlau (above) was often crowned by an elaborate, ornamental gable.*

A pointed arched portal, *decorated with ceramic borders, was a typical feature of many village churches.*

Main portal

Gables with tiled decorations *and intricate openwork, such as this gable of the south chapel of the Nikolaikirche in Wismar, are a feature of many Lower Pomeranian churches.*

The vast twin-towered façade symbolizes the power of its founders – wealthy Lübeck patricians.

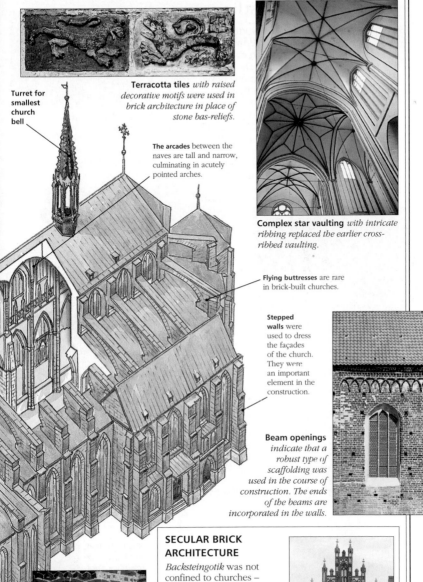

Terracotta tiles *with raised decorative motifs were used in brick architecture in place of stone bas-reliefs.*

Turret for smallest church bell

The arcades between the naves are tall and narrow, culminating in acutely pointed arches.

Complex star vaulting *with intricate ribbing replaced the earlier cross-ribbed vaulting.*

Flying buttresses are rare in brick-built churches.

Stepped walls were used to dress the façades of the church. They were an important element in the construction.

Beam openings *indicate that a robust type of scaffolding was used in the course of construction. The ends of the beams are incorporated in the walls.*

Friezes on the arcades, *such as this interlaced motif made from brick, are frequently used as a decorative element, even in village churches.*

SECULAR BRICK ARCHITECTURE

Backsteingotik was not confined to churches – this style was used in magnificent town halls, weigh-houses, gateways and houses, mostly on narrow plots, with elaborate gables decorated with glazed bricks and white plasterwork.

Gothic house on the market square in Greifswald

The German Coastline

The waters of two seas – the North Sea and the
Baltic Sea – lap on northern Germany's shores,
linked by the Kiel Canal, which cuts across the
base of the Jutland peninsula. The cool climate
on the coast makes for short summers yet, on a
sunny day, the beaches are packed with
holidaymakers, and a holiday here can have a lot
to offer. Heiligendamm was the first seaside
resort to be established in Germany, in 1783 by a
duke of Mecklenburg. By the end of the 19th
century, spas with elegant villas, promenades
and piers were springing up everywhere. A
popular attraction are the *Strandkörbe* –
huge wickerwork beach chairs.

The sand dunes *form
part of a nature reserve
in the northern part of
Sylt, the largest of the
North Frisian islands.*

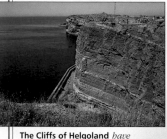

The Cliffs of Helgoland *have
a characteristic reddish hue
indicating the red sandstone
from which they are composed.*

Sylt

NORDFRIESISCHE INSELN

NORDFRIESLAND

Helgoland

Flensburg

Schleswig

Rendsburg

Kiel

Neumünster

NORDSEE (NORTH SEA)

OSTFRIESLAND

Wilhelmshaven

Emden

Oldenburg

Itzehoe

Elmshorn

Pinneberg

Hamburg

Reinbek

Bremerhaven

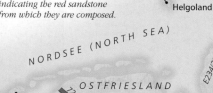

The Kiel Canal,
*known in Ger-
many as the Nord-
Ostsee-Kanal, was
constructed in
1887–95. Around
40,000 vessels pass
through the canal
every year.*

Borkum, *one of the East Frisian
islands, was once inhabited by
whalers. Garden fences were
often constructed from whale
bones, and some have survived
to the present day.*

Bremerhaven *is a vast port at the
mouth of the Weser river. It was constructed from 1827 to support the
port of Bremen, which is located
farther inland, away from the sea.*

Stralsund, *a Hanseatic harbour town with a medieval lay-out, has a large number of well-preserved historic monuments.*

On the small, flat island of Hiddensee *all car traffic is banned. The island was much loved by the writer Gerhart Hauptmann, who lies buried here in the local cemetery.*

THE COASTLINE

The hinterland of the Baltic region is generally flat and sandy, but in some areas it is steep and rocky. For visitors the greatest draw are the islands: Rügen with its steep chalky cliffs, Usedom with its wide, sandy beaches and Hiddensee. Off the lowlands and the marshy coastal region in the hinterland of the North Sea coast extends the chain of Frisian islands.

The beach at Ahlbeck *and the pier with its restaurant are the greatest attractions on the island of Usedom, at the mouth of the Oder river.*

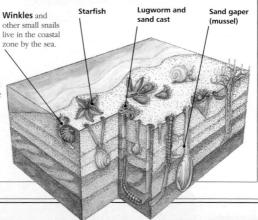

207

OSTSEE (BALTIC SEA)

•Bergen
RÜGEN

Stralsund

ODERBUCHT

Ribnitz-
- Damgarten

96

LÜBECKER BUCHT

105

•Rostock

E251/96

•Greifswald

20

103

109

Wismar

Anklam•

Güstrow

104

Ueckermünde

Schwerin•

Rügen, *famous for its unusual chalky cliff formations, was immortalized by Caspar David Friedrich and continues to inspire artists.*

| 0 km | 60 |
| 0 miles | 60 |

CROSS-SECTION OF WATT

The Watt is a flat, boggy stretch of coastline, up to several kilometres wide, which is covered by the sea as the tide comes in, and laid bare as it goes out again. The Watt landscape is fairly monotonous, but it is fascinating to observe the rich flora and fauna, which has adapted to cope with life both underwater and exposed to the air.

Winkles and other small snails live in the coastal zone by the sea.

Starfish

Lugworm and sand cast

Sand gaper (mussel)

LOWER SAXONY, HAMBURG AND BREMEN

T*hree federal states – Lower Saxony and the independent city states of Hamburg and Bremen – cover an enormous terrain, embracing the whole of northwestern Germany. For the visitor they provide a series of memorable snapshots: the mighty cosmopolitan port of Hamburg, enchanting towns and villages with half-timbered houses and the blooming heather of the Lüneburger Heide.*

Lower Saxony was formed in the 19th century through the merging of the kingdom of Hannover with the duchy of Brunswick, Oldenburg and Schaumburg-Lippe and other parts of northern Germany. The second-largest German state after Bavaria, it only ranks fourth in terms of the number of its inhabitants, being less densely populated than other states.

Lower Saxony is characterized by lowlands that become hillier in the south, culminating in the Harz Mountains. The only large cities are Hannover, a modern centre renowned for its trade fairs and for hosting Expo 2000, and Braunschweig, a venerable town that cherishes its link with the Saxon king Heinrich der Löwe, its first important ruler. The Romanesque splendour of Hildesheim is a magnet for visitors, as are the Renaissance centres along the Weser River including Hameln, the charming towns of Celle, Lüneburg and Einbeck, and Wolfenbüttel, Stadthagen and Bückeburg which contain some remarkable Mannerist works of art.

Nature lovers will enjoy excursions to the Lüneburger Heide or paddling in the endless expanses of mud-flats in the North Sea. Tourists are also attracted by the sandy beaches of the East Frisian islands, as well as the solitary rock of the island of Helgoland.

The "free and Hanseatic" towns of Hamburg and Bremen rejoice in a different atmosphere, urban and urbane, tolerant and multicultural, based on centuries of trade with the world.

The glorious moorlands of the Lüneburger Heide, with tall juniper bushes and flowering heathers

◁ The charming Gänselieselbrunnen (goose girl fountain) in the market square in Göttingen

Exploring Lower Saxony, Hamburg and Bremen

Hamburg and Bremen, the region's largest cities, are
also the most convenient bases for tourists, offering
accommodation in every price category.
The most attractive area in this region is the southeastern section, extending to the foothills of the
Harz Mountains with picturesque towns, such as
the university town of Göttingen,
Romanesque Hildesheim or the
stunningly beautiful mer-
chant town of Goslar.
A visit to the seaside
and an excursion to
the islands are
also enjoyable.

SEE ALSO

• *Where to Stay* pp513–16

• *Where to Eat* pp552–4

The crowning feature of the
bay window of the Dempter-
haus in Hameln

The massive edifice of the Neues Rathaus in Hannover

KEY

▬	Motorway
▬	Main road
▭	Minor road
▬	Road under construction
▬	Main railway
—	Minor railway
▬	National border
▬	Regional border

GETTING AROUND

There are international airports in Hamburg, Bremen and Hannover. A network of motorways links Lower Saxony with Scandinavia (via Schleswig-Holstein), and with the rest of western Europe (via the Netherlands or southern Germany). There are good ferry connections between Hamburg and Harwich (England). An extensive rail network makes the entire state accessible, although bus connections are limited.

The Grosse Wallanlagen Park in Hamburg, laid out along the city's former fortifications

| 0 km | | 40 |
| 0 miles | | 40 |

Ostfriesische Inseln (East Frisian Islands) ➊

Road map B2. 🚢 *Emden-Borkum, Norden-Norddeich to Juist and Norderney, Nessmersiel-Baltrum, Bensersiel-Langeoog, Neuharlingersiel-Spiekeroog, Harlesiel-Wangerooge.* ℹ️ *(0180) 20 20 96.* **www**.die-nordsee.de

Moormuseum in Elisabethfehn, Ostfriesland

A long the North Sea Coast extends the belt of East Frisian Islands consisting of, from west to east: Borkum, Juist, Norderney, Baltrum, Langeoog, Spiekeroog and Wangerooge. All around them is the **Nationalpark Niedersächsisches Wattenmeer**, a large national park established to protect the unique ecosystem of the shallow seas. At low tide it turns into vast mud-flats, extending to the horizon. This is the time to tour the Watt, as it is known locally, either by horse-drawn carriage or barefoot – always making sure to return before the tide comes in!

The islands themselves, with their beautiful sandy beaches, sand dunes and healthy climate, are among the most popular holiday destinations in Germany.

The car-free island Juist, a 17-km (11-mile) strip of land less than 500 m (1,640 ft) wide, and Norderney with its main town of the same name are the most interesting islands. Neo-Classical villas recall the days when such figures as Heinrich Heine and Otto von Bismarck spent their holidays here. It is also worth

visiting Wangerooge, another island where cars are banned. Three lighthouses – Westturm, Alter Leuchtturm and Neuer Leuchtturm – indicate the island's role in the navigation of the Weser River estuary.

Ostfriesland (East Frisia) ➋

Road map B2. 🚉 *Emden, Leer, Norden.* ℹ️ *(01805) 20 20 96 or (04931) 93 83 200.* **www**.die-nordsee.de 🎪 *Kiewittmarkt (end Mar); Altstadtfest (Aug).*

East Frisia is a peninsula near the border with the Netherlands and the Jadebusen bay, at Wilhelmshaven. This is a land of flat meadows, grazing cows and windmills.

Emden, the region's capital, has an attractive town hall resembling that in Antwerp, and a town centre crossed by many canals. The **Nannen-Kunsthalle Emden**, founded in the early 1990s by Henri Nannen, publisher of the magazine *Stern*, holds a remarkable collection of 19th-century paintings, including the works of many German Expressionists such as Emil Nolde, Max Beckmann and Oskar Kokoschka.

Another attraction is the **Moor- und Fehnmuseum** (moor and fen museum) in Elisabethfehn, which is dedicated to the extraction of peat. Its exhibits include the world's largest plough, as well as the story of Jever, the local beer. Also worth visiting are the Renaissance palace whose reception hall has a ceiling with sunken panels, and next

to the parish church the wood and stone tomb of the Frisian leader Edo Wiemken, made in 1561– 4 by master craftsmen from Antwerp.

🏛 Nannen-Kunsthalle Emden
Hinter dem Rahmen 13. **Tel** *(04921) 975 00.* ⏱ *10am–8pm Tue, 10am–5pm Wed–Fri, 11am–5pm Sat & Sun.* ⬛ *1 May, 25 & 31 Dec.* 📷

🏛 Moor- und Fehnmuseum
Oldenburger-Str. 1. **Tel** *(04499) 22 22.* ⏱ *end Mar–end Oct: 10am–6pm Tue–Sun & bank holidays.*

Clemenswerth ➌

Road map B3. 🚉 *Sögel or Lathen.* ℹ️ *Papenburg, Rathausstr. 2 (04961-839 60).* **Schloss Tel** *05952-93 23 25.* ⏱ *Apr–Oct: 10am–6pm Tue–Sun.* ⬛ *winter.*

Emsland, to the south of East Frisia, extends along the Dutch border, a poor area since time immemorial, with moors and boglands. Only the discovery of oil in the 20th century engineered its progress. Sögel, 33 km (21 miles) south of Greater Papenburg, has the region's greatest attraction, the palatial hunting lodge or schloss Clemenswerth, built from 1737– 49. In search of solitude, the elector and archbishop of Cologne Clemens August commissioned the lodge from Johan Conrad Schlaun. The design was modelled on the pavilion-pagoda of Nymphenburg in Munich. Altogether it comprises seven pavilions with mansard roofs and a chapel. All the brick buildings were laid out on a green lawn, creating a star shape around the palace. Inside there is a museum of the region.

Nationalpark Niedersächsisches Wattenmeer in the Greefsiel area

Oldenburg ❹

Road map B2. 🏘 *155,000.* 🚆
ℹ️ *Kleine Kirchenstr. 10 (01805-938 333).* 🎉 *Hafenfest (7 days after Whitsun); Altstadtfest (end Aug); Kramermarkt (Sep/Oct).*

A thousand years old, and once part of Denmark, this town remained the seat of a duchy until 1918.

The **Lambertikirche**, in the central market square, is a late-Gothic hall-church with a Neo-Classical rotunda added in 1797. The **Schloss**, the ducal residence, displays a similar marriage of styles, particularly Baroque and Neo-Classical. The **Landesmuseum für Kunst und Kulturgeschichte** (state museum of art and culture), based in the castle, is known mainly for its collection of paintings assembled by Wilhelm Tischbein, who lived here for 25 years. The affiliated **Augusteum**, a Neo-Renaissance building in a picturesque spot, holds the museum's modern collection.

🏛 **Landesmuseum für Kunst und Kulturgeschichte**
Damm 1. **Tel** *(0441) 220 73 00.*
⏰ *9am–5pm Tue, Wed & Fri, 9am–8pm Thu, 10am–5pm Sat & Sun.*
⏰ *1 Jan, Good Friday, Easter, 1 May, 24, 25 & 31 Dec.* 📷

Environs
The small spa town of **Bad Zwischenahn** is worth a visit. Its star attraction is the Gothic St Johanniskirche with frescoes from 1512.

A windmill in the open-air museum in Cloppenburg

Cloppenburg ❺

Road map B2. 🏘 *29,000.*
ℹ️ *Eschstr. 29 (04471-152 56).*
🎉 *Mariä Geburtsmarkt (Sep).*

The small market town of Cloppenburg boasts the **Museumsdorf**, the oldest open-air museum in Germany, established in 1934. On a vast site, 50 architectural monuments from all over Lower Saxony have been assembled. There are houses, including charming examples of the half-timbered style of Wehlburg, windmills and a small 17th-century church from Klein-Escherde near Hildesheim.

To the east of Cloppenburg lies Visbek. Here the visitor is taken back to the Stone Age, with megalithic graves from 3,500 to 1,800 BC, including the 80-m (262-ft) long grave known as "Visbeker Bräutigam" (bridegroom) and the even larger, 100-m (321-ft) long "Visbeker Braut" (bride).

🏛 **Museumsdorf Cloppenburg**
Bether Straße 6. **Tel** *(04471) 948 40.* ⏰ *Mar–Oct: 9am–6pm daily, Nov–Feb: 9am–4:30pm daily.* 📷

Osnabrück ❻

Road map B3. 🏘 *157,000.* 🚆
ℹ️ *Bierstr. 22–23 (0541-32 32 202).*

This Westphalian town has been a bishop's see since the time of Charlemagne. In 1648, negotiations took place here between representatives of Sweden and the Protestant duchies of the Reich. The signing of the Peace of Westphalia in 1648, which ended the Thirty Years' War, was announced from the town hall steps. It was also the birthplace of the writer Erich Maria Remarque in 1899.

Despite damage in World War II, the **Dom St Peter**, Osnabrück's 13th-century cathedral, is worth visiting. It has a bronze baptismal font and enormous triumphal cross, and the late-Gothic Snetlage-Altar of the Crucifixion. From here a short walk takes the visitor to the market square, Marienkirche and the Gothic **Rathaus** (town hall), with a sculpture of Charlemagne.

Epitaph for Albert von Bevessen in the Dom in Osnabrück

Environs South of Osnabrück is the western part of the Teutoburger Wald (Teutoburg Forest). The spa town of **Bad Iburg**, 12 km (8 miles) to the south of Osnabrück, has a monumental Benedictine monastery and bishop's palace. The Rittersaal (knights' hall) is worth seeing, with its giant ceiling fresco depicting an architectural fantasy of foreshortened perspectives.

The Schloss in Oldenburg, featuring Baroque and Neo-Classical styles

Bremen

Bremen, together with its deep-water port Bremerhaven, constitutes a separate town state. Not so much a
bustling modern metropolis as a peaceful country
town, it is conscious of its historical origins dating back
to Charlemagne. The townscape is not dominated by
the port as in Hamburg, but by the old town with its
magnificent cathedral and town hall. Bremen enjoyed
prosperity from 1358 when it joined the Hanseatic
League, its wealth based on the coffee and wool trade.
Today, Bremen still benefits from its port, which ships
around 700,000 cars a year.

Statue of the Bremen Town Musicians, by Gerhard Marcks

Gabled houses and the statue of Roland in the Marktplatz

Exploring Bremen

Most of Bremen's tourist
attractions are in the old town,
on the east bank of the Weser
River. The area is easy to
pick out on a map as it is
surrounded by a green belt,
established when the town's
fortifications were demolished.
The Überseemuseum (eth-
nography museum) is close to
the old town, and trams run
to Schwachhausen, where the
Focke-Museum is based.

🏛 Marktplatz

On the main square of Medieval Bremen stand the town
hall and the cathedral, and,
on the west side, several
gabled houses. This lovely
view is slightly marred by
the unattractive 1960s Haus
der Bürgerschaft, the state
parliament building.

In front of the town hall
stands a 10-m (32-ft) statue of
Roland, dating from 1404. It
is the largest of many similar
statues in German towns, and
the prototype for others. A
nephew of Charlemagne,
Roland symbolizes a town's

independence. His gaze is
directed toward the cathedral,
the residence of the bishop,
who frequently sought to
restrict Bremen's autonomy.
Roland's sword of justice
symbolizes the judiciary's
independence, and the
engraved motto confirms the
emperor's edict, conferring
town rights onto Bremen.

The second, more recent
(1953) monument in the
square is dedicated to the
Bremen Town Musicians – a
donkey, dog, cat and cockerel,

who according to the Grimm
fairy tale trekked to Bremen.

🏛 Rathaus

Marktplatz. **Tel** *(0421) 30 80 00.*
⬜ *11am–noon 3pm, 4pm Mon–Sat,
11am–noon Sun.* 🎫

The original Gothic building
dating from the years 1405–10
was clad with a magnificent
Renaissance façade, one of
the finest examples of Weser
Renaissance architecture in
northern Germany, designed
by Lüder von Bentheim. He
masterfully incorporated the
Gothic figures of Charle-
magne and seven Electors, as
well as four prophets and
four wise men. In the 40-m
(131-ft) Große Halle (great
hall) new laws were passed,
as symbolized by the fresco
(1932) of Solomon's court.
Among its many other
treasures is the meticulously
crafted Renaissance spiral
staircase. On the western side
of the town hall is the
entrance to the "Ratskeller"
where you can sample 600
different wines, and delight in
the murals from 1927, by the
Impressionist Max Slevogt.

The late-Renaissance façade of Bremen's Rathaus

🏛 Schütting

Marktplatz.

On the southwestern side of Marktplatz stands this mansion used by the Merchants' Guild for their conventions. It was built in 1537–9 by the Antwerp architect Johann der Buschener in Dutch Mannerist style. The eastern gable, more classically Renaissance in style, is the work of the local builder Carsten Husmann.

The Mannerist Schütting, a meeting place for merchants

🏛 Dom

Tower and "Bleikeller":
🕐 Easter–1 Nov: 10am–5pm Mon–Fri, 10am–2pm Sat, 2–5pm Sun.

This magnificent Romanesque cathedral with its vast twin-towered façade dates from the 11th century. Over the years it was extensively refurbished. At the end of the 19th century, while the southern tower was rebuilt, the façade was also reconstructed and a tower was added at the junction of the naves. Inside, it is worth looking at the sandstone bas-reliefs which divide the western choir stalls as well as fragments of Gothic stalls that were destroyed in the 19th century, with scenes of the Passion and the battle

of Judas Machabeus. There is also a Baroque pulpit paid for by Christina the Queen of Sweden in 1638, and numerous multi-coloured memorials, including one to Segebad Clüver by the entrance to the north tower (1457). The larger eastern crypt has interesting Romanesque capitals, while in the second eastern crypt visitors can admire the oldest Bremen sculpture of Christ the Omnipotent (1050) as well as the baptismal font. The latter has 38 bas-reliefs, and a bowl supported by four lions with riders. In the so-called "Bleikeller" (lead cellar) underneath the former church cloisters, eight perfectly preserved mummies are on show.

Bas-reliefs on the western choir stalls in the Dom

BREMEN TOWN CENTRE

0 metres 500

0 yards 500

Key to Symbols *see back flap*

⚜ Böttcherstraße

Paula-Modersohn-Becker-Museum and **Roseliushaus**
Böttcherstr. 6–10. **Tel** *(0421) 336 50 77.* ☐ *11am–6pm Tue–Sun.*

This once insignificant lane where coopers lived was transformed into Art Deco style in 1926–30 by Ludwig Roselius, a wealthy coffee merchant. The National Socialists preserved the street as an example of degenerate art. At the entrance to the street is a bas-relief by Bernhard Hoetger from 1920, of the Archangel Michael fighting a dragon.

Archangel Michael fighting a dragon, on a bas-relief in Böttcherstrasse

The **Paula-Modersohn-Becker-Museum**, built in the Expressionist style, contains an art museum, while in the neighbouring 16th-century **Roseliushaus** the original period interiors can be admired. The street's other attraction is a carillon which chimes tuneful melodies every day at noon, 3pm and 6pm.

⚜ Schnoorviertel

Spielzeugmuseum im Schnoor
Schnoor 24. **Tel** *(0421) 32 03 82.* ☐ *11am–6:30pm Mon–Fri, 11am–7pm Sat; 1 Apr–31 Dec: 11am–6pm Sun.*

The Schnoorviertel is a historic district of small houses dating from the 15th–18th centuries. One of Bremen's poorest areas before World War II, it miraculously escaped destruction. It has

been restored gradually since 1958 and now teems with restaurants, cafés, souvenir shops and tourists. In the centre of the district is the Gothic **Johanniskirche**, which once belonged to the Franciscans. In accordance with the order's rules it has no tower, although this is compensated for by a decorative gable on the western façade, and three levels of arched alcoves and herringbone brickwork. The **Spielzeugmuseum** (toy museum) nearby is also worth visiting.

🏛 Kunsthalle

Am Wall 207. **Tel** *(0421) 32 90 80.* ☐ *10am–9pm Tue, 10am–5pm Wed–Sun.* 🖼

On the edge of the old town is this art gallery, which actually lost most of its collection to Russia during World War II. The pieces that remained, as well as works subsequently acquired, make the collection

of great importance. There are works by Dürer, Altdorfer, Rubens, Jan Breughel, van Dyck and Rembrandt. There is also an excellent French section, with works by Delacroix, Denis, Monet and Manet, as well as 19th- and 20th-century German painters such as Beckmann and Kirchner. At the heart of the collection are about 40 paintings by Paula Modersohn-Becker.

🏛 Übersee-Museum

Bahnhofplatz 13. **Tel** *(0421) 160 38 190.* ☐ *9am–6pm Tue–Fri, 10am–6pm Sat & Sun.* 🖼

This museum of overseas countries transports the visitor to faraway destinations. Founded in 1891, it was originally a museum of German colonialism and is now dedicated to the culture of non-European nations. Of special interest are exhibits on Pacific cultures, with life-sized models of houses and boats from the Solomon Islands.

🏛 Focke-Museum

Schwachhauser-Heerstr. 240. **Tel** *(0421) 361 35 75.* ☐ *10am–9pm Tue, 10am–5pm Wed–Sun.* 🖼

The excellent collections of this museum compensate for its distant location. Founded in 1918, when the history museum was amalgamated with the decorative arts museum, it presents Bremen's art and culture from the Middle Ages to the present day. Exhibits from patrician houses and original sculptures from the façade of the town hall testify to the wealth of the Hanseatic town. Other sections are devoted to the archaeology of the region as well as to whaling and emigration to the US in the 19th and 20th centuries.

The nearby Rhododendronpark offers a pleasant respite from the museums. It includes 1,600 varieties of rhododendron which become a sea of flowers from late April to June.

Environs

Three places in the Bremen area are particularly worth a detour. About 50 km (31 miles) to the north lies Bremen's deep-sea harbour **Bremerhaven**, with the

Camille Pissarro, *Girl lying on a grassy slope*, Kunsthalle

PAULA MODERSOHN-BECKER (1876–1907)

A pupil of Fritz Mackensen and wife of Otto Modersohn, Paula Modersohn-Becker was the most significant artistic figure in Worpswede. She learned about the Impressionist use of colour during visits to Paris, and her own unique

sensibility made her a precursor of Expressionism. She became famous for her naturalistic paintings of poor, starving and even dying country folk. She died in childbirth, aged only 31, and this is how she was commemorated on her tombstone, in the peaceful village cemetery in Worpswede, by the sculptor Bernhard Hoetger.

Girl playing a flute in birch woods (1905)

Exhibits in the Große Kunstschau in Worpswede near Bremen

Deutsches Schifffahrtsmuseum. This wonderful, marine museum, designed by the renowned architect Hans Scharoun, displays both originals and models of a wide range of ships, dating from the Roman Empire to the present day. A special hall displays the *Hanse Kogge,* a merchant ship dredged from the bottom of the Weser River in 1962. This type of ship was capable of holding 120 tons of cargo, and handled the entire merchandise of northern Europe during the late Middle Ages. Displayed outside, in the open-air part of the museum, are the last great German sailing boat *Seute Deern,* the polar ship *Grönland* and *Wilhelm Bauer,* a U-boat from World War II.

The small village of **Worpswede**, northeast of Bremen, takes the visitor into the world of art. From 1889 until the end of World War II it was a famous artists' colony,

situated in the middle of peat bogs. Apart from poets, such as Rainer Maria Rilke, and such architects as Bernhard Hoetger, the fame of this village rested principally on the painters: Fritz Mackensen, Otto Modersohn, Hans am Ende, Fritz Overbeck and Heinrich Vogeler. Unquestionably the greatest artist in Worpswede was Paula Modersohn-Becker, whose sad fairy-tale world of rustic subjects cannot be defined within one style. Work by the founding members is on display in the **Große Kunstschau and the Worpsweder Kunsthalle**.

Verden an der Aller, the picturesque bishops' residence and once a free town of the Reich, is known to sports enthusiasts thanks to its horse-racing tracks, training centres and stadiums, and the **Deutsches Pferdemuseum**

(horse museum), with a large collection of equestrian artifacts. Seven horse auctions are held in the town each year, and the most important are in April and October.

Apart from horses, Verden an der Aller has a picturesque town centre with small houses, the Andreaskirche, a church with the famous brass tomb of bishop Yso, as well as the Johanniskirche with a rainbow-arched wall dating from the 18th century.

Above the town rises the Dom with a large, steep roof. The hall of this cathedral, a modification of earlier basilicas, is architecturally interesting, with a multi-sided presbytery, a passageway dating from 1268–1311 and Romanesque cloisters and a tower. North of the cathedral is the Domherrenhaus, housing the Historisches Museum, with exhibits on regional history and archaeological and ethnographic departments.

🏛 **Deutsches Schifffahrtsmuseum**
Bremerhaven, Hans-Scharoun-Platz 1.
Tel (0471) 482 070. ☐ *Apr–Oct:*
10am–6pm daily; Nov–Mar: 10–6pm
Tue–Sun. ● *24, 25 & 31 Dec.* 📷

🏛 **Große Kunstschau**
Worpswede. Lindenallee 3 & 5.
Tel (04792) 13 02. ☐ *10am–5pm*
(to 6pm mid-Mar–mid-Nov) daily. 📷

🏛 **Worpsweder Kunsthalle**
Bergstr. 17. *Tel (04792) 12 77.*
☐ *Apr–Oct: 10am–6pm daily;*
Nov–Mar: 11am–6pm daily. 📷

🏛 **Deutsches Pferdemuseum**
Holzmarkt 9. *Tel (04231) 80 71*
40. ☐ *10am–5pm Tue–Sun.*

The Dom in Verden an der Aller, with its unusually large roof

Hamburg

Crest on the town hall

Germany's second largest city, Hamburg has an openness to the world and a variety of architectural styles in its districts, making it a fascinating place to visit. For many years, Hamburg was a leading member of the Hanseatic League and an independent trading town, and in 1945 it became a city-state of the Federal Republic. Visitors are attracted by Hamburg's enormous port, situated right in the centre of the city, colourful entertainments in the red-light district St Pauli, many attractive parks and lakes as well as the warm welcome extended by the locals who, on first encounter, may seem a little cool.

A fountain in the Neo-Renaissance Rathausmarkt

Exploring Hamburg

The best way to get around Hamburg is by metro (U-Bahn and S-Bahn), using an all-day ticket (Tageskarte) since parking space is scarce. The city centre can be explored on foot, including the area between the main railway station and the lake, along with the rest of the old town, the port and Hamburg's two largest museums.

🚇 Rathausmarkt

The symbol of Hamburg is the enormous Neo-Renaissance town hall, the fifth in the city's history. Previous town halls were destroyed by wars as well as a catastrophic fire in 1842. Little remains of the old town. The city's current appearance is characterized by 19th-century style as well as Modernism. The town hall itself, with its ornamental halls, is worth visiting.

Door knocker on St Petrikirche

The town hall square is enclosed on one side by Alsterfleet. Originally a small river, it is today one of numerous canals which have given Hamburg the name "Venice of the North". A monument in memory of the victims of World War I is the work of the artist Ernst Barlach. Between Rathausmarkt and Gänsemarkt runs a network of elegantly roofed shopping arcades. These were built in the 19th century, and have since been continually extended.

🚇 Alster

Elegant arcades lead from the Rathausmarkt to Binnenalster, a large lake in the middle of the city. Like the much larger Außenalster lake further north, it was created by damming the Alster River. On a sunny day, the Jungfernstieg, an elegant boulevard running the length of the Alster, is a pleasant place for a walk. Great views of the city can be had from the café in the Alsterpavilion. There is a small quay from which boats depart for the "Alsterrundfahrt", an excursion which takes the visitor all the way to the Außenalster and to smaller canals with views of the villas in the north of Hamburg and the cityscape of the centre with its five main towers.

🔒 St Petrikirche

Mönckebergstr. *Tel (040) 325 74 00.* 🕐 10am–6:30pm Mon, Tues, Thu, Fri, 10am–7pm Wed, 10am–5pm Sat, 9am–9pm Sun.
The church of St Petri, originally Gothic, was extensively rebuilt in the Neo-Gothic style after the Great Fire of 1842. The Grabower Altar that once belonged to the church has been transferred to the Kunsthalle *(see pp436–7)*. Tourists can still admire the Gothic sculpture of the Madonna, dating from 1470.

🚇 Jakobikirche

Jakobikirchhof 22. *Tel (040) 303 73 70.* 🕐 Oct–Mar: 11am–5pm Mon–Sat; Apr–Sep 10am–5pm Mon–Sat.
The church of St Jacobi, from 1340, was bombed during World War II, and subsequently rebuilt in its original style. Its captivating interior includes the largest Baroque

The main altar in Jakobikirche

For hotels and restaurants in this region see pp513–16 and pp552–4

organ in northern Germany, the work of Arp Schnitger. The triptych of St Luke in the presbytery of the southern nave, a magnificent example of late-Gothic art, was originally created in 1499 for Hamburg's cathedral, which was pulled down in 1804.

🏛 Kontorhausviertel

Deichtorhallen Deichtorstr. 1–2 **Tel** (040) 32 10 30. ⬭ 11am–6pm Tue–Sun (during exhibitions).

After World War I a district of commercial offices known as Kontorhausviertel was built between Steinstraße and Messberg. The **Chilehaus**, built by Fritz Höger in 1922–4, was an experiment in creating a traditional brick building with a Modernist design. This ten-storey building, with its pointed eastern façade resembling a ship's bow, became internationally famous as a symbol of Expressionist architecture.

Nearby are the enormous **Deichtorhallen**, market halls of the port built in 1911–12. Turned into dramatic exhibition halls in 1997, they are now used for major art exhibitions.

The Expressionist Chilehaus in Kontorhausviertel

🏛 Speicherstadt

Deutsches Zollmuseum Alter Wandrahm 16a. **Tel** (040) 30 08 76 11. ⬭ 10am–5pm Tue–Sun.

The atmosphere of the giant warehouse district by the port will seem depressing to some, charming to others. Located within the toll-free area of the port, this district is reached after crossing the customs post. It is the largest complex of warehouses in the world. The Neo-Gothic buildings, dating from the end of the 19th century, are separated by canals. They still serve as

storerooms for coffee, tea and carpets, waiting here in customs-free limbo until the owners are ready to sell them. Recently listed as one of the city's historic monuments, Speicherstadt is waiting for a new owner and a new purpose. The **Deutsches Zollmuseum** (German customs museum), temporarily located here by Kornhausbrücke, (corn house bridge), tells the story of customs and excise over the past hundred years.

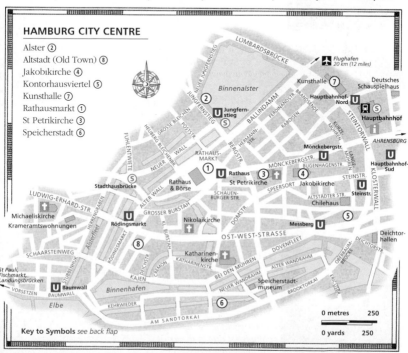

HAMBURG CITY CENTRE

Alster ②
Altstadt (Old Town) ⑧
Jakobikirche ④
Kontorhausviertel ⑤
Kunsthalle ⑦
Rathausmarkt ①
St Petrikirche ③
Speicherstadt ⑥

Key to Symbols see back flap

| 0 metres | 250 |
| 0 yards | 250 |

Kunsthalle

The most interesting art gallery in
northern Germany, the Kunsthalle in
Hamburg has a tradition dating back to
1817, when the Kunstverein (friends of the
fine arts), proud of its middle-class, non-
aristocratic background, was established.
The museum opened to the public in 1869.
The collection has a standard chronological
review of European art movements, with
an emphasis on 19th-century German
Romantics, with works by Caspar David
Friedrich and Philipp Otto Runge. A four-
storey extension, the Galerie der Gegenwart
(contemporary gallery), was built in 1996
to a design by the architect O M Ungers. The
building is reached by an underground link
from the basement of the main gallery.

The Polar Sea (1823–4)
*Caspar David Friedrich's dramatic
seascape, with a sinking ship in
the background behind the
rising flow, is loaded
with symbolism.*

★ **Hannah and Simeon in the
Temple** (c.1627) *Thanks to his
mastery of a sense of drama,
Rembrandt succeeded in depicting
the psychological make-up of his
elderly subjects, who have
recognized the Saviour in
an unspoken message
conveyed to the
temple by Mary
and Joseph.*

**High Altar
of St Peter in
Hamburg** (1383)
*This panelled
painting,
displaying a
stunning wealth of
detail, was produced by
Master Bertram of Minden,
the first artist in Germany to
be identified by his name.*

★ **Morning** (1808)
*This painting by Philipp
Otto Runge centres around
Aurora, goddess of dawn,
and was intended to be
part of a series called
"Times of the Day". The
other works were never
completed due to the artist's
untimely death aged 33.*

Main
entrance

Ground
floor

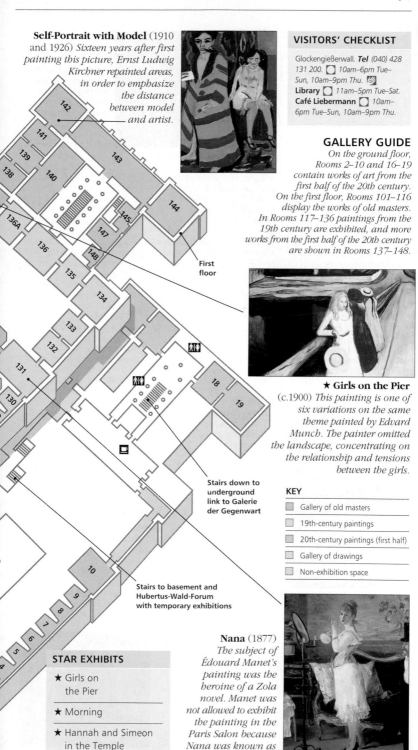

Self-Portrait with Model (1910 and 1926) *Sixteen years after first painting this picture, Ernst Ludwig Kirchner repainted areas, in order to emphasize the distance between model and artist.*

142
141
139
138
140
143
136A
136
144
145
147
148
135
134
133
132
131
130

First floor

GALLERY GUIDE
On the ground floor, Rooms 2–10 and 16–19 contain works of art from the first half of the 20th century. On the first floor, Rooms 101–116 display the works of old masters. In Rooms 117–136 paintings from the 19th century are exhibited, and more works from the first half of the 20th century are shown in Rooms 137–148.

★ **Girls on the Pier**
(c.1900) *This painting is one of six variations on the same theme painted by Edvard Munch. The painter omitted the landscape, concentrating on the relationship and tensions between the girls.*

18
19

Stairs down to underground link to Galerie der Gegenwart

KEY
☐ Gallery of old masters
☐ 19th-century paintings
☐ 20th-century paintings (first half)
☐ Gallery of drawings
☐ Non-exhibition space

10
9
8
7
6
5
4

Stairs to basement and Hubertus-Wald-Forum with temporary exhibitions

STAR EXHIBITS
★ Girls on the Pier
★ Morning
★ Hannah and Simeon in the Temple

Nana (1877) *The subject of Édouard Manet's painting was the heroine of a Zola novel. Manet was not allowed to exhibit the painting in the Paris Salon because Nana was known as a Parisian courtesan.*

🏛 Altstadt (Old Town)

Hamburg's old town extends to the south of the Rathaus (town hall) but, following the Great Fire of 1842 and bombing during World War II, only a few original buildings remain. **Katharinenkirche** (St Catherine's), with its characteristic tower, was begun in the 13th century and completed in the 17th century. It has been restored after damage in World War II. Of the neighbouring Neo-Gothic **Nikolaikirche** only a single tower remained after 1945, the Nikolaiturm, which is the third tallest in Germany. It serves as a monument to the tragic consequences of war.

Deichstrasse is one of a few surviving streets in the old town, with the original façades visible from both the road and the canal (the best view is from Hohe Brücke, a bridge). One of the many famous restaurants is at No. 25, "Zum Brandanfang", where The Great Fire of 1842 was said to have broken out, which eventually destroyed most of the city.

Ornate Baroque pulpit in Hamburg's Michaeliskirche

⛪ Michaeliskirche

Observation tower *Tel* (040) 37 67 81 00. ◯ *Apr–Sep: 9am–6pm Mon–Sat, 11am–5:30pm Sun; Oct–Mar: 10am–5pm Mon–Sat, 11am–5:30pm Sun.*

The massive Baroque church of St Michaelis, visible from afar with its 132-m (433-ft) tower (the "Michel"), is the main symbol of Hamburg. The interior is preserved in a white, grey and gold colour

The neon-lit Reeperbahn in St Pauli

scheme, and some of the fittings are made from tropical wood. The observation platform affords splendid views of the city and its harbour.

🏛 Krameramtswohnungen

Krayenkamp 10. *Tel* (040) 37 50 19 88. ◯ *10am–5pm Tue–Sun.*
Near the Michaeliskirche a section of the old town, the Krameramtswohnungen, has miraculously survived. These half-timbered houses, linked by a courtyard, were funded by the merchants' guild and built to house the widows of shopkeepers. Today they are occupied by tourist shops, cafés and restaurants.

🚢 The Port

Cap San Diego *Tel* (040) 36 42 09. ◯ *10am–6pm daily.* **Rickmer Rickmers** *Tel* (040) 319 59 59. ◯ *10am–6pm daily.*
Situated 104 km (62 miles) inland along the Elbe River, Hamburg is Europe's second largest port after Rotterdam,

and the port dominates the panorama. Every year 12,000 ships dock here from 90 countries. From the U3 Baumwall metro station it is best to walk to **Landungsbrücken**, past the museum ships moored here: the freighter *Cap San Diego* and the sailing boat *Rickmer Rickmers* (1896). Landungsbrücken is a 200-m (656-ft) long building from where the passenger ferries depart. A tour of the harbour is highly recommended. Near Landungsbrücken, in a copperdomed building, is the entrance to Alter Elbtunnel (the old tunnel under the Elbe) where people and cars are lowered in a giant lift.

🏛 St Pauli

Infamous around the world, this area is also known as **Reeperbahn**, after the main street. It is a world of nightclubs and bars, pubs and theatres, sex clubs and brothels. It is here, in Hamburg's red-light district, that some teenage seasonal workers from Liverpool, the Beatles, started their careers. On Herbertstrasse, scantily clad women offer their services behind a metal barrier – women and those under 18 are forbidden entrance. St Pauli

---

FISCHMARKT – A MARKET FOR EVERYTHING

This is an attraction for early risers or for those who never get to bed at all. From 5am (7am in winter) on Sundays the Auktionshalle (auction hall) and the nearby waterside turn into a colourful market place. Fishermen returning from the sea with their freshly caught fish compete with noisy greengrocers offering their wares and bric-à-brac merchants setting out stalls. Thousands of tourists mingle with sailors and ladies of the night relaxing with a cup of steaming mulled wine after a hard night's work in St Pauli. Here and there you can hear Plattdeutsch being spoken, the northern patois. Morning mass at 10am used to mark the end of this colourful spectacle, but today's public lingers on and then hurries off to bed instead of church.

Bric-à-brac on sale at a market stall in Fischmarkt

For hotels and restaurants in this region see pp513–16 and pp552–4

even has an Erotic-Museum, where next to the exhibits are reproductions of works by artists from Rembrandt to Picasso, which are said to "prove" that everything revolves around the female posterior.

Environs
The magnificent palace in **Ahrensburg** (1595), 23 km (14 miles) to the northeast, has Baroque and Rococo interiors open to visitors.

Façade of Schloss Ahrensburg, flanked by towers

Altes Land ⑨

Road map C2.

On the flood plains stretching for more than 30 km (19 miles) between Hamburg and Stade, along the Lower Elbe River, is the Altes Land (old land). This area is fertile and has the largest number

of orchards in Germany. Many visitors come here in May, when cherry and apple tree blossom turns everything into a sea of white and pink. In this riot of colour stand sturdy red-brick houses with white half-timbered panels, thatched roofs and carved gates. The most beautiful villages are **Neuenfelde**, **Jork**, **Borstel**, **Steinkirchen** and **Hollern**, with their richly furnished Baroque churches.

Stade ⑩

Road map C2. 🏛 *47,000.*
🚆 *U3 to Neugraben, then by train or catamaran from Landungs-brücken.* ℹ️ *Hansestrasse 16 (04141-40 91 70).*

This medieval Hanseatic town has retained most of its half-timbered buildings, with the most attractive in the **Alter Hafen** (old harbour). There is a also a quaint crane and the **Schwedenspeicher** (Swedish granary) dating from the Swedish occupation during the Thirty Years' War (1692–1705). It is now home to the **Schwedenspeicher-Museum**, Stade's regional museum with exhibits on the town's history and defence system, including wheels from 700 BC, which were part of a Bronze-Age cart. Nearby, an interesting building at Am Wasser West 7 houses the **Kaufmann Collection**, with works by Worpswede artists. The entire old

The Baroque portal of the Dutch-influenced Rathaus in Stade

town is surrounded by preserved modern fortifications. Other attractions are the **Bürgermeister-Hintze-Haus** at Am Wasser West 23, a house built for the mayor, Hintze, in 1617–46, and the exquisite Baroque **Rathaus** (town hall) from 1667, its design revealing Dutch influence.

It is also worth visiting two Gothic churches: **St Wilhadi** from the 14th century which boasts an interesting Gothic hall and a leaning tower, and **St Cosmas and Damiani**, founded after the Great Fire of 1659, with marvellous Baroque furnishings.

🏛 **Schwedenspeicher-Museum**
Am Wasser West 39. **Tel** *(04141) 32 22.* ⏰ *10am–5pm Tue–Fri, 10am–6pm Sat & Sun.* 📷

The half-timbered houses along the waterside of Alter Hafen in Stade

Lüneburg ⓫

Road map D2. 👥 *70,000.*
🏛 ℹ *Rathaus, Am Markt (04131-
207 66 20).* **www**.lueneburg.de

It is hard to believe that this
small, former Hanseatic town
was once one of the weal-
thiest in Germany. Its
prosperity was founded on
salt mines. Opened in 956,
they provided work for more
than 2,000 people by the late
Middle Ages and were the
largest industry in Europe.
    Lüneburg's most important
monument is the **Rathaus**
(town hall). The interior
is even more intriguing
than the frequently re-
built façade, in particular the Großer Ratssaal
(the main hall) with its
Gothic stained-glass
windows and 16th-cen-
tury frescoes of the Last
Judgement, as well as
the Große Ratsstube
(council chamber) with
Renaissance woodwork
by Albert von Soest.
The **Museum im Rathaus**
(town hall museum) holds a
remarkable collection of
municipal silverware.
    Johnniskirche, one of
Lüneburg's three Gothic churches, stands on Am Sande.
It has a 108-m (354-ft) west
tower, which leans more than
2 m (6 ft) from the perpendicular. In one of its five naves
there is a panelled painting
dating from 1482–5, the
masterful work of the German
painter Hinrik Funhof. Also
interesting is the soaring
basilica of **Michaeliskirche**,
consecrated in 1409.

Not far from here is the old
port on the Ilmenau River. On
Lüner Straße stands the **Altes
Kaufhaus**, a former herring
warehouse with a Baroque
façade. The 14th-century
wooden crane was rebuilt in
the 18th century. It was used
to load salt onto ships. The
decorative wavy brick lines
(Taustäbe) on many of the
old buildings are charac-
teristic of the town.

🏛 **Museum im Rathaus**
Am Markt. **Tel** *(04131) 30 92 30.*
⏰ *10am–5pm daily (by tour only).*
⬤ *1 Jan, 24–26 & 31 Dec.* 📷

A typical farmstead in Lüneburger Heide

Lüneburger Heide ⓬

Road map D2. ℹ *Lüneburg, Barck-
hausenstr. 35 (01805-20 07 05).*

South of Hamburg, between
the rivers Elbe and Aller,
is a large sprawling area of
heathland, grazed by heifers
and sheep and buzzing with
bees in the heathers and pine
forests. Until the Middle Ages,
this area was covered by
dense mixed forests, but
these were felled in order to
satisfy demand for wood in

the saltworks of Lüneburg.
The half-stepped terrain
provides grazing land for
Heidschnucken, the local
breed of sheep. The heather
moors are best seen at the
**Naturschutzpark Lünebur-
ger Heide**, a large area of
nature reserve founded in
1921. From the village of
Undeloh it is best to continue
by foot, bike or carriage to
the traditional village of
Wilsede. From Wilsede it is
not far to Wilseder Berg, the
highest peak of this moraine
region. The view of the surrounding countryside is particularly beautiful at the end of
August, when the purple
heather is blooming.

Soltau ⓭

Road map C3. 👥 *23,000.* ℹ *Am
Alten Stadtgraben 3 (05191-82 82 82).*

The main attraction of the
town of Soltau is **Heidepark
Soltau**, a vast funfair with
trains, water rides and a
genuine Mississippi steam-
boat. For nature lovers, the
Vogelpark Walsrode, 20 km
(12 miles) southwest of Soltau,
may be a more attractive alternative. It holds about 1,000
species of birds from every
continent, from penguins to
birds of paradise. Aviaries,
some 12-m (40-ft) tall, seek to
simulate an impression of the
birds' natural environment.

🦢 **Heidepark Soltau**
Tel *(05191) 91 91.* ⏰ *Apr–Oct:
9am–6pm daily (admission till 4pm).*
🦢 **Vogelpark Walsrode**
Tel *(05161) 604 40.* ⏰ *Mar–Oct:
9am–7pm daily.*

Environs:
In grim contrast to both parks
stands **Bergen-Belsen**, a
concentration camp built by
the National Socialists in the
moorland of Osterheide, about
30 km (19 miles) south of
Soltau. A monument and
small museum commemorate
the place where 50,000
people were murdered,
among them Anne Frank.

🏛 **Gedenkstelle Bergen-Belsen**
Lohheide. **Tel** *(05051) 60 11.*
⏰ *9am–6pm daily.*

Eighteenth-century wooden crane in Lüneburg

For hotels and restaurants in this region see pp513–16 and pp552–4

Vogelpark Walsrode – a paradise with 1,000 different bird species

Celle ⑭

Road map C3. 🏢 74,000.
🚉 Bahnhofplatz. 🛈 Markt 14–16
(05141-12 12).
www.region-celle.de

Between the years 1378 and 1705, Celle was the seat of distant relations of the Welf family, the reigning dynasty in the Duchy of Brunswick-Lüneburg. The **Schloss** (castle), rebuilt in Renaissance style after 1533, has a preserved eastern façade with octagonal towers at the corners, gables and bay windows. It is one of the most important early-Renaissance buildings in Germany. The Gothic chapel is worth visiting. It was rebuilt in a Mannerist style to a design by Martin de Vos, who painted 76 of its paintings, including the famous *Crucifixion* (end of the 16th century).

Celle prides itself on 500 half-timbered houses, with the most interesting ones in picturesque Kalandgasse and Zöllnerstrasse. **Hoppner Haus**, at Poststrasse 8, is richly decorated with

reliefs of mythological beasts. Equally interesting is the painted decoration of the **Rathaus** (town hall), a great example of Weser Renaissance (*see p453*) from 1579. From the **Stadtkirche** church tower great views unfold. The Baroque **Synagoge**, beyond the old town, is the only one surviving in northern Germany.

♣ **Schloss**
Tel (05141) 12 373. ⬜ Apr–Oct: 11am, noon, 1, 2 & 3pm Tue–Sun; Nov–Mar: 11am & 3pm Tue–Sun. 🎧

⛪ **Stadtkirche**
Tel (05141) 7735. ⬜ 10am–6pm Tue–Sat. **Tower:** Apr–Oct: 10–11:45am 2–4:45pm Tue–Sat.

⭐ **Synagoge**
Im Kreise 24. ⬜ 3–5pm Tue–Thu, 9–11am Fri, 11am–1pm Sun.

Environs:
The town of **Wietze**, 11 km (7 miles) west of Celle, has been a centre of petroleum since 1858. The **Deutsches Erdölmuseum Wietze** provides a very interesting overview on the history of oil extraction. The neighbouring village of **Wienhausen** has a Cistercian

Kloster (monastery) with a beautiful 13th–14th century church. Worth seeing are its Gothic frescoes, the presbytery vaults and the 14th- and 15th-century tapestries.

🏛 **Deutsches Erdölmuseum**
Schwarzer Weg 7–9. *Tel* (05146) 92 340. ⬜ Mar–Oct: 10am–5pm Tue–Sun; Jun–Aug: 10am–6pm Tue–Sun. 🎧

⛪ **Wienhausen Kloster**
Tel (05149) 357. ⬜ Apr–Oct: 10 & 11am, 2–5pm Tue–Sat, noon–5pm Sun. 🎧

Wolfsburg ⑮

Road map D3. 🏢 123,000. 🚉
🛈 Willy-Brandt-Platz 3 (05361-14 333).

During the 1930s, this small village began to develop into a sizeable town, based around the Volkswagen car works. Production of the "people's car" was conceived by Hitler – every German was to be able to afford this inexpensive car, designed by Ferdinand Porsche. The model reached its peak during the post-war economic boom years. The **Volkswagenwerk** factory is open to visitors.

Wolfsburg also has some outstanding examples of modern architecture: a cultural centre designed by Alvara Aalto, a city theatre designed by Hans Scharoun and a planetarium.

🏭 **Volkswagenwerk Autostadt**
Stadtbrücke. *Tel* (0800) 28 86 78 23. ⬜ 9am–8pm (to 6pm Apr–Oct) daily. 🎧 guided tours every 15 mins

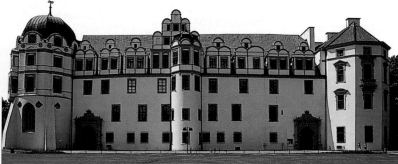
The façade of the Schloss with octagonal towers at the corners, in Celle

The Renaissance Schloss in Stadthagen

Stadthagen 🔟

Road map C3. 👥 23,800. 🚉
ℹ️ *Am Markt 1 (05721-92 60 70).*

The counts of Schaumburg-Lippe used the Renaissance **Schloss** (castle) as their private residence. Apart from this and the town hall, the main attraction is the church of **St Martini** which has an early Baroque mausoleum of Ernst zu Holstein-Schaumburg built onto its eastern wall. Adrian de Vries, court artist to Rudolf II in Prague, created a masterful monument of bronze figures.

🔼 St Martini
Schulstr.18. ⬜ *3–5pm Wed & Fri.*

Environs
A gem of Romanesque architecture can be found at **Idensen** near Wunsdorf, 22 km (14 miles) from Stadthagen. The church interior (1120) is entirely painted with scenes from the Old and New Testaments, and there is a vast, Byzantine-style image of Christ's Enthronement (*maiestas domini*) on the vaulted ceiling of the apsis.

Bückeburg 🔢

Road map C3. 👥 21,000. 🚉
ℹ️ *Schlossplatz 5 (05722-20 61 81).*

In the 16th century this town became the capital of the principality of Schaumburg-Lippe. The philosopher Johann Gottfried von Herder was the preacher here. The **Stadtkirche** (town church), one of the first Protestant churches in Germany, is a pinnacle of Mannerism with

its fantasy façade. Another attraction is the **Schloss** with its enchanting chapel. The Goldener Saal (golden hall), from 1605, has a Götterpforte (portal of the divinities) and a beautiful panelled ceiling.

🔼 Stadtkirche
Lange Str. **Tel** *(05722) 957 70.*
⬜ *15 Apr–15 Oct: 3–5pm Mon; 10:30am–noon, 3–5pm Tue–Fri, 3–5pm Sun; 16 Oct–14 Apr 2:30–4:30pm Wed & Sun.*

⛪ Schloss
Tel *(05722) 50 39.* ⬜ *Apr–Sep: 9:30am–6pm; Oct–Mar: 9:30am–5pm.*

The opulent Goldener Saal in Schloss Bückeburg

Braunschweig (Brunswick) 🔢

Road map E3. 👥 240,000. 🚉
ℹ️ *Vor der Burg 1 (0531-27 35 50).*
🎵 *Festival of Chamber Music (May); Medieval Fair (May/Jun).*

An important commercial and political centre from the early Middle Ages, Braunschweig was chosen as town of residence by Heinrich der Löwe (Henry the Lion), ruler of Saxony

and Bavaria. A member of the Welf family, he eventually lost in his struggle against the German emperor.

Very different in character but equally famous was Till Eulenspiegel, an ordinary man who poked fun at dim-witted citizens, the aristocracy and the clergy. His exploits were fictionalized in the 16th century, and he was immortalized with a fountain on Bäckerklint Square.

Braunschweig's continued decline culminated in the almost total destruction of the town in 1944. During reconstruction, the concept of the "Traditionsinsel" was developed: small islands of reconstructed historic monuments adrift in a sea of modernism.

A tour of the town is best started from Burgplatz (castle square). Here is the **Burglöwe**, the monument of a lion funded by Heinrich in 1166 (the original is in a museum). Symbolizing Heinrich's rule, it was the first such sculpture to be erected since Roman days. The **Dom** (cathedral), Romanesque in style but modified, is well worth seeing. In the north nave, an extension, are unusual turned pillars, and in the transept and presbytery are 13th-century frescoes. Its marvellous treasures include a gigantic seven-armed bronze candlestick, the tomb of Heinrich and his wife Mathilde, the Crucifix of Imerward and a wooden cross with the figure of Christ modelled on the sculpture of *Voltosanto* in Lucca. Visitors can also see the column of the Passion with the figure of Christ, the work of Hans Witten.

To the west of the cathedral lies the **Altstadtmarkt** (old town market). Here are the L-shaped **Rathaus** (town hall), with a two-storey open cloister, and the Gothic church

The Burglöwe, Heinrich der Löwe's monument in Braunschweig

of **St Martini**. The beautiful **Gewandhaus** (cloth hall), rebuilt in the Renaissance, is also worth seeing.

East of the cathedral is the **Herzog-Anton-Ulrich-Museum**, the oldest in Germany. It was opened to the public as a gallery by Duke Anton Ulrich and holds a variety of gems such as Rembrandt's *Family Portrait*, a Giorgioni self-portrait and Vermeer van Delft's *Girl with a Glass of Wine*.

🏛 **Dom**
Burgplatz. 🕐 *10am–5pm daily.*

🏛 **St Martini**
Altstadtmarkt. ***Tel** (0531) 161 21.* 🕐 *10am–1pm daily.*

🏛 **Herzog-Anton-Ulrich-Museum**
Museumsstr. 1. ***Tel** (0531) 122 50.* 🕐 *10am–5pm Tue & Thu–Sun, 1pm–8pm Wed.* 🏷

The richly decorated portal of the Gewandhaus in Braunschweig

Environs

In **Königslutter**, 35 km (22 miles) east of Braunschweig, Emperor Lothar initiated the building of the Benedictine **Abteikirche**, a monastery church and later his burial place. The portal with figures of lions, a frieze with figures of fishermen, and the cloisters reflect the taste of the times and the northern Italian origin of architects and sculptors; only the frescoes are late 19th-century additions.

Helmstedt, 45 km (28 miles) to the east, is unjustifiably only associated with the former border crossing between East and West Germany. In 1576,

The Marienbrunnen fountain on Altstadtmarkt in Braunschweig

Duke Julius of Brunswick founded the Julius Academy, one of Germany's most popular Protestant universities, where the Italian philosopher Giordano Bruno taught. Juleum (1592–7), the main building, has a central tower and two decorative gables. It is now home to the **Kreisheimatmuseum**, a regional museum and library.

🏛 **Abteikirche**
Königslutter. 🕐 *9am–6pm daily, in winter until 5pm.*

🏛 **Kreisheimatmuseum**
Helmstedt. ***Tel** (05351) 121 14 81.* 🕐 *9–11am, 3–5pm Mon–Fri, 3–5pm Sat, 11am–12:30pm Sun.* **Library** 🕐 *3–5pm Tue, Thu.*

Wolfenbüttel ⓳

Road map E3. 🚉 *53,000.* 🚌 ℹ️ *Stadtmarkt 7 (05331-86 280).* 🎭 *Theaterfest (Jul/Aug); Altstadtfest (Aug).*

This small town has had a remarkably turbulent past. From 1432 until 1753 the Welf dukes moved their seat here from Braunschweig. In the 16th century, innovative town design introduced wide avenues and spacious squares. Largely unscathed by World War II attacks, the town has 500 historic half-timbered houses, and a magnificent library. The **Herzog-August-Bibliothek** contains 130,000 volumes, including the most valuable book in the

world, Heinrich der Löwe's Gospel book. Associated with the town are the philosopher Gottfried Wilhelm Leibniz and writer Gotthold Ephraim Lessing. The **Lessinghaus** houses a literature museum.

The centre of the town is dominated by the **Schloss**, the largest castle in Lower Saxony, refurbished in the Baroque style in 1714–16. It houses the **Schlossmuseum** with regional items such as furniture and tapestries. The Venussaal (hall of Venus) has beautiful Baroque ceiling frescoes. Opposite the castle is the **Zeughaus** (armoury), built in 1613–19 to a design by Paul Francke.

Continuing eastwards the visitor will get to the **Hauptkirche**, the 16th-century church dedicated to *Beatae Mariae Virginis*, the ducal pantheon and the leading example of Protestant Mannerist architecture. Begun in 1608, the church's façade has delicate reliefs, while the interior reveals an unusual combination of styles.

⚜ **Schloss and Schloss-museum**
Schlossplatz 13. ***Tel** (05331) 924 60.* 🕐 *10am–5pm Tue–Sun.* **Lessinghaus, Museum & Zeughaus Tel** *(05331) 80 80.* 🕐 *11am–5pm Tue–Sun.* **Herzog-August-Bibliothek** 🕐 *8am–8pm Mon–Fri, 9am–1pm Sat,* 🔒 *24 & 31 Dec.* 🏷

🏛 **Hauptkirche**
Michael-Praetorius-Platz 9. ***Tel** (05331) 72 055.* 🕐 *9am–noon, 2–5pm Tue & Thu.*

Baroque façade of Schloss Wolfenbüttel

Hannover (Hanover) 🔟

The capital of Lower Saxony, Hannover does not at first glance seem particularly exciting, but appearances can be deceptive: the town boasts interesting architecture in the historic centre, magnificent Baroque gardens and one of Europe's most important museums of modern art. Hannover's past was marked by its dynastic links with England, sharing the same ruler during the years 1714–1837. Annual industrial trade fairs have earned the town an international reputation, and in 2000 Hannover hosted the international exhibition Expo 2000 which attracted 18 million visitors.

Exploring Hannover

After the near-total destruction of the old town in 1944, many historic monuments have been rebuilt, and large green spaces encourage the visitor to explore the town on foot. It is best to follow an extensive circuit, starting from and returning to the railway station. The Baroque gardens at Herrenhausen in the northwest of the town are reached by metro (U-Bahn 4, 5).

🎭 Opernhaus

Opernplatz 1. *Tel* (0511) 99 99 11 11.
The opera house was built in 1845–57 by George Ludwig Friedrich Laves, Hannover's most important architect, to a fine Neo-Classical design. Particularly charming is the façade with portico columns.

🏛 Niedersächsisches Landesmuseum

Willy-Brandt-Allee 5. *Tel* (0511) 980 76 66. ◷ 10am–5pm Tue–Sun, 10am–7pm Thu. 🖼
The most interesting part of the state museum of Lower Saxony is the picture gallery, which holds excellent German medieval and Renaissance paintings (Dürer, Spranger, Cranach), a good section with Dutch and Flemish paintings (Rubens, Rembrandt, van Dyck) as well as German paintings of the 19th and 20th centuries, with fine examples of Romanticism and Impressionism (Friedrich, Corinth, Liebermann).

🏛 Sprengel Museum

Kurt-Schwitters-Platz 1. *Tel* (0511) 16 84 38 75. ◷ 10am–8pm Tue, 10am–6pm Wed–Sun. 🖼
One of Europe's finest museums of modern art, the Sprengel-Museum reflects the city's role as an artists' mecca in the 1920s, before the National Socialists destroyed works of art that they designated as "degenerate". Hannover's controversial artist Kurt Schwitters worked here, as did El Lissitzky, whose *Kabinett der Abstrakten* (school of abstraction, 1928, reconstructed) is worth seeing. Funded by Bernhard Sprengel, a chocolate magnate, the museum was built in 1979, and holds works by Munch, Chagall and Picasso, as well as many more recent artists, including Christo.

The museum is located by Maschsee, a large artifical lake created in the centre of the city in 1936. During the summer it teems with motor and sailing boats, while Hanoverians stroll around its banks.

Mueller's *The Lovers* (1920), in the Sprengel-Museum

🏛 Neues Rathaus

Trammplatz 2. *Tel* (0511) 168 45 333. **Dome** ◷ Apr–Oct: 9:30am–6pm Mon–Fri, 10am–6pm Sat & Sun.
The gigantic town hall symbolizes the lofty ambitions of the wealthier citizens at the beginning of the 20th century. It was built from 1901–13, on more than 6,000 beech pillars, modelled on a Baroque palace with a central dome, and decorated with Neo-Gothic and Secessionist detail. The Swiss artist Ferdinand Hodler created a vast painting entitled *Einigkeit* (unity) for the Debating Hall, which depicts the arrival of Protestantism in the town in 1533. A unique oblique lift takes you up to the dome from where there are wonderful views.

🏛 Leineschloss

Hinrich-Wilhelm-Kopf-Platz.
In the historic city centre by the Leine River stands the Leineschloss, a 17th-century palace completely rebuilt by the local architect Laves between 1817 and 1842. It had to be rebuilt again after destruction in World War II, and now serves as headquarters for the Niedersächsischer

Façade of the vast Neues Rathaus, with its central dome

For hotels and restaurants in this region see pp513–16 and pp552–4

Interior of the church of St Georg und St Jacobus, in Marktplatz

Landtag (Lower Saxony state parliament). The porticos on the façade were modelled on ancient Greek temples.

🏛 Marktplatz

Although the houses on this square had to be almost completely rebuilt after World War II, this is one of the best examples of 15th-century red-brick architecture, with amazing gables with projections as well as figurative friezes of glazed terracotta. Nearby, the Marktkirche St Georg und St

Jacobus (church of St George and St Jacob) features a 14th-century nave with a characteristic four-pinnacled tower. The most valuable object among its furnishings is the Gothic altar, with scenes of the Passion and copper engravings by the renowned artist Martin Schongauer.

⚜ Herrenhäuser Gärten

Despite having been razed to the ground during World War II, the gardens in Hannover's Herrenhausen district are among the most beautiful Baroque gardens in Germany. They were established by Duchess Sophie von der Pfalz, daughter of Elizabeth Stuart and mother of England's

VISITORS' CHECKLIST

Road map C3. 522,000.
Ernst-August-Platz. *Ernst-August-Platz 8 (0511-123 45-111).*
Sat. *Schützenfest (Jun/Jul).*
www.hannover.de

George I. The Großer Garten, the most important of the four gardens, has a formal layout modelled on 17th- and 18th-century Dutch parks. It is a botanical garden with fountains, including the Große Fontäne, the tallest in Europe with a 82-m (269-ft) water spout. There are grottoes, mazes, sculptures and decorative urns, and the hedges are some 21 km (13 miles) long.

The stunningly beautiful Baroque gardens in Herrenhausen

HANNOVER CITY CENTRE

Leineschloss ⑤
Marktplatz ⑥
Neues Rathaus ④
Niedersächsisches Landesmuseum ②
Opernhaus ①
Sprengel Museum ③

0 m   300
0 yards   300

Key to Symbols see back flap

Hildesheim ㉑

The undisputed capital of Romanesque culture, the old town of Hildesheim was transformed into a heap of rubble by heavy bombing on 22 March 1945. The most important monuments have now been recreated, with mixed results, surrounded by modern developments. Two churches, the Michaeliskirche and the Dom St. Mariä, are UNESCO World Heritage sites, and the Roemer-Pelizaeus-Museum of Egyptian Culture also makes a visit to Hildesheim worthwhile.

Wedekindhaus, a beautiful half-timbered house on Marktplatz

Exploring Hildesheim

Contrary to received wisdom, the city is best visited on foot. Visitors can park in the centre, for example near the church of St Michael, and then explore the main sights from here. A round tour, including the museums, should not take longer than around 4–5 hours. It is also possible to follow the Rosenroute (rose trail) around town which is marked on the pavements by white roses.

🏛 Marktplatz

Since gaining civic rights in the 11th century, the heart of the bishopric town has been its market square. Every detail has now been faithfully reconstructed, and it is easy to forget that the square looked totally different only a few years ago. In 1987, the Knochenhaueramtshaus (butchers' guild hall) was rebuilt, the largest and most famous half-timbered house in Germany, dating from 1529. Opposite are the Gothic town hall and the Tempelhaus, an original 15th-century building with round turrets and a half-timbered annexe, added in 1591. Reliefs depict the story of the Prodigal Son.

🔒 Andreaskirche

Andreasplatz. ⏰ Apr–Sep: 9am–6pm Mon–Fri, 9am–4pm Sat, 11:30am–4pm Sun; Oct–Mar: 10am–4pm Mon–Sat, 11:30–4pm Sun. **Tower** May–Oct: Mon–Sat, noon–4pm Sun.
The reconstructed Gothic church of St Andrew is notable for the brightness and the quality of the light that passes through its vast windows, as well as its soaring proportions. The 115-m (377-ft) tower was added in the 19th century.

🔒 Michaeliskirche

Michaelisplatz. **Tel** (05121) 34 410. ⏰ Apr–Oct: 8am–6pm Mon–Sat, noon–6pm Sun; Nov–Mar: 9am–4pm Mon–Sat, noon–4pm Sun.
Built on the instructions of Bishop Bernward, the church is a textbook example of what became known as the Ottonian style, the early Romanesque culture of the Otto dynasty. Its characteristic feature is the streamlined simplicity of interior and exterior, with square pillars intersecting with the naves. The sarcophagus of the founder, St Bernward, is in the crypt in the western part of the church.

Luckily, a rare painted 12th-century ceiling was removed during World War II and thus largely survived. It depicts the story of Redemption, from Adam and Eve through to Mary and the Saviour.

🏛 Roemer-Pelizaeus-Museum

Am Steine 1. **Tel** (05121) 93 690. ⏰ 10am–6pm daily.

Bas-relief on the façade of Andreaskirche

The pride of this museum is the Ancient Egyptian collection, one of the best in Europe, which includes the burial figures of Hem Om and the writer Heti from the Old Kingdom (c.2600 BC). It also has fine collections of Chinese porcelain and Inca artefacts, and it is famed for its temporary exhibitions on ancient cultures.

🔒 Dom St Mariä

Domhof. **Tel** (05121) 179 17 60. ⏰ 15 Mar–15 Oct: 9:30am–5pm Mon–Sat, noon–5pm Sun; 16 Oct–14 Mar: 10am–4:30pm Mon–Sat, noon–5pm Sun.
During a hunting expedition in 815, Ludwig der Fromme (the devout), son of Charlemagne, allegedly hung relics of the Virgin Mary on a tree. When he tried to remove them they would not budge – which he took to be a heavenly sign that a church should be founded on this site and a town alongside it. The Tausendjähriger Rosenstock (1,000-year-old rose) of this legend grows to this day

Presbytery of Michaeliskirche

◁ View over Hann's rooftops, Münden

The Bernwardsäule in the Dom St. Mariä – a huge bronze column

in the cathedral's apse, and even survived bombing. The cathedral was reconstructed after World War II, using a model of the church's 11th-century appearance.

Original works of art bear witness to the cathedral's foundry which flourished under bishop Bernward. Bronze double doors depict the Old Testament version of the Creation on one side, and the life of Christ according to the New Testament on the other. The Bernward-

säule, a huge bronze column from 1022, was once topped by a crucifix. The column, with scenes from the life of Christ arranged as a spiralling picture story, recalls the column of Emperor Trajan in Rome. Two further important works of art are a chandelier from 1060, with a diameter of 3 m (10 ft), and a baptismal font (c.1225) based on the personifications of the four rivers of the Garden of Eden.

⛪ Godehardkirche

Godehardsplatz. **Tel** (05121) 34578.
☐ Apr–Sep: 9am–6pm Mon–Fri, 9am–5pm Sat, noon–6pm Sun; Oct–Mar: 9am–4:30pm Mon–Sat, noon–4:30pm Sun.

This church is dedicated to Bernward's successor, bishop Godehard, who like him has been included in the canon of saints. Built in 1133–72, it is typical of local architecture, and also recalls the earlier church of St Michaelis. It has interesting carved capitals as well as a northern doorway with the Blessed Jesus Christ accompanied by St Godehard and St Epiphany.

⛪ Mauritiuskirche

Moritzberg.
Another Romanesque church worth visiting in Hildesheim

VISITORS' CHECKLIST

Road map C3. 🚇 106,000. 🚉 Bahnhofsplatz. 🛈 Rathausstr. 18–20 (05121-179 80). 🎷 Jazz-Time (before Whitsun); Weinfest (May); Klosterkonzert (Jul); Bauernmarkt (Sep); Drachenflugtag (Oct). www.hildesheim.de

is the church of St Maurice, west of the centre. Founded by bishop Hezilo and built in the years 1058–68, the church has enchanting cloisters, dating from the 12th century, and the sarcophagus of the founder of the church.

Presbytery of the massive Godehardkirche, flanked by towers

HILDESHEIM CITY CENTRE

Andreaskirche ②
Dom St. Mariä ⑤
Godehardkirche ⑥
Marktplatz ①
Michaeliskirche ③
Roemer-Pelizaeus-
    Museum ④

0 metres   300
0 yards   300

Key to Symbols see back flap

Street-by-Street: Goslar ㉔

Goslar, at the foot of the Harz mountains, is a captivating town with 1,800 charming, half-timbered houses, the largest number in Germany. For 300 years the Holy Roman Emperors of Germany resided in Goslar, a member of the Hanseatic League also known as "the treasure chest of the North". Goslar's main source of wealth was the nearby mine in Rammelsberg, where zinc, copper and especially silver were mined. The townscape has remained largely unchanged, making it a great tourist attraction as well as a UNESCO world heritage site.

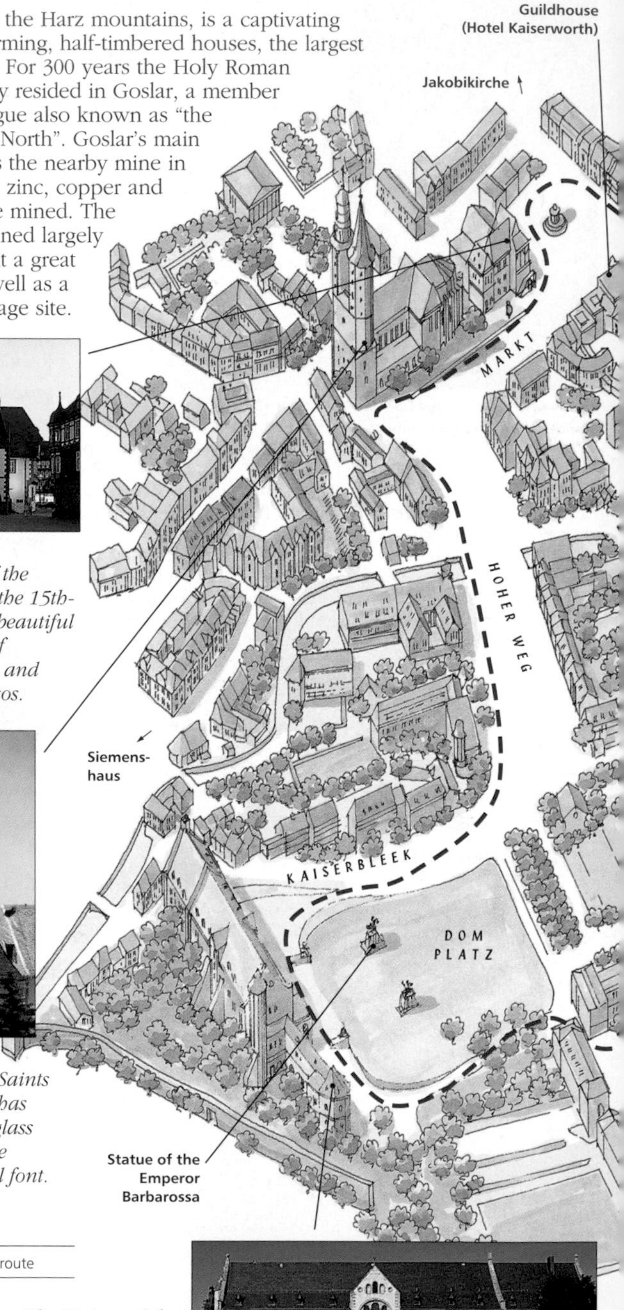

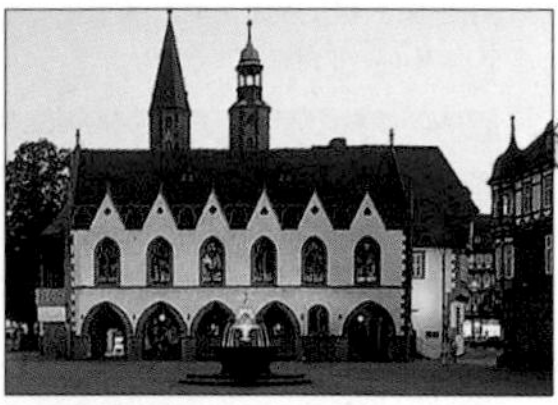

Guildhouse (Hotel Kaiserworth)
Jakobikirche
MARKT
HOHER WEG
Siemenshaus
KAISERBLEEK
DOM PLATZ
Statue of the Emperor Barbarossa

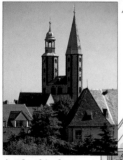

★ Rathaus

On the western side of the market square stands the 15th-century town hall. Its beautiful Huldigungsaal (hall of homage) has a ceiling and walls with Gothic frescos.

★ Pfarrkirche

The Gothic Church of Saints Cosmas and Damian has Romanesque stained-glass windows and a bronze Renaissance baptismal font.

KEY

– – – Suggested route

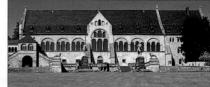

The Kaiserpfalz

The Emperors' palace is a stone building (1005–15), largely rebuilt in the 19th century. The chapel and the Emperors' hall with its superb paintings are worth seeing.

For hotels and restaurants in this region see pp513–16 and pp552–4

★ Historic Half-Timbered Houses

Many charming half-timbered buildings from various periods have survived in Goslar, creating compact rows of houses in the streets of the city centre.

0 meters   50

0 yards   50

→ St Annen-Stift

MASSTRASSE

🏠 Siemenshaus
Schreiberstraße 12. **Tel** *(05321) 238 37.* ⏰ *10am–noon Tue & Thu.*
This half-timbered house, one of the most attractive, was once owned by the Siemens family who have their roots in Goslar. The former brewery on this site is open to visitors.

🏠 St Peter and St Paul
Frankenberger Platz.
Located in the Frankenberg neighbourhood, this was one of 47 churches which once stood in the town. It was built in the 12th century, and the tympanum of the south portal dates from this period. Extensively refurbished, the church prides itself on its magnificent Baroque furnishings.

🏠 St Jakobi
Jakobi-Kirchhof. **Tel** *(05321) 235 33.* ⏰ *10am–4pm daily.*
The present appearance of this church, the only Catholic one in Goslar, is the result of Gothic additions, although the structure of the walls remains Romanesque. The famous work of art in the church is the *Pietà* by Hans von Witten, but it is also worth looking at the wall paintings, the organ and the baptismal font.

🏠 Neuwerkkirche
Rosentorstraße 27a. **Tel** *(05321) 228 39.* ⏰ *Apr–Oct: 10am–noon & 2:30–4:30pm Mon–Sat, 2:30–4:30pm Sun.*
This impressive late-Romanesque church was built in the 12th–13th centuries for the Cistercian Order, although the surviving monastic buildings date from the early 18th century. Inside, the wall paintings and the choir partition are of interest. The church is surrounded by a peaceful garden.

The train in the Bergbaumuseum in Rammelsberg

🏠 Breites Tor
Breite Straße.
Some parts of the defensive system, dating mainly from c.1500, are well preserved. This "wide gate", which can be seen on the eastern approach of the town, is the most imposing part.

🏠 St Annen-Stift
Glockengießerstraße 65. **Tel** *(05321) 398 700.* ⏰ *11am–1pm & 2–4pm Mon–Thu, 11am–1pm Fri & Sat.*
The hospice of St Anna for orphans, the elderly and infirm still fulfills the same function. Behind its picturesque façade is a beautiful small chapel with superb paintings on a wooden ceiling.

🏛 Bergbaumuseum Rammelsberg
Bergtal 19. **Tel** *(05321) 75 00.* ⏰ *9am–6pm daily*
Goslar's mining museum is based in the 10th-century silver mine. One of the oldest surviving industrial structures in the world, it was entered in UNESCO's list of world heritage sites. On display are the mining tools and utensils that were used in various periods. Visitors can take a train ride through the mine and learn about the history of mining.

The above-ground buildings of the silver mine in Rammelsberg

Einbeck ㉓

Road map C3. 🏛 *29,400.* 🚉
🛈 *Rathaus, Marktplatz 6 (05561-91 61 21).* **www**.einbeck.de

In the Middle Ages, this town had 600 breweries – more than houses – and today it is still known for its beers; Bockbier, the famous German strong beer, was invented here. Burned down in 1540 and 1549, the town was subsequently rebuilt in a uniformly Renaissance style. The historic town centre is enclosed by the city walls. More than 100 half-timbered houses have survived to this day. **Eickesches Haus** (Marktstraße 13) is particularly eye-catching, with a sculpted façade based on biblical and Classical stories. Other picturesque houses can be found in Tiedexer Straße and in **Markt-platz**. The latter boasts the **Rathaus** (town hall) and the **Rats-waage** (municipal weigh house) and **Ratsapotheke** (chemist). The tower of the neighbouring **Pfarrkirche St Jakobi** (parish church) leans 1.5 m (5 ft) from the perpendicular. In 1741, a Baroque façade was added to hide this.

Stone crest on Göttingen's Rathaus

Environs
15 km (9 miles) from Einbeck is the spa town of **Bad Gandersheim**. It grew up around a Benedictine monastery established here in 852, which in the 10th century was the home of Roswitha von Gandersheim, the first known German poet.

Göttingen ㉔

Road map C4. 🏛 *129,000.* 🚉
🛈 *Altes Rathaus, Markt 9 (0551-499 800).* 🎭 *Händel-fest (Jun); Literaturherbst (Oct), Jazzfestival (Nov); student festivals, such as Stiftungsfest.* **www**.goettingen.de

Along with Tübingen, Marburg and Heidelberg, Göttingen is one of the most renowned German university towns. Established in 1737 by the English King George II, who was also the ruler of Hannover, the university taught the sons of wealthy German, English and Russian aristocrats. Important cultural figures worked here, including the writer Heinrich Heine, the brothers Grimm and the explorer Alexander von Humboldt. Göttingen's reputation as an educational centre continues today, partly due to the establishment of the Max Planck Institute, named after the scientist who was born in the city and developed the quantum theory.

Göttingen is a lively town thanks to its student population, with dozens of cafés, cosmopolitan restaurants and bars. University buildings are scattered all over town, and the **Aula**, a Neo-Classical Assembly Hall, is worth a visit. On the Marktplatz in the town centre stands the **Rathaus** (town hall) with a Gothic stone façade. The **Gänseliesel-brunnen**, the goose girl fountain, in front dates from 1901. It is kissed by students who have passed their exams, and much loved by tourists.

From the southeastern end of the market square, Göttingen's four main churches can be seen: St Michael to the south, St Johannis to the west, St Albani to the east and St Jakobi to the north. The latter two boast late-Gothic altars worth visiting. Together, they testify to Göttingen's early importance in the Middle Ages.

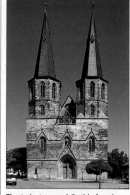

The twin-towered Gothic façade of St Cyriakus in Duderstadt

Duderstadt ㉕

Road map C4. 🏛 *24,500.* 🚉
🛈 *Marktstr. 66 (05527-84 12 00).*

To the south of the Harz mountains, not far from the former border with East Germany, lies this often overlooked gem. A walk around the medieval town is best started on **Obermarkt** (upper market). Here stands the half-timbered **Rathaus** (town hall), with an interesting façade and spiky towers. Inside it has exhibition halls and a cultural centre. East of the town hall rises the Catholic **Probsteikirche St Cyriakus** with its rich interior of altars and 15 Baroque statues. **St Servatius**, its Protestant counterpart, combines Gothic architecture with a Secessionist interior. Nearby is the **Westertorturm**, the only surviving town gate. Its strangely spiralling finial is not a decorative feature, but the consequence of a weakness in its design.

The Gothic Rathaus on Marktplatz in Göttingen

The Weser Renaissance Trail ㉖

The Weser Renaissance is an architectural and decorative style of northern Germany, dating from the mid-16th to the mid-17th century. Its tall roofs and gables were inspired by Dutch architecture, although it has many original features: the *Zwerchhäuser* (bay windows, one or more storeys high), the *Utlucht* (protruding sections of the façade), lavish decorations and multi-wing castles, some with spiral staircases in their towers.

Hameln ①

Rattenfängerhaus (rat catcher's house), Hochzeitshaus (wedding house) and Demptersches Haus (Dempsters' house) are good examples of the Weser Renaissance style. The Romanesque-Gothic Münster (collegiate church) is also worth seeing.

Bevern ③

Another gem of the Weser Renaissance style, the castle in Bevern, near Holzminden, was built from Prussian stone in the years 1602–12. It has four wings as well as two towers in the corners of its courtyard.

Hämelschenburg ②

The castle, built in 1588–1612, is a three-winged building, surrounded by a moat. It has an impressive exterior with towers and decorative gables; its original interiors are also preserved.

Münden ④

The principal buildings that exemplify the Weser Renaissance style are the town hall and the castle, now a regional museum with a collection of ceramics. Fragments of a Renaissance fresco of Duke Eryk II of Calenberg can also be admired here.

0 km   20

0 miles   20

TIPS FOR DRIVERS

Starting point: Hameln.
Length: 112 km (70 miles).
Stopping-off places: good restaurants and bistros can be found in all the towns and villages along the route.

SCHLESWIG-HOLSTEIN

*S*chleswig-Holstein is the northernmost German state, situated between the Baltic and the North Sea and bordered by the Elbe River and Denmark. Weather-beaten by the unstable marine climate, the Gothic brick buildings of Lübeck, queen of the Baltic coast, testify equally to the turbulent history of this region. Today, tourists visit Schleswig-Holstein for its wide sandy beaches and impressive lakes.

Originally, this state comprised two territories: Schleswig in the north, which was inhabited by Germanic tribes (Angles, Saxons, Vikings and Danes) in the Middle Ages, and Holstein in the south, mainly populated by Slavs, who converted to Christianity as late as the 12th century. Its more recent history was characterized by struggles between the Hanseatic towns and the rulers of Denmark. In the 18th century, the entire region, from Altona in the south (now part of Hamburg) to Kolding in the north, belonged to Denmark, but in 1866 it was annexed to Bismarck's Prussia. In 1920, the political borders that exist today were established when Denmark regained the northern part of Schleswig after a plebiscite, leaving a significant Danish minority on the German side.

Schleswig-Holstein is principally an agricultural region, and less densely populated than any other state in Germany. Art lovers are mainly drawn to Lübeck, the most powerful Hanseatic town in the Baltic during the Middle Ages. Lübeck's old town, an architectural gem, has now been listed as a world heritage site by UNESCO. Other places offer surprises aplenty – the visitor will be captivated by the Romanesque churches around Flensburg, while the magnificent countryside more than compensates for the lack of major cultural monuments. A walk through the national park of Schleswig-Holsteinisches Wattenmeer, the moving sand dunes of the elegant island of Sylt, or a romantic sunset on the lake shores in Plön will leave lasting impressions.

The moated Renaissance Wasserschloss in Glücksburg

◁ Idyllic landscape with a lighthouse on Sylt island

Exploring Schleswig-Holstein

Undoubtedly the greatest attraction in this two-part state is Lübeck, and at least one day should be set aside to visit this town. Kiel is a popular destination during the annual Kieler Woche, the world's largest sailing festival. The sun-kissed island of Sylt invites the visitor to linger for a few days, while the stunning scenery of Helgoland is best explored in a one-day trip from Cuxhaven or Büsum. Hotels in the larger towns, such as Schleswig, Kiel or Flensburg, and many provincial boarding houses, provide a good base for excursions.

0 km   25
o miles   25

Buildings in Plön, in the Holstein Switzerland Nature Reserve

GETTING AROUND

The nearest international airport is Hamburg. Two motorways bisect Schleswig-Holstein: leaving Hamburg and the long queues for the Elbe Tunnel behind, the E47 (No 7) takes the visitor to Kiel and via Flensburg on to the Danish peninsula of Jutland, while the E22 (turning off the E47) leads via Lübeck to the Danish capital, Copenhagen.

The lake at Westensee Nature Reserve, where visitors can experience the captivating nature and wildlife close up

SIGHTS AT A GLANCE

KEY

══ Motorway

━━ Main road

⋯⋯ Minor road

▬▬ Main railway

━ Minor railway

▬▬ National border

▬▬ Regional border

Ferries departing for excursions from the harbour in Kiel

Helgoland ❶

For lovers of spices in Germany, it may have seemed a bad deal when in 1890 Germany received Helgoland from Britain in return for Zanzibar, but the island is nevertheless worth a visit. Farthest out in the open sea (50 km/31 miles from the mainland), the island always had great strategic importance, and after 1945, Britain used it as a bombing target before it was returned to Germany in 1952. Today its fresh air and spectacular red cliffs attract thousands of tourists.

VISITORS' CHECKLIST

Road map B1. 🚶 1,900. 🚢 Bremerhaven, Cuxhaven and Wilhelmshaven. 🚩 Lung Wai 28 (04725-81 37 11 & 14). **www**.helgoland.de

Lange Anna ③
Tall Anna, measuring about 40 m (131ft) high, is the best known red sandstone cliff. Nearby is the Lummenfelsen, which is the smallest nature reserve in Germany.

Port ①
On the flat part of the island is Unterland, a small post-war town with 1,900 inhabitants and a port. Fishermen store their nets in the colourful little houses, referred to as Hummerbuden (lobster huts).

Oberland ②
In the upper part of the island stands the Nikolai-kirche, dating from 1959. Close by, and worth a visit, are 16th-century tombs.

0 metres   100
0 yards   100

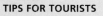

KEY

– – – Suggested route

TIPS FOR TOURISTS

Starting point: the port of Helgoland
Length: 1.7 km (1.1 miles).
Stopping places: there are numerous restaurants, bars and cafés all over the island .

Glückstadt ❷

Road map C2. *12,000.* *Große Nübelstraße 31 (04124-93 75 85).*

The Danish king, Christian IV, founded this little town in 1617 and although less impressive than Hamburg, the town is worth a visit for its layout – roads radiate out from the hexagonal market square, once surrounded by fortifications. On the square stands the reconstructed 17th-century town hall as well as the Baroque Stadtkirche (town church). In 1648, parts of the duchy of Holstein were transferred to Glückstadt. Most of the palaces built to house the Dukes survived, for example the Palais Werner with its amazing ballroom. The regional **museum** is now in Brockdorf-Palais, another palace from 1632.

Detlefsen-Museum
Am Fleth 43. ***Tel*** *(04124) 93 76 30.* *2pm–5pm Wed, 2pm–6pm Thu, Fri, Sat, 2pm–5pm Sun.*

Meldorf ❸

Road map C1. *7,500.* *Nordermarkt 10 (04832-97 800).*

Meldorf has preserved the **Dithmarscher Dom**, its cathedral, a 13th-century basilica with an exterior extensively rebuilt in the 19th century. The vaulting in the transept, resembling a cupola, is decorated with Gothic frescos, depicting the legends of saints Catherine, Christopher and Nicholas. There is a richly decorated dividing wall (1603) and a grand triptych of the Crucifixion (c.1520).

The port and waterfront of Flensburg

Sylt ❹

Road map B1. *50,000.* *in Westerland.* *Westerland, Stephanstraße 6 (04651-820 20).*

The island of Sylt, the largest of the North Frisian islands, has long attracted wealthy German visitors. The 50-km (31-mile) long island offers a rich variety of landscapes: white, sandy beaches, shifting sand dunes near List, towering up to 25 m (82ft) high, steep shorelines, the Rotes Kliff (red cliff) near Kampen and the Watt, the endless expanse of mudflats in the national park, Schleswig-Holsteinisches Wattenmeer. **Westerland** is Sylt's main town, and its promenade, Friedrichstraße, is "the" place to be seen. There is also an interesting casino in a former Secessionist spa building.

Flensburg ❺

Road map C1. *84,500.* *Rathausstraße 1 (0461-909 09 20).* *Rum-Regatta in Flensburger Förde (May).*

The most northerly town in Germany, Flensburg was an important trading centre in the 16th century with 200 ships, although at times it belonged to Denmark. The **Nordertor** (northern gate), dating from 1595, is an emblem of the city. The shipping museum is fascinating while the Marienkirche has a Renaissance altar, sculptures and the painting *The Last Supper* (1598). Nearby is the **Heilig-Geist-Kirche** (church of the Holy Ghost), which has belonged to the town's Danish community since 1588. Other interesting churches are **Nikolaikirche** which boasts a magnificent Renaissance organ, and Johanniskirche with a vaulted ceiling dating from around 1500. Its painted scenes show people disguised as animals, which was a covert way of criticizing the church and the system of indulgences.

Environs

Schloss Glücksburg, 9 km (6 miles) northeast of Flensburg, a square castle with massive corner towers on a granite base, was built from 1582–7. Visit its captivating castle chapel, the Roter Saal (red hall) with its low vaulting, and the valuable collection of 18th-century tapestries from Brussels. The artist Emil Nolde lived and worked in **Seebüll**, west of Flensburg, from the age of 20 until his death in 1956.

The sandy beaches of the North Frisian island of Sylt, extending far to the horizon

For hotels and restaurants in this region see pp516–17 and pp555–6

The inner courtyard of Schloss Gottorf in Schleswig

Schleswig **6**

Road map C1. 🚶 *27,000.* 🚌
ℹ️ *Plessenstr. 7 (04621-98 16 16).*
🎭 *Schleswig-Holstein Musik Festival throughout the region (Jul/Aug); Wikinger-Tage (Aug every other year).*

The main seat of the Vikings, Schleswig became a bishop's see as early as 947, and from 1544 to 1713 it was the residence of the dukes of Schleswig-Holstein-Gottorf, once related to the rulers of Denmark and Russia. They resided in **Schloss Gottorf**, a castle with four wings which now houses the **Schleswig-Holsteinisches Landes-museum** (regional museum) as well as northern Germany's most famous archaeological museum, the **Archäologi-sches Landesmuseum**,

exhibiting the *Moorleichen*, prehistoric corpses preserved in peat. It is also worth seeing the two-storey chapel (1590).

The **Dom** (cathedral) was built in stages between the 12th and 15th centuries. Its largest treasure is the Bordes-holmer Altar, a triptych altar carved by Hans Brüggemann in 1514–21. A masterpiece of Gothic carving, it is 12 m (39 ft) high and comprises 392 figures; the only one to look straight at the visitor is the sculptor himself, bearded and hat askew (in the house of Abraham and Melchisede).

Visitors can also walk around the historic fishermen's district of **Holm**, and visit the **Wikinger-Museum Haithabu**, about 4 km (2 miles) from the town centre. The fortifications have survived in the grounds

of this historic Viking settle-ment. The museum is housed in a modern building, which looks like an upturned boat. Exhibits include the depiction of Viking life, models of boats, jewellery and everyday items.

🏛 **Schloss Gottorf/ Schleswig-Holsteinisches Landesmuseum/Archäologi-sches Landesmuseum**
***Tel** (04621) 81 30.* ⏺ *Apr–Oct: 10am–6pm daily; Nov–Mar: 10am–4pm Tue–Fri (to 5pm Sat & Sun).*

🏛 **Wikinger-Museum Haithabu**
***Tel** (04621) 81 32 22.* ⏺ *Apr–Oct: 9am–5pm daily; Nov–Mar: 10am–4pm Tue–Sun.*

Kiel **7**

Road map C1. 🚶 *245,000.* 🚌
ℹ️ *Andreas-Gayk-Straße 31 (01805-65 67 00).* **Town hall** ⏺ *9am–6pm Mon–Fri, 9am–1pm Sat.* 🎭 *Kieler Woche (end Jun).*

Located at the end of the Kieler Förde inlet, Kiel marks the beginning of the Nord-Ostsee-Kanal (Kiel Canal), in service since 1895, with two giant locks. Ferries depart from Kiel for Scandinavia, and in the summer the "Kieler Woche" turns the town into a mecca for yachtsmen from around the world.

A walk along the Schweden-Kai (embankment) and sur-roundings will take visitors to the vast **Rathaus** (town hall), dating from the beginning of the 20th century, and the **Nikolaikirche** (church of St Nicholas) which was rebuilt after the devastation of World War II, with its baptismal font and Gothic altar. Ernst Bar-lach created *Geistkämpfer*, the sculpture outside the church, which symbolizes the triumph

ROMANESQUE BAPTISMAL FONTS

There are few places in the world where visitors can see as many Romanesque baptismal fonts as in Angeln. Generally fashioned from granite, they have been preserved in enchanting 12th-century churches, which can be visited by following a 63-km (39-mile) route along the roads linking Flensburg and Schleswig, Munkbrarup, Sörup, Norder-brarup, Süderbrarup and finally Ulsnis.

Font in the church in Borbry

Font in the church in Munkbrarup

Font in the church in Sörup

A house in Kiel's Schleswig-Holsteinisches Freilichtmuseum

of mind over matter. Pieces of the sculpture, which had been cut up by the National Socialists, were found and reassembled after the war.

The most interesting of Kiel's many museums is the **Schleswig-Holsteinisches Freilichtmuseum**, an open-air museum in Molfsee, 6 km (4 miles) from the centre of Kiel, where German rural architecture from the 16th– 19th centuries is on show. Pottery, basket-making and baking are demonstrated, and the products are sold here.

🏛 **Schleswig-Holsteinisches Freilichtmuseum**
Hamburger Landstraße 97. *Tel* (0431) 65 96 60. ⬜ Apr–Oct: 9am–6pm daily; Nov–Mar: 11am–4pm Sun & public holidays. 📷

Holsteinische Schweiz (Holstein's Switzerland) ❽

Road map D1. 🚌 🛈 Bad Malente, Kurverwaltung, Strand-Allee 75A (04523-20 01 00). 🎷 Jazz-Festival in Plön (May); open-air opera during Sommerspiele in Eutin.

The morain hills, which reach a height of 164 m (538 ft), and 140 lakes are the reasons why this area is known as Holstein's Switzerland. The best means of transport here is the bicycle, allowing visitors to appreciate the beauty of nature and the wealth of the fauna – ornithologists have counted 200 species of birds. The main centre of this holiday area is **Plön** on the

The 17th-century Schloss in Plön, in Holstein's Switzerland

EMIL NOLDE (1867–1956)

Born Emil Hansen, this great artist later adopted the name of the town in which he was born. After studying art in Copenhagen, Munich and Paris, Nolde devoted himself to painting, and was also successful in the graphic arts. From 1906–7 he belonged to the Expressionist group *Die Brücke*. He is known particularly for his use of vivid colours and highly expressive features, embuing his subjects with great emotion. Rejected and forbidden to paint by the National Socialists as an exponent of "degenerate art", Nolde settled and continued to paint in Seebüll, where a house was built for him to his own designs.

Großer Plöner See (large Plön lake). Nearby is **Preetz**, an old shoemakers' town, which has a towerless Gothic church that belonged to a former Benedictine monastery. Older still is the Romanesque church in **Bosau**, a small town in a picturesque location on the Großer Plöner See. It was the first bishopric in this area, and home to Vizelin – the apostle of the Slavs.

It is also worth visiting **Eutin**, a small town full of picturesque buildings, which is sometimes referred to as the "Weimar of the north". The original Schloss, a brick structure with four wings, was built in the Middle Ages as the residence of the Lübeck bishops, but it was substantially altered in the years 1716–27. Worth seeing inside are the palace chapel, the Blauer Salon (blue salon) with Rococo stucco work, as well as paintings by Johann Heinrich Wilhelm Tischbein, which were inspired by the *Iliad* and the *Odyssey,* epic poems written by Homer.

The Dom in Ratzeburg

Ratzeburg ❾

Road map D2. 🚍 12,500. 🚌 🛈 Schlosswiese 7 (04541-85 85 65 or 800 080).

Ratzeburg, situated on an island in the Großer Ratzeburger See, is linked with the mainland by three causeways. The town was named after Ratibor, the duke of the Elbe River area. Henry the Lion established a missionary bishopric here in 1154, and later it became the residence of the Lauenburg dukes.

The **Dom** (cathedral) is one of the earliest examples of brick architecture, a style that was imported from Lombardy. The southern vestibule of the Romanesque basilica is particularly impressive – with herringbone-pattern brickwork and lines of black tiles as interior decoration. The Romanesque stalls, a 13th-century crucifix in a rainbow arch, the ducal gallery above the nave and the Baroque altar in the southern transept are some of its treasures.

Street-by-Street: Lübeck ⑩

This "specific nest", as Lübeck was described by its
most famous resident, Thomas Mann, is well worth a
visit. The most important town in the Baltic basin by
the end of the Middle Ages, it is now a magnet for fans
of Backsteingotik, Gothic brick architecture which has
been elevated to a national style. In Lübeck it is easy to
see why: church interiors, the façades of buildings, the
city gates, the unique town hall and even the Medieval
hospital resemble pictures from an illustrated history of
architecture brought to life. Despite a few blunders, the
city has been beautifully rebuilt after World War II and
enjoys a positive revival.

Rathaus
*Germany's most famous
brick town hall, dating
from 1226, has unusual
walls and turrets.*

Buddenbrookhaus
*This beautiful Gothic
building was once
the home of Nobel-
prize-winning
author Thomas
Mann. It now
houses a
museum
dedicated to
the Mann family.*

Heiligen-Geist-
Hospital

★ Marienkirche
*St Mary's Church, larger than the
cathedral and situated behind the
town hall, holds great art treasures.*

Holstentor
*This gate, once the only entrance
into Lübeck, was built by Hinrich
Helmstede in the years 1466–78,
based on Flemish designs. It has
become the emblem of the town.*

Petrikirche
The church of St
Peter, from the
first half of the
14th century, is
Lübeck's only
five-naved church.

KEY

– – – Suggested route

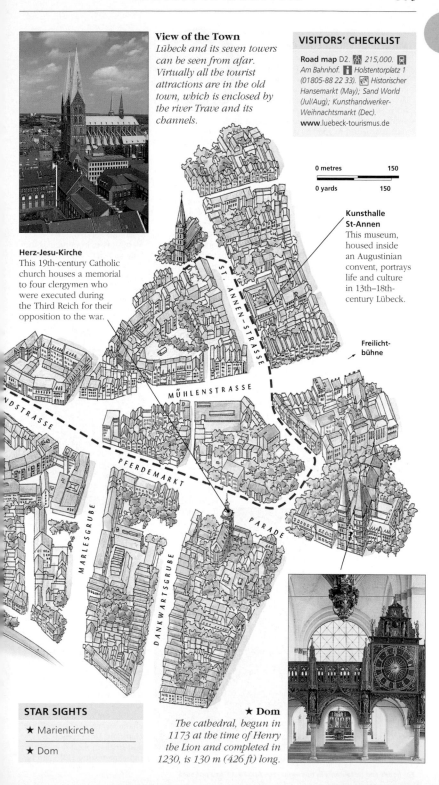

View of the Town
Lübeck and its seven towers can be seen from afar. Virtually all the tourist attractions are in the old town, which is enclosed by the river Trave and its channels.

| 0 metres | 150 |
| 0 yards | 150 |

Kunsthalle St-Annen
This museum, housed inside an Augustinian convent, portrays life and culture in 13th–18th-century Lübeck.

Herz-Jesu-Kirche
This 19th-century Catholic church houses a memorial to four clergymen who were executed during the Third Reich for their opposition to the war.

Freilicht-bühne

ST. ANNEN-STRASSE

MÜHLENSTRASSE

...NDSTRASSE

PFERDEMARKT

MARLESGRUBE

DANKWARTSGRUBE

PARADE

STAR SIGHTS

★ Marienkirche

★ Dom

★ Dom
The cathedral, begun in 1173 at the time of Henry the Lion and completed in 1230, is 130 m (426 ft) long.

MARZIPAN FROM LUBECK

A favourite present from Lübeck is marzipan, which has been popular throughout Europe since the 19th century. The sweets are made from two-thirds sweet almonds imported from Venice and one-third sugar and aromatic oils. The Persians referred to it as *marsaban*, and in 1530 its name was recorded for the first time in Lübeck as *Martzapaen*. From 1806, the Niederegger patisserie perfected the recipe; they established a patisserie on Breite Strasse which operates to this day.

Exploring Lübeck

All the most important monuments, with the exception of the Holstentor, are situated within the old town, which is best explored on foot.

🔒 Marienkirche

⏰ 9am–5pm daily, in winter to 3pm.
St Mary's church was constructed by the Lübeckers as a monument to themselves. The twin-towered basilica with transept and a passageway around the polygon-shaped presbytery is the brick modification of a Neo-Classical French cathedral.

Its vast interior boasts the highest vaulted brick ceiling in the world (40 m/131 ft) which dominates the other interior features. These include a 10 m (32 ft) bronze Holy Sacrament (1476–9); a baptismal font in the main nave dating from 1337; the altar dedicated to the Virgin Mary in the Sängerkapelle (singers' chapel) made in Antwerp in 1518; and the main, late-Gothic Swarte-Altar with the Madonna. The Brief-kapelle, the south-western side chapel built around 1310, is one of the earliest examples of star vaulting in Europe.

In one of the towers, the shattered fragments of the church bells have been left embedded in the floor where they fell during the bombing in 1942; the present bells are from St Catherine's in Gdansk.

🏛 Buddenbrook-Haus

Heinrich-und Thomas-Mann-Zentrum, Mengstr. 4. **Tel** (0451) 122 41 92. ⏰ Jan–Mar: 11am–5pm daily; Apr–Dec: 10am–6pm daily. 🔒 24, 25, 31 Dec. 🎫
Literature lovers will wish to visit the Buddenbrook house. Behind its Rococo façade from 1758 is a museum devoted to the Mann family, the great writers who lived here in 1841–91. It is here that Thomas Mann wrote the family saga of the Buddenbrooks, after whom the house is named, and for which he was awarded the Nobel Prize in 1929. The centre exhibits

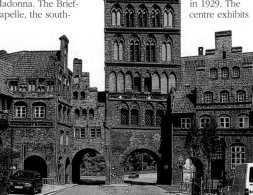

The multi-storey Burgtor, crowned by a Baroque cupola

documents relating to this famous family, in particular to Thomas and Heinrich Mann, concentrating on their time in Lübeck and their emigration and exile after 1933.

🏛 Schabbelhaus

Mengstraße 48 & 52.
Originally the western, wealthier half of Lübeck had many patrician houses, facing the streets with their ornate brick gables. Many of these were damaged in the bombing raids of March 1942, but after World War II they were carefully restored. The most interesting buildings survived in Mengstrasse, in particular the famous Schabbelhaus at No. 48. Built in 1558, this house gained a magnificent Baroque hall in the 18th century. Today it is an attraction in its own right as well as a restaurant.

Stepped gables of the Haus der Schiffergesellschaft

🏛 Haus der Schiffergesellschaft

Breite Straße 2.
The house of the Marine Guild, which dates from 1535, has a splendid interior and now houses one of the city's most elegant restaurants. The façade has stepped gables and terraces/forecourts, typical of Lübeck.

🏛 Füchtingshof

Glockengießerstr. 23.
The eastern part of the town is of an entirely different character: narrow streets link charming Höfe (courtyards) and small, modest houses. The most interesting Höfe can be

For hotels and restaurants in this region see pp516–17 and pp555–6

The faςade of the Gothic Heiliger-Geist-Hospital, with its spiky towers

found at numbers 23 and 39. The Baroque portal of the Füchtingshof, at No. 23, leads to houses which, from 1639, were built for the widows of merchants and captains.

🏰 Burgtor
On the northern limits of the old town stands the castle gate, a second surviving gate of the historic fortifications. A Baroque finial was added to the gate in 1685. The five storeys of the tower are decorated with uniform rows of windows and windbreaks.

✚ Heiliger-Geist-Hospital
Große Burgstr. **Tel** *(0451) 79 07-841.* ☐ *Apr–Sep: 10am–5pm Tue–Sun; Oct–Mar: 10am–4pm Tue–Sun.*
The Holy Ghost hospital is the best preserved Medieval building of its type in central Europe. Built in the shape of the letter T, it has a shorter western section with a twin-aisled hall-church (c. 1286), containing frescos of *Christ and the Madonna on Solomon's Throne* and *Majestas Domini*. The second storey contains the actual hospice. In 1820, small cubicles were created for the elderly, who lived here until 1970.

🔒 Jakobikirche
This 15th-century church, which suffered only insignificant damage during World War II, has preserved its original, mainly Baroque features. Of particular note are the main altar as well as the side altar in the south chapel. The latter was established around 1500 by the mayor, Heinrich Brömbse,

and depicts a scene of the Crucifixion carved in sandstone. Both the small and the large organ originate from the 15th century.

🔒 Katharinenkirche
Königstraße. **Museumskirche St. Katharinen** *Tel (0451) 122 41 80.* ☐ *May–Oct: 10am–1pm, 2–5pm Tue–Sun.*
St Catherine's, the only surviving monastic church, was built by the Franciscans, as is apparent from the absence of a tower and its monastic gallery in the presbytery of the main nave. The western façade, with its glazed brickwork, is of a high artistic quality. In the 20th century, sculptures carved by Ernst Barlach were added (*Woman in the Wind, Beggar on Crutches* and *The Singing Novitiate*). On the western side hangs the painting of *The*

The bright interior of the Gothic Dom

Resurrection of Lazarus by Jacopo Tintoretto, bought by a wealthy patrician; the sculpture of St George and the dragon is a copy of the famous original by the Lübeck artist Bernt Notke, which is now in Stockholm.

🏛 Kunsthalle St-Annen
St-Annen-str. 15. **Tel** *(0451) 122 41 37.* ☐ *Apr–Sep: 10am–5pm Tue–Sun, 10am–5pm Sat & Sun; Oct–Mar: 10am–4pm Tue–Fri, 11am–5pm Sat–Sun.* ● *Easter, 24, 25, 31 Dec.* 🖐
The Augustinian convent houses unusual Lübeck art treasures. There is an impressive number of wooden Gothic altars, commissioned by wealthy families for their private chapels in one of the five churches. The altars were supposed to bring them eternal salvation after death, and to symbolize the wealth and prestige of the family during their lifetime. Gems of the collection are the Hans Memling altar with Christ's Passion, and the external side wings of the Schonenfahrer Altar by Bernt Notke.

🔒 Dom
☐ *Apr–Oct: 10am–6pm daily; Nov–Mar: 10am–4pm daily.*
The cathedral, completed in 1341, takes the form of a Gothic hall-church. Its most precious possession is the Triumphal Cross sculpted from a 17-m (55-ft) oak tree by Bernt Notke, a celebrated local artist. The giant figures, resplendent with emotion, include Adam and Eve, as well as the founder, bishop Albert Krummedick. Among numerous memorials, that dedicated to bishop Heinrich Bocholt, made from bronze, stands out. Additionally, two valuable sculptures can be seen; *Holy Mary Mother of God* with a crown composed of stars, as well as the *Beautiful Madonna* in the southern nave (1509). Note the bronze baptismal font by Lorenz Grove from 1455, with its three kneeling angels.

MECKLENBURG-LOWER POMERANIA

The medieval towns of Schwerin, Wismar, Rostock and Stralsund, as well as several magnificent architectural monuments, provide reason enough to visit this part of Germany, yet it also offers a largely untouched landscape of forests and lakes. Along the Baltic coastline, tourists delight in the beautiful sandy beaches of Darß or Usedom, but above all they head for the island of Rügen, with its famous white cliffs.

Mecklenburg-Vorpommern (Lower Pomerania), a mosaic of regions, can look back on an eventful history. In the 12th century, indigenous Slav tribes were colonized and converted to Christianity. The region became part of the Holy Roman Empire and German colonialism resulted in the Slavs' rapid assimilation. In the Middle Ages, several towns became rich trading centres and joined the Hanseatic League. From the 18th century, the Swedish Empire was the most powerful political force in this part of Europe. It ruled Wismar, Rügen and Stralsund until 1803 and 1815 respectively, when the territories became part of Prussia, and later the German Reich. During World War II the Baltic towns suffered terrible destruction and then from neglect under the German Democratic Republic: in 1953 all the hotels were nationalized and the unique buildings in the Hanseatic towns were left to decay or were destroyed.

After eunification, although still one of the poorest states in Germany, Mecklenburg-Lower Pomerania today has become an idyllic holiday destination. Improvements in the infrastructure, new hotels and restaurants have brought positive change, and it has much to offer. Nature lovers, walkers and cyclists, for example, can enjoy the Mecklenburg lake district and the island of Rügen. Fans of architecture will find a wealth of interest in the palace in Ludwigslust and the castle of Güstrow, as well as the Gothic brick architecture in town halls, churches and smaller buildings.

The beautiful white chalk cliffs on the island of Rügen sweep down to the blue Baltic Sea

◁ The superb Schloss of Schwerin, on an island in the middle of Schwerin lake

Exploring Mecklenburg-Lower Pomerania

This is a large region with only minor roads so visitors are well advised to allow extra time to explore it. The area can be divided into three: the west, stopping off in pretty Wismar or charming Schwerin with its fairy-tale castle; the centre, with the major port of Rostock as a base, and the east, which can be explored from Stralsund or Greifswald. In the central Mecklenburger Seenplatte is Müritz National Park, a vast area of lakes and forests that is ideal for camping, walking and sailing. It is also a good plan to set aside a few days for relaxation on the sandy beaches of Darß, Zingst, Usedom or Rügen.

Mecklenburg's glorious beaches

SIGHTS AT A GLANCE

Anklam **14**
Bad Doberan **5**
Gadebusch **3**
Greifswald **12**
Güstrow **6**
Ludwigslust **2**
Neubrandenburg **7**
Rostock p476 **9**
Rügen pp478–9 **11**
Schwerin pp470–71 **1**
Stralsund p477 **10**
Usedom **15**
Wismar **4**
Wolgast **13**

Excursions

Nationalpark Müritz **8**

SEE ALSO

• *Where to Stay* pp517–19

• *Where to Eat* p556–7

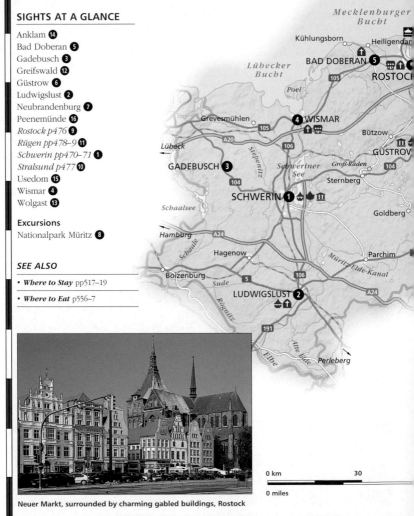

Neuer Markt, surrounded by charming gabled buildings, Rostock

0 km   30

0 miles

GETTING AROUND

International flights land at Hamburg and Berlin, domestic flights at Rostock and Heringsdorf on Usedom. Ferries go from Denmark, Sweden and Lithuania to Sassnitz and Rostock, and the E55 motorway runs from the south to Schwerin and Rostock.

Rügen, lit by dawn sunlight

Kap Arkona
Hiddensee
Sassnitz
RÜGEN
Prerow
Darss
Zingst
Waase
11
Bergen
Ahrenshoop
Barth
96
Putbus
105
10 STRALSUND
Ribnitz-Damgarten
Greifswalder Bodden
194
96
16 PEENEMÜNDE
Grimmen
Wieck
12
13 WOLGAST
Recknitz
110
A20
GREIFSWALD
109
111
Gnoien
111
Heringsdorf
Ahlbeck
USEDOM
ECKLENBURG-
Demmin
Peene
110
15
VORPOMMERN
ANKLAM 14
Usedom
Kummerower See
Oderhaff
Teterow
Malchin
96
Zarow
Ueckermünde
Malchiner See
Basedow
Reuterstadt
197
108
Friedland
104
Uecker
Randow
NATIONALPARK MÜRITZ
NEUBRANDENBURG
7
109
Waren
192
A20
Pasewalk
Malchow
8
Tollensesee
Stargard
104
Müritzsee
198
Szczecin
198
Neustrelitz
198
A11
Mirow
96
Berlin
Wittstock
Seenplatte
Berlin

KEY

- Motorway
- Main road
- Minor road
- Road under construction
- Main railway
- Minor railway
- National border
- Regional border

The attractive cloisters of Schloss Güstrow

Schwerin ❶

Despite protests from Rostock, the smaller town of
Schwerin was chosen as the capital of the newly united
state of Mecklenburg-Lower Pomerania. This was an
inspired choice as the town is picturesquely situated
amid several lakes, with a fairy-tale castle on an island,
and an enchanting old town with many Neo-Classical
and historic buildings that survived World War II largely
unscathed. Apart from a brief spell, the Mecklenburg
dukes resided in Schwerin from 1318–1918. Intellectual
life flourished here in the 16th century and
so the city is known as "Florence
of the North".

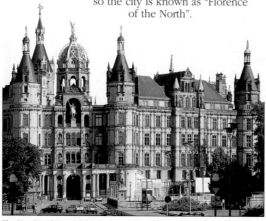

The Neo-Renaissance Schloss on an island in Schweriner See

Exploring Schwerin
The old town of Schwerin is
situated between Pfaffenteich
railway station and Schweriner See, a vast 65-sq km (25-
sq mile) lake. All the town's
most important tourist attractions can easily be visited on
foot. Close by to the north is
Schelf, which was once a
separate town.

♣ Schloss
Schlossinsel. *Tel (0385) 52 52 920.*
☐ *15 Apr–14 Oct: 10am–6pm
daily; 15 Oct–14 Apr: 10am–5pm
Tue–Sun.*
Situated on Burg Island, this
castle is often referred to as
the "Neuschwanstein of
Mecklenburg", after the
famous Bavarian castle. The
Schweriner Schloss was in
fact largely built in 1843–57 to
an eclectic design by Georg
Adolph Demmler and Fried-
rich August Stüler, who were
inspired by the turrets of
Château Chambord in France.
Major refurbishment tried to
recreate some of the castle's
original Renaissance features,

of which only the ceramic
decorations have remained.
Inside, the castle chapel built
by Johan Batista Parra in
1560–63 has survived. The
elegant rooms in the castle –
Thronsaal (throne chamber),
Ahnengalerie (ancestral gallery), Rote Audienz (red auditorium), Speisesaal (dining
chamber) – are decorated
with gilded stucco work. Despite the proliferation of their
styles these rooms delight
visitors, transporting them
back to the 19th century.

♣ Burg-und Schlossgarten
The remaining part of the
island is occupied by the
Burggarten (fortress garden),
which has an orangery and
an artificial grotto, built from
granite around 1850. A bridge
leads to the larger Schlossgarten (castle garden) which
is a favourite place for the
town's inhabitants to relax.
The Kreuzkanal, a canal
built in 1748–56, one of the
garden's axes, is lined with
copies of Baroque statues

including the *Four Seasons*,
created by the renowned
sculptor of the Dresden
Zwinger, Balthasar Permoser.

🏛 Staatliches Museum
Am Alten Garten 3. *Tel (0385) 595
80.* ☐ *10am–6pm (to 5pm mid-Oct–
mid-Apr) daily.* ● *24 & 31 Dec.* 🖼
The state museum stands in
Alter Garten, one of the most
attractive squares in Germany,
where the waters beautifully
reflect the castle and the Neo-
Renaissance theatre. The
museum, which features lions
on its façade and a portico
with Ionic columns, houses
an art collection based on that
of Duke Christian Ludwig II, a
lasting testimony to his taste
and erudition. Apart from
works by German artists such
as Cranach, Liebermann and
Corinth, and the Dutch
painters Hals and Fabritius, it
holds works by many French
artists. This includes 34
paintings by Jean-Baptiste
Oudry, who was court painter
to Ludwig XIV, as well as a
good selection of paintings by
the much more recent Dadaist
artist Marcel Duchamp.

🏯 Marktplatz
The town hall square is surrounded by the homes of
wealthy citizens, often with
19th-century façades concealing older walls. This is true of
the Gothic town hall, which is
hidden under an English
mock-Tudor-style façade.
Demmler was the architect
who is responsible for
numerous Neo-Renaissance

Venus and Amor (1527) by Lucas
Cranach in the Staatliches Museum

The Dom and houses in Schwerin

and Neo-Gothic buildings, the showpieces of Schwerin. One of the outstanding buildings in the market square is Neues Gebäude on the north side. This "new building" is a covered market from 1783–5, with a showpiece façade comprising 12 Doric columns.

🔒 Dom St Maria und St Johannes

Am Dom 4. *Tel (0385) 56 50 14.*
Tower ☐ *Oct–Apr: 11am–2pm Mon–Sat, noon–3pm Sun; Apr–Oct: 10am–5pm Mon–Sat, noon–5pm Sun.* 📷
This cathedral is regarded as the most important work of Gothic brick architecture in the Baltic region, in spite of its Neo-Gothic tower, which affords a marvellous view of the entire town. The basilica, dating from 1240–1416, with its wide transept and passageway

around the presbytery and its wreath of chapels, is reminiscent of the design of French cathedrals. A small number of outstanding original features remain in the cathedral, which compare well with the finest works from Antwerp during this time. They include the wooden late-Gothic multi-panelled Crucifixion worked in sandstone, the 14th-century baptismal font, a memorial to Duchess Helen of Mecklenburg created by the Vischer workshop in Nuremberg, as well as the tombstones of Duke Christopher and his wife (1595).

🏛 Freilichtmuseum Schwerin-Mueß

Alte Crivitzer Landstraße 13.
Tel *(0385) 208 41-0.* ☐ *May–Oct: 10am–6pm Tue–Sun.* 📷
The museum contains a collection of Mecklenburg folk architecture, including 17 houses of the 17th–19th centuries, which strive to recreate the look of an original village. Combine a visit to this open-air museum with a leisurely day on the beach in nearby Zippendorf.

Houses of an earlier era in open-air Freilichtmuseum in Schwerin-Mueß

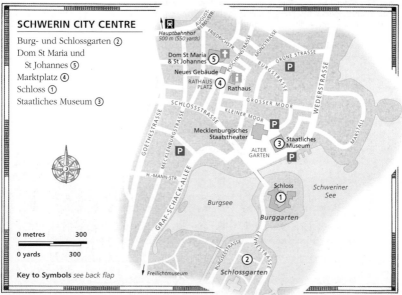

SCHWERIN CITY CENTRE

Burg- und Schlossgarten ②
Dom St Maria und
    St Johannes ⑤
Marktplatz ④
Schloss ①
Staatliches Museum ③

0 metres   300
0 yards   300

Key to Symbols *see back flap*

One of 24 waterfalls in Ludwigslust Park

Ludwigslust ❷

Road map D2. 🏠 *12,600.*
🚉 *north of centre, 15 min. walk.*
ℹ️ *Schlossstr. 36 (03874-52 62 51).*

At the beginning of the 18th century, the small village of Klenow was founded here, which from 1765 grew into a town. The town was laid out around the **Schloss**, residence of the dukes of Mecklenburg-Schwerin until 1837. The "Versailles of Mecklenburg" is in fact quite different from its French namesake. The Baroque palace was built entirely in brick, concealed beneath sandstone from the Ruda hills. The ornate interior, particularly the elegant Goldener Saal (gold hall), was decorated in Ludwigsluster Carton, a type of papier-mâché, in order to cut costs.

In the mid-19th century, the vast **Schlosspark** was redesigned by Peter Joseph Lenné as an English-style landscaped garden. On a scenic walk round the garden, the visitor can discover some 24 waterfalls, a canal, artificial ruins, a stone bridge and the mausoleum of Helena Pavlovna, daughter of Tsar Peter I,

who died tragically young. In the town you will find the Protestant **Stadtkirche**, built in 1765–70 to look like an antique temple. In the presbytery is a giant mural, *The Adoration of the Shepherds.*

🏛 **Schloss**
Tel *(03874) 57 19 0.* ⏰ *15 Apr–14 Oct: 10am–6pm Tue–Sun; 15 Oct–14 Apr: 10am– 5pm Tue–Sun.* 🚫 *24, 31 Dec.* ♿

🏛 **Stadtkirche**
Tel *(03874) 219 68.* ⏰ *Mar–Oct: 11am–4pm Tue–Sat, 3–4pm Sun.*

Gadebusch ❸

Road map D2. 🏠 *6,600.* 🚉
ℹ️ *Lübsche Str. 5 (03886-29 76).*

This small town, situated right next to the former East–West border, has two interesting historic monuments. The **Stadtkirche**, which dates from 1220, is the oldest brick church in Mecklenburg. Its cross vaulting, chunky pillars and goblet-shaped capitals are Romanesque in style. One of its most precious pieces is the bronze baptismal font (1450). Angels hold the bowl, on which 22 scenes of the Passion were sculpted by an unknown artist.

In the 16th and 17th centuries, the **Schloss** was the

Baptismal font in the Stadtkirche in Gadebusch

residence of distant relations of the dukes of Mecklenburg. Resembling the castle in Wismar, it is decorated with glazed reliefs and pilasters. It is not open to visitors.

Wismar ❹

Road map D2. 🏠 *55,000.* 🚉
ℹ️ *Am Markt 11 (03841-194 33).*

Wismar is undoubtedly one of the most attractive towns in Mecklenburg. During the Middle Ages, it was an important Hanseatic centre, as evidenced by the monumental brick church, which is completely out of proportion with the provincial town of today. After the Thirty Years' War, in 1648, the Swedes were established in the town, and rebuilt it as the strongest fortress in Europe. In 1803 they leased Wismar to Mecklenburg, but never claimed it back.

The town centre has a grand market square measuring 100 x 100 m (328 x 328 ft), with **Wasserspiele** (water feature), a Dutch-Renaissance pavilion from 1602 in the centre. Water was piped here from a source 4 km (2 miles) away, until 1897, to supply 220 private and 16 public buildings. The most beautiful house on the square is the **Alter Schwede** (old Swede), built about 1380, with a protruding Gothic

The Baroque residence of the dukes of Mecklenburg-Schwerin in Ludwigslust

For hotels and restaurants in this region see pp517–19 and pp556–7

Alter Schwede and Wasserspiele in the market square in Wismar

brick gable. To the west of the market there are two churches, which act as sad examples of the GDR's neglect of its historical legacy. The reconstruction of the **Georgenkirche**, badly damaged in World War II, was begun in 1989, and it will soon be returned to its former glory. The **Marienkirche** has only one surviving tower – the ruined nave was blown up in 1960. Nearby lies the **Fürstenhof**, residence of the dukes of Wismar. The north wing is the most interesting – its Mannerist style was inspired by the Italian town of Ferrari and northern European ceramic traditions (such as Lübeck workshop). The magnificent sandstone portal is flanked by pairs of intertwined fauns. **Nikolaikirche** is a gem of Wismar architecture. Spared in World War II, the façade of this late-Gothic basilica from the 14th and 15th centuries is decorated with glazed friezes of mythological creatures, saints and, at the peak of the transept, a huge rose window. The proportions of the interior and the height of the vaulted main

pair of fauns om the portal Fürstenhof in Wismar

nave measuring 37 m (121 ft) are captivating. Some of the interior fixtures and fittings came from other churches in the city, which were either ruined or no longer exist, including the so-called Krämeraltar with a sculpture of the *Beautiful Madonna and Child* (c.1420). The room by the tower has the most complete cycle of frescos in the region (c.1450).

Bad Doberan ❺

Road map D1. 🏠 *11,900.* 🚉
ℹ️ *Severingstr 6 (038203-621 54).*

When Duke Henry Borwin was hunting deer, a passing swan reportedly shouted "*Dobr Dobr*" (a good location) as the deer fell. Borwin duly founded the most important Cistercian monastery of the Baltic region here. The **Münster** was built in 1295–1368, with a severe interior and a small bell, in accordance with the order's rules which stipulate that no tower should be built. The interior is fascinating, its walls surfaced in red, with white plasterwork and colourful ribbing. Most of the original fixtures and fittings have survived almost intact. Among the treasures are a vast, gilded panelled painting, produced in Lübeck in 1310, a 12-m (39-ft) Holy Sacrament made from oak, a small cupboard holding the chalice and relics from an earlier Romanesque

building, as well as a statue of the Virgin Mary. Beautiful tombs mark the resting places of the rulers of Mecklenburg, of the Danish Queen Margaret, and Albrecht, King of Sweden, who died in 1412. Visitors can walk around the outside of the church which has a pleasant lawn. Beyond you can find a small octagonal building, beautifully decorated with glazed brickwork – this lovely piece of 13th-century architecture is the morgue.

A stroll around the health spa is also recommended. Right in its centre it has two early 19th-century pavilions with Chinese features – an ideal place for a coffee break.

Environs
Another adventure the visitor could try is a trip on the "Molli", a narrow-gauge railway that links Bad Doberan with Heiligendamm and Kühlungsborn, where there is a 4-km (2-mile) long beach. On the way, a little gem of 13th-century country architecture, the church in **Stefenshagen**, calls for a visit. On its south portal, see the terracotta figures of the Apostles. Across the presbytery runs a brickwork relief with mythological creatures.

🔒 **Doberaner Münster**
Klosterstraße 2. **Tel** *(038203) 627 16.* ⏲ *May–Sep: 9am–6pm Mon–Sat, noon 6pm Sun; Mar, Apr, Oct: 10am–5pm Mon–Sat, noon–5pm Sun; Nov–Feb: 10am–4pm Mon–Sat; noon–4pm Sun.* 🎫 *daily.*

The monumental Cistercian Münster in Bad Doberan

The imposing Schloss, dominating the skyline of Güstrow

Güstrow **6**

Road map D2. 🚍 *32,500.* 🚆
ℹ *Domstr. 9 (01805-68 10 68).*

Güstrow is one of the most harmonious towns of the former German Democratic Republic, with an attractive old town, unmarred by pre-fabricated tower blocks. All the most important monuments are within easy reach. The town is dominated by the **Schloss**, built from 1558 by Franz Parr, a member of a renowned family of sculptors and architects from northern Italy. German, Italian and Dutch elements come together here, including fantastical chimneys and two-storey arcades in the courtyards. The architect's brother decorated the Festsaal (ballroom) with a hunting frieze – the stucco heads of the deer have real antlers.

In the nearby **Dom**, a brick cathedral of the 13th and 14th centuries, there is a fascinating Gothic altar (c.1500). Look for the vast figures of the Apostles on the pillars of the nave and the 16th century tomb of Duke Ulrich and his two wives, with a large genealogical family tree of all three of them. In the north nave hangs the burly *Schwebende* (Hovering Angel), a remarkable work by Ernst Barlach, who lived here from 1910 until his death in 1938. He described his works to Bertolt Brecht as: "beautiful without beautifying, sizeable without enlarging, harmon-

ious without smoothness, and full of vitality without brutality". Barlach's work bore the brunt of National Socialist condemnation – the original *Schwebende* was melted down and made into cannons but the copy that replaced it was made from the original plaster cast. Other works by Barlach can be seen in the museum dedicated to him.

It is worth concluding a visit to this town in the market, near which rises the **Pfarrkirche St Marien**. This church has a magnificent high altar, a panelled work of art with painted wings by Belgian artists (c.1522).

Environs
The open-air museum in **Groß-Raden**, near Sternberg, is popular with tourists as well as archaeology students. A village has been re-created with houses, workshops and a system of fortifications.

🏛 **Archäologisches Freilichtmuseum**
Groß-Raden. *Tel* (03847) 22 52.
◯ *Apr–Oct: 10am–5:30pm daily; Nov–Mar: 10am–4:30pm Tue–Sun.* ◯ *24 Dec.*

Neubrandenburg **7**

Road map E2. 🚍 *75 000.* 🚆
ℹ *Stargader Str. 17 (0395-194 33).*

Founded in 1248 as a sister town to Brandenburg on the Havel, the town was laid out in the form of a regular oval. It prospered as a trading centre until the Thirty Years' War, after which it fell into disrepair. As a result it now has what is probably the only example of post-World War II concrete tower blocks surrounded by medieval town walls, which have survived virtually intact. The walls extend for 2.3 km (2515 yds), originally with a keep open to the interior, and subsequently interspersed with half-timbered houses, known as **Wiekhäuser** (there were once 58, of which 24 survive). Of the four city gates the most interesting are **Friedländer Tor** (begun in 1300), with inner and outer gateways and a tower, as well as Neues and Stargarder Tor, decorated on the town side with mysterious terracotta figures of women with raised hands (c.1350).

In the town centre stands the Medieval **Marienkirche**, which was damaged during World War II and is now restored as a concert hall.

Environs
The castle in **Stargard**, some 10 km (6 miles) to the south, is the oldest secular building in Mecklenburg. Its 4 m (13 ft) walls were begun in 1200; the residence in 1236. Today it houses a youth hostel.

A typical half-timbered Wiekhaus in the town wall in Neubrandenburg

Nationalpark Müritz ⓼

There are about a thousand lakes between Schwerin and Neubrandenburg; the largest of these is Müritzsee, to the east of which a national park was established in 1990. A particularly attractive part of the lake district is the so-called Mecklenburgische Schweiz (Swiss Mecklenburg), with its hilly moraines, such as Ostberg, 115 m (377 ft) above sea level. Tourists are attracted by the breathtaking scenery, perfect conditions for water sports and fascinating castles and palaces.

VISITORS' CHECKLIST

Road map E2. ℹ *Waren, Neuer Markt 21. (03991-66 61 83); Neustrelitz, Strelitzerstr. 1 (03981-25 31 19).*

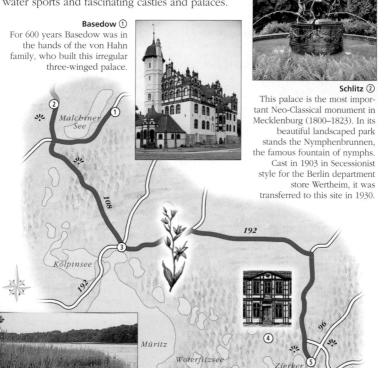

Basedow ①
For 600 years Basedow was in the hands of the von Hahn family, who built this irregular three-winged palace.

Schlitz ②
This palace is the most important Neo-Classical monument in Mecklenburg (1800–1823). In its beautiful landscaped park stands the Nymphenbrunnen, the famous fountain of nymphs. Cast in 1903 in Secessionist style for the Berlin department store Wertheim, it was transferred to this site in 1930.

Müritzsee ④
Müritzsee (meaning "small sea") is, at 115 sq km (44 sq miles), the second largest lake in Germany after Lake Constance.

KEY

▬	Tour route
▬	Scenic route
═	Minor road
▬	River, lake
☀	Viewpoint

Neustrelitz ⑤
The palace (1712) was the seat of distant relations of the Mecklenburg-Strelitz dukes who established the town and its church, and after 1733 resided here.

0 km   15

0 miles   15

Waren ③
Waren, an ideal base for tourists, is close to Binnen-müritz with its beaches and shops with watersports equipment for sale or hire.

Rostock **9**

The history of the most important German port in the Baltic has been turbulent. This prosperous Hanseatic town had established trade links with distant ports such as Bergen (Norway), Riga (Latvia) and Bruges (Belgium) as early as the 15th century. In 1419 the first university in northern Europe was founded here, and it flourished again in the 19th century. After it suffered heavy damage in the Allied air raids of 1942, Rostock was rebuilt on a grand scale as the GDR's showpiece.

VISITORS' CHECKLIST

Road map D1. 200,000.
Neuer Markt 3.
(0381-381 22 22).
www.rostock.de
Warnemünder Woche (Jul),
Hansesail (Aug).

Kröpelinerstraße – a promenade with 17th century houses

Exploring Rostock

A visit to the town is best started from the Neuer Markt (new market), from where the most important monuments can easily be reached on foot.

🏛 Rathaus

The town hall, on Neuer Markt, has a Baroque façade (added in 1727–9), from which seven Gothic towers of the original building emerge. At the rear of the building, in Große Wasserstraße, it is worth seeking out Kerkoffhaus, the best preserved Gothic house in Rostock with a splendidly ornate façade featuring glazed brickwork, dating from 1470.

🏛 Steintor

A few minutes south of Neuer Markt is the Steintor, the best known of the gates in the old city wall. One of only three surviving gates of the original fortifications (at one time with 22 gates), it received its characteristic crowning feature during the Renaissance.

🏛 Marienkirche

Am Ziegenmarkt 4. **Tel** (0381) 492 33 96. ☐ phone to check times.
This church, meant to exceed the height of its Lübeck counterpart, was completed in the mid-15th century, after almost 250 years of construction. The nave, built after the original roof had collapsed, has an untypical, short body, while the massive western tower is as wide as three naves. Interconnected swathes of glazing decorate the exterior of the church, while much of the whitewashed interior features star vaulting. The main attraction is the astronomical clock, constructed in 1472 by maestro Düringer of

Baptismal font in the Marienkirche

Nuremberg. Its mechanism will show the correct time and date until 2017. Every afternoon its clockwork apostles parade before the tourists.

🏛 Kröpelinerstraße

The most popular street in the city is lined by houses from the 17th to the 19th centuries. In summer students congregate around the "Brunnen der Lebensfreude" (fountain of happiness) on the Universitätsplatz (university square). The main university building was built in the years 1867–70 in Neo-Renaissance style. The southern part of the square is occupied by a palace with a beautiful Baroque hall where concerts are performed. A Neo-Classical annexe with a Doric colonnade (1823) stands nearby. A statue on the square commemorates the town's most famous resident, Field Marshal Blücher, who helped defeat Napoleon at Waterloo.

Environs

Between Rostock and Stralsund lies a delightful coastal area. The peninsula, with the three former islands of **Fischland**, **Darß** and **Zingst**, attracts visitors to its quiet, beautiful beaches and splendid natural scenery. Particularly attractive are the villages of **Ahrenshoop**, which was originally an artists' colony, **Prerow**, which has traditional fishermen's houses and churches, and **Wieck**, with its charming thatched houses. A national park has been established here, and includes Darß and its magnificent forest, Zingst, the west coast of Rügen and the island of Hiddensee.

The richly decorated pulpit in the Marienkirche

Stralsund ⑩

After Lübeck, Stralsund is the most interesting Hanseatic town in northern Germany. During its history, it has had to defend its independence against Lübeck, Denmark, Holland and Sweden. In the Thirty Years' War, General Wallenstein vowed that he would take the town even if it was chained to heaven – but he failed. Subsequently, Lower Pomerania stayed under Swedish rule for 200 years until 1815, when it became Prussian. Despite its turbulent history, 811 protected buildings survived in the old town, among them some truly remarkable examples of architecture.

The Rathaus with its small turrets

Exploring Stralsund

The town centre of Stralsund is surrounded by water on all sides – in the north by the Strelasund bay, and on the other sides by lakes formed in the moats of the former bastions, Knieperteich and Frankenteich. All the most interesting historic monuments are easily accessible on foot from here.

⚜ Alter Markt

The old market square affords the best view of the filigree façade of the town hall, beyond which stands the vast edifice of St Michael's church. It is surrounded by houses from various eras, of which the two most important are the Gothic Wulflamhaus, and the Commandantenhaus, Baroque headquarters of the town's former Swedish commandant. The Rathaus dates from the 13th century with a 14th-century façade and ground-floor arcades, and resembles the one in Lübeck. In 1370 the Hanseatic League

Portal of the Nikolaikirche

and the defeated Danish king signed a peace treaty here.

The Nikolaikirche, built from 1270–1360, was inspired by French Gothic cathedrals as well as the Marienkirche in Lübeck. It has rare free-standing flying buttresses in brick, which are much more unusual than in stone. Inside there are several intriguing furnishings, for example, the statue of St Anna (c.1290), an astronomical clock (1394), as well as fragments of the Novgorod stall with various fascinating scenes including one of hunting for sables. The Baroque main altar was designed in 1708 by renowned Berlin architect and sculptor Andreas Schlüter.

🏛 Kulturhistorisches Museum

Mönchstr. 25/27
Tel *(03831) 287 90.*
🕐 *10am–5pm Tue–Sun.*
📷
The Katharinenkloster, a former 15th-century Dominican abbey, now houses two museums. Its abbey rooms provide an appropriate setting for historic exhibitions – the refectory has vaults supported by stylish columns – including copies of the famous Viking treasure from Hiddensee and a collection of 18th- and 19th-century toys and dolls' houses. A branch of the Museum, in Böttcherstraße, has a collection devoted to village life, folklore and costumes of the Baltic region.

🏛 Deutsches Museum für Meereskunde und Fischerei

Tel *(03831) 265 00.* 🕐 *Oct–May: 10am–5pm daily; Jun–Sep: 10am–6pm daily.* 🔴 *24, 31 Dec.* 📷
Highlights of this museum of the sea and fishing, based in a former convent, include colourful aquariums and a 16-m (52-ft) long skeleton of a whale. It is also a scientific establishment researching the life of sea organisms.

🔒 Marienkirche

Tower 🕐 *May–Oct: 10am–5pm Mon–Sat, 11:30am–5pm Sun; Nov–Mar: 10am–noon, 2–4pm Mon–Fri, 10am–noon Sat, 2:30–4pm Sun; Apr: 10am–4pm Mon–Sat, 2:30–4pm Sun.* **Organ concerts:** *summer: 11am Mon–Wed, Fri–Sun.* 📷
Dominating the Neuer Mark is the town's largest church, St Mary's, built in 1383–1473, with an octagonal tower (with good views of Stralsund). Star vaulting lightens the impact of the monumental 99-m (325-ft) high interior. Main attractions are Gothic frescos, carved wooden figures of saints and a late-Gothic baptismal font. The huge Baroque organ is used for concerts in summer.

Marienkirche with its dominant, octagonal tower

Rügen ⓫

The largest of Germany's islands at 926 sq km (357 sq miles), Rügen is also the most beautiful and diverse, boasting steep cliffs next to sandy beaches and a hilly hinterland with forests and peat bogs. The island is only 50 km (31 miles) across, yet its rugged coastline extends for hundreds of miles. The Huns once ruled here, and their tombs can still be seen. It was fortified by the Slavs, then ruled by Danes and Swedes. In 1815 Rügen came under Prussian rule, and in 1936 it was linked to the mainland by the 1 km- (0.6 mile-) long Rügendamm.

Kap Arkona
An attractive walk around the rugged cape, 46 m (150 ft) high, passes the ruins of the Jaromar ancestral home and a temple to the Slav god Svantevit.

Hiddensee
This small island is accessible from Stralsund or Schaprode on Rügen. Horse-drawn carts and bikes replace cars in this oasis of tranquillity.

KEY

▬	Motorway
═	Main road
☀	Viewpoint

★ Waase
At this typical fishing village on the island of Ummanz, an unusual work of art has survived: an altarpiece from Antwerp, from around 1520.

STAR SIGHTS

★ Nationalpark Jasmund

★ Putbus

★ Waase

Jasmund Peninsula

The northeast of the peninsula is occupied by the Stubnitz forest of oak and beech trees, which continues down to the sea, interrupted by dazzling white chalk cliffs. The symbol of Rügen, they inspired artists like Caspar David Friedrich.

★ **Nationalpark Jasmund**

An attractive walk starts at the viewpoint of Königsstuhl (king's seat; 119 m/390 ft), continues along the Hochuferweg (cliff-top walk), past Victoriasicht and Wissower Klinken viewpoints, to end at Sassnitz.

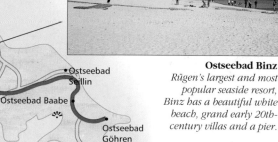

Ostseebad Binz

Rügen's largest and most popular seaside resort, Binz has a beautiful white beach, grand early 20th-century villas and a pier.

★ **Putbus**

This elegant late Neo-Classical town was planned after 1807 on the model of Bad Doberan. Its centrepiece is the theatre, which was built in 1819 to a design by Wilhelm Steinbach.

0 km   5

0 miles   5

(map labels) romper Wiek · Lohme · Glowe · NATIONAL PARK JASMUND · Sagard · Sassnitz · oßer under dden · JASMUND · Kleiner Jasmunder Bodden · Prorer Wiek · en · Ostseebad Binz · Ostseebad Sellin · Ostseebad Baabe · Putbus · Ostseebad Göhren · Rügischer Bodden · Greifswalder Bodden

Greifswald ⑫

Road map E1. 🏛 *54,000.* ⊞ 🛈
*Rathaus Am Markt (03834-52 13
80).* 🎵 *Musical concerts
"Greifswalder Bachwochen" (Jun);
Jazz Evenings in Eldena (Jul);
Fischerfest (Jul).*

This former Hanseatic town is
situated 5 km (3 miles) from
the Bay of Greifswald. From
afar the picturesque silhouette
of the town with its three
church towers, nicknamed Fat
Mary, Little Jakob and Long
Michael, appears like a
painting by Caspar David
Friedrich – the town's most
famous resident – come to life.
Charm pervades the old town,
its architectural mix resulting
from 40 years of East German
rule. Greifswald, an important
academic centre and market
town, has geared up more for
tourism since 1989. It is certainly worth a visit – a short
walk from east to west will
enable the visitor to see all
the most important
monuments in town.

The 14th-century **Marienkirche** has a vast square tower,
giving it a rather squat appearance and its nickname, Fat
Mary. Inside, the church
contains the remains of frescos
and an amazing Renaissance
pulpit depicting the Reformation figures of Luther, Bugenhagen and Melanchthon. The

city museum has a collection
of paintings by Caspar David
Friedrich, including his famous
landscapes of the ruined
monastery of Eldena, *Ruined
Eldena in the Riesengebirge*,
which he transposed to the
mountains of present-day
Poland and Czech Republic.

The market square with its
Baroque town hall is surrounded by patrician houses, with
exemplary rich brickwork
façades (particularly numbers
11 and 13). Nearby rises the
vast **Dom St Nikolai**. The cathedral's octagonal tower, topped
with a Baroque helm, affords
extensive views of the town.
The Rubenow-Bild (1460), one
of the paintings inside, depicts
the founding professor of
Greifswald's university in front
of Mary, Mother of God.

Environs
Wieck, an attractive working
fishing village, is now
incorporated into Greifswald. It
has a drawbridge dating from
1887, reminiscent of typical
Dutch bridges. The Cistercian
monastery of **Eldena**, just 1
km (0.6 mile) south of Wieck
district, was made famous by
the Romantic paintings of
Caspar David Friedrich. The
monastery was founded in
1199 and plundered by the
Swedes in 1637. Its ruined red
walls amid the green grass and
trees look wildly romantic.

**Alter Speicher – the half-timbered
granary in Wolgast**

Wolgast ⑬

Road map E1. 🏛 *15,000.* ⊞
🛈 *Rathausplatz 10 (03836-60 01 18).*

From 1295 the seat of the
Pomeranian-Wolgast dukes,
Wolgast castle was destroyed
in 1713, when Peter the Great
ordered the town to be burned
down. An interesting building
still remaining is the 12-sided
cemetery chapel with star
vaulting, which is supported
by a single column. The most
valuable work of art can now
be seen in **Pfarrkirche St Petri**,
a 14th-century parish church.
Dating from the turn of the

Renovated houses around the Fischmarkt in Greifswald

For hotels and restaurants in this region see pp517–19 and pp556–7

17th to the 18th century, the *Totentanz* frieze is an imitation of the famous *Dance of Death* by Hans Holbein in Basle. Another notable artifact is the epitaph of Duke Philip I, crafted in 1560 by the Saxon artist Wolf Hilinger.

Other attractions in the town are the **Alter Speicher**, an 80 m- (262 ft-) long half-timbered granary (Burgstraße, 1836), and the family home of Philipp Otto Runge, famous romantic painter and adopted son of Hamburg.

🏛 Philipp-Otto-Runge-Gedenkstätte
Kronwieckstraße 45. **Tel** (03836) 20 30 41. ☐ *Jun–Aug: 10am–6pm Mon–Fri, 10am–2pm Sat, Sun; Sep–May: 10am–5pm Mon–Fri, 10am–2pm Sat.*

One of the models in the Otto Lilienthal-Museum in Anklam

Anklam ⓮

Road map E2. 🏠 *16,400.* 🚉
🛈 *Markt 3, Rathaus (03971-835 154).*

A former Hanseatic town, Anklam's erstwhile importance is revealed by its vast defensive walls, in which is set the mid=15th century city gate, **Steintor**. It is worth visiting the Gothic **Marien-kirche**. Inside, the church's octagonal pillars and the arches of its arcades are paint-ed with graceful figures, which reveal a Lübeck influence. A museum recalls the life and inventions of Otto Lilienthal, born here in 1848. After observing storks, he built a flying machine and completed his first flight in 1891. In total he created 2000 machines, none of which flew further than 350 m (1148 ft).

Fishing boat on the beach at Usedom

🏛 Otto-Lilienthal-Museum
Ellbogenstraße 1. **Tel** (03971) 24 55 00. ☐ *Jun–Sep: 10am–5pm daily; Oct & May: 10am–5pm Tue–Fri, 1pm–5pm Sat & Sun; Nov–Apr: 11am–3:30pm Wed–Fri, 1pm–3:30pm Sat.*

Usedom ⓰

Road map E1. 🚉 🛈 *Heringsdorf, Kurverwaltung, Kulmstr. 33 (038378-24 51); Ahlbeck, Kurverwaltung, Dünenstr. 45 (038378x-244 97).*

The island, named after the village of Usedom and separated from the mainland by the Peenestrom, is the second largest in Germany at 445 sq km (172 sq miles). A small corner in the east was incorporated into Poland after 1945. Usedom is almost as attractive as Rügen, possessing white beaches, forests, peat bogs and bays overgrown with rushes in the south. It is linked with the mainland by two drawbridges (near Anklam and Wolgast). The resorts follow one another like pearls on a string: Bansin, Heringsdorf and Bad Ahlbeck, known as the "three sisters", are connected by a wide beach. At the beginning of the 20th century they evolved into elegant holiday resorts, with white villas, hotels and boarding houses, as typical of seaside resorts. Worth a visit is the industrialist Oechler's house in Heringsdorf

(Delbrückstr. 5), which has an antique appearance with mosaics on its façade. During the past few years, the early 20th-century piers in all three spas have been rebuilt and restored. The longest, in Heringsdorf, is also the second largest in Europe, after one in Poland. The Marienkirche, one of the island's main attractions, was erected in the 19th century.

Peenemünde ⓯

Road map E1. 🏠 *650.*

Historically the most interesting spot on the island of Usedom is the **museum** at Peenemünde, based on military territory. It demonstrates the evolution of space travel, pioneered at this research station since 1936. During World War II, long-distance rockets, powered by liquid fuel and known as V-2 *(Vergeltungswaffe;* retaliatory weapon), were produced here, which inflicted heavy damage on London and Antwerp in 1944. After the war, the chief engineer, Wernher von Braun, worked for NASA and helped develop the Apollo rockets.

🏛 Historisch-technisches Informationszentrum
Am Kraftwerk. **Tel** (038371) 205 73. ☐ *Apr–Oct: 9am–6pm daily (Jun–Sep: also Mon); Oct–Mar: 10am–4pm Tue–Sun.*

V-2 rocket in Peenemünde

TRAVELLERS' NEEDS

WHERE TO STAY

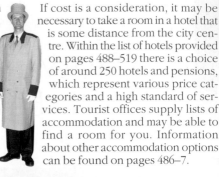

It is relatively easy to find a room in a hotel or pension in Germany, even in small towns or large villages. The range of prices for a night's accommodation is wide, depending on the standard of services offered and the location of the establishment. In smaller towns located in attractive tourist areas, you can also find rooms to rent at a reasonable rate in private homes. In large towns and cities it is harder to find inexpensive accommodation.

If cost is a consideration, it may be necessary to take a room in a hotel that is some distance from the city centre. Within the list of hotels provided on pages 488–519 there is a choice of around 250 hotels and pensions, which represent various price categories and a high standard of services. Tourist offices supply lists of accommodation and may be able to find a room for you. Information about other accommodation options can be found on pages 486–7.

The atmospheric lobby of the Kempinski Hotel, Berlin *(see p490)*

THE RANGE OF HOTELS

German hotels are awarded stars following the same system that is used in other countries, with the number of stars awarded depending on the facilities offered by the hotel rather than the standard of service. This means that it may be possible to enjoy a more pleasant stay in a small hotel that has only a single star than in a three-star hotel that offers lifts, a swimming pool, restaurant and business centre, but where refurbishment is long overdue.

If the name of the hotel includes the appellation *"Garni"*, this indicates that there is not a restaurant on the premises, but only a dining room where breakfast is served. *"Apartmenthotel"* means that the establishment is comprised of suites that include equipped kitchens or a kitchen annexe. The price of suites is such that it is not worth booking them for just one night, although a booking of several days for a family or group of friends can turn out to be very economical.

Standards vary enormously between hotels. In large cities there will be no difficulty in finding a deluxe (and, of course, expensive) hotel, which typically will be part of an international chain. The choice of less expensive accommodation usually, though not necessarily always, entails accepting a lower standard of service or a less convenient location.

Away from cities, high prices generally apply to rooms in comfortable hotels in particularly peaceful and beautiful locations, or to those provided within historic palaces or villas. Smaller hotels in such areas usually offer good accommodation at very affordable prices, where visitors can enjoy their stay in small, but cosy and comfortable rooms.

HOW TO BOOK

As in other countries, hotel accommodation can be booked directly by telephone, letter or fax, as well as by e-mail or through the Internet. Reservations can be made directly with the hotel or through a local tourist office. They may request written confirmation of the booking, and will almost certainly ask for a credit card number. Tell the owners what time you will be turning up, and let them know if you are delayed, in order not to lose the room.

For those who have not pre-booked, the local tourist office can usually find a hotel room or provide information about rooms in private homes. They are also a good source of advice about the availability of other accommodation options in the area.

Entrance of Opera Hotel, Munich

The deluxe Hotel Vier Jahreszeiten in Hamburg *(see p514)*

INTERNATIONAL AND GERMAN CHAIN HOTELS

Throughout Germany there are hotels belonging to virtually all the well-known international chains, as well as to German national chains. Many places in Germany have an IBIS, which can be relied on to provide inexpensive, usually two-star accommodation. In season, they offer a double room for little more than €51.

Somewhat more expensive, and of a higher standard, are hotels belonging to the Best Western chain. Their excellent standard of service, combined with an affordable price, ensures their popularity with tourists. Hotels belonging to the Sorat group are also recommended. Their standard is similar to that of Best Western establishments and can be two-, three- or even four-star, but their premises always have interesting interiors, designed by renowned architects. Many hotels belonging to chains are, in fact, four- or deluxe five-star. Among the finest are the Kempinski and Vier Jahreszeiten hotels. In addition to these, there is no shortage of hotels belonging to chains such as Hilton, Holiday Inn, Inter-Continental, Mercure, Ramada and Hyatt Regency.

HOTELS IN HISTORIC BUILDINGS

Germany, like many other countries, has numerous palaces, castles and other historic buildings that have been converted into hotels. Often the name *Schlosshotel* is used to indicate that an establishment is a hotel

within a palace. Many of these hotels are members of international organizations, such as **European Castle Hotels and Restaurants** or **Romantik Hotels und Restaurants**, who can provide further information.

Sign for the four-star Parkhotel in Dortmund

HOTEL PRICES

In Germany, a complicated hotel categorization system operates, with a diverse range of prices depending on the season, as well as on various events that are taking place. In summer resort areas, it is obviously most expensive during the summer, while in large cities visited frequently for business the most expensive seasons are spring and autumn. In cities where commercial fairs are held, prices may double during the

most popular fairs – for example, in Berlin during the tourist fair ITB, in Hanover during the information-computer fair CEBIT and in Frankfurt during the car and publishing fairs. It is the same, of course, in Munich during the October beer festival.

Many hotels offer significant reductions at weekends, and often there is the opportunity of a discount for those who turn up without a reservation. Prices can also sometimes be negotiated for longer bookings, especially during periods when business is slack.

ADDITIONAL COSTS

Tax is included in the basic price of a hotel room, but tips should be given for additional services such as having your baggage taken to your room or having theatre tickets reserved for you. Additional costs can come as a surprise when you settle your bill. In the most expensive hotels, for example, breakfast is not included in the cost of the room. Most hotels have their own parking facilities, but the cost may be unacceptably high. Check in advance the cost of making direct-dialled telephone calls from the hotel room, as well as the commission charged by the hotel for cashing traveller's cheques and the rate offered when exchanging currency. Using the mini-bar and pay-to-view TV channels in your room can also prove to be expensive.

Swimming pool in the Grand Hotel Esplanade in Berlin

The picturesque Alte Wirt Hotel in Bernau

PENSIONEN AND GASTHOFE

A *Gasthof* is a traditional inn with a restaurant on the ground floor and rooms to rent on the upper floor. A wide range of establishments is covered by this simple description, however, from small, inexpensive, family-run hotels, with modestly equipped rooms, to the most luxurious and elegant accommodation in an exquisitely restored country inn.

Pensionen are less formal establishments than hotels and are typically run by a family. They usually provide modest accommodation, breakfast and a pleasant family atmosphere. They are always comfortable and very clean, at affordable prices.

INEXPENSIVE ACCOMMODATION

Germany has a very widely developed chain of youth hostels *(Jugendherberge)* and these provide the cheapest option for an overnight stay. A youth hostel can be found in every large town, as well as in small holiday centres. The most attractive are those that are located in old castles, beautiful villas or other historic buildings. Most hostels are of a high standard. Accommodation may be provided in double and triple rooms, as well as in dormitories. In order to be eligible to use youth hostels, you must carry a valid membership card of the Youth Hostels

Association. Membership is available from the YHA of your own country. The fee for overnight accommodation with breakfast is around €13.50–25. Unless you are carrying a sheet sleeping bag with you, you must hire one at the hostel, for which an additional charge will be made. The hostels are usually closed during the day, so you must ensure that all arrangements connected with your stay are arranged before 9am or after 4–4:30pm. In large cities during the high season, when demand for beds is particularly heavy, your stay may be limited to 2–3 days. Apart from in Bavaria, overnight accommodation is open to everyone who is in possession of a valid membership card. In Bavaria, however, young people are given priority, but older people can stay too (although for an additional charge), as can families with young children.

Guesthouse near Neuschwanstein

Private accommodation offers another inexpensive option. In attractive tourist areas, it is common for owners of larger villas and private houses to rent rooms to tourists, often offering breakfast as well. Houses with rooms available to rent are indicated by the sign *Fremdenzimmer* or *Zimmer frei*. Details of such accommodation can be obtained and booked in tourist information offices.

During the summer months, students may also benefit from acommodation in student hotels that otherwise house university students during term times in German university towns. Again, information about such accommodation may be obtained from tourist offices.

Mountain hut at Feldberg, Black Forest

AGROTOURISM

Agrotourism is very popular in Germany, and has become an attractive and low-cost alternative holiday, particularly for families with children. The rooms that are available are of a perfectly acceptable standard and meals can often also be provided by the farmers.

For younger children, and especially those from towns and cities, it is a great thrill to observe the daily work on a farm and to have contact with farm animals. Often, farmers who take holidaymakers keep a number of different animals on the farm. They may also offer the possibility of horse-riding, or hiring bicycles, a boat or fishing tackle, so that a full programme of outdoor activities can be enjoyed. Agrotourist holidays can be booked through **Zentrale für den Landurlaub Landschriften** and by **Agrartour GmbH**.

MOUNTAIN HOSTELS

Mountainous regions of Germany are generally well prepared to accommodate walkers. Shelters, hostels and mountain hotels can be found not only along Alpine trails, but also in the Thuringian Forest, the Black Forest and the Harz Mountains. Details about such accommodation can be obtained from local tourist information bureaux.

CAMPING

Travelling with a camping trailer, camper van or just a tent continues to be very popular in Germany, with a highly developed network of more than 2,000 camping sites throughout the country. Of a generally high standard, sites are equipped with wash-rooms and kitchens. There is usually a shop and café and some have swimming pools.

DISABLED TRAVELLERS

Virtually all hotels of a higher standard are equipped to accommodate disabled guests. At least one entrance will

have ramp access, and a few rooms will have bathrooms adapted to the needs of those who are confined to a wheel-chair. Facilities for the disabled are worse in lower-category hotels, where specially adapted fixtures and fittings are rarer. In such hotels, you may have to negotiate steep stairs, as many rooms are located on the upper floors of buildings.

In order to receive additional help during a journey, a disabled person can contact the **Bundesarbeits-gemeinschaft Hilfe für Behinderte e.V.**, or the **Bundesverband Selbsthilfe Körperbehinderter e.V.**

A mountain shelter in Oybin, Saxony

TRAVELLING WITH CHILDREN

Travelling with children through Germany should not present any problems. In most hotels, facilities such as cots and high chairs can be

obtained and there is often no additional accommodation charge for a young child. In better hotels, a few hours of babysitting for the children can usually be booked. Few hotels, however, provide children's playrooms. The standard equipment in every restaurant includes a high chair for toddlers, while menus always include the option of children's portions.

DIRECTORY

Choosing a Hotel

Hotels have been selected across a wide price range for facilities, good value and location. All rooms have private bath, TV, air conditioning and are wheelchair accessible unless otherwise indicated. Most have internet access, and, in some cases, fitness facilities may be offsite. The hotels are listed by area. For map references, *see pp114–15*.

PRICE CATEGORIES
Price categories are for a standard double room for one night in peak season, including tax, service charges and breakfast:

€ under 75 euros
€€ 75–125 euros
€€€ 125–175 euros
€€€€ 175–225 euros
€€€€€ over 225 euros

BERLIN

EASTERN CENTRE Hotel am Anhalter Bahnhof   €€
Stresemannstraße 36, 10963 **Tel** *(030) 251 03 42* **Fax** *(030) 251 48 97* **Rooms** *45*   **Map** *4 B4*

This small and friendly hotel is situated in an old apartment block. Its low prices only apply to rooms without bathrooms; expect to pay more for en suite bathrooms. The more expensive rooms face onto an attractive courtyard. **www.hotel-anhalter-bahnhof.de**

EASTERN CENTRE Alexander Plaza Berlin   €€€
Rosenstraße 1, 10178 **Tel** *(030) 240 010* **Fax** *(030) 240 017 77* **Rooms** *92*   **Map** *5 D1*

This top-quality hotel, opened in 1997, is located near the S-Bahn station Hackescher Markt. Rooms in the late 19th-century building, an intriguing mixture of stucco ceilings, glass and steel, are large, comfortable and full of light, with soundproof windows. There is a nice lobby bar and café. **www.alexander-plaza.com**

EASTERN CENTRE Art'otel Berlin Mitte   €€€
Wallstraße 70–73, 10179 **Tel** *(030) 240 620* **Fax** *(030) 240 622 22* **Rooms** *109*   **Map** *5 E3*

Overlooking the Spree river, this upmarket hotel is well priced and one of the most popular establishments in Mitte. Inside, it is modern with simple and elegant furniture. In summer there is a café on a riverboat tied to the riverbank. The hotel is popular with young, culture-oriented guests. **www.artotel.de**

EASTERN CENTRE Derag Residenz Hotel Henriette   €€€€
Neue Rossstraße 13, 10179 **Tel** *(030) 246 009 00* **Fax** *(030) 246 009 40* **Rooms** *54*   **Map** *5 E3*

The small and intimate Henriette is the nicest – and the most unknown – of the many Derag hotels in town. Although built recently, it exudes an incredibly elegant, historic flair, with oak furniture, precious carpets and beds. The hotel provides excellent service. **www.deraghotels.de**

EASTERN CENTRE Hotel Gendarm   €€€€
Charlottenstraße 61, 10117 **Tel** *(030) 206 06 60* **Fax** *(030) 206 066 66* **Rooms** *27*   **Map** *4 C3*

The Gendarm's reputation as one of the best and most popular smaller hotels in Berlin is more than justified. An excellent service, a great location off Gendarmenmarkt and traditional, elegantly furnished rooms make this a serious competitor of the big five-star hotels nearby. **www.hotel-gendarm-berlin.de**

EASTERN CENTRE Mövenpick Hotel Berlin   €€€€
Schöneberger Straße 3, 10963 **Tel** *(030) 230 060* **Fax** *(030) 230 061 99* **Rooms** *243*   **Map** *4 B4*

The brand-new Mövenpick is a surprisingly nice hotel in the rough, but fascinating, neighbourhood of Kreuzberg. The spacious designer rooms all have modern office and entertainment amenities. The deluxe rooms under the roof are particularly cosy. **www.moevenpick-berlin.com**

EASTERN CENTRE Das Dorint Hotel am Gendarmenmarkt   €€€€€
Charlottenstraße 50–52, 10117 **Tel** *(030) 203 750* **Fax** *(030) 203 751 00* **Rooms** *92*   **Map** *4 C3*

This flagship establishment of the German hotel brand, Dorint, offers well-furnished rooms and an excellent service. Conveniently located near the Gendarmenmarkt, not far from Unter den Linden. The Aigner restaurant downstairs specializes in good Austrian food. **www.dorint.de**

EASTERN CENTRE Westin Grand   €€€€€
Friedrichstraße 158–164, 10117 **Tel** *(030) 202 70* **Fax** *(030) 202 733 62* **Rooms** *358*   **Map** *4 C2*

A lavish hotel built at the end of the 19th century in Empire and Secessionist styles. The main hall is particularly impressive, with a huge atrium and a stunning staircase. It is close to most historic sites as well as a variety of good restaurants and cafés. **www.westin-grand.de**

WESTERN CENTRE A & O Hostel am Zoo   €
Joachimsthaler Straße 1–3, 10623 **Tel** *(030) 889 135-0* **Fax** *(030) 889 135-40* **Rooms** *550*   **Map** *2 B4*

Located in a former Aldi budget grocery store, this hostel is a favourite among budget travellers looking for a cheap night's sleep. Conveniently located opposite the Zoo railway station, it offers packages such as combined hostel and dancing club weekends, which appeal to the younger guests. **www.aohostels.com**

Key to Symbols *see back cover flap*

WESTERN CENTRE Hotel Astoria
⌧ ♿ €€

Fasanenstraße 2, 10623 **Tel** *(030) 312 40 67* **Fax** *(030) 312 50 27* **Rooms** *32* **Map** *2 A4*

Managed by the same family for three generations, this intimate hotel occupies a 19th-century building and is considered to be one of the best of its kind in town. The rooms are comfortable and the lack of a restaurant is made up for by the hotel's proximity to Savignyplatz. **www.hotelastoria.de**

WESTERN CENTRE Remter
⌧ €€

Marburger Straße 17, 10789 **Tel** *(030) 235 08 80* **Fax** *(030) 213 86 12* **Rooms** *31* **Map** *2 B5*

This is a pleasant, quiet hotel and is well located for tourists – close to the historic Kaiser-Wilhelm-Gedächtnis-Kirche. Although the prices for its rooms are not the cheapest in Berlin, the Remter is one of the best-value hotels in this central location. **www.hotel-remter-berlin.de**

WESTERN CENTRE Arte Luise Kunsthotel
⌧ 🎫 €€€

Luisenstraße 19, 10117 **Tel** *(030) 284 480* **Fax** *(030) 284 484 48* **Rooms** *47* **Map** *1 E3*

An authentic Berlin artist's hotel, the Künstlerheim (literally "home for artists") welcomes the artsy crowd into individually designed rooms, created by various German artists, in an early 19th-century house. It is steps away from the Scheunenviertel and offers great service. **www.luise-berlin.com**

WESTERN CENTRE Berlin Marriott Hotel
⌧ 🍴 ♨ 🏋 🖭 🎫 €€€

Inge-Beisheim-Platz 1, 10785 **Tel** *(030) 220 000* **Fax** *(030) 220 001 000* **Rooms** *379* **Map** *4 A3*

The Marriott at the Beisheim-Center near Potsdamer Platz is an elegant four-star hotel with a towering entrance atrium. Its spacious rooms offer lovely views of the green Tiergarten and the government district. You get the same facilities for less than half the rate of the adjacent Ritz-Carlton. **www.marriott.de**

WESTERN CENTRE Hotel Albrechtshof
⌧ 🍴 €€€

Albrechtstraße 8, 10117 **Tel** *(030) 308 860* **Fax** *(030) 308 861 00* **Rooms** *101* **Map** *1 F3*

This charming hotel is situated near the Spree river, in a modernized, early 19th-century building. It offers not only a bar, restaurant and banqueting hall, but a chapel as well. Internet access is available in all of the spacious rooms, and the service is personal and warm. Weekend discounts are available. **www.hotel-albrechtshof.de**

WESTERN CENTRE Crowne Plaza Berlin City
⌧ 🍴 ♨ 🏋 🖭 🎫 €€€€

Nürnberger Straße 65, 10787 **Tel** *(030) 210 070* **Fax** *(030) 213 20 09* **Rooms** *423* **Map** *2 C5*

This luxurious hotel is located near Kaiser-Wilhelm-Gedächtnis-Kirche and Tauentzienstraße. It has a swimming pool, a good restaurant, large rooms with all the usual amenities and a pleasing atmosphere. It offers special weekend rates combined with sightseeing tours. **www.cp-berlin.de**

WESTERN CENTRE Grand Hotel Esplanade Berlin
⌧ 🍴 ♨ 🏋 🖭 🎫 €€€€

Lützowufer 15, 10785 **Tel** *(030) 254 780* **Fax** *(030) 254 788 222* **Rooms** *385* **Map** *3 D4*

A modern, lavish establishment overlooking the Landwehrkanal, the hotel has well-furnished rooms that attract prominent guests. Harry's New York Bar is famous and the Harlekin restaurant is one of the city's best. The hotel's boat offers trips along the rivers. **www.esplanade.de**

WESTERN CENTRE Hotel Brandenburger Hof
⌧ 🍴 ♿ €€€€

Eislebener Straße 14, 10789 **Tel** *(030) 214 050* **Fax** *(030) 214 051 00* **Rooms** *72* **Map** *2 B5*

An intimate family atmosphere, impeccable service and quiet luxurious rooms make this one of the most desirable top-notch hotels in Berlin. The enchanting building has been restored and rooms feature Bauhaus furniture. The Michelin-awarded restaurant, Die Quadriga, is a must *(see p527)*. **www.brandenburger-hof.com**

WESTERN CENTRE Kempinski Hotel Bristol Berlin
⌧ 🍴 ♨ 🏋 🖭 🎫 €€€€€

Kurfürstendamm 27, 10719 **Tel** *(030) 884 340* **Fax** *(030) 883 60 75* **Rooms** *301* **Map** *2 B4*

One of Berlin's most famous hotels, the Kempinski was redecorated in the 1990s and has a classic interior. Its luxurious rooms are very comfortable and 18 rooms have wheelchair access. Its famous restaurant, Kempinski-Grill, serves international cuisine. **www.kempinskiberlin.de**

FURTHER AFIELD Hotel-Pension Kastanienhof
⌧ €

Kastanienallee 65, 10119 **Tel** *(030) 44 30 50* **Fax** *(030) 443 051 11* **Rooms** *35*

The Kastanienhof is a budget *Pension* hidden in a fully restored, typical Berlin tenement house. Its location is perfect for exploring the clubbing scene in Prenzlauer Berg. The rooms are surprisingly nice and come equipped with a hairdryer, mini bar and safe. **www.hotel-kastanienhof-berlin.de**

FURTHER AFIELD Pension Niebuhr
€

Niebuhrstraße 74, 10629 **Tel** *(030) 324 95 95* **Fax** *(030) 324 80 21* **Rooms** *12*

One of the smallest and most inexpensive *Pensionen* in all of Charlottenburg, the Niebuhr has only 12 tastefully and comfortably furnished rooms. The location is perfect for exploring the district. Breakfast is served in your room. **www.pension-niebuhr.de**

FURTHER AFIELD Art Hotel Charlottenburger Hof
🍴 €€

Stuttgarter Platz 14, 10627 **Tel** *(030) 329 070* **Fax** *(030) 323 37 23* **Rooms** *46*

A must for any traveller looking for a real Berlin experience, the Charlottenburger Hof is a successful version of a traditional *Hotelpension* for young tourists. The individually designed rooms are decorated with art by Mondrian and the staff are very helpful. **www.charlottenburger-hof.de**

FURTHER AFIELD Dolce Berlin Müggelsee

Müggelheimer Damm 145, 12559 **Tel** *(030) 658 820* **Fax** *(030) 658 822 63* **Rooms** *176*

This is an excellent hotel, far from the hustle and bustle of the city. Tucked away in the greenery of the Müggelsee in Köpenick, it is perfect for a relaxed stay. Rooms are fairly spacious, and all of the three guest floors are decorated differently in Italian, Asian and German styles. **www.dolceberlin.de**

FURTHER AFIELD Honigmond

Tieckstraße 11, 10115 **Tel** *(030) 284 45 50* **Fax** *(030) 284 455 11* **Rooms** *40*

Map *1 F2*

The Honigmond is great for exploring the Mitte and Prenzlauer Berg arts scenes. Originally a traditional 19th-century tenement house with a courtyard, it has individuallly designed rooms, some of which feature four-poster beds and parquet floors, while other rooms entice you with their summerhouse feel. **www.honigmond.de**

FURTHER AFIELD Hotel Luisenhof

Köpernicker Straße 92, 10179 **Tel** *(030) 241 59 06* **Fax** *(030) 279 29 83* **Rooms** *27*

Map *5 F3*

Situated at the Märkisches Museum, this hotel occupies the oldest building (built in 1882) in this part of Berlin. Extensive restoration has created a charming hotel with attractive rooms and a delightful restaurant in the cellar. Given its size and decor, the Luisenhof makes for a great deal. **www.luisenhof.de**

FURTHER AFIELD Schlossparkhotel

Heubnerweg 2a, 14059 **Tel** *(030) 326 90 30* **Fax** *(030) 326 903 600* **Rooms** *39*

The modern Schlossparkhotel is part of a private clinic and is known as a very pleasant and small, but top-class, hotel near the beautiful gardens of Schlosspark Charlottenburg, making this the only downtown hotel in a green setting. Request a room with a balcony overlooking the gardens. The S-Bahn Westend is nearby. **www.schlossparkhotel.de**

FURTHER AFIELD Schlosshotel in Grunewald

Brahmsstraße 10, 14193 **Tel** *(030) 895 840* **Fax** *(030) 895 848 00* **Rooms** *54*

This exclusive hotel was formerly a palace, built in 1912 for Walter von Pannwitz, the Kaiser's personal lawyer. The contemporary interiors were created by Karl Lagerfeld. and the lobby's magnificent coffered ceiling is breathtaking. The hotel's restaurant, the Vivaldi *(see p528),* is very popular. **www.schlosshotelberlin.com**

BRANDENBURG

BRANDENBURG Kurth's Landgasthaus und Hotel

Dorfstraße 3–4, 14778 **Tel** *(033836) 40 24 5* **Fax** *(033836) 49 71 2* **Rooms** *14*

The vines spilling out of the upstairs windows are somehow very inviting, especially in this lovely lakeside location. Inside, light bright decoration and furniture counteracts cramped rooms, and the dark exposed beams in the attic are charming. **www.kurths-landgasthaus.de**

BRANDENBURG Villa Lindenhof

Chausseestraße 21, 14774 **Tel** *(03381) 40 43 0* **Fax** *(03381) 40 43 33* **Rooms** *16*

This is a very traditional establishment with old-fashioned wooden furniture and chiffon curtains. It is a more homely experience than the larger, chain hotels would offer. They also have a restaurant that has tables in the garden in the summer months. **www.lindenhof-plaue.de**

BRANDENBURG Axxon Hotel

Magdeburger Landstraße 228, 14770 **Tel** *(03381) 32 10* **Fax** *(03381) 32 11 11* **Rooms** *119*

Not too far from the lake, though the hotel's location is not so picturesque. The rooms are comfortable, if a little small, but the fitness area is vast and well equipped. They have four apartments, which have a cosy quality and are well suited to families. **www.axxon-hotel.de**

CHORIN Neue Klosterschänke

Neue Klosterallee 12, 16230 **Tel** *(033366) 53 10* **Fax** *(033366) 53 14 1* **Rooms** *14*

A hilltop rural setting offers wonderful views over the tops of trees and across a lake, and as you would expect in such a setting, the outside is more important and impressive than the inside. The slightly unimpressive façade disguises a comfortable but not overly fashionable interior. **www.neue-klosterschaenke.de/**

COTTBUS Ahorn Hotel & Restaurant

Bautzener Str. 134 / 135, 3050 **Tel** *(0355) 47 80 00* **Fax** *(0355) 47 80 04 0* **Rooms** *21*

This is a well-run hotel and restaurant. The guest rooms are decorated in an uncluttered and smart manner, and have the usual amenities you would expect. There is also an added attraction of a pleasant beer garden in which to relax after a day's sightseeing. **www.ahorn-hotel.com**

COTTBUS Radisson SAS Hotel Cottbus

Vetschauerstr. 12, 3048 **Tel** *(0355) 47 61 0* **Fax** *(0355) 47 61 90 0* **Rooms** *241*

This hotel is as comfortable as it is possible to be with its stylish and well-appointed wood-panelled rooms, and as you would expect from this global hotel chain, there is a full range of facilities, amenities and services. All expectations will be met willingly by the courteous and helpful staff. **www.radissonsas.com**

Key to Price Guide *see p488* **Key to Symbols** *see back cover flap*

COTTBUS Sorat Hotel

Schlosskirchplatz 2, D-03046 **Tel** *(0355) 78 44 0* **Fax** *(0355) 78 44 24 4* **Rooms** *101*

Whoever designed the interior of this place managed to achieve a style that is very modern, but not overly trendy or at all aloof. As such it is all very welcoming, tidy and pleasant, and replete with comforts and all the usual amenities found in these larger chain hotels. **www.sorat-hotels.com/hotel/cottbus.html**

JUTERBORG Zum Goldenen Stern

Markt 14, 14913 **Tel** *(03372) 40 14 76* **Fax** *(03372) 40 16 14* **Rooms** *29*

The rooms here are fresh, breezy and fun, and the garden-style furniture scattered about makes you feel as though you are outside. They will even serve your breakfast in a glass-encased winter garden. A pleasant change from more formal hotels. They also rent in-line skates. **www.hotel-goldenen-stern.de**

LEHNIN Hotel Restaurant Markgraf Lehnin

Friedenstr. 13, 14797 **Tel** *(03382) 76 50* **Fax** *(03382) 76 54 30* **Rooms** *40*

A comfortable, rambling and family-friendly hotel that should appeal to pretty much everyone. Rooms are simple and comfortable. Sauna, solarium, spa and other well-being and beauty services are offered, as is a large conference hall. Overall, it is a pleasant and welcoming place. **www.hotel-markgraf.de**

NEURUPPIN Am Alten Rhin

Friedrich-Engels-Straße 12, 16827 **Tel** *(03391) 76 50* **Fax** *(03391) 76 51 5* **Rooms** *33*

Here you will find sturdy, wooden, cottage-like furniture in clean bright rooms. It all adds up to simple, honest comfort. The hotel is located only a short distance from a river and lake, which encourages the guests to get out and enjoy the surroundings. **www.hotel-am-alten-rhin.de**

NEURUPPIN Altes Casino

Dudweilerstraße 20, 66287 **Tel** *(06897) 96 57 0* **Fax** *(06897) 96 57 57* **Rooms** *12*

Rooms are a little spartan and basic, but they have made an effort to brighten the place up with contemporary and colourful decor and furnishings. They have a good restaurant and there is a pleasant outdoor eating area. Simple, but pleasant and good value. **www.altescasino.com**

NEURUPPIN Hotel Fontane

Seeufer 20, 16816 **Tel** *(03391) 40 35 0* **Fax** *(03391) 40 35 24 59* **Rooms** *140*

Nestled on the edge of Ruppiner See, this hotel could almost be classed as a resort, especially with the addition of a sauna facility that appears to hover over the lake. Rooms are classy and have the standard conveniences expected in a resort-style hotel, and most overlook the lake. **www.hotel-fontane.com**

POTSDAM art'otel Potsdam

Zeppelinstraße 136, D-14471 **Tel** *(0331) 98 15 0* **Fax** *(0331) 98 15 55 5* **Rooms** *123*

This hotel is just a stone's throw from Sanssouci, and is a palace packed with art in its own right. Although the hotel is very bright and modern, it still has a natural feel with exposed wooden beams here and there. Abstract art features quite extensively in the decoration. **www.artotel.de/potsdam/potsdam.html**

POTSDAM Mercure Potsdam

Lange Bruecke, 14467 **Tel** *(0331) 27 22* **Fax** *(0331) 27 20 23 3* **Rooms** *210*

This chain hotel is conveniently located near the train station. Inside, it sticks to the international Accor hotels recipe of maximum comfort from pleasingly minimalist design. Everything is neat, tidy and smartly tucked away, and all the amenities you would expect are provided. **www.mercure.com**

POTSDAM Relexa Schlosshotel Cecilienhof

Neuer Garten, 14469 **Tel** *(0331) 37 05 0* **Fax** *(0331) 29 24 98* **Rooms** *41*

This is an extraordinary place that retains the atmosphere of a lordly manor rather than a hotel. Thankfully, if the luxury is all too much, you can head to the courtyard (in summer, at least) where there are normal chairs, without padding, rather than the luxurious thrones scattered throughout the rest of the hotel. **www.relexa-hotels.de**

POTSDAM NH Voltaire Hotel

Friedrich-Ebert Straße 88, 14467 **Tel** *(0331) 23 17 0* **Fax** *(0331) 23 17 10 0* **Rooms** *156*

A grand and gracious façade hides rooms that have a modern style and all the usual modern amenities such as cable television, mini bar, wireless internet and an in-room safe. Other facilities include a sauna, solarium and spa, as well as on-site parking. **www.nh-hotels.com**

WITTSTOCK Scharfenberger Krug

Scharfenberg 28, 16909 **Tel** *(03394) 71 24 17* **Fax** *(03394) 44 37 15* **Rooms** *10*

Located on the Scharfenberg hill, which was the site of the bloodiest battle of the Thirty Years' War (1618–48), this hotel's accommodation is a little cramped, especially in the attic rooms, but it is also home to all manner of medieval memorabilia. **www.scharfenberger-krug.de**

WITTSTOCK Seehotel Ichlim

Am Nebelsee 1, 17248 **Tel** *(039827) 30 26 4* **Fax** *(033966) 60 25 3* **Rooms** *29*

This is an enormous barn-shaped building on the side of a lake with large, pleasantly decorated, comfortable rooms, plenty of health and beauty services, and all manner of water sports on offer. There is even a jetty and a small private beach. **www.seehotel-ichlim.de**

SAXONY-ANHALT

BERNBURG Parkhotel Bernburg

Aderstedter Str. 1, 6406 **Tel** *(03471) 362-0* **Fax** *(03471) 362-111* **Rooms** *111*

This hotel represents a clever and competent compromise between a business-class and a tourist-style hotel. Everything is very smart and comfortable, but there is still a very welcoming sense of homely warmth that makes it a nice place to stay. **www.parkhotel-bernburg.de**

DESSAU Steigenberger Hotel Fürst Leopold

Friedensplatz, 6844 **Tel** *(0340) 25 15 0* **Fax** *(0340) 25 15 17 7* **Rooms** *204*

This hotel's design is heavily influenced by Bauhaus, with rooms that are similarly unfussy and functional. Anything that will not enhance your productivity or comfort has been left out, but earthy-toned walls and plants add a restful and natural touch. There is also a vast sauna and spa area. **www.dessau.steigenberger.de**

DESSAU NH Hotel

Zerbster Straße 29, 6844 **Tel** *(034) 02 51 40* **Fax** *(034) 02 51 41 00* **Rooms** *152*

Like all the hotels in this trendy global chain, the NH here is clean, smart and very stylish. Space tends to be used very well, and even though some rooms are not large, they do not feel cramped. The hotel also features a classy restaurant, casual-style bar and sauna. **www.nh-hotels.com**

HALBERSTADT Parkhotel Unter den Linden

Klamrothstr. 2, 38820 **Tel** *(03941) 62 54 0* **Fax** *(03941) 62 54 44 4* **Rooms** *43*

Every room in this hotel is unique, some with bay windows, some with balconies and others with interior arches. It gives a sense of history and character to the building that adds a nice touch to your stay. They even have a sauna in the attic. It also has an excellent restaurant of the same name *(see p531)*. **www.pudl.de**

HALLE Kempinski Hotel & Congress Centre Rotes Ross

Leipziger Straße 76, 6108 **Tel** *(0345) 23 34 30* **Fax** *(0345) 23 34 36 99* **Rooms** *88*

Style and elegance are the hallmarks of this historic hotel located in the heart of Halle. The guest rooms are replete with luxury and also have a lovely and unique charm. Other highlights include an excellent restaurant and superb fitness and wellbeing area. **www.kempinski-halle.de**

ILSENBURG Zu Den Rothen Forellen

Marktplatz 2, 38871 **Tel** *(039452) 93 93* **Fax** *(039452) 93 99* **Rooms** *52*

A stunning hotel located in a lovely setting right beside a lake. The guest rooms have a rich, warm and elegant cottage charm, the pool and spa area is sparkling, and the restaurant is an attraction it its own right *(see p531)*. Overall, this hotel is a delightful discovery. **www.rotheforelle.de**

MAGDEBURG Classik Hotel Magdeburg

Leipziger Chaussee 141, 39120 **Tel** *(0391) 62 90 0* **Fax** *(0391) 62 90 51 9* **Rooms** *109*

There is a fresh and friendly appeal about this big yellow building. Rooms are by no means large, but are brightly furnished and have a spacious and airy feel thanks to lots of colourful touches. The restaurant is smart without being stifling, and there is a pleasant lobby area with an open fire. **www.classik-hotel.de**

MAGDEBURG Hotel Ratswaage

Ratswaageplatz 1–4, 39104 **Tel** *(0391) 59 26 0* **Fax** *(0391) 56 19 61 5* **Rooms** *174*

Although the outside of this hotel is somewhat austerely functional, there is plenty of comfort and luxury inside. Rooms have a bright, warm feeling and a simple homely charm. There is also a good swimming pool and sauna where you can pass the time. **www.ratswaage.de**

MAGDEBURG Herrenkrug Parkhotel

Herrenkrug 3, 39114 **Tel** *(0391) 85 080* **Fax** *(0391) 85 08 50 1* **Rooms** *147*

This attractive hotel provides a very tidy arrangement of cosy rooms in a lovely big house situated in the middle of a big park. All the expected comforts and a full range of amenities are offered in a happy marriage of old and new styles. **www.herrenkrug.de**

MAGDEBURG Maritim Hotel

87 Otto-Von-Guericke Straße, 39104 **Tel** *(0391) 59 49 0* **Fax** *(0391) 59 49 99 0* **Rooms** *514*

This hotel has a striking, ultra-modern exterior with a distinctive glass cylinder entrance. Inside it is a stylish delight. The central hall is breathtaking and the suites are amazing. It has a choice of restaurants and also a pool. A very professional establishment. **www.maritim.de**

MERSEBURG Radisson SAS

Oberaltenburg 4, 6217 **Tel** *(03461) 45 20 0* **Fax** *(03461) 45 21 00* **Rooms** *132*

As you would expect from a top hotel chain, this establishment has all the amenities (including a solarium) and is superbly run. It is well worth asking for a room with a view, because the hotel is on a hill and has splendid views of the palace and gardens. The Belle Epoque restaurant is highly recommended *(see p531)*. **www.radissonsas.com**

Key to Price Guide *see p488* **Key to Symbols** *see back cover flap*

NAUMBURG Gasthaus Zur Henne

Henne 1, 6618 **Tel** *(03445) 23 26 0* **Fax** *(3445) 23 26 26* **Rooms** *15*

A very welcoming and friendly place situated in a building that is very much like a country manor. The restrained decor is in keeping with the traditional country feel, but it has a modern twist. It also has an excellent restaurant. **www.gasthaus-zur-henne.de**

NAUMBURG Stadt Aachen

Markt 11, 6618 **Tel** *(03445) 24 70* **Fax** *(03445) 24 71 30* **Rooms** *38*

This hotel is in an excellent location close to the market square. The building itself looks rather historic but has been renovated to meet modern hospitality standards. The rooms are large and bright and scattered with pleasant furniture. **www.hotel-stadt-aachen.de**

NAUMBURG Zur alten Schmiede

Lindenring 36/37, 6618 **Tel** *(03445) 24 36 0* **Fax** *(03445) 24 36 66* **Rooms** *36*

What was an 18th-century blacksmith's workshop has been knocked down and replaced with a hotel and restaurant, both of which have been designed to retain the historic feel combined with modern convenience and quality. Accommodation is pleasantly simple with touches of rustic charm. **www.hotel-zur-alten-schmiede.de**

QUEDLINBURG Hotel Domschatz

Mühlenstraße 20, 6484 **Tel** *(03946) 70 52 70* **Fax** *(03946) 70 52 71* **Rooms** *15*

This is a distinctive lime-green Fachwerk building – a rescued dilapidated historic house – which is now home to 15 modern and warmly decorated guest rooms. The staff also arrange some interesting special offers, packages and tours. **www.quedlinburg-hoteldomschatz.de**

STENDAL Altstadt-Hotel

Breite Straße 60, 39576 **Tel** *(03931) 69 89 0* **Fax** *(03931) 69 89 39* **Rooms** *28*

This mid-range family-run hotel is centrally located. It has themed decor – plenty of wood panelling and pastel-patterned furniture – which makes you feel that you could be on a boat at sea. The guest rooms come with safes and cable television. Parking is also available. **www.altstadthotelstendal.de**

TANGERMÜNDE Ringhotel Schwarzer Adler

Lange Straße 52, 39590 **Tel** *(039322) 96 0* **Fax** *(039322) 36 42* **Rooms** *56*

The guest rooms here are filled with comforts encased in floral wallpaper and furnishings. Other facilities at the hotel are a bit more practical but no less pleasing, with the attractive glass-roofed dining room being of particular note. **www.schwarzer-adler-tangermuende.de**

WERNIGERODE Ringhotel Weisser Hirsch

Marktplatz 5, 38855 **Tel** *(03943) 60 20 20* **Fax** *(03943) 63 31 39* **Rooms** *54*

While the smart reception suggests that this is a business-class hotel, the rooms are more homely than you might expect, although not at all short on luxury. Merely staying in such a grand Fachwerk building in this great location would be pleasant enough, but the hotel's comforts are also very appealing. **www.hotel-weisser-hirsch.de**

WITTENBERG Stadthotel Wittenberg

Schloßstraße 2, 6886 **Tel** *(03491) 42 04 34 4* **Fax** *(03491) 42 04 34 5* **Rooms** *17*

The location is a big plus here, as you can walk to most of the interesting sights and attractions from the hotel. The rooms themselves have a very warm appearance and are fitted with the standard conveniences such as Internet access and satellite television. The staff are very helpful. **www.stadthotel-wittenberg.de**

WÖRLITZ Wörlitzer Hof

Markt 96, 6786 **Tel** *(034905) 41 10* **Fax** *(034905) 41 122* **Rooms** *50*

Located adjacent to a pleasant square with trees and a little fountain, this hotel has a calm and welcoming feel. This cosy feel continues in the rooms, which, though a little plain, are not short on the standard comforts. The beer garden under the lime trees is its most attractive feature. **www.woerlitzer-hof.de**

SAXONY

BAUTZEN Villa Antonia

Lessingstraße 1, 2625 **Tel** *(03591) 50 10 20* **Fax** *(03591) 50 10 44* **Rooms** *13*

This late 1890s villa, located in a quiet and up-market part of town, is a historic monument that was once owned by a concert pianist. It has since been refreshed and renovated and is now this small hotel which is straightforward but pleasant and comfortable. **www.hotel-villa-antonia.de**

BAUTZEN Goldener Adler

Hauptmarkt 4, 2625 **Tel** *(03591) 48 66 0* **Fax** *(03591) 48 66 20* **Rooms** *30*

Ideal for those who like light and space as the rooms have high ceilings and simple, smart furnishings. It is a nice contrast to the cosy feeling of its adjoining wine cellar and curved-roofed beer hall and restaurant. The historic charm of the original 1540s building has been retained. **www.goldeneradler.de**

CHEMNITZ Günnewig Hotel Chemnitzer Hof
€€

Theaterplatz 4, 9111 **Tel** *(0371) 68 40* **Fax** *(0371) 67 62 58 7* **Rooms** *98*

This late-1920s building has been renovated to its former glory. The foyer is gleaming and grand, although the period charm is lost in the rooms themselves which are merely tidy and stylish. All rooms have wireless Internet, safes and satellite television. **www.guennewig.de**

CHEMNITZ Ringhotel Schlosshotel Klaffenbach
€€

Wasserschloßweg 6, 9123 **Tel** *(0371) 26 11 0* **Fax** *(0371) 26 11 10 0* **Rooms** *46*

A turreted fairy-tale hotel flanked by two wings of more modest buildings. The rooms vary from simple standards to some very interesting options. Easily the most attractive aspect of the hotel is the location right in the historic centre of Chemnitz. **www.schlosshotel-klaffenbach.de**

CHEMNITZ Mercure Hotel Kongress Chemnitz
€€€

Brueckenstraße 19, 9111 **Tel** *(0371) 68 30* **Fax** *(0371) 68 35 05* **Rooms** *386*

This hotel is located in a striking glass tower and has rooms which are simple and have all the amenities you would expect from a hotel that is owned by an international chain. Hotel facilities include meeting rooms, conference rooms, a fitness room and a sauna. An airport shuttle is also available. **www.mercure.com**

DRESDEN Landhotel Dresden
€

Fritz-Meinhardt-Straße 105, 1239 **Tel** *(0351) 28 03 0* **Fax** *(0351) 28 03 13 0* **Rooms** *43*

An uncomplicated and simple establishment which is not short on comforts. There is an easygoing and relaxed atmosphere to this hotel, which can be a refreshing change from some of the more stiff, classy places. Every morning, guests may help themselves to a "coffee to go" to perk them up for the day ahead. **www.landhotel-dresden.de**

DRESDEN art'otel Dresden Design Hotel
€€€

Ostra-Allee 33, 1067 **Tel** *(0351) 49 22 0* **Fax** *(0351) 49 22 77 7* **Rooms** *174*

A very distinctive hotel with modern art, daring design and bright colours. All the guest rooms have modern conveniences and comforts, including air conditioning, satellite and pay television, and wireless Internet – as well as plenty of art on the walls. **www.artotels.de**

DRESDEN Romantik Hotel Pattis
€€€

Merbitzer Straße 53, 1157 **Tel** *(0351) 42 55 0* **Fax** *(0351) 42 55 25 5* **Rooms** *46*

This is very much a family-run hotel (pictures, birth dates and other family information are given on the website) and offers a rather effective mix of business-class standards and personal touches that will make you feel both important and relaxed at the same time. **www.pattis.de**

DRESDEN Steigenberger Hotel de Saxe
€€€

Neumarkt 9, 1067 **Tel** *(0351) 43 86 0* **Fax** *(0351) 43 86 88 8* **Rooms** *185*

Even the simple rooms are vast and elegant and offer Internet, satellite television, safes and the usual list of comforts and conveniences. There is a definite sense of sparkle and fresh opulence in the dining areas. This is a very refined establishment. **www.desaxe-dresden.steigenberger.de**

FREIBERG Silberhof
€

Silberhofstraße 1, 9599 **Tel** *(03731) 26 88 0* **Fax** *(03731) 26 88 78* **Rooms** *30*

The rooms in this interesting-looking building are decorated in a distinctive style somewhat influenced by rococo themes with lots of gleaming satin and white-painted wood. All the usual modern amenities are on offer as well, such as satellite television, Internet access and mini bars in all rooms. **www.silberhof.de**

FREIBURG Colombi Hotel
€€€€

Rotteckring 16, 79098 **Tel** *(0761) 21 06 0* **Fax** *(0761) 31 41 0* **Rooms** *120*

A truly impressive hotel that successfully combines friendliness and impressive luxury. It is extraordinary and of a standard that has rightfully earned it a string of awards and put it among the ranks of some of the best hotels in the world. **www.colombi.de**

GÖRLITZ Sorat Hotel Görlitz
€€

Struvestraße 1, 2826 **Tel** *(03581) 40 65 77* **Fax** *(03581) 40 65 79* **Rooms** *46*

The rooms are decorated in an Art Nouveau style with colourful modern furniture and a touch of flair. There are smoking and non-smoking rooms available with basic services. Best of all though, it is in an ideal location next to the Marienplatz and Görlitz's department store. **www.sorat-hotels.com**

KAMENZ Goldner Hirsch
€€

Markt 10, 1917 **Tel** *(03578) 78 35 0* **Fax** *(03578) 78 35 59 9* **Rooms** *30*

Established in 1550 and one of the few buildings in the city that was not destroyed in the 1842 fires, there is a successful mixture of old and new in this hotel. The rooms are simple but classy and comfortable, and there are two restaurants and a beer garden. **www.hotel-goldner-hirsch.de**

LEIPZIG Alt-Connewitz Hotel - Restaurant
€

Meusdorfer Straße 47a, 4277 **Tel** *(0341) 30 13 77 0* **Fax** *(0341) 30 13 80 0* **Rooms** *33*

A simple and straightforward hotel with very reasonable prices. The comfortable guest rooms have a fresh, clean decor and include Internet access and TV. They also have a good restaurant with a serviceable selection of wines. **www.alt-connewitz.de**

Key to Price Guide *see p488* **Key to Symbols** *see back cover flap*

LEIPZIG Hotel Fürstenhof ⬚⬚⬚⬚⬚⬚ €€

Tröndlinring 8, 4105 **Tel** *(0341) 14 00* **Fax** *(0341) 14 03 70 0* **Rooms** *92*

A hotel with a bright and confident classiness. Its rooms are colourfully decorated and furnished, and tall slim windows offer plenty of light and a feeling of space. All rooms have a mini bar and satellite television, but the ones that overlook the courtyard are worth requesting. A bold and luxurious hotel. **www.luxurycollection.com/fuerstenhof**

LEIPZIG Leipzig Marriott Hotel ⬚⬚⬚⬚ €€

Am Hallischen Tor 1, 4109 **Tel** *(0341) 96 53 0* **Fax** *(0341) 96 53 99 9* **Rooms** *231*

Dark wood and richly patterned carpets and furnishings create an environment in which you can nestle in warmth and comfort. It can feel a bit old fashioned, but services such as Internet access and air conditioning ensure that it is not. The hotel is well located in the historic part of town and just across from the train station. **www.marriott.com**

LEIPZIG Westin Leipzig ⬚⬚⬚⬚⬚⬚ €€

15 Gerber Straße, 4105 **Tel** *(0341) 98 80* **Fax** *(0341) 98 81 22 9* **Rooms** *436*

The beds are the big attraction here. They have what is called a Heavenly Bed which features a special mattress and four layers of covers. The guest rooms are richly and tastefully decorated. An equally stylish "fitness" bar and pool are also available. **http://aktuelles.westin.de/leipzig**

MEISSEN Hotel Andree ⬚⬚⬚⬚ €€

Ferdinandstraße 2, 1662 **Tel** *(03521) 75 50* **Fax** *(03521) 75 51 30* **Rooms** *86*

This hotel is in the centre of town but in a quiet location. The guest rooms are decorated and furnished in a simple and uncomplicated style. The excellent restaurant is certainly worth a visit because it serves a good variety of local cuisine. **www.hotel-andree.de**

MORITZBURG Landhaus Moritzburg ⬚⬚⬚⬚ €

Schlossallee 37, 1468 **Tel** *(0035207) 89 69 0* **Fax** *(0035207) 89 69 19* **Rooms** *17*

A good away-from-it-all option, where you can stay in an attic-style room and look out over meadows. The rooms range from cosy to spacious, and have an almost Scandinavian feel to them. There is a decent restaurant, including terrace dining in the pleasant garden in warmer months. **www.landhaus-moritzburg.de**

PIRNA Romantik Hotel Deutsches Haus ⬚⬚⬚ €€

Niedere Burgstraße 1, 1796 **Tel** *(03501) 46 88 0* **Fax** *(03501) 46 88 20* **Rooms** *40*

A charming, historic place occupying three Renaissance houses. There is also a lovely, atmospheric brick vault cellar and highly recommended restaurant, Deutsches Haus *(see p534)*. There are beautiful riverside walks nearby along the banks of the Elbe. **www.romantikhotel-pirna.de**

ZITTAU Schwarzer Bär ⬚ €

Ottokarplatz 12, 2763 **Tel** *(03583) 55 10* **Fax** *(03583) 55 11 11* **Rooms** *16*

The Black Bear is so named because the landlord in 1694 was expelled for keeping a black bear. This is a homely and very pleasant place with attractive, simply decorated guest rooms and a reputable restaurant. **www.hotel-schwarzer-baer.de**

ZWICKAU Achat Hotel ⬚⬚⬚ €€

Leipziger Straße 180, 8058 **Tel** *(0375) 87 20* **Fax** *(0375) 87 29 99* **Rooms** *202*

A full range of all the services and facilities you would expect in a smart, modern hotel. The rooms are simple, clean and comfortable, with just a subtle sprinkling of charm. An ideal place to stay if you are not interested in splashing out on luxuries. **www.achat-hotel.de**

THURINGIA

ALTENBURG Altenburger Hof ⬚⬚⬚⬚ €

Schmöllnsche Landstraße 8, 4600 **Tel** *(03447) 58 40* **Fax** *(03447) 58 44 99* **Rooms** *140*

The guest rooms are decorated in a straightforward, clean, modern style, with long vertical striped curtains, neutral tones and simple furniture. All rooms have desks and Internet connections. The hotel has a good restaurant and cocktail bar, as well as a sauna and wellbeing area. **www.altenburger-hof.de**

ALTENBURG Parkhotel am Grossen Teich ⬚⬚ €

August-Bebel-Str. 16/17, 4600 **Tel** *(03447) 58 30* **Fax** *(03447) 58 34 44* **Rooms** *65*

This hotel used to be a hat factory, and there is a definite air of gentle refinement here. The guest rooms are well equipped, including satellite television, mini bar and marble decorated bathrooms. The staff are friendly and there is an excellent restaurant. **www.parkhotel-altenburg.de**

EISENACH Steigenberger Hotel Thuringer Hof ⬚⬚⬚⬚⬚ €€

Karlsplatz 11, 99817 **Tel** *(03691) 28 0* **Fax** *(03691) 28 19 0* **Rooms** *127*

If you want to combine art and hospitality the Steigenberger hotel is the right place. There are paintings and wooden sculptures in the lobby, and the modern rooms are just as elegant. Some have a beautiful view over the castle and surrounding area. The restaurant serves delicate Asian cuisine. **www.eisenach.steigenberger.de**

EISENACH Hotel auf der Wartburg
⊞ 🍴 🏃 ▤   €€€€€

Wartburg Castle, 99817 **Tel** *(03691) 79 70* **Fax** *(03691) 79 71 00* **Rooms** *35*

A little castle perched high on a cliff. Expect nothing but the best, and then have your expectations exceeded. The individually decorated rooms are well equipped, including wireless Internet access. Cosiness, palatial luxury and a great view are all combined here. **www.wartburghotel.de**

ERFURT Grand Hotel am Dom
⊞ 🍴 🏃 📺 ▤   €€€

Theaterplatz 2, 99084 **Tel** *(0361) 64 45 0* **Fax** *(0361) 64 45 10 0* **Rooms** *160*

The towering glass box entrance hints at the business-class quality of the hotel. Rooms have that smart and tidy muted-brown and burgundy decoration style that offers at once warmth and respectability. All rooms have safes, mini bars, satellite and pay television and internet access. **www.accorhotels.com**

ERFURT Zumnorde
🍴   €€€

Anger 50/51, 99084 **Tel** *(0361) 56 80 0* **Fax** *(0361) 56 80 40 0* **Rooms** *50*

Stately rooms with muted style and quality polished wood furniture. The hotel is located in the historic centre of town near the Mariendom and St Severi. It also offers special discounts through its website, particularly for weekend visits. **www.hotel-zumnorde.de**

ERFURT-APFELSTADT Park Inn
⊞ 🍴 📺   €€

Riedweg 1, 99192 **Tel** *(0362) 02 85 0* **Fax** *(0362) 02 85 41 0* **Rooms** *96*

This colourful hotel has a bright, fresh and friendly atmosphere, and is a nice compromise between the needs of business travellers and tourists. It has a health centre with sauna, gym and solarium, and conference facilities. Rooms also have satellite and pay television and Internet access. **www.parkinn.com**

GERA Courtyard by Marriott
⊞ 🍴 📺 ▤   €

Gutenbergstraße 2a, 7548 **Tel** *(0365) 29 09 0* **Fax** *(0365) 29 09 10 0* **Rooms** *165*

The rooms here are all pretty generous in terms of space, and are decorated in a mildly lively and colourful way. Wireless internet access operates throughout the hotel. The location is quiet and almost has a residential feeling about it. **www.marriott.com**

GOTHA Hotel am Schlosspark
⊞ 🍴 ▤   €€

Lindenauallee 20, 99867 **Tel** *(03621) 44 20* **Fax** *(03621) 44 24 52* **Rooms** *95*

With parts of the hotel being set in a greenhouse-style glass box, there is a summery feeling to this place at any time of year. Guest rooms have all the facilities that one would expect of a four-star hotel. The hotel's restaurant of the same name is pleasant *(see p535)*, and a spa and sauna are also available. **www.hotel-am-schlosspark.de**

GREIZ Schlossberg Hotel
⊞ 🍴 🏃 ▤   €

Marienstr. 1–5, 7973 **Tel** *(03661) 62 21 23* **Fax** *(03661) 62 21 66* **Rooms** *33*

Guest rooms are light and uncomplicated, and all have mini bar and television and many have wireless Internet access. There is a Greek restaurant in the hotel, while there is another restaurant offering traditional regional fare just a few minutes' stroll away. **www.schlossberghotel-greiz.de**

JENA Jembo Park
🍴 📺   €

Rudolstädter Str. 93, 7745 **Tel** *(03641) 68 50* **Fax** *(03641) 68 52 99* **Rooms** *48*

For accommodation that is attached to a bowling alley and pub, it looks surprisingly good. This is an easygoing kind of place that is often used for wedding receptions and parties, and offers a no-nonsense straightforward kind of comfort. **www.jembo.de**

MÜHLHAUSEN Mirage Hotel
⊞ 🍴 🏃 📺   €

Karl-Marx-Str. 9, 99974 **Tel** *(03601) 43 90* **Fax** *(03601) 43 91 50* **Rooms** *77*

Things are very clean and simple here in a business-like way. The guest rooms are very stylish with muted colours and minimal furniture. All rooms have satellite television and wireless Internet access. It is situated in the perfect location for the old town and all the best sights of Mühlhausen. **www.mirage-hotel.de**

OBERHOF Treff Hotel Panorama
⊞ 🍴 ≋ 🏃 📺 ▤   €€

Theodor-Neubauer-Straße 29, 98559 **Tel** *(036842) 50 0* **Fax** *(036842) 22 55 1* **Rooms** *409*

This huge hotel offers stunning architecture and a huge range of activities, especially for children. Set in parkland, it rises out of the woods like a pyramid. There are tennis, squash and badminton courts as well as an indoor climbing gym. **www.treff-hotel-panorama.de**

WEIMAR Hotel Anna Amalia
⊞ 🏃   €

Geleitstraße 8–12, 99423 **Tel** *(03643) 49 56 0* **Fax** *(03643) 49 56 99* **Rooms** *51*

Conveniently located within strolling distance of all the things you may wish to see while in town. The interior is supposed to follow the theme of Goethe's Italian travels, but really this does not extend beyond naming the rooms after Italian cities. The rooms and apartments are comfortably furnished. **www.hotel-anna-amalia.de**

WEIMAR Hotel Elephant
⊞ 🍴 🏃   €

Markt 19, 99423 **Tel** *(03643) 80 20* **Fax** *(03643) 80 26 10* **Rooms** *99*

Despite the hotel's name, the style here is very refined and stately. Everything is squared-off, neat, respectable and comfortable. All rooms also have original artworks, and the hotel has a tradition of being a meeting place for artists, poets and intellectuals. **www.luxurycollection.com/elephant**

Key to Price Guide *see p488* **Key to Symbols** *see back cover flap*

WEIMAR Ringhotel Kaiserin Augusta

Carl-August-Allee 17, 99423 Tel (03643) 23 40 Fax (03643) 23 44 44 Rooms 134

An elegant-looking old building that has guest rooms that either look out across the old part of town or onto a courtyard. All rooms are decorated in light colours and feel spacious and airy, and are tidy and comfortable without feeling too stiff or formal. **www.hotel-kaiserin-augusta.de**

WEIMAR Dorint am Goethepark

Beethovenplatz 1–2, 99423 Tel (03643) 87 20 Fax (03643) 87 21 00 Rooms 143

A three-minute walk to the historic town centre, this rather interesting building offers a good mix of comfort and convenience, and also combines the old and the new in a surprising but effective way. The building itself consists of a new, modern style construction that sits between two classical mansions. **www.accorhotels.com**

WEIMAR Grand Hotel Russischer Hof zu Weimar

Goetheplatz 2, 99423 Tel (03643) 77 40 Fax (03643) 77 48 40 Rooms 126

A place of tradition and time-honoured luxury, this hotel has gleaming floors, an astrological grandfather clock, polished wood, heavy curtains tied back with tasselled golden ropes, textured walls and ceilings, and a range of fine dining options. It is really rather grand. **www.russischerhof.com**

MUNICH

Insel Mühle

Von-Kahr-Straße 87, 80999 Tel (089) 81010 Fax (089) 812 0571 Rooms 38

This hotel has a dreamy romantic setting in an old mill in beautiful gardens by a small river. The style is simple, country and comfortable. There is also an excellent restaurant, beer garden, wine cellar and bar. Choose tables in shady spots, under trees, or simply relax and wander around the grounds. **www.insel-muehle.com**

Am Siegestor

Akademienstraße 5, 80799 Tel (089) 399550 Rooms 20

The building where the hotel stands became a hotel in 1950 and still houses the original lift, one of Munich's oldest hotel lifts, dating back to the late 1800s. It is situated close to the lively Schwabing scene with good shops, bars and restaurants. Guest rooms are simple but adequate. **www.siegestor.de**

Dorint Novotel

Hochstraße 11, 81669 Tel (089) 661070 Fax (089) 66107 999 Rooms 305

A very contemporary four-star hotel with simple, sleek, bright decor. The welcoming breakfast room has large floral photographs. There is also a spacious pool and relaxation room plus fitness area. Its central location means that you can walk to Marienplatz, the Gasteig cultural centre or museums. **www.novotel.com**

Gästehaus Englischer Garten

Liebergeselstraße 8, 80802 Tel (089) 3839410 Fax (089) 38394-133 Rooms 25

A cosy little guesthouse with pleasant, if small rooms. The hotel is quiet and family run. Longer-stay apartments are also available, offering more space and a balcony. Once a watermill, the now listed building has a lovely garden where you can sit out and enjoy breakfast. **www.hotelenglischergarten.de**

Hotel am Nockherberg

Nockherstraße 38a, 81541 Tel (089) 6230010 Fax (089) 623 00129 Rooms 38

Modern, small, neat and clean sums up this hotel. What it lacks in stylish design it makes up for in convenient location, being close to the river Isar, Deutsches Museum and Gasteig cultural centre. The decor is simple but comfortable in neutral tones. A welcoming and friendly place. **www.nockherberg.de**

Advokat

Baaderstraße 1, 80469 Tel (089) 216310 Fax (089) 216310 Rooms 50

Advokat is the designer sister hotel of the Admiral. It is situated right in the trendy artistic quarter where you can find nice boutiques and great cafés. The decor throughout is in an elegant, classic style, with lots of paintings, flowers, sculptures and contemporary design. Minimal but stylish. There is a small roof terrace. **www.hotel-advokat.de**

Cosmopolitan Hotel

Hohenzollernstraße 5, 80801 Tel (089) 383810 Fax (089) 38381-111 Rooms 71 **Map 2 C1**

A contemporary hotel in a quieter side street in the fashionable Schwabing district. There is a modern design feel throughout and rooms have Ligne Roset furniture. Enjoy breakfast on the outdoor terrace in warmer weather. It is located just a short walk from the English Garden. **www.geisel-privathotels.de**

Hotel am Viktualienmarkt

Utzschneiderstraße 14, 80469 Tel (089) 23110 90 Fax (089) 23110955 Rooms 27 **Map 2 B5**

A very central location near the famous fruit and vegetable market, Viktualienmarkt. It is simple and basic, but comfortable. The rooms are modern with floral or striped fabric furnishings and plenty of green. The hotel also owns the café a few doors down. **www.hotel-am-viktualienmarkt.de**

Olympic

Hans-Sachs-Straße 4, 80469 **Tel** *(089) 231890* **Fax** *(089) 23189199* **Rooms** *38*

A small hotel with neo-Baroque appeal and stylish, arty charm in the heart of the creative area. It is favoured by artists, photographers and fashion designers. The decor is Italian modern classic with an art gallery lobby. Most rooms look out onto an inner courtyard, offering a peaceful atmosphere. **www.hotel-olympic.de**

Splendid-Dollmann

Thierschstraße 49, 80538 **Tel** *(089) 238080* **Fax** *(089) 23808 365* **Rooms** *36*   **Map** *3 D4*

The Splendid has an English town house feel to it. Expect a traditional and charming hotel in quiet Lehel, an old quarter of the town rich in tradition. It offers a restaurant, babysitting service and a lovely small garden, library and bar. The guest rooms are elegant and have antique furniture. **www.hotel-splendid-dollmann.de**

Admiral

Kohlstraße 9, 80469 **Tel** *(089) 216350* **Fax** *(089) 293674* **Rooms** *33*

Situated just around the corner from the Deutsches Museum this small four-star hotel offers traditional style, efficient staff, a wonderful breakfast buffet, some rooms with balconies overlooking the garden and a bar for evening drinks. Caters for families too. Tranquil location not far from the river Isar. **www.hotel-admiral.de**

Anna

Schützenstraße 1, 80335 **Tel** *(089) 599940* **Fax** *(089) 599 94333* **Rooms** *73*   **Map** *1 F4*

A very design-conscious hotel in the heart of Munich with a gold-coloured reception desk, designer seating in the café, bar and restaurant, and pillars, a wonderful chandelier and purple sofas in the lounge. Try the innovative cuisine with Euro-Asian inspiration. It is located just ten minutes by foot from Marienplatz. **www.geisel-privathotels.de**

Asam Hotel

Josephspitalstraße 3, 80331 **Tel** *(089) 2309700* **Fax** *(089) 23097097* **Rooms** *24*   **Map** *1 F5*

A popular hotel among celebrities, it offers good service and a certain level of style. Guest rooms have marble bathrooms and you can choose from international cuisine in the hotel's own Speisekammer restaurant and enjoy cocktails in the bar. The surrounding streets are quiet at night. **www.hotel-asam.de**

Cortiina

Ledererstraße 8, 80331 **Tel** *(089) 2422490* **Fax** *(089) 2422 49100* **Rooms** *39*   **Map** *2 C4*

You might be forgiven for thinking the hotel lobby is an art gallery. A favourite among the fashionable and design set, there is a stylish bar and oak panelling in the rooms, and it is located right in the heart of the city. They can provide a babysitter and daily newspapers are complimentary. **www.cortiina.com**

Das Palace

Trogerstraße 21, 81675 **Tel** *(089) 419710* **Fax** *(089) 41971-819* **Rooms** *74*

This rather noble hotel has become a haven for culture lovers and artists. It has a lovely garden, an adorable roof garden and a smart restaurant. Children are more than welcome, and guests are treated to mineral water and fruit on arrival. A great hotel bar, plus sauna, massage and fitness area. **www.muenchenpalace.de**

Hotel Excelsior

Schützenstraße 11, 80335 **Tel** *(089) 551370* **Fax** *(089) 55137121* **Rooms** *114*   **Map** *1 F4*

A four-star, first-class hotel in a central location. There is an Italian influence not only in the hotel's design but also in the cuisine. It prides itself on an excellent choice of top Italian wines in the Geisel's Vinothek wine restaurant. Guests can also use the facilities in its partner hotel Königshof. **www.geisel-privathotels.de**

Hotel Ritzi

Maria-Theresa-Straße 2a, 81675 **Tel** *(089) 4195030* **Fax** *(089) 41950350* **Rooms** *25*   **Map** *3 F5*

A stylish ambience greets you at Ritzi. The guest rooms are all individually decorated, with a global traveller feel, such as sea blue with beach mementoes, African inspired, zen oriental, white regency or warm Moroccan. A wonderful Mediterranean restaurant and a cosy lounge and bar with Art Deco styling. **www.hotel-ritzi.de**

Maritim

Goethestraße 7, 80336 **Tel** *(089) 552350* **Fax** *(089) 55235-900* **Rooms** *347*   **Map** *1 E4*

A good central location near the shops, theatre and not far from the main station, this hotel is also handy for the famous Oktoberfest fairground. The hotel has two restaurants, a piano bar, sauna and steam bath. The large indoor pool has panoramic views from the top floor. A classic large hotel. **www.maritim.de**

Opera

St-Anna-Straße 10, 80538 **Tel** *(089) 2104940* **Fax** *(089) 21049477* **Rooms** *25*   **Map** *3 D4*

Tucked in a side street close to the designer shops is Hotel Opera in a smart town house. It has a beautiful façade and Italian Renaissance courtyard. Enjoy the peace and quiet in the lovely garden or try some of the French, German or Italian specialities in the fine restaurant Gandl *(see p536)*. The guest rooms are all different. **www.hotel-opera.de**

Bayerischer Hof

Promenadeplatz 2–6, 80333 **Tel** *(089) 21200* **Fax** *(089) 2120906* **Rooms** *395*   **Map** *2 A3*

A large luxurious hotel in a prominent central location near the best shops, museums, opera house, theatres and restaurants. Elegant rooms with swathes of fabrics mixing plaids and florals in a country-house style. It also has a spa, three restaurants, including the Garden Restaurant *(see p537)*, and a great bar. **www.bayerischerhof.de**

Key to Price Guide *see p488* **Key to Symbols** *see back cover flap*

Hotel Königshof

🖥️🍴♨️📺☰ €€€€€

Karlsplatz 25, 80335 **Tel** *(089) 551360* **Fax** *(089) 551360* **Rooms** *87*
Map *1 F3*

A renowned hotel with classical elegance, first-class service, comfort and an internationally acclaimed cuisine in its Michelin-starred restaurant of the same name *(see p537)*. This is top class luxury in a central location, close to the shops and museums. Make use of the fitness, sauna and wellbeing area. **www.geisel-privathotels.de**

Kempinski Hotel Vier Jahreszeiten

🖥️🍴♨️♨️📺☰ €€€€€

Maximilianstraße 17, 80539 **Tel** *(089) 21250* **Fax** *(089) 2125 2000* **Rooms** *308*
Map *2 C4*

The top address in Munich (built for King Maximilian II in 1858) nestled among the designer stores on Maximilianstraße. Excellent service, gastronomy and bars. A stunning entrance hall in rich gold and reds sets the tone. The pool and wellness floor was completely revamped in 2006. **www.kempinski-vierjahreszeiten.de**

Mandarin Oriental

🖥️🍴♨️♨️📺☰ €€€€€

Neuturmstraße 1, 80331 **Tel** *(089) 290980* **Fax** *(089) 222539* **Rooms** *73*
Map *2 C4*

This centrally located, luxury Munich property offers spacious rooms, marble bathrooms with separate bath and shower and panoramic views of the city from the rooftop terrace's heated swimming pool. Dine in the fine Mark's restaurant with its Michelin star, or alfresco on the terrace. **www.mandarinoriental.com/munich**

BAVARIA

ALTOTTING Zur Post

🖥️🍴♨️📺 €€

Kapellplatz 2, 84503 **Tel** *(08671) 5040* **Fax** *(08671) 6214* **Rooms** *93*

Located in the heart of a charming small town on one of Germany's oldest squares, the rooms here are classically elegant with fine wooden furniture, some with views over church spires. Guests can also enjoy several restaurants, as well as a pool with sauna and steam bath. **www.zurpostaltoetting.de**

ANSBACH Bürger-Palais

🍴 €€

Neustadt 48, 91522 **Tel** *(0981) 95132* **Fax** *(08671) 95600* **Rooms** *12*

Ornate and Baroque in style with a lovely garden and terrace. The restaurant is Bavarian rustic with stained-glass windows and waitresses in traditional costume. Period furniture, chandeliers and original fireplaces enhance the ambience. Prices go up during Bach week from the end of July to early August. **www.hotel-buergerpalais.com**

ASCHAFFENBURG Wilder Mann

🖥️🍴📺 €€

Löherstraße 51, 63739 **Tel** *(06021) 3020* **Fax** *(06021) 302234* **Rooms** *74*

The Wilder Mann dates back to a 16th-century inn at the old bridge over the river Main. It has no-fuss, comfortable modern rooms and its restaurant of the same name *(see p538)* serves good quality regional food and you can even eat up on the roof terrace. There is also a spa area. **www.hotel-wilder-mann.de**

ASCHAU IM CHIEMGAU Residenz Heinz Winkler

🖥️🍴♨️📺 €€€

Kirchplatz 1, 83229 **Tel** *(08052) 17990* **Fax** *(08052) 1799-66* **Rooms** *32*

A culinary destination for real gourmands. Masterchef Heinz Winkler took over the original Post Hotel here in 1989. The former medieval building now has luxurious rooms plus invigorating and rejuvenating spa treatments. Enjoy the great terrace and garden. **www.residenz-heinz-winkler.de**

AUGSBURG Dom Hotel

🖥️♨️📺📺 €€

Frauentorstraße 8, 86152 **Tel** *(0821) 343930* **Fax** *(0821) 343930* **Rooms** *52*

A recently restored historic hotel near the cathedral and within walking distance of all the sights and local restaurants. An extra plus is the pool, sauna and fitness area. The Dom has been family owned for four generations and lies in a quiet side street by the Bischofsmauer, which is the old town wall. **www.domhotel-augsburg.de**

AUGSBURG Romantikhotel Augsburger Hof

🖥️🍴📺 €€

Auf dem Kreuz 2, 86152 **Tel** *(0821) 343050* **Fax** *(0821) 3430-55* **Rooms** *36*

Located opposite Mozart's house in the centre of Augsburg. The old building has been recently renovated and is a five-minute walk from the pedestrian zone. The clean, fresh, contemporary rooms are decorated in a smart rustic, country-house style. Regional Swabian food is served in the fine restaurant. **www.augsburger-hof.de**

AUGSBURG Steigenberger Drei Mohren

🖥️🍴 €€€

Maximilianstraße 40, 86150 **Tel** *(0821) 50360* **Fax** *(0821) 157864* **Rooms** *105*

In the heart of the historic old town, it is an excellent base for visiting all the sights. Well-appointed rooms contain antiques and old paintings. It also has an excellent restaurant. A short walk from the museum, theatre and palaces. Comfort and high quality service. **www.augsburg.steigenberger.de**

BAMBERG Alt Ringlein

🖥️🍴📺 €€

Dominikanerstraße 9, 96049 **Tel** *(0951) 95320* **Fax** *(0951) 9532500* **Rooms** *33*

A pleasant and comfortable hotel in Bamberg's centre. Enjoy the choice of Franconian meals in its restaurant of the same name *(see p538)* and try one of several local beers, including their own home-brewed one. In the wing dating back to 1296 they have Franconian styled rooms. Make sure you spend time in the nice beer garden. **www.alt-ringlein.com**

BAMBERG Welcome Hotel Residenzschloss €€€
Untere Sandstraße 32, 96049 **Tel** *(0951) 60910* **Fax** *(0951) 6091701* **Rooms** *184*

This hotel has classic rooms in a listed building on the banks of the river Regnitz. Now a spa and conference hotel, it began life as a hospital back in 1789. Guests can choose between two restaurants, and there is also a piano bar and small chapel, which sometimes holds classical concerts. **www.residenzschloss.com**

BAYREUTH Bayerischer Hof €€
Bahnhofstraße 14, 95444 **Tel** *(0921) 78600* **Fax** *(0951) 7860560* **Rooms** *50*

A luxury hotel within walking distance of the Oberfrankenhalle and Festival Hall for the famous Wagner Festspiele music festival. It offers spacious elegant rooms, a French bistro, a restaurant, a pool and sauna, garden area, sun terrace and also a roof terrace. **www.bayerischer-hof.de**

BAYREUTH Lohmühle €€
Badstraße 37, 95444 **Tel** *(0921) 53060* **Fax** *(0951) 5306469* **Rooms** *42*

Located on the banks of the pretty Mülbach river, this privately owned three-star hotel offers a peaceful setting and classic contemporary decor in a half-timbered house close to the pedestrianized area. Expect traditional Franconian hospitality and fresh, locally-caught fish on the restaurant menu. **www.hotel-lohmuehle.de**

BAYREUTH Ramada Hotel Residenzschloss €€
Erlanger Straße 37, 95444 **Tel** *(0921) 75850* **Fax** *(0951) 7585601* **Rooms** *102*

This tastefully appointed four-star hotel, located on the edge of town, has a light airy restaurant looking out onto the garden. You can sample regional and international food from the menu. Wireless Internet is available and you can make use of the hotel's own fitness club with sauna and whirlpool. **www.ramada.de**

BERG, LAKE STARNBERG Seehotel Leoni €€€
Assenbucher Straße 44, 82335 **Tel** *(08151) 5060* **Fax** *(08151) 506140* **Rooms** *67*

A stylish modern building with an Italian flair. The design conscious decor mixes cool cream rooms with a hint of colour. It has a superb garden and sits directly on Lake Starnberg in Berg. There is a good restaurant, spa and pool, and a wonderful panorama from the veranda and sun terraces. **www.starnbergersee-hotel.com**

BURGHAUSEN Landhotel Reisingers Bayerische Alm €€
Robert-Koch-Str. 211, 84489 **Tel** *(08677) 9820* **Fax** *(08677) 982200* **Rooms** *23*

A superior family-run hotel in Burghausen, overlooking Europe's longest castle and old town. Enjoy excellent food in the hotel's beautiful beer garden of the same name *(see p539)*. Amenities include Wireless Internet, free parking and anti-allergy beds, a garden of the five senses and healthy or macrobiotic menus. **www.bayerischealm.de**

COBURG Festungshof €
Festungshof 1, 96450 **Tel** *(09561) 80290* **Fax** *(09561) 802933* **Rooms** *14*

The Festungshof offers simple but adequate rooms in a comfortable rustic style. Located at the foot of the Coburg fortress, it dates back to 1337 and boasts great views across the surrounding countryside. Eat traditional Franconian fare in the wood-panelled Wallensteinstube or the large beer garden. **www.hotel-festungshof.de**

COBURG Hotel Weinstube Gerberhof €
Gerbergaße 1, 96450 **Tel** *(09561) 871187* **Fax** *(09561) 871189* **Rooms** *8*

The small Gerberhof is an old corner house steeped in tradition and history, from exposed beams to a typical regional wine tavern with rustic decor. You can enjoy regional cuisine but also some Thai specials. Situated at the edge of the pedestrianized area, it is a good spot from which to explore Coburg. **www.hotel-gerberhof.de**

COBURG Goldene Traube €€€
Am Viktoriabrunnen 2, 96450 **Tel** *(09561) 8760* **Fax** *(09561) 876222* **Rooms** *72*

Centrally located, this friendly hotel was established in 1756. The smart, classic restaurant prides itself on its good regional and creative cuisine, as well as its selection of wines. Rooms are cosy and comfortable, and there is also a steam room, sauna, whirlpool and a lovely summer terrace. **www.goldenetraube.com**

DACHAU Zieglerbräu €
Konrad-Adenauer-Straße 8, 85221 **Tel** *(08131) 454396* **Fax** *(08131) 4543 9898* **Rooms** *12*

In the middle of Dachau's old town, the Zieglerbräu has undergone a pleasant transformation. Major and much needed renovation has brought it into the 21st century. Rooms are bright, colourful, comfortable and fresh. As well as beer from its own brewery, it offers guests typical Bavarian and international food. **www.zieglerbraeu.com**

DINKELSBÜHL Deutsches Haus €€
Weinmarkt 3, 91550 **Tel** *(09851) 6058* **Fax** *(09851) 7911* **Rooms** *18*

The building dates back to 1440. Its famous half-timbered German High Renaissance façade is one of the best in the region. With classic old-style rooms, modern facilities and an excellent restaurant of the same name *(see p539)*, the town of Dinkelsbuhl is a highlight on the Romantic Road from Würzburg to the Alps. **www.deutsches-haus-dkb.de**

EICHSTÄTT Adler Hotel €€
Marktplatz 22–24, 85072 **Tel** *(08421) 6767* **Fax** *(08421) 8283* **Rooms** *28*

Double studios overlook the Baroque market square at the front and the town wall to the rear. Centrally located but quiet nonetheless. The rooms are furnished in a rather simple style but are clean and comfortable. The listed building retains a certain traditional atmosphere. **www.adler-eichstaett.de**

Key to Price Guide *see p488* **Key to Symbols** *see back cover flap*

FREISING Isar Hotel
Isarstraße 4, 85356 **Tel** *(08161) 8650* **Fax** *(08161) 8655 55* **Rooms** *56*

A family-owned hotel which is welcoming and centrally situated by the river Isar close to the old town. It has German country-style wooden decor and offers wireless Internet access in the lobby, as well as a bar and a restaurant specializing in Asian food. Bike hire is available plus a sauna and massage and beauty treatments. **www.isarhotel.de**

FÜSSEN Alpenblick
Uferstraße 10, 87629 **Tel** *(08362) 50570* **Fax** *(08362) 505773* **Rooms** *61*

Come to this hotel for the stunning view across the lake and Alps more than the style, which is quite cosy and chintzy. Füssen lies close to King Ludwig II's beautiful and famous castles. Opportunities for hiking, fishing, cycling or sauna, steam bath and solarium are all nearby. **www.alpenblick.de**

FÜSSEN Treff Hotel Luitpoldpark
Luitpoldstraße 1–3, 87629 **Tel** *(08362) 9040* **Fax** *(08362) 904678* **Rooms** *131*

A majestic pale pink building with modern classic decor. It is in the heart of Füssen, surrounded by Allgäu's Alps, lakes and the pretty park, the King's Nook. Choose from four top restaurants serving Bavarian cuisine *(see p540)*. The hotel also boasts a large Fit and Fun athletic centre. **www.luitpoldpark-hotel.de**

GARMISCH-PARTENKIRCHEN Garmischer Hof
Chamonixstraße 10, 82467 **Tel** *(08821) 9110* **Fax** *(08821) 51440* **Rooms** *54*

Located close to the centre of town, Garmischer Hof is a traditional chalet-style hotel which is elegant, if a little dated. From the balconies of south-facing rooms you get a good view of the surrounding mountains and it is quiet at night. The hotel also boasts a garden and a restaurant with a summer terrace. **www.garmischer-hof.de**

GARMISCH-PARTENKIRCHEN Hotel Bavaria
Partnachstraße 51, 82467 **Tel** *(08821) 3466* **Fax** *(08821) 76466* **Rooms** *32*

Bavaria is a small family-run hotel near the centre of Garmisch, offering guests old-fashioned charm and hospitality. It has a wonderful garden and you can even fish in the hotel's peaceful stretch of river. The guest rooms are tastefully decorated. **www.hotel-bavaria-garmisch.com**

GARMISCH-PARTENKIRCHEN Post-Hotel Partenkirchen
Ludwigstraße 49, 82467 **Tel** *(08821) 93630* **Fax** *(08821) 9363 2222* **Rooms** *58*

The oldest and most traditional building in town is located in the pedestrianized area. King Ludwig II housed his generals here. It has antique wooden furniture, traditional Bavarian style, rich colours, compact and cosy rooms, a lovely garden terrace with mountain views and an elegant restaurant. **www.post-hotel.de**

INGOLSTADT Ara Hotel
Schollstraße 10a, 85055 **Tel** *(0841) 95430* **Fax** *(0841) 9543444* **Rooms** *95*

The family-run Ara Hotel is near the centre of Ingolstadt. It is a large crimson-coloured hotel in a contemporary building with outdoor sun terrace and compact comfortable rooms. Also, non-smoking and disabled rooms are available. The Italian restaurant, La Tosca, is light and spacious. **www.hotel-ara.de**

KEMPTEN Bayerischer Hof
Füssener Straße 96, 87437 **Tel** *(0831) 57180* **Fax** *(0831) 5718100* **Rooms** *51*

A four-star hotel in a traditional house in the centre of Kempten. It offers rooms with views over the park or river, a complimentary bottle of mineral water, Internet access, a Bavarian restaurant and beer garden, plus a small fitness area. The hotel also has a pretty garden and terrace for use in summer. **www.bayerischerhof-kempten.de**

LANDSHUT Romantik Hotel Fürstenhof
Stethaimer Straße 3, 84034 **Tel** *(0871) 92550* **Fax** *(0871) 925544* **Rooms** *24*

An elegant and classic hotel with a romantic and regal aura, set in a beautiful Art Nouveau villa in the centre of Landshut. This hotel offers a sauna and a peaceful garden. The very good restaurant has one Michelin star and provides healthy cuisine using fresh local produce such as duck and venison. **www.romantikhotels.com/landshut**

LINDAU Reutemann Seegarten
Ludwigstraße 21, 88131 **Tel** *(08382) 9150* **Tel** *(08382) 915591* **Rooms** *64*

A great setting right on the promenade of this pretty town on Lake Constance. There is a lovely view of the Austrian Alps across the lake from the balconies and terrace or bar. Fitness and wellbeing facilities plus an open-air pool can be used in the sister hotel next door. Make the most of the hotel's bikes. **www.reutemann-lindau.de**

LINDAU Bayerischer Hof
Seepromenade, 88131 **Tel** *(08382) 9150* **Fax** *(08382) 915591* **Rooms** *97*

A luxurious Neo-Classical building dating back to 1854, located on the harbour front which has spacious rooms and suites, good service and excellent fitness, pool, sauna and wellbeing facilities. Enjoy the international cuisine in the restaurant of the same name *(see p540)* and unforgettable lake views from the bar. **www.bayerischerhof-lindau.de**

LINDAU Villino
Hoyerberg 34, 88131 **Tel** *(08382) 93450* **Fax** *(08382) 934512* **Rooms** *18*

Located behind Lindau in the bordering village of Hoyern, on the Hoyerberg hill. Culture and haute cuisine are paramount in this idyllic country residence set in a beautiful garden. Its restaurant of the same name *(see p540)* offers cuisine inspired by Asian-Italian fusion. There is a peaceful terrace, spa and wireless Internet access. **www.villino.de**

MURNAU AM STAFFELSEE Alpenhof Murnau €€€€€
Ramsachstraße 8, 82418 **Tel** *(08841) 4910* **Fax** *(08841) 491100* **Rooms** *60*

A top class spa and chalet-style retreat between Garmisch and Munich, close to Oberammergau which borders the Murnauer Moos nature reserve, overlooking the majestic Alps and Lake Staffel. It is an idyllic setting. Enjoy the renowned cuisine in the Reiterzimmer restaurant. **www.alpenhof-murnau.com**

NEUBURG AN DER DONAU Neuwirt €
Färberstraße 88, 86633 **Tel** *(08431) 2078* **Fax** *(08431) 38643* **Rooms** *24*

A traditional and typical small Bavarian hotel with a cosy feel. It has a *Stube* tavern and a spacious beer garden in a sunny courtyard, partly undercover. The guest rooms are simply decorated with a rustic charm and are adequate and clean. **www.neuwirt-neuburg.de**

NEU-ULM Römer Villa €€
Parkstraße 1, 89231 **Tel** *(0731) 800040* **Fax** *(0731) 80004-50* **Rooms** *23*

A beautiful, elegant building like a French turreted manor house, set back from the road on the edge of a park. It has a lofty, vaulted reception, lounge with open fire, wine bar, high quality restaurant and a winter garden. The classic, traditionally furnished guest rooms come with a balcony or terrace. **www.roemer-villa.de**

NÜRNBERG Burghotel €€
Lammgaße 3, 90403 **Tel** *(0911) 238890* **Fax** *(0911) 2388 9100* **Rooms** *58*

Charming simple rooms filled with light offer some great views over the roofs of the old town. Burghotel has traces of ancient castle life, such as armour and coats-of-arms. There is also a lounge with an open fire, rustic bar, sun terrace and sauna. **www.altstadthotels-nuernberg.de**

NÜRNBERG Romantik Hotel am Josephplatz €€
Josephsplatz 30–32, 90403 **Tel** *(0911) 214470* **Fax** *(0911) 21447-200* **Rooms** *36*

A romantic hotel dating back to 1675 located within walking distance of Nürnberg's old centre. There are small apartments which would suit a family. Enjoy the good breakfast buffet, roof terrace, sauna, solarium, fitness room and winter garden. There are also several restaurants close by. **www.romantikhotels.com/Nuernberg**

NÜRNBERG Maritim Hotel Nürnberg €€€€
Frauentorgraben 11, 90443 **Tel** *(0911) 23630* **Fax** *(0911) 2363 823* **Rooms** *316*

The Maritim has a slightly corporate feel (it is run by a large German chain), but has an excellent central location opposite the ancient city wall. There are good swimming and wellbeing facilities plus a choice of restaurants – Stube for international cuisine, the Blauer Salon café or the piano bar. **www.maritim.de**

OBERAMMERGAU Turmwirt €
Ettalerstraße 2, 82487 **Tel** *(08822) 92600* **Fax** *(08822) 1437* **Rooms** *22*

Built in the Bavarian country-house style and owned by the same family for three generations, this small hotel has a welcoming wooden reception area with antique chests and rugs. It has a sun terrace and outdoor tables under chestnut trees, an *à la carte* restaurant and a café. **www.turmwirt.de**

OBERSTDORF Kappeler Haus €
Am Seeler 2, 87561 **Tel** *(08322) 96860* **Fax** *(08322) 968613* **Rooms** *45*

This chalet-style hotel in the Allgäu Alps is located in the heart of Obertsdorf, the southern-most village in Germany. An in-house beautician is on hand to pamper guests. Music recitals take place in the hotel, too. There is also a garden and pool and it is set in a quiet location. **www.kappeler-haus.de**

PASSAU Residenz €€
Fritz-Schäffer-Promenade, 94032 **Tel** *(0851) 989020* **Fax** *(0851) 98902200* **Rooms** *45*

A fabulous river setting with great views of castle, boats and the Danube plays host to this historic building offering comfort and a lovely little terrace. Built in the 15th century, it has a history of river trade and travellers. The town square is very close as are the boats for taking trips down the Danube. **www.residenz-passau.de**

PASSAU Passauer Wolf €€€
Rindermarkt 6–8, 94032 **Tel** *(0851) 931510* **Fax** *(0851) 9315150* **Rooms** *41*

This hotel is located in the old town of Passau, next to the pedestrian precinct and on the banks of the Danube. The St Stephan cathedral and several museums and unique sights are within walking distance. Choose between rooms with a view over the river, the old town or the courtyard. **www.hotel-passauer-wolf.de**

REGENSBURG Bischofshof am Dom €€€
Krauterermarkt 3, 93047 **Tel** *(0941) 5 84 60* **Fax** *(0941) 5846 146* **Rooms** *55*

Situated opposite the cathedral, this rustic-style hotel boasts an elegant, renowned restaurant, David (*see p541*). The rooms have a romantic style with pretty country-house fabrics in florals and stripes. It has a quiet location looking out onto the side street or courtyard. All rooms are individually decorated. **www.hotel-bischofshof.de**

REGENSBURG Sorat Inselhotel €€€€
Müllerstraße 7, 93059 **Tel** *(0941) 81040* **Fax** *(0941) 810 4444* **Rooms** *75*

This is a contemporary, comfortable and well-established hotel in a central location with lovely town views over the river. Enjoy the restaurant Brandner, lobby bar with full-length window and views downstream, plus spa, fitness centre and wireless Internet. **www.sorat-hotels.com/de/hotel/regensburg**

Key to Price Guide *see p488* **Key to Symbols** *see back cover flap*

ROTHENBURG OB DER TAUBER Gasthaus am Siebersturm   ◫ 🚶   €

Spitalgaße 6, 91541 **Tel** *(09861) 3355* **Fax** *(09861) 933823* **Rooms** *9*

A friendly and family-run hotel with romantic medieval charm near the old tower that serves good quality hearty Franconian meals in its own little restaurant. Some rooms look out over the famous Tauber valley. Splash out on a room with a four-poster, or stick to the more affordable standard doubles. **www.siebersturm.de**

ROTHENBURG OB DER TAUBER Prinzhotel   ◫◫   €€

An der Hofstett 3, 91541 **Tel** *(09861) 9750* **Fax** *(09861) 97575* **Rooms** *52*

Within the old town walls, this historic hotel is in a very quiet location surrounded by the town's medieval history. All the sights are within walking distance. The hotel's restaurant serves Franconian–Italian cuisine. Parking is available in front of the hotel. **www.prinzhotel.rothenburg.de**

WERNBERG Hotel Burg Wernberg   ◫◫🚶◫   €€€€

Sclossberg 10, 92633 **Tel** *(09604) 9390* **Fax** *(09604) 939139* **Rooms** *25*

Housed in a 12th-century turreted castle, now fully restored with all the modern comforts, this hotel has an unusual romantic, fairy-tale setting on a hill. The rooms are decorated in a Gothic style and amenities include a sauna, cigar lounge, Internet access. Some rooms have four poster beds. **www.relaischateaux.com/burgwernberg**

WÜRZBURG/ HOCHBERG Minotel Zum Lamm   ◫◫🚶   €€

Hauptstraße 76, 97204 **Tel** *(0931) 3045630* **Fax** *(0931) 408973* **Rooms** *37*

The hotel lies in Höchberg, outside the baroque centre of Würzburg and offers guests a typical Franconian hospitality and great gourmet food. It also boasts a lovely courtyard and garden. Guests are spoiled with great food and wine, and it is popular with cyclists, motorcyclists and hikers touring the area. **www.lamm-hoechberg.de**

BADEN-WURTTEMBERG

BADEN-BADEN Tannenhof   ◫◫   €€

Hans-Bredow-Straße 20, 76530 **Tel** *(07221) 300990* **Rooms** *27*

The Tannenhof has a wonderful, peaceful and idyllic setting with panoramic views. It is a great place to relax, whether in the garden, on the sun terrace, lawn or in the sauna and solarium. The house restaurant, Piemonte *(see p542)*, specializes in Northern Italian food and wines. **www.hotel-tannenhof-baden-baden.de**

BADEN-BADEN Hotel Belle Epoque   ◫◫   €€€€

Maria-Viktoria-Straße 2c, 76530 **Tel** *(07221) 300660* **Rooms** *16*

Housed in a beautiful Neo-Renaissance villa surrounded by its own verdant park, all the rooms and suites in this hotel are decorated with original furniture from the Belle Epoque period. An elegant hotel with excellent service. **www.hotel-belle-epoque.de**

BADEN-BADEN Steigenberger Badischer Hof   ◫◫◫◫   €€€€

Lange Straße 47, 76530 **Tel** *(07221) 9340* **Rooms** *139*

Baden-Baden's oldest hotel offering palatial grandeur with palms, pillars and plants. Some of the guest rooms have balconies, while others have thermal water pumped into the bathrooms. There are also indoor and outdoor thermal pools, plus a medical spa. **www.badischer-hof.steigenberger.de**

BADEN MERGENTHEIM Hotel Gästehaus Alte Münze   ◫   €

Münzgasse 12, 97980 **Tel** *(07931) 5660* **Rooms** *30*

In a quiet location near the Knight's Castle in the centre of town, this hotel has light, airy and modern, if simply decorated, guest rooms. There is also a cosy familiar breakfast room for guests with lots of plants. Discover the rich history of the area, the powers of the mineral water and enjoy walks in the surrounding countryside. **www.hotelaltemuenze.de**

BADEN MERGENTHEIM Hotel Victoria   ◫◫◫   €€€

Poststraße 2–4, 97980 **Tel** *(07931) 5930* **Rooms** *78*

An intimate and highly-regarded spa hotel located in the centre close to the Kurpark thermal baths. It has well-equipped rooms and wine buffs will appreciate the Vinothek restaurant and enjoy sampling some of the 400 top wines from France and Italy, which you can buy in the shop along with olive oils. **www.victoria-hotel.de**

BRUCHSAL Ritter   ◫◫   €€

Au in den Buchen 73, 83 & 92, 76646 **Tel** *(07257) 880* **Rooms** *55*

The Hotel Ritter is comprised of several houses with pleasant and comfortable guest rooms. Try a cool beer and barbecue in the beer garden or dine in the Brasserie. The hotel also offers a sauna and fitness area. Close to a beautiful Baroque castle and within a day-trip distance of Heidelberg. **www.ritterbruchsal.de**

ESSLINGEN Am Schelztor   ◫🚶◫   €€

Schelztor 5, 73728 **Tel** *(0711) 39 69 640* **Rooms** *33*

A small, personal, family-run hotel with a historic touch, this hotel boasts a panoramic view of the vineyards of Esslingen and the castle. Close to the station and large cinema complex. Relax in the Finnish sauna or use the fitness room. There is a good restaurant nearby in a converted stable. Families are welcome. **www.hotel-am-schelztor.de**

FREIBURG IM BERISGAU Zum Roten Bären

Oberlinden 12, 79098 **Tel** *(0761) 387 870* **Rooms** *25*

Situated in a building that dates back to the 12th century, just minutes form the centre of Freiburg, this hotel also has a lovely traditional *Stube*, a tavern-style restaurant serving regional seasonal food. The guest rooms are comfortable and there is also a peaceful courtyard. **www.roter-baeren.de**

FREIBURG IM BERISGAU Colombi Hotel

Rotteckring 16, Am Colombi Park, 79098 **Tel** *(0761) 21060* **Rooms** *117*

This is a hotel offering elegant luxury and style, excellent service and a quiet, central location. It faces a park with a small castle and is not far from the Freiburg monuments. In addition to an award-winning gourmet restaurant, café, bar and tavern, the hotel has a pool, sauna and beauty spa, and other sports facilities nearby. **www.colombi.de**

HEIDELBERG Hotel Heidelberg

Heuauerweg 35–37, 69124 **Tel** *(06221) 71040* **Rooms** *40*

This hotel is located 6 km (4 miles) from Heidelberg's centre and castle in a relaxed setting with a beer garden and sun terrace. The guest rooms are comfortable with traditional wooden furniture, wireless Internet access and some have balconies. There is also a sauna and steam room. Families welcome. **www.hotel-erna.de**

HEIDELBERG Holländer Hof

Neckarstaden 66, 69117 **Tel** *(06221) 60500* **Rooms** *39*

An old house in the centre of town with a pretty façade and classic, elegant rooms, this hotel is within easy reach of the famous castle and not far from the shops, restaurants, churches and pedestrianized area of Heidelberg. It is also close to where boat rides are run up and down the Neckar. **www.hollaender-hof.de**

HEIDELBERG Die Hirschgasse

Hirschgasse 3, 69120 **Tel** *(06221) 4540* **Rooms** *20*

First mentioned in 1472, Hirschgasse has a sense of history. The hotel boasts innovative chefs in its non-smoking restaurants, the very smart Le Gourmet and the Mensurstube, and a tavern, which has been the meeting place for Heidelberg's student fraternities for centuries. **www.hirschgasse.de**

HEIDELBERG Europäischer Hof Hotel Europa

Friedrich-Ebert-Anlage 1, 69117 **Tel** *(06221) 5150* **Rooms** *118*

The best in the area this hotel has luxurious suites, high quality rooms, courteous and helpful staff, à la carte dinners in the Kurfürstenstube, a terrace overlooking a garden, a shopping arcade and the Panorama spa and fitness club. There is everything you could possibly want to make it a memorable stay. **www.europaeischerhof.com**

HEILBRONN Ringhotel Burkhardt

Lohtorstraße 7, 74072 **Tel** *(07131) 62240* **Rooms** *80*

A modern concrete, steel and glass building, convenient for the romantic old centre of town. The rooms are comfortable and clean and the design is contemporary throughout. Very close to the public swimming baths with saunas. The hotel's restaurant, Vinopolitan, serves typical Swabian fare. **www.burkhardt-ringhotel.de**

KARLSRUHE Alfa Garni

Bürgerstraße 4, 76133 **Tel** *(0721) 29926* **Rooms** *36*

This small city hotel is right on Ludwigsplatz in the heart of Karlsruhe. The modern, light-filled building has comfortable rooms and art prints in the hallways. Enjoy the local cafés and restaurants with Mediterranean flair in the town centre, a few minutes by foot from the hotel. **www.alfa-karlsruhe.com**

KARLSRUHE Renaissance

Mendelssohnplatz, 76131 **Tel** *(0721) 37170* **Rooms** *215*

This is a recently renovated building with good location and facilities. It is not ideal for families as it has quite a business-like atmosphere. The Baroque castle, botanic gardens and zoo are close. Baden-Baden's casino and health spa are also not far away. Rooms are modern and functional. **www.renaissancehotels.com**

KONSTANZ Barbarrossa

Obermarkt 8–12, 78462 **Tel** *(07531) 128990* **Rooms** *50*

Centrally located in the heart of the old town, this is where in 1183, Emperor Friedrich I, known as Barbarossa (Red Beard) signed a peace treaty with Lombardy. It has a very old painted façade, terrace seating at the front, stylish modern rooms and bright décor with red accents. **www.barbarossa-hotel.com**

KONSTANZ Steigenberger Inselhotel

Auf der Insel 1, 78462 **Tel** *(07531) 1250* **Rooms** *102*

Situated on its own private island at the edge of the old town, right on Lake Constance, the Inselhotel is housed in a former Dominican monastery. The cloisters and murals have been preserved. Rooms, service and cuisine are all to the highest standard. **www.konstanz.steigenberger.de**

KONSTANZ Villa Barleben am See

Seestraße 16, 78464 **Tel** *(07531) 942330* **Rooms** *8*

Set in a wonderful spot right by the lake, this hotel is housed in a beautiful villa with antique furniture and ornaments, a cultivated atmosphere and a lovely terrace restaurant on summer evenings for hotel and outside guests. The guest rooms with a lake view are more expensive but worth the cost. **www.hotel-barleben.de**

LUDWIGSBURG Nestor

Stuttgarter Straße 35/2, 71638 **Tel** *(07141) 9670* **Rooms** *179*

This listed building in central Ludwigsburg, not far from the Baroque castle, the Friedenskirche church and market square, used to be a bakery. The guest rooms are modern; suites and executive doubles are also available. The hotel also has a sauna, solarium and fitness area. **www.nestor-hotels.de**

LUDWIGSBURG Schlosshotel Monrepos

Domäne Monrepos 22, 71634 **Tel** *(07141) 3020* **Rooms** *80*

Whether you want to laze on the pretty garden terrace under the chestnut trees, take a stroll around the Monrepos castle grounds, swim in the hotel's pool, have a massage or enjoy the culinary delights in one of the three restaurants, Monrepos is a peaceful and beautiful place to relax. **www.schlosshotel-monrepos.de**

MANNHEIM Maritim Parkhotel

Friedrichsplatz 2, 68165 **Tel** *(0621) 15880* **Rooms** *173*

A traditional hotel with an impressive façade situated on Friedrichsplatz with its historical buildings dating back to the Art Nouveau era. This elegant hotel has a palatial foyer, a fine vaulted restaurant, spacious rooms, an indoor swimming pool and marbled bathrooms, all set in wonderful parkland. **www.maritim.de**

MARBACH Parkhotel

Schillerhöhe 14, 71672 **Tel** *(07144) 9050* **Rooms** *56*

Set in lush parkland with great views overlooking the Neckar valley and close to the Schiller Museum and the German literature archive, this hotel is ideally located and its lovely restaurant Schillerhöhe *(see p544)* allows you to dine out on the terrace in warmer weather to watch the beautiful sunset. **www.parkhotel-schillerhoehe.de**

RAVENSBURG Romantik Hotel Waldhorn

Marienplatz 15, 88212 **Tel** *(0751) 36120* **Rooms** *30*

A family-run hotel (five generations) in Ravensburg's pedestrianized area. The hotel has a fine gourmet restaurant serving delicious game and fish dishes. Its stylish, modern rooms are comfortable and classic with contemporary touches. Romantic, old and full of tradition but with all the comforts you would expect. **www.waldhorn.de**

ROTTWEIL Hotel Haus zum Sternen

Hauptstraße 60, 78628 **Tel** *(0741) 53300* **Rooms** *11*

One of Rottweil's oldest stone houses, dating from 1278, this hotel is located in the heart of the historic town. It has many historic features, including an old wine cellar, which can be seen from the basement Platinum Bar. The rooms a mix of old charm and modern comfort. It has an excellent restaurant of the same name *(see p544)*. **www.haus-zum-sternen.de**

SALEM Reck's Hotel Restaurant

Bahnhofstraße 111, 88682 **Tel** *(07553) 201* **Rooms** *20*

A high class hotel with the famous Reck's restaurant *(see p544)*, close to Lake Constance in beautiful countryside, this hotel has pleasant, comfortable rooms with period furniture and views out over the orchard. The fine restaurant offers a renowned cuisine of fresh, regional and seasonal food, including fish from the lake. **www.recks-hotel.de**

SCHWÄBISCH GMUND Hotel Einhorn

Rinderbachergasse 10, 73525 **Tel** *(07171) 63023* **Rooms** *18*

This Baroque hotel is bright, elegant and modern, it is housed in an old building with a Roman entrance and modern facilities, such as wireless Internet access. It also boasts the Barbarossa jazz bar and the brick-vaulted Barbarossakeller restaurant, plus a separate summer café, Einhorn, in the old town. **www.hotel-einhorn-centre.com**

STUTTGART Hansa Hotel

Silberburgstraße 114–116, 70176 **Tel** *(0711) 6567800* **Fax** *(0711) 617349* **Rooms** *80*

This is located near the pedestrianized area, so it is a good central base for exploring the Swabian capital of Stuttgart. It is also close to shops, restaurants, the station and museums. There is Internet access, bike hire, a restaurant, Petrarca, offering Mediterranean specials, and a beer garden. **www.hansa-stuttgart.de**

STUTTGART Kronen Hotel

Kronenstraße 48, 70174 **Tel** *(0711) 22510* **Rooms** *80*

Located in a quiet spot, but still with easy access to the railway station, this hotel has a nice garden with terrace. Enjoy the great breakfast buffet in the modern breakfast room, looking out onto a palmed terrace. Guests can also take drinks at the little lobby bar or use the hotel sauna. **www.kronenhotel-stuttgart.de**

STUTTGART Hotel am Schlossgarten

Schillerstraße 23, 70173 **Tel** *(0711) 20260* **Rooms** *116*

A modern hotel in the extensive Schlossgarten parklands. It has luxurious rooms and suites with elegant floral furnishings. There are several dining options, such as the gourmet French restaurant, the Zirbelstube, or classic, light modern and regional food in the hotel restaurant. **www.hotelschlossgarten.com**

TÜBINGEN Krone

Uhlandstraße 1, 72072 **Tel** *(07071) 13310* **Fax** *(07071) 133132* **Rooms** *48*

A good place to stay to capture the romance and medieval feel of Tübingen's past, Krone has elegant, comfortable rooms and a refined restaurant, and has been in the same family for over a century. Sample typical regional dishes in the fine Uhlandstube restaurant or try the less formal Ludwig's for coffees and light meals. **www.krone-tuebingen.de**

ULM-LEHR Engel

Loherstraße 35, 89081 **Tel** *(0731) 140400* **Fax** *(0731) 14040-300* **Rooms** *46*

A modern hotel located outside the centre of Ulm in the quieter suburb of Lehr, the rooms are clean and comfortable with simple decor. There is also a sauna and solarium, a bar and a restaurant. The owners also took over a local fish farm, so the fish dishes on the menu come highly recommended. **www.hotel-engel-ulm.de**

WEINGARTEN Walk'sches Haus

Marktplatz 7, 76356 **Tel** *(07244) 70370* **Fax** *(07244) 703740* **Rooms** *26*

This hotel is in a 16th-century half-timbered house. The original walls dated back to 1509, but it was rebuilt after damage in the Thirty Years' War (1618–48). It also has a wonderful little French restaurant with tables in the garden. The cuisine is light, contemporary and original. Internet access is available in the rooms. **www.walksches-haus.de**

RHINELAND-PALATINATE AND SAARLAND

BAD HONNEF Avendi Hotel

Hauptstraße 22, 53604 **Tel** *(02224) 1890* **Fax** *(02224) 189189* **Rooms** *101*

This hotel sits regally overlooking the Rhine. There is a large fitness and wellbeing area, including an indoor pool. Creatively decorated and comfortable rooms have all the modern trappings. There is a restaurant as well as a bistro, which specializes more in drinks and small snacks than main meals. **www.avendi.de**

BAD NEUENAHR Steigenberger Hotel

Kurgartenstraße 1, 53474 **Tel** *(02641) 9410* **Fax** *(02641) 941410* **Rooms** *224*

Architecturally impressive and very comfortable, the genteel rooms here are spacious and furnished with antiques. There is a restaurant, café, cocktail lounge and beer garden. There is also a golf course 2.5 km away, and the hotel has lockers for stowing golf bags and has the facility to book tee-times. **www.bad-neuenahr.steigenberger.de**

DUDENHOFEN Hotel Zum Goldenen Lamm

Landauer Straße 2, 67373 **Tel** *(06232) 95001* **Fax** *(06232) 98502* **Rooms** *29*

A colourful and classy hotel in a quiet part of Dudenhofen, the bright and airy rooms are decorated in warm, Mediterranean colours. This theme continues into their garden restaurant which serves Greek-style food. Their restaurant inside focuses on seafood dishes. **www.info-lamm.de**

KOBLENZ Top Hotel Krämer Garni

Kardinal-Krementz-Straße 12, 56073 **Tel** *(0261) 406200* **Fax** *(0261) 41340* **Rooms** *25*

A comfortable and new hotel, with a touch of the traditional German style. The rooms have a 1990s feel about them, and fresh flowers are a colourful touch which contrast well with the somewhat minimalist decor. The service is friendly and enhances the personal atmosphere of the hotel. **www.tophotel-k.de**

KOBLENZ Diehl's Hotel

Rheinsteigufer 1, 56077 **Tel** *(0261) 97070* **Fax** *(0261) 9707213* **Rooms** *57*

Located on the banks of the Rhine and opposite where the Rhine and the Mosel rivers meet, this hotel has a terrace overlooking this beautiful area, and all guest rooms have a similar view. There is restaurant serving creative international cuisine, as well as banquet facilities for large functions such as weddings. **www.diehls-hotel.de**

KOBLENZ Mercure

Julius-Wegeler-Straße 6, 56068 **Tel** *(0261) 1360* **Fax** *(0261) 1361199* **Rooms** *169*

There is a home-like feeling to the colourful and comfortable rooms, which also offer nice views. The hotel has an elegant restaurant and a stylish lounge bar. There is also a good view from the higher floors of the hotel looking over Koblenz and the surrounding district. **www.mercure.com**

KOBLENZ Hotel Scholz

Moselweißer Straße 121, 56073 **Tel** *(0261) 94260* **Fax** *(0261) 942626* **Rooms** *67*

The oldest family-run hotel in Koblenz, it has been in the family for three generations. The present generation conducted extensive renovations and modernization. The small rooms are comfortable and well equipped. There is a rustic restaurant serving traditional German cuisine in an unmistakably German setting. **www.hotelscholz.de**

LAHNSTEIN Mercure Hotel Lahnstein

Rhein-Höhen Weg/Zu den Thermen 1, 56112 **Tel** *(02621) 9120* **Fax** *(02621) 912100* **Rooms** *227*

Located in a park which has beautiful footpaths. There are tennis courts nearby, and tennis lessons can be arranged for guests. The hotel has two restaurants with stunning views over the city, as well as a café and comfortable lounge bar. Their pool and wellness area has recently been renovated. **www.mercure.de**

MAINZ Dorint Novotel Mainz

Augustusstraße 6, 55131 **Tel** *(06131) 9540* **Fax** *(06131) 954100* **Rooms** *217*

The bright and well-equipped rooms are very comfortable, and there is a spacious and relaxing pool area. Their restaurant offers elegant dining and a must-see wine bar, Kasematten, which is situated in a 17th-century vaulted cellar, providing a distinctive atmosphere for wine tastings. **www.dorint.com**

Key to Price Guide *see p488* **Key to Symbols** *see back cover flap*

MAINZ Favorite Parkhotel 🖥️🍴🏊🏋️📺🗄️ €€€
Karl-Weiser-Straße 1, 55131 **Tel** *(06131) 80150* **Fax** *(06131) 8015420* **Rooms** *122*

There is a pleasant surprise around every door here. Apart from the ultra-comfortable rooms and suites, there is a greenhouse with different varieties of palms, a gourmet restaurant and a beer garden that is a favourite meeting place for locals as well as guests. **www.favorite-mainz.de**

MARIA LAACH SeeHotel Maria Laach 🖥️🍴🏊🏋️📺🗄️ €€€
Ortsteil Maria Laach, 56653 **Tel** *(02652) 5840* **Fax** *(02652) 584522* **Rooms** *69*

Situated near a 900-year old monastery, this hotel scores highly for relaxation and comfort. Beautiful lake views, a pleasant café with terrace seating in their winter garden as well as a high-class restaurant of the same name *(see p546)*, serving delicate regional and seasonal dishes, make this a delightfully comfortable place to stay. **www.maria-laach.de/seehotel**

NIEDERZISSEN Hotel am Bowenberg €
Auf Brohl 7, 56651 **Tel** *(02636) 6217* **Fax** *(02636) 8317* **Rooms** *9*

A quaint hotel set amidst peaceful countryside, some of the rooms here have balconies overlooking the tree tops surrounding the hotel, and there is a library with a big fireplace, which is the perfect place for contemplating the next day's activities. It is close to the city centre and nearby tennis courts. **www.hotel-am-bowenberg.de**

RÖMERBERG Gasthof Zum Engel 🍴 €
Berghäuser Straße 36, 67354 **Tel** *(06232) 60120* **Fax** *(06232) 601230* **Rooms** *10*

A cute little guesthouse with a long history, this is the oldest inhabited house in the town, and was used as the bishop's residence in the 16th century. There are ten warm, bright and friendly rooms to choose from. The restaurant serves traditional German food, and offers a large wine list of local and international wines. **www.zumengel.de**

RÜSSELSHEIM Columbia Hotel 🖥️🍴🏊🏋️📺🗄️ €€€
Stahlstraße 2–4, 65428 **Tel** *(06142) 8760* **Fax** *(06142) 876805* **Rooms** *150*

A hotel with a high level of service and excellent facilities. A favourite with both business guests and tourists. Each room is styled with warm colours and wooden furniture. There is a well-stocked gym and a landscaped pool. The main restaurant is French in style. They also have a bistro and lounge bar. **www.columbia-hotels.de**

SAARBRÜCKEN Hotel am Triller 🖥️🍴🏊🏋️📺 €€€
Trillerweg 57, 66117 **Tel** *(0681) 580000* **Fax** *(0681) 58000303* **Rooms** *110*

An artistically inclined hotel with a lot to offer, the top floor suites here are astronomically themed, and have been named after constellations. The design merely begins here. Other themes include Moulin Rouge and The Four Seasons. There is a pool and an extensive wellness area. It is a ten-minute walk to the town centre. **www.hotel-am-triller.de**

SAARBRÜCKEN Victor's Residenz-hotel 🖥️🍴🏋️📺 €€€
Deutschmühlental, 66117 **Tel** *(0681) 588210* **Fax** *(0681) 58821199* **Rooms** *145*

This hotel is close to the French border and reflects the French influence well. It is surrounded by a forest and next to a lake. The atrium lobby is impressive and leads into their own casino and cocktail lounge. There is a luxurious wellness area and a restaurant that serves gourmet French cuisine. **www.victors.de**

SPEYER Bistumshaus St. Ludwig 🖥️🍴🏋️ €
Johannsstraße 8, 67346 **Tel** *(06232) 6098* **Fax** *(06232) 609600* **Rooms** *61*

Constructed on the site of a 14th-century monastery and adjacent to St Ludwig's church, which dates back to the 13th century, this hotel is centrally located for exploring the city. Rooms are cosy and compact. It also has extensive facilities for business guests. The restaurant can cater for large functions. **www.bistumshaus.de**

SPEYER Hotel A Wartturm 🍴 €
Landwehrstraße 28, 67346 **Tel** *(06232) 64330* **Fax** *(06232) 643321* **Rooms** *17*

Named after an old defence tower that dates back to 1451, this hotel is not, however, housed in the tower. It does offer comfortable rooms, though, some of which have balconies overlooking a garden. There is also a very cheerful wine bar that oozes character, where you may also enjoy light meals. **www.hotel-amwartturm.de**

SPEYER Domhof 🖥️🍴 €€
Bauhof 3, 67346 **Tel** *(06232) 13290* **Fax** *(06232) 132990* **Rooms** *49*

Here you will find very spacious rooms that have been decorated with a refined taste. The hotel is set in a quiet area that has a calm and serene atmosphere. The elegant restaurant offers creative cuisine and the beer garden is a sanctuary of traditional German beer drinking. **www.domhof.de**

SPEYER Lindner Hotel & Spa Binshof 🖥️🍴🏊🏋️📺🗄️ €€€€€
Binshof 1, 67346 **Tel** *(06232) 6470* **Fax** *(06232) 647199* **Rooms** *135*

The focus of this hotel is on the wellness and spa facilities, which should not be missed. All tastes are catered for in this huge spa complex. The guest rooms are just as luxuriously furnished, and there is a restaurant that serves fantastic Mediterranean food. **www.lindner.de**

TRIER Hotel Blesius Garten 🖥️🍴🏊🏋️ €€
Olewigerstraße 135, 54295 **Tel** *(0651) 36060* **Fax** *(0651) 360633* **Rooms** *62*

This is a unique hotel with beautiful rooms. It dates back to the 18th century, although it has kept itself modern through renovations. The winter garden restaurant has an open fireplace and they operate a terrace in the summer months. They also have their own brewery. **www.blesius-garten.de**

TRIER Hotel Eurener Hof

Eurener-Straße 171, 54294 **Tel** *(0651) 82400* **Fax** *(0651) 800900* **Rooms** *86*

An ostentatious building, standing on the corner of the street. Many of the rooms have small balconies and the corner rooms have wonderful views. There is a delightful garden terrace where you can enjoy breakfast. Elegant and comfortable rooms and a majestic dining area, where you can sample their fine cuisine. **www.eurener-hof.de**

TRIER Römischer Kaiser

Porta-Nigra-Platz 6, 54292 **Tel** *(0651) 9770100* **Fax** *(0651) 97701999* **Rooms** *43*

This hotel is housed in part of a historic building in the illustrious Porta Nigra Square. First mentioned in 1885, the hotel was refurbished in 1994, and now offers a decadent retreat in the heart of Trier. The rooms are tastefully furnished and spacious. It has a highly recommended restaurant of the same name *(see p546)*. **www.hotels-trier.de**

TRIER Mercure Hotel Trier Porta Nigra

Porta-Nigra-Platz 1, 54292 **Tel** *(0651) 27010* **Fax** *(0651) 2701170* **Rooms** *106*

One of the largest hotels in Trier, it is well situated and furnished with all the comforts that you could expect, including a fitness centre, wellness area and spa facilities. The surrounding area is littered with historical sights and buildings. Their restaurant is well known and there is an imaginatively decorated bar. **www.dorint.de**

ZWEIBRUCKEN Romantik Hotel Landschloss Fasanerie

Fasanerie 1, 66482 **Tel** *(06332) 9730* **Fax** *(06332) 973111* **Rooms** *50*

Only 45 minutes by car to either Luxembourg or France, this hotel has a relaxing rose garden filled with many different varieties of the flower. The rooms all have wonderful views; the suites and loft apartments look out onto the garden and forest. There is an indoor pool and a Michelin-starred restaurant. **www.landschloss-fasanerie.de**

HESSE

ALSFELD Zum Schwalbennest

Pfarrwiesenweg 12–14, 36304 **Tel** *(06631) 911440* **Fax** *(06631) 71081* **Rooms** *65*

First constructed in 1968, the "Swallow's Nest" is a serene and cheerful place to stay. It has comfortable rooms, a rustic restaurant, relaxed beer garden and is within an easy walking distance of the centre of Alsfeld. There is even a dance floor for those fond of a waltz or two. **www.hotel-schwalbennest.de**

BAD HOMBURG ParkHotel

Kaiser-Friedrich-Promenade 53–55, 61348 **Tel** *(06172) 8010* **Fax** *(06172) 801400* **Rooms** *123*

A very pleasant, privately-owned hotel, where the beds are very inviting and the rooms are decorated with a sense of colour and with an eye for comfort. The hotel offers baby beds and babysitters can be arranged at reception. There are two restaurants, one Italian and one Chinese. **www.parkhotel-bad-homburg.de**

BAD HOMBURG Maritim Kurhaushotel

Ludwigstraße 3, 61348 **Tel** *(06172) 6600* **Fax** *(06172) 660100* **Rooms** *158*

Right next door to a peaceful park, some of the rooms here have balconies overlooking the trees, and all are impeccably decorated. There is a nice pool for laps, and golfing facilities for the enthusiasts. They have a bistro, bar and a good restaurant which caters to the vegetarian palate. **www.maritim.de**

DARMSTADT Hotel an der Mathildenhöhe

Spessartring 53, 64287 **Tel** *(06151) 49840* **Fax** *(06151) 498450* **Rooms** *23*

A small hotel that combines a central location with a peaceful ambience, each of the rooms here have balconies and are quite large with all the modern necessities available. There is a definite family environment here, and they offer a babysitting service through reception. **www.hotel-mathildenhoehe.de**

DARMSTADT Jagdschloss Kranichstein

Kranichsteiner Straße 261, 64289 **Tel** *(06151) 97790* **Fax** *(06151) 977920* **Rooms** *15*

Housed in one of the most beautiful Renaissance castles in the region, this hotel offers a unique experience. A perfect setting for a wedding reception, the hotel often finds all 15 of their rooms booked by wedding parties. The grounds are stunning and well kept, and there is a beautiful forest nearby. **www.hotel-jagdschloss-kranichstein.de**

DIEZ City Hotel Diez

Bergstraße 8, 65582 **Tel** *(06432) 921569* **Fax** *(06432) 921570* **Rooms** *20*

A small hotel with a vibrant feel, the rooms here are relatively small but comfortable all the same. They have a barbecue grill in the garden area, as well as a rustic restaurant inside. Although a small hotel, there is also a well-equipped pool and a fitness and wellness area. **www.city-hotel-diez.de**

ELTVILLE AM RHEIN Kronenschlösschen

Rheinallee, 65347 **Tel** *(06723) 640* **Fax** *(06723) 7663* **Rooms** *18*

The hotel fits beautifully in the little village of Eltville. The rooms are stylish and charming, each having its own individual shape and furnishings. The bathrooms are works of art. The restaurant serves very elegant cuisine, as does the bistro, which may tempt those less inclined to empty their wallet. **www.kronenschloesschen.de**

Key to Price Guide *see p488* **Key to Symbols** *see back cover flap*

FRANKFURT Arabella Sheraton Grand Hotel
🛗🍽🏊🛗📺🗐 €€€€€

Konrad-Adenauer-Straße 7, 60313 **Tel** *(069) 29810* **Fax** *(069) 2981810* **Rooms** *378*

There is everything here that you could want from a hotel, and possibly more. Ultra-comfortable rooms, fantastic location and elegant and classy cuisine at the Peninsula Atrium restaurant *(see p547)* all wrapped up in an extremely stylish package. The amenities are reflected in the price, so bear that in mind. **www.arabella-sheraton.de**

FRANKFURT AM MAIN Frankfurt Hotel Savoy
🛗🍽🏊🛗📺🗐 €€

Wiesenhüttenstraße 42, 60329 **Tel** *(069) 273960* **Fax** *(069) 27396795* **Rooms** *144*

This hotel has a classy attitude. Situated in a convenient location for trade fairs and with good access to the airport, guests will find the hotel itself a charming place to explore. There is a swimming pool on the top floor, which offers a rare and beautiful skyline view of Frankfurt am Main. **www.savoyhotel.de**

FRANKFURT AM MAIN Hotel Borger
€€

Triebstraße 51, 60388 **Tel** *(06109) 30900* **Fax** *(06109) 309030* **Rooms** *36*

A family-styled hotel with a comfortable atmosphere and a convenient location, the rooms here offer the basic amenities, and the hotel is the perfect base for exploring the city and surrounding areas. The villa has been in the family for over a hundred years and was renovated late in the 20th century. **www.hotel-borger.de**

FRANKFURT AM MAIN Hessischer Hof
🛗🍽🛗📺🗐 €€€€€

Friedrich Ebert Anlage 40, 60325 **Tel** *(069) 75400* **Fax** *(069) 75402924* **Rooms** *117*

An exquisitely styled hotel with a sense of class. The rooms are styled either in a modern manner or with more of an antique feel about them, with some of the suites furnished with pieces from the Prince of Hesse. The restaurant and bar compliment each other well. **www.hessischer-hof.de**

FRANKFURT AM MAIN Steigenberger Frankfurter Hof
🛗🍽🛗📺🗐 €€€€€

Am Kaiserplatz, 60311 **Tel** *(069) 21502* **Fax** *(069) 2150900* **Rooms** *321*

A very large and comprehensive hotel where everything you desire is catered for and is done in style. The rooms are impeccable and the restaurants are among the best in the city. It is situated less than a kilometre away from the main station and has very helpful and friendly staff. **www.frankfurter-hof.steigenberger.de**

FULDA Maritim Hotel am Schlossgarten
🛗🍽🏊🛗📺🗐 €€€

Pauluspromenad 2, 36037 **Tel** *(0661) 2820* **Fax** *(0661) 282499* **Rooms** *112*

An ostentatious hotel with a refined atmosphere, some of the upper floors here have balconies with great views, and all the guest rooms are spacious and luxurious. There are two restaurants in unique settings: one in an intimate wine cellar; the other in a historic hall with Baroque styling. They also have a good pool area. **www.maritim.de**

KASSEL Hotel Residenz Domus
🛗 €€

Erzbergerstraße 1–5, 34117 **Tel** *(0561) 703330* **Fax** *(0561) 70333498* **Rooms** *55*

An intimate hotel that gives each guest a feeling of being personally looked after, the Art Nouveau design of the Domus's rooms betrays the modern comforts that are offered. In addition though, there is also an old-fashioned gambling room with a pool table. **www.hotel-domus-kassel.de**

KASSEL Schlosshotel Bad Wilhelmshöhe
🛗🍽🛗📺🗐 €€

Schlosspark 8, 34131 **Tel** *(0561) 30880* **Fax** *(0561) 3088428* **Rooms** *101*

Dating back to 1767, this hotel is situated in one of the most exclusive areas of Kassel. There are beautiful grounds to wander through and a plethora of wellness programmes to enjoy. The guest rooms are refined and relaxing, and the suites are spacious and opulent without being garish and over-exuberant. **www.schlosshotel-kassel.de**

KASSEL Adesso Hotel Astoria
🛗 €€€€

Friedrich-Ebert-Straße 135, 34119 **Tel** *(0561) 72830* **Fax** *(0561) 7283199* **Rooms** *40*

Friendly and comfortable service with bright and airy rooms, this is quite a well-located hotel that satisfies guests of all types, be it for business, visiting the many museums in the area or exploring the region. There are very good conference facilities here, with six dedicated rooms and extensive inclusive packages. **www.adesso-hotels.de**

LIMBURG Romantik Hotel Zimmermann
🍽 €€

Blumenröder Straße 1, 65549 **Tel** *(06431) 4611* **Fax** *(06431) 41314* **Rooms** *20*

Different styles in each of the rooms, ornate furnishings and a restful environment all make this hotel an ideal base for all types of guest. Each bathroom is fitted with Italian marble, and for the convenience of business guests there is wireless Internet access throughout the hotel. **www.romantikhotel-zimmermann.de**

MARBURG Waldecker Hof
🛗🏊🛗📺 €€

Bahnhofstraße 23, 35037 **Tel** *(06421) 60090* **Fax** *(06421) 600959* **Rooms** *40*

A comfortable and pleasant hotel with a nice pool and fitness area, the hotel itself is still family run, and the service reflects a high level of care that has been put into creating a welcoming atmosphere for guests. The delicious buffet breakfast is great. Situated close to the main train station. **www.waldecker-hof-marburg.de**

MARBURG Vila Vita Hotel & Residenz Rosenpark
🛗🍽🏊🛗📺🗐 €€€€

Rosenstraße 18–28, 35037 **Tel** *(06421) 60050* **Fax** *(06421) 6005100* **Rooms** *138*

Ostentatious and elegant at the same time, the glass dome in the lobby lends a palatial quality to the hotel, as does the impeccable service. There are 30 apartments also available, which is why it is also called "Residenz". There are three restaurants to choose from, as well as a wine cellar and lounge bar. **www.vilavitahotels.com**

RÜDESHEIM AM RHEIN Jagdschloss Niederwald   €€€
Am Niederwald 1, 65385 **Tel** *(06722) 71060* **Fax** *(06722) 7106666* **Rooms** *52*

Set in a historic hunting castle, this hotel offers all that you could wish for, including a tennis court and swimming pool. Its restaurant has a terrace with a panoramic view, and the wine cellar has the best wines from the region. The cocktail bar serves a very nice Long Island Ice Tea. **www.niederwald.de**

WEILBURG Schlosshotel Weilburg   €€
Am Schloss, 35781 **Tel** *(06471) 50900* **Fax** *(06471) 5090111* **Rooms** *50*

This castle from the Renaissance period provides a luxurious place to rest one's weary head. Apart from the beautiful architecture and design of the hotel itself, the surrounding area exudes a sense of history. The rooms are tastefully decorated and spacious. It has an excellent restaurant, Alte Reitschule *(see p548)*. **www.schlosshotel-weilburg.de**

WETZLAR Landhotel Naunheimer Mühle   €€
Mühle 2, 35584 **Tel** *(06441) 93530* **Fax** *(06441) 935393* **Rooms** *33*

Set in a quiet area adjacent to the Lahn, the hotel itself was once mill-powered by the flowing waters. With an intimate design mixed with a traditional slanting towards comfort, the rustic restaurant serves cuisine from the region. The terrace and outside seating area is a great place to relax. **www.naunheimer-muehle.de**

WIESBADEN Klee am Park   €€€
Parkstraße 4, 65189 **Tel** *(0611) 90010* **Fax** *(0611) 9001310* **Rooms** *60*

Recently renovated and enlarged, most rooms here have their own balcony, offering a wonderful view over Wiesbaden. The restaurant serves delicious international dishes, and the surrounding park is the perfect place to burn off some calories from over-indulging. **www.klee-am-park.de**

WIESBADEN Nassauer Hof   €€€€€
Kaiser-Friedrich-Platz 3, 65183 **Tel** *(0611) 1330* **Fax** *(0611) 133632* **Rooms** *139*

This exclusive hotel offers eight different grades of superb rooms, all the way up to the presidential suite. The architecture and design brings a historic sense of aristocratic opulence, and yet this marries with the modern amenities. The wellness area and restaurant attracts many non-residential guests. **www.nassauer-hof.de**

NORTH RHINE-WESTPHALIA

AACHEN Holiday Inn   €€
Krefelder Straße 221, 52070 **Tel** *(0241) 18030* **Fax** *(0241) 1803444* **Rooms** *99*

With good service and a friendly atmosphere, this hotel has a similar layout to most Holiday Inns. You can expect comfortable rooms with good amenities, which in this hotel includes wireless Internet access throughout. There is a restaurant, bistro and a beer garden is used in the warmer months. **www.aachen-holiday-inn.de**

AACHEN Best Western Hotel Royal garni   €€€
Jülicher Straße 1, 52070 **Tel** *(0241) 182280* **Fax** *(0241) 18228699* **Rooms** *35*

Centrally located, this hotel makes a good base for business meetings, trade fairs and sightseeing tours into the city and surrounding area. The rooms have a minimalist style and the suites come with private terraces and kitchenettes. The Aachener Cathedral lies within half a kilometre of the front door. **www.royal.bestwestern.de**

AACHEN Dorint Sofitel Quellenhof Aachen   €€€€
Monheimsallee 52, 52062 **Tel** *(0241) 91320* **Fax** *(0241) 9132100* **Rooms** *185*

A grand hotel in every sense of the word, the elegant rooms and suites here are just the tip of the iceberg. The sauna, swimming pool and fitness area are stunning, as is the restaurant which offers Mediterranean-style food and sprawls out onto a terrace with a wonderful view of the park. **www.dorint.com**

BIELEFELD Ambiente Hotel Rütli   €
Osningstraße 245, 33605 **Tel** *(0521) 92120* **Fax** *(0521) 9212445* **Rooms** *73*

This restful hotel set in parklands dates back to 1908 and was restored in 1993. The interior has been modernized, along with the luxurious rooms. There is a fantastic beer garden and terrace area, which is perfect for relaxing in after returning from a hike in the surrounding woods. Another highlight is the restaurant. **www.ruetli.de**

BIELEFELD Brenner Hotel Diekmann   €€
Otto-Brenner-Straße 133, 33607 **Tel** *(0521) 29990* **Fax** *(0521) 299 9220* **Rooms** *65*

A quaint little hotel with a homespun charm, there is a small bowling alley here which adds to the unique character of the hotel. There is also a restaurant that caters to large groups and functions, as well as a bar with lots of traditional paraphernalia on the walls and a beer garden outside. **www.brenner-hotel.de**

BONN Schlosshotel Kommende Ramersdorf   €€
Oberkasslerstraße 10, 53227 **Tel** *(0228) 440734* **Fax** *(0228) 444400* **Rooms** *18*

Situated in a fairytale castle, the rooms and hallways here are filled with antiques and works of art that help set it apart from other hotels. There is a medieval feel to the hotel, and each room is individual. The restaurant is also worth a visit. **www.schlosshotel-kommende-ramersdorf.de**

BONN Kaiser Karl 🔢 €€€
*Vorgebirgsstraße 56, 53119 **Tel** (0228) 985570 **Fax** (0228) 9855777 **Rooms** 42*

Exquisitely decorated rooms and a keen eye for details make this hotel a welcome oasis of leisure and pleasure. All rooms cater to those with allergies. Many famous guests have passed through the doors, and more than a few have tinkled the keys of the piano in the old-fashioned and dignified bar. **www.kaiser-karl-hotel-bonn.de**

BONN Hilton Bonn 🔢 €€€€
*Berliner Freiheit 2, 53111 **Tel** (0228) 72690 **Fax** (0228) 7269700 **Rooms** 252*

With spacious and classy rooms equipped with all the modern conveniences you would expect, the hotel caters well for families, as does their wellness and fitness area. They have a nice pool and gym, which is the perfect place to burn off the calories consumed in the fantastic, Mediterranean-style restaurant. **www.hilton.de/bonn**

BONN Dorint Sofitel Venusberg 🔢 €€€€€
*An der Casselruhe 1, 53127 **Tel** (0228) 2880 **Fax** (0228) 288288 **Rooms** 85*

This hotel sits on the banks of the Rhine and has colourful and decadent rooms that overlook the surrounding forest. There are a number of sporting facilities in the area, such as golf and tennis, and there is a jogging track inside the hotel for fitness fans. **www.dorint.de**

DETMOLD Lippischer Hof 🔢 €€
*Willy-Brandt-Platz 1, 32756 **Tel** (05231) 9360 **Fax** (05231) 24470 **Rooms** 25*

There is an attractive view from the windows of this hotel, set in the heart of Detmold. It has a deceptive simplicity with a high level of comfort and service. The restaurant is quite romantic, and on occasion there are functions held in the larger rooms used for conferences with set menus. **www.hotellippischerhof.de**

DÜSSELDORF Hotel Weidenhof 🔢 €
*Oststraße 87, 40210 **Tel** (0211) 1306460 **Fax** (0211) 13064619 **Rooms** 36*

A ten-minute walk from all the central sights, there is a genteel charm to the rooms here, which are tastefully decorated with subtlety. It is a relatively small hotel but one that attracts many returning guests. There are six apartments which are well suited to families and small groups. **www.hotelweidenhof.de**

DÜSSELDORF Ibis Hauptbahnhof 🔢 €€
*Konrad-Adenauer-Platz 14, 40210 **Tel** (0211) 16720 **Fax** (0211) 1672101 **Rooms** 166*

A hotel with all the basic comforts and necessities, this hotel has a nice little bar near the modern lobby and wireless Internet throughtout. The location is one of the best in Düsseldorf for access to the train station and general sightseeing. Guaranteed to deliver exceptional value. **www.ibishotel.com**

DÜSSELDORF Madison I 🔢 €€
*Graf-Adolf-Straße 94, 40210 **Tel** (0211) 16850 **Fax** (0211) 1685328 **Rooms** 100*

There is a sporting and fitness centre connected to the hotel, which is very extensive and well equipped. Each room is tastefully decorated with warm colours and cosy furniture. There is a bistro with a terrace for the warmer months and another bistro in the hotel. **www.madison-hotels.de**

DÜSSELDORF Steigenberger ParkHotel 🔢 €€€€
*Königsallee 1a, 40212 **Tel** (0211) 13810 **Fax** (0211) 1381592 **Rooms** 130*

This is an elegant hotel with delicately styled rooms, some of which are furnished with antiques while retaining a high level of comfort at the same time. Well situated, close to the Altstadt and the Rhine, a highlight here is the restaurant, which has a diverse menu and an extensive wine list. **www.duesseldorf.steigenberger.de**

ESSEN Astoria Hotel 🔢 €€
*Wilhelm-Nieswandt-Allee 175, 45326 **Tel** (0201) 83584 **Fax** (0201) 8358040 **Rooms** 102*

With new, intimate and colourful rooms in a modern building that has recently been renovated and expanded, this hotel is ideally placed for sightseeing and visiting the business districts. For functions there is the facility to arrange catering for the outside areas of the hotel, which are leafy and peaceful. **www.astoria-hotels.de**

ESSEN Welcome Hotel 🔢 €€
*Schützenbahn 58, 45127 **Tel** (0201) 17790 **Fax** (0201) 1779199 **Rooms** 176*

A very modern and colourful hotel, the rooms here are filled with everything you could desire, and the beds are soft and comfortable. They can cater for people suffering sensitive allergies, for whom it would be better to avoid their beautiful but pollinated garden restaurant which operates in summer. **www.welcome-to-essen.de**

ESSEN Scandic Hotel 🔢 €€€
*Theodor Althoff Straße 5, 45133 **Tel** (0201) 7690 **Fax** (0201) 7691143 **Rooms** 293*

Close to the fairgrounds and other central locations, this hotel has become popular among business guests. There is a colourful lounge and lobby area, and very large facilities for conferences, including a hall. They also have a pool, fitness area and indoor skittles. **www.scandic-hotels.com/essen**

ESSEN Schlosshotel Hugenpoet 🔢 €€€€€
*August-Thyssen-Straße 51, 45219 **Tel** (02054) 12040 **Fax** (02054) 120450 **Rooms** 25*

Built on ruins that date back to 778, this castle-hotel is amongst the finest in the region. Each room is guaranteed to captivate the attention, and the wedding suite is furnished with antiques from the 16th century. There are two fantastic restaurants, each serving delicious cuisine from around the world. **www.hugenpoet.de**

HOXTER Ringhotel Niedersachsen

Gruben-Straße 3–7, 37671 **Tel** *(05271) 6880* **Fax** *(05271) 688444* **Rooms** *80*

Set in a beautiful area this hotel has an expansive wellness and spa area, with a sizeable swimming pool. Some of the guest rooms have an unorthodox style to them, with big wooden beams. The hotel also boasts four restaurants to keep your taste buds occupied. **www.hotelniedersachsen.de**

KÖLN Hotel Kosmos

Waldecker Straße 11–15, 51065 **Tel** *(0221) 67090* **Fax** *(0221) 6709321* **Rooms** *161*

Set in an otherwise dull area this hotel is an oasis of comfort and hospitality. The air-conditioned rooms are spacious and well equipped. The hotel is still family run and great care has gone into retaining its charm. They have a large pool and good fitness facilities. It attracts mostly business guests for trade fairs. **www.kosmos-hotel-koeln.de**

KÖLN Hyatt Regency

Kennedy-Ufer 2a, 50679 **Tel** *(0221) 8281234* **Fax** *(0221) 8281370* **Rooms** *306*

One of the best hotels in Germany, this Hyatt has a prime location perfect both for crossing the bridge into the Old Town and visiting the trade fairs. All tastes are catered for and the view over the Rhine and the Old Town is unparalleled. **www.cologne.regency.hyatt.de**

KÖLN Hotel im Wasserturm

Kaygasse 2, 50676 **Tel** *(0221) 20080* **Fax** *(0221) 2008888* **Rooms** *88*

Integrated into a historic water tower in the heart of Cologne, this top class hotel is one of the most distinctive in the city. The building's shape has spawned oddly shaped rooms, some with two levels. On the 11th floor is an opulent restaurant, La Vision *(see p551)*, that has been awarded a Michelin star. **www.hotel-im-wasserturm.de**

KÖLN Intercontinental

Pipinstraße 1, 50667 **Tel** *(0221) 28060* **Fax** *(0221) 28061111* **Rooms** *262*

Opened in 2003, this new Intercontinental is one of the most refined hotels in the city. It is very close to the Old Town, and an easy walking distance from the trade fairs. The bars, restaurants and cocktail lounges have become famous by themselves, and the fitness/pool area is state of the art. **www.koeln.intercontinental.com**

KÖLN Jolly Hotel MediaPark

Im MediaPark 8b, 50670 **Tel** *(0221) 27150* **Fax** *(0221) 2715999* **Rooms** *217*

Part of an Italian chain of hotels, this one displays the subtle and refined styling that serves them well. There are luxurious and comfortable rooms and facilities, situated in the MediaPark, next to the tall tower. There are excellent fitness and wellness facilities, and guests receive discounts at the nearby Holmes gym. **www.jollyhotels.de**

LEMGO Im Borke

Salzufler Straße 132, 32657 **Tel** *(05266) 1691* **Fax** *(05266) 1231* **Rooms** *37*

Here you will find a peaceful atmosphere that is well-suited to families. A lot of care has been put into making this hotel a welcome and friendly place to stay, and it has paid off. There is a restaurant of the same name *(see p551)* serving international cuisine in a traditional environment, and there is also a bowling alley downstairs. **www.hotel-im-borke.de**

MÜNSTER Schloss Wilkinghege

Steinfurter Straße 374, 48159 **Tel** *(0251) 213045* **Fax** *(0251) 212898* **Rooms** *35*

A successful blend of modern comfort and historic charm, the top suite here has been furnished with antiques, and the bathroom adorned with Philip Starck fixtures. The restaurant serves refined cuisine with a subtle French flair. Next door there is a golf course and tennis courts. **www.schloss-wilkinghege.de**

MÜNSTER Romantik Hotel Hof zur Linde

Handorfer Werseufer 1, 48157 **Tel** *(0251) 32750* **Fax** *(0251) 328209* **Rooms** *48*

Built on the banks of the Werse river, with magnificent views and plenty of room to stroll around, this is about as authentic as a farm cottage hotel gets. There are suites and cottages with their own fireplaces and the restaurant serves high quality dishes, seasoned with herbs fresh from the hotel's own garden. **www.hof-zur-linde.de**

SIEGEN Best Western Parkhotel Siegen

Koblenzer Straße 135, 57072 **Tel** *(0271) 33810* **Fax** *((0271) 3381450* **Rooms** *88*

A hotspot for business guests, the area around this hotel is quiet and serene, which makes for a relaxing atmosphere. The rooms and suites are quite modern and stylishly furnished. The ideal evening involves their sauna and steam room, the cocktail lounge and a leisurely stroll to a nearby restaurant. **www.parkhotel-siegen.bestwestern.de**

WINTERBERG Steymann

Mollenkotten 195, 59955 **Tel** *(02981) 929540* **Fax** *(02981) 9295450* **Rooms** *35*

This hotel is suited to families and a mature clientèle. It has pleasant rooms, all with balconies. Those wishing to make this a base for exploring the beautiful scenery can return to the relaxing pool and sauna before sampling the local cuisine in the restaurant and, of course, using the bowling alley. **www.hotel-steymann.de**

WUPPERTAL Intercity Wuppertal

Döppersberg 50, 42103 **Tel** *(0202) 43060* **Fax** *(0202) 456959* **Rooms** *160*

Close to the main train station and the attractions of the town centre, as well as the business district, this hotel is well set-up for business guests, with wireless Internet access in each corner of the hotel and extensive conference facilities. The cocktail bar and restaurant lack atmosphere, although the cuisine is rewarding. **www.intercityhotel.de**

Key to Price Guide *see p488* **Key to Symbols** *see back cover flap*

LOWER SAXONY, HAMBURG AND BREMEN

BREMEN Landhaus Radler Garni

Kastanienweg 17, 27404 **Tel** *(04281) 98820* **Fax** *(04281) 988210* **Rooms** *16*

A family-owned and managed hotel, this place is a little distant from the centre of Bremen, but offers a peaceful atmosphere that is appreciated by families. There is a playground for children and the surrounding area is perfect for cycling and exploring on foot. Nestled in the rear is a well-maintained little garden. **www.landhaus-radler.de**

BREMEN Landhaus Höpkens Ruh

Oberneulander Landstraße 69, 28355 **Tel** *(0421) 205853* **Fax** *(0421) 2058545* **Rooms** *8*

A small, stylish hotel with decor emulating the French country style, each of the eight rooms here is individually furnished, which will be obvious when you see the level of detail that has been applied. Set in parkland with a good restaurant serving seasonal and regional cuisine. **www.hoepkens-ruh.de**

BREMEN Lichtsinn

Rembertistraße 11, 28203 **Tel** *(0421) 368070* **Fax** *(0421) 327287* **Rooms** *35*

Very spacious and genteel, with a splash of home-style comfort, this hotel is family owned and has a sedate elegance that symbolizes German hospitality. Each room is individually furnished and quite tastefully so, with some having a more modern decor than others. The river is a few minutes walk away. **www.hotel-lichtsinn.de**

BREMEN Best Western Zur Post

Bahnhofsplatz 11, 28195 **Tel** *(0421) 30590* **Fax** *(0421) 3059591* **Rooms** *170*

There is an undercurrent of understated unorthodoxy here, although it all works very well. Some of the rooms have imaginative murals and decoration, and the bar is worthy of admiration for its colour and style. The hotel is in the heart of the city, and sits right outside the central train station. **www.zurpost.bestwestern.de**

BREMEN Hilton Bremen

Böttcherstraße 2, 28195 **Tel** *(0421) 36960* **Fax** *(0421) 3696960* **Rooms** *235*

Generous and exuberant rooms and services, with a great location next to the river and the marketplace square in the centre. It is also a stone's throw away from the Casino Bremen, which lures many guests to its ritzy opulence. There are impressive fitness facilities and a relaxing pool area. **www.hilton.de/bremen**

BREMEN Park Hotel

Im Bürgerpark, 28209 **Tel** *(0421) 34080* **Fax** *(0421) 3408602* **Rooms** *177*

Opulent and expansive, the Park Hotel brings to life all your dreams of luxury and comfort. The grounds are well sculpted and spectacular, as are the rooms which are guaranteed to make you feel relaxed. There are several restaurants, bars and bistros, so take your pick. **www.park-hotel-bremen.de**

BÜCKEBURG Große Klus

Am Klusbrink 19, 31675 **Tel** *(05722) 95120* **Fax** *(05722) 951250* **Rooms** *31*

Situated in a serene forested area you are assured of a peaceful sojourn here. The building itself dates back to the 1700s, though the rooms are quite modern. There is a restaurant serving seasonal and local cuisine and their beer garden serves the house's own beer, which is brewed in the hotel microbrewery. **www.kluesker.de**

CELLE Hotel am Braunen Hirsch

Münzstraße 9c, 29223 **Tel** *(05141) 93930* **Fax** *(05141) 939350* **Rooms** *24*

Primarily famous for the historic restaurant next door, this hotel has a lot to offer the weary traveller. With comfortable and spacious rooms that are sunny and cheerful, and architecture that is angular and sharp, affecting the layout of the rooms, every corner of this hotel has its own character and charm. **www.hotelambraunhirsch.de**

CELLE Fürstenhof Celle

Hannoversche Straße 55–56, 29221 **Tel** *(05141) 2010* **Fax** *(05141) 201120* **Rooms** *73*

Seated amidst history in beautiful Celle, this top class hotel is a comprehensive palace of comfort. Their Michelin-starred gourmet restaurant, Endtenfang *(see p552)*, attracts guests from all over the region. Enjoy authentic Italian fare at the rustic Palio restaurant. There is also an impressive fitness area. **www.fuerstenhof-celle.de**

CLOPPENBURG Park Hotel

Burgstraße 8, 49661 **Tel** *(04471) 6614* **Fax** *(04471) 6617* **Rooms** *51*

Restful, cheerful and quiet, lying close to the Soeste river and near to the centre of Cloppenberg, this makes a good nest for fledgling explorers new to the town. There is a golf course, tennis courts and a skittle alley nearby for sportier guests, and a sauna bath for the more contemplative ones. **www.parkhotel-cloppenburg.de**

DUDERSTADT Zum Löwen

Marktstraße 30, 37115 **Tel** *(05527) 3072* **Fax** *(05527) 72630* **Rooms** *42*

Renowned also for its restaurant, this hotel provides a comfortable respite from the larger chain hotels. Some of the rooms have balconies, from which guests can view the beautiful city of Duderstadt. The restaurant serves regional German cuisine, and there is an intimate cellar bar. **www.hotelzumloewen.de**

EINBECK Der Schwan

Tiedexerstraße 1, 37574 **Tel** *(05561) 4609* **Fax** *(05561) 72366* **Rooms** *12*

Set amongst the romantic buildings of Einbeck, and providing a central location from which to discover the town, the rooms here are quite comfortable and all tinged with pink. The restaurant offers creative and experimental cuisine, which is both delicious and artistic. **www.schwan-einbeck.de**

GOSLAR Treff Hotel Das Brusttuch

Hoher Weg 1, 38640 **Tel** *(05321) 34600* **Fax** *(05321) 346099* **Rooms** *13*

The building is part of the UNESCO-protected Altstadt in Goslar. Although the building itself is over 480 years old, it has been successfully renovated to provide all the modern comforts. There is a large restaurant in the hotel and a swimming pool for guests. The rooms are spacious and quaint. **www.treff-hotels.de**

GOSLAR Der Achtermann

Rosentorstraße 20, 38640 **Tel** *(05321) 70000* **Fax** *(05321) 7000999* **Rooms** *152*

A touch of the modern in a historic city, this hotel is decorated in an Art Deco style with an efficiency that sets a high standard. The pool and sauna area is quite large and well equipped, offering yoga and massages. There is a restaurant and a nice little café outside with seating in the shade of trees. **www.der-achtermann.de**

GÖTTINGEN Intercity Göttingen

Bahnhofsallee 1a, 37081 **Tel** *(0551) 52110* **Fax** *(0551) 5211500* **Rooms** *145*

Not far from the main train station and in easy walking distance of the centre and attractions, this hotel has neat and tidy rooms that lack a little individuality. There are good facilities in the rooms, however, and for business guests there are a number of conference rooms and halls. **www.intercityhotel.de**

GÖTTINGEN Romantik-Hotel Gebhard

Goetheallee 22–23, 37073 **Tel** *(0551) 49680* **Fax** *(0551) 4968110* **Rooms** *63*

Popular amongst business guests, Gebhard Hotel is also fantastically located close to both the centre of town and the main train station. Warm and luxurious rooms make for a comfortable stay, and the little restaurant provides a romantic atmosphere. There is also a sauna and whirlpool. **www.gebhardshotel.de**

HAMBURG Central Hotel

Präsident-Krahn-Straße 15, 22765 **Tel** *(040) 306150* **Fax** *(040) 383049* **Rooms** *35*

Opposite the Hamburg-Altona train station and close to the city centre, this hotel is in a trendy part of Hamburg, and is surrounded by a vibrant nightlife. The rooms are compact and modern. There are two well-known theatres nearby, and the hotel often has information about what is showing. **www.hamburg-erleben.de**

HAMBURG Holiday Inn Kieler Strasse Hotel

Kieler Straße 333, 22525 **Tel** *(040) 547400* **Fax** *(040) 54740100* **Rooms** *105*

A futuristic and expansive lobby greets guests, who tend to be a mixture of both business people and tourists. The location is well serviced by public transport, although coming by car is useful for exploring the city in the evening. The hotel also serves a tasty breakfast in the mornings. **www.hamburg-kielerstrasse.holiday-inn.de**

HAMBURG Crown Plaza Hamburg

Graumannsweg 10, 22087 **Tel** *(040) 228060* **Fax** *(040) 2208704* **Rooms** *285*

Close to the main train station and the trade fair areas and renovated in 2002, this Crown Plaza is packed full of facilities such as an indoor pool, full fitness area, restaurant, cocktail lounge and more. There are good amenities for families and children accompanied by their parents eat for free in the restaurant. **www.ichotelsgroup.com**

HAMBURG Europäischer Hof

Kirchenallee 45, 20099 **Tel** *(040) 248248* **Fax** *(040) 24824799* **Rooms** *320*

A hotel and wellness retreat combined, this hotel has a huge water slide, squash courts, golf simulator, sauna and more. The hotel was destroyed in World War II, but was rebuilt to exacting standards soon after. There are three restaurants and a piano bar with live music, as well as an atmospheric wine cellar for functions. **www.europaeischer-hof.de**

HAMBURG Dorint Sofitel am Alten Wall

Alter Wall 40, 20457 **Tel** *(040) 369500* **Fax** *(040) 369501000* **Rooms** *241*

There is a somewhat Japanese-inspired minimalist style to this beautiful hotel. Wonderfully located next to a canal with a terrace literally on top of the water. Every whim is catered for here, including business services and conference facilities. There is an unorthodox and cool styling to the indoor pool. **www.dorint.com**

HAMBURG Kempinski Hotel Atlantic Hamburg

An Der Alster 72, 20099 **Tel** *(040) 28880* **Fax** *(040) 247129* **Rooms** *252*

Luxurious and refined, offering the best in service and comfort, some rooms and suites here overlook the nearby lake. They have an ultra-modern fitness and wellbeing area, as well as two restaurants serving international and Chinese cuisine. There is also a small private cinema, which is a little pricey. **www.kempinski.com**

HAMBURG Vier Jahreszeiten

Neuer Jungfernstieg 9–14, 20354 **Tel** *(040) 34940* **Fax** *(040) 34942600* **Rooms** *156*

Elegance and style reign in this hotel. Many rooms overlook the Alstersee and some have a private balcony. Each room is individually furnished with both antiques and modern pieces. There are a number of bars and restaurants in the hotel, one of which has been awarded a Michelin star. **www.raffles-hvj.de**

Key to Price Guide *see p488* **Key to Symbols** *see back cover flap*

HANNOVER Best Western Parkhotel Kronsberg €€€

Gut Kronsberg 1, 30539 Tel (0511) 87400 Fax (0511) 867112 Rooms 200

Conveniently located opposite the fairground, the hotel has become a favourite with business guests. With lots of light and space, the lobby is crowned with a glass dome. There is a mixture of room styles which are all comfortable and spacious. The restaurants and bistros offer character and good food. **www.kronsberg.bestwestern.de**

HANNOVER Hotel Kaiserhof €€€

Ernst-August-Platz 4, 30159 Tel (0511) 36830 Fax (0511) 3683114 Rooms 78

Housed in a historic building constructed in 1915, this hotel has been well preserved. There is a subtle French style to the tastefully detailed rooms. It is located opposite the main train station and close to the city centre. The restaurant is highly acclaimed, and serves trout that they raise themselves in a courtyard fountain. **www.centralhotel.de**

HANNOVER Dorint Novotel Hannover €€€€

Podbielskistraße 21–23, 30163 Tel (0511) 39040 Fax (0511) 3904100 Rooms 206

Housed in an old biscuit factory, this hotel has luxurious amenities and guest rooms, with a playground for children, as well as a babysitting service if required. It also has extensive conference facilities, indeed one conference room still retains some old machinery from the factory days. **www.dorint.de**

HILDESHEIM Parkhotel Berghölzchen €€

Am Berghölzchen 1, 31139 Tel (05121) 9790 Fax (05121) 979400 Rooms 80

This hotel dates back to 1770 when it began as a restaurant, which is still the jewel in their crown, serving regional delicacies. It has spacious and well-equipped rooms. A cosy beer garden operates in the warmer months. There is also the facility for long-term renting rooms. **www.berghoelzchen.de**

HOHEGING Hotel-Restaurant Waldesruh €

Am Baumweg 2, 49685 Tel (04471) 94850 Fax (04471) 948516 Rooms 22

This peaceful little hotel is nestled amongst trees and pastures. Tennis courts are available for guest use and there is a golf course nearby. The recently refurbished rooms are cosy and offer the basic comforts. The restaurant serves regional cuisine, with a reasonable selection for vegetarians. **www.waldesruhhotel.de**

KÖNIGSLUTTER Avalon Hotelpark Königshof €€

Braunschweigerstraße 21a, 38154 Tel (05353) 5030 Fax (05353) 503244 Rooms 174

This is a spread-out hotel with a lot of amenities, including tennis courts, swimming pool and bowling alley. They have 15 conference rooms, with many conference packages that include spa treatments and sporting facilities. The restaurant, Merlin *(see p554)*, serves regional cuisine, and there is also a disco. **www.hotelpark-koenigshof.de**

LAUENAU Hotel Montana Lauenau €

Hanomagstraße 1, 31867 Tel (05043) 91190 Fax (05043) 9119100 Rooms 53

A handy hotel that scores well with visitors arriving by car. The hotel and the rooms have a calm quality about them and the beds are very soft and inviting. This is a modest hotel, although it is truly comfortable and offers a pleasant stay. The restaurant is really no more than a convenience. **www.montana-hotels.de**

LÜNEBURG Bremer Hof €€

Lüner Straße 12, 21335 Tel (04131) 2240 Fax (04131) 224224 Rooms 53

A family affair since 1889, the Bremer Hof has been serving up comfort and hospitality unceasingly. Individually styled, some rooms incorporate the dark wooden structural beams into their design. It stands in the shadow of St Nicolai church, and is within easy walking distance of the town centre. **www.bremer-hof.de**

OLDENBURG Heide €€

Melkbrink 49–51, 26121 Tel (0441) 8040 Fax (0441) 884060 Rooms 92

Chic yet comfortable, the style of the lobby here is an insight into the design of the rooms, with a contrast of dark and light colours accentuating space. The hotel is quite modern and is popular with business guests. Their elegant restaurant serves international and seasonal dishes, and has a large wine cellar. **www.dormotel-heide.de**

OSNABRÜCK Steigenberger Hotel Remarque €€

Natruper-Tor-Wall 1, 49076 Tel (0541) 60960 Fax (0541) 6096600 Rooms 156

Named after German author Erich Remarque (1898–1970), whose works can be found in their elegant library, you can request a room here with a water bed. The restaurant, Vila Real, is highly acclaimed and has a very comprehensive wine list. The hotel also has a wine shop where they sometimes hold wine tastings. **www.hotelremarque.de**

OSNABRÜCK Walhalla €€

Bierstraße 24, 49074 Tel (0541) 34910 Fax (0541) 3491144 Rooms 66

Built in 1690 and recently renovated, the Walhalla is almost a museum of architecture. The loft has been converted into spacious and beautiful suites, while their standard rooms are also dapper and spacious. There is a peaceful beer garden and two restaurants. **www.hotel-walhalla.de**

WOLFENBÜTTEL Hotel Golden Tulip €€

Bahnhofsstraße 9, 38300 Tel (05331) 98860 Fax (05331) 988661 Rooms 48

Close to the centre of Wolfenbüttel. An airy lobby awaits you, as does the prompt and friendly service. There is a cinema and bowling alley on the premises, as well as an American-style restaurant. They also have a nice terrace where you may dine in the summer months. **www.goldentulipwolfenbuettel.de**

WOLFENBÜTTEL Parkhotel Altes Kaffeehaus   €€
Harztorwall 18, 38300 **Tel** *(05331) 8880* **Fax** *(05331) 888100* **Rooms** *75*

This hotel hosts a mixture of the modern and traditional. While the rooms are a little generic, the atmosphere around the hotel is friendly. The beer garden is popular in the summer months, and the wine cellar offers an opportunity to sample local wines. The French restaurant of the same name is also worth a visit *(see p554)*. **www.parkhotel-wolfenbuettel.de**

WOLFSBURG Brackstedter Mühle   €€
Zum Kühlen Grunde 2, 38448 **Tel** *(05366) 900* **Fax** *(05366) 9050* **Rooms** *50*

Set in the peaceful German countryside, each room here is unique due to the development and refurbishment of the hotel. There are banquet facilities offering delicacies such as suckling pig and other traditional dishes. It also has a beautiful winter garden with a glass roof. **www.brackstedter-muehle.de**

WOLFSBURG Tryp Hotel   €€€
Willy-Brandt-Platz 2, 38440 **Tel** *(05361) 899000* **Fax** *(05361) 899444* **Rooms** *121*

With well-designed and spacious rooms and suites that have an early 1990s colour scheme, this hotel is close to the Volkswagen plant and theme park. There is a classy restaurant with an extensive wine list. In the summer months they operate an outdoor terrace. **www.solmelia.com**

SCHLESWIG-HOLSTEIN

BAD MALENTE Gartenhotel Weisser Hof   €€€
Vossstraße 45, 23714 **Tel** *(04523) 99250* **Fax** *(04523) 6899* **Rooms** *18*

A small hotel with a big heart. Family owned and family run, there is also a high level of professionalism here. The rooms are bright and spacious, and there is an excellent restaurant of the same name *(see p555)*. They have a nice pool and wellness area and there is a nearby golf course. The garden has ample space for children to play. **www.weisserhof.de**

FLENSBURG Am Wasserturm   €
Blasberg 13, 24943 **Tel** *(0461) 3150600* **Fax** *(0461) 312287* **Rooms** *34*

Located in a quiet area – you are guaranteed to get a peaceful night sleep here – and furnished in a reserved and tasteful manner, this hotel caters to large groups and offers special rates for 15 people and up. The breakfast is diverse and satisfying, and you can enjoy it out on the terrace. **www.hotel-am-wasserturm.com**

HELGOLAND Atoll   €€€
Lung Wai, 27498 **Tel** *(04725) 8000* **Fax** *(04725) 800444* **Rooms** *50*

This is the hotel of tomorrow, designed in a futuristic and creative manner. Each room is a work of art, with colour blending well with a minimalistic style. Situated overlooking the water, many rooms have a wonderful view. The restaurant serves fantastic fresh seafood dishes as well as international cuisine. **www.atoll.de**

KIEL Kieler Yacht-Club   €€€
Hindenburgufer 70, 24105 **Tel** *(0431) 88130* **Fax** *(0431) 8813444* **Rooms** *57*

The rooms here have picturesque sea views and some have balconies or are connected to terraces. Close to all the water-related activities and attractions. They also have quite large conference facilities and offer extensive packages. The restaurant serves some of the freshest seafood in town. **www.hotelkieleryachtclub.de**

KIEL Maritim Hotel Bellevue   €€€
Bismarckallee 2, 24105 **Tel** *(0431) 38940* **Fax** *(0431) 3894790* **Rooms** *89*

With a uniquely styled lobby and foyer that reflects a desire to break away from convention, there is a spectacular panoramic view from the hotel. The terrace also provides a great view and dining is available. The cocktail bar is quite swanky, with an extensive cocktail menu. **www.maritim.de**

LÜBECK Radisson SAS Senator Hotel   €€
Willy-Brandt-Allee 6, 23554 **Tel** *(0451) 1420* **Fax** *(0451) 1422222* **Rooms** *224*

Overlooking the river and close to the centre, the rooms here are very comfortable and bright. There are many facilities to keep children occupied and when accompanied by parents they eat in the restaurant free. Along with the restaurant, there is a cocktail bar, a café and a tavern with adjoining beer garden. **www.senatorhotel.de**

LÜBECK Kaiserhof   €€€
Kronsforder Allee 11–13, 23560 **Tel** *(0451) 703301* **Fax** *(0451) 795083* **Rooms** *58*

Sitting in the middle of the "island", you could not ask for a better location. Close to historic attractions and museums, some guest rooms here have a balcony. Their restaurant focuses on fish and there is an elegant banquet hall which is often used for weddings and other functions. **www.kaiserhof-luebeck.de**

OEVERSEE Romantik Hotel Historischer Krug   €€
Grazer Platz 1, 24988 **Tel** *(04630) 9400* **Fax** *(04630) 780* **Rooms** *60*

This hotel has been in the same family since 1815, and has a history that goes back to the 16th century. It is a sanctuary of relaxation and luxury, providing massages, beauty treatments, spas and saunas. They also have a nice restaurant and terrace. **www.historischer-krug.de**

RATZEBURG Der Seehof

Lüneburger Damm 1–3, 23909 **Tel** *(04541) 860100* **Fax** *(04541) 860102* **Rooms** *50*

This hotel is situated so close to the water it is practically floating. There are magnificent water views from the rooms, some of which have large terraces and balconies. The restaurant specializes in fish and other seafood, although their regional dishes are spectacular as well. The wellness area is quite comprehensive. **www.derseehof.de**

SCHLESWIG Waldschlösschen

Kolonnenweg 152, 24837 **Tel** *(04621) 3830* **Fax** *(04621) 383105* **Rooms** *117*

Lying a little out of town, there are many opportunities for walking, cycling and exploring. The rooms are large and tastefully furnished. Access to the wellness area and swimming pool is included in the rates. There are two restaurants and a chic lounge bar. **www.hotel-waldschloesschen.de**

SYLT Lindner Hotel Windrose

Strandstraße 21–23, 25996 **Tel** *(0211) 5997310* **Fax** *(0211) 5997348* **Rooms** *91*

Only a few short steps away from the beach, the wellness and pool area here is impressive and offers treatments of curative Sylt mud. The bar and restaurant is decorated in an old-fashioned style. The food is less ornate but still delicious and has earned the restaurant several accolades. **www.lindner.de**

SYLT Benen-Diken-Hof

Süderstraße 3, 25980 **Tel** *(04651) 93830* **Fax** *(04651) 9383183* **Rooms** *40*

A delightful country hotel with all the amenities of an inner-city hotel. The hotel also specializes in the rental of apartments for longer stays, while it is still possible to rent their studio apartments for short stays. There is a golf course in the area and the pool is very elegant, with terrace seating outside. **www.benen-diken-hof.de**

SYLT Miramar

Friedrichstraße 43, 25980 **Tel** *(04651) 8550* **Fax** *(04651) 855222* **Rooms** *67*

Perched overlooking the sandy beach and with scintillating views, some rooms here have balconies and each is individually designed and furnished. Their wellness and pool area provides massages and manicures. There is also a seafood-oriented restaurant. **www.hotel-miramar.de**

TIMMENDORFER STRAND Maritim Seehotel

Strandallee 73, 23669 **Tel** *(04503) 6050* **Fax** *(04503) 6052450* **Rooms** *248*

The shores of the Baltic Sea lap at the door of this magnificent hotel. All the floors have great views, with the rear-facing rooms overlooking the parklands. Some of the rooms also have amazing corner balconies. There is a huge wellness area, as well as an indoor and an outdoor pool if the sea is not enough for you. **www.maritim.de**

TRAVEMÜNDE Hotel Columbia Casino

Kaiserallee 1, 23570 **Tel** *(04502) 3080* **Fax** *(04502) 308333* **Rooms** *73*

This hotel has variously styled rooms that are all superbly furnished and detailed. Some rooms have a sea view and terrace. The conference and function facilities are stunning and there is an elegant ballroom. There is a choice of three restaurants with an emphasis on seafood, and there is a golf course nearby. **www.columbia-hotels.de**

TRAVEMÜNDE/LÜBECK Maritim Strandhotel

Trelleborgallee 2, 23570 **Tel** *(04502) 890* **Fax** *(04502) 892020* **Rooms** *240*

The hotel sits at the mouth of the estuary and enjoys superb panoramic views. Some of the guest rooms have balconies. The café on the 35th floor has an amazing view over the surrounding district and Baltic Sea and attracts guests from outside the hotel. **www.maritim.de**

MECKLENBURG-LOWER POMERANIA

ANKLAM Hotel am Stadtwall

Demminer Straße 5, 17389 **Tel** *(03971) 83 31 36* **Fax** *(03971) 83 31 37* **Rooms** *18*

A cheap and cheerful place, this hotel welcomes cyclists and those who like fishing, and will happily and securely accommodate bicycles and tackle. The building itself looks something like an old British school, which is rather charming. **www.hotel-am-stadtwall.de**

BAD DOBERAN Hotel Friedrich Franz Palais

August-Bebel-Straße 2, 18209 **Tel** *(038203) 63 03 6* **Fax** *(038203) 62 12 6* **Rooms** *50*

The Laura Ashley-inspired rooms here, with lots of floral and frilly bits, are certainly very comfortable. All rooms have generously sized beds, overflowing with fluffy pillows and quilts, as well as mini bars and satellite television. Some overlook a monastery garden, while others peer over a town park. **www.friedrich-franz-palais.de**

DARGUN Hotel am Klostersee

Am Klosterdamm 3, 17159 **Tel** *(039959) 25 20* **Fax** *(039959) 25 22 8* **Rooms** *26*

Located near a monastery lake and ideal for an active family holiday, there is plenty for kids to do here and there are a couple of different restaurant options nearby. The rooms are comfortably decorated, but are by no means the main attraction. **www.klostersee-hotel.de**

GREIFSWALD VCH Hotel Greifswald

Wilhelm-Holtz-Straße 5–8, 17489 **Tel** *(03834) 51 60* **Fax** *(03834) 51 65 16* **Rooms** *122*

This is an extensive hotel with not only rooms but also 48 apartments for longer stays, or for family groups. The rooms are basic yet adequate. There are a number of buildings housing the amenities and rooms. You can guarantee privacy here and the staff are friendly. **www.vchhotel-greifswald.de**

GREIFSWALD Kronprinz Hotel Greifswald

22 Lange Straße, 17489 **Tel** *(03834) 79 00* **Fax** *(03834) 79 01 11* **Rooms** *31*

Set in a good location in the town centre and close to the cathedral, the rooms here are uncluttered and clean, with simple wooden furniture and patterned bedspreads. They also have a mini bar and television, but are otherwise a bit short on features – you just get the basics. **www.hotelkronprinz.de**

GREIFSWALD Parkhotel Greifswald

Pappelallee 1, 17489 **Tel** *(03834) 87 40* **Fax** *(03834) 87 45 55* **Rooms** *62*

This is a business-cum-tourist hotel that offers a competent compromise between the needs of those who are working and those who are relaxing. All rooms have a desk, but otherwise it is all pretty laid-back. The attic rooms have a lovely charm to them, with exposed beams adding a nice sense of character. **www.parkhotel-greifswald.de**

GÜSTROW Kurhaus am Inselsee

Heidburg 1, 18273 **Tel** *(03843) 85 00* **Fax** *(03843) 85 01 00* **Rooms** *39*

A very relaxing hotel in a peaceful, sleepy setting. One of the more lavish hotels in the area, the wellness treatments and packages are very attractive. The rooms are comfortable and some offer a nice view of the surrounding countryside. The garden terrace has a great atmosphere, especially in the afternoons. **www.kurhaus-guestrow.de**

HEILIGENDAMM Kempinski Grand Hotel Heiligendamm

Prof.-Dr.-Vogel-Straße 16–18, 18209 **Tel** *(038203) 74 00* **Fax** *(038203) 74 07 47 4* **Rooms** *225*

This is an opulent hotel with such stately buildings and a lovely seaside location that it is easy to simply relax and embrace it all. There are five big buildings, one of which is a castle, and all of which offer rooms that effortlessly combine class and comfort. This hotel is entirely unique. **www.kempinski-heiligendamm.com**

INSEL RÜGEN Hotel am Meer & Spa

Strandpromenade 34, 18609 **Tel** *(038393) 44 0* **Fax** *(038393) 44 44 4* **Rooms** *60*

A beautiful hotel in a fantastic position, just off the beach, the rooms here are stunning, offering a maritime theme. Each floor has its own theme colour, and different wood types to match. The wellness and fitness area is quite new, and expansive. You will definitely find yourself relaxing the moment you arrive. **www.hotel-am-meer.de**

MECKLENBURG Hotel Vier Jahreszeiten Binz

Zeppelinstraße 8, 18609 **Tel** *(038393) 500* **Fax** *(038393) 50430* **Rooms** *76*

Not far from the centre of Binz, and a short distance from the beach, the rooms here have a very bright and fresh style, while still retaining some classic, smart (almost naval) formality. This is a very polished and classy hotel in a lovely beachside town. **www.jahreszeiten-hotels.de**

NEUBRANDENBURG Landhotel Broda

Oelmühlenstraße 29, 17033 **Tel** *(0395) 569170* **Fax** *(0395) 5691729* **Rooms** *13*

There is a summery holiday atmosphere here but the standard of service and inclusion of conference facilities place it in the business-class category. All rooms have a terrace or balcony, satellite television and are wheelchair-friendly (spacious and uncluttered). **www.landhotel-broda.de**

PREROW TOP CountryLine Hotel Waldschloesschen

Bernsteinweg 4, 18375 **Tel** *(038233) 61 70* **Fax** *(038233) 61 74 03* **Rooms** *33*

You will have to walk 300 m (980 ft) if you want to stroll on sandy Baltic Sea beaches, but while in the hotel you will enjoy the luxury of what was once a lavish private residence. Rooms are scattered among three buildings and all are tastefully decorated and offer good basic facilities. **www.topinternational.com**

ROSTOCK Courtyard by Marriott

Kropeliner/Schwaansche Str. 6, 18055 **Tel** *(0381) 49 70 0* **Fax** *(0381) 49 70 700* **Rooms** *148*

This is really something extraordinary, combining an old-town square historic frontage with a direct link to a gleaming, modern shopping centre. It is a business-class hotel and so offers all the usual facilities for business guests, but it would also be quite a treat for tourists. **www.marriott.com**

ROSTOCK Godewind

Warnemünder Straße 5, 18146 **Tel** *(0381) 60 95 70* **Fax** *(0381) 60 95 71 11* **Rooms** *58*

In a location that takes advantage of the landscape around the southern coast of the Baltic Sea, this family-run complex consists of a hotel, restaurant and apartments. The guest rooms have a relaxed feel about them and some have a balcony. **www.hotel-godewind.de**

ROSTOCK Sonne Hotel Rostock

Neuer Markt 2, 18055 **Tel** *(0381) 49 73 0* **Fax** *(0381) 49 73 35 1* **Rooms** *111*

This is a 200-year-old building on the market square that was renovated and reopened as a hotel in 1998. All the modern conveniences are here, such as wireless Internet access, while the historic feel has been maintained with some specially designed furniture. There are a range of beauty and wellness services. **www.rostock.steigenberger.de**

Key to Price Guide *see p488* **Key to Symbols** *see back cover flap*

ROSTOCK Trihotel

Am Schweizer Wald Tessiner Straße 103, 18055 **Tel** *(0381) 65 97 0* **Fax** *(0381) 65 97 60 0* **Rooms** *101*

All the rooms here are laid out and furnished a little differently, but they are all cosy, comfortable and furnished with a bit more adventure than you would expect to find in a business-class or chain hotel. There is also a full range of health and spa treatments and facilities available. **www.trihotel-rostock.de**

ROSTOCK Neptun Hotel Rostock

Seestraße 19, 18119 **Tel** *(0381) 77 78 71* **Fax** *(0381) 77 74 00* **Rooms** *338*

As you would expect from a luxury resort located right on the beach, every room has a balcony with a sea view. The rooms are decently decorated and all offer excellent facilities. The resort has a full range of health, fitness and fun services. **www.hotel-neptun.de**

RÜGEN Landhotel Herrenhaus

Bohlendorf bei Wiek, 18556 **Tel** *(038391) 77 0* **Fax** *(038391) 70 28 0* **Rooms** *22*

This is not a hotel, it is a home. It looks like it has been handed down through generations. The rooms are bright and clean and have simple period-style furniture. There is a terrace, café (with home-made cakes and toffees) and a fireplace room for warming toes and reading a good book in winter. **www.bohlen-dorf.de**

RÜGEN Villa Sano

Strandstraße 12–14, 18586 **Tel** *(038303) 12 66 0* **Fax** *(038303) 12 66 99 9* **Rooms** *46*

Aimed at families and only a five-minute walk from the beach, this is a good option for those wanting to combine more than one room to form a family suite (there are interconnecting doors) without paying the high beachside prices. They also offer services such as playrooms and child-minding. **www.villasano.de**

RÜGEN Cliff-Hotel

Siedlung am Wald, 18586 **Tel** *(038303) 82 14* **Fax** *(038303) 84 95* **Rooms** *256*

This is a very stylish and refined hotel, with most rooms having plump cushions, ochre, gold and burgundy colour schemes and no shortage of luxury. The location is also superb, as it is in a large resort estate with its own beach (accessible via an elevator) and not far from the impressive Sellin Pier. **www.cliff-hotel.de**

RÜGEN DorintResorts Binz

Strandpromenade 58, 18609 **Tel** *(038393) 43 0* **Fax** *(038393) 43 10 0* **Rooms** *63*

With crisp linen, sparkling water, a sandy beach and high standards of service, this is a luxury treat with a nautical theme and big windows that overlook the sea. Rooms also have air conditioning and wireless Internet access. Dining options include balconies and terraces, also with sea views. **www.accorhotels.com**

SCHWERIN Fritz Hotel

Dorfstraße 3b, 19061 **Tel** *(0385) 64 63 70* **Fax** *(0385) 64 63 79 9* **Rooms** *22*

This is a big and welcoming building in a huge garden. There is a lot of greenery about, and the garden has a pond. The rooms are simply decorated, with pastel-pink bedding. The large park-like setting is extremely relaxing and appealing. **www.fritz-hotel.de**

SCHWERIN Ramada Hotel Schwerin

Am Grünen Tal 39, 19063 **Tel** *(0385) 39 92 0* **Fax** *(0385) 39 92 18 8* **Rooms** *78*

What seems to be a straightforward breeze-block building houses a good, efficient hotel that ticks all the boxes and meets all expectations. Rooms are sparingly comfortable and there is a gym, sauna and spa. The hotel is a 15-minute tram ride form the historic centre of Schwerin. **www.ramada.de**

SCHWERIN Speicher am Ziegelsee

Speicherstraße 11, 19055 **Tel** *(0385) 50 03 0* **Fax** *(0385) 503111* **Rooms** *78*

You could use this place to define "cosy". Lots of natural materials and warm colours create a soothing atmosphere. Stone fireplaces, terracotta tiles, wood and wicker furniture suggest a place that you could almost nest in. Of course, there are also plenty of facilities and services, and a lovely waterside location. **www.speicher-hotel.de**

STRALSUND Zum Seeblick

Barhöft, Am Hafen, 18445 **Tel** *(038323) 45 00* **Fax** *(038323) 45 05 4* **Rooms** *38*

The name of this hotel means "sea view", and indeed some (but not all) of the rooms do have rather nice sea views. There are actually two separate buildings that can accommodate guests, both of which seem to be of pretty much equal standard with basic but comfortable rooms. **www.hotel-zum-seeblick.m-vp.de**

USEDOM Residenz Waldoase

Waldoase 1, 17419 **Tel** *(038378) 50 22 0* **Fax** *(038378) 50 29 9* **Rooms** *45*

Fresh and light on the outside, cosy and warm on the inside, this hotel combines the best of a seaside and forest location, and is ideal for families. Bicycle rental is available and picnic hampers can be organized. Families, including those with young children, are welcome and well catered for. **www.usedom-touristik.de**

WARNEMUENDE KurPark Hotel

Kurhausstraße 4, 18119 **Tel** *(0381) 44 02 99 0* **Fax** *(0381) 44 02 99 9* **Rooms** *18*

This is a hotel situated in a rather lovely old house. There is a choice of "English, Mediterranean (and) Louis-Philippe-style" guest rooms, but the only real difference is the pattern on the duvet cover. The best way to choose a room is to ask for one with a balcony. **www.kur-park-hotel.de**

WHERE TO EAT

German cuisine does not enjoy the same reputation as that of, say, France, but nevertheless you can eat very well here. There are many establishments that specialize in regional cuisine, which, although somewhat heavy, is always very appetizing. It is also easy to find good restaurants serving ethnic cuisine, such as Italian, Greek, Indian, Chinese, Thai or Turkish. In the past few years, some

The crest of the Forsthaus Paulsborn restaurant in Berlin

fine restaurants have opened. Run by renowned master chefs, they serve excellent cuisine of the very highest European standards.

From the many thousands of restaurants throughout Germany, we have chosen the finest for inclusion in this guidebook, with a view to catering for a variety of budgets. Detailed information on the selected restaurants can be found on pp526–57.

TYPES OF RESTAURANTS

The term *Restaurant* is used to define both restaurants offering exquisite cuisine and excellent service, at steep prices, and popular local establishments with affordable prices. The word *Gasthaus* usually indicates a traditional style of inn that specializes in straightforward regional cuisine. In many towns, there is a *Ratskeller* established in the cellar of the town hall. These are usually good, not overly expensive restaurants serving dishes that represent the regional cuisine. They usually have atmospheric, stylized interiors that are well adapted to the vaulted, dark spaces of the historic cellars. A *Weinstube* is a wine bar, where good, usually local, wine is served. Often decent

food is also available here. A *Bierstube* is similar in style, except that the beverage is beer. The term *Café* has a variety of connotations in Germany. This is a place that serves an excellent breakfast with various options in the mornings, while from noon they offer lunch dishes. The choice is usually somewhat heavy, though varied. In addition, at any time of the day and evening, customers can have a coffee here, eat some ice cream or a cake, drink beer or some other alcoholic beverage. In the evenings there is often music.

A typical venue in which you can spend an evening is a *Kneipe*. In terms of its atmosphere, this is somewhat reminiscent of an English pub. Patrons generally come here to have a drink, but there are usually a few hot dishes on offer to appease their hunger. Self-service venues offering snacks are known as *Imbiss*. These can have a very varied character, from a stall serving baked sausages and cans of drink, to elegant kiosks offering a large choice of salads and fast food. These kiosks are often run by immigrants. In fact in most large German towns there are numerous kiosks serving Arabic, Turkish, Chinese and American food. If shoppers feel the need for a snack, they might like to take

advantage of the restaurant or cafeteria facilities in department stores. These are usually self-service establishments known as *Stehcafé*, which means "Stand Up Café".

Entrance to a *Gasthaus* near the cathedral in Cologne

WHAT AND WHEN TO EAT

Breakfast is usually a hearty affair with various types of bread accompanied by cheese, sausages and marmalade. On Sundays brunch is served in most places until 2pm: this is a combination of breakfast and lunch, in the form of a Swedish buffet. During the lunch period (between noon and 2pm) most establishments serve an excellent salad or a bowl of filling soup, while many restaurants offer a special fixed-price menu that is significantly cheaper than in the evenings. Restaurants start to fill up in the evenings between 6 and 7pm, although dinner is most usually eaten after 8pm.

Altdeutsche Weinstube in Dörrenbach

Wine festival in Alter Hof in Munich

OPENING HOURS

Cafés generally open from 9am, while restaurants are open from noon, sometimes with a break from 3 to 6pm. The most expensive places do not open until dinner time and are frequently closed for one day during the week.

A street stall serving snacks of freshly cooked sausages

MENU

In most good restaurants the menu is written in German and English, and sometimes also in French. In cafés and less expensive restaurants, the menu may be handwritten, in which case the staff may be able to help with a translation. In many of the less expensive places there is, in addition to the regular menu, a daily menu with attractive seasonal dishes. Sometimes the chef's special offers are written on a blackboard. In all restaurants and cafés, a menu showing prices will be displayed outside the establishment.

RESERVATIONS

Making a prior reservation is essential in all the best restaurants while in most good and medium standard restaurants it is advisable to do so, particularly on a Friday or Saturday night. If you have not made a reservation, try one of the popular restaurant complexes where you can usually get a table.

PRICES AND TIPS

The cost of restaurant meals in Germany is unusually diverse depending on location. A three-course meal without alcohol can be found for around €10–13, but in the centre of larger cities a minimum of €18–22 would be more usual. In a luxury restaurant, the bill for a six-course meal, without drinks, can cost in excess of €76. The price of alcoholic drinks also varies, but beer is the cheapest drink.

Prices include service and tax, but it is usual to leave a tip – generally around 10 per cent of the total bill. When paying for a meal by credit card, the tip can be added to the total. Restaurants and cafés that accept credit cards usually display the logos of acceptable cards near the entrance. Before ordering, it is best to find out whether a minimum charge is applied to customers who wish to pay their bill by credit card.

DRESS CODE

Germans usually prefer to dress comfortably, casually and practically, preferring a sporty style to more formal attire. When going out in the evenings, many women – regardless of their age – wear trousers and comfortable low-heeled shoes, though some prefer elegant dresses. Men generally wear jackets and ties only during office hours.

Going to a restaurant does not require any particular preparation unless you wish to go to a luxurious, gourmet restaurant, for which you will probably have to book up to two months in advance.

Formal interior of a restaurant in Berlin

CHILDREN

Restaurants usually provide high chairs for toddlers and, particularly during the lunch period, there will be light dishes for children – or you can order small portions.

VEGETARIANS

Increasingly, Germans are turning to vegetarianism, although the number of vegetarian restaurants is still limited. However, a few vegetarian dishes can usually be found on most menus. If necessary, choose a restaurant that serves a national cuisine in which there is no shortage of vegetarian dishes – for example Indian or Thai.

DISABLED VISITORS

If a table with wheelchair access is required, it is best to specify this when making the reservation. At the same time, check whether toilets are easily accessible.

Picnicking – a popular form of relaxation in Germany

The Flavours of Germany

Germany is famous for its hearty sausages, meats, breads, beer and wine. But German cuisine is much more regionally varied than many visitors might imagine. In addition to standard high-calorie plates, young chefs are coming up with creative new versions of German classics and old regional recipes. The key to this new trend is the fresh German produce found at colourful farmers' markets and old-world stores in quaint little towns around the country. Locally grown vegetables, pork, poultry and game, as well as freshwater and ocean fish, freshly made breads, cakes and dumplings are usually of a very high standard.

Harzer Roller and
Emmenthaler cheeses

Coffee and cakes at a typical city *Konditorei* (café)

NORTHERN AND EASTERN GERMANY

The frugality and hardships of life in the northern and East German lowlands and coast are reflected in the hearty fish- and game-based dishes found in this region. Ocean fish like halibut, sea bass, cod, herring or plaice feature in local dishes like Hamburg's *Finkenwerder*

Scholle (plaice fried with North Sea shrimps and bacon), as do freshwater fish such as pike-perch (a Berlin-Brandenburg favourite) or trout, served as *Grüne Forelle* or *Forelle Müllerin Art*, two herb-oriented recipes for roasted trout. Warming winter soups and stews such as lentil or potato soup or *Pichelsteiner Eintopf* (a one-pot dish with meat, potatoes and vegetables

cooked in broth) are omnipresent – as is the famous potato salad, which is served in numerous ways. In East Germany, Thuringian and Saxonian cuisines have made a stunning comeback with *Thüringer Bratwurst* (spicy, roasted sausage served with hot mustard), *Sauerbraten* (roast beef marinated in vinegar) and some of Germany's best cakes, such as *Dresdner Christstollen*

Mehrkornbrötchen (mixed grain roll)

Laugenbrötchen (salty sourdough rolls)

Berliner Landbrot (mild rye bread)

Grau-Oder Mischbrot (wholewheat)

Semmel (milk-dough roll)

Selection of typical German loaves and bread rolls

CLASSIC GERMAN FOOD

Many of the classic German dishes revolve around meat, particularly pork and poultry. Berliners and North Germans love *Kasseler Nacken*, a salted and dried slice of pork, served with mashed potatoes and *Sauerkraut*, while Bavarians prefer roast pork knuckle. There are delicious fish recipes, too, with Hamburg and Northern Germany leading the way. Ocean fish dishes like *Matjes* (salted herring with onions and cream served with baked potatoes) are now enjoyed throughout the country, as are freshwater fish and even sweet river crabs. German pasta and dumplings, along with soups, and a great selection of desserts and cakes round up any classic German menu.

Pork salamis

Maultaschen, large pasta parcels, are stuffed with a meat or vegetable filling and served in soup or with butter.

Display of traditional German sausages in a Berlin butcher's shop

(Christmas cake with raisins, nuts and marzipan) or *Baumkuchen* (a very sweet, multi-layered pyramid cake covered in chocolate glaze).

WESTERN AND SOUTHERN GERMANY

This part of Germany, and in particular the German wine regions around the rivers Rhine, Mosel and Neckar, has always had a love of superb, often French-influenced, gourmet feasts. Alsace-Lorraine is a fascinating hotch-potch of French and German cooking. Regions such as the Pfalz, Schwaben, Franken, the Black Forest and many others, have also developed their own, very distinctive, delicious and often very hearty cuisines. The Pfalz, for example, is famous for its *Pfälzer*

Saumagen, a sow's stomach filled with sausage, herbs and potatoes; the Schwaben are known for their *Maultaschen* and an endless varieties of *Spätzle* (curly pasta); and the Franken for their *Nürnberger Rostbratwürstchen* (little

Fresh vegetables from the Brandenberg region

spicy roast sausages), various fish dishes, using rare types such as sheatfish, and perhaps the best gingerbread found anywhere in the country. In the far southeast, Austrian and Eastern European influences are evident in great goulash and dumpling dishes. But pride of place possibly goes to the Bavarians, whose hearty, no-nonsense dishes are what the world considers to be German cuisine. Here, sweet *Weißwürstchen* (white sausages with a beer pretzel) are enjoyed in the morning, often with a beer, while dinner might be soup with liver dumplings, roast pork, *Sauerkraut* and a pile of potato dumplings.

NEW GERMAN CUISINE

In the early 1970s, chefs like Eckart Witzigmann broke free of the high-carb diet of postwar times, and cooked light, delicate "nouvelle" German dishes with superb ingredients in innovative combinations. Witzigmann, still Germany's most popular chef, won the first three German Michelin stars in 1979. A new generation of chefs calling themselves "Junge Wilde" (young wild) are still enjoying the shock waves today: healthy, international cooking is the norm in restaurants and homes, and almost no traditional recipe is sacrosanct.

Zanderfilet, *or Havel-Zander, is delicious pan-fried pike-perch served with a vegetable sauce, onions and potatoes.*

Schweinshaxe *is roast pork knuckle, best accompanied by Sauerkraut, potato dumplings and a good, strong beer.*

Rote Grütze *mixes summer berries with spices and red wine, which is set into a jelly and topped with cream.*

What to Drink

Throughout Germany, beer is undoubtedly the most popular drink, and each region has its own beer-brewing traditions. However, the country is also renowned for excellent wines, which are produced in the south. The most well known are Mosel and Rhine wines, although these are not necessarily better than Franconian wines. Stronger spirits and liqueurs are also available, as are some very pleasant non-alcoholic cold drinks.

Shop in Eberbach stocked with wine from the adjoining monastery

HOT DRINKS

In German establishments there is no difficulty in getting a cup of tea *(Tee)*, but don't be surprised if the waiter asks whether you mean mint tea *(Pfefferminztee)* or camomile *(Kamillentee)*, since herbal infusions are popular in Germany. To be sure of being served Indian tea, it is advisable to specify *Schwarztee* when placing the order.

Herbal infusions include mint and camomile tea

Coffee is another popular drink. In general, filter coffee, which is fairly mild, is served. For customers who prefer a stronger coffee, it is best to order an espresso.

NON-ALCOHOLIC COLD DRINKS

Various types of carbonated drinks and fruit juices – ubiquitous throughout Europe and the US – are popular, and an extensive choice is available in every café and restaurant in Germany. A refreshing non-alcoholic drink is *Apfel-Schorle*, which is apple juice mixed with equal proportions of sparkling mineral water. (The alcoholic version is *Wein-Schorle*, which is wine mixed with mineral water.) Another popular non-alcoholic drink is *Spezi*, which is a mixture of cola and Fanta.

Although tap water is generally safe to drink, it is not usually served with restaurant meals. To order a bottle of mineral water, ask for *Mineralwasser*, adding the phrase "*stilles Wasser*" if still water is preferred.

Mineralwasser (Mineral water)

Limonade (Lemonade)

Apfel-Schorle

SPIRITS AND LIQUEURS

Strong spirits are often drunk after heavy meals, particularly pork dishes. It is best to order one of the popular drinks distilled from rye or wheat, such as *Doppel Korn*. Brandy (known as *Weinbrand*) is also produced in Germany. Liqueurs are also popular, as is a spirit flavoured with herbs and roots (known as bitters). Among the most popular are *Kümmerling* and *Jägermeister* while, in Berlin, *Kaulzdorfer Kräuter Likör* is served. In many restaurants various kinds of whisky can be ordered, including well-known Scottish and Irish brands and popular American bourbons, but connoisseurs may miss their personal favourites. Italian restaurants often serve grappa, a grape spirit, after a meal, while in Greek restaurants ouzo – an aniseed spirit – may be offered.

Bitter-sweet spirit, Jägermeister

Herbal/root-flavour spirit, Kümmerling

Weizen Doppel Korn (rye spirit)

WINES

Germany is renowned for its excellent white wines, particularly those made from the Riesling grape. Among the most highly prized wines are those from the Rheingau region. Lovers of red wine might like to try Assmannshausen Spätburgunder wine, which is produced from the Pinot Noir grape.

Germany has a system of classifying wines into three groups according to their quality: the lowest quality is *Tafelwein*, then *Qualitätswein* and the highest quality *Qualitätswein mit Prädikat*. The latter includes wines produced from appropriately selected grapes, which is always confirmed on the bottle label. The term *Trocken* indicates a dry style, *Halbtrocken*, semi-dry and *Süss* means sweet. Very good sparkling wines, known as *Sekt*, are also produced in Germany

Mainstockheimer Hofstück Spätburgunder

Spätburgunder from the Rheingau region

Riesling Schloss Vollrads

BEERS

Beermat with brewery logo

Each region of Germany has its own beer-brewing tradition: the most popular breweries in the north are Jever in Freesia and Beck's in Bremen, along with Bitburger, Warsteiner and Karlsberg. In the Rhine region, the biggest producers are DAB from Dortmund and König in Duisburg. In Berlin, Schultheiss, Berliner Kindl and Engelhardt compete for the primary position, while in Dresden the principal beers are produced by a brewery in Radeberg. However, Bavaria is by far the major brewing centre – the names of the breweries Löwenbräu, Hofbräu and Paulaner are known to every beer lover around the world. The most commonly drunk beer is Pils, a bottom-fermented lager of the pilsner type. Brown ales are also popular, particularly in the south. Schwarzbier, a top-fermented brown ale of over 4 per cent alcohol, is increasingly popular. Weizenbier, a bitter top-fermented beer, also has many fans, as has Bock, which is strong, at around 6 per cent alcohol.

Löwenbräu beer

König Ludwig Dunkel beer

Schultheiss beer

Wheat beer mixed with fruit juice, Berliner Weisse mit Schuss – speciality of Berlin

Franziskaner Hefe Weissbier beer

A tankard of beer with the essential head of foam

Choosing a Restaurant

The restaurants in this guide have been selected across a wide range of price categories for their good value, exceptional food and interesting location. This chart lists the restaurants by region, in chapter order. Map references for Berlin restaurants correspond with the Berlin Street Finder, *see pp114–19*.

PRICE CATEGORIES
The following price ranges are for a three-course meal for one, including a half-bottle of house wine, tax and service:
€ under 30 euros
€€ 30–45 euros
€€€ 45–60 euros
€€€€ 60–90 euros
€€€€€ over 90 euros

BERLIN

EASTERN CENTRE Historische Weinstuben   €€
Poststraße 23, 10178 **Tel** *(030) 242 41 07*   **Map** *5 E2*

This popular wine bar is housed in one of the most decorative buildings of the Nicolaiviertel. Traditional dishes from Berlin, such as *Kohl* or *Rinderrouladen* (rolled and roasted stuffed beef), can be accompanied by a drink from a small but exquisite wine list of 50 mostly German vintages.

EASTERN CENTRE Oxymoron   €€
Rosenthaler Straße 40–41, 10178 **Tel** *(030) 283 918 86*   **Map** *5 D1*

This fashionable restaurant, with its distinctive red-and-gold interior reminiscent of a 19th-century salon, has mainly Mediterranean and light German dishes on the menu. For lunch, dine at a table in the courtyard, which is the most beautiful inside historic Hackesche Höfe, and enjoy excellent fare at a reasonable price.

EASTERN CENTRE XII Apostel   €€
Georgenstraße 2, 10117 **Tel** *(030) 201 02 22*   **Map** *4 C1*

Picturesquely situated in the old arcade of an S-Bahn railway bridge near Museum Island, this restaurant offers popular Italian cuisine. The thin, crispy pizza creations from a stone oven are a speciality here, and are named after the 12 apostles. Ironically, Judas is the most sumptuous.

EASTERN CENTRE Brauhaus Georgbräu   €€€
Spreeufer 4, 10178 **Tel** *(030) 242 42 44*   **Map** *5 E2*

At first sight, this restaurant looks like a typical tourist trap with large tables, big dining halls and masses of people, but you should not be fooled. If you are not a fan of sausages, try *Brauhausknüller*, a Berlin dish with pork knuckle, mashed split peas, *Sauerkraut* and potatoes with cold beer.

EASTERN CENTRE Zum Nussbaum   €€€
Am Nussbaum 3, 10178 **Tel** *(030) 242 30 95*   **Map** *5 E2*

Situated in an alley in the Nicolaiviertel, this is a reconstruction of a 16th-century country inn, serving traditional Berlin cuisine, with tender pork knuckle, rollmops or *Berliner Boulette*, a spicy hamburger pattie without a bun. In summer, dine in its garden and enjoy the various brands of local beer.

EASTERN CENTRE Ermeler-Haus Factory & Bar   €€€€
Märkisches Ufer 10, 10179 **Tel** *(030) 240 620*   **Map** *5 E3*

Good regional cuisine in a modern style, with a Mediterranean flair. The restaurant is part of the gastronomic complex of Art'otel (*see p488*) and is situated in a stylishly decorated basement. After a good fill of beef fillet with fried potatoes and green beans, or green salad with filled rabbit neck, enjoy a cocktail at the bar.

EASTERN CENTRE Lutter & Wegner   €€€€
Charlottenstraße 56, 10117 **Tel** *(030) 202 954 17*   **Map** *4 C3*

The first restaurant to start the revitalization of the gourmet scene in the historic centre of Eastern Berlin. A fine German champagne brand until today, it now serves delicious German–Austrian food. The huge *Wiener Schnitzel* with potato salad, best served lukewarm, is a delight as are the duck and goose specialities in winter.

EASTERN CENTRE Sale E Tabacchi   €€€€
Kochstraße 18, 10969 **Tel** *(030) 252 11 55*   **Map** *4 C4*

The Sale E Tabacchi offers reliable Italian food (but almost never pizza) in a dark, cosy Kreuzberg interior. In summer, the courtyard is the preferred dining area, mostly frequented by politicians and journalists from the neighbouring newspaper companies. For lunch, try one of the inexpensive three-course meals.

EASTERN CENTRE Vau   €€€€€
Jägerstraße 54–55, 10117 **Tel** *(030) 202 97 30*   **Map** *4 B2*

This restaurant stands out with its elegant and unpretentious interior. The excellent and imaginative Austrian- and French-based dishes are created by Berlin's star chef, Kolja Kleeberg. The service is welcoming and there is a selection of good wines. The small courtyard is used during lunch.

Key to Symbols *see back cover flap*

WESTERN CENTRE Nolle

Georgenstraße 203, 10117 **Tel** *(030) 208 26 55*

€€

Map *4 C1*

The Nolle is a pleasantly decorated, 1920s-style Berlin restaurant tucked way under the S-Bahn tracks. The lush greenery around the place, the elegantly appointed tables and candlelight make a perfect setting for its international and German dishes. The *Schnitzel* selection is impressive.

WESTERN CENTRE Café Einstein

Kurfürstenstraße 58, 10785 **Tel** *(030) 261 50 96*

€€€

Map *3 D4*

This Berlin landmark is located in an elegant villa once owned by a German movie star. The old-fashioned waiters are dressed in black suits and bow ties, while the fine Viennese food has *fin-de-siècle* Austrian charm. All the traditional dishes are good, but the *Wiener Schnitzel* and *Gulasch* are exceptional.

WESTERN CENTRE Ganymed

Schiffbauerdamm 5, 10117 **Tel** *(030) 285 852 42*

€€€

Map *4 B1*

A good-quality brasserie restaurant in charming surroundings with a small garden and views of the Spree river. The chef favours fish dishes, including Berlin fish specialities, but also offers traditional French fare such as steak tartare, fresh scallops sauteéd in white wine, and a good cheese selection.

WESTERN CENTRE Desbrosses

Potsdamer Platz 3, 10785 **Tel** *(030) 337 776 400*

€€€€

Map *4 A3*

Desbrosses has the most authentic French brasserie interior in all of Berlin. Dark wood-panelled walls, comfortable, plush leather bistro chairs, an open show kitchen and recordings of Piaf, all make for a real French experience. A must here is the seafood platter.

WESTERN CENTRE Käfer im Bundestag

Reichstag, Platz der Republik, 10557 **Tel** *(030) 226 299 33*

€€€€

Map *4 A2*

A favourite dining place of the Mitte district, thanks to its unique location on the rooftop of the Reichstag, right next to Sir Norman Foster's cupola. The German cooking is creative and true to the owner, German catering star Käfer. Service is impeccable. Book ahead for lunch.

WESTERN CENTRE Kuchi

Kantstraße 30, 10623 **Tel** *(030) 315 078 15*

€€€

Map *2 A4*

Kuchi, one of the best value Japanese restaurants in Berlin, offers excellent sushi and regional dishes. A simple, unpretentious Asian interior and a welcoming service make it the ideal venue for a dinner for two. The dim sum rotation and the sampler are particularly tasty. Reservations advised.

WESTERN CENTRE Die Quadriga

Eislebener Straße 14, 10789 **Tel** *(030) 214 050*

€€€€€

Map *2 B5*

Hotel Brandenburger Hof's *(see p489)* most obvious attraction is this gourmet restaurant, one of Berlin's best. This cosy establishment serves unusual French dishes accompanied by perfect service. Chef Bobby Bräuer loves fresh produce from France and carefully reinvents traditional and international dishes. Book ahead.

WESTERN CENTRE Hugo's

Budapester Straße 2, 10787 **Tel** *(030) 260 212 63*

€€€€€

Map *2 C4*

This newly opened restaurant, in the Inter-Continental Hotel, is one of the best in Berlin. Unusual French and international dishes are prepared with a German influence. The fish and seafood dishes are proof of the chef's real mastery. An attraction is the restaurant's rooftop location with great views. Reservations necessary.

WESTERN CENTRE Midtown Grill

Ebert Straße 3, 10785 **Tel** *(030) 220 006 410*

€€€€€

Map *4 A3*

Steak and fresh seafood are the order of the day at this restaurant. While waiting for your dinner, you can watch the chefs in the open show kitchen, enjoy vintages from one of Berlin's best wine menus and listen to jazz. The service is very friendly, though somewhat slow when the restaurant is full.

FURTHER AFIELD Angkor Wat

Seelingstraße 34–36, 14059 **Tel** *(030) 325 59 94*

€€

A striking restaurant with a gaudy interior that used to be an insider's secret. The menu offers aromatic dishes that often include an array of delicate spices and coconut milk, typical of Cambodian cuisine. It integrates recipes from Vietnam, Thailand and other Asian countries. The service is friendly and forthcoming.

FURTHER AFIELD Merhaba

Wissmannstraße 32, 12049 **Tel** *(030) 692 17 13*

€€

People from all over Berlin come to this charming restaurant to join the local Turks and Germans who enjoy the food served here. Even if you are not particularly hungry, you will not be able to resist the various appetizers. There is outdoor dining in summer and belly dancing on Fridays and Saturdays.

FURTHER AFIELD Grunewaldturm

Havelchaussee 61, 14193 **Tel** *(030) 300 07 30*

€€€

Combining a meal in this restaurant with a trip to Grunewald Forest is a fine way to spend an afternoon. The menu mostly offers game or hearty meat dishes but also serves some local fish such as perch. Lunch or supper with wonderful views is an ideal end for this kind of outing.

FURTHER AFIELD Restauration 1900

🖼️▯🏠 €€€

Husemannstraße 1, 10435 **Tel** *(030) 442 24 94*

One of the oldest and most traditional in this part of Berlin, this restaurant welcomes its guests into a simple dining room with an outstanding historic bar counter and other antiques. It offers light cuisine with some dishes of German origin and a large selection for vegetarians. The terrace looks over to Husemannstraße.

FURTHER AFIELD Wirtshaus Moorlake

🖼️🏠 €€€

Moorlakeweg 1, 14109 **Tel** *(030) 805 58 09*

Situated on the secluded bank of the Havel river this historic restaurant serves German dishes. Although it is worth trying all the game dishes on its menu, the most highly recommended are game ragout with cranberries and buttered *Spätzle*, and the barbeque sampler, Moorlake with pork fillets and sauce bearnaise.

FURTHER AFIELD Maxwell

▯🏠 €€€€

Bergstraße 22, 10115 **Tel** *(030) 280 71 21*

This highly regarded, up-market and very well-known restaurant offers exquisite Berlin and German food with Mediterranean influences. The Maxwell always guarantees a laid-back and unpretentious atmosphere with a friendly, helpful service. There is a cheaper menu for lunch but only a few affordable wines.

FURTHER AFIELD Ana e Bruno

▯🏠 €€€€€

Sophie-Charlotten-Straße 101, 14059 **Tel** *(030) 325 71 10*

One of the best Italian restaurants in Berlin. An elegant interior creates the perfect atmosphere to sample the magnificent creations prepared by the chef. Everything is delicious, including the roast sturgeon in Mediterranean sauce. Menus given to women omit prices, but provide a calorie count for each dish.

FURTHER AFIELD Mutter

🖼️♿🏠 €€€€€

Hohenstaufenstraße 4, 10781 **Tel** *(030) 216 49 90*

True to its name, Mutter (German for "mother") serves generous portions to its patrons, mostly students. A fixture of the bustling Winterfeldplatz nightlife scene, it offers cool Caribbean drinks and an eclectic mix of some traditional German, Italian and Asian dishes, with an emphasis on sushi and Thai food.

FURTHER AFIELD Remise im Schloss Klein-Glienicke

▯🏠 €€€€€

Königstraße 36, 14109 **Tel** *(030) 805 40 00*

This is the ideal place for an elegant meal on the outskirts of Berlin. Now run by Franz Raneberger, one of Berlin's most prominent chefs, the restaurant offers excellent German cuisine, with perch, crayfish and game, all prepared with a dose of imagination. The restaurant is also a good choice for lunch.

FURTHER AFIELD Vivaldi

▯🏠 €€€€€

Brahmsstraße 10, 14193 **Tel** *(030) 895 845 20*

A luxurious restaurant in the expensive Schlosshotel *(see p490)*. The interior, designed by Karl Lagerfeld, features panelled walls, gold leaf and chandeliers. Due to many changes in the management, the restaurant has lost its gourmet standard, but still makes for a pleasant evening with exquisite French food. Book ahead.

BRANDENBURG

BRANDENBURG Bismarck Terrassen

♿🖼️▯🏠 €

Bergstraße 20, 14770 **Tel** *(03381) 300 9 39*

Typical and modern Brandenburg dishes in a historic but fun setting. This restaurant is located in the oldest quarter of Brandenburg and is managed by an intriguing and passionate group. Various *flambé* dishes as well as roasted pork are favourites. Extensive wine and beer list. Enjoy traditional music during holidays and some weekends.

BRANDENBURG Kartoffelkäfer

🖼️▯👶🏠 €

Steinstraße 56, 14776 **Tel** *(03381) 22 41 18*

Excellent address for lovers of potato-based dishes. Located in the heart of the central district of the city, most dishes at this restaurant include potato as one of the main ingredients. There is a rustic but cosy atmosphere and many child-friendly services are available. Reservations not required, but call in advance if your party is larger then six people.

BRANDENBURG Sorat Hotel Brandenburg

🏠 €

Altstädtischer Markt 1, 14770 **Tel** *(03381) 59 70*

The intimate, yet refined setting at this efficient restaurant reminds one of an old English-style mansion. White table cloths, wooden floors and black leather seating welcome you along with the delicious smells wafting from the kitchen. Try the Brandenburg *Teller* dishes – roulade of venison, wild stuffed mushrooms and potato chard gratin.

CHORIN Alte Klosterschänke

🖼️🖼️🏠 €

Am Amt 9, 16230 **Tel** *(033366) 530 100*

Famed throughout the region for its highly polished service, this charming restaurant is located inside a 270-year-old half-timbered building. Surrounded by trees, the small garden is a great place to sit during the summer and enjoy the dishes from their extensive menu. Call ahead if there are more than six in your party.

Key to Price Guide *see p526* **Key to Symbols** *see back cover flap*

CHORIN Haus Chorin 🖻🚉🎽 €€

Neue Klosterallee 10, 16230 **Tel** *(033366) 500*

This hotel-restaurant is based in a stylish Art Nouveau villa situated on the shores of a lake. Several regional and national specialities are on the menu, including pork fillet with honey on paprika and *Häckerle* (fish salad). Most of the vegetables on the menu come from local organic farmers and are delivered daily.

COTTBUS Mosquito 🖻🎽 €

Altmarkt 22, 3046 **Tel** *(0355) 2 88 90 444*

A South American twist on the café, bar and restaurant experience in Cottbus. Join the staff at Mosquito every day for happy hour or on Tuesdays for drink specials (a different one each month). Live music during the week and on special occasions. There is a lovely brunch on Sundays from 10am to 3pm. Try the chilli olive bread.

COTTBUS Cavalierhaus Branitz 🍷🎽 €€

Zum Kavalierhaus 8, 3042 **Tel** *(0355) 71 50 00*

Located in the centre of Branitzer Park, this beautiful and refined restaurant is a great place for dessert as well as dinner. Sample the delectable *Pückler torte* or wonderful *Pückler Eis* dessert for a taste of what keeps local patrons returning for more. They have wonderful wines from all over the world and the service is excellent.

COTTBUS Best Western Parkhotel Branitz 🎽 €€€€€

Heinrich-Zille Str., 3042 **Tel** *(0355) 751 00*

Located in the Best Western Parkhotel Branitz. This restaurant is renowned for its excellent service and high quality dishes, with German specialities the focus of the menu. Lighter choices are on the menu as well. End your day with a glass of wine or a draught beer: several varieties of both are on offer.

LEHNIN Rittergut Krahne 🚉🎽 €€

Hauptstraße 6a, 14797 **Tel** *(033 835) 602 87*

A uniquely different eatery with a fetish for knights and swords. The extensive menu features wild boar and other local specialities, as well as dishes from assorted regions of the world. Try the baked apple with walnut ice cream for dessert. Reservations for larger groups are recommended. Parking is available for your car or horse.

LEHNIN Markgraf ♿🚉🍷🎽 €€€€€

Friedenstr. 13, 14797 **Tel** *(03382) 76 50*

This restaurant belongs to the Hotel Markgraf *(see p491)*. Austrian cuisine is the house standard and to a high standard by the head chef. Enjoy a glass of Austrian wine or German beer with your meal or alone after a long day. Outside tables are available during the summer when the weather is pleasant.

LÜBBENAU Hotel Schloss Lübbenau 🚉🍷🎽 €€€€

Schloßbezirk 6, 0-3332 **Tel** *(03542) 87 30*

An award-winning restaurant connected to a four-star hotel of the same name. The menu emphasizes fresh produce as well as delightful meat and fish dishes. Most items combine the flair of international cuisine with local ingredients. Furnishings are more old English than German. Sit on the terrace during breakfast and enjoy the view.

NEUHARDENBURG Parkhotel Schloss Wulkow 🍷🎽 €€€€

Hauptstr. 24, 15320 **Tel** *(033476) 580*

This restaurant is based in the Parkhotel Schloss Wulkow, which was an imperial palace and is close to a nature preserve and natural lake. They use fresh produce and meats from local producers. The extensive wine list includes bottles from all over the world. The decor is quite elaborate, including crystal chandeliers.

NEURUPPIN Altes Kasino am See ♿🚉🎽 €

Seeufer 11 / 12, 16816 **Tel** *(0339) 130 59*

Enjoy breakfast or drinks in the atrium of this cosy 100-year-old eatery. This hotel-restaurant sits directly by the water and is home to some of the most relaxing views of the area. A good selection of game and fish dishes is available. Try the fish plate for a sample of different varieties and preparation methods of the local catch.

NEURUPPIN Bootshaus 🚉👥🎽 €

Hans Thörner Str. 17, 16816 **Tel** *(0339) 1856979*

This restaurant is right by the river and next to guest rooms owned by the same proprietors. A great place for families. Delicious, no-nonsense German food reminiscent of home cooking, though there are few vegetarian items on the menu. A charming breakfast buffet is available on weekends or for special occasions.

ORANIENBURG Gasthaus Charlottenhof 🚉🎽 €

Neulöwenberger Straße 26, 16775 **Tel** *(0330) 94 50 417*

A quiet, intimate restaurant attached to the Gasthaus Charlottenhof hotel. The outdoor seating area is great in summer. Regional cuisine dominates the menu and features several pork and fish dishes. Try one of the delicious soups for something light but filling. There is bar seating for single guests or a quick drink.

ORANIENBURG Galerie ♿🎽 €€

André-Pican-Straße 23, 16515 **Tel** *(0330) 169 00*

This restaurant is in the excellent Stadthotel Oranienburg. Fresh flowers and interesting art help add to the welcoming ambience. It is well lit and appropriately decorated and the staff are friendly and well dressed. It is also child and family friendly. The bar is popular with business travellers, but does not stay open late.

POTSDAM Froschkasten   🔲🍴🚭   €

Kiezstraße 3–4, 14467 **Tel** *(0331) 291315*

Connected to a hotel of the same name, this restaurant is decorated with Old Berlin-style furnishings. The friendly, attentive service is usually speedy but uncompromising. Try one of the celebrated fish or traditional Brandenburg dishes for dinner. A separate room is available for large parties or groups.

POTSDAM Krongut Bornstedt   📇🔲🍴🚭   €€

Ribbeckstr. 6–7, 14469 **Tel** *(0331) 550 65 0*

Enjoy dining in this 400-year-old wine cellar, brewery and café on this former Prussian royal estate. Guests can enjoy regal dishes such as "Freidrich's *Leibspeise*", potato soup with bacon. The "Chocolate Balmoral", a chocolate beverage made from pure milk chocolate and derived from an English recipe is a must for all visitors to the café.

POTSDAM Speckers Gaststätte zur Ratswaage   ♿🔲🍴🚭   €€€

Am Neuen Markt 10, 14467 **Tel** *(0331) 280 43 11*

French-influenced cuisine reigns supreme at this restaurant located in the centre of the city. Modern decor with fresh and elegant touches produces a charming, comfortable but unpretentious dining experience. Family run and famous for its excellent service as well as exquisite menu. Produce arrives to the restaurant fresh daily from local producers.

POTSDAM Bayrisches Haus   🔲🍴🚭   €€€€

Im Wildpark 1, Potsdam (West), 14471 **Tel** *(0331) 550 50*

This restaurant is in a top class hotel of the same name. It is famed for its luxury, service and French-inspired cuisine. Extensive menu offers meals in predetermined courses, a great option for those looking for a mix of house specialities. Fresh flowers abound year round. Enjoy the terrace in summer with its great views.

POTSDAM Restaurant Juliette   ♿🍴🚭   €€€€€

Jägerstraße 39, 14467 **Tel** *(0331) 270 17 91*

A French restaurant with all the romantic trimmings you would expect – candles, white tablecloths and a lit fireplace. French food traditionalists beware, the decorated and imaginative chef serves up both traditional and experimental cuisine. Try the ever-popular *crème brûlée* for dessert. There are vegetarian options on the menu.

WANDLITZ SeePark Wandlitz   🔲🍴🚭   €€€€

Kirchstr. 10 (Hinter der alten Dorfkirche am See), 16348 **Tel** *(0333) 977 50*

This Mediterranean-style restaurant also offers German fare. All the dishes are prepared with locally grown produce. Steak fillet with a sage, ham and almond stuffed Spanish onion is a culinary highlight. They have an extensive wine list, including superb wines that are only available by the glass. Open for lunch and dinner.

WITTSTOCK Stadt Hamburg   📇🔲🚹🚭   €€€€

Röbeler Str. 25, 16909 **Tel** *(03394) 404 60*

This restaurant is regarded in the region as a good eatery for travellers or those with children in tow. It is tastefully furnished and the service is good. The menu has limited options for vegetarians. Open for both lunch and dinner, it can get busy during national holidays and local events.

SAXONY-ANHALT

BERNBURG Zille Stube   📇   €€€€€

Siedlung 37a, 0-6406 **Tel** *(03471) 33 31 90*

A very traditional, quaint and unfussy German restaurant, although more like a pub. Dark, hardwood furniture and friendly staff are standard. They specialize mostly in traditional German cuisine and beers. Look out for regional artisan crafts throughout as well as paintings by various local artists.

BLANKENBURG Hotelrestaurant Viktoria Luise   🍴🚭   €€€

Hasselfelder Str. 8, 38889 **Tel** *(03944) 91170*

Less than 20 minutes from the Harz National Park, this restaurant is a great location for health-conscious diners. All dishes are home-made regional creations centred on fresh ingredients. There are several vegetarian offerings, including many organic options. Delightful fish and duck courses. There is also a wine cellar with a lovely terrace.

DESSAU Teehäuschen   📇♿🔲🚭   €

Im Grünen der Stadt-Im Stadt Park, 0-6844 **Tel** *(0340) 21 49 96*

A lovely garden surrounds this teahouse in the Stadtpark area. For over 30 years, patrons have enjoyed the wide variety of teas, cakes and light meals made fresh daily, though more substantial meals are also on offer. Everything is delicious. Larger parties are welcome, but call ahead for more information. Closed Mon.

DESSAU Kornhaus   🚭   €€

Kornhausstr. 146, 0-6846 **Tel** *(0340) 640 41 41*

The proprietors of Kornhaus are in love with food and hope to share their passion with all their guests. Try one of the three-course meals or order *à la carte*. There are organic items on the menu and several options for vegetarians or others with dietary concerns. For dessert, try the *Rote Grütze* with vanilla sauce.

Key to Price Guide *see p526* **Key to Symbols** *see back cover flap*

DESSAU Weinstuben Paechterhaus

Kirchstr. 1, 0-6846 **Tel** *(0340) 650 1447*

Set in a half-timbered house over 300 years old, this wine *Stube* has much on offer for patrons. The food menu focuses on interesting flavour combinations and textures, while the wine menu offers a little something for everyone. A popular place throughout the region for its relaxed atmosphere and expert staff.

HALBERSTADT Parkhotel Unter den Linden

Klamrothstr. 2, 38820 **Tel** *(03941) 625 40*

The restaurant of the Parkhotel Unter den Linden *(see p492)*. The service here is great and the staff are very friendly. They have an international menu with German influences. The wine list is extensive and there is a wine cellar on the property. Try the French apple tart with home-made champagne rice for dessert.

HALLE Dorint Hotel Charlottenhof

Dorotheenstraße 12, 0-6108 **Tel** *(0345) 292 30*

This restaurant belongs to the Dorint Hotel Charlottenhof, which is located in the city centre. Guests can watch their food being elegantly prepared while in the restaurant dining area. The food is above average and served by friendly and knowledgeable staff. There is also a pleasant hotel bar.

HALLE Enchilada

Universitätsring 6, 0-6108 **Tel** *(0345) 686 77 55*

A Mexican themed bar-restaurant near the university. It is geared towards the younger crowd or those looking for a taste of something different. The focus is more on drinks than food. However, the food is good and temperature adjustable for those not so keen on spicy food. Happy hour daily from 6pm to 9pm.

ILSENBURG Landhaus "Zu den Rothen Forellen"

Marktplatz 2, 38871 **Tel** *(39452) 93 93*

In a delightful setting by a lake close to the Hochharz nature preserve – come here for a relaxing dining experience. Restored in 1995, the 400-year-old structure is home to a restaurant and hotel *(see p492)*. Sit directly by the lake for dinner if you dine outside. The staff are very friendly and knowledgeable.

MAGDEBURG Le Frog

Heinrich-Heine-Platz 1, 39114 **Tel** *(0391) 53 13 55 6*

This brassiere and lounge is a cool place to eat or sip one of the local brews. It is located in the middle of Stadtpark, which is a local hotspot catering to a fun and vibrant crowd. They have a buffet brunch on Sundays with several tasty treats and magnificent creations. The beer garden seats over 400 people and there is a large terrace as well.

MAGDEBURG Tokio Haus

Johannes-Göderitz-Straße 27, 39130 **Tel** *(0391) 506 94 93*

A bit harder to find, but well worth the effort to locate for the delicious Japanese food at this locally-owned restaurant. There are many varieties of sushi on the menu, including *maki* and *sashimi*. The lunch menu is a good choice for those watching their budget or looking for a variety to sample. Closed Tue.

MAGDEBURG Amsterdam

Olvenstedter Str. 9, 39108 **Tel** *(0391) 662 86 80*

There is a bistro-type atmosphere at this very hip address near the centre. Several beers are on offer and a smaller wine selection. Try the "Do-It-Yourself" breakfast menu where guests can mix and match items for a set price. The French cheese plate or one of the other international dishes are great for something lighter in the evening.

MERSEBURG Shoalin

Am Airpark 3, 6217 **Tel** *(03461) 34 28 78*

Chinese and Thai foods are served at this spacious restaurant located near a city garden. Typical Chinese decor predominates, but the service is affable. Try one of the duck dishes for something different or ask for something spicy if you prefer a meal with bite. There are several vegetarian options. Closed Mon.

MERSEBURG Belle Epoque

Oberaltenburg 4, 6217 **Tel** *(03461) 452 00*

An exquisite restaurant in the Radisson SAS Hotel Halle-Merseburg *(see p492)*, which is located on the cathedral hill. They specialize in Scandinavian and German cuisine, as well as a few international dishes. Interesting decor and very good service. The café includes a terrace. The Raben bar is a highlight for business travellers.

NAUMBURG Zur alten Schmiede

Lindenring 36/37, 6618 **Tel** *(03445) 243 60*

A delightful, traditional restaurant in the wine-producing region of the Saale-Unstrut. It is located in the town centre and the current structure dates back to 1700 when it was used as a blacksmith's shop. Excellent location for sampling some of the local wines and regional food specialities. There is a romantic fire on colder evenings.

QUEDLINBURG Romantik Hotel am Brühl

Billungstr. 11, 0-6484 **Tel** *(03946) 961 80*

Famed for its service, menu and extensive wine list, this restaurant is a great option for those in town or staying near by. Wines available include varieties from France, Italy, California and, of course, regional favourites. A glorious inner courtyard is wonderfully relaxing on clear days, so eat outside if possible.

QUEDLINBURG Weinkeller Theophano   🔲🍷🚭   €€€€

Markt 13–14, 0-6484 **Tel** *(3946) 96300*

A family-owned establishment. This 400-year-old wine cellar is a restored structure with sandstone vaulted ceilings. The staff are welcoming and friendly and the lighting is soft. The menu combines German as well as international dishes and is refreshingly seasonal, with many items only offered during peak season. Very popular with the locals.

STENDAL Altstadt-Hotel   🖥🚭   €€

Breite Str. 60, 39576 **Tel** *(03931) 698 90*

A quaint but pleasant place to enjoy a meal or light snack. Open for both lunch and dinner, this hotel *(see p493)* and restaurant is located in the centre of town. Tastefully furnished and relaxing, you can sit outside in good weather. The menu offers international and German dishes, although there are few options for those with special dietary needs.

TANGERMÜENDE Kutscherstübchen   🖥🚭   €€

Lange Str. 52, 39590 **Tel** *(039322) 23 91*

Part of the historic Schwarzer Adler Hotel *(see p493)*, this is a nice family-friendly restaurant. Pleasantly furnished and tranquil, most meals are served in generous portions with the focus on regional fare, although some international ingredients and cooking methods influence the menu.

WERNIGERODE Gothisches Haus   🖥🍷🚭   €€

Marktplatz 2, 38855 **Tel** *(03943) 67 50*

This restaurant is connected to a mid-sized four-star hotel of the same name. The main train station is approximately one kilometre away. Enjoy dining among the half-timbered houses in the centre of this wonderfully romantic town. The restaurant includes a bar, outdoor seating area and wine tavern (they have an extensive wine list).

WITTENBURG Grüne Tanne   🚭   €€

Am Teich 1, 0-6896 **Tel** *(03491) 62 90*

Located on the outskirts of town, this former knight's manor is over 400 years old. This pleasant restaurant, based in a hotel of the same name, serves above average traditional and regional German dishes. They have a small but good wine list. Open for dinner from 5:30pm on weekdays and for lunch from 11am.

WITTENBURG Glücksburger Schlosskeller   🔲🍷🚭   €€€€€

Am Schlossplatz 1, 0-6886 **Tel** *(03491) 40 65 92*

Located in the rustic, vaulted basement of a 16th-century house, this place is sure to please anyone looking for something traditional and cosy with its fascinating decor. The menu includes time-honoured German and Saxonian fare. Various regional and national beers are on offer, as well as wines. The staff dress in medieval costumes.

SAXONY

AUGUSTUSBURG Café Friedrich   🔲🖥🚸🚭   €€

Hans-Planer-Str. 1, 0-9573 **Tel** *(037291) 66 66*

Over 100 years of family tradition await you at this lovely café, which is situated in a hilly, picturesque part of the town with amazing views of Castle Augustusburg. They offer both lighter and heavier dishes, and their desserts, especially cakes, are to die for. There is a play area for children in the garden.

BAD MUSKAU Am Schlossbrunnen   🔲♿🚭   €€

Köbelner Str. 68, 0-2953 **Tel** *(035771) 5230*

Operated by the Wieczorek family, this hotel and restaurant sits on the edge of town. It has a delightful interior. Both regional and international dishes are served, with a focus on fish, most of it caught locally in the heathland lakes. Also, try one of the steak dishes or the excellent *Fürst-Puckler* ice cream, which is a local speciality.

BAUTZEN Bautzener Brauhaus   🔲🖥🚭   €

Thomas-Mann-Str. 7 , 0-2625 **Tel** *(03591) 49 14 56*

As the name of this eatery suggests, this is one of the local brew houses. Choose from several varieties of beer, including *Schwarzbier*, or black beer, and the original *Pilsner*. Enjoy your beer either on site, or take some home. The menu offers mostly standard German fare but at good prices. Tours of the brewery are also available.

BAUTZEN Residence   🔲🖥🚭   €€€€€

Wilthener Str. 32, 0-2625 **Tel** *(03591) 35 57 00*

Situated close to the historic centre of town, this newer, sensibly decorated hotel and restaurant has a menu mainly offering no-nonsense meals at affordable prices. Regional cuisine and international dishes available. The main dining area has lot of sun in summer, although not uncomfortably so. There is also a large sun terrace.

CHEMNITZ Sächsischer Hof   🖥🚭   €

Brühl 26, 0-9111 **Tel** *(0371) 461 480*

This restaurant is in a hotel of the same name. They offer international and regional dishes made with a creative flair. Crème sauces, salads and fish entrées dominate the menu. The service is first rate and the staff extremely friendly. Dark wood furniture and greenery greet you inside, as does a bar. Some credit cards are accepted.

Key to Price Guide *see p526* **Key to Symbols** *see back cover flap*

CHEMNITZ Glashaus €€
Salzstr. 56, 0-9113 **Tel** *(0371) 334 10*

Based in the Renaissance Hotel and surrounded by lush greenery, this restaurant offers great views of the old town and the restaurant pond. International dishes are served in this lovely, modern venue, which rivals any botanical garden. There is also an attractive terrace and various seasonal events available to guests.

DRESDEN Sophienkeller €
Taschenberg 3, 0-1067 **Tel** *(0351) 49 72 60*

One of the most popular and lively restaurants in Dresden. It is one of three eateries located in the Taschenbergpalais. Come here for the re-created rustic atmosphere of an 18th-century beer cellar. They have authentic regional cuisine on the menu. The staff wear period costumes. Ask to sit at the indoor carousel table.

DRESDEN Cuchi €€
Wallgäßchen 5, 0-1097 **Tel** *(0351) 862 75 80*

Chinese, Vietnamese and Japanese fusion cuisine all under one roof. The sushi menu is extensive, as are the wine and beer lists. Try one of the meals served in a wok. The Chillout Garden lives up to its name and is very relaxing and calm. Open daily at noon Monday to Thursday. Evening reservations are recommended.

DRESDEN Intermezzo €€€
Taschenberg 3, 0-1067 **Tel** *(0351) 49 12 0*

This restaurant is in the Kempinski Taschenbergpalais and serves unconventional dishes with a touch of the Mediterranean. Try one of the delicious salads or soups for lunch. Desserts are also worth noting as is the extensive wine list. The dining area of the hotel also includes an American-style bar, café and other dining options.

DRESDEN Das Caroussel €€€€€
Rähnitzgasse 19, 0-1097 **Tel** *(0351) 800 30*

The hotel and restaurant are based within a recently restored Baroque palace in the historic city centre, dating from the 18th century. Famed in the region as one of the best restaurants in Saxony, dine on French cuisine while sipping one of the first-class wines. Truly spectacular.

KAMENZ Goldener Hirsch Ratskeller €
Markt 10, 1917 **Tel** *(03578) 78350*

The restaurant of the Goldener Hirsch hotel *(see p494)*, which is in the market square. This elegant establishment serves exquisite Italian dishes. The rustic Ratskeller, which serves traditional German fare, is also recommended. Reservations are not usually required, but call ahead if your party is large.

LEIPZIG Zest €
Bornnaische Str. 54, 4277 **Tel** *(0341) 2319126*

A fresh and creative take on meatless international fusion food. Try one of the wildly imaginative and intriguing vegetarian dishes, such as spinach risotto balls with a cashew nut crust and coconut crème. The rosemary lemon cake is also tempting and worth sampling. An extensive wine list. Open daily at 11am.

LEIPZIG Kaiser Maximilian €€€
Neumarkt 9, 4109 **Tel** *(0341) 355 33 333*

A bright restaurant, pleasantly decorated and with small recesses for the tables, the menu here is largely influenced by Italian dishes, but several regions of the world are also represented, and changes every other week, ensuring that the best in-season produce is used for the head chef's fabulous new creations.

LEIPZIG La Mirabelle €€€
Gohlisertrasse 11, 4105 **Tel** *(0341) 590 29 81*

A typical French restaurant with lots of goat's cheese and wine on the menu. Ask for the seasonal or special dishes during dinner. A refined and stylish place. Reservations are not required but recommended. Open for lunch Monday to Friday from 11:30am and for dinner every evening from 6pm.

LEIPZIG Michaelis €€€€
Paul-Gruner-Str. 44, 4107 **Tel** *(0341) 26780*

This is a restaurant based in a hotel situated in a building that dates back over 100 years. Look for the usual, mostly European cuisine as well as local specialities. The well-lit dining area is intimate and nice in good weather. There is a child-friendly seating area and menu, although there are few options for those with special dietary needs.

LEIPZIG Medici €€€€€
Nikolaikirchhof 5, 4109 **Tel** *(0341) 211 38 78*

A hip, up-market restaurant located in the centre of the city. The menu focuses on the Mediterranean with fresh, high quality ingredients, especially vegetables and fish. Take your pick of lighter or heavier meals. The wine list is certainly better than average. Open daily at noon and closed between 3pm and 6pm.

MEISSEN Bauernhäusel €€
Oberspaarer Str. 20, 1662 **Tel** *03521 / 73 33 17*

Join the traditional, uniform-wearing and friendly staff at this historic pub in Meissen. Wine is the top drink on offer and is very good. The menu is traditional German, with some French, Austrian, Italian, English and American influences. Open Tuesday to Sunday (brunch on some Sundays).

MEISSEN Mercure Grandhotel Meissen €€

Hafenstr. 27–31, 1662 **Tel** *(03521) 722 50*

This classy hotel-restaurant, based in a large Art Nouveau villa on the bank of the Elbe, serves regional and international food. Look for a wide selection of fish dishes on the menu. Their wine list is superb. Guests can also dine in the café, which has a terrace, or in the intimate hotel bar.

MORITZBURG BEI DRESDEN Churfürstliche Waldschaenke €€€€€

Große Fasanenstr., 1468 **Tel** *(035207) 860-0*

This restaurant, in the Waldschänke Hotel and near a former pheasantry, serves regional German and European food. There is a good choice of game dishes on the menu. There is a large wine selection to choose from, including brands from the immediate vicinity and other parts of the region. Large parties can be accommodated, but call ahead.

PIRNA Deutsches Haus €

Niedere Burgstr. 1, 1796 **Tel** *(03501) 46 880*

This modern restaurant, part of a hotel belonging to the Romantik Hotels chain *(see p495)*, is highly rated and very popular with locals. The food is mostly German with some international influences. Reservations are rarely needed, but call ahead on extended holiday weekends or if your party has special needs.

PIRNA Escobar €

Obere Burgstr. 1, 1796 **Tel** *(03501) 582773*

Nestled in a building over 80 years old, which was recently renovated. Visit this café, bar and restaurant for a decor reminiscent of 1950s South America. The South American influence continues on the menu with dishes such as fish curry with plantain fillets. Brunch buffet every Sunday beginning at 10am.

TORGAU Central-Hotel €

Friedrichokatz 8, 4860 **Tel** *(03421) 732 80*

This attractively furnished but modest restaurant is based in a hotel of the same name. It specializes in cuisine from Baden, so come here for food that is uncomplicated but delightful – the desserts are especially good. However, there are few vegetarian options. The service is courteous and attentive. Open for both lunch and dinner.

ZITTAU Riedel €

Frieenstr. 23, 2763 **Tel** *(03583) 68 60*

Serving German foods from several regions, this hotel-restaurant is a good place to sample all things German. There are several grilled and roasted pork dishes on the menu. Relax in the beautiful and comfortable beer garden in good weather or enjoy a pint of one of the many beers on offer in the Bavarian-style pub.

ZWICKAU Drei Schwaene €€

Heinrich-Heine-Str. 69, 8058 **Tel** *(0375) 204 76 50*

A lovely French restaurant. Lots of fresh flowers on the tables make your dining experience intimate as well as first class. As expected, the wine list is phenomenal and focuses mostly on French producers. Reservations are recommended for dinner. There are very few vegetarian options on the menu, but ask your waiter for house selections.

THURINGIA

ALTENBURG Altenburger Hof €

Schmöllnsche Landstr. 8, 4600 **Tel** *(03447) 58 40*

The Altenburger Hof Hotel *(see p495)* restaurant is typical of many in the region. Expect good service and decent quality food at affordable prices. The café is also fairly standard, but charming all the same. The hotel also has a bar. As in most regions of Germany, hotel bars often close earlier than you might expect.

EISENACH Café Lackner & Julian's Restaurant €

Johannisstr. 22, 99817 **Tel** *(03691) 78 45 50*

A family-owned (since 1929) café plus adjoining restaurant. It has a very tranquil outdoor seating area, so sit outside if the weather is nice. Service is exceptional and the staff are very knowledgeable about the menu and surrounding area. It can get busy during dinner, so call ahead if you want to guarantee a table.

EISENACH Eisenacherhof €€

Katharinenstr. 11–13, 99817 **Tel** *(03691) 293 90*

A Mediterranean restaurant and pizzeria in the Eisenacherhof Hotel. The pasta is made fresh and to order. A second restaurant, the Lutter, specializes in German cuisine from various regions. Try one of the many pork or fish dishes. The wine list is decent. There is also a pleasant hotel bar, a café with a terrace and an in-house disco some nights.

ERFURT Anger Maier €

Schlösserstr. 8, 99084 **Tel** *(0361) 566 10 58*

Do not let the low prices at this restaurant fool you, this is the perfect place to enjoy a meal during your trip. The walls of the restaurant are decorated with photos of former patrons and family members. The outdoor seating area has lots of colourful shrubbery. They also have a charming dark wood bar.

Key to Price Guide *see p526* **Key to Symbols** *see back cover flap*

ERFURT Naumburgischer Keller

Michaelisstr. 49, 99084 **Tel** *(0361) 540 24 50*

A restaurant located in a half-timbered building over 300 years old. The culinary focus is on Thuringian food and local beers. Try the *Rostbrätel*, or roasted meat with braised onions, as an entrée. The special Christmas menu features typical regional Christmas fare. The wine list has an excellent selection.

ERFURT Zum alten Schwan

Gotthardtstr. 27, 99084 **Tel** *(0361) 674 00*

Situated in the historic city centre of Erfurt, this restaurant is housed in the Sorant Hotel. The cooking is of a very high standard and there is a wide selection of dishes on offer. Choose one of the lighter dishes if you are not hungry enough for a full meal, such as fresh salads or light but filling soups.

ERFURT Alboth's Restaurant im Kaisersaal

Futterstr. 15/16, 99084 **Tel** *(0361) 568 82 07*

Very fancy and highly rated. This restaurant, located in the hotel Kaisersaal, has earned its reputation as one of the city's classiest places to dine. Top-notch wine list. The innovative head chef creates memorable meals using ultra-fresh ingredients and international food preparation techniques. Superb desserts.

ERFURT Köstritzer "Zum güldenen Rade"

Marktstr. 50, 99084 **Tel** *(0361) 5 61 35 06*

There is a little something here for everyone, especially those with discriminating tastes, with the very international menu – try something Asian or French. There are several vegetarian dishes on the menu as well as typical German and local fare. Dark woods and plush colours abound. Wheelchair accessible and family friendly.

GERA li_be

Humboldtstr. 22, 7545 **Tel** *(0365) 5519395*

This is a very chic and hip bistro. The chef focuses on the art of food and the staff on the art of service and both do a terrific job. An international menu centred on European cuisine, but also branching into some other areas of the globe. Sip a cocktail at the bar to relax after a long day. There is live music on the weekends.

GOTHA Hotel am Schlosspark

LIndenauallee 20, 99867 **Tel** *(03621) 44 20*

A relaxing hotel *(see p496)* restaurant enhanced by the indoor foliage and sunny outdoor surroundings in good weather. Enjoy coffee or your favourite beer while sitting in the outdoor seating area. They offer both classic regional fare and international dishes. The restaurant is situated at the end of the castle park.

JENA Schwarzer Bär

Lutherplatz 2, 7743 **Tel** *(03641) 40 60*

A hotel and restaurant in a historic building near the University of Jena. Eat in the same place Martin Luther once stayed. Choose this restaurant if you are looking for simple, modern and regional food. Try the Goethe menu, which has leg of lamb, puréed potato soup with sausages and two delicious desserts.

JENA Scala

Leutragraben 1, 7743 **Tel** *(036 41) 35 66 660*

A wonderful restaurant located on the 28th floor of the former GDR tower and affording a panoramic view of the city. Try the fillet of bass on a saffron risotto with a white wine sauce. The restaurant also includes conference rooms, all named after famous cities around the world. Highly recommended.

MÜHLHAUSEN Brauhaus zum Löwen

Kornmarkt 3, 99974 **Tel** *(03601) 4710*

This local brewery serves its own beer in the restaurant and pub. Most of the food is traditional German and so there are few vegetarian options. Try one of the *bretzels* or sausages as a snack, or any of the main courses for something more substantial. The hotel is also adjacent to the dining areas.

SAALFELD Obstgut Gehlen

Hohe Str. 1, 7318 **Tel** *(03671) 20 27*

This restaurant and hotel are based in a beautiful Art Nouveau building located some distance outside the town. A range of dishes are prepared in the intimate restaurant, including food from France and several of Germany's regions. The wine list is respectable, with several wines from France, Italy and Germany on offer.

SCHMOLLN Hotel Restaurant Bellevue

Am Pfefferberg 7, 4626 **Tel** *(034491) 70 00*

An award-winning restaurant, based in a hotel of the same name. The atmosphere is refined with crisp tablecloths, silver cutlery and nice indoor greenery. Views from the terrace are astounding. The menu focuses almost exclusively on continental cuisine, with some non-European influences. A very good wine list.

WEIMAR Brasserie Central

Rollplatz 8a, 99423 **Tel** *(03643) 85 27 74*

Typical French provincial cuisine with some international influences, mostly German and Italian. Sweet or savoury crêpes are made to order. The menu changes constantly, so check with the staff for current offerings. They have a vast wine list, so it is a great place to try a new wine or enjoy an old favourite.

WEIMAR Wolff's Art Hotel and Restaurant ⬆🏠🍴🛗 €

Freiherr-vom-Stein-Allee 3a/b, 99425 **Tel** *(03643) 540 60*

As you would expect with a name like Art Hotel and Restaurant, there is lots of art on display here for guests to enjoy. Both the Art Hotel and its restaurant are furnished in the style created by the Bauhaus School. The menu includes foods from all regions of the world, with an emphasis on European cuisine.

WEIMAR Anna Amalia ⬆🏠🍴🛗 €€€€

Markt 19, 99423 **Tel** *(03643) 80 20*

This restaurant has a venerable tradition, with famous customers such as Richard Wagner and Thomas Mann, and remains popular to this day. You will enjoy some of the finest Italian cooking in all of Thuringia, with an ever-evolving menu. The interior is decorated in Art Deco style. Service is first class.

MUNICH

Königsquelle ⬆🏠 €

Baaderplatz 2, 80469 **Tel** *(089) 220071*

A must for whisky lovers who flock here for the whisky bar. The food here ranges from homely and simple to refined high-class cooking. The veal *Wiener Schnitzel* comes highly recommended. A warm friendly atmosphere with good reliable service. The range of beers and wines is also good. It is popular so it is best to book ahead.

Ruffini 🍴⬆🏠🛗 €€

Orffstraße 22–24, 80637 **Tel** *(089) 161160*

With 25 years of experience behind it, Ruffini is a well-established address for good regional Italian cuisine. Try the organic roast pork with rosemary potatoes or penne with Italian smoked sausage, tomatoes and paprika. It is also popular as a bright, sleek café and patisserie. By evening the guests come for the good Italian wine and food.

Vanilla Lounge ⬆ €€

Bayerstr. 3–5, 80335 **Tel** *(089) 51262222*

In the heart of Schwabing, Munich's laid-back hip and arty district, you will find this modern café-bar-restaurant. The relaxed feel reigns all day. It is trendy and comfortable, with a club-like decor with changeable lights and colours. Try this coffee bar cum lounge for relaxed and tasty dinners.

Yum €€

Utzschneiderstraße 6, 80469 **Tel** *(089) 23230660* **Map** *2 B5*

A very fashionable and trendy Thai kitchen and bar. The interior is dark – black walls, orchids and spotlit gilt buddhas – chilled and full of glamorous media types. The food is wonderfully presented. Sample authentic Thai curry with coconut sauce, stir fries and spicy fish soups. A great atmosphere, even if the food takes a while to arrive.

Zum Franziskaner ⬆🏠🍴 €€

Residenzstraße 9, Perusastraße 5, 80331 **Tel** *(089) 2318120* **Map** *2 B4*

Rich in tradition and one of the best places to head for typical Bavarian specials. Their home-made white sausage, *Wießwurst* is famous in Munich. Also, try the Bavarian meatloaf with mustard, fillet of ox, plus a variety of salads and vegetarian dishes. Being the brewery's restaurant, you must try the Franziskaner beer, originally brewed by monks.

Al Pino ⬆🏠🛗 €€€

Franz-Hals-Straße 3, 81479 **Tel** *(089) 799885*

Excellent Italian dishes mastered by chef Valerio Scopel, open for lunch (except Sunday) or dinner. It has an understated decor, where portraits reminiscent of the Medici line the walls. Try the red mullet on fennel purée, zucchini flower ravioli in saffron butter and green apple mousse on cassis cream.

Dallmayr 🍴 €€€

Dienerstraße 14–15, 80331 **Tel** *(089) 2135100* **Map** *2 B4*

Dallmayr is a Munich institution, famous for its coffee house and café. The elegant restaurant offers delicious treats such as zucchini flowers with lobster on a bed of ratatouille in curry sauce, plus a selection of superb wines. Very popular with locals and tourists for its high level of service, patisserie and cuisine.

Gandl ⬆🏠 €€€

St-Anna-Platz 1, 80538 **Tel** *(089) 162525* **Map** *3 D4*

Gandl is the hotel restaurant of the attractive Opera Hotel *(see p498)*, serving light Italian cuisine at midday and a fine French cuisine in the evenings. Depending on the time of year, you can eat by the open fire or on the lovely terrace. Excellent starters, steak, lamb, fish and duck dishes followed by French cheeses are available.

Nektar ⬆🛗 €€€

Stubenvollstraße 1, 81667 **Tel** *(089) 45911311*

A contemporary, decadent experience awaits at Nektar. A supper club atmosphere where you eat several courses while reclining, with performances in-between. Everything is white, emphasizing the futuristic lighting, design, chilled music and video projections. Daily changing menus and good Old World wines. Book ahead.

Key to Price Guide *see p526* **Key to Symbols** *see back cover flap*

Spatenhaus
€€€

An der Oper, Residenzstraße 12, 80333 **Tel** *(089) 2907060*   **Map** *2 B4*

A classic place to sample traditional high quality Bavarian cuisine, part of the renowned Kuffler company. The First Floor is more informal, while the Second Floor is more sophisticated and has great views of the Opera House. Specials include the stuffed breast of veal or meatballs with home-made potato salad or a slow baked cabbage roll.

Acetaia
€€€€

Nymphenburgerstraße 215, 80639 **Tel** *(089) 13929077*

This small and narrow, friendly and stylish restaurant has a small menu based entirely around balsamic vinegar. Try the cauliflower soup and home-made ravioli filled with riccotta cheese and mushrooms or pecorino, topped with a drop of the real 25-year-old balsamic vinegar from Modena. There are seats out front in the summer.

Austernkeller
€€€€

Stollbergstraße 11, 80539 **Tel** *(089) 298787*   **Map** *2 C4*

Munich's famous seafood restaurant specializes in oysters. The cuisine is typically French and uses the freshest catch of the day. Be sure to ask for the daily specials. Well established with a great reputation for over 25 years, the scallops and French onion soup are highly recommended. There is a romantic and intimate feel.

Broeding
€€€€

Schulstraße 9, 80634 **Tel** *(089) 164238*

Broeding is a fine restaurant and also an Austrian wine importer. There is a daily changing five-course set menu (fish every first Wednesday in the month) and a list of top quality wines. Set up by a sommelier and a chef who share a passion for excellent food and wine. Small but simply the best. Book well ahead.

Dukatz
€€€€

Salvatorplatz 1, 80331 **Tel** *(089) 2919600*   **Map** *2 B3*

A cultural spot in Munich's Literaturhaus ("house of literature"), this restaurant has won accolades for its food and reasonable pricing. The bistro serves an excellent choice of light Mediterranean dishes with seasonal menus, which change on a daily basis. Meat or fish with vegetables or salads are available in a mouthwatering variety of dishes.

Garden Restaurant
€€€€

Promenadenplatz 2–6, 80333 **Tel** *(089) 2120993*   **Map** *2 A3*

The elegant option within Munich's gorgeous luxury hotel Bayerischer Hof *(see p498)*, this lovely roof garden restaurant offers fabulous views across the city. The menu and decor are inspired by the southern Mediterranean. Try the grilled wild salmon, pan-fried *foie gras*, orange and braised fennel ravioli, veal, lamb or fish dishes.

Lenbach
€€€€

Ottostraße 6, 80333 **Tel** *(089) 5491300*   **Map** *1 F3*

One of the city's best restaurants in a Renaissance building with interiors by Sir Terence Conran in the theme of the seven deadly sins. Specialities of the house include *osso bucco* of veal with chipolino and artichokes, asparagus ravioli *au gratin* with raspberry and chervil. Choose from the three halls, the bar, gallery or terrace.

Acquarello
€€€€€

Mühlbaurstraße 36, 81677 **Tel** *(089) 4704848*

This restaurant serves fabulous Michelin-starred Italian cuisine using fresh ingredients and special seasonings. Ask chef and owner Mario for his wine recommendations. Try the tortelli of figs and *foie gras*, squab with red wine, walnut and parsley sauce followed by lemon ricotta tart. There is typically Italian kitsch decor and excellent food.

Bistro Terrine
€€€€

Amalienstraße 89, 80799 **Tel** *(089) 281780*   **Map** *2 B1*

Bistro Terrine is Tantris' younger sister and a high quality restaurant. They specialize in delicious low-calorie dishes and especially good are the lamb and fish. There is also a lovely garden terrace and children are welcome. It is light, bright and very stylish with antique beaded lamps. Located in the lively studenty area of Schwabing.

Ederer
€€€€€

Kardinal-Faulhaber-Straße 10, 80333 **Tel** *(089) 24231310*   **Map** *2 B3*

A first-floor restaurant within the Fünf Höfe building opposite a large bank. Excellent fish and seafood is available, such as terrine of sardines and sweet peppers or pea soup and gambas, all fresh from the market. Also, over 500 great wines from their cellar. Diners can enjoy the courtyard terrace in summer.

Käfer Schänke
€€€€€

Prinzregentenstraße 73, 81675 **Tel** *(089) 4168247*

Michael Käfer's renowned gourmet restaurant attracts a mix of politicians and artsy and business types. Open all day from 11am for lunch and dinner whenever you want. There are cosy, intimate dining rooms in contemporary chic mixed with traditional Bavaria – hunting room, opera room and a lounge with an open fire.

Königshof
€€€€€

Karlsplatz 25, 80336 **Tel** *(089) 551360*   **Map** *1 F4*

A Michelin-starred gourmet restaurant in the hotel of the same name *(see p499)*. Chef Martin Fauster creates wonderful food such as medallion of venison with chanterelles and cabbage, fillet of sea bass with artichoke fond and ravioli or crème brûlée and liquorice ice cream with poached pear. There is a refined atmosphere.

Mark's Restaurant Mandarin Oriental   🔥💺♿   €€€€€
Neuturmstraße 1, 80331 **Tel** *(089) 2909862*   **Map** *2 C4*

Fine dining in sumptuous surroundings is offered here. There is a special monthly menu and over 400 wines to choose from. Located on the mezzanine overlooking the lobby, sample resident chef Mario Corti's lavish dishes, such as white halibut in wild garlic fumet and artichoke or medaillon of beef fillet with green asparagus are second to none.

Tantris   🖼💺   €€€€€
Johann-Fichte Straße 7, 80805 **Tel** *(089) 3619590*

A classic establishment and a Munich institution for over 30 years. Designed in a 1970s style it offers gourmet menus, a high standard of luxury and also has two Michelin stars, a garden and a terrace. Booking is essential. Try the specials, aubergine and sardine terrine with pesto or lukewarm salmon in leek purée and brown butter.

BAVARIA

ANSBACH Drechsels-Stuben   💺   €€
Am Drechselsgarten 1, 91522 **Tel** *(0981) 89020*

Within the Best Western Hotel, the Drechsels-Stuben offers guests great views over the town and area. The cuisine is based on fresh seasonal produce, with a German leaning but also serves some international dishes. The menu changes weekly and offers meat, fish and vegetable combinations. There is also a café and outdoor terrace seating.

ASCHAFFENBURG Post   💺🖼♿   €
Goldbacher Straße 19–21, 63739 **Tel** *(06021) 33 40*

Right in the heart of Aschaffenburg is the Post Hotel. Its fancy restaurant with gilt decor, pillars and quiet and slightly private niches serves Mediterranean, regional and often traditional cuisine. It has won several accolades for its gourmet menu. Bavarian specialities come highly recommended, especially the *Wiener Schnitzel*.

ASCHAFFENBURG Restaurant Hotel Wilder Mann   💺🖼♿🔥   €€€
Löherstraße 51, 63739 **Tel** *(06021) 3020*

Good quality regional and seasonal cuisine, especially fresh fish from the basin and the Wilder Man Steak platter. It also offers an extensive wine list, specializing in German and international wines. As part of a hotel *(see p499)*, it dates back to a 16th-century inn at the bridge over the river Main. They have a roof terrace.

ASCHAU IM CHIEMGAU Heinz Winkler   💺🖼♿🔥   €€€€
Kirchplatz 1, 83229 **Tel** *(08052) 17990*

Masterchef Heinz Winkler took over the original Post Hotel here in 1989 *(see p499)*. He has created a culinary destination for real gourmands with a wonderful Alpine backdrop by the Chiemsee. Dine in palatial surroundings in the Venetian lounge, garden salon, winter garden or loggia terrace. Exceptional food and wine.

AUGSBURG Kaiman   💺♿   €€
Ludwigstraße 19, 86251 **Tel** *(0821) 7808140*

Kaiman is a young, lively and fashionable spot in the centre of Augsburg. Its contemporary concept is a chilled lounge with extravagant food. The cuisine is healthy Pan-Asian with European touches for modern global nomads who like to dine with music in a relaxed dark candlelit atmosphere. How about Caipirinha chicken or ostrich steaks?

AUGSBURG Die Ecke   💺🖼🔥   €€€
Elias-Holl-Platz 2, 86150 **Tel** *(0821) 510600*

A fine Swabian-Bavarian restaurant famous for its innovative dishes with waller, the European or wels catfish, such as baked with horseradish on vegetables and rice with a Riesling sauce. Another house special is the roast lamb in Pommery and mustard crust on shallot sauce, beans and potato gratin. They also have excellent wines.

AUGSBURG Magnolia Restaurant im Glaspalast   💺🖼♿🔥   €€€
Beim Glaspalast 1, 86153 **Tel** *(0821) 3199999*

Magnolia offers a refined, modern international menu. It is housed in a listed industrial glass building, alongside original works of art. The menu changes weekly. Try the tuna tartar with caviar *crème fraîche* and rocket, or Provençale fillet of beef with *foie gras*. Fish dishes are equally impressive, as are much simpler creations.

AUGSBURG August   💺🖼♿🔥   €€€€€
Frauentorstraße 27, 86152 **Tel** *(0821) 35279*

Expect great cuisine at August, but what makes it special is the complexity and artistry in preparation and combinations. The food is painstakingly prepared using fresh seasonal vegetables, fish, seafood and game. Everything is incredibly light and has strong aromas as well as colours. Untypically delicate for Bavaria.

BAMBERG Alt Ringlein   🖼   €
Dominikanerstraße 9, 96049 **Tel** *(0951) 95320*

In the heart of Bamberg's Old Town, this hotel *(see p499)* and restaurant serves up Franconian specialities accompanied by the famous Bamberg beers. Tables outdoors in summer in the beer garden with a view of the cathedral. The wing housing the restaurant dates back over 700 years.

Key to Price Guide *see p526* **Key to Symbols** *see back cover flap*

BAMBERG St Nepomuk   ⬧   €€
Obere Mühlbrücke 9, 96049 **Tel** *(0951) 98420*

Dine in a traditional restaurant which has been a staple in the community for centuries. Good selection of game and fish dishes as well as accompanying local wines and beers. The cuisine is generally international. Part of a former mill, it has a charming atmosphere and great views across the river and the town.

BAYREUTH Oskar   ⬧⬧   €€
Maximilianstraße 33, 95444 **Tel** *(0921) 5160553*

A traditional institution in Bayreuth, this popular spot draws the crowds for its lively bar which often hosts comedy shows. Fine old dining rooms serve a good selection of regional Franconian food at reasonable prices. A great atmosphere and friendly young staff. Housed in the former town hall right on the marketplace in the heart of town.

BAYREUTH Restaurant Lohmühle   ⬧⬧⬧   €€
Badstraße 37, 95444 **Tel** *(0921) 53060*

Freshwater fish is the speciality here, all fattened up and caught in the restaurant's own pond. Look out for trout, carp and blue wels catfish on the menu. There is also a good choice of regional Franconian wines to complement the food. Just a stroll from the town centre, it is housed in a quaint old tannery at the edge of a babbling brook.

BAYREUTH Schlossgaststätte Eremitage   ⬧⬧⬧⬧   €€€
Eremitage 6, 95448 **Tel** *(0921) 799970*

An incredibly beautiful setting in the castle where there is also a terrace for alfresco summer dining, an orangerie for the afternoon or aperitifs and a café. Excellent cuisine, service and international wines. Highly recommended is the fine perch, or steak in balsamic and shallott sauce with rocket roast potatoes. The desserts are also exquisite.

BAYREUTH Jagdschloss Thiergarten   ⬧⬧⬧⬧   €€€€
Oberthiergärtner Straße 36, 95448 **Tel** *(09209) 9840*

This romantic setting is popular for special occasions as well as romantic dinners. The castle provides a cosy tavern, with a hunting lodge feel, serving traditional game dishes, or the more formal, elegant Schloss restaurant serving nouvelle cuisine. Try the tuna *carpaccio*, fish, duck, lobster or lamb.

BAYRISCHZELL Der Alpenhof   ⬧⬧⬧⬧   €€€€
Osterhofen 1, 83735 **Tel** *(08023) 90650*

High quality, Michelin-starred Bavarian and international specials. Fish, game, meat, vegetables and superb desserts. Situated south of Munich near the Austrian border, in an Alpine village close to the Tegernsee and with splendid Alpine views. There is a very welcoming comfortable atmosphere.

BURGHAUSEN Bayerische Alm   ⬧⬧⬧⬧   €€€
Robert-Koch-Str. 211, 84489 **Tel** *(08677) 9820*

Guests come here not only for the excellent Austrian and Mediterranean specialties, but also for the unrivalled view of Europe's longest castle with the Alps as a backdrop. Dine outdoors in the beer garden or on the terraces in warm weather. Local produce is favoured. Part of the Landhotel Reisingers Bayerische Alm *(see p500)*.

COBURG Der Kräutergarten & Die Petersilie   ⬧⬧   €€
Rosenauer Straße 30c, 96450 **Tel** *(09561) 26080*

A fine roast lamb in herbs and garlic served with French beans and potato gratin is one of the house specials, as is the rainbow trout in Riesling sauce. A fine establishment on the edge of Coburg with an authentic, cosy and rustic interior. Herbs play the lead role in the cuisine here, hence the name Kräutergarten, "herb garden".

DINKELSBÜHL Zum kleinen Obristen   ⬧⬧   €
Dr.Martin-Luther-Straße 1, 91550 **Tel** *(09851) 57700*

A superb restaurant located in the centre of the old town in Hotel Eisenkrug's ancient vaulted rooms. Gastronomic delights range from exotically spiced dishes to regional homely cuisine. The chef's seasonal specialities include game from September to March and asparagus in spring. There is a good selection of regional wines.

DINKELSBÜHL Deutsches Haus   ⬧   €€
Weinmarkt 3, 91550 **Tel** *(09851) 6058*

An impressive patrician's house dating back to 1440 is the setting for this hotel *(see p500)* and restaurant. Traditional German food with home-made specialities and light creative dishes are served in three different rooms, as well as outside in summer. Choose from high quality meat, fish and vegetables. The whole place is steeped in history.

EICHSTÄTT Klosterstuben   €€
Pedettistraße 26, 85072 **Tel** *(08421) 98000*

Klosterstuben is well known throughout the region for its fine cuisine. Chef Walter Seitz prepares a mix of excellent Bavarian specials, international as well as vegetarian dishes. Old beams and a tiled stove remind you of the building's history. A small, modern hotel-restaurant with good service and a homely, rustic feel right in the heart of Eichstätt.

FREISING Zur Alten Schießstätte   ⬧⬧⬧   €€
Dr.-v.-Daller-Straße 1-3, 85356 **Tel** *(08161) 5320*

Within the Dorint hotel in Freising, this restaurant has a good and well-deserved reputation for high quality Bavarian cuisine. Just a stroll from the historic centre of the town, which is close to Munich's airport and 30 minutes from Munich city centre. It has a 470-year-old vaulted beer cellar and a beer garden under chestnut trees.

FÜSSEN Alpenblick ●

Uferstraße 10, 87629 **Tel** *(08362) 50570*

The hotel Alpenblick's *(see p501)* regional restaurant specializes in fish from Lake Hopfen and offers some stunning views across the lake and Alps. In a cosy Bavarian traditional atmosphere you can choose between the indoor restaurant, winter garden or large terrace. In addition to fish there are several *Schnitzel* and *Bratwurst* options.

FÜSSEN Treff Hotel Luitpoldpark

Luitpoldstraße, 87629 **Tel** *(08362) 9040*

This magnificent hotel *(see p501)* offers various gastronomic treats, from the elegant restaurant Kurfürst von Bayern with its Bavarian specialities and international gourmet cuisine, to the cosy and traditional tavern Lautenmacher Stube, the Viennese café or even a Mexican restaurant.

GARMISCH-PARTENKIRCHEN Reindl's

Bahnhofstraße 15, 82467 **Tel** *(08821) 943870*

This top restaurant is found in the Partenkirchner Hof Hotel. With a long-standing tradition of fine cuisine, excellent service and refined atmosphere, the current chef presents a Bavarian menu with a classic French leaning. From the marinated wild salmon to veal kidneys, rack of lamb or venison, expect great quality and some wonderful wines.

GARMISCH-PARTENKIRCHEN Best Western Hotel Obermühle

Mühlstraße 22, 82467 **Tel** *(08821) 7040*

The Mühlenstube restaurant in the Best Western Hotel Obermühle is a mere five-minute stroll from the centre of Garmisch, and boasts magnificent views of Mt Zugspitz and other Alpine peaks. Open for both lunch and dinner, it offers an international menu, as well as the Mill Wheel bar (Mühlradl) where you can feast on Bavarian specialities.

GARMISCH-PARTENKIRCHEN Grand Hotel Sonnenbichl

Burgstraße 97, 82467 **Tel** *(08821) 7020*

Set in fabulous Alpine scenery, Grand Hotel Sonnenbichl's fine gourmet restaurant is called the Blue Salon. The impressive Art Nouveau building offers magnificent views of the mountains. In sunny weather guests can dine out on the terrace. The Blue Salon serves a fine variety of international dishes in classic elegant decor.

HAINDLFING NEAR FREISING Gasthaus Landbrecht

Freisinger Straße 1, 85354 **Tel** *(08167) 8926*

The *à la carte* menu offers a choice of regional gourmet specials. The meat, fish and vegetable dishes change with the season. This small, familiar restaurant is located in a quiet spot just north of Freising town. Country touches include features such as wood panelling and traditional tiled stoves. Parking available. Open Wednesday to Sunday.

INGOLSTADT Hummel

Feldkirchener Straße 59, 85055 **Tel** *(0841) 954530*

A charming and friendly family-run hotel and restaurant close to the old town. The contemporary decor adds to the relaxed feel. Open to non-hotel guests, the restaurant, which takes the owners' family name, serves both Italian and international cuisine, either *à la carte* or from fixed menus. Try the wonderful potato soup or smoked trout.

KEMPTEN Peterhof

Salzstraße 1, 87435 **Tel** *(0831) 53440*

The Peterhof hotel is conveniently located in the heart of Kempten, next to the historical city centre and the pedestrianized area. It has a smart, modern restaurant which serves a variety of Italian dishes. It is familiar, informal and contemporary. Enjoy several light courses with Italian wine, rounded off by a great espresso.

LANDSHUT Schloss Schönbrunn

Schönbrunn 1, 84036 **Tel** *(0871) 95220*

Situated just outside Landshut in a magnificent pale pink 17th-century Bavarian castle, this classic, vaulted hotel and restaurant is the place to try some good old-fashioned Bavarian cooking. The hearty meals in traditional style form the basis of the menu, but the chef also serves international dishes. Wonderful beer garden too.

LINDAU Alte Post

Fischergasse 3, 88131 **Tel** *(08382) 93460*

This attractive family-run restaurant was built in 1700 and offers diners a roof terrace, tables alfresco in the secluded square or indoor dining in a cosy room. Located in a quiet corner of the old town on the island. Local produce is used to create a variety of simple to gourmet meals with a hint of tradition. Families with children are welcome.

LINDAU Villino

Hoyerberg 34, 88131 **Tel** *(08382) 93450*

Run by the young family Fischer, the Villino hotel and its restaurant *(see p501)* have a wonderfully warm atmosphere. Close to the lake in an idyllic garden setting, you can dine on the peaceful terrace under the shade of the trees. Enjoy the high quality dishes that combine the cuisines of Asia and Italy.

LINDAU Bayerischer Hof

Seepromenade, 88131 **Tel** *(08382) 9150*

For a classic *grande dame*-style hotel dining room, decked out in the finest swathes of rich fabrics, head to Bayerischer Hof Hotel's *(see p501)* restaurant. It serves excellent formal cuisine with a service to match, and superb views across Lake Constance, which are especially stunning from the terrace in summer.

Key to Price Guide *see p526* **Key to Symbols** *see back cover flap*

NEUBURG AN DER DONAU Zum Klosterbräu €€€
Kirchplatz 1, 86633 **Tel** *(08431) 67750*

A well-established restaurant dating back to 1744, it is run by a young family and a creative chef. You can either dine in the slightly more private Jakobsstube for a romantic meal, or the cosy Gaststube specializing in typical high quality Bavarian cuisine and a Sunday roast. There is also a romantic garden for alfresco dining in fine weather.

NEU-ULM Landhof Meinl €€€
Marbacher Straße 4, 89233 **Tel** *(0731) 70520*

This hotel-restaurant has a welcoming rustic feel with a touch of modern elegance. Set in quiet country surroundings (part of the so-called Silence hotel chain), the food served here is influenced by Swabian Alb cuisine. Try the lovely fresh salads with fish or chicken breast, or turkey in creamed pepper sauce with pan-fried potato *rösti*.

NÜRNBERG Sebald €€€€
Weinmarkt 14, 90403 **Tel** *(0911) 381303*

A smart contemporary restaurant in the centre of the old town. The chef combines his global experience to serve appetizing dishes with a German and Italian predominance, from *vitello tonnato* to clear oxtail soup, scallops, *Wiener Schnitzel*, fish and meat dishes. The cuisine does not disappoint. It is very popular, so be sure to book.

NÜRNBERG Wonka €€€€
Johannisstraße 38, 90419 **Tel** *(0911) 396215*

A true gem, housed in a former bakery. It offers an excellent range of tasty dishes with a slightly exotic flair, from soups to fish, seafood and desserts. Good, friendly service and a wine list with each wine offered by the glass. Moderate prices for the city and highly recommended for the atmosphere and food.

NÜRNBERG Essigbrätlein €€€€€
Weinmarkt 3, 90403 **Tel** *(0911) 225131*

Just a stroll away from the main market square, this small intimate restaurant only has 20 tables so booking ahead is essential. Tightly packed, cosy and familiar, there is excellent food, staff and wines. You can choose from the daily changing menu or let the head waiter and sommelier advise you. Delicious fish dishes plus exquisite desserts.

OBERAMMERGAU Böld €€€
König-Ludwig-Straße 10, 82427 **Tel** *(08822) 9120*

The restaurant in this classic chalet-style hotel offers traditional Bavarian hospitality. Expect a warm welcome, rustic but smart decor and good quality fare based on regional recipes and fresh local produce. You can decide between the restaurant, bar or sun terrace. It has a spectacular view of the surrounding mountains.

OBERSTDORF Exquisit €€€
Prinzenstraße 17, 87561 **Tel** *(08322) 96330*

Set in an Alpine paradise with terraces overlooking sweeping lawns where guests can relax and dine in summer. A cosy country-style Bavarian restaurant, decked out in blue plaid, with very attentive, friendly but unobtrusive waiting staff. The cuisine is varied, from gourmet to low calorie, just let them know what you prefer.

PASSAU Christophorus Stüberl €
Pfaffengasse 7, 94032 **Tel** *(0851) 7568090*

For hearty home cooking head to the old-fashioned Christophorus Stüberl in a narrow old street in the heart of Passau. In addition to traditional regional cuisine they offer international dishes such as steaks and fish. It is nestled in a cobbled street between the cathedral and the Danube and the owners also sell fine Italian gourmet products.

PASSAU Heilig-Geist-Stift Stiftskeller €€€
Heilig-Geist-Gasse 4, 94032 **Tel** *(0851) 2607*

Dark wood panelling throughout with a historical feel and old tiled stoves. Dinner is served in the hunting room or bishop's room, where coats of arms, hunting trophies and old prints adorn the walls. This rustic restaurant and wine bar specialize in Bavarian food. Try the freshwater fish caught in the local rivers. Closed Wednesday.

REGENSBURG Rosenpalais €€€
Minoritenweg 20, 93047 **Tel** *(0941) 5997579*

The ground floor of this beautiful palace is taken over by the restaurant. The delightful Baroque rooms on the first floor are only used for special occasions. There are high ceilings, cool simple rooms, elegant style, large windows and a rose garden. The high standard of cuisine has its roots in the local Oberpfalz cooking with game and meat dishes dominating.

REGENSBURG Restaurant Gänsbauer €€€€
Keplerstraße10, 93047 **Tel** *(0941) 57858*

A light Mediterranean cuisine is served in this historic spot with a long-standing reputation as one of the town's best restaurants. Whether you try the duck, fish, meat or seafood, it will not disappoint. There is a lovely little romantic courtyard garden too. They offer wine tastings in their wine store, Stehladl, plus cookery courses. Closed Sunday.

REGENSBURG David €€€€€
Krauterermarkt 3, 93047 **Tel** *(0941) 5 84 60*

A lovely first-rate restaurant in the Bischofshof am Dom hotel *(see p502)* in the centre of town, it takes its name from the story of David and Goliath – murals of which, dating back to 1573, can be admired on the building's façade. They provide classic gourmet food and there are great views from the roof terrace.

ROTHENBURG OB DER TAUBER Gerberhaus Cafe

Spitalgasse 25, 91541 **Tel** *(09861) 94900*

Try a local Franconian specialty such as *Nürnberger Bratwürstl mit Sauerkraut* (Nürnberg sausages with Sauerkraut) in the lovely beer garden of the Hotel Gerberhaus, below the city wall. The popular café offers great pastries and cappuccino. Other light meals are served accompanied by local wine from the Tauber valley.

ROTHENBURG OB DER TAUER Eisenhut

Herrngasse 3–7, 91541 **Tel** *(09861) 7050*

A delicately pretty restaurant in the very old Eisenhut hotel. The dining room is reminiscent of an aristocratic country manor with antique furniture, rugs, paintings and elegant table decorations. It overlooks the tranquil garden at the back. Enjoy regional and international specials, local wines and music from the hotel's piano bar in the next room.

WERNBERG-KOBLITZ Kastell

Hotel Burg Wernberg, Schlossberg 10, 92533 **Tel** *(09604) 9390*

Kastell has the well-deserved accolade of two Michelin stars. Choose from a superb gourmet menu under the fine vaulted ceilings of the moated Wernberg castle. Expect the whole works surrounding the great food, from excellent service to silver, porcelain and refined wine. Situated in a quiet setting, there is a garden restaurant too.

WÜRZBURG Nikolaushof

Spittelbergweg, 97082 **Tel** *(0931) 797500*

Welcoming and stylish, this modern restaurant in warm Mediterranean tones sits atop a hill near a chapel overlooking the town. Enjoy the view of the lights at night through the large front windows or look out across the roofs of Würzburg from the shady terrace in summer. Dine on international and regional Franconian specialities.

WÜRZBURG Zum Lamm

Hauptstraße 76, 97204 **Tel** *(0931) 3045630*

The Lamb is a well-known restaurant in the region. Established back in 1732 it used to serve crusaders. Today, the guests are both locals and tourists who come for the Franconian and international cuisine, the cosy feel and the romantic courtyard garden in summer. The emphasis is on locally farmed produce and seasonal recipes.

WÜRZBURG Schloss Steinburg

Auf dem Steinberg, 97080 **Tel** *(0931) 97020*

The romantic Steinburg castle provides the attractive setting for this hotel and restaurant. It boasts fabulous views over the town from the garden terrace in fine weather. Steeped in history the castle was first mentioned in 1236. Enjoy German gourmet specialities with excellent service. Perhaps book a romantic candlelit dinner for two.

BADEN-WURTTEMBERG

BADEN-BADEN Laterne

Gernsbacher Straße 10–12, 76530 **Tel** *(07221) 29999*

Housed in a typical 300-year-old building of the region, this hotel-restaurant is right in the pedestrianized area. The interior is rustic in style and cosy. Expect Baden cuisine and wine, including specials such as *Sauerbraten*, smoked trout or *Spätzle* noodles in cheese sauce. Outdoor tables are set up in summer.

BADEN-BADEN Stahlbad

Augustaplatz 2, 76530 **Tel** *(07221) 24569*

A well-established elegant and romantic restaurant just a few steps from the Kurhaus in the centre of Baden-Baden. The chef combines the fresh local produce with a French flair. Try the warm goose liver with apple purée, crayfish with an asparagus *ragout* or venison medallions with cranberries, chestnuts and *Spätzle*. It has a lovely terrace.

BADEN-BADEN Piemonte

Hans-Bredow-Straße 20, 76530 **Tel** *(07221) 300990*

An attractive restaurant within the Tannenhof hotel *(see p503)* overlooking Baden-Baden in the foothills of the Black Forest. It is set in peaceful surroundings away from the tourist bustle and has a small stylish dining room. It was refurbished in early 2006. The chef re-creates Northern Italian cuisine with some Piedmontese specials.

BADEN-BADEN-NEUWEIER Restaurant im Schloss Neuweier

Mauerbergstraße 21, 76534 **Tel** *(07223) 9570555*

In 2004 German chef, Armin Röttele, took over the Neuweier castle with his wife, where they offer rooms as well as a fantastic restaurant. Try the castle's own fine wine and gourmet delights such as roast saddle of suckling-pig in an orange cumin crust with asparagus risotto, or smoked sole on a basil purée, and some amazing cheeses.

BADEN-BADEN-NEUWEIER Zum Alde Gott

Weinstraße 10, 76534 **Tel** *(07223) 5513*

The vineyards of Neuweier are the lovely setting for this family-run, traditional German restaurant. Dishes include regional specials cooked with a light touch, such as home-made goose-liver pâté, pheasant with kale purée and chestnuts and figs in beer batter. To accompany the food ask for their great selection of Baden wines.

Key to Price Guide *see p526* **Key to Symbols** *see back cover flap*

BRAUNSBACH Schloss Döttingen €€
Buchsteige 2, 74542 **Tel** *(07906) 1010*

A romantic, relaxing atmosphere reigns in this hotel-restaurant, which is part of Schloss Döttingen, a 12th-century hunting lodge. Choose between the elegant restaurant, the wine bar, café, terrace on balmy evenings or drawing rooms with open fire on cold nights. Enjoy regional Hohenlohe specialities, especially the locally farmed meat.

FREIBURG Enoteca €€€€
Gerberau 21, 79098 **Tel** *(0761) 3899130*

With 20 years of experience, Enoteca is one of Freiburg's leading restaurants. It offers a high level of light but classic Italian cuisine, where the emphasis is on simplicity and wonderful fresh produce. There are several menus to choose from, a simple choice, the fish menu, daily menu or à la carte. The dining room is stylish and understated.

HEIDELBERG Schlossweinstube Schönmehls €€€€
Im Schlosshof, 69117 **Tel** *(06221) 97970*

In the magnificent old Heidelberg castle, this stylish and spacious restaurant offers modern cuisine of international and regional dishes. Good choices are fish, duck or game. For a special treat book a candlelit dinner for two. There is also a lovely terrace to dine outdoors on warm evenings. There are fish and vegetarian menus.

HEIDELBERG Simplicissimus €€€€
Ingrimstraße 16, 69117 **Tel** *(06221) 183336*

Owing to the busy central location in Heidelberg's old town, booking is recommended. Tourists and locals flock here for the simple but outstanding cuisine, combining regional fresh produce, French flavours and good wines. Sit in the intimate dining room or in the flower-filled courtyard. Wine-tasting events take place every first Friday of the month.

HEILBRONN Grüner Kranz €€
Lohtorstraße 9, 74072 **Tel** *(07131) 96170*

This friendly little town hotel has a lovely restaurant where you can sample some simple local Swabian specialities as well as more international gourmet dishes. Run by a young couple who welcome families and young children, there are good local beef dishes on the menu, plus salads and local *Spätzle* noodles. Be sure to try one of the region's wines.

KARLSRUHE Ketterer €€€
Bahnhofplatz 14–16, 76137 **Tel** *(0721) 3715112*

The impressive Residenz hotel with its solid pillared arcade is home to the smart Ketterer restaurant. Locally grown Wurttemberg asparagus is a house speciality, worked into a variety of dishes when in season. Other typical favourites are the pork in gravy and the doughy *Spätzle* noodles which crop up all over the region. Also has a bistro and terrace.

KARLSRUHE Oberländer Weinstube €€€€€
Akademiestraße 7, 76133 **Tel** *(0721) 25066*

Tradition and service rank high in this well-established family-run restaurant. The wood-panelled interior with tiled corner stoves provides a cosy atmosphere. The creative modern chef offers star-rated combinations using traditional recipes with modern flair. For example, salmon and perch roulade on pearl barley risotto with wild garlic butter.

KARLSRUHE-DURLACH Zum Ochsen €€€€€
Pfinzstraße 64, 76227 **Tel** *(0721) 943860*

The menu at the renowned Zum Ochsen is dominated by French dishes. The fish is delicate and the cuisine creative. Try the Breton red mullet fillets on fennel salad, glazed dove breast on chanterelle mushrooms or marinated lamb fillets on Provençale vegetable salad. The lobster salad in warm orange butter is a house special.

KONSTANZ Die Bleiche €€
Bleicherstraße 8, 78467 **Tel** *(07531) 9422860*

Housed in a former bleaching factory owned by the local tent company Stromeyer, this restaurant features lofty rooms, friendly service and a great beer garden in summer. You look right onto the Rhine flowing past. A variety of regional dishes are served and they also offer an affordable lunchtime buffet. Sundays is a brunch buffet and Thursdays a fish buffet.

KONSTANZ Rheinterasse €€
Spanierstraße 5, 78467 **Tel** *(07531) 56093*

A wonderful setting next to the Rhine public bathing spot. Very popular in the summer especially with families as the children can play on the lawns next door. Also favoured by the fashionable who come for coffees, dinner or music in the early hours. It has the best terrace from which to watch the sunset. International cuisine and good wines.

LUDWIGSBURG Goldener Pflug €€
Dorfstraße 4–6, 71636 **Tel** *(07141) 44110*

A friendly, informal little restaurant, part of the hotel of the same name. The Golden Plough serves a wide choice of familiar regional dishes with both a daily and standard menu. Try the local variety of soup with *Maultaschen* (filled noodle parcels) or the beef roasted in onions and red wine. The cheese *Spätzle* noodles are particularly good.

MANNHEIM Gasthof zum Ochsen €€
Hauptstraße 70, 68259 **Tel** *(0621) 799550*

Housed in a listed building dating back to 1632, this restaurant can be found in the Freudenheim area of Mannheim. Despite its age, it offers a contemporary atmosphere, simple styling and a warm welcome. The menu changes seasonally. Excellent fish dishes, locally farmed ox and a fine mixed grill.

MANNHEIM Hahnhof   €€€€
Keplerstraße 32, 68165 **Tel** *(0621) 447455*

Conveniently located just a stroll from the Arts Centre in central Mannheim, the Hahnhof is a rustic and convivial place to eat. Expect old stained-glass windows, chequered tablecloths and geraniums in the windows. It offers friendly service, good wines and regional seasonal specials, such as Viennese cutlets, truffles, game and fresh fish.

MARBACH Schillerhöhe   €€
Schillerhöhe 12, 71672 **Tel** *(07144) 85590*

A timeless elegance fills the Schillerhöhe. The international gourmet cuisine makes it the best in the area. Enjoy a meal either by candlelight or on the terrace with a view across the Neckar valley. Delicious salads with barbary duck breast or scallops on.a bed of fresh crisp leaves. We also recommend the various fish, from snapper to bass.

RAVENSBURG Gasthof Engel   €
Marienplatz 71, 88212 **Tel** *(0751) 23484*

A traditional establishment, a favourite with visitors since 1878. In the heart of the pedestrianized area, it is a good place to stop for a meal while touring the town. Typical Swabian specials are on offer, plus regional beers and wines. Sit outdoors in front of the little guesthouse in summer. Good for either lunch or dinner.

RAVENSBURG Bärengarten   €€
Schützenstraße 21, 88212 **Tel** *(0751) 353092*

Conveniently located right in the town centre. It has the oldest and nicest beer garden in town plus a playground. Choose between menus with several courses or simple regional cooking, accompanied by local wines and beers. Good for the regional onion roast, *Maultaschen*, *Spätzle* noodles with cheese and sausage salad.

ROTTWEIL Haus zum Sternen   €€
Hauptstraße 60, 78628 **Tel** *(0741) 53300*

High quality cuisine taking inspiration from traditional recipes and local home cooking is offered in this restaurant in the hotel of the same name *(see p505)*. House specials include beef consommé with herb pancake strips, Swabian onion roast beef with *Spätzle* dough noodles followed by apple pie and vanilla ice cream.

SALEM Gasthof Schwanen   €€€
Am Salemer Schloss, 88682 **Tel** *(07553) 283*

Located within the famous local wine estate of the Margrave of Baden. In addition to the fine home-grown wines, the food, too, has a true local essence. The seasonal menu offers wonderful venison and fish caught in the Margrave's hunting park and fish hatcheries. An elegant contemporary take on traditional rustic style.

SALEM Salmannsweiler Hof   €€€
Salmannsweilerweg 5, 88682 **Tel** *(07553) 7450*

This half-timbered house provides a relaxed rustic atmosphere, whether you dine indoors or on the terrace. Fish and the home-grown vegetables are recommended. They also have a good house schnapps. Try the large bowl of organic salad, freshly picked on the premises. They serve some good locally produced wines.

SALEM Reck's   €€€€
Bahnhofstraße 111, 88682 **Tel** *(07553) 201*

This restaurant is in a hotel *(see p505)* just outside Salem in the beautiful landscape behind Lake Constance. All food is reared and grown locally, then lovingly prepared and presented. The owner-chef learned his trade in France and is now supported by his daughter, who has also trained at top places. Sophisticated dining with fresh, regional cooking.

SCHWÄBISCH GMÜND Gmünder Geigerle   €€€
Türlensteg 9, 73525 **Tel** *(07171) 359701*

The restaurant is part of the Pelikan hotel which is in the old town. A modern unassuming building with friendly staff and a choice of international dishes on the menu. The bright open dining room wins no prizes for its design or style, but the menu offers good Swabian specialities as well as cooking inspired from around the world.

SCHWÄBISCH GMÜND Stadtgarten   €€€€
Rektor-Klaus-Straße 9, 73525 **Tel** *(07171) 69024*

This excellent restaurant is located in a modern building in the town's official gardens. For lunch or dinner you can choose dishes such as beef *carpaccio*, scallops, bouillabaisse and wonderful fish or meat. Fine local wines accompany the food. There is also a pretty Rococco lodge in the gardens with a wine tavern and lovely summer terrace.

STUTTGART Hotel Traube   €€€
Brabandtgasse 2, 70599 **Tel** *(0711) 458920*

Steeped in history, the Traube is a half-timbered, small hotel in Plieningen, a village just outside Stuttgart. From its antique furniture to old doors, cobblestones and gabled roof, it exudes a romantic charm. The wood-panelled dining room is cosy indoors and the summer terrace is a pretty alternative. Good Swabian game and fish.

STUTTGART Schlossgastronomie Solitude   €€€
Solitude 2, 70197 **Tel** *(0711) 692025*

An impressive sprawling rococo castle from 1775 is the setting for this restaurant. The elegant restaurant offers dinners only. The chef concentrates on French cuisine with light dishes using fresh local produce, but also serves regional specials and international cooking. It has a lovely garden terrace. Closed Monday.

Key to Price Guide *see p526* **Key to Symbols** *see back cover flap*

STUTTGART Trattoria da Loretta
€€€

Büchsenstraße 24, 70173 **Tel** *(0711) 2804507*

Loretta Petti opened her homely Tuscan Trattoria in 2005, after years running speciality food stores in Stuttgart. She cooks her way into the hearts of local Italophiles who love the regional cooking from her homeland. It is open, modern, laid-back and simple, in both design and cuisine.

STUTTGART Cube
€€€€

Kleiner Schlossplatz 1, 70173 **Tel** *(0711) 2804441*

A gastronomic delight within Stuttgart's modern art museum. The vast glass cube houses this excellent restaurant for cultured dining on the fourth floor. Minimal, stylish and cosmopolitan, the Pacific Rim cuisine in the evenings offers fusion dishes such as honey-and-soya-glazed duck breast on chilli-vanilla cabbage.

TÜBINGEN Carat
€€€

Wöhrdstraße 7, 72072 **Tel** *(07071) 139100*

Fine dining at the edge of the river in the heart of Tübingen. The modern hotel has floor-to-ceiling windows on the river side. It is just minutes across the bridge from the old town centre. Choose between a fine light regional cuisine or a coastal Mediterranean-style cuisine. There is a garden terrace in summer. Closed Sunday.

WEINGARTEN Altdorfer Hof
€€€

Burachstraße 12, 88250 **Tel** *(0751) 50090*

This opulent hotel and restaurant offers an exquisite menu of Swabian dishes. The decor is rather over the top with flounces, ruches, swirls, swans and rococo touches, but the quality of the food is excellent. From the fish to lamb and veal, all dishes are classically cooked and presented with a touch of exotic flair. Close to Ravensburg.

RHINELAND-PALATINATE AND SAARLAND

BESCHEID Zur Malerklause
€€€€

Im Hofecken 2, 54413 **Tel** *(06509) 558*

There is a low-key serenity about the restaurant. The menu is changes often to make the most of seasonal ingredients. The cuisine varies from German to French and Mediterranean. The goose-liver terrine is particularly rich and exuberant. There are over 300 wines in the cellar and an enthusiastic sommelier to help in your choice.

BOLLENDORF Restaurant Bellevue
€€€

Sonnenbergalle 1, 54669 **Tel** *(06526) 92800*

The view from the dining area is spectacular and there is also a terrace. There are a number of different menus and special menus, such as Asian and game. The cuisine is mainly German and it is a good place to sample the local and regional dishes. Located in the Waldhotel Sonnenberg.

DIEBLICH Halferschenke
€€€

Hauptstraße 63, 56332 **Tel** *(02607) 1008*

Located not far from the river, in a quiet area, the cuisine is international with some really fantastic Mediterranean dishes. The chef is happy to explore new tastes and has "surprise" menus for patrons, even going so far as to select accompanying wines. There is a nice terrace and beer garden.

HEIDESHEIM Crevette
€€€

Budenheimer Weg 61, 55262 **Tel** *(06132) 5270*

This is a spectacular palace of seafood. The restaurant is quite extensive, with a number of beautiful and atmospheric dining areas both inside and out. The staff are very friendly and helpful when deciding which white wine best accompanies their fantastic paella.

KOBLENZ Da Vinci
€€

Firmungstraße, 56068 **Tel** *(0261) 9215444*

An Italian restaurant with a sophisticated atmosphere and superb cuisine. There are often functions held here, such as wine tastings and fashion shows. The walls are covered with paintings and there is often soft music playing. The fresh ingredients and traditional Italian dishes have made this new restaurant popular amongst the locals.

KOBLENZ Loup de mer
€€€

Neustadt 12, 88250 **Tel** *(0261) 9114546*

This could possibly be the best seafood restaurant in Koblenz. The dishes are imaginative and comprehensive and not restricted to fish. The menu also contains tasty dishes for vegetarians and non-fish eaters. Their *loup de mer* dish, after which the restaurant is named, is divine. There is a great dining area outside on their terrace.

MAINZ EisGrub-Bräu
€€

Weissliliengsasse 1a, 55116 **Tel** *(06131) 221104*

Just a short distance from the Dom, this restaurant/beer hall is teeming with charm. They brew several kinds of beer, serving them to enthusiastic patrons who love the bustling ambience. Famous for their huge steaks, there is also a buffet in the cellar that is a great way to sample the various regional dishes they prepare.

MAINZ Der Halbe Mond

In der Witz 12, 55252 **Tel** *(06134) 23913*

A tiny restaurant offering some very special creations. Because there are only five tables it is a good idea to make reservations first. The dishes have a refined flavour and a French influence. The night is not complete without sampling their white and dark chocolate mousse with caramelized hazelnuts.

MARIA LAACH Seespiegel-Seehotel Maria Laach

Orsteil Maria Laach, 56653 **Tel** *(02652) 584512*

This unique and well-respected restaurant is located in a hotel *(see p507)* close to a 900-year-old monastery, which provides the kitchen with fresh produce. Seafood has a starring role on the menu, although their lamb fillet salad is tempting and seductive. The chef is sympathetic to vegetarians and provides them with fantastic fare.

NEUNKIRCHEN Hostellerie Bacher

Limbacher Straße 2, 66539 **Tel** *(06821) 31314*

Set in a stylish hotel, this is an elegant and impressive restaurant. Apart from the traditional elegance of the dining area there is also a wonderful winter garden, which has a glass roof and looks out onto the garden. The chef creates innovative cuisine that defies categorization and which is imaginatively presented.

SAARBRÜCKEN Schloss Halberg

Am Halberg, 66121 **Tel** *(0681) 63181*

Fantastically positioned in Halberg castle, the inside blends a modern design with the historic atmosphere of the castle and creates a wonderful environment. The cuisine is decidedly French in style, and the desserts are just gorgeous. Try the flambé. There is a terrace for outside dining in the warmer months.

SAARBRÜCKEN Villa Weismüller Restaurant Quack

Gersweilerstraße 43a, 66117 **Tel** *(0681) 52153*

An extensive restaurant with a number of different rooms, some of which are available for private functions. Apart from the restaurant there is a lounge, a beer garden and a brasserie. The restaurant is popular with the locals as well as travellers. The menu is quite large and comprehensive. Their salads are diverse and very filling.

SPEYER Feuerbachhaus

Allerheiligenstraße 9, 67346 **Tel** *(06232) 70448*

The birthplace of the German painter Anselm Feuerbach (1829–80). This wine bar/restaurant is part of a museum about him. Some rooms are dedicated to art. The menu is rather limited, although quite tasty and the wine list has many good German wines, particularly whites. There is a garden area with tables.

SPEYER Backmulde

Karmelitersstraße 11–13, 67346 **Tel** *(06232) 71577*

The creative cuisine mixed with a traditional French approach produces interesting dishes. The menu is constantly changing and the chef makes good use of seasonal produce. Their set menu always delights guests and sometimes helps them investigate cuisine they might otherwise not choose. They have a huge and superb wine list.

SPEYER Zweierlei

Johannesstraße 1, 67346 **Tel** *(06232) 61110*

There is a calm ambience in this restaurant. The cuisine is mostly German and regional, with a few surprises thrown in. The service is great and they are very happy to help when it comes to the selection of both the dishes and the wine. The restaurant has a modern design that complements the eating experience.

ST INGBERT Die Alter Brauerei

Kaiserstraße 101, 66386 **Tel** *(06894) 92860*

Positioned in a historic building dating back to the 18th century, this restaurant has a very intimate ambience. The outside appears rustic, yet the inside reveals a modern design, which is reflected in the New German cuisine that has earned the chef a Michelin Bib Gourmand. Quite a good selection of German wines.

THOLEY Im Hotellerie Hubertus

Metzer Straße 1, 66636 **Tel** *(06853) 91030*

Part of the Hotellerie Hubertus, there is also a café and wine bar. This gourmet restaurant serves light, French-style dishes, using the freshest ingredients from the region. The chef gives much sought-after cooking lessons for the true fans. There is an open fireplace in the main dining area, which creates an intimate and romantic atmosphere.

TRIER Römischer Kaiser-Taverne

Porta-Nigra-Platz 6, 54292 **Tel** *(0651) 97700*

This restaurant is inside the Römischer Kaiser hotel *(see p508)*, which is located at the edge of a scenic square in Trier. The specials are often interesting and tasty, especially the game dishes. There is an extensive wine list that has a number of international wines as well as a good selection of German wines. It is best to book on the weekends.

TRIER Pfeffermühle

Zurlaubener Ufer 76, 54292 **Tel** *(0651) 26133*

This restaurant overlooks the Mosel river and has a great view that can be enjoyed from their terrace in the warmer months. The building dates back to the 19th century and provides an intimate location to enjoy their international cuisine. The terrace is a little more sociable, as there are more tables outside.

Key to Price Guide *see p526* **Key to Symbols** *see back cover flap*

HESSE

ALSFELD Krone
Schellengasse 2, 36304 **Tel** *(06631) 4041*

Consistently great service and delicious food. The speciality would have to be the game dishes, which are always being refined and perfected. The dining area is relatively small and yet spacious at the same time, and the size ensures that the waiters and waitresses deliver a more personalized service.

BAD HOMBURG Charly's Bistro
Kaiser-Friedrich-Promenade 69–75, 61348 **Tel** *(06172) 181 648*

Decorated and designed to evoke an atmosphere of a Parisian boulevard, the menu explores many types of cuisine and is not limited to France. The wine list is vast, with over 130 different varieties to choose from. The restaurant is located in the Steigenberger hotel and is quite large, seating over 140 diners.

BAD WILDUNGEN Wickenhof
Bilsteinstraße 67, 34537 **Tel** *(05621) 5190*

You know it as soon as you step in the door; you are in waffle country. Wall-to-wall waffles here, with over 100 varieties. The cuisine is not restricted to the mighty waffle, though, with many regional dishes in very generous proportions for hungry people. Along with the main restaurant there is a nice terrace and beer garden.

DARMSTADT Bockshaut
Kirchstraße 7–9, 64283 **Tel** *(06151) 99670*

This rustic restaurant, whose name means "Goat's skin", is housed in an old tannery dating back to the 16th century. The menu is filled with traditional dishes from the region, so lovers of *Sauerkraut* and *Blutwurst* will be happy, as will vegetarians who are thoughtfully provided with a number of great dishes. It has distinctive old wooden furnishings.

EGELSBACH Schuhbeck's Check Inn
Ausserhalb 20, 63329 **Tel** *(06103) 4859380*

Located next to a domestic airfield, with spectacular views of the runway. The restaurant itself is housed in an old hangar. The food is mostly regional, with a few hints of Asian and Mediterranean influences. There are a number of good vegetarian dishes. There is also a microbrewery and beer garden.

ELTVILLE AM RHEIN Wintergarten
Hauptstraße 43, 65346 **Tel** *(06123) 6760*

There are three restaurants in this historic castle, all possessing their own style and flair. The winter garden is in a beautiful glasshouse that has a great view of the garden and castle. The menu is small, though quite diverse, with interesting and creative dishes that have a slight leaning towards an Italian theme.

FISCHBACHTAL Landhaus Baur
Lippmannweg 15, 64405 **Tel** *(06166) 8313*

This elegant and refined restaurant is in the Landhaus Baur hotel. The menu is a little restricted and not suited to vegetarians, but still excellent. The dining areas are very comfortable and relaxed, with an outstanding level of service. The lunch menus are often less expensive.

FRANKFURT AM MAIN Peninsula Atrium
Konrad-Adenauer-Straße 7, 60313 **Tel** *(069) 2981-174*

Located in the Arabella Sheraton Hotel *(see p509)* this is an atmospheric, international restaurant. There are several restaurants in the hotel offering different cuisines – this one focuses on the Mediterranean. It has a high-ceiling glass cupola which adds to the elegant ambience. The chefs prepare the food in view of the diners.

FRANKFURT AM MAIN Zum Schwarzen Stern
Römerberg 6, 60311 **Tel** *(069) 291279*

A restaurant serving traditional fare as well as international dishes. There is a specific menu section called "Grandmother's recipes" which caters to the taste for regional cuisine. It is located next to the cathedral in a very old building and there are references to it dating back to 1453.

FRANKFURT AM MAIN Alte-Kanzlei
Niedenau 50, 60325 **Tel** *(069) 721424*

An Italian restaurant doing justice to its heritage. There is an intimate and refined atmosphere inside that emphasizes and complements the rich cuisine. The whole menu is appetizing, but their duck breast with sweet and sour sauce is worthy of high praise. The service is very good and one can expect high standards here.

FRANKFURT AM MAIN Tigerpalast
Heiligkreuzgasse 16–20, 60313 **Tel** *(069) 92002225*

It is a rare restaurant indeed that is coupled with a variety show and awarded a Michelin star. They serve light Mediterranean dishes with flair and passion. The walls are adorned with show posters from all over the world. It is common for guests to combine dining in the restaurant with watching the show.

FULDA Dachsbau
Pfandhausstraße 8, 36037 **Tel** *(0661) 74112*

Creative and elegant cuisine with inspired presentation is served here. Guests can feel the chef's personality in each of the dishes, which have French and regional influences. There is a large selection of wines to choose from, both German and international. The atmosphere in the restaurant is intimate and friendly, with an eclectic decor.

GIESSEN Köhler "Klemens"
Westenlage 33–35, 35390 **Tel** *(0641) 979990*

The hotel and adjoining restaurant is family owned and they take pride in the service they provide. The Klemens restaurant does not fail to deliver. Fantastic international cuisine with a French leaning is complemented by the extensive wine selection. There is also a wine bar with a huge selection of wines.

KASSEL Zum Steinernen Schweinchen
Konrad-Adenauer-Straße 117, 34132 **Tel** *(0561) 940480*

The gourmet restaurant inside the Zum Steineren Schweinchen will delight and seduce you. There is a beautiful glass-enclosed dining area that offers diners views out into the garden. Their cuisine has become very highly acclaimed, and they now offer classes on how to perfect such dishes as their grilled lamb fillets on a bed of polenta.

LIMBURG Wirsthaus Obermühle
Am Huttig 3, 65549 **Tel** *(06431) 27927*

This cosy traditional restaurant is located next to an old mill dating back to the 12th century with the waters of the Lahn river flowing past. The wheel of the mill still moves on occasion, which can make the beer garden a little noisy, although the inside is peaceful. The food is excellent and reflects an ongoing evolution of German cuisine.

MARBURG Das Kleine Restaurant
Barfüssertor 25, 35037 **Tel** *(06421) 22293*

True to its name, this is a small restaurant although there is much in the way of flavour and style. There is a blend of French and German approaches to the food, with eclectic ingredients and creative presentation. The wine list extends to a very impressive, if not intimidating, 450 wines.

MICHELSTADT Drei Hasen
Braunstraße 5, 64720 **Tel** *(06061) 71017*

Its name means "three hares" and this hotel-restaurant is renowned in the area for its traditional ambience as well as its delectable regional cuisine, specifically the fish dishes. The interior has a strong rustic charm that fits the cuisine perfectly. They also have an extensive beer garden which is served by the same kitchen.

OFFENBACH Frezzini`s
Bieberer Straße 47, 63065 **Tel** *(06982) 360606*

Specializing in Mediterranean and Italian cuisine, the Frezzini family has created a beautiful and elegant restaurant. Their fish dishes are very popular, and it is near impossible not to try the tiramisu. The area is a little drab, which makes the serenity and elegance of the restaurant a welcome contrast. The wine list has many Italian wines.

RÜDESHEIM AM RHEIN Krone
Rheinuferstraße 10, 65385 **Tel** *(06722) 4030*

You will find a high standard of elegance and good service in this historic restaurant. The walls are covered with old paintings and the dining area is furnished with antiques. The international-style dishes creatively combine ingredients. However, a very hungry person might find that full satisfaction comes at a high cost.

WEILBURG Alte Reitschule
Langgasse 25, 35781 **Tel** *(06471) 5090 717*

This restaurant is located in the Schlosshotel Weilburg *(see p510)* and serves international and regional dishes in a picturesque setting. There is a terrace with outside seating that offers patrons a wonderful view of the castle and surrounding area. The restaurant often has offers on Sundays with reasonably priced set menus.

WETZLAR Der Postreiter
Parisergasse 20–22, 35578 **Tel** *(06441) 9030*

One of three restaurants in the Bürgerhof Hotel. This one serves international cuisine which makes the most of seasonally available produce. Their fish dishes are fresh and highly acclaimed, and there are some great vegetarian courses as well. The staff are happy to help you choose from their comprehensive wine list.

WIESBADEN Domäne
Domäne, 65205 **Tel** *(0611) 737460*

A comfortable and relaxing restaurant with a Mediterranean style to the design and menu. The tables are decorated with fresh flowers, and there is seating in the beautiful garden. The restaurant is set in a complex comprising a bakery, guesthouse and farmlands, which provide the restaurant with most of its fresh produce.

WIESBADEN Kaefers Bistro
Kurhausplatz 1, 65189 **Tel** *(0611) 536200*

There is a busy atmosphere in this French-style bistro. The restaurant seats over 200 guests and it has no difficulty filling those seats. The food marries German portions and produce with a French subtlety, balancing the two with a good variety of wines from the region. There is often live music and they have a large terrace for outside dining.

Key to Price Guide *see p526* **Key to Symbols** *see back cover flap*

NORTH RHINE-WESTPHALIA

AACHEN Schloss Schönau
Schönauer Allee 15, 52072 **Tel** *(0241) 173577*

Set in a castle dating from the 11th century, this restaurant has become well known for its set menus. The decor is stunning and opulent, rather apt for the inside of a castle. The chef likes seafood and the menu has a wide variety of different dishes. The Schloss itself is set in parkland and the restaurant has scenic views of the surrounding area.

AACHEN St. Benedikt
Benediktusplatz 12, 52076 **Tel** *(02408) 2888*

This gourmet restaurant has a cottage feel about it, and provides an elegant atmosphere in which to enjoy the great cuisine. In spring the façade of the restaurant is covered with flowers and the inside is no less attractive, with antique chairs and oil paintings on the walls.

BAD HONNEF Alexander's Restaurant
Alexander-von-Humboldt-Straße 20, 53604 **Tel** *(02224) 771 400*

Named after Alexander von Humboldt (1769–1859), the famous scientist and explorer, this restaurant is located in the Seminaris Hotel and offers international cuisine with a few regional dishes thrown in. If you are new to German traditional cuisine you should try their *Rievkoche*, fried potato cakes served with apple sauce.

BIELEFELD Westfälische Hofstube
Niedernholz 2, 33699 **Tel** *(0521) 20900*

Located in the Oldentruper Hof Hotel, along with two other restaurants, the name suggests the cuisine, with the focus squarely on regional and traditional dishes from the Westphalia area, though there are international dishes on the menu as well. The service is warm and friendly and the atmosphere is comfortable.

BONN Zur Lindenwirtin Aennchen
Aennchenplatz 2, 53173 **Tel** *(0228) 0312051*

The interior is very ornate and the stylish setting creates an intimate and romantic atmosphere. The kitchen produces international dishes with a leaning towards France. Their carefully chosen wine list encompasses great wines from nine different countries. The service is impeccable and polite.

BONN-BAD GODESBERG Halbedel's Gasthaus
Rheinallee 47, 53173 **Tel** *(0228) 354253*

A stone's throw from the Rhine in an exclusive part of town in a nondescript villa. The chef concocts fantastic and interesting international cuisine and is constantly inventing new dishes. They cater to the serious wine lover, too, with more than 700 different wines. The service is first rate.

BRÜHL Seerose
Römerstraße 1–7, 50321 **Tel** *(02232) 2040*

This restaurant is in the Ramada Treff hotel, which is situated between Bonn and Cologne in a forested area. They prepare international food in a modern and colourfully designed dining area. Nearby is the Schloss Brühl which often hosts outdoor concerts of classical music.

DETMOLD Speisekeller im Rosental
Am Schlossplatz 7, 32756 **Tel** *(05231) 22267*

The decor of this modern gourmet restaurant has a warm Tuscan feeling about it. Vegetarians, so often overlooked, will be very satisfied with the large variety of delicious meals available. Much effort has gone into creating a good environment for dining and the service is excellent. In summer the terrace is open and has a view over the park.

DORTMUND Boomerang Australian Pub & Grill
Kuckelke 20, 44135 **Tel** *(0231) 5862911*

Lots of steak, lots of fried things and lots of beer. Such is the perception of Australian cuisine, and this restaurant is not bursting the bubble. The food is rigorous and heavy, and comes in impressive proportions. The atmosphere is unique and cheerful in a typically Australian manner.

DÜSSELDORF Libanon Restaurant
Berger Straße 19–21, 40213 **Tel** *(0211) 134917*

Guests are greeted by beautiful Middle-Eastern flair and style at this popular Lebanese restaurant. There is a large selection of authentic dishes with generous portions. The kitchen also caters for large functions of 20 or more people. There are belly-dancing shows in the evenings, adding to the already authentic atmosphere.

DÜSSELDORF Savini
Stromstraße 47, 40221 **Tel** *(0211) 393931*

This Italian restaurant is located in the harbour area of Düsseldorf and is very popular, so it is advised to book well in advance. The popularity is well deserved and their pasta dishes are just great – a particular favourite is the gnocchi with mascarpone spinach sauce. There is a good wine list as well.

DÜSSELDORF Canonicus
Neusser Tor 16, 40625 **Tel** *(0211) 289644*

Located in a house, each room is tasteful and intimate. They have a Western-oriented menu and an Eastern (Asian) menu, both of which offer the best of each world. The wine list is excellent, especially the French reds, including a 1986 Château Lafite Rothschild.

DÜSSELDORF Im Schiffchen
Kaiserswerther Markt 9, 40489 **Tel** *(0211) 401050*

Reservations should be made months in advance to this fabulous restaurant. It is one of only five restaurants in Germany to have been awarded three Michelin stars. The thoroughly informed staff will guide you through their extensive and creative menu, as well as their 900-strong wine list.

ESSEN Bonne Auberge
Witteringstraße 92, 45130 **Tel** *(0201) 783999*

French cuisine with various influences is offered here. Carpaccio is one of their strengths, with eight different varieties. Situated in the heart of Essen, just a few blocks from the Stadtgarten. The decor is stylish and modern, incorporating the architecture into the design and ambience. Friendly staff and a well-stocked wine cellar.

ESSEN Casino Zollverein
Gelsenkirchener Straße 181, 45309 **Tel** *(0201) 830240*

Located in an old mine, this casino and restaurant have a unique character. The styling and design is trendy, as is the food. They claim to "keep in touch" with the traditional miner's food, although the fillet of ostrich would probably not have appeared in the lunchbox of the average miner.

ESSEN Big Easy
Viehofer Platz 2, 45127 **Tel** *(0201) 202828*

This restaurant is a New Orleans-style venue, with live music and some great Cajun cooking, strong flavours and many interesting herbs and spices. The chef strays into many cuisines, from Indian to Thai, which creates an interesting menu that is always changing. You can also listen to some good jazz bands during your meal.

ESSEN Résidence
Auf der Forst 1, 45219 **Tel** *(02054) 8911*

Located in the beautiful Résidence Hotel, this restaurant attracts patrons from all over Germany. The holder of two Michelin stars, the chef produces irresistible cuisine that never fails to impress, particularly the fish dishes. The chef also gives private cooking lessons and is happy to chat with diners.

HAGEN Felsengarten
Wasserloses Tal 4, 58093 **Tel** *(02331) 3911 200*

This restaurant serves a wide variety of international dishes and caters to different tastes. The kitchen puts a lot of effort into the presentation of the food. The restaurant is located in the Mercure Hotel and there is an accompanying beer garden and terrace, which is pleasant in the summer months. It has modern, bright decor.

HÖXTER Entenfang
Godelheimer Straße 16, 37671 **Tel** *(05271) 97080*

An elegant restaurant with friendly staff, the cuisine is mainly French, with a few fantastic international dishes thrown in. Located in the Weserberghof Hotel, there is also live music on some evenings which creates a romantic mood. The dining area is characteristically German. The chef gives private cooking courses.

KÖLN Restaurant Pöttgen
Landmannstraße 19, 50825 **Tel** *(0221) 555246*

This traditional and cheerful restaurant has been in the Pöttgen family for four generations and is still going strong. The history of the restaurant and family can be seen in the charming decor. The food is always very tasty and is fantastic value. The chef has kept some dishes from the menus of his ancestors'.

KÖLN Fischers
Hohenstaufenring 53, 50674 **Tel** *(0221) 3108470*

This restaurant revolves around wine. The cellar is vastly stocked and they operate a wine club as well. The dining area is spacious and simple, which suits the cuisine which is earthy and focuses on fresh produce. They also have a wine bar and terrace, which is very pleasant in the evenings.

KÖLN Il Carpaccio
Lindenstraße 5, 50674 **Tel** *(0221) 236487*

This is one of the best-known Italian restaurants in Cologne. One of their secrets is the top-quality ingredients they use – always fresh and authentic. Their home-made pasta is quite simply fantastic. Every Friday and Saturday there is live music. Great food, stylish design and a good wine selection.

KÖLN Landhaus Kuckuck
Olympiaweg 2, 50933 **Tel** *(0221) 485360*

This restaurant is located in a quiet part of Cologne and has a reputation for its fine cuisine as well as its very extensive wine cellar. The menu is changed frequently and the chef makes good use of seasonal produce. The outside seating area has a very pleasant ambience. They are happy to cater for large functions and groups.

Key to Price Guide *see p526* **Key to Symbols** *see back cover flap*

KÖLN L'escalier

Brüsseler Straße 11, 50674 **Tel** *(0221) 2053998*

A French restaurant with a passion for cuisine. The elegant entrance reflects the style of the establishment, which is confirmed by the stylish dining area. Delicious food is on offer, especially the game dishes, and the service is fantastic. A special treat is their soufflé which takes 45 minutes to prepare, so be prepared for a wait.

KÖLN Börsen-Restaurant Maître

Unter Sachsenhausen 10–26, 50667 **Tel** *(0221) 133021*

A very elegant and romantic restaurant in the shadow of the Cologne Dom cathedral. The kitchen produces high quality French cuisine in a stunning location. The stylish yet comfortable dining area is an ideal place for a romantic evening, and it is a good idea to book ahead because it can suddenly become busy.

KÖLN La Vision

Kaygasse 2, 50676 **Tel** *(0221) 200 800*

Seated like a crown on the Hotel Im Wasserturm *(see p512)*, La Vision is on the top floor with a beautiful view over Cologne. The fine French cuisine is complemented by the outstanding wine list. The quality of the entire dining experience has earned the restaurant a Michelin star. There is also a terrace with panoramic views.

LEMGO Im Borke

Salzufler-Straße 132, 32657 **Tel** *(05266) 1691*

Housed in the Im Borke hotel *(see p512)*, this rustic little restaurant has a cosy charm. On the weekends it has a bustling and friendly atmosphere and attracts many people from the surrounding region. The menu is mainly regional cuisine with a number of international dishes as well, including some great Indian dishes.

MONSHAU Wiesenthal

Laufenstraße 82, 52156 **Tel** *(02472) 860*

The dining area of this restaurant is pleasant, mixing modernity with a refined style. Along with a bistro, the restaurant is located in the Carat Hotel. The cuisine is New German and the menu is changed often, with creative specials incorporating seasonal produce from the region.

MÜNSTER Alter Pulverturm

Breul 9, 8143 **Tel** *(0251) 45830*

This restaurant is where the old powder tower was sited, hence the name. The spot is quiet and peaceful and the adjoining beer garden is a great place to relax or meet friends before dining at the restaurant. They have an extensive menu with a variety of cuisines, including some very nice vegetarian dishes.

MÜNSTER Landhaus Eggert

Zur Haskenau 81, 48157 **Tel** *(0251) 328040*

The hotel and restaurant are family owned and run, and there is a personal approach to the service. The chef produces fantastic and varied menus, exploring international cuisine while also showcasing the region's best dishes. The setting is a peaceful country area and the hotel was once a farm.

MÜNSTER Villa Medici

Ostmarkstraße 15, 48145 **Tel** *(0251) 34218*

Boasting a simple design and imaginative food, this place is one of the best Italian restaurants in Germany. The dishes are wonderfully balanced and the presentation is genuinely exciting. There is a sophisticated simplicity to the cuisine, and the same can be said for the decor of the dining area, with colourful art contrasting the white walls.

PADERBORN Balthasar

Warburger Straße 28, 33098 **Tel** *(05251) 24448*

The kitchen in this attractive and modern restaurant enthusiastically mixes art with food. The chef uses a variety of interesting ingredients to create new and imaginative dishes, and also suggests wines that would complement the food. The extensive wine list includes a 1928 Sauternes.

TROISDORF Restaurant Forsthaus Telegraph

Mauspfad 3, 53842 **Tel** *(02241) 76649*

This restaurant serves international dishes in a very refined setting. The sauces are rich and diverse, with the chef combining the best of all styles and cuisines. The restaurant operates a catering service as well as a food outlet. It has become extremely popular because of its ever-changing and innovative menus, so book ahead.

WUPPERTAL Scarpati

Scheffelstraße 41, 42327 **Tel** *(0202) 784074*

As the name suggests, this restaurant and hotel has Italian heritage and does it proud with their cuisine and service. Their pasta dishes are fresh and rich; definitely worth the calories. The ambience is relaxed and intimate, and the dining area has a pleasant view over the garden. There are rooms for private dinners and functions.

XANTEN Hotel van Bebber

Klever Straße 21, 46509 **Tel** *(02801) 6623*

Located in the hotel of the same name, this restaurant produces excellent traditional regional cuisine. Particular favourites among the locals are the chef's fish dishes. Apart from their traditionally styled dining area they also have a unique wine cellar with occasional live piano performances.

LOWER SAXONY, HAMBURG AND BREMEN

BAHRENFELD Graceland
Stresemannstraße 374, 22761 **Tel** *(040) 89963100*

Cajun and Creole cooking, with more than a dash of an American influence, is on offer here. The food is really tasty and incorporates some spicy Central American cuisine as well. There is often live music and sometimes dancing at the restaurant, which has quite a large capacity. They do takeaway as well, if you need that fried catfish to go.

BRAUNSCHWEIG (BRUNSWICK) Herrendorf
Am Magnitor 1, 38100 **Tel** *(0531) 47130*

Proclaiming itself to cater to "everybody's gums", this restaurant does a fine job living up to this proclamation. Housed in a building that dates back to 1476, it is part of the Stadthotel Magnitor, and is quite modern in design. The kitchen produces great regional fare, sometimes straying into French territory with their sauces.

BREMEN Westfalia-Bierlachs
Langemarckstraße 38–42, 28199 **Tel** *(0421) 59020*

This charming restaurant has a number of different menus for different events and evenings. Their goose dishes are just fabulous and extensive, but their true speciality is fish. The decor is traditional and the atmosphere friendly. The restaurant itself is located in the Hotel Westfalia, which is a ten-minute walk from the town centre.

BREMEN L'Orchidée
Am Markt, 28195 **Tel** *(0421) 3059888*

L'Orchidée is housed in the oldest operating wine cellar in Germany, established over 600 years ago. There is a wine bar which offers over 1,000 different wines. The restaurant serves great international food in a truly magnificent dining area, complete with wood-panelled walls, chandeliers and wall paintings.

BREMEN Das Kleine Lokal
Besselstraße 40, 28203 **Tel** *(0421) 7949084*

Each dish is a surprise at this modern restaurant. The creative presentation is reinforced by the unorthodox plate designs and perfectly suited to the stylish design of the dining area. The portions are petite and delicious. The sommelier is thoroughly knowledgeable and helpfully chatty.

BREMEN Meierei
Im Bürgerpark, 28209 **Tel** *(0421) 3408619*

This restaurant was first opened in 1881. There is a Mediterranean flavour running through the menu, however, one should not overlook their fabulous rabbit *ragout*. The inside is inviting with a warm fireplace in the dining area which is dominated by earth tones. There is a large wine selection, especially Italian wines.

BÜCKEBURG Ambiente
Herminstraße 11, 31675 **Tel** *(05722) 9670*

True to its name, the Ambiente restaurant (in the hotel of the same name) has a very serene and enjoyable dining area, with high glass ceilings and lots of indoor plants. The cuisine is mainly German and Italian, with large portions. As well as the great dining area there is a little garden where guests may dine in the warmer months.

CELLE Camelot
Am Heiligen Kreuz 6, 29221 **Tel** *(05141) 6400*

Step back into the Middle Ages at Camelot, into what at first seems to be a redecorated dungeon. This restaurant creates an atmosphere emulating the days of knights and knaves, with cuisine to match. If you crave game dishes this is definitely the place for you. There are a number of shows in the evenings, fire-eating being just one example.

CELLE Endtenfang
Hannoversche Straße 55–56, 29221 **Tel** *(05141) 2010*

Located in the Fürstenhof Celle *(see p513)*, this is one of the most highly acclaimed restaurants in town. The chef produces fantastic French cuisine, with a number of Mediterranean influences as well. It has been awarded a Michelin star, not only for the great food but also for the outstanding service and unique location.

CLOPPENBURG Restaurant Margaux
Lange Straße 66, 49661 **Tel** *(04471) 2484*

This restaurant is located in the Hotel Schäfer. The young chef at this restaurant has a passion for cooking and it shows in the cuisine. There is a variety of different styles and ingredients to enjoy, with a special highlight being the bouillabaisse. There is a warm and friendly atmosphere.

EPPENDORF jus
Lehmweg 30, 20251 **Tel** *(040) 42949654*

Seasonally influenced dishes with its finger on the pulse of modern cuisine. The chef marries traditional ingredients with subtlety and confidence. It is a small restaurant, still new but it is fast building a healthy reputation. Because of its size and popularity, it is becoming necessary to make reservations.

Key to Price Guide *see p526* **Key to Symbols** *see back cover flap*

GOTTINGEN Restaurant Gaudi
€€€

Rote Straße 16, 37073 **Tel** *(0551) 5313001*

Dedicated to the life and works of the Spanish architect Antoni Gaudí (1852–1926), this restaurant provides some fine Spanish and Mediterranean cuisine. Apart from the exquisite fish dishes they also have a great tapas selection, which is popular at lunchtime. The design is unorthodox, just like Gaudi himself.

HAMBURG Au Quai
€€

Grosse Elbstraße 145, 22767 **Tel** *(040) 38037730*

Housed in a refurbished cold storage depot, the conversion has resulted in a fantastic place to try the best of Hamburg's seafood. Operated by a brother and sister, the kitchen reflects their heritage with great Mediterranean dishes and a subtle French influence that works well with the delicate fish-dominated menu.

HAMBURG Restaurant Nido
€€

Cremon 35–36, 20547 **Tel** *(040) 51310317*

Primarily focusing on Austrian cuisine, the chef makes fun little detours into Asian delicacies, and has a separate sushi menu accompanying the traditional menu. The design of the restaurant has also taken an Asiatic detour, which complements the fresh Japanese cuisine. The lunchtime menu is popular amongst business people.

HAMBURG Rive
€€

Van-Der-Smissen-Straße 1, 22767 **Tel** *(040) 3805919*

A great restaurant situated by the water, the dining area and terrace boast fantastic views of the harbour, which creates a romantic ambience. The kitchen prepares a lot of fish dishes, including a number of sushi and sashimi courses. There is a comprehensive wine list, incorporating many regional German wines.

HAMBURG Calla
€€€

Heiligengeistbrücke 4, 20459 **Tel** *(040) 368060*

The Calla is in the Steigenberger hotel along with a bistro and piano bar, which has live music. The high windows and open plan design create a bright atmosphere. The walls have been adorned with the designs of a Chinese restaurant. The menu has a very Asian flair to it, mixing a little European influence in as well.

HAMBURG Fischmarkt
€€€

Ditmar-Koel-Straße 1, 20459 **Tel** *(040) 363809*

A bustling, friendly restaurant where they create some very exciting fish dishes. Housed inside the fish market after which it is named, the restaurant is popular among tourists who visit the area. The ambience inside is relaxed yet professional, with great staff who are very helpful when it comes to selecting dishes.

HAMBURG Indochine
€€€

Neumühlen 11, 22763 **Tel** *(040) 39807880*

Opened in 2002, this restaurant is devoted to the cuisine of Southeast Asia. Many people come in groups and share the entrées and main courses as is the custom in the region. The set menus, while a bit pricier, are very well chosen. A good restaurant for vegetarians.

HAMBURG Fischereihafen-Restaurant
€€€€

Grosse Elbstraße 143, 22767 **Tel** *(040) 381816*

This is the place to go for fresh, delicious seafood (though other dishes are offered). The large menu is changed often to suit the seasons. The terrace overlooks the water and has one of the best views in the harbour. The list of famous guests is longer than the extensive wine list and reflects the great food and outstanding service.

HAMBURG Fischküche
€€€€

Kajen 12, 20459 **Tel** *(040) 365631*

Fresh fish and seafood are the fare in this restaurant. The decor leaves no doubt of the influence of the sea in this place, and the staff seem to know more about seafood than most fishermen. The crab dishes have earned the chef renown amongst the locals and visitors to the harbour. The wine list has been chosen with care.

HAMBURG Jacobs Restaurant
€€€€€

Elbchaussee 401–403, 22609 **Tel** *(040) 822550*

This restaurant, situated in the beautiful Hotel Louis C. Jacob, is among the best in the city. The cuisine is international with a definite French infusion. There is also a wine cellar that keeps connoisseurs happily occupied for hours, with the help of the master sommelier. There is an adjacent wine bar and a terrace.

HAMBURG Tafelhaus
€€€€€

Neumühlen 17, 22763 **Tel** *(040) 892760*

The chef in this elegant restaurant produces fantastic and innovative cuisine from all over the world. Of special renown are his Asiatic dishes. The terrace overlooks the harbour, although the dining area offers the more romantic atmosphere. The chef also gives cooking lessons to enthusiastic students.

HANNOVER Die Insel
€€€

Rudolf-von-Bennigsen-Ufer 81, 30519 **Tel** *(0511) 831214*

There is a picturesque view of nearby Lake Masch from the dining area. This restaurant attracts customers from the music industry to politics. The cuisine is hard to pin down, with some great regional dishes as well as some great oriental creations. The food is matched by the equally impressive wine selection.

HANNOVER Hindenburg Klassik   🔲🔁   €€€
Gneisenaustraße 55, 30175 **Tel** *(0511) 858588*

This restaurant has been set-up in a way to reflect a traditional Italian eating area with long tables to accommodate the largest of families. There is a comprehensive specials menu that changes daily, and there is always their fantastic home-made pasta, which makes this place a favourite among the locals.

HANNOVER Clichy   🔲🔁🔲🔁   €€€€
Weißekreuzstraße 31, 30161 **Tel** *(0511) 312447*

The chef here conjures up some fantastic traditional German and French dishes. With rich sauces and strong flavours, the menu is forceful and entertaining. The staff are courteous and very helpful when it comes to choosing from the menu and wine list. Quite a busy restaurant, so make reservations.

HANNOVER Landhaus Ammann   🔲🔁   €€€€
Hildesheimer Straße 185, 30173 **Tel** *(0511) 830818*

This restaurant is in the Landhaus Ammann hotel, which is an elegant establishment in the heart of Hannover. The seasoned chef creates delicious, well-balanced dishes from the best ingredients and produce. The wine cellar is perhaps one of the best stocked in Germany, with some very rare wines.

HANNOVER Restaurant Titus   🔲🔁🔁   €€€€
Wiehbergstraße 98, 30519 **Tel** *(0511) 835524*

This restaurant has one of the more unorthodox restaurant interiors. The fabulous creations that come out of the kitchen keep pace with the decor. The grilled venison in bitter chocolate is but one example of the innovative and experimental cuisine. They have a terrace which is open in the warmer months.

HANNOVER Gallo Nero   🔲🔁   €€€€€
Gross-Buchholzer Kirchweg 72b, 30655 **Tel** *(0511) 5463434*

The "Black Rooster" offers top-quality Northern Italian cuisine, ranging from basic flavours and produce to more refined sauces and spices. The interior of the restaurant resembles a Tuscan art gallery, which gives a very intimate and unique atmosphere to enjoy their unpretentious food. They have a large selection of Italian wines.

HANNOVER Le Chalet   🔲🔁   €€€€€
Isernhagener Straße 21, 30161 **Tel** *(0511) 319588*

An intimate dining experience in an elegant part of town. The French cuisine has won popularity amongst patrons with their rich sauces and exquisite salads. The staff blend into the background until they are needed, at which time they seem to materialize out of thin air. This is particularly helpful when selecting wines, as they are experts.

KÖNIGSLUTTER Merlin   🔲🔁   €€
Braunschweigerstraße 21a, 38154 **Tel** *(05353) 5030*

Part of the beautiful Königshof Hotel (*see p515*), the Merlin is internationally recognized for its fantastic cuisine and character. During the day the high windows create a bright, open atmosphere and at night time the dark surrounds give a feeling of intimacy. The staff are generous with their time and the service is very good.

OLDENBURG Kiebitz-Stube   🔲🔁   €
Europaplatz 4-6, 26123 **Tel** *(0441) 8080*

There are a few bistros and restaurants in the City Club Hotel, with the Kiebitz-Stube being the most elegant. There is a formal atmosphere in the evenings, with well-constructed set menus, but lunchtime is less formal. A terrace opens out over a peaceful garden, where it is possible to dine in the warmer months.

OSNABRÜCK Vila Real   🔲🔁   €€€€€
Natruper-Tor-Wall 1, 49076 **Tel** *(0541) 609627*

An innovative restaurant that combines fresh ingredients with imagination. The chef alternates between Italian and Mediterranean cuisine and succeeds in every domain. The crayfish ravioli is just sublime. There is a large selection of wines, which is partly due to the adjoining Enoteca wine shop, which also has tapas evenings and wine tastings.

STADTHAGEN Fischhaus Blanke   🔲🔁   €€€€
Rathauspassage 5, 31655 **Tel** *(05721) 81786*

This restaurant has been serving the freshest seafood in town for over 80 years. They serve a vast variety of different fish, shellfish and everything else that lives in water. It is unpretentious and cosy, and the food speaks for itself. The owners have a seafood outlet which supplies superbly fresh produce for the restaurant.

WOLFENBÜTTEL Parkhotel Altes Kaffeehaus   🔲🔁   €€
Harztorwall 18, 38300 **Tel** *(05331) 8880*

Part of the Parkhotel (*see p516*), the Altes Kaffeehaus is quite an elegant restaurant, offering good value cuisine with a number of vegetarian dishes. There is a wine grotto in the cellar which is quite attractive and has a vaulted brick roof that adds to the ambience. The overall cuisine is basic, regional fare with large portions.

WOLFSBURG La Fontaine   🔲🔁   €€€€€
Gifhorner Straße 25, 38442 **Tel** *(05362) 9400*

La Fontaine serves cuisine that refuses to be categorized, combining the best of all styles and ingredients. A speciality is combining regional and international produce and ingredients to create innovative new tastes, and their venison with Shiitake mushrooms is a good example. There is a dining terrace open in the summer months.

Key to Price Guide *see p526* **Key to Symbols** *see back cover flap*

SCHLESWIG-HOLSTEIN

AHRENSBURG Berlin Milljöh   🔲   €
Große Straße 15, 22926 **Tel** *(04102) 52919*

This happy little restaurant is a fantastic place to enjoy local dishes at very affordable prices. More a tavern than a restaurant, the food is still satisfying and authentic. The atmosphere is a little dark because of the worn wooden furnishings, though it does have a comfortable and friendly ambience.

AHRENSBURG Le Marron   🔲🔲🔲🔲   €€€
Lübecker Straße 10a, 22926 **Tel** *(04102) 2300*

Le Marron is in the Park Hotel Ahrensburg. The restaurant scores highly among international critics, especially for its fantastic and friendly service. The food is diverse with influences from all over the culinary spectrum. There is also a comfortable winter garden. They welcome families and there is a playroom for children.

BAD MALENTE Gartenhotel Weisser Hof   🔲🔲   €€
Vossstraße 45, 23714 **Tel** *(04523) 99250*

Set in a peaceful rural environment, this restaurant is a cosy place to sample the regional food. There is a warm and friendly atmosphere and the portions are generous. It is part of the Weisser Hof hotel *(see p516)*, which is situated in parkland. Many customers combine a trip to the relaxing wellness area in the hotel with a visit to the restaurant.

FLENSBURG Rôtisserie   🔲🔲   €
Alte Zollstraße 44, 24955 **Tel** *(0461) 7020*

This restaurant delivers elegance and flair in both its traditional German cuisine and service. Located in the Hotel des Nordens, there is a French theme running through the design of the dining area, which is both spacious and intimate. The hotel is just a short drive from Flensburg, on the Danish border.

FLENSBURG Im Alten Speicher   🔲   €€€
Speicherlinie 44, 24937 **Tel** *(0461) 12018*

Generous portions and delicious seafood dishes. This is quite a large restaurant with a number of dining rooms and areas. They are well set-up for functions and large groups, and have a catering service as well. There is a somewhat understated outside terrace, which is best enjoyed in the afternoons.

KIEL Im Park Parkrestaurant   🔲🔲   €€€
Niemannsweg 102, 24105 **Tel** *(0431) 88110*

Set in a peaceful wooded area, with a beautiful landscaped garden, Parkrestaurant is in the Parkhotel Kieler Kaufmann. The terrace has wonderful sea views. The cuisine is New German, although there is a dedicated regional set menu that showcases the best of the local fare. There is also a good wine selection.

LÜBECK Historischer Weinkeller   🔲🔲   €€€
Koberg 6–8, 23552 **Tel** *(0451) 76234*

This unique restaurant is located in an 800-year-old wine cellar under a historic hospital. There is a medieval tone to the restaurant, which has retained the ambience of its heritage while at the same time creating a light and friendly atmosphere. Their game dishes have won the hearts of locals and tourists.

LÜBECK Wullenwever   🔲🔲   €€€€€
Beckergrube 71, 23552 **Tel** *(0451) 704333*

A very elegant restaurant that offers a number of unique rooms and dining areas, the chef is liberal with his creations, happily giving out recipes to interested patrons. The set menus have been artfully chosen to give a perfect balance of tastes, and there are wine suggestions for each dish. It has become rather well-known, so book ahead.

RATZEBURG Hansa Hotel   🔲🔲   €€
Schrangenstraße 25, 23909 **Tel** *(04541) 2094*

The Hansa hotel and restaurant is in a quiet area on an island in Ratzeburg. The menu changes every fortnight and makes good use of seasonal vegetables and fish. The dining area is relatively small, which creates a mellow atmosphere and emphasizes the polite and unobtrusive service of the friendly staff.

SCHLESWIG Strandhalle   🔲🔲   €€
Strandweg 2, 24837 **Tel** *(04621) 9090*

This is a cheerful restaurant in a pleasant hotel. There is a definite family atmosphere and the restaurant is often booked for celebrations and functions. The restaurant and hotel are family owned and the staff are very welcoming. An open fireplace creates a cosy feeling in the wintertime and a beautiful terrace is used in the summer.

SIEK Alte Schule   🔲🔲🔲   €€€€
Hauptstraße 44, 22962 **Tel** *(04107) 9114*

Located in an old schoolhouse, this restaurant has been going strong for close to 30 years now and has been run by two successive generations. It serves mostly regional and German dishes, with some French affiliations. There are a few good vegetarian meals and a very good wine list with many German and French producers.

SYLT Stadt Hamburg   €€€
Strandstraße 2, 25980 **Tel** *(04651) 8580*

There is a bistro and gourmet restaurant in the Stadt Hamburg hotel, both offering interesting and varied cuisine. The gourmet area focuses on French and Mediterranean dishes, while the bistro explores the regional side. There is also a relaxing fireplace lounge which can be enjoyed before and after meals.

SYLT Fährhaus   €€€€€
Heefwai 1, 25980 **Tel** *(04651) 93970*

This highly regarded restaurant has become one of the best on Sylt and is justifiably popular. The young chef, who has been awarded a Michelin star, creates miracles with contrasting flavours and ingredients. The sommelier is happy to guide you through the 780 wines they have in the cellar.

SYLT Restaurant Jörg Müller   €€€€€
Süderstraße 8, 25980 **Tel** *(04651) 27788*

This leading restaurant is one of the most famous on the island, and attracts customers from all over Europe. The dining area is comfortable and unpretentious. The hotel is secondary in status to the restaurant and there are many packages incorporating dining. There is also cheerful and enthusiastic service.

UETERSEN La Cave   €€€
Marktstraße 2, 25436 **Tel** *(04122) 3640*

This restaurant delivers gourmet cuisine from Southern France and the Mediterranean. Of particular renown are their fish dishes, which are constantly changing in keeping with seasonal availability. The staff are helpful and friendly. As you would expect, they have a good selection of French wines.

MECKLENBURG-LOWER POMERANIA

AHLBECK Villa Auguste Viktoria   €
Bismarkstr. 1–2, 17419 **Tel** *(038378) 24 10*

This adorable restaurant is located in the hotel of the same name. Friendly and knowledgeable staff cater to guests with first-rate attention. Ask for one of the daily house specials or something from the menu. The emphasis is on fish dishes, but many other items can also be recommended. Children are welcome.

BAD DOBERAN Residenz   €€€
Prof.-Dr.-Vogel-Str. 16–18, Heiligendamm, 18209 **Tel** *(038203) 740 6210*

A comfortable restaurant in the Residenz Hotel, which is part of the Romantik hotel chain. The extensive menu includes regional and national dishes, as well as cuisine from the four corners of the globe, with an emphasis on European. The wine and beer lists are respectable.

DASSOW Schloss-Restaurant Schloß Lütgenhof   €€€€
Ulmenweg 10, 23942 **Tel** *(38826) 8250*

Dine like royalty at this castle by the Baltic Sea. A magnificent dining area is completed by fine cutlery, crisp tablecloths and chandeliers. The menu highlights modern versions of more traditional regional and international dishes. Try the *Tournedos à la Rossini*, or Austrian pancakes with raisins and baked plums.

GREIFSWALD Wallensteinkeller   €
Hafenstr. 12b, 18439 **Tel** *(03831) 309274*

This is one of two rustic restaurants in the region owned by the same proprietor. Finger foods and soups feature on the menu as well as potatoes and roasted pork entrées. Enjoy one of the many draught beers. The staff are friendly and there is an engaging atmosphere (look for the authentic suit of armour near the entrance).

GUSTROW Marktkrug   €
Markt 14, 18273 **Tel** *(03843) 68 12 82*

This restaurant is situated in the centre of town and has two floors and a relaxing beer garden. The delicious food reminds you of typical Mecklenburgian home-cooked meals. Plums are very popular in regional gastronomy and you will find them here in abundance. Try the *Meckelbörger Rippenbraten*.

HERINGSDORF Kräuterstuben   €€
Puschkinstr. 10, 17424 **Tel** *(038378) 26 50*

The elegant restaurant is part of the Oasis Hotel and includes a café with relaxing terrace and a chic bistro. The food is high quality and very tasty. Come in summer and lounge in one of the beach chairs for hire and enjoy the sun as cold cocktails, beers or other drinks are served.

NEUBRANDENBURG Sankt Georg   €
St-Georg-Str. 6, 17033 **Tel** *(0395) 544 37 88*

The restaurant of the St Georg Hotel is conveniently situated on the edge of town, towards Rostock, next to the Treptow Gate. Guests can sample regional dishes or enjoy the classic German tradition of sipping beer in the beer garden in good weather. The staff are incredibly friendly and good-humoured.

Key to Price Guide *see p526* **Key to Symbols** *see back cover flap*

NEUBRANDENBURG Zur Alten Münze
Burg 5, Burg Stargard, 17094 **Tel** *(039603) 27 00*

A beautiful provincial estate with a wine *Stube* and restaurant on site. Step back in time and enjoy centuries-old traditions in this very uncomplicated eatery. The selection of wines is very good. The dishes on offer are typical of the region and high quality, made with the freshest of ingredients.

RALSWIEK/RÜGEN Schlossrestaurant Ralswiek
Parkstr. 35, 18528 **Tel** *(03838) 20 32 0*

This restaurant is in the Hotel Ralswiek, which is a former castle. Service is very attentive and the staff are warm and welcoming. The menu offers dishes based on international cuisine. Desserts include lemon panna cotta with wild berries and a wonderful tiramisu – both are very highly recommended.

ROSTOCK Silo 4
Am Strande 3d, 18055 **Tel** *(0381) 458 58 00*

This restaurant is right by the water and overlooks the docks. It has plenty of windows and great views. The service is courteous and they have a great wine list, including wines from Spain, Italy, Germany and South Africa. Check out the very cool bar, which radiates different colours of light during the evening.

ROSTOCK Zur Kogge
Wokrenter Str. 27, 18055 **Tel** *(0381) 4934493*

This restaurant is part of the oldest guesthouse in Rostock. The establishment's long history and resulting memorabilia decorate the walls. As you would expect, fish and seafood dominate the menu and are prepared well. Some vegetarian options can be found on the menu. There are several wines to choose from.

ROSTOCK Chezann
Mühlenstr. 28, 18119 **Tel** *(0381) 5107177*

A wonderfully modern bistro near the Seepromenade. Its atmosphere is tranquil and chic. Warm lighting and fresh flowers help create a fine dining experience. Try one of the game or fish dishes, and the desserts are incredibly good. A full vegetarian menu is available. They have an extensive wine list. Highly recommended.

RÜGEN Poseidon
Lottumstr. 1, 18609 **Tel** *(038393) 26 69*

A large and spacious restaurant where you can enjoy your meal in the restaurant or on the terrace in good weather. The focus is on Italian and German cooking with good quality ingredients. Advance booking is usually not required in the evenings, but it is preferred that larger parties should call in advance.

RÜGEN Orangerie
Zeppelinstr. 8, 18609 **Tel** *(038393) 50444*

A small, elegant restaurant in the Hotel Vier Jahreszeiten, specializing in traditional fish dishes, served in varying styles. The menu focuses on both healthy as well as more indulgent dishes, so something is available for all tastes. Renowned locally for both its menu and clientèle, reservations are advisable, especially at the weekends.

SCHWERIN Zum Stadtkrug
Wismarsche Straße 126, 19053 **Tel** *(0385) 5936693*

A microbrewery built in 1936 where tradition is central – the beer is still brewed in accordance to 1516 brewery laws. The decor is rustic and antique but comfortable. Try one of the regional dishes or unique internationally influenced entrées. The restaurant also has a beer garden. Take a look at the copper brewing tanks.

SCHWERIN Weinhaus Uhle
Schusterstr. 13–15, 19055 **Tel** *(0385) 562956*

This traditional restaurant is one of the best in town and is situated near the castle, theatre and cathedral. Excellent regional and French dishes are served in the chic restaurant, the knight's hall and the wine hall. The *Mecklenburger Zander* (pike-perch) is worth trying. They have some excellent wines – a great destination for connoisseurs.

SCHWERIN Schröter´s
Schliemannstr. 2, 19055 **Tel** *(0385) 5507698*

Stylish and chic, this address in Schwerin is a great place to eat. They produce some of the most interesting and innovative flavour combinations in the region. The cuisine is international, though mostly European, and its reputation for excellent cooking is well-deserved. The wine list includes mostly European producers and is very good.

STRALSUND Tafelfreuden
Jungfernstieg 5a, 18437 **Tel** *(03831) 29 92 60*

This modern restaurant is situated in a converted house. The unpretentious decor creates a tranquil and comfortable atmosphere. The menu focuses on German and Mediterranean dishes. Try the *Zarzuela*, a Spanish fish soup, as a starter or one of the pork dishes. A children's menu is also available.

WISMAR Stadt Hamburg
Am Markt 24, 23966 **Tel** *(03841) 23 90*

This hotel-restaurant is conveniently situated near the market square. They serve filling German dishes, as well as lighter Mediterranean cuisine. There are several vegetarian options on the menu. Join other guests on the terrace for amazing views of the city. They welcome children and the restaurant has wheelchair access.

SHOPPING IN GERMANY

Germany is known for its regional handicrafts, high quality manufacturing, good wines and beers, as well as wonderful bread, cakes and fresh produce. Make sure you sample some of the various cakes from the Konditorei. Organic food and produce is also big in Germany, more so than elsewhere in Europe. All towns have the usual international brands of clothing and accessories,

Black Forest cuckoo clock

as do German department stores. The food markets are a real treat for seasonal local produce and are a meeting place for locals once or twice a week. The pedestrian precinct is also common in German town centres where there is usually a department store, a post office, boutiques and a weekly market, as well as cosy cafés and ice-cream parlours. Often it is considered the social hub of the town.

OPENING HOURS

It was only in 1996 that the law was relaxed and shops were allowed to remain open until 8pm weekdays and until 4pm Saturdays. As a general rule, shops open between 9–10am and close at 8pm. Department stores are also open until 8pm. In smaller towns, shops will often close at lunchtime from 12:30–2:30pm and in the evening at 6:30pm. On the last four Saturdays leading up to Christmas, shops stay open until 6pm (known as a "long Saturday"). The only shops opening at all on Sundays are some of the bakeries and cake shops, and only then for a few hours in the morning. Everything shuts on public holidays. Outside these hours the only places open are petrol stations or railway kiosks. Dispensing chemists work on a rota so that there is always one open 24 hours in each town. Each chemist displays a sign in the window saying which one is on duty.

METHODS OF PAYMENT AND VAT REFUNDS

Cash is widely used for small items and at markets. Large department stores take credit cards, as do international chains of boutiques. Smaller shops will only accept the local E-Card or debit card and no cheques, so visitors are advised to use cash where credit cards are not taken. Cash machines are widely available, though some are inside the bank and only accessible during opening hours.

Visitors from countries outside the EU can claim a VAT refund (*Mehrwertsteuer*) in shops displaying the Tax-Free sign. Ask for a special form to be completed and, on leaving the country, all forms have to be stamped for a refund at the border, which may be given on the spot or sent to your address. Goods bought tax-free must remain unopened in the original packaging for a valid refund at the border.

SALES

End of season goods are sold off at a discounted price during the twice-yearly sales (*Schlussverkauf*) – in summer at the end of July and in winter at the end of January. Depending on trading, discounts of 30 to 70 per cent may be given.

Food market in Munich selling fresh local farmers' produce

GREEN SHOPPING

Germans are very ecologically aware when it comes to shopping and recycling. They buy locally when it comes to basics and fresh fruit and vegetables, supporting local farmers and small businesses. Shoppers can be seen all over the country with their wicker shopping baskets at markets and local stores, and any additional bags are reusable cotton totes, rather than plastic bags. Cotton bags are also available to buy at cash desks in every supermarket or department store, and you are always asked if you need a plastic bag or whether you can do without. Organic shopping has boomed. Several organic supermarkets

One of Germany's very popular organic supermarkets

have opened up in the cities, selling fresh and packaged food, cosmetics, clothing and household goods.

FASHION

What Germany does best in the way of clothing and accessories is casualwear, jeanswear, sportswear and outerwear. Typical brands originating in Germany are Esprit, S. Oliver, Hugo Boss, Bogner, Adidas and Puma. German fashion design is classic, purist and discreet.

Although it is not on a par with Italy or France, well-known names on the international scene include Jil Sander, Strenesse, Wolfgang Joop, Escada and the famous couturier Karl Lagerfeld. Classic department store chains are Karstadt and Galeria Kaufhof, and independent ones are Ludwig Beck in Munich and KaDeWe in Berlin. Speciality stores (*Fachhandel*) are still common in German towns, especially for leather goods and homeware. International chains have a high presence, though mixed brand boutiques are still thriving.

Factory outlets are another way of getting hold of German design, albeit for seconds or reduced goods. Metzingen has a high concentration – Hugo Boss was the first outlet, followed by Bogner, Jil Sander and Escada. Other stores worth trying here are Villeroy & Boch in Mettlach and Puma in Herzogenaurach.

High Fashion in KaDeWe department store, Berlin

REGIONAL PRODUCTS

There are many high quality regional products on sale throughout Germany which make ideal souvenirs. The most common are glass from Saxony and Bavaria, porcelain and ceramics from Meissen in Saxony, and gourmet products and intricate carved wooden objects, such as cuckoo clocks, from the Black Forest. Traditional toys, dolls and dolls houses are common around the Nürnberg area with its long standing reputation of toy manufacturing and traditional Christmas markets. In terms of food, marzipan is a speciality of Lübeck, gingerbread comes from Nürnberg, jams from the Black Forest, cheese from Allgäu, ham from Westphalia, and each region has its own special sausages.

MARKETS

Once or twice a week, local farmers set up their stalls in town centres in the market square or a car park. They sell farm produce from the

Gingerbread *(Lebkuchen)* on sale at a market stall

region, as well as imported goods, such as exotic fruits. It is a colourful, lively sight full of local flavour. Flea markets are also popular all over Germany.

FOOD AND DRINK

Wine and beer are readily available at supermarkets. Specialist wine stores are also common in most towns. Germans drink a lot of sparkling water at home, often mixed with the widely produced sparkling apple juice (*Apfelsaft-schorle*), as well as beer, wine and other soft drinks. All these are bought at the wholesaler (*Getränkemarkt*) with a deposit on bottles and crates. Local food is best sought in the markets, though supermarkets and specialist delicatessen offer a good choice as well.

Traditonal beer tankard

SIZE CHART

Women's dresses, coats and skirts

European	36	38	40	42	44	46	48
British	10	12	14	16	18	20	22
American	8	10	12	14	16	18	20

Women's shoes

European	36	37	38	39	40	41
British	3	4	5	6	7	8
American	5	6	7	8	9	10

Men's suits

European	44	46	48	50	52	54	56	58 (size)
British	34	36	38	40	42	44	46	48 (inches)
American	34	36	38	40	42	44	46	48 (inches)

Men's shirts (collar size)

European	36	38	39	41	42	43	44	45 (cm)
British	14	15	15½	16	16½	17	17½	18 (inches)
American	14	15	15½	16	16½	17	17½	18 (inches)

Men's shoes

European	39	40	41	42	43	44	45	46
British	6	7	7½	8	9	10	11	12
American	7	7½	8	8½	9½	10½	11	11½

OUTDOOR ACTIVITIES AND SPECIALIST HOLIDAYS

Germany is home to some of the most active holiday-makers in the world, so it is certainly fitting that there is an abundance of leisure activities available throughout the country. Outdoor pursuits of every kind are readily accessible, from mountain sports, such as climbing, skiing and hiking, to water sports,

Holiday-makers on a yacht

such as sailing, water-skiing and diving. Numerous other, slightly less adventurous activities such as golf, tennis, biking and spas are available and all are thoroughly organized and regulated. Any regional tourist office can provide you with detailed information and advice about planning your outdoor activities.

Walking in the Trettachtal valley in the Bavarian Alps

GENERAL SPORTING INFORMATION

The **Deutscher Sportbund** can provide a great deal of general information about sport in Germany.

WALKING AND HIKING

Walking trails are everywhere in Germany, from the most demanding of Alpine trails to gentler excursions in the Erzgebirge *(see p166)*, Thuringian Forest *(see pp190–91)* and the Black Forest *(see pp326–7)*.

Before setting off on an expedition you should get maps showing the walking trails in your chosen region. Detailed information can be obtained from the **Deutscher Volkssportverband e.V.** (German Sports Federation) or the **Deutscher Wander-verband** (German Hiking Club). Guided walking excursions can also be organized through the local

tourist offices or by contacting the **Verband Deutscher Gebirgs- und Wandervereine e.V.** (German Mountaineering and Hiking Club). The **DAV Summit Club** is also a very useful source of information.

CYCLING

Cycling is a great way of enjoying the German countryside. In most towns and tourist areas, bicycles can be hired for just a few days or for a week or more. A bike can easily be transported on trains and on the urban U-Bahn or S-Bahn trains for a minimal fee. You will find that most towns and cities are bike-friendly with cycle lanes and plenty of bike stands. For those interested in mountain biking and more adventurous cycling there are many great places to visit, and the **ADFC (Allgemeiner Deutscher Fahrrad-Club)** (German Cycling Federation) can supply maps, guidebooks and advice.

WATER SPORTS

Germans enjoy all kinds of water sports. Water-skiing and wake-boarding are extremely popular, especially at lakes equipped with static towing lines, where you pay an hourly fee and can take as many trips skiing around the lake as you want. The **Deutscher Wasserski- und Wakeboard Verband e.V.** can provide detailed advice on locations and prices.

There is excellent sailing in the lakeland areas of Mecklenburg *(see pp468–9)*, the coastal regions and on Lake Constance *(see pp320–21)*. As is the case in most countries, you must demonstrate sailing knowledge before being allowed to hire a full-sized boat or small catamaran by showing a valid sailing licence. To find out more about sailing locations, boat hires and regulations, contact the **Deutscher Segler-Verband e.V.** There are also plenty of opportunities for

Cyclists outside a tavern in Rhineland-Palatinate

scuba diving, mostly centred on the lakes or the protected coastal regions. The **Verband Deutscher Sporttaucher (VDST) e.V.** (German Divers' Association) can provide up-to-date advice.

Canoe trips can be taken on many of the country's rivers – from calm and picturesque stretches of water and the canals of the Spreewald *(see p141)*, to exhilarating adventures in rapidly flowing Alpine streams that demand professional skill.

GOLF AND TENNIS

Over the last decade or so golf has become hugely popular in Germany and the number of courses has increased. Golf is usually played at a club, however.

Golfing on the Castle Hotel course in Kronberg, Hesse

You usually need to prove a certain level of golfing proficiency before you are allowed onto the course. This can be achieved by showing a membership card from a course or club back home. Alternatively, look for one of the "Pay & Play" courses, which can be found throughout the country and usually have only six holes. For further information contact the **Deutscher Golf Verband e.V.**

Most large German towns have tennis courts that can be hired for a few hours and there is almost always a private tennis club in all the sizeable towns and cities. For more information on how to make a booking, contact the **Deutscher Tennis Bund e.V.**

Canoeing on a stretch of the River Main in Miltenberg

SKIING AND MOUNTAIN SPORTS

The most renowned centre for skiing is still Garmish-Partenkirchen *(see p280)*. Other regions such as the Black Forest *(see pp326–7)* and the Erzgebirge *(see p166)* also offer skiing. Some of the larger cities have indoor skiing halls, though they are a poor substitute for the Alps *(see pp204–5)*. Cross-country skiing is also popular, and there are many well-prepared routes. Information can be obtained from local tourist information offices or contact the **Deutschen Skiverbandes e.V. DSV Haus des Ski** (German Ski Association).

The Alps are the centre of German climbing. Here you can find sport climbers mixing with Alpinists. The Allgäu region is probably the most well-known place for climbers but challenges can also be found in the Ries basin. The **Verband Deutscher Berg- und Skiführer (VDBS)** (Association of German Mountain and Ski Guides) can help you with hiring a guide.

Interesting rock formations that provide memorable challenges are not only to be found in the Alps, but throughout Germany. Places such as the Harz Forest *(see p147)*, Fichtelgebirge and the Schwäbische Alb *(see pp300–1)* are all outstanding places for sport climbing. Also, you can find indoor climbing gyms in most cities. The **Deutsche Alpine Verein (DAV) Bundesgeschäftsste lle** (German Alpine Association) can help with all your climbing requirements.

NATIONAL PARKS

Germany has a richly varied landscape, from mountains to coasts, and has many nature reserves, biosphere reserves and national parks. From the swamp-like Spreewald *(see p141)* to the lush forests and mountain peaks of the Bavarian Forest *(see p257)*, each park has its own spectacular natural characteristics and offers a range of different visitor services and facilities.

All parks have sign-posted trails and most have special maps for walking, biking or jogging tours. These are also excellent locations for observing and enjoying the flora and fauna of Germany's various regions. Many parks have notices posted to inform visitors about the animals and plants indigenous to the area. To find out more about the various locations and holidays available in Germany's national parks and nature reserves contact the **Verband Deutscher Naturparke** or **Europarc Deutschland e.V.**

Mountain sports in the Schildenstein Mangfall mountains

CAMPING AND CARAVANNING

During the months of July, August and September there are a great many foreign holiday-makers on Germany's Autobahns heading for the camping parks. The word "camping" in Germany means primarily caravanning, not pitching a tent. Most sites are privately owned and offer a lot of extras. The majority have wash facilities, snack stands or restaurants as well as small shops and play-grounds. The more upscale parks will offer electricity as well as group activities, caravans and bungalows for hire. To find out more contact the **Deutscher Camping-Club e.V.** Tent-pitching holidays are also possible and this is strongly regulated in order to avoid misuse of national parks. Tents are often allowed in the camping parks mentioned above and many national parks have places set aside for tents and campfires. **Backpacker Network Germany e.V.** is a good resource for information about camping.

Spielgau, the well-known hiking spot in the Bavarian Forest

HISTORIC AND SCENIC ROUTES

Germany has over 50 official driving routes. These routes highlight the best features of an individual region. The following are just a few of many excellent drives. The **Burgenstraße e.V** (Castle Road) is over 1,000 km (620 miles) long, from Mannheim *(see p294)* through Bavaria to Prague. It offers plenty of romantic castles and historical

Burgenstraße (Castle Road) scenic route following the Rhine

sites. The **Deutsche Märchenstraße** (Fairytale Route) covers more than 600 km (370 miles) from Bremen *(see pp430–33)* to Hanau *(see p377)*, linking more than 70 towns and villages associated with the Brothers Grimm and the realm of fairytales, sagas, myths and legends. The **Deutsche Weinstraße e.V.** (Wine Route) *(see p347)* is 85 km (52 miles) and runs from Bad Dürkheim to Bad Berzabern. The **Touristik Arbeitsgemeinschaft Romantische Straße** (Romantic Road) is Germany's most famous and popular tourist route. It runs for 350 km (217 miles) through a rich and varied landscape along the River Main to the Alps. The **Tourismusverband Ruppiner Land e.V. "Deutsche Tonstraße"** (Ceramics Route) is a circular route running 215 km (134 miles) through the Ruppiner Land area of northern Brandenburg *(see pp130–31)*.

SPECIALIST HOLIDAYS

Language tours offer you the chance to immerse yourself in German culture. Living arrangements range from homes to hotels and hostels, depending upon budget. The **Goethe Institute** is the best place for information on this type of holiday.

Wine holidays are becoming more commonplace because German wines are coming back into popularity. Most winemakers offer tastings and small meals, but some also

offer packaged holidays. To find out more about wine holidays contact **Deutsches Weininstitut GmbH** or **Viniversität – Die Weinschule GmbH**.

There are equestrian centres in many parts of Germany where visitors can ride under supervision or head off on their own. Specialized weekends or week-long riding vacations are available throughout Germany. More information can be obtained from the **Deutsche Reiterliche Vereinigung e. V**.

SPA VACATIONS

Germany has more than 350 health and spa resorts, as well as numerous hotels and holiday centres, where your wellbeing is the top priority. Cultural delights, culinary experiences, sights of historical importance and physical activites all form part of the German philosophy of looking after yourself, known as "Das Wellness". Health and fitness breaks are available all year round and facilities vary from the minimalist ultra-modern to marble and gold imperial luxury, with everything in between. Each region has something special to offer, though some of the most well-known spas are in the Black Forest *(see pp326–7)*, on the East Frisian Islands *(see p428)* and in Schleswig-Holstein *(see pp455–65)*. The **Deutscher Heilbäder-verband e. V.** can help you find the right spa and holiday package.

Wine from the Mosel

DIRECTORY

GENERAL SPORTING INFORMATION

Deutscher Sportbund
Otto-Fleck-Schneise 12,
Frankfurt am Main.
Tel (069) 67 000.
www.dsb.de

WALKING AND HIKING

DAV Summit Club
Am Perlacher Forst 186,
81545 München.
Tel (089) 64 24 00.

Deutscher Volkssportverband e.V.
Fabrikstraße 8,
D-84503 Altötting.
Tel (086) 71 80 71.
www.dvv-wandern.de

Deutscher Wanderverband
Wilhelmshöher Allee
157–159, D-34121 Kassel.
Tel (0561) 938 730.
www.dtwanderverband.de

Verband Deutscher Gebirgs- und Wandervereine e.V.
Wilhelmshöher Allee
157–159, 34121 Kassel.
Tel (0561) 938 730.
www.wanderverband.de

CYCLING

ADFC (Allgemeiner Deutscher Fahrrad-Club)
Bundesgeschäftsstelle,
Postfach 10 77 47,
28077 Bremen.
Tel (0421) 34 62 90.
www.adfc.de

WATER SPORTS

Deutscher Segler-Verband e.V.
Gründgensstr. 18,
22309 Hamburg.
Tel (040) 632 00 90.
www.dsv.org

Deutscher Wasserski- und Wakeboard Verband e.V.
Gründgensstr. 18,
D-22309 Hamburg.
Tel (040) 63 99 87 32.
www.wasserski-online.de

Verband Deutsche Sporttaucher (VDST) e.V.
Bundesgeschäftsstelle,
Berliner Str. 312,
63067 Offenbach.
Tel (069) 9819025.
www.vdst.de

GOLF AND TENNIS

Deutscher Golf Verband e.V.
Postfach 21 06,
65011 Wiesbaden.
Tel (0611) 990 200.
www.golf.de/dgv

Deutscher Tennis Bund e.V.
Hallerstraße 89,
20149 Hamburg.
Tel (040) 411780.
www.dtb-tennis.de

SKIING AND MOUNTAIN SPORTS

Deutsche Alpine Verein (DAV) Bundesgeschäftsste lle
Von-Kahr-Str. 2–4,
80997 München.
Tel (089) 140030.
www.alpenverein.de

Deutschen Skiverbandes e.V., DSV Haus des Ski
Am Erwin-Himmelseher-Platz Hubertusstraße 1,
D-82152 Planegg.
Tel. (089) 857900.
www.ski-online.de

Verband Deutscher Berg- und Skiführer (VDBS)
Untersbergstr. 34,
83451 Piding.
Tel. (08651) 71221.
www.bergfuehrer-verband.de

NATIONAL PARKS

Europarc Deutschland e.V.
Friedrichstraße 60,
D-10117 Berlin.
Tel (030) 28878820.
www.europarc-deutschland.de

Verband Deutscher Naturparke
Görresstraße 15,
D-53113 Bonn.
Tel (0228) 9212860.
www.naturparke.de

CAMPING AND CARAVANNING

Backpacker Network Germany e.V.
Max-Brauer-Allee 277,
22769 Hamburg.
Tel (040) 43 18 23 10.
www.backpacker
network.de/home/

Deutscher Camping-Club e.V.
Mandlstraße 28,
80802 München.
Tel (089) 3801420.
www.camping-club.de

HISTORIC AND SCENIC ROUTES

Burgenstraße e.V
(Castle Road)
Allee 28,
D-74072 Heilbronn.
Tel (07131) 5640 28.
www.burgenstrasse.de

Deutsche Märchenstraße
(Fairytale Route)
Obere Königsstraße 15,
34117 Kassel.
Tel (0561) 70 7707.
www.deutsche-maerchenstrasse.de

Deutsche Weinstraße e.V.
(Wine Route)
Martin-Luther-Str. 69,
67433 Neustadt an der Weinstraße.
Tel (06321) 912333.
www.deutsche-weinstrasse.de

Tourismusverband Ruppiner Land e.V. "Deutsche Tonstraße"
(Ceramics Route)
Fischbänenstr. 8,
16816 Neuruppin.
www.deutsche-tonstrasse.de

Touristik Arbeitsgemein-schaft Romantische Straße
(Romantic Road)
Waaggässlein 1,
91550 Dinkelsbühl.
Tel (09851) 551387.
www.romantischestrasse.de

SPECIALIST HOLIDAYS

Deutsche Reiterliche Vereinigung e.V
Freiherr von
Langen-Straße 13,
48231 Warendorf.
Tel (025 81) 63 620.
www.pferd-aktuell.de
www.fn-dokr.de

Deutsches Weininstitut GmbH
Gutenbergplatz 3–5,
55116 Mainz.
Tel (06131) 28290.

Goethe Institute
Dachauer Straße 122,
80637 München.
(Postal address: P.O. Box
19 04 19, 80604
München).
Tel (089) 159210.
www.goethe.de

50 Princes Gate,
Exhibition Road,
London SW7 2PH.
*Tel (020) 7596 4000 or
(020) 7594 0240.*

Viniversität – Die Weinschule GmbH
Haus Meer 2,
D-40667 Meerbusch.
Tel (02132) 75680.
www.viniversitaet.de

SPA VACATIONS

Deutscher Heilbäderverband e. V.
Schumannstraße 111,
53113 Bonn.
Tel (0228) 201 200.
www.deutscher-heilbaederverband.de

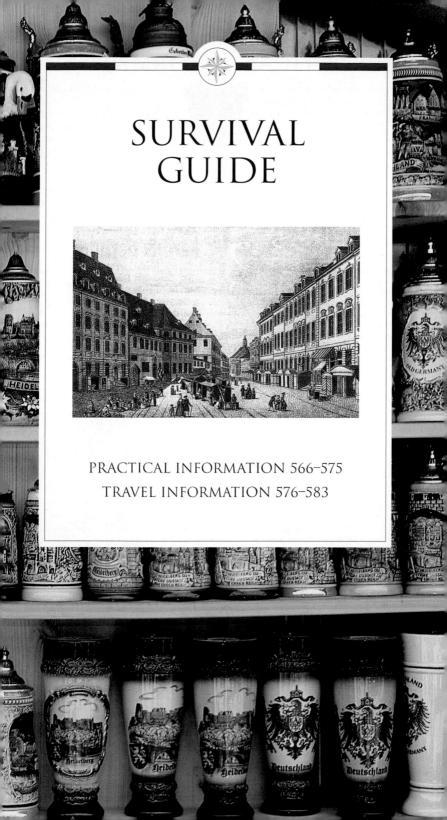

SURVIVAL GUIDE

PRACTICAL INFORMATION

Germany is a country that is particularly well prepared to receive visitors. Every town, large and small, has a helpful tourist information centre that can offer help with finding accommodation and providing information about local restaurants, attractions and activities. Virtually all the larger cities also have Internet web sites where up-to-date information on hotels, restaurants, museums and historic monuments can be

Posters advertising future events

readily accessed. The country is served by an excellent public transport system and a first-rate network of roads and motorways, which makes getting around quick and easy. There is a plentiful supply of comfortable, affordable tourist accommodation in Germany, but it is worth bearing in mind that hotels can become booked up quickly during the festivals and fairs that occur throughout the year in different parts of the country.

WHEN TO VISIT

In Germany, a pleasant and relaxing vacation can be enjoyed at any time of the year. When planning to visit cities and historic monuments, however, it is best to come in the spring or early autumn, particularly in the south of the country where it can be very warm. July and August are the ideal months for spending a restful holiday by the sea, in the lake districts or in the mountains. Arriving in Bavaria during the second half of September provides the opportunity to take part in the Oktoberfest. In December everybody is preoccupied with frantic Christmas shopping, while, in the winter, skiing is a popular pursuit in the Black Forest, the Alps and the Harz Mountains.

Increased traffic on the roads depends on the dates of school holidays, which are set independently in each

Typical information plaques on historic buildings

state. It can also be quite busy at the start of the "long weekends" that occur at Easter, Whitsun and around other national public holidays.

VISA REGULATIONS

Citizens of countries that are members of the European Union, the US, Canada, Australia, and New Zealand do not require a visa to visit Germany, so long as their stay does not exceed three months duration. Visitors from South Africa will need a visa. In addition, citizens of many EU countries do not require a passport to enter Germany, though a national ID card is necessary.

CUSTOMS REGULATIONS

German regulations totally prohibit the importation of drugs, animals and exotic plants that are under special protection. There are also

regulations that restrict the importation of cigarettes. An adult may bring in 200 cigarettes or 100 cigars, and 250g (9oz) of tobacco, as well as one litre of spirits and two litres of wine. You can also import up to 5kg (11lb) of foodstuffs, but not animal products which are forbidden. Beyond these limits, goods must be cleared by Customs when entering the country.

Tourist information office in Rottweil, Baden-Wurttemberg

TOURIST INFORMATION

A very well-developed network of tourist information centres exists in Germany. These are generally run by the city or regional tourist authorities, *Verkehrsamt*. They provide information on accommodation, addresses and opening hours of historic monuments and museums, cruises, organized excursions and city tours, as well as brochures covering the most important tourist information.

Tourists on an excursion with a guide

◁ Beer tankards from Heidelberg

They sell useful guide books, maps and postcards and may be able to find and book you a hotel room.

OPENING HOURS

Opening hours of shops, offices and other businesses depend to a great extent on the size of the town. In larger cities, the usual office opening hours are from around 9am until 6pm. Banks operate much shorter hours *(see p572)*. In smaller towns, however, nothing tends to open until 10am, and many businesses close from 1–2pm for lunch. Visitors must also bear in mind that there is a compulsory and virtually total ban on trading on Saturday afternoons, Sundays and on public holidays. Restrictions also limit the opening hours of shops *(see p558–9)*.

MUSEUMS AND HISTORIC MONUMENTS

Museums in Germany are generally open from 9am until 6pm, and in smaller places from 10am until 5pm or even 4pm. Some museums, however, do close at lunchtime. Once a week, usually on Wednesdays or Thursdays, some museums may be open somewhat longer, while on Mondays they may be closed. Larger churches in major cities are accessible to tourists throughout the whole day. In smaller places, visiting may only be possible after making prior arrangements. There may be a notice on the door of the church advising visitors whom to contact in order to obtain the key.

Publications providing information on cultural events

ADMISSION TICKET PRICES

The price of admission to museums and historic monuments can be high. For example, entrance to a small regional museum may cost €1–€1.5, to a large state-run museum around €2.5–€3, while a private or residential venue may charge as much as €5. Admission to smaller churches is usually free but a fee may be charged in certain cathedrals and monastic churches. There may also be a fee to see the church treasury, where the most valuable exhibits are displayed.

High fees are charged at large entertainment complexes: for example, you may have to pay €10–€15 for a tour of a film studio.

EMBASSIES AND CONSULATES

The embassies of several countries, including the UK and US, are located in Berlin. Consulates are also based in other major German cities.

Illustrated admission tickets for tourist attractions

DIRECTORY

EMBASSIES

Australia
Wallstraße 76–79, 10179 Berlin.
Tel (030) 880 08 80.
Fax (030) 880 08 8-210.
www.australian-embassy.de

Canada
Leipziger Platz 17, 10117 Berlin.
Tel (030) 20 31 20.
Fax (030) 20 31 25 90.
www.kanada-info.de

Republic of Ireland
Friedrichstraße 200, 10117 Berlin.
Tel (030) 22 07 20.
Fax (030) 22 07 22 99.
www.botschaft-irland.de

New Zealand
Friedrichstraße 60, 10117 Berlin.
Tel (030) 20 62 10.
Fax (030) 20 62 11 14.
www.nzembassy.com

South Africa
Tiergartenstraße 18,
10785 Berlin.
Tel (030) 22 07 30.
Fax (030) 22 07 31 90.
www.suedafrika.org

United Kingdom
Embassy
Wilhelmstraße 70, 10117 Berlin.
Tel (030) 20 45 70.
Fax (030) 20 45 75 79.
www.britischebotschaft.de

Consulate
Harvestehuder Weg 8a,
20148 Hamburg.
Tel (040) 448 03 20.
Fax (040) 410 72 59.

United States of America
Embassy
Neustädtische Kirchstraße 4-5,
10117 Berlin.
Tel (030) 238 51 74:
Fax (030) 238 62 90.
www.usembassy.de

Consulate
Königinstraße 5, 80539 Munich.
Tel (089) 288 80.
Fax (089) 28 30 47.

TOURIST OFFICE

BTM – Berlin Tourist Information
Tel (030) 25 00 25.
www.berlin-tourist-information.de

German National Tourist Office
PO Box 2695, London, W1A 3TN.
Tel (020) 731 70908.
www.germany-tourism.de

Practical Information

A kiosk selling newspapers and cigarettes

DISABLED VISITORS

Germany is a country that is relatively well prepared to receive disabled travellers. Large museums and important historic monuments have special ramps or lifts for people who are confined to wheelchairs. Offices and banks are also accessible to wheelchair users, and there are usually lifts at railway stations and larger underground stations. A large proportion of public transport vehicles have been adapted to take wheelchair passengers. Most hotels, especially the higher grades, offer suitably equipped bedrooms. For visitors who use wheelchairs, there are usually specially designed toilet facilities within public toilets in car parks, railway stations and airports. A handicapped person may, however, still have problems in gaining access to some places, such as small museums, certain historic monuments and to toilets in restaurants, which are often located in the cellar. Contact **NatKo** for further useful information.

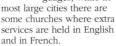

Sign for public toilets, including facilities for disabled visitors

RELIGION

In a country with profound historical influences, the dominant religion varies from area to area and from state to state, depending on which faith was chosen by local rulers in the past. Today, the southern states are predominantly Catholic while, in the north, Protestantism is more common. However, with a migrating population, this historical division has begun to change. The 20th century brought a huge influx of people of other faiths: the Muslim population now numbers several millions. Where large communities of ethnic minorities exist, services are held in their languages, while in most large cities there are some churches where extra services are held in English and in French.

EVERYDAY CUSTOMS

Germans, and particularly the older generation, attach great importance to courteous behaviour. You constantly hear *"Guten Tag"* when entering a shop, and *"Auf Wiedersehen"* – or the more youthful *"Tschüss"* when leaving. Germans are also very punctual and consider even a small delay to be very impolite. Arriving somewhat earlier than arranged for an engagement is regarded as courteous.

It is also important to adapt to German regulations. It is a violation, for example, to cross the road when there is a red light showing, even if the road is clear, and can result in an official reprimand.

Among younger Germans, however, shifts in traditional ideas of politeness can be observed. Older people and women are no longer treated with such respect and are no longer automatically offered seats on public transport by younger passengers. Another notable change is the huge tolerance now shown towards even the most unruly children by parents and other adults.

LANGUAGE

Although all Germans do speak German, many of them use dialects that are virtually incomprehensible, even to those from neighbouring regions. The most difficult dialects to understand are often considered to be those of southern Germany, particularly Bavarian and Schwabian, but Frisian and Saxon dialects are also likely to cause severe communication problems for visitors.

Travellers can usually be understood in Germany by speaking English, particularly in larger cities and in places that are frequented by foreign tourists and holidaymakers.

NEWSPAPERS

Publications can be bought not only in kiosks, but also in automatic vending machines. In the evenings, papers are distributed in bars

A national and a regional German newspaper

and restaurants by news-vendors. Current newspapers are usually available in cafés. Every state has its own titles. In Berlin the most popular newspapers are *Berliner Zeitung, Der Tagesspiegel* and *Die Tageszeitung*. In southern Germany it is *Süddeutsche Zeitung*. Highly respected throughout Germany is the *Frankfurter Allgemeine Zeitung*, while the most widely read is *Bild*.

Foreign language publications, such as *International Herald Tribune, The Guardian, Le Monde, El País, Neue Zürcher Zeitung* and *Corriere della Sera*, are available at kiosks, railway stations and airports, as well as in more expensive hotels.

Information sign

Slot for coins

Pull lever to obtain newspaper after inserting coins

Automatic newspaper vending machine

TIME

Germany uses Central European Time (GMT plus one hour). Clocks move forward one hour on the last Sunday in March and back on the last Sunday in October.

WEIGHTS AND MEASURES

The metric system of measurement is used in Germany. Note that half a kilogram is expressed by the word *Pfund*. In contrast to UK usage, decimals are indicated by a comma and thousands by a point: thus 10,000.50 (UK) = 10.000,50.

ELECTRICITY

The electrical system in Germany provides 220V, 50 Hz AC, except in some hotel bathrooms where a lower current is provided as a standard safety measure. UK 220V appliances can be plugged into German sockets with an adaptor. However US 110V appliances will have to be used with a transformer.

WOMEN TRAVELLING ALONE

A woman travelling on her own will not surprise anyone in Germany and only the usual safety precautions need be taken, particularly in large cities at night. However, it is best to avoid certain areas in towns where there is a lively nightlife – for example the *Reeperbahn* in Hamburg. Hitchhiking is quite popular in Germany, but a better option for single women may be to use the services of *Mitfahrzentrale (see p581)*.

TRAVELLING WITH CHILDREN

Travelling with children is common in Germany and consequently their needs are well catered for. Restaurants can usually provide a high chair for a toddler and offer a special *Kindermenu* with small portions. Public toilets at railway stations, airports and in motorway service stations, as well as in many museums and stores, usually offer a separate facility for mothers and babies. The majority of hotels and guest houses offer discounts for

Phantasialand, Brühl, a popular children's entertainment park

children *(see p487)*. Discounts or even free travel for the youngest children are available on various forms of transport and there are similar concessions in most museums. In many German cities it is possible to purchase family tickets that provide substantial discounts on fares and admission fees.

An international student identity card, the ISIC card

INFORMATION FOR YOUNG PEOPLE

During a stay in Germany it is worth carrying an International Student Identity Card (ISIC), which entitles holders to a 50 per cent discount in certain museums and reductions when buying some theatre tickets. It also allows students to get useful discounts on air tickets and certain urban public transport.

In the larger towns and cities there are special information bureaux for young people, where legal advice and support on such issues as education and employment is available.

DIRECTORY

INFORMATION FOR DISABLED VISITORS

Directions Unlimited
123 Green Lane, Bedford Hills, NY 10507, USA.
Tel (800) 533 53 43.

Holiday Care
Tourism For All, The Hawkins Suite, Enham Place, Enham Alamein, Andover SP11 6JS, UK.
Tel 0845 1249971.
www.holidaycare.org

NatKo e.V. (Nationale Koordinationsstelle Tourismus für Alle)
Kirchfeldstr. 140, 40215 Düsseldorf. *Tel* (0211) 336 80 01.
www.natko.de

Security and Health

Pharmacy sign

As in other countries, visitors are far safer in small towns and villages in Germany than in big cities, where extra vigilance must be taken against pickpockets – particularly when travelling on public transport during rush hour. It is worth using a money belt or other means of concealing your money and documents. Taking out medical insurance cover is always advisable when travelling abroad, but for minor health problems that do not require the services of a doctor, pharmacists are a good and easily accessible source of assistance.

Characteristically coloured white and green police van

POLICE

Green is the predominant colour of German police uniforms and signs. Motorized police units, *Verkehrspolizei*, which look after safety on the streets, roads and motorways, are distinguished by their white caps, while uniformed policemen patrolling city streets have a cap that is the same colour as their uniform. However, the police who are

Policeman and policewoman

responsible for criminal offences, *Kriminalpolizei*, are generally dressed in plain clothes. They will produce their identification and insignia as necessary.

In towns, urban police in navy-blue uniforms are in evidence. Their role is, above all, to catch motorists who have parked illegally or have failed to pay the appropriate parking fee. Such traffic offences may incur on-the-spot fines and rigorous checking of documents.

PERSONAL PROPERTY

Police sign

The most serious threat for a tourist is always the pickpocket. This type of thief tends to prowl in crowded places, such as railway platforms, in the carriages of trains and on buses. They also frequent popular tourist sights and any events where large groups of people are likely to gather. When setting off on an excursion it is best to leave valuable items and documents in the hotel safe.

Conceal valuable items, such as cameras and audio equipment, under clothing and carry cash in a money belt. Park your car in the hotel car park whenever possible and never leave valuable items in the vehicle, especially if it has to be left in the street overnight.

ACCIDENTS AND EMERGENCIES

If an accident or a serious breakdown occurs on the motorway, it is best to use one of the special telephones that are set out at regular intervals along the hard shoulder *(see p580)*. Throughout the whole of Germany there is a special emergency number, *112*, which will be answered by an operator who is an experienced member of a rescue team. Among their responsibilities are informing the appropriate emergency services. Every telephone, including mobile phones, will allow callers to connect free of charge to this number.

Thefts and burglaries must be reported immediately to the criminal police. If a crime is committed on the platform of the S-Bahn or the U-Bahn, the appropriate emergency alarm button can be used to summon assistance. Special alarm buttons, within small red boxes, also provide a direct connection with the fire brigade *(Feuerwehr)*. These alarm buttons are usually located in prominent positions on the streets and in large department stores.

In the case of more serious problems, such as loss of passport, visitors should turn to their Consulate *(see p567)*. Officials in a consulate are available to help travellers in case they need to acquire a replacement passport, obtain legal advice, hire the services of a translator or assistance in contacting their family. In some circumstances, they may even be able to arrange for financial loans to finance the purchase of a ticket home.

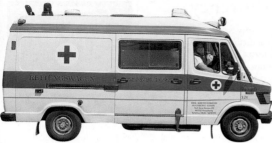
Ambulance of the paramedic rescue services

LOST AND STOLEN PROPERTY

Before leaving home it is advisable to take out an insurance policy to cover property against loss or theft. Theft must be reported to the police immediately and a certificate obtained to confirm that the loss has been needed if an insurance claim is submitted.

If property has been lost, it is worth asking at a lost property office (*Fundbüro*). These exist in every German city. The railway network has its own lost property offices – *Fundbüro der Deutschen Bahn AG* – as do the urban transport systems in individual towns.

Alarm button for the fire brigade

MEDICAL ASSISTANCE

Citizens of countries within the European Union do not have to take out medical insurance in order to obtain free medical care in Germany. In order to avail themselves

of these reciprocal arrangements, however, visitors must obtain a European Health Insurance Card (EHIC) – the form is available from post offices. However, it is still advisable to take out some form of health insurance. If plans include taking part in any sporting activities, particularly dangerous sports, make sure that the policy has a clause guaranteeing the refund of costs if rescue services are involved – for example mountain rescue services. This type of insurance is usually much more expensive.

In case of serious illness, it is necessary to call an ambulance who will take the patient to the nearest hospital out-patient clinic. In large hotels medical care is often provided on the premises. For minor accidents it is best to turn to a pharmacy (*Apotheke*).

HEALTH

Germany poses no health hazards for the traveller. The country is well served with hospitals and there are no prevalent diseases. No vaccinations are required when entering the country.

Visitors who require pre-scribed medication should ensure that they take enough to cover their stay, as it may not be available locally.

Throughout the whole of Germany, tap water is safe to drink. In department stores, pharmacies and large banks there are water tanks with plastic cups, which can be used free of charge.

Entrance to a pharmacy in Heidelberg

PHARMACIES

Pharmacies in Germany are indicated by a stylized letter "A" (*Apotheke*) and are usually open from 8am–6pm; in small towns they may close from 1–3pm. In larger towns there is always a rota and this is displayed in the window of each pharmacy with a note of addresses. Information on rota pharmacies may also be obtained from tourist offices.

PUBLIC CONVENIENCES

In large cities, public toilets (often automatic cubicles) can usually be found without much difficulty. Instructions on how to use these facilities are given in several languages on the doors of the cubicles. Public toilets can also usually be found in museums, cafés, restaurants and department stores. Men's toilets are marked *Herren* and ladies' *Damen* or *Frauen*.

DIRECTORY

EMERGENCY SERVICES

Fire Brigade and Police
Tel 110.

Ambulance
Tel 19222 (plus the area code if using a mobile).

Airborne Rescue Club (Deutsche Rettungsflugwacht)
Tel (0711) 700 70.

Emergency Poison Help Line
Tel (0761) 192 40.

LOST PROPERTY

Fundbüro der Deutschen Bahn AG
Tel (01805) 99 05 99.

Zentrales Fundbüro Berlin
Platz der Luftbrücke 6, Berlin.
Tel (030) 7560 31 01.

Banks and Local Currency

Logo of the ReiseBank

Until recently some credit cards, including Visa, were not quite as popular in Germany as in other countries. This has now changed, however, and tourists should have no problems. In cities and towns cash can be obtained from automatic cash points (ATMs) and foreign currency exchanged at a bank and currency exchange point.

One of Germany's many bureaux de change

CHANGING CURRENCY

There are no limits on the amount of foreign currency that can be brought into the country. Travellers generally use travellers' cheques or credit cards, both of which minimize problems in case of loss or theft.

Foreign currency can be exchanged in a bank or exchange bureau, *Wechselstube*. Both offer a similar rate of exchange, but they usually charge a commission. It is best to check this before undertaking a transaction in order to confirm how much you will have to pay. Most banks have quite inconvenient opening hours: they are open Monday–Friday, from 9am–3:30pm, with a break for lunch between noon and 1pm. Once a week (usually on a Thursday) they are open until 6pm. Opening hours may be a little longer in larger cities. It is advisable to take advantage of the services offered by a branch of the ReiseBank as soon as you arrive – these are

Automatic cash machine

located in airports and railway stations. Currency exchange counters are usually located near railway stations or in places frequented by tourists. These have longer opening hours than banks, but may have less favourable exchange and commission rates.

Foreign currency can be exchanged at special automatic cash points, which can generally be found at larger airports, railway stations and in city centres that are visited by tourists. Cash can also always be exchanged at hotel reception desks, but check the exchange rate before going ahead as the rate may be quite low.

TRAVELLERS' CHEQUES

Travellers' cheques can be used to pay for goods and services, or to settle hotel bills, but it is often better to pay by cash. Cheques can be cashed in banks and currency exchange bureaux, but it should be remembered that

it is most advantageous to exchange them for local currency. Therefore it is a good idea to purchase travellers' cheques in Euro denominations.

Logo of Deutsche Bank, one of the biggest banks in Germany

CREDIT CARDS

Credit cards can be used to pay bills in most hotels and restaurants, in all department stores and in most shops – a fact that is always confirmed by a sticker with the credit card logo on the door or by the cash till. Sometimes, especially in restaurants and cafés, there is a compulsory minimum limit that can be paid by credit card. It is advisable, therefore, to check the situation before ordering just a drink or snack, since it may not be possible to pay for small amounts by credit card.

In busy parts of town and in commercial centres, it is easy to find a cash point that accepts credit cards, but note that some of these accept only Master-

DIRECTORY

**LOST CREDIT CARDS/
TRAVELLERS' CHEQUES**

American Express
Tel (069) 97 97 10 00.

Diner's Club
Tel (069) 66 16 60.

EC and Bank Cards
Tel (069) 74 09 87.

MasterCard
Tel (069) 79 33 19 10.

VISA
Tel (0800) 81 49 100.

The Bayerische Vereinsbank in Munich

Card. Lost credit cards or travellers' cheques should be reported immediately to a bank or the issuing organization.

CURRENCY

The deutschmark was the sole German currency until 2002. On 1 January 2002, the Euro, common currency of the European Union, was introduced into general circulation. Twelve countries have replaced their traditional currencies with the Euro: Austria, Belgium, Finland, France, Germany, Greece, Ireland, Italy, Luxembourg, Netherlands, Portugal and Spain chose to join the new currency; the UK, Denmark and Sweden stayed out, with an option to review their decision. All the old currencies were phased out by mid-2002.

Euro Bank Notes
Euro bank notes have seven denominations. The 5-euro note (grey in colour) is the smallest, followed by the 10-euro note (pink), 20-euro note (blue), 50-euro note (orange), 100-euro note (green), 200-euro note (yellow) and 500-euro note (purple). All notes show the 12 stars of the European Union.

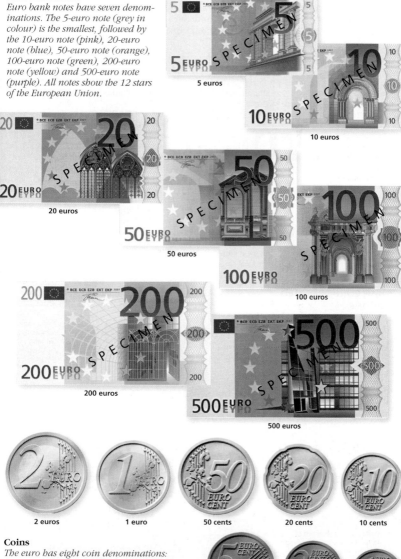

5 euros

10 euros

20 euros

50 euros

100 euros

200 euros

500 euros

2 euros

1 euro

50 cents

20 cents

10 cents

Coins
The euro has eight coin denominations: 2 euros and 1 euro; 50 cents, 20 cents, 10 cents, 5 cents, 2 cents and 1 cent. The 2- and 1-euro coins are both silver and gold in colour. The 50-, 20- and 10-cent coins are gold. The 5-, 2- and 1-cent coins are bronze.

5 cents

2 cents

1 cent

Communications

A rare, antique mail-box

The postal and telecommunications services in Germany work very efficiently. Though it may be necessary to queue for a few minutes in the post office, letters and postcards are usually delivered within the country in 24 hours. There are no problems using the telephone. Telephones can be found on every street corner, in U- and S-Bahn stations, and in virtually every restaurant and café. The distinctive yellow mail-boxes are also a common sight.

Every public phone should be equipped with a set of telephone directories, but these often go missing.

Telephone boxes marked with the word "*National*" can only be used to ring numbers with German dialling codes, but overseas calls can be made from other phones.

Telephone calls can be made from hotel rooms, but the cost of these will be much greater than those made from public telephone boxes. It is worth checking with your hotel first.

Telephone calls can also be made at post offices: there, calls are booked at a window marked "*Ferngespräche*".

USING THE TELEPHONE

Germany's public telephones are serviced by *Deutsche Telekom*. The oldest types are coin-operated and require a minimum deposit, which is the cost of a single local call. Smaller denomination coins are not accepted. Unused coins are returned, but no change is given. It is far more convenient to use a telephone card, which can be purchased at post offices, priced €5, 10 and 20. Alternatively, travellers may purchase an international phone card before leaving home. While using a phone card in a public phone, an illuminated display will show the amount of credit still remaining on the card. Card-operated public phones can be found in many busy areas of towns and cities. In order to use them it is necessary to dial in a personal pin number.

Many phone boxes have their own telephone number. This means that they can receive incoming calls, so that a caller can be called back if his money or card runs out.

Deutsche Telekom sign

TARIFFS

Depending on the time and day, different tariffs apply to local telephone calls, as well as to intercity and inter-national calls. The most expensive period to make a call is between 7am and 6pm. Calls cost less between 6pm and 9pm, and, later in the evening, they are even cheaper. Likewise, telephone calls are cheaper at weekends than on weekdays.

USING A COIN-OPERATED TELEPHONE

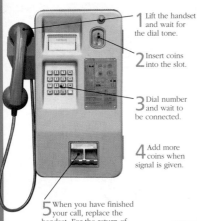

1 Lift the handset and wait for the dial tone.

2 Insert coins into the slot.

3 Dial number and wait to be connected.

4 Add more coins when signal is given.

5 When you have finished your call, replace the handset. For the return of unused coins, press the button above the slot where you inserted the coins.

USING A CARD-OPERATED TELEPHONE

1 Lift the handset and wait for the dial tone.

2 Choose the appropriate language.

3 Insert the card as instructed. The illuminated display will show the amount of credit remaining.

4 Dial the number and wait to be connected.

5 After finishing the call replace the handset. Withdraw the card by pressing the green button.

Colourful chip telephone card (back and front)

MOBILE TELEPHONES

A mobile (cellular) telephone can prove invaluable on holiday, especially for phoning ahead to book hotel rooms or when taking part in mountain sports or travelling in remote areas. Before leaving home, travellers should discuss their requirements with their network provider, including which countries are to be visited. The different options can be explained and the most suitable tariff selected. Charges vary according to the facilities and coverage offered.

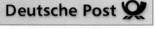

The logo of the German postal service

POSTAL SERVICES

Just as in other countries, registered mail, telegrams and parcels can be sent from post offices. As well as stamps, post offices also sell phone cards, postcards, envelopes and cartons in which to send items by post. Letters sent *Poste Restante* are usually issued from post offices near railway stations. Such correspondance should be marked with the words "*Postlagernde Briefe/Sendungen*". In order to collect mail, a passport or other form of identification will have to be produced.

SENDING A LETTER

Stamps for letters and postcards can be bought at a post office, and sometimes they are sold along with postcards. Stamps can also be bought from automatic stamp machines. Before posting a letter in a mail-box, check what is written on the box. Some mail-boxes have two slots – one marked for local post only, the other for all other destinations.

POST OFFICES

Post offices in Germany are indicated by the word "*Post*", while mail-boxes and the official *Deutsche Post* logo are a distinctive yellow colour. In large towns, post offices are usually open from 8am until 6pm, and from 8am until noon on Saturdays. Branches with longer opening hours, and which are often also open on Sundays, can be found at most airports and large railway stations. In smaller towns, post offices are often located in local shops.

POSTAL ADDRESSES

In Germany, the postal code of five digits is an important part of the address, allowing a more precise location than simply the street name and house number. In cities, for example, different sections of long streets will have different

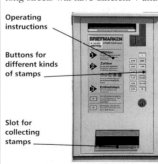

Operating instructions

Buttons for different kinds of stamps

Slot for collecting stamps

Street vending machine selling postage stamps and telephone cards

Entrance to one of the post offices in Bonn

postal codes. In multiple-occupancy buildings, the number of individual apartments is not given in the address. Instead, mail is delivered according to the name cards at the entrance to the building. Consequently, in order to send mail to a person who is staying in someone else's house, it is necessary to write at the top of the envelope the name of the main occupant, preceded by the letters "c/o" (care of).

THE INTERNET AND E-MAIL

The internet and e-mail have become increasingly popular and essential as a means of communication, and they can be especially useful for people who are abroad on holiday or business. As a result, many hotels now offer guests access to the Internet and e-mail facilities. Internet cafés, where online access can be obtained for a small fee, can be found in most towns and cities, while computers can often be hired by the hour in commercial centres.

Information plaque indicating the collection times

Opening for long-distance mail

Opening for local letters

The most typical style of mail-box seen in Germany

USEFUL TELEPHONE NUMBERS

- Directory enquiries, national numbers: 11 833.
- Directory enquiries, international numbers: 11 834.
- International calls: Dial 00, wait for dialling tone, then dial country code, area code + number, omitting first 0.
- Country codes: UK 44; Eire 353; Canada and US 1; Australia 61; South Africa 27; New Zealand 64.

TRAVEL INFORMATION

Travelling in Germany is very quick and easy. In every large city there is an airport, most of which offer international connections. The whole of Germany is linked by a dense network of motorways, while main roads are of a high standard and are well signposted. Rail travel throughout the country is comfortable

Lufthansa plane

and reliable; for longer journeys it is worth taking advantage of the fast connections offered by InterCity Express (ICE). Buses are also comfortable and efficient and are particularly useful in rural areas not served by rail. In German cities, trams, buses and sometimes underground rail systems provide useful services.

ARRIVING BY AIR

Germany's most important airports are Frankfurt am Main, Munich and Düsseldorf, from where connecting flights can be made to other German cities. The country's national carrier is Lufthansa, which operates regular, scheduled flights to most of the world's major destinations. British Airways also offers regular, scheduled flights to Germany from London (Heathrow and Gatwick) as well as from several regional airports in the United Kingdom.

The US is well served with flights to German cities, particularly to Berlin and to Frankfurt, which is Germany's largest airport and one of the busiest in Europe. Direct flights are usually available from major US cities, including New York (JFK), Washington DC, Boston, Chicago, San Francisco and Los Angeles.

Although Canada does not have many direct flights to Germany, AirCanada operates a regular flight from Toronto to Frankfurt while Canadian offers a direct flight from Vancouver to Frankfurt.

DOMESTIC FLIGHTS

In addition to Lufthansa, there are a number of other smaller carriers in Germany. These include Deutsche BA, which is a subsidiary of British Airways. These carriers often offer cheaper fares than Lufthansa on internal routes, as well as providing air links with small airports, such as Augsburg, Dortmund and Erfurt, that would not be economically viable for Lufthansa to operate.

AIR FARES

The cost of scheduled airfares can vary considerably, so it is always worth checking whether any carriers are offering special promotional fares. When buying a ticket it is worth finding out about any price reductions for children, young people and elderly passengers. Students and passengers under the age of 26 are often eligible for discounts. If the journey is going to be undertaken by a larger group, then it would be worth checking whether

Control tower at Munich's international airport

this qualifies for a group discount on the fare or a free ticket for the group leader.

It should also be borne in mind that fares vary depending on whether travellers are able to confirm their return date when buying the ticket. The cheapest scheduled ticket is an APEX, which requires booking well in advance, staying over a Saturday night,

Car park and airport building at Tegel airport, Berlin

View of runway and airport buildings at Frankfurt airport

and a fixed return date. Once booked, these tickets cannot be altered or cancelled, so it is wise to take out insurance to cover the loss if travel plans have to be changed.

The cheapest fares are often those offered by the new low-cost, no-frills airlines, or by discount agents. The latter are usually for seats on charter or scheduled flights.

INTERNATIONAL AIRPORTS

The largest German airports are Frankfurt am Main and Munich. The gigantic airport in Frankfurt comprises two huge terminals, which are connected by a fast over-ground railway. Both terminals are comprehensively equipped with everything that a traveller could possibly require. If you do have some free time it is worth watching the planes as they take off and land, and which form long queues at peak times.

The airport in Munich is somewhat smaller but still very popular. The terminal extends along one axis, with the result that if you have to change planes, you have to take a long walk along a corridor to make the transfer.

Among the busiest airports are Düsseldorf, Cologne-Bonn and Berlin, which actually has three airports, Tempelhof, Tegel and Schönefeld.

DIRECTORY

AIRLINES

Air Canada
Tel (069) 27 11 51 11.
www.aircanada.com

British Airways
Tel (01805) 26 65 22.
www.britishairways.com

Delta Air Lines
Tel (01803) 33 78 80.
www.delta.com

Deutsche BA
Tel (01805) 35 93 22.
www.deutsche-ba.de/

Lufthansa
Tel (01805) 83 84 26.
www.lufthansa.com

Qantas
Tel (01805) 25 06 20.
www.qantas.com

United Airlines
Tel (069) 50 07 03 87.
www.unitedairlines.com

AIRPORT	INFORMATION	DISTANCE FROM CENTRE	JOURNEY TIME TO CENTRE BY TAXI	JOURNEY TIME TO CENTRE BY PUBLIC TRANSPORT
Berlin Tegel	(0180) 500 01 86	8 km (5 miles)	25 min	Bus: 25 min
Berlin Tempelhof	(0180) 500 01 86	5 km (3 miles)	20 min	U-Bahn: 15 min
Berlin Schönefeld	(0180) 500 01 86	20 km (12 miles)	45 min	S-Bahn: 35 min
Bremen-Neuenland	(0421) 559 50	3.5 km (2 miles)	15 min	Tram: 17 min
Dresden	(0351) 881 33 60	9 km (5.5miles)	25 min	Bus: 30 min
Düsseldorf	(0211) 42 10	8 km (5 miles)	25 min	S-Bahn: 13 min
Frankfurt am Main	(01805) 372 46 36	10 km (6 miles)	20 min	Train: 11 min S-Bahn: 10 min
Hamburg	(040) 50 75 25 57	13 km (8 miles)	30 min	Bus: 30 min
Hannover	(0511) 97 70	12 km (7.5 miles)	20 min	S-Bahn: 13 min
Cologne-Bonn	(02203) 40 400 1	Bonn: 28 km (17.5 miles) Cologne: 17 km (10.5 miles)	Bonn: 15 min Cologne: 20 min	Bus to Bonn: 35 min Bus to Cologne: 45 min
Leipzig	(0341) 224 11 55	18 km (11 miles)	30 min	Bus: 30 min
Munich	(089) 97 52 13 13	40 km (25 miles)	45 min	S-Bahn: 40 min Bus: 45 min
Nürnberg	(0911) 937 00	6 km (4 miles)	20 min	Bus: 45 min U-Bahn: 12 min
Stuttgart	(0711) 94 80	18 km (11 miles)	25 min	S-Bahn: 30 min

Travelling by Train, Ferry and Ship

Logo of German railways (Deutsche Bahn)

Travelling around Germany by train is not the cheapest form of transport, but it is undoubtedly one of the most comfortable. German trains are renowned for their punctuality, safety and cleanliness, though in high season visitors may feel that these are a little overrated. The fastest are InterCity-Express (ICE) trains. Germany is also well served by ports to which ferries and passenger ships operate.

Narrow-gauge tourist railway service in the Harz mountains

GETTING TO GERMANY BY TRAIN

Travelling by train from the UK generally costs more than flying, as well as taking longer. Main routes are via Dover to Ostend or Harwich to Hook of Holland. From either of these ports, connections to Berlin, Frankfurt and other German cities are made. An alternative is to travel to Brussels by Eurostar and make a connection there.

certain stations, and offer an express service. When travelling over shorter distances it is best to take the Regional-Express (RE) trains.

GERMAN TRAINS

The fastest trains, InterCity Express (ICE), are aerodynamically designed, painted white, with air-conditioning in coaches and airline-style seats. Unfortunately, there is not much room for luggage. They can travel at more than 200 kph (125 mph), which means that a journey from Hamburg to Munich takes only a few hours. ICE trains operate on just a few routes linking the country's largest cities. Somewhat slower and less expensive are the InterCity (IC) trains, which stop only at

TICKETS

Deutsche Bahn railway workers

Train fares are quite expensive in Germany and in express trains there is a compulsory surcharge, *Zuschlag*. It is not essential to reserve seats, but in the high season it is a good idea to do so and charges are not exorbitant. One way to travel more cheaply is to buy a *BahnCard*, which gives a 25 per cent discount. Deutsche Bahn have many seasonal special offers, so it is advisable to book in advance.

When planning a lengthy stay in Germany and travelling around the country, it is worth acquiring an InterRail card, which is available to every European citizen, regardless of age. Every year the variety of discounted fares to which this card entitles the bearer is extended, so that it is worth checking out the full range. The price of the card depends on the age of the

traveller. Schoolchildren and students are entitled to a reduced rate. The cost also depends on which countries are to be visited. An InterRail card that is valid for travel in Germany is also valid for Austria, Switzerland and Denmark. InterRail cards can be obtained from Rail Europe or from some travel agents.

During the summer season in Germany, various discounts and special offers are introduced – for example, weekend tickets, family, group and so on, so it is worth making enquiries about these before setting off on a train journey.

RESERVATIONS

Train tickets can be bought and reservations made in travel agents or at the railway station at the *Reisezentrum*, which at the same time acts as an information centre. Tickets can also be reserved by telephone or through the Internet, where a detailed timetable can be viewed. Using this facility, it is simple to plan the appropriate routes for your journey yourself.

RAILWAY STATIONS

In Germany, many railway stations are magnificent, historic buildings with vast halls covering the platforms. Among the most beautiful is

DIRECTORY

RAILWAY INFORMATION

National Rail Enquiries
Tel (01805) 33 10 50.

Deutsche Bahn
www.bahn.de
www.deutsche-bahn.de

The fastest and most comfortable German train – InterCity Express

TRAIN ROUTES IN GERMANY

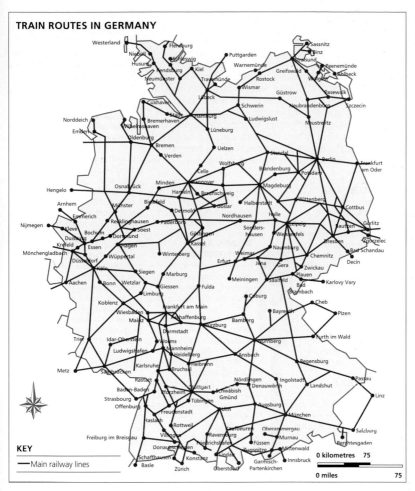

KEY

— Main railway lines

0 kilometres 75

0 miles 75

the main station in Leipzig. In large towns, railway stations are generally located in the centre. They include dozens of shops (often open on Sundays), car rental firms, hotel reservation bureaux, and other services, such as cash points, left luggage provision and public toilets with shower facilities.

TRAVELLING BY FERRY AND SHIP

Visitors travelling to Germany by car from the UK will have to decide which crossing to use (unless using the Channel Tunnel). This will depend to some extent on which part of Germany is to be visited. The crossings

from Dover to Ostend, in Belgium, or to Calais, in France, are the shortest, while the Harwich to Hook of Holland route is useful for those travelling from further north. There are also two ferry services to Hamburg, operated by Scandinavian Seaways – one from Harwich and one from North Shields, near Newcastle-upon-Tyne.

There are many links between German ports and other countries. Color Line from Oslo (Norway) to Kiel; Scand-lines from Trelleborg, (Sweden) to Rostock and Trelleborg to Sassnitz, and also from Denmark: Gedser to Rostock, Rødby to Puttgarden and Rønne (Bornholm) to Sassnitz; DFDs Seaways operates from Harwich to Cuxhaven.

Ship taking passengers to Helgoland

Travelling by Car and Bus

Sign for parking ticket machine

The fastest and most comfortable way of travelling around Germany is to use the motorways. The excellent network of toll-free routes guarantees fast progress over longer distances, while a well-maintained system of main roads enables you to reach interesting places throughout the country. Motorways have the advantage of regularly sited service stations, where travellers can stop for fuel and something to eat. On lesser roads and in remote areas, petrol stations may be few and far between.

ARRIVING BY CAR

There are many border crossings into Germany and providing that you carry the necessary documents and your car does not look disreputable, you should experience a minimum of delay and formalities. EU citizens do not have to make a Customs declaration on arrival, but there are limits on the amount of duty-free goods that can be brought in *(see p566).*

WHAT TO TAKE

Visitors travelling by car in Germany must carry a valid driving licence as well as their vehicle's registration document and insurance policy. Before leaving home check with your insurance company whether your policy will cover you while you are in Germany. If may be necessary to obtain a Green Card to extend the cover for the duration of your stay.

The car must carry a plate indicating country of origin, and it must also be equipped with a red warning triangle for use in case of breakdown.

Seatbelts are compulsory and children under 12 must sit in the back, with babies and toddlers in child-seats.

ROADS AND MOTORWAYS

The German motorway network is extensive. They are all toll-free and have regularly spaced petrol stations, as well as parking facilities with toilets, restaurants and motels. Ranging along the hard shoulder are yellow poles with emergency buttons, which can be used to call for help in the event of a breakdown or accident. An *Autobahn* (motorway) is indicated by the letter "A" followed by a number – some also have a letter "E" and a number, denoting that the road crosses the German border. A *Bundesstraße* (main road) is indicated by the letter "B" and a number.

Motorway telephone

ADDITIONAL ROAD SIGNS

In addition to internationally understood road signs on German roads, there are also written signs that clarify the meaning of the sign above.

A selection of traffic signs on German roads

On motorways, for example, a yellow triangular warning sign with a row of cars is a warning about the possibility of traffic jams, which may be accompanied by the word *"Stau"*. On mountain roads, a warning sign showing a car tyre wrapped in a chain will be accompanied by the word *"Schnee"*, which warns against driving without chains when there is snow.

A diversion is indicated by the colour yellow and the word *"Umleitung"*, while the diversion route is indicated by the letter "U" followed by the number of the road. A sign with the slogan *"Baustelle"* (meaning "refurbishment") always precedes the stretch that is being renovated.

A sign showing a horizontal blue arrow with the word *"Einbahnstrasse"* indicates a one-way street.

RULES OF THE ROAD

Germans on the whole drive in accordance with the regulations. They are generally courteous, but they can be a little aggressive, particularly on motorways. German drivers hurtle along the outside lane at very great speed and get very annoyed if they have to slow down because of other drivers. Visitors should be particularly careful when first starting to drive in Germany, especially if they are unused to driving on the right. Bear in mind that being caught exceeding the speed limit incurs a large fine.

In the event of an accident on the motorway, or if a traffic jam necessitates an abrupt reduction in speed, drivers should turn on their flashing emergency lights to warn drivers behind of impending danger.

Petrol station at a motorway service area

Parking-ticket Machine

Automatic parking-ticket machines like this issue receipts that are placed on the inside of the windscreen. There are also parking meters with a timer, which allow parking for up to 2 hours.

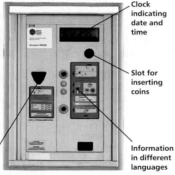

Ticket is dispensed from here

Clock indicating date and time

Slot for inserting coins

Information in different languages

DRIVING IN TOWNS

Finding a place in which to park is not easy: it is often best to use a multi-storey car park, which is indicated by "*Parkhaus*"; the word "*Frei*" indicates that parking spaces are available. It is never worth leaving your car in a prohibited area – a traffic warden will arrive immediately, impose a fine and arrange for the car to be towed away. Retrieving an impounded car is expensive and difficult.

Cars left in a controlled parking zone must either display a parking ticket or be parked validly at a meter.

ROAD TRAFFIC REGULATIONS

In Germany, the same road traffic regulations apply as in most European countries. For example, all passengers must wear a seat-belt and children under the age of 12 must travel in the back seats. Driving after drinking a small amount of alcohol is allowed, but if you cause an accident, the consequences will be more severe if a breathalyzer shows the presence of alcohol in your blood. In built-up areas the speed limit is 50 km/h (31 mph); beyond this it

is 100 km/h (62 mph), and on motorways there is no overall limit. Many drivers drive at speeds exceeding 200 km/h (125 mph). When travelling with a caravan or camping trailer outside built-up areas, drivers should not exceed 70 km/h (44 mph), and on motorways 100 km/h (62 mph). Road traffic police are strict about imposing fines for breaches of speed restrictions.

Drivers can incur fines for driving too close to the vehicle in front and for parking in prohibited areas as well as for breaking the speed limits.

HIRING A CAR

Representatives of car-hire firms can be found at airports, railway stations and in more expensive hotels. In order to hire a car, drivers need to produce their passport and driving licence and to be over 18. In some cases, they may be required to have an international driving licence.

HITCH-HIKING

Hitch-hiking is a popular way of travelling, particularly among young people. A safer method of finding a lift or a travelling companion is to

make use of the services of Mitfahrzentralen, a contact agency for drivers who offer spare seats on a journey for an agreed fee. Check addresses and telephone numbers in local telephone directories.

ARRIVING BY COACH

Travelling to Germany by coach from the UK is not a very attractive option as the journey is long and fares are not particularly cheap. Routes are operated by Eurolines.

TRAVELLING BY COACH

There is a good network of inter-city coach services in Germany, though journeys are generally no cheaper than travelling by train. Most towns have a *Zentraler Omnibus Bahnhof* (ZOB) close to the train station. It is here that most bus services originate and where service timetables can be obtained and tickets purchased. Many local coach services also operate from the central bus station, although suburban areas have their own services to the centre of town. It is best to ask at the tourist information centre for information about getting to your destination.

DIRECTORY

CAR HIRE

Avis
Tel (06171) 68 18 00 or (01805) 21 77 02.

Hertz
Tel (01805) 93 88 14.

Sixt Rent-a-Car
Tel (01805) 25 25 25.

ROADSIDE ASSISTANCE

Central Information ADAC
Tel (01805) 10 11 12.

Road Assistance ADAC
Tel (01802) 22 22 22.

ACE
Tel (01802) 34 35 36.

Comfortable, long-distance, double-decker coach

Transport in Cities

The S-Bahn logo

Getting around Germany's huge cities is not easy and the historic centres are best visited on foot. Large towns often suffer from traffic congestion and it can be difficult to find vacant parking places. It is advisable to leave your car in a car park on the outskirts and travel around using the fast railway (S-Bahn), underground (U-Bahn), trams or city buses. The latter operate frequent, timetabled services and can usually avoid traffic jams as they have the advantage of travelling along specially designated traffic lanes.

The city rail line, Schwebebahn, in Wuppertal

TAXIS

Taxis offer a comfortable though expensive way of getting around towns and cities. If several people share a cab, however, this can work out cheaper than using the bus or train. Every taxi vehicle, regardless of make, is a cream colour and has a "TAXI" sign on the roof; this will be illuminated if the taxi is free. Cabs can be hailed on the street or booked by telephone. They can also be picked up at a taxi rank, though these are rare. If the rank is empty, a cab can be called for from the telephone there.

The fare for the journey is calculated by an illuminated meter on the dashboard. The same rates apply during the week, at weekends and at night, for journeys within the city limits.

Telephone at a taxi rank

TRAVELLING ON THE U-BAHN AND S-BAHN

All the big German cities have a network of fast connections by underground railway (U-Bahn) and by rail (S-Bahn). The U-Bahn offers frequent services – in peak hours every 3–5 minutes – and individual stations are situated quite close to each other. The S-Bahn offers less frequent services, every 10 or 20 minutes, while the stations are quite markedly apart. Generally the S- and U-Bahn use the same tickets, as do buses and trams. Various

types of ticket can be bought from ticket machines located by the entrance to stations; the tickets must be punched in the red punching machine situated nearby. On German railway stations there are no regulatory measures, such as ticket-operated barriers, so it is easy for unscrupulous passengers to get onto a train without a ticket. However it is not worth trying to do this as trains are patrolled by ticket inspectors, often dressed in civilian clothes, who start checking tickets once a train has left the station. Fines for travelling without a ticket are very high.

U-Bahn stations are indicated by square signs with a white "U" on a dark blue background, while S-Bahn stations have round signs with a white "S" on a green background. On maps of the network, each line of the U- and S-Bahn is marked in a different colour and has its own number. The direction of

the route is indicated by the name of the station at which the route terminates. On every station platform a display shows the destination of the next incoming train. A white circle or oval on the map indicates an interchange station. On every station you will find town maps and maps of the transport network displayed in prominent positions. Maps are also displayed in carriages.

Carriage doors on U- and S-Bahn trains are operated manually, but they close automatically. At major stations a member of staff gives the signal for trains to leave the station. Passengers are not allowed to board the train after his cry of "*Zurück-bleiben!*" – which means that the doors are about to close. Throughout the journey, the names of the next stations are announced, while in modern trains these are usually also indicated on illuminated displays in the carriages.

Automatic Ticket Machine

To use this machine, select the appropriate ticket by pressing a button. Insert the amount of money indicated by the display. Your ticket and change will then be delivered.

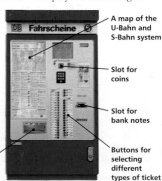

A map of the U-Bahn and S-Bahn system

Slot for coins

Slot for bank notes

Buttons for selecting different types of ticket

Opening, from which tickets and change are delivered

Tram and Bus Stop Sign

At every stop, a board displays the numbers and destinations of trams and buses that stop there. Timetables and maps of the public transport system are also displayed.

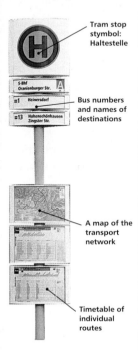

Tram stop stymbol: Haltestelle

Bus numbers and names of destinations

A map of the transport network

Timetable of individual routes

BUSES

Bus routes have individual timetables, which are displayed on boards at bus stops. Maps showing each stage of the route are also displayed there. As well as a route number, buses also have a sign indicating where their particular route ends. This is useful as some buses operate on shorter routes outside peak hours.

During the journey, the bus driver generally announces the name of the bus stop that the bus is approaching. In the centre of town, this is not so important, as in heavy traffic the bus stops at every bus stop as a matter of course. However, further away from the city centre or in periods where the traffic is not so heavy, you have to listen out for these announcements.

At many bus stops, the driver will pull in only on request, so passengers must press the "Halt" button in plenty of time to warn the driver that they wish to alight.

TRAMS

Trams are a comfortable means of urban transport, with the advantage that they do not get stuck in traffic jams. The same tickets as for buses and S-Bahn can be used.

TICKETS

For the purpose of public transport charges, large cities are generally divided into zones, with the cost of a ticket depending on which zones are travelled through during a journey.

In many cities a single-use ticket is valid for two hours, and during this time you can use all the modes of transport available, including the S- and U-Bahn, even changing routes several times. However, using this type of ticket is the most expensive way to travel. In addition to these standard tickets (*Normaltarif*), there are also cheaper tickets available (*Kurzstrecke*), which limit you to short distances. In many German cities you can also buy tickets in the form of a strip, which has to be punched according to the length of the journey.

Children who have not reached the age of 14 are eligible for a reduced rate (*Ermäßigungstarif*), while toddlers up to the age of six travel free. Children's push-chairs and dogs will often be carried on public transport without any extra charge.

A modern type of tram that operates in German cities

There are many other types of tickets and travelcards – for example a one-day ticket (*Tageskarte*), a one-day group ticket (*Gruppentageskarte*), and a weekly ticket (*7-Tage-Karte*). Some towns issue a *WelcomeCard* that allows for three days' travel around town as well as giving many discounts in museums.

Bicycles parked near the entrance to the Hofgarten in Munich

BICYCLES

Bicycles are a popular form of transport in Germany. There are numerous cycle lanes and many junctions have special lights for cyclists. In front of virtually every office, bank and school there is a bicycle stand, although these should be used only for a short period and, of course, the bicycle still needs to be secured against theft. Bicycles can be transported on the S-Bahn, although owners will need to get on the train at the appropriate door and stand their vehicle in the designated place. Bicycles can be hired at the station or other hire places (*Fahrradverleib*).

A city bus in Munich

General Index

Acknowledgements

Dorling Kindersley and Wiedza i Życie would like to thank the following people for their help in preparing this guide:

Additional Text
Michał Jaranowski, Barbara Sudnik-Wójcicka, Grażyna Winiarska, Konrad Gruda, Bożena Steinborn

Additional Photographs
Amin Akhtar, Francesca Bondy, Maciej Bronarski, Demetrio Carrasco, Witold Danilkiewicz, Grzegorz Kłosowski, Renata and Marek Kosińscy, Sergiusz Michalski, Nils Meyer, Ian O'Leary, Jürgen Scheunemann, Andrzej Zygmuntowicz and Ireneusz Winnicki, Władysław Wisławski

Publishing Manager
Helen Townsend

Managing Art Editor
Kate Poole

Consultant
Gerhard Bruschke

Factcheckers
Barbara Sobeck, Jürgen Scheunemann

Director of Publishing
Gillian Allan

Editorial and Design Assistance
Sam Atkinson, Sonal Bhatt, Hilary Bird, Arwen Burnett, Susi Cheshire, Sherry Collins, Lucinda Cooke, Jo Cowen, Conrad Van Dyk, Marcus Hardy, Lucinda Hawksley, Victoria Heyworth-Dunne, Jacky Jackson, Jeroen van Marle, Claire Marsden, Ferdie McDonald, Sam Merrell, Rebecca Milner, Casper Morris, Sangita Patel, Marianne Petrou, Dave Pugh, Simon Ryder, Sadie Smith, Andrew Szudek, Leah Tether, Karen Villabona, Stewart J. Wild

The publisher would also like to thank all the people and institutions who allowed photographs belonging to them to be reproduced, as well as granting permission to use photographs from their archives:

Archäologische Staatssammlung in Munich; Arthothek (Jürgen Hinrichsowi); Bavaria Filmstadt; Bayerisches Nationalmuseum in Munich; Bildarchiv Preussischer Kulturbesitz in Berlin (Heidrun Klein); Bildvorlagen Römerschatz – Gäubodenmuseum Straubing (Dr. Prammer); Bischöfliches Dom- und Diözesanmuseum Mainz (Dr. Hansowi-Jurgenowi Kotzurowi); Brecht-Weigel-Gedenkstätte in Berlin (Elke Pfeil); Bridgeman Art Library; Bröhan-Museum in Berlin (Ingrid Jagr and Frau Betzker); Brücke-Museum in Berlin; Brüder-Grimm-Museum in Kassel; Corbis; Das Domkapitel (Gertraut Mockel, Büro Dr Georg Minkenberg); Deutsches Apothekenmuseum in Heidelberg; Deutsches Historisches Museum in Berlin (Kathi Rumlow); Deutsche Press Agentur (dpa) in Berlin (Tanija Teichmann); Deutsches Museum in Munich (Sigrid Schneider and Marlene Schwarz); Deutsches Schiffahrtsmuseum in Bremerhaven (Hansowi-Walterowi Kewelohowi); Deutsches Tapetenmuseum Kassel (Sabine Thümmler); Deutsches Technikmuseum Berlin (Renate Förster); Diözesanmuseum in Bamberg (Birgit Kandora); Dombauverwaltung des Metropolitankapitels Köln (Birgit Lambert); Dresden Museum für Geschichte der Stadt Dresden (Dr. Christel Wünsch); Flash Press Media (Sylwii Wilgockiej); Forschungs- und Gedenkstätte Normannenstraße (Stasi-Museum) in Berlin (Andrei Holland-Moritz); Fürstlich Hohenzollernsche Schlossverwaltung in Sigmaringen (Heldze Boban); Gemäldegalerie Alte Meister (Steffi Reh); Gemäldegalerie Neue Meister (Gisela Mehnert); Germanisches Nationalmuseum in Nuremberg (Hermanowi Maué); Hamburger Bahnhof in Berlin; Hamburger Kunsthalle; Hessisches Landesmuseum Kassel; Käthe-Kollwitz-Museum in Berlin (A. Ingrid Findell); Komische Oper Berlin (Gaby Hofmann); Kunstmuseum

Düsseldorf (Anne-Marie Katins); Kunstsammlungen Paula Modersohn in Bremen (Hubertusowi Morgenthalowi); Kunstsammlungen zu Weimar (Angelice Goder); Kunstverlag Maria Laach (Helmutowi Keipowi); Kurdirektion des Berchtesgadener Landes (Vroni Aigner, Birgit Tica); Landesmuseum Trier (Margot Redwanz); LBB Photo Archives (Dyrektorowi Christophowi Kalischowi); Linden-Museum Stuttgart, Staatliches Museum für Völkerkunde (Dr. Doris Kurelli); Lutherstube in Wittenberg (Jutcie Strehle); Markgräfliches Opernhaus in Bayreuth; Mercedes-Benz-Museum in Stuttgart; Museum am Ostwall in Dortmund; Museum der Bildenden Künste in Leipzig (Roswitha Engel); Museum Folkwang in Essen, Stadt Essen (Mr Hildebrandowi); Museum of the City of Berlin; Porzellansammlung (Ulrike Maltschew); Rheinisches Landesmuseum Bonn (Dr Gerhard Bauchhenß); Rüstkammer (Yvonne Brandt); Schlösserverwaltung in Munich (Frau Gerum); Seebul Ada und Emil Nolde (Dr Andreasowi Fluckowi); Staatliche Graphische Sammlung in Munich (Wiebke Tomaschek); Staatliche Kunstsammlungen Dresden, Albertinum,Grünes Gewölbe; Staatliche Porzellan-Manufaktur Meißen GMBH (Christine Mangold); Staatliche Schlösser und Gärten, Pforzheim (Herr Braunowi); Staatsarchiv Hamburg (Kathrin Berger); Staatsgalerie Stuttgart (Frau Fönnauer); Städelsches Kunstinstitut in Frankfurt am Main (Elisabeth Heinemann); Stadt Köln, Wallraf-Richartz-Museum in Cologne (Dr Roswitha Neu-Kock and Dr Mai); Stadtmuseum in Munich; Stiftung Luthergedenkstätten in Sachsen-Anhalt; Stiftung Preussische Schlösser und Gärten Berlin (Carli Kamarze); Superstock Polska Sp. z.o.o. (Elżbiecie Gajewskiej); Von der Heydt-Museum Wuppertal (Margarecie Janz); Wartburg-Stiftung in Eisenach (Petrze Wilke); Zefa (Ewie Kozłowskiej)

The publisher would also like to thank the following for their assistance on the guide:
Joanna Minz for coordinating information, Tamara and Jacek Draber for their help with correspondence and telephone contacts, Jürgen Christoffer of Deutscher Wetterdienst for meteorological information.

Picture Credits
t = top; tl = top left; tlb = top left below; tc = top centre; tcb = top centre below; tr = top right; tra = top right above; trb = top right below; cl = centre left; cla = centre left above; clb = centre left below; c = centre; ca = centre above; cb = centre below; cr = centre right; cra = centre right above; cbr = centre bottom right; crb = centre right below; bl = bottom left; blb = bottom left below; bc = bottom centre; br = bottom right; bra = bottom right above; brb = bottom right below; b = bottom

Aachener Dom (Copyright: Domkapitel Aachen – photo. Ann Münchow) 396t, 396ca, 396cb, 396t (Skarbiec), 397ca, 397cb, 397br, 397bl; **Alamy Images**: alwaysstock, LLC/Michael Hill 562tr; archivberlin Fotoagentur GmbH/J. Henkelmann 107tl; Arco Images 12tr, 558cr; Jon Arnold Images/Walter Bibikow 22t; BL Images Ltd 10cl, 231cr; David R. Frazier Photolibrary, Inc. 12bc; FAN travelstock/Sabine Lubenow 11c, 11tl, 560br, 561cl; Iconotexc/Ettore Venturini 559tr; imagebroker/Manfred Bail 231tl; imagebroker/Michael Fischer 561br; imagebroker/Stephan Goerlich 232tc; ImageState/Pictor International 11br; Andre Jenny 230cr; Stan Kujawa 13tr; Yadid Levy 230bl, 522cl; Werner Otto 13br, 142; Gillian Price 560cl; John Stark 10br; **Albertinum** (Dresden) 172t; **Allianz Arena München Stadion GmbH** 233tl; **Amt für Stadtmarketing und Touristik, Limburg** 362cla; **Archäologische Staatssammlung** (Munich) 219d; **Artothek** 30t, 30b, 31cla, 31blb, 54t, 176ca, 176cb, 176b, 177t, 177ca, 177cb, 177b, 175cb, 222cb, 261b, 436t, 436b, 437t, 437cb, 444t; Joachim Blauel 31bra, 50t, 222t, 222b, 223cb, 260t, 294cr; Blauel/Gnamm 218t, 222ca, 223t, 223ca, 259tr; Bayer d'Mitko 223d; Sophie-R. Gnamm 226; Alexander Koch 31trb; Christoph Sandig 470d; G. Westermann 432b, 437t. **Basic AG** 558bl; **Bavaria Filmstadt** 227t; **Bayerische Staatsoper** Wilfried Hösl 232bl; **Berlin Tourismus Marketing GmbH** www.berlin-

tourist-information.de 97br; **BerlinerFestspiele** Bianka
Gobel 109tl; **Brecht-Weigel-Gedenkstätte** (Berlin) 101c;
Bridgeman Art Library 34br, 103t; **Britstock** 328–329;
Bronarski Maciej 334t, 350t, 350c, 350b, 351t, 351ca,
351cb, 351b; **Bröhan-Museum** (Berlin) 96t; **Brüder-
Grimm-Museum** (Kassel) 364tr, 368tr (© Staatliche
Museum Kassel).

Corbis 28tr, 28bra, 28blb, 172c (© Jack Fields/Corbis),
446–447 (©Bob Krist/Corbis), 454 (© Nilk Wheeler/Corbis);
Corbis Sygma/Annebicque Bernard 523tl; Michael
S.Yamashita 523c; Zefa/Frank Lukasseck 182; Zefa/Herbert
Spichtinger 232cr; **Danilkiewicz Witold** 425b, 466, 474t;
Deutsches Apothekenmuseum (Heidelberg) 298tr;
Deutsches Technikmuseum Berlin 81b; **Deutsches
Historisches Museum Berlin** (Zeughaus) 26b, 28c, 34ca,
34cla, 34clb, 34crb, 34br, 35cla, 35tlb, 35tr, 35clb, 35cb,
35crb, 35cbr (Holz & Kunststoff), 36 cla, 46, 52tl (R.
Bemke), 52tr (Jurgen Liepe), 52c, 52b (A.C. Theil), 53t (R.
Boemke), 54b, 55t, 55cla, 56cl, 60b, 61bl, 126tr, 126b,
127t; **Deutsches Museum** (Munich) 228–229 (all images);
Deutsches Schifffahrtsmuseum Bremerhaven 50d;
Diözesanmuseum (Bamberg) 251t; **dpa** 26tra, 27tl, 27tr,
27cra, 27crb, 27br, 27bl, 28tl, 28tr, 35cla, 35cra, 35bl, 36tr,
60ca, 139t, 109t, 205tl, 293t, 461t; Jens Büttner 61t; Claus
Felix 43b; Matthias Hiekel 40b; Peter Förster 40t; Wulf
Hirschberger 41b; Ralf Hirschberger 38b; Peer Grimm 22tr;
Frank Leonhardt 39t; Wolfgang Kluge 28b; Wolfgang
Kumm 61br; Kay Nietfeld 38t, 39t; Frank Mächler 41t;
Carsten Rehder 38t; Wulf Pfeiffer 41d; Martin Schutt 42t,
181d; Roland Scheidemann 43t; Ingo Wagner 61t; Heinz
Wieseler 42b; **DK Images** Posteritati/Judith Miller 112cl;
Dresden Museum für Geschichte der Stadt Dresden 55crb;
Eisenach-Wartburg Stiftung 186cla, 186cla, 186clb,
186crb, 187c.

Foto-Thueringen Barbara Neumann 122c.

Gäubodenmuseum Straubing 47bl; **Germanisches
Nationalmuseum** (Nuremberg) 260–61 (all images);
Getty Images Tina & Horst Herzig 561tr; **Grünes
Gewölbe** (Dresden) 172t. **Hamburger Bahnhof** (Berlin)
93bl; **Hamburger Kunsthalle** (Hamburg) 30cla, 436t;
Hessisches Landesmuseum Kassel 364tl, 364b
(© Staatliche Museum Kassel Deutsches Tapetenmuseum).

KaDeWe store, Berlin 559bl; Quelle 559bl; **Käthe-
Kollwitz-Museum** (Berlin) 87t; **Klosowski Grzegorz**
24cra; **Kloster Maulbronn** 302t, 302b, 303cla, 303crb,
303b; **Kölner Dom** 402tl, 402c, 402b, 403t, 403ca, 403cb,
403bl, 403br (© Dombauarchiv Köln, Matz und Schenk);
Komische Oper (Berlin) Monika Ritterhaus 108b, 108br;
Kosińscy, Renata and Marek 24clb, 24bra, 24blb, 25cla,
25tlb, 25blb, 204tl, 205ca, 205tr, 205cl, 205cr, 205br;
Kunstmuseum Düsseldorf 30clb; **Kunstsammlungen
Paula Modersohn** 433tl; **Kunstverlag Maria Laach**
334b, 358tl, 358tr, 358ca, 359t, 359ca, 359cb, 359b;
Kurdirektion des Berchtesgadener Landes Storto,
Leonberg 276b. **Landesmuseum Trier** Thomas Zühmer
342t; **Linden Museum für Völkerkunde** (Stuttgart)
310tlb; **Lübeck and Travemuende Tourist-Service
GmbH** HLTS 462cla; **Ludwigsburg – Schloss** 306ca,
306cb, 306b, 307t; **Lutherstube** (Wittenberg) 127t. **Mainz
– Dom** 335b (© M. Hankel-Studio); **Mercedes-Benz-
Museum** (Stuttgart) 310tra; **Meyer Nils** 60cb; **Michalski
Sergiusz** 20t;**Mittelalterliches Museum** (Rothenburg ob
der Tauber) 262br; **Museum der Bildenden Künste**
(Leipzig) 51t (MdbK, Gerstenberger 1994); **Museum**

Folkwang (Essen) 31t; **Museum für Naturkunde**
(Berlin) 93br; **Museum am Ostwall** (Dortmund) 390t;
Musikinstrumenten-Museum (Berlin) 85ca.
Nationalmuseum (Munich) 219t. **Opernhaus** (Bayreuth)
252t. **Philharmonie** (Berlin) 85t; **Popkomm GmbH**
109bc; **Presse- und Informationsamt des Landes
Berlin** BTM/Drewes 92bl; BTM/Koch 92cla; G. Schneider
43t. **Rheinisches Landesmuseum Bonn** 408t; **Robert
Harding Picture Library** H P Merten 13cl; **Rosas Dance
Company, Belgium** Herman Sorgeloos 109cr.
Schauspielhaus (Konzerthaus Berlin) 72d; **Schloss
Sigmaringen** 315b; **Karsten Schirmer** 108cl;
Schlösserverwaltung (Munich) 246ca, 247t, 247ca,
247cb, 247b, 282t, 282ca, 282cb, 282b; **Schneider
Guenter** 62–3; **Sea Life München** 233cr; **Slips Fashion,
Munich** 230tc; **STA Travel** 569tr; **Staatsarchiv Hamburg**
50–51; **Staatliche Museen Preußischer Kulturbesitz**
(Berlin) 48c, 55br, 56–7, 57tl, 57br, 58t, 58cra, 58clb, 58b,
59t, 59bl, 59br, 60t, 64br, 65cra, 75t, 76ca, 77t, 89t, 90cb,
91clb, 98cla, 104t, 124tl, 125brb; Hans-Joachim Bartsch
49c, 49b, 55bl; Jorg P. Anders 84c, 84b, 88b, 90tr, 90tl,
90ca, 90b, 91t, 91cra, 91d; Grammes 48br; Klaus Göken
56b, 59c, 76b, 77d; Erich Lessing 74clb, 76t, 77cb
Jurgen Liepe 75c, 76cb; Georg Niedermeister 77ca; Arne
Psille 47br, 48tr, 48bl; Steinkopf 84tr; **Staatliche
Porzellan-Manufaktur Meißen GMBH** 34cra, 124tr,
124cra, 124clb, 124b, 125t, 125bra, Klaus Tänzer 125cra;
Staatsgalerie Stuttgart 311ca, 311tlb, 312t, 312b, 313t,
313ca, 313cb, 313b; **Städelsches Kunstinstitut** (Frankfurt
am Main) 378t, 378c, 378b, 379t, 379ca, 379cb, 379b;
Stadtmuseum Berlin 69c, 71t; Hans-Joachim Bartsch 53bl;
Stadtmuseum (Munich) 69c, 214tl; Hans-Joachim
Bartsch 5t; Sudnik 25crb; **Stasi-Museum** (Berlin) 102b;
Stiftung Preussische Schlösser und Gärten Berlin 54c,
98cl, 99ca, 99b, 99crb, 135cr, 136b, 139b; **Superstock
Polska Sp. zo.o.** 324t
Tourist Office – Altötting 270t, 270b. **Wallraf-Richartz-
Museum** (Cologne) 404t, 404ca, 404cb, 404b, 405t, 405c,
405br, 405bl (© Rheinisches Bildarchiv);
www.dresden.de Christoph Münch 168u; **Zeta** 25cl,
202–3c, 387b, 412–13, 422bra, 422t, 423b, 433b, 450t,
450c, 451tl, 451tr, 451b, 453b, 478t; Bloemendal 5t; Damm
21b, 398b, 288, 394b, 451tra, 467d; Eckstein 23b, 423tl,
423tr, 477b; Freytag 19b, 204tr, 327t; Haenel 1, 33tcb,
456b, 469t, 481t; Kehrer 25cr; Kinne 406t, 406b; Kohlhas
409t; Leidort 15t, 15b; Rossenbach 8–9, 322–3, 398c, 410b,
411t, 412–13, 459b, 470t, Rose 411t; Steeger 423t;
Streichan 352–3, 363t, 383b; Svenja-Foto 394t, 403cra;
Waldkirch 450t; M. Winkel 402tr; **Zwinger** (Dresden)
174t, 174cb, 175b; Gemäldegalerie Alte Meister 176t.

Jacket
Front - Corbis: Derek Croucher main image; DK Images:
Pawel Wojcik clb. Back - Alamy Images: ImageState/Pictor
International cla; DK Images: Dorota and Maiusz
Jarymowicz tl, clb, bl. Spine - Corbis: Derek Croucher t;
DK Images: Dorota and Maiusz Jarymowicz b.

Front Endpaper
Alamy Images: Werner Otto R tc; Corbis: Zefa/Frank
Lukasseck R clb.

All other images © Dorling Kindersley.
For further information see: www.dkimages.com

SPECIAL EDITIONS OF DK TRAVEL GUIDES

Phrasebook

In an Emergency

Where is the telephone?	Wo ist das Telefon?	voh ist duss tel-e-fone?
Help!	Hilfe!	**hilf**-uh
Please call a doctor	Bitte rufen Sie einen Arzt	**bitt**-uh **roof**'n zee ine-en artst
Please call the police	Bitte rufen Sie die Polizei	**bitt**-uh **roof**'n zee dee poli-**tsy**
Please call the fire brigade	Bitte rufen Sie die Feuerwehr	**bitt**-uh roof'n zee dee **foyer**-vayr
Stop!	Halt!	**hult**

Communication Essentials

Yes	Ja	**yah**
No	Nein	**nine**
Please	Bitte	**bitt**-uh
Thank you	Danke	dunk-uh
Excuse me	Verzeihung	fair-**tsy**-hoong
Hello (good day)	Guten Tag	**goot**-en tahk
Goodbye	Auf Wiedersehen	owf-**veed**-er-zay-ern
Good evening	Guten Abend	goot'n **ahb**'nt
Good night	Gute Nacht	goot-uh **nukht**
Until tomorrow	Bis morgen	biss **morg**'n
See you	Tschüss	chooss
What is that?	Was ist das?	voss ist duss
Why?	Warum?	var-**room**
Where?	Wo?	**voh**
When?	Wann?	**vunn**
today	heute	**hoyt**-uh
tomorrow	morgen	**morg**'n
month	Monat	**mohn**-aht
night	Nacht	**nukht**
afternoon	Nachmittag	**nahkh**-mit-tahk
morning	Morgen	**morg**'n
year	Jahr	yar
there	dort	**dort**
here	hier	**hear**
week	Woche	**vokh**-uh
yesterday	gestern	**gest**'n
evening	Abend	**ahb**'nt

Useful Phrases

How are you? (informal)	Wie geht's?	vee gayts
Fine, thanks	Danke, es geht mir gut	dunk-uh, es gayt meer goot
Until later	Bis später	biss **shpay**-ter
Where is/are?	Wo ist/sind...?	voh ist/sind
How far is it to...?	Wie weit ist es...?	vee **vite** ist ess
Do you speak English?	Sprechen Sie Englisch?	shpresh'n zee **eng**-glish
I don't understand	Ich verstehe nicht	ish fair-**shtay**-uh nisht
Could you speak more slowly?	Könnten Sie langsamer sprechen?	**kurnt**-en zee **lung**-zam-er **shpresh**'n

Useful Words

large	gross	**grohss**
small	klein	**kline**
hot	heiss	**hyce**
cold	kalt	**kult**
good	gut	**goot**
bad	böse/schlecht	**burss**-uh/**shlesht**
open	geöffnet	g'**urff**-nett
closed	geschlossen	g'**shloss**'n
left	links	**links**
right	rechts	**reshts**
straight ahead	geradeaus	g'**rah**-der-**owss**

Making a Telephone Call

I would like to make a phone call	Ich möchte telefonieren	ish mer-shtuh tel-e-fon-**eer**'n
I'll try again later	Ich versuche es später noch einmal	ish fair-zookh-uh es **shpay**-ter nokh ine-mull
Can I leave a message?	Kann ich eine Nachricht hinterlassen?	kan ish **ine**-uh nakh-risht hint-er-**lahss**-en
answer phone	Anrufbeantworter	an-roof-be-**ahnt**-vort-er
telephone card	Telefonkarte	tel-e-**fohn**-kart-uh
receiver	Hörer	**hur**-er
mobile	Handy	han-dee
engaged (busy)	besetzt	b'zetst
wrong number	Falsche Verbindung	falsh-uh fair-**bin**-doong

Sightseeing

library	Bibliothek	bib-leo-**tek**
entrance ticket	Eintrittskarte	ine-tritz-**kart**-uh
cemetery	Friedhof	**freed**-hofe
train station	Bahnhof	**barn**-hofe
gallery	Galerie	**gall**-er-ree
information	Auskunft	**owss**-koonft
church	Kirche	**keersh**-uh
garden	Garten	**gart**'n
palace/castle	Palast/Schloss	pallast/shloss
place (square)	Platz	**plats**
bus stop	Haltestelle	**hal**-te-shtel-uh
national holiday	Nationalfeiertag	nats-yon-**ahl**-fire-tahk
theatre	Theater	tay-**aht**-er
free admission	Eintritt frei	ine-tritt fry

Shopping

Do you have/ Is there...?	Gibt es...?	geept ess
How much does it cost?	Was kostet das?	voss **kost**'t duss?
When do you open/ close?	Wann öffnen Sie? schließen Sie?	vunn **off**'n zee **shlees**'n zee
this	das	duss
expensive	teuer	**toy**-er
cheap	preiswert	**price**-vurt
size	Größe	**gruhs**-uh
number	Nummer	**noom**-er
colour	Farbe	**farb**-uh
brown	braun	brown
black	schwarz	**shvarts**
red	rot	**roht**
blue	blau	**blau**
green	grün	**groon**
yellow	gelb	**gelp**

Types of Shop

antique shop	Antiquariat	antik-**var**-yat
chemist (pharmacy)	Apotheke	appo-**tay**-kuh
bank	Bank	**bunk**
market	Markt	**markt**
travel agency	Reisebüro	**rye**-zer-boo-roe
department store	Warenhaus	**vahr**'n-hows
chemist's, drugstore	Drogerie	droog-er-**ree**
hairdresser	Friseur	freezz-**er**
newspaper kiosk	Zeitungskiosk	tsytoongs-kee-osk
bookshop	Buchhandlung	**bookh**-hant-loong

bakery	Bäckerei	beck-er-**eye**
post office	Post	posst
shop/store	Geschäft/Laden	gush-**eft/lard**'n
film processing shop	Photogeschäft	**fo**-to-gush-**eft**
self-service shop	Selbstbedienungs-laden	selpst-bed-**ee**-nungs-lard'n
shoe shop	Schuhladen	shoo-lard'n
clothes shop	Kleiderladen, Boutique	klyder-lard'n, boo-**teek**-uh
food shop	Lebensmittel-geschäft	**lay**-bens-mittel-gush-eft
glass, porcelain	Glas, Porzellan	**glars**, **Port-sellahn**

Staying in a Hotel

Do you have any vacancies?	Haben Sie noch Zimmer frei?	harb'n zee nokh **tsimm**-er-fry
with twin beds?	mit zwei Betten?	mitt tsvy bett'n
with a double bed?	mit einem Doppelbett?	mitt ine'm **dopp**'l-bet
with a bath?	mit Bad?	mitt **bart**
with a shower?	mit Dusche?	mitt **doosh**-uh
I have a reservation	Ich habe eine Reservierung	ish **harb**-uh rez-er-**veer**-oong
key	Schlüssel	shlooss'l
porter	Pförtner	**pfert**-ner

Eating Out

Do you have a table for...?	Haben Sie einen Tisch für...?	harb'n zee tish foor
I would like to reserve a table	Ich möchte eine Reservierung machen	ish **mer**-shtuh ine-uh rezer-**veer**-oong makh'n
I'm a vegetarian	Ich bin Vegetarier	ish bin vegg-er-**tah**-ree-er
Waiter!	Herr Ober!	hair **oh**-bare!
The bill (check), please	Die Rechnung, bitte	dee **resh**-noong bitt-uh
breakfast	Frühstück	**froo**-shtock
lunch	Mittagessen	**mit**-targ-ess'n
dinner	Abendessen	**arb**'nt-ess'n
bottle	Flasche	**flush**-uh
dish of the day	Tagesgericht	**tahg**-es-gur-isht
main dish	Hauptgericht	**howpt**-gur-isht
dessert	Nachtisch	**nahkh**-tish
cup	Tasse	**tass**-uh
wine list	Weinkarte	vine-**kart**-uh
tankard	Krug	khroog
glass	Glas	**glars**
spoon	Löffel	**lerff'l**
teaspoon	Teelöffel	tay-**lerff'l**
tip	Trinkgeld	**trink**-gelt
knife	Messer	**mess**-er
starter (appetizer)	Vorspeise	for-**shpize**-uh
the bill	Rechnung	**resh**-noong
plate	Teller	**tell**-er
fork	Gabel	**gahb**'l

Menu Decoder

Aal	**arl**	eel
Apfel	**upf'l**	apple
Apfelschorle	**upf'l**-shoorl-uh	apple juice with sparkling mineral water
Apfelsine	**upf'l**-seen-uh	orange
Aprikose	upri-**kawz**-uh	apricot
Artischocke	arti-**shokh**-uh	artichoke
Aubergine (eggplant)	or-ber-**jeen**-uh	aubergine
Banane	bar-**narn**-uh	banana
Beefsteack	**beef**-stayk	steak
Bier	beer	beer
Bockwurst	**bokh**-voorst	a type of sausage
Bohnensuppe	burn-en-zoop-uh	bean soup
Branntwein	brant-vine	spirits
Bratkartoffeln	brat-kar-toff'ln	fried potatoes
Bratwurst	brat-voorst	fried sausage
Brötchen	bret-tchen	bread roll
Brot	brot	bread
Brühe	bruh-uh	broth
Butter	**boot**-ter	butter
Champignon	**shum**-pin-yong	mushroom
Currywurst	**kha**-ree-voorst	sausage with curry sauce
Dill	**dill**	dill
Ei	**eye**	egg
Eis	**ice**	ice/ ice cream
Ente	**ent**-uh	duck
Erdbeeren	ayrt-**beer**'n	strawberries
Fisch	**fish**	fish
Forelle	for-**ell**-uh	trout
Frikadelle	Frika-dayl-uh	rissole/hamburger
Gans	ganns	goose
Garnele	**gar**-nayl-uh	prawn/shrimp
gebraten	g'**braat**'n	fried
gegrillt	g'**grilt**	grilled
gekocht	g'**kokht**	boiled
geräuchert	g'**rowk**-ert	smoked
Geflügel	g'**floog**'l	poultry
Gemüse	g'**mooz**-uh	vegetables
Grütze	**grurt**-ser	groats, gruel
Gulasch	**goo**-lush	goulash
Gurke	**goork**-uh	gherkin
Hammelbraten	hamm'l-**braat**'n	roast mutton
Hähnchen	haynsh'n	chicken
Hering	**hair**-ing	herring
Himbeeren	him-beer'n	raspberries
Honig	**hoe**-nikh	honey
Kaffee	kaf-**fay**	coffee
Kalbfleisch	kalp-flysh	veal
Kaninchen	ka-**neensh**'n	rabbit
Karpfen	**karpf**'n	carp
Kartoffelpüree	kar-toff'l-poor-ay	mashed potatoes
Käse	**kayz**-uh	cheese
Kaviar	**kar**-vee-ar	caviar
Knoblauch	k'**nob**-lowkh	garlic
Knödel	k'**nerd**'l	noodle
Kohl	**koal**	cabbage
Kopfsalat	**kopf**-zal-aat	lettuce
Krebs	**krayps**	crab
Kuchen	**kookh**'n	cake
Lachs	**lahkhs**	salmon
Leber	**lay**-ber	liver
mariniert	mari-neert	marinated
Marmelade	marmer-**lard**-uh	marmalade, jam
Meerrettich	may-re-tish	horseradish
Milch	**milsh**	milk
Mineralwasser	minn-er-**arl**-vuss-er	mineral water
Möhre	**mer**-uh	carrot
Nuss	**nooss**	nut
Öl	**erl**	oil
Olive	o-**leev**-uh	olive
Petersilie	payt-er-**zee**-li-uh	parsley
Pfeffer	**pfeff**-er	pepper
Pfirsich	**pfir**-zish	peach
Pflaumen	**pflow**-men	plum
Pommes frites	pomm-**fritt**	chips/ French fries
Quark	kvark	soft cheese
Radieschen	ra-**deesh**'n	radish
Rinderbraten	**rind**-er-brat'n	joint of beef
Rinderroulade	**rind**-er-roo-lard-uh	beef olive
Rindfleisch	**rint**-flysh	beef
Rippchen	**rip**-sh'n	cured pork rib
Rotkohl	roht-koal	red cabbage
Rüben	rhoob'n	turnip
Rührei	**rhoo**-er-eye	scrambled eggs
Saft	**zuft**	juice
Salat	zal-aat	salad
Salz	**zults**	salt

Salzkartoffeln	zults-kar-toff'l	boiled potatoes	18	achtzehn	**uhkht**-tsayn
Sauerkirschen	zow-er-**keersh**'n	cherries	19	neunzehn	**noyn**-tsayn
Sauerkraut	zow-er-krowt	sauerkraut	20	zwanzig	**tsvunn**-tsig
Sekt	**zekt**	sparkling wine	21	einundzwanzig	**ine**-oont-tsvunn-tsig
Senf	**zenf**	mustard			
scharf	sharf	spicy	30	dreißig	**dry**-sig
Schaschlik	shash-lik	kebab	40	vierzig	**feer**-sig
Schlagsahne	shlahgg-zarn-uh	whipped cream	50	fünfzig	**foonf**-tsig
Schnittlauch	shnit-lowhkh	chives	60	sechzig	**zex**-tsig
Schnitzel	**shnitz**'l	veal or pork cutlet	70	siebzig	**zeep**-tsig
Schweinefleisch	**shvine**-flysh	pork	80	achtzig	**uhkht**-tsig
Spargel	**shparg**'l	asparagus	90	neunzig	**noyn**-tsig
Spiegelei	shpeeg'l-eye	fried egg	100	hundert	**hoond**'t
Spinat	shpin-art	spinach	1000	tausend	**towz**'nt
Tee	**tay**	tea	1 000 000	eine Million	**ine**-uh **mill**-yon
Tomate	tom-art-uh	tomato			
Wassermelone	vuss-er-me-lohn-uh	watermelon	**Time**		
Wein	**vine**	wine			
Weintrauben	vine-trowb'n	grapes	one minute	eine Minute	**ine**-uh min-**oot**-uh
Wiener Würstchen	veen-er voorst-sh'n	frankfurter	one hour	eine Stunde	**ine**-uh **shtoond**-uh
Zander	**tsan**-der	pike-perch	half an hour	eine halbe Stunde	**ine**-uh hullb-uh **shtoond**-uh
Zitrone	tsi-trohn-uh	lemon			
Zucker	**tsook**-er	sugar	Monday	Montag	**mohn**-targ
Zwieback	tsvee-bak	rusk	Tuesday	Dienstag	**deens**-targ
Zwiebel	**tsveeb**'l	onion	Wednesday	Mittwoch	**mitt**-vokh
			Thursday	Donnerstag	**donn**-ers-targ
			Friday	Freitag	**fry**-targ
Numbers			Saturday	Samstag/ Sonnabend	**zums**-targ zonn-ah-bent
0	null	**nool**	Sunday	Sonntag	**zon**-targ
1	eins	**eye'ns**	January	Januar	**yan**-ooar
2	zwei	**tsvy**	February	Februar	**fay**-brooar
3	drei	**dry**	March	März	**mairts**
4	vier	**feer**	April	April	april
5	fünf	**foonf**	May	Mai	my
6	sechs	**zex**	June	Juni	**yoo**-ni
7	sieben	**zeeb**'n	July	Juli	**yoo**-lee
8	acht	**uhkht**	August	August	ow-**goost**
9	neun	**noyn**	September	September	zep-**tem**-ber
10	zehn	**tsayn**	October	Oktober	ok-toh-ber
11	elf	**elf**	November	November	no-**vem**-ber
12	zwölf	**tserlf**	December	Dezember	day-**tsem**-ber
13	dreizehn	**dry**-tsayn	spring	Frühling	**froo**-ling
14	vierzehn	**feer**-tsayn	summer	Sommer	**zomm**-er
15	fünfzehn	**foonf**-tsayn	autumn (fall)	Herbst	**hairpst**
16	sechzehn	**zex**-tsayn	winter	Winter	**vint**-er
17	siebzehn	**zeep**-tsayn			

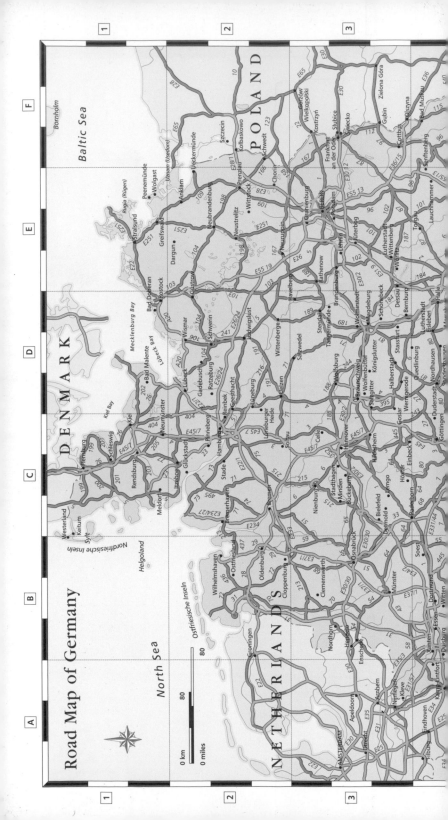

Road Map of Germany